The Economy of
Early America

PUBLISHED IN COOPERATION WITH
THE LIBRARY COMPANY OF PHILADELPHIA

THE PENNSYLVANIA STATE UNIVERSITY PRESS
UNIVERSITY PARK, PENNSYLVANIA

The Economy of
Early America

HISTORICAL PERSPECTIVES
& NEW DIRECTIONS

EDITED BY

Cathy Matson

Library of Congress Cataloging-in-Publication Data

The economy of early America : historical perspectives
and new directions / edited by Cathy Matson.
     p.   cm.
Includes index.
"Published in cooperation with The Library Company
of Philadelphia."
ISBN 978-0-271-02711-1 (cloth : alk. paper)
ISBN 978-0-271-02765-4 (pbk : alk. paper)
1. United States—Economic conditions—To 1865.
2. United States—Economic conditions—1865–1918.
3. Great Britain—Colonies—America—Economic
conditions.
I. Matson, Cathy D., 1951– .

HC104.E25 2006
330.973′02—dc22
2005026097

The Pennsylvania State University Press
is a member of the Association of
American University Presses.

It is the policy of
The Pennsylvania State University Press
to use acid-free paper. Publications on
uncoated stock satisfy the minimum
requirements of American National
Standard for Information Sciences—
Permanence of Paper for Printed Library
Materials, ANSI Z39.48–1992.

FRONTISPIECE: *Louis L. Peck Manufacturer & Dealer in Burning
Fluid Varnishes, Pine Oil . . .* (detail). Chromolithograph
printed in Philadelphia by Wagner and McGuigan, c. 1855.
Library Company of Philadelphia.

Contents

PREFACE   vii

1   A House of Many Mansions: Some Thoughts on the
    Field of Economic History   1
    Cathy Matson

2   Rethinking *The Economy of British America*   71
    David Hancock

3   Colonial America's Mestizo Agriculture   107
    Russell R. Menard

4   Peopling, Producing, and Consuming in Early
    British America   124
    Lorena S. Walsh

5   Indentured Servitude in Perspective: European
    Migration into North America and the Composition
    of the Early American Labor Force, 1600–1775   146
    Christopher Tomlins

6   Capitalism, Slavery, and Benjamin Franklin's
    American Revolution   183
    David Waldstreicher

7   Moneyless in Pennsylvania: Privatization and the
    Depression of the 1780s   218
    Terry Bouton

8   Creative Destruction: The Forgotten Legacy of the
    Hessian Fly   236
    Brooke Hunter

9   The Panic of 1819 and the Political Economy of
    Sectionalism   263
    Daniel S. Dupre

10 Toward a Social History of the Corporation:
    Shareholding in Pennsylvania, 1800–1840   294
    John Majewski

11 Small-Producer Capitalism in Early
    National Philadelphia   317
    Donna J. Rilling

12 The Unfree Origins of American Capitalism   335
    Seth Rockman

LIST OF CONTRIBUTORS   363
INDEX   365

Preface

Eleven chapters in this volume began as papers prepared for distribution and discussion at the first conference of the Program in Early American Economy and Society (PEAES) in April 2001. The two-day conference, ambitiously titled "The Past and Future of Early American Economic History: Needs and Opportunities," discussed, in all, twenty-two papers that offered varied perspectives on economic history written since 1985, and suggested directions for future research. Conference participants were asked to self-consciously place their work in the context of both previous scholarship and today's debates, and to lay this work before an open forum of people from many academic disciplines. In keeping with the economy program's objectives of nurturing the study of economic issues from the colonial through the antebellum era, using an expansive definition of "economic history," the authors in this volume offer diverse approaches and arguments. I wrote the introductory chapter separately in order to provide a much longer range assessment of economic history's contested terrain, and to offer a bird's-eye view of the many directions that the historiography of this field has taken.

At the outset, some conference participants were asked to assess a particular pathbreaking contribution or a long-standing point of view; some were asked to evaluate a field of scholarship; and some were asked to explain how their empirical research and conceptual approach to an economic issue adds fresh insights to the field. The authors bring to this volume their training and inspiration from various methodologies that originate in economic theory and econometrics, but also include cultural studies, political economy, and social and intellectual history. Their arguments are at once sweeping and particular. As with all good history, economic or otherwise, some chapters emulate and expand upon the spadework of historians who preceded them, while others engage in current dialogues or explicitly seek to redirect work in economic history toward new questions and evidence. Some reconsider past scholars' contributions to the field; others investigate new subjects or new places of negotiation and development that have not been considered "economic" in the past. Although readers may see the imprint of traditional economic history from time to time, most of the authors in this volume are immersed in scholarly dialogues that PEAES has sought to promote, dialogues about a broadly conceived role in the field of economic history for the Atlantic world economy, regional comparisons of colonial and early national development, the relationship of emerging economic institutions to early America's rapid ascent in the global economy, the nature of population and migration patterns, popular perceptions of credit and debt, the role of age and gender in household economies, labor and production relations, and many other topics.

The present volume does not attempt to provide a synthesis of all current work in economic history, and the authors do not agree on one interpretation of the historical past in economic terms, especially on such matters as the pace and character of economic growth, the nature and significance of a "transition to capitalism" or a "market revolution," or the assumptions we make about economic rationality, markets, or the role of governments. However, while the essays do not encompass all the issues or approaches in the field of economic history, they do represent certain bands of light along a rich spectrum of recent work that illuminate our past contributions and point toward new "needs and opportunities" in scholarship on the economy of British North America down to the 1850s. As a result, each essay places at the reader's fingertips valuable sources for understanding past and current debates, as well as areas in need of further investigation.

Cathy Matson, Professor of History, University of Delaware, and PEAES Director

Chapter One

A House of Many Mansions: Some Thoughts on the Field of Economic History

CATHY MATSON

Since its recognizable origins near the end of the nineteenth century, economic history has negotiated an uneasy coexistence between the two professional disciplines from which it came, history and economics. For years, the American Economic Association, which was founded in 1885, had a decidedly historical orientation and met annually along with the American Historical Association. The mainstream of scholarship produced by economic historians in that generation, whether they held positions in academia or in public institutions, came from a venerable tradition of narrative writing. Arguably, this historical tradition stretched back to the eighteenth century's Scottish Enlightenment authors, Adam Smith, James Steuart, David Hume, and James Millar, and the nineteenth century's David Ricardo, John Stuart Mill, Karl Marx, and many others. In newly industrializing America, economic historians hailed from training that included literature and philosophy, or service to labor and government agencies, and some of them bequeathed a solid corpus of work highlighting the accomplishments of inventors, entrepreneurs, corporate founders, union leaders, and other highly visible individuals. Others produced an impressive array of encyclopedic studies on the roles of the imperial, state, and federal governments in shaping economies, all with a more historical than statistical or mathematical orientation.[1]

I am indebted to Kate Carté-Engel, Timothy Hack, Christian Koot, Brian Luskey, Brian Schoen, and Ted Sickler for their conceptual insights and numerous reading assignments.

1. For valuable reviews of these developments, see John Higham, *History: Professional Scholarship in America* (Englewood Cliffs, N.J.: Prentice-Hall, 1965), especially chapter 2; Dorothy Ross, *The Origins of American Social Science* (New York: Cambridge University Press, 1991), chapter 6, for the 1880s to roughly World War I, and 407–27 for the 1920s; and Geoffrey M. Hodgson, *How Economics Forgot History: The Problem of Historical Specificity in Social Science* (New York: Routledge, 2001). For reflections on the role of economic history in a

A gathering momentum across the social sciences at the turn of the century provoked divisions that had been latent in the young discipline of economic history. Armed with a belief in the ability of scholars to unearth and analyze large bodies of data, and in the conviction that such "scientific" work would lead to more precise knowledge about the past, many economic historians became eager to leave behind the stories of heroic battles, political icons, and compendia of legislative facts in order to investigate aggregates of more ordinary people. A new fascination with mathematical and behavioral models held out the promise of escaping the impressionism of personal biography and the teleology of progress that characterized much of the previous generation's narratives, even those fundamentally grounded in economic events and transformations. Explicit economic models, argued scholars trained as "marginalists," would give systematic meaning to people working, migrating, spending, investing, and otherwise making economic choices within large communities and nations. In place of historical subjects who, in traditional narrative history, spoke in their own words or could be known through close study of the world immediately around them, this new social scientific subject would be one among great numbers of people in broad contexts. Much of this thinking was brought together in Alfred Marshall's *Principles of Economics* (1890), a work that linked marginalist analysis of price equilibriums to certain classical writings about individual behavior in supply-demand markets. In the early twentieth century, much of the profession, still small in number, was captivated by the apparent certainties offered in Marshall's neoclassical market analysis and enthusiastically generated increasingly sophisticated bodies of data. Along the way, however, Marshallians proposed a very narrow set of assumptions about how and why people generated wealth. Their neoclassical findings documented an optimistic unfolding of unfettered competitive capitalist markets under the aegis of ingenious policymakers, strong nation-states, and similarly motivated producers and consumers.[2]

By World War I the theory and practice of Marshallians dominated economics departments, while the investigation of more broadly conceived economic processes retreated more deeply into history departments. Historians freely debated whether economic modeling could incorporate the ups and downs of markets, the turning points that set economies on new trajectories, or the unpredictable characteristics of human behavior. Many in this non-Marshallian

broader context, see Eric Hobsbawm, *On History* (New York: New Press, 1997), chapters 5–8. See also the commentary in Albert O. Hirschman, *Essays in Trespassing: Economics to Politics and Beyond* (New York: Cambridge University Press, 1981).

2. Economic perspectives were present in a variety of early twentieth-century studies. See, e.g., those of Charles McLean Andrews, Herbert Levi Osgood, E. R. A. Seligman (who was a powerful influence on Charles Beard early in the century), John R. Commons, and Richard T. Ely. For Alfred Marshall, see especially his *Principles of Economics* (London: Macmillan, 1890); and a study of his impact in Phyllis Deane, *The Evolution of Economic Ideas* (New York: Cambridge University Press, 1978), chapter 3.

majority had been trained in the narrative strategies of historical writing that lingered well into the twentieth century. Some were drawn to Thorstein Veblen's radical, historically grounded studies of "conspicuous consumption," in which he argued for the primacy of economic factors and social class in setting cultural trends, a view with widespread appeal for economic historians leaning toward socialism, nationalization of industry, or the efficacy of political revolution during these years. Others who rejected the neoclassical emphasis on rather uniform human behavior in markets looked at the reality of social dislocation in the early twentieth century through the lens of nineteenth-century Marxism's "materialist conception of history" (though often they did not subscribe to its political solutions).[3]

Still others found in the early twentieth-century writings of sociologist Max Weber another compelling argument against Marshallians. Weber placed particular emphasis on the economically creative values and attitudes of rationality, order, diligence, efficiency, and deferred pleasure in Protestant populations. Many economic historians saw in his work a powerful explanation for the rise of industrial capitalism—or at least a compelling complement to mathematical measures of trade, prices, money flows, and the like. Weber's explanation of why certain nations passed from an era of commercial "merchant capitalism" to industrialization held sway over many economic historians investigating long eras of transformation, especially North America's apparently deep "spirit" of enterprise, institutional sophistication, and high civic consciousness. Weber's "Protestant ethic" was often translated—even by the best economic historians—into a sweeping explanation of American economic development and national character down through World War II.[4] Recently, Weber's appeal is on the rise again.

Elements of these early twentieth-century theoretical sources, as well as the rising tide of public progressive reform and academic social science, cemented the confidence of economic historians of the post–World War I era known as "institutionalists." Together, they parted company permanently from the narrative traditions derived from literature and philosophy, and distinguished themselves from neoclassicists by arguing that not a theorized market individual

3. See Veblen's culminating work, *The Theory of the Leisure Class* (New York: Modern Library, 1934); Joseph Dorfman, *Thorstein Veblen and His America* (Cambridge: Harvard University Press, 1934), chapters 1–2; Ross, *Origins of American Social Science*, 204–16. Postwar economic history often moved in tandem with "Progressive" scholarship.

4. Max Weber, *The Protestant Ethic and the Spirit of Capitalism* (1905; London: G. Allen and Unwin, 1930). Weber's explanatory power would rise again during the 1990s; see, e.g., Joyce Appleby, "The Vexed Story of Capitalism Told by American Historians," *Journal of the Early Republic* 21 (Spring 2001): 1–19; David Landes, *The Wealth and Poverty of Nations* (New York: W. W. Norton, 1998); Gordon S. Wood, *The Radicalism of the American Revolution* (New York: Knopf, 1992); and Stephen Innes, *Creating the Commonwealth: The Economic Culture of Puritan New England* (New York: W. W. Norton, 1995). Innis finds a "civic ecology" in New England not matched elsewhere in North America.

or unfettered market system, but rather the real life of governments, labor groups, corporate entities, and other shifting collectives of social interests created the constraints and opportunities for economic development.[5] During the interwar years in particular, institutionalists developed increasingly detailed understandings of social change in their studies of policymaking and interest-group decision making that affected social outcomes in time- or place-specific ways in American history. Institutionalists seemed to offer humanistic social applications for the study of economic issues, and to broaden the subject matter under scrutiny from elite business and political leaders to wide layers of historical agents. The commanding figures of Frederick Jackson Turner and Charles Beard, for example, acknowledged being deeply influenced by these early economic historians, and later Progressive economic historians of the 1930s built an even stronger case for the primacy of economic "forces" in American development. In bold departures from their teachers—including Turner and Beard—younger Progressive institutionalists demanded solid empirical bases in scholarship and stronger statements about the uneven nature of American economic development, and its unequal results, which in turn required bold governmental corrective intervention. This insistence on the "scientific" economic measurement of class and social structure informed much economic history into the 1950s.[6]

Equally important, the gap between rigorous mathematical modeling conducted in economic departments, on the one hand, and institutional and social studies done in history departments, on the other, found no middle ground during these years. Indeed, the gap widened after World War II. In the shadow of their memories of world depression followed by world war, many economists grew increasingly concerned about banking and monetarist policies. Much work took place under the auspices of granting agencies such as the Rockefeller Foundation. During the 1940s, the Committee on Research in Economic History, within the Social Science Research Council, also began using mathematical modeling to study the role of federal and local governments in furthering economic development. The work of scholars such as Carter Goodrich, which blended both mathematical appreciations of economic development and historical sensitivity to the "mixed enterprise" of individual entrepreneurs, private

5. Thomas C. Cochran, "Research in American Economic History: A Thirty-Year View," *Mid-America* 29 (January 1947): 1–29.

6. For the ties between economic historians, especially those at Johns Hopkins University and Columbia University, and the Progressive movement, see Higham, *History,* chapter 2. John Hicks was one of many of Progressive historians in the 1930s emphasizing "economic forces," as was Louis Hacker; see, too, the thirteen-volume series, *A History of American Life,* edited by Arthur M. Schlesinger Sr. and Dixon Ryan Fox (New York, 1927–44), which gives an "economic interpretation" without econometric or neoclassical modeling; Arthur M. Schlesinger Jr.'s Pulitzer Prize–winning *Age of Jackson* (Boston: Little, Brown, 1945); W. T. Baxter, *The House of Hancock: Business in Boston, 1724–1775* (New York: Russell and Russell, 1945); and Kenneth W. Porter, *The Jacksons and the Lees: Two Generations of Massachusetts Merchants, 1765–1844,* 2 vols. (Cambridge: Harvard University Press, 1937).

corporations, and local or state governments, would be appreciated fully only in later decades.[7]

The rift between econometrics and economic history became even more obvious with the emergence of "new economic history" during the 1950s. Following World War II, Walter W. Rostow and others were searching for ways to explain economic development, especially the surges of production and consumption marking America's entry into an industrial era, by looking beyond the simple cause-and-effect developments spurred by invention, technology, or banking, and beyond simple measures of capitalist investment in the economy. Rostow proposed ways to analyze very large and diverse sectors of economic development, according to an emphasis on the investment potential (GNP minus consumed goods and government expenditures) of millions of Americans. In 1960 he proposed that an economy sometimes reached a "take-off" point at which populations could sustain a sufficient amount of investment over income levels to propel it into significantly higher levels of "growth." In America's case, the takeoff of sustained economic growth owed more to investment in the railroads—and the mining, manufacturing, employment, migration, marketing, and other "linkages" they spawned during the nineteenth century—than to any other development.[8]

Rightly or wrongly, Rostow's growth theory bolstered prevailing postwar policymakers' ideological preoccupation with American exceptionalism and "first worldism" in international affairs. But aside from its timely appearance amid the rising cold war thinking in America, the theory was hailed immediately by academic economic historians who saw its potential for explaining cycles of development and long-range growth. As the field of "new economic history" grew outward from its core of brilliant practitioners at Purdue University, it shifted focus from applied and policy matters to topics that historians had been investigating for some time. In doing so, new economic historians were

---

7. While many writers assert that this split was evident, as well, by the clustering of scholars in history and economics departments, with very little cross-fertilization of research by the 1950s, this generalization needs study. For the attack on economic history by intellectual and political historians in the late 1940s and 1950s, see Higham, *History,* chapter 6. For an example of the strain of econometric work during the 1940s, spearheaded by Edwin F. Gay, Carter Goodrich, Robert Lively, and Arthur H. Cole, among others, see, e.g., Lively, "The American System," *Business History Review* 29 (March 1955): 81–96.

8. Walter Rostow, *The Stages of Economic Growth: A Non-Communist Manifesto* (Cambridge: Harvard University Press, 1960); Susan P. Lee and Peter Passel, *A New Economic View of American History* (New York: W. W. Norton, 1979), introduction; Robert W. Fogel, "'Scientific' History and Traditional History," in *Which Road to the Past?* ed. Robert W. Fogel and G. R. Elton (New Haven: Yale University Press, 1983), 23–34; and Eric H. Monkkonen, ed., *Engaging the Past: The Uses of History Across the Social Sciences* (Durham: Duke University Press: 1994). Among the vanguard of scholars emphasizing a quantitative rather than a narrative approach to economic history, and pitting their view against both Progressive and Marxist models, were Rostow, Simon Kuznets, and young Douglass North. See, e.g., Douglass C. North, "The State of Economic History," *American Economic Review* 55 (May 1965): 86–91.

able to point at the unfortunate inclination of social scientists to assume too much about causal linkages between events and results; new economic historians, including many who supported Rostow's stages-of-growth model generally, demanded that historians formulate more explicit research questions, use counterfactual analysis, propose testable hypotheses within the context of a rigorously established model, and provide adequate empirical evidence that could bear mathematical testing. Even lacking the data to construct econometric models, they argued, the exercise of asking counterfactual questions—what if something else had happened, some other choice been made?—would salvage historical inquiries from overgeneralization. We will return to the fruits of new economic history shortly.

Alongside the emergence of takeoff models and new economic history, another kind of interpretation of long-term economic development was revitalized in the three post–World War II decades: the "staples thesis." During the 1930s Canadian historian Harold Innes pioneered work supporting his contention that dominant export commodities—such as furs, rice, indigo, and tobacco, but stretched by later scholars to include wheat, timber, and other commodities—and the labor relations requiring their production set the tone for economic relations, personal fortunes, regional and imperial development, and much of the social and cultural life of developing areas. By the 1950s the staples thesis was somewhat modified by models of economic stages and structural linkages within and between nations or empires, bearing some resemblance to emerging new economic historians' models. Through "backward linkages," staples influenced craft labor, shipbuilding, internal transport, insurance services, and other activities geared to getting crops to points of processing, packaging, exporting, and consumption. Through "forward" and "final demand" linkages, staples spurred the creation of mills, stores, and shops that provided goods and credit to surrounding producers, and prompted the work of a host of itinerant peddlers, weavers, and distributors in these diversifying economies. Dependence on outside credit and bound labor typically accompanied North American staples production, and the vagaries of international prices and markets conditioned the pace and character of economic development. Only after the American Revolution, according to the staples approach, did the onset of manufacturing and interregional specialization begin to mitigate North Americans' determinant role of producing for export and external demand.[9]

9. An invaluable summary of staples thesis work down to 1985 is in John J. McCusker and Russell R. Menard, *The Economy of British America, 1607–1789* (Chapel Hill: University of North Carolina Press, 1985). While the staples thesis strongly influenced economic historians, and Progressive scholars' "economic forces" sustained a following, a rising group of intellectual historians, to whom the profession would bow by the late 1940s, recoiled from "economic determinism." For an example of a deterministic behavioral approach attributing the nation's economic rise to a single American character, see David M. Potter, *People of Plenty: Economic Abundance and the American Character* (Chicago: University of Chicago Press, 1954).

Within a few short years new economic historians were challenging numerous long-standing interpretations of the early American past. Some tackled the Turner thesis by looking at internal improvements and westward migration in econometric ways; others revised thinking about antebellum slavery by studying its productivity; still others reached beyond local pictures of the past to find trends in birth, marriage, family size, death, income, wages, and landholding in large populations. Robert Fogel's controversial grand exercise in counterfactual analysis of antebellum railroads argued that it was not the locomotive steam engine and ribbons of newly laid railroad track, but rather the country's rising agricultural productivity—whether by slave-based plantation expansion, tenancy and indentures, or freeholders and hired labor in the early Republic— that spurred the most consequential economic growth of the era. New economic historians also began to explain the structures of market demand with greater sophistication; to identify major turning points in colonial agricultural production and international trade; to offer much-needed portraits of early American capital formation; and to glimpse household consumption before industrialization. Computer-generated databases, they argued, would bring to light the silent and "inarticulate" actors whose lives were but small pinpoints of light in mountains of statistics that cumulatively became beacons of historical interpretation. Among their most consequential, and most controversial, investigations is the ongoing measurement of per capita income and wealth, or gross per capita product for different places and times, in early America. But the staples approach also attracted a number of new researchers who wished to study long-term price swings and commodities exchange. In either case, their findings diminished the impact of technological breakthroughs on farming and craft production, cultural influences on business organization, and sudden economies of scale before the late antebellum era; instead, their work pointed toward a subtle "thickening" of economic change in agricultural yields, commercial exchange, and rising incomes over time, until a qualitative takeoff toward industrialization and urbanization was measurable. At its most extreme, postwar new economic history furthered the field of cliometrics, a resolutely mathematical and hypothesis-driven approach to many of these issues.[10]

10. An early example of cliometric work is A. H. Conrad and J. R. Meyer, "The Economics of Slavery in the Ante-Bellum South," *Journal of Political Economy* 66 (April 1958), 95–130; a few years later Robert Fogel and Stanley Engerman drew fire with *Time on the Cross: The Economics of American Negro Slavery*, 2 vols. (Boston: Little, Brown, 1974), while Douglass C. North's important study, *The Economic Growth of the United States, 1790–1860* (Englewood Cliffs, N.J.: Prentice-Hall, 1961), held that "U.S. growth was the evolution of a market economy where the behavior of prices of goods, services and productive factors was the major element in any explanation of economic change" (68). For summaries of cliometric work on early America, see Ida Altman and James Horn, eds., *"To Make America": European Emigration in the Early Modern Period* (Berkeley and Los Angeles: University of California Press, 1991); and David W. Galenson, "The Settlement and Growth of the Colonies: Population, Labor, and Economic Development," in *The Cambridge Economic History of the United States*, 3 vols., ed. Stanley L. Engerman and Robert E. Gallman (New York: Cambridge University Press, 1996)

By the mid-1960s new economic history had become a fertile and provocative field of study. But the gap between the disciplines of history and economics continued to thwart mutually beneficial dialogue, and critics soon challenged research questions, methodologies, and conclusions put forward by new economic historians. The problem was not the "scientific" understandings of historical issues made possible by computer-generated findings; nor was it the introduction of counterfactual inquiry into historical discourse. Many economic historians acknowledged the value of these contributions. But they retreated emphatically from many of the theoretical assumptions and research claims of new economic historians and became more insistent on the primacy of human agency, shifting demographics, local productivity, systems of authority and culture, and uneven institutional growth in North America's early economy. More and more these economic historians focused on the consequences of economic development for social and cultural inequality, rather than on the processes of development per se.

Their work was strongly influenced during the 1960s and 1970s by the emergence of the new social history, which itself warmed to theories that would have particular resonance for economic historians. One school of these new social historians, the *Annales* scholars who were a product of European intellectual turmoil arising out of World War I, gained an important hearing among American economic historians by the 1960s. Fernand Braudel's magisterial work on price movements, inflationary eras, and the vagaries of agricultural productivity over *longue durees* produced a storm of historical reinterpretation about the emergence of empires, popular uprisings, the relationships between demography and social well-being, and the halting rise of industrialization. Inspired by this expansive perspective, which permitted historians to write about the economic patterns that emerged from a multitude of local experiences without having to posit a necessarily profit-maximizing individual, numerous American historians got to work. Their topics were familiar to new economic historians: price series and commodities movements for a number of places and eras; trends in population growth and expansion; and the mechanisms of demand and supply, production and consumption, per capita incomes and wealth in early America. But they rejected causal determinism, linear outcomes, and universal economic motives; instead, they adopted from the *Annalistes* a perspective insisting on varieties of cultural patterns, local geographies, and other variables affecting economic outcomes over time. Some scholars hailed this approach as the basis for shifting the focus of American history away from either a series of discrete developmental moments or an unproblematic "rise of American civilization," and

---

(hereafter *CEHUS*), 1:169–89, 420–21. For a spirited defense of responsible cliometrics, see Fogel, "'Scientific' History and Traditional History," 23–34.

toward portraits of interconnectedness of human experience over long stretches of time.[11]

Dependency theory, originally applied to studies of Africa and Latin America, also exerted a strong influence on many American economic historians. Positing that it was in the nature of capitalist globalization to favor nations in the most advanced sectors, whose capital in turn underdeveloped the nations in what we used to call the "Third World," dependency writers offered new tools for constructing a critique of neoclassical assumptions. Imperial and North American colonial markets, they argued, did not level out over time; "peripheral" parts of the world had failed to benefit materially from the rise of a global economy to the extent that imperial centers had. Work by numerous economic historians during the 1960s and 1970s seemed to confirm that the early American economy had developed unevenly from within, as well, and had left great numbers of citizens behind. And, in a reversal of Weber's insistence on the power of culture to shape economies, most dependency writers insisted that the economic relationships of markets, exchange, and consumption generated cultural beliefs.[12]

Cultural anthropology also complemented the methodological strategies of economic historians who eschewed neoclassical research during the 1960s and 1970s. The synthetic and historically grounded studies of Eric Wolf, who combined elements of Marxist theory and a sweeping staples approach to the development of "people without history" in the Western Hemisphere, and of Elwin Service, who investigated the economies of far-flung non-European and "premodern" empires and state systems, offered compelling support to North American scholars who distinguished between historically distinct kinds of economic relationships and motivations rather than the uniform exchanging, producing, and consuming individual. Clifford Geertz, whose discursive strategy of "thick description" proposed ways to give scanty bodies of evidence, nontraditional artifacts, and unrecorded information rich interpretive significance, provided still more methodological direction in the search for changing economic patterns. Mary Douglass established that the consumption of worldly goods did not spring from an innate desire to use or own things but was largely socially determined. And, perhaps most provocatively of all, Marshall Sahlins set off a wave of discussion about how a "domestic mode of production," present in earliest human times, disproved neoclassical theories of economic behavior.[13]

11. Fernand Braudel's influence on American scholarship flourished especially after the appearance of his *Capitalism and Material Life, 1400–1800*, trans. Miriam Kochan (New York: Harper and Row, 1973).

12. E.g., Andre Gunder Frank, *World Accumulation, 1492–1789* (New York: Monthly Review Press, 1978).

13. Eric Wolf, *Europe and the People Without History* (Berkeley and Los Angeles: University of California Press, 1983); Elman Service, *Primitive Social Organization: An Evolutionary Perspective* (New York: Random House, 1962); Clifford Geertz, *Local Knowledge: Further Essays in Interpretive Anthropology*

In sociology, Immanuel Wallerstein's "world systems" model was among the most influential historically grounded theories of economic development to challenge neoclassical interpretations for a generation of graduate students. In his ambitious research agenda, Wallerstein set out to correct the Enlightenment focus of Western historians on a European "core," and instead to integrate all major regions of the world into a view that gave equal weight to its "periphery." Braudel's effort to write a total history had resulted in a highly regional and western European compendium that traced only faintly the global connections of the early modern era; Geertz and others offered deep appreciations of only "local knowledge." Wallerstein's promise to economic historians of the 1970s was to explain how European imperial elites more successfully appropriated surplus from subordinate populations than those of China or Africa could have. Wallerstein proposed that the early modern era's world system was based not on the luxury trades—the focus of numerous staples thesis approaches—and consumption at the top of the social ladder, but rather on the ways that productive enterprise was organized and controlled from top to bottom. It soon became clear to many economic historians, however, that Europe remained the dominant agent in this analysis, and that little was yet known about the economic history of production and consumption at the level of a world system. More recently, Andre Gunder Frank has offered a thousand-year perspective on a truly global network of trade, war, and economic diplomacy, and Atlantic-world scholarship (about which more below) has been providing important correctives to Wallerstein's model in recent years.[14]

By the mid-1970s, three kinds of withering criticism against new economic history reinforced the rift between econometricians and historians. One critique emanated from the collective weight of the new social historians, most of whom were attracted to one or more of the theoretical models just outlined and who perceived that economists—in particular, cliometricians—made unwarranted claims about statistical exactitude. Critics of the staples approach, for example, pointed out that many long-range generalizations about colonial America were based not on exacting measures of quantifiable data but on qualitative assessments and uneven numbers in the historical record. The staples approach failed to appreciate fully the diverse sources of capital and credit, fits and starts of productivity, deep regional distinctions, and nonstaples foci of economic activity

(New York: Basic Books, 1983); Mary Douglas and Baron Isherwood, *The World of Goods: Towards an Anthropology of Consumption* (New York: Basic Books, 1979); and Marshall Sahlins, *Stone Age Economics* (Chicago: University of Chicago Press, 1972).

14. Immanuel Wallerstein, *The Modern World System: Capitalist Agriculture and the Origins of the European World-Economy in the Sixteenth Century* (New York: Academic Press, 1974). One of the most direct recent challenges to Wallerstein's approach comes from Andre Gunder Frank, an early dependency theorist, in *(Re)Orient: Global Economy in the Asian Age* (Berkeley and Los Angeles: University of California Press, 2001).

by large numbers of people. Others argued that even plentiful data might fail to explain the causal relationships economic historians should be exploring. Exceptions and twists of events that did not fit the model were ignored in some instances; specific and unique moments were neglected; and the irrationality and misfortunes of particular human choices lay outside the concerns of many cliometricians.[15]

A second critique emerged in the 1970s, as a large number of trained academics began to doubt the virtue of America's efforts to redeem other parts of the world to its own liberal economic character and, by extension, began to question the characterization of the early American economy as capitalist "since the first ships." Some argued against profits-first farm families or rationally calculating merchants; some eschewed the presumed cliometric faith in self-correcting impersonal markets by sharpening their own understanding of markets as systems of social relationships, and capitalism as a historically specific set of economic arrangements. Human agents in marketplaces and market relations, they wrote widely, often practiced "safety-first" production and exchange, lived with customs and cultural constraints, showed aversion to risk, and sought "competency" rather than competition. Scholars investigating the causes and consequences of industrialization in the early national era began to recast our views of when it occurred and how it changed American life, and found that no general model, no overriding set of characteristics, explains industrialization. There were just too many false starts, failures, and roads not taken to posit a model for getting from one point in time to another, too much culture to account for, too much institutional indeterminacy to posit generalized economic growth.[16]

A third development was the weakening of cliometrics at the hands of its own practitioners. Against those who clung to belief in the power of numbers to explain human behavior, many economic historians admitted that rigorous theory could not always be applied to intractable and complicated economic issues. As Lance Davis explained years ago, new economic historians, at their best, explicitly unveiled assumptions and demanded empirical evidence put through the rigors of models that held out the promise of explaining historical change, when other scholars, for the most part, only described it. At their worst, new

---

15. For new social history critiques of the econometric analysis of one issue, slavery, see Paul David et al., *Reckoning with Slavery: A Critical Study in the Quantitative History of American Slavery* (New York: Oxford University Press, 1976); and Herbert Gutman et al., *Slavery and the Numbers Game: A Critique of Time on the Cross* (Urbana: University of Illinois Press, 1975). For a systematic critique of the staples thesis using new social historians' objections, see Marc Egnal, *New World Economies: The Growth of the Thirteen Colonies and Early Canada* (New York: Oxford University Press, 1998). For a sensitive effort to balance econometric analysis and its critics, see Claudia Goldin, *Understanding the Gender Gap: An Economic History of American Women* (New York: Oxford University Press, 1990).

16. For a review of work on colonial North America, see Allan Kulikoff, *From British Peasants to Colonial American Farmers* (Chapel Hill: University of North Carolina Press, 2000), especially chapter 5, and further discussion below.

economic historians created irrelevant models and asked less than useful questions. Others agreed that neoclassical theory and econometric models could not explain economic growth, especially in early modern North America, when there were too many variables and questions, and too few data to quantify human economic behavior. Moreover, few new economic historians had the tools and patience to take on the Herculean task of challenging certain master narratives in economic history about the development of settler communities, the unfolding commerce and agriculture, the rise of banking and manufacturing, and the eventual industrialization of America. Their measurements were mostly useful for only short-run behavior of economic variables; long periods of time introduced problems of reliability and commensurability of data, and the causes of long-term change are always multiple, often social and cultural, and difficult to introduce into quantitative measurements. In short, understanding most historical issues required the toolbox of social scientists more broadly speaking.[17]

By 1985, roughly a century after its professional appearance, the field of economic history seemed to be at a crossroads. A previous generation of historians had created historiographical chaos that introduced new interpretive frameworks, called for more meaningful wholes and consequential interpretations, grappled with shifting lines of class and community, and incorporated peripheries into metropolitan cores, rural places into urban spheres, new settlement into imperial frameworks, and marginal peoples into dominant cultures. By 1985, while many of their fellow historians were being transported into the empire of discourse, culture, and identity studies and the "linguistic turn," a number of economic historians demonstrated the virtues of incorporating new perspectives from economic culture, political economy, regional and comparative studies, as well as both consumer and market revolutions. Most of them started not with impersonal markets and forces but with the human choices, authority, causation, indeterminacy, and negotiation that are less quantifiable and evince messier patterns over time.[18] By the time John J. McCusker and Russell R. Menard's synthetic volume, *The Economy of British America,* appeared in 1985, scholars were partially "answering the call" the authors issued for new research, but they were largely reaching beyond the methodological scope of the volume to revise our

17. E.g., Lance Davis, "'And It Will Never Be Literature'—The New Economic History: A Critique," *Explorations in Entrepreneurial History* 6 (1968): 75–92; and Joel Mokyr, "Introduction: The New Economic History and the Industrial Revolution," in *The British Industrial Revolution: An Economic Perspective,* ed. Joel Mokyr, 2d ed. (Boulder: Westview Press, 1998), 1–127. For an early critique of Robert Fogel's cliometric counterfactual analysis of railroad development from within the discipline, see the work of Fritz Redlich, who argues that instead of asking how railroads could have been dispensed with, a historian would ask why and how they were built in that era. See also Fogel, "'Scientific' History and Traditional History."

18. E.g., Jack P. Greene, "Interpretive Frameworks: The Quest for Intellectual Order in Early American History," *William and Mary Quarterly* 48 (October 1991): 515–30. For a review of "the uses of history" to economists, see Hugh Rockoff, "History and Economics," in Monkkonen, *Engaging the Past,* 48–76. See also McCusker and Menard, *Economy of British America.*

understandings of Atlantic-world commerce, hemispheric cultural encounters, the processes of Creolization, the nature of informal local exchange, the nature of economic federalism, varieties of labor systems, middle grounds, composite farms, moral capitalists, and debtors who were also creditors.

A rich diversity of work in economic history was beginning to make our questions and methodologies explicit, our evidence open to scrutiny, and our claims reasonable, as new economic history had urged us to do. But it also tended to recoil from reducing human behavior to laws, asserting instead that chance, irrationality, error, and the complexity of human behavior require cultural, social, and political assessments of meaning. The 2001 PEAES conference recognized, and the essays in this volume confirm, the need to continue blending conversations across disciplines. A conversation that has been difficult since its inception in the 1880s still has not produced the deep collaboration needed, and the benefits to both sides have thus been modest. But perhaps it is in the conversation itself—and the complicated, negotiated, indeterminate variety of economic lives it discusses—that we will find the most fruitful contributions and potential for more work. Let us review three large chronological areas in which the conversation has continued since 1985.

Colonial North America

By 1985 many of the quantitative characteristics of the colonial and early national economy had been incorporated into narrative surveys, some of which became standard volumes for undergraduate and graduate study. At the center of McCusker and Menard's immensely influential contribution to our understanding of early North America's economic history were the commercial foundations of early settlement and colonial networks within the British empire, including dependence on world prices, investment in shipping and transport and insurance, overseas demand and colonial distribution networks necessary outside the colonies to ensure success, the credit relations of colonists with a wide range of correspondents, and employment and profits made possible by the commerce that produced the ascent toward material comfort. Their massive compendium of scholarly literature was set in a lively narrative accessible to quantifiers and non-quantifiers alike, and while their approach contained unmistakable notes of neoclassical analysis, it permitted room for the social-theory models prevalent during the decades preceding their synthesis. Their rich footnotes cite biographies of prominent merchants, narratives centered on the production and exchange of commodities, work about imperial economies whose mercantile states furthered or restrained particular opportunities, the political economy and economic culture of colonial economic development, and much more. They adopted a central tenet of new economic history by limiting much of their examination to "the production and distribution of wealth," which they considered "the central interest of most economic historians." Above all, their salutary efforts to complicate the staples approach established a model for many economic historians who are still investigating the ways that export-driven demand affected colonists' development, as well as how staples production and exchange steered colonists toward the labor systems they chose and set them on a course of debt and dependency in the empire, from which, many scholars argue, only the Revolution released them. Despite the shortcomings of the staples thesis, McCusker and Menard demonstrated the value of analyzing how the particular staple(s) of a region had profound "forward and backward linkages" to the nature of labor relations, the generation of wealth, communication and distribution systems, the extent of internal development, and much more. For example, it was the inability of northern colonists to produce staples that forced them into more diverse economic activities that may not have been among their initial preferences. Even in particular parts of the Chesapeake, planters may have been discouraged by the fluctuations of staples markets and turned to a mix of crops, livestock, and petty craft production to compensate.[19]

Although McCusker and Menard centered their approach to colonial economic history on the era's commerce in goods and people, their synthesis hardly glimpsed the tremendous outpouring of scholarship in the revitalized and flourishing field of Atlantic-world studies that was gaining momentum. Already, graduate teaching and conference programs offer new chronologies for developments within the early modern era; new journals and intellectual clearinghouses are refocusing thinking about peripheries and frontier, inviting new conceptualizations of power across national and cultural boundaries, and seriously

19. McCusker and Menard, *Economy of British America,* especially the introduction. At the 2001 PEAES conference, participants on the panel "Are We Answering the Call? Assessing the Impact of *The Economy of British America*" were asked to assess the authors' contribution to our understanding of the state of economic history in 1985 and its framework for future scholarship. Panelists included McCusker, Menard, Peter Coclanis, David Hancock, and Lorena Walsh. Hancock's, Walsh's, and Menard's contributions are revised for this volume and include reviews of the literature; Coclanis's essay appears as Peter A. Coclanis, "In Retrospect: McCusker and Menard's *Economy of British America,*" in *Reviews in American History* 30 (June 2002): 183–97. See also John J. McCusker, *Mercantilism and the Economic History of the Early Modern World* (New York: Cambridge University Press, 1997). Surveys that cross disciplines include Edwin J. Perkins, *The Economy of Colonial America* (New York: Columbia University Press, 1980); Stuart Bruchey, *The Roots of American Economic Growth, 1607–1861: An Essay in Social Causation* (New York: Harper and Row, 1965); and Gary M. Walton and James F. Shepherd, *The Economic Rise of Early America* (Cambridge: Cambridge University Press, 1979). Jacob Price's work on the Chesapeake tobacco trade, and the entrepreneurship and imperial connections it engendered, was an important model for a generation of scholars; see, e.g., *Overseas Trade and Traders: Essays on Some Commercial, Financial, and Political Challenges Facing British Atlantic Merchants, 1660–1775,* (New York: Variorum, 1996), and the review of this work in John J. McCusker and Kenneth Morgan, eds., *The Early Modern Atlantic Economy* (New York: Cambridge University Press, 2000), introduction. Another model for Chesapeake studies is Russell R. Menard, "The Tobacco Industry in the Chesapeake Colonies, 1617–71: An Interpretation," *Research in Economic History* 5 (1980): 109–77; and see the literature reviewed in the chapters in this volume by Lorena Walsh, Russell Menard, and David Hancock.

challenging older perspectives about North American emulation of the British economy *and* colonial economic exceptionalism.

Some of this work treats familiar methodologies in imaginative ways. To give but one example, Marc Egnal has incorporated work on the international price swings and foreign demand for North American staples into a larger portrait of merchants, farmers, and planters making decisions about what to produce and how to trade. He combines models of sectoral long swings of development, which were shaped by changes in the terms of trade (the ratio between export prices and import prices) and capital flows throughout large economic units such as the British Empire or an entire colonial system of economic relations, with explanations for the opportunities and constraints of concrete regional, local, and subsistence economies. The consequence, he argues, is to put faces on the economic agents who are otherwise obscured by analyses of goods and prices in the staples approach, to illuminate the ups and downs of markets, and to show not only *what* happened, but *why.*[20]

Other economic historians have embraced Atlantic-world studies because the field has encouraged a more definitive departure from traditional methodologies and subjects of analysis. Responding to the reality of nonnational and antinational developments around the world, and to the "linguistic turn" in academia, they have turned from once dominant analyses of a single empire or region and toward transnational studies and comparative imperial perspectives. Some, following in Wallerstein's footsteps, have turned from a staples focus on dominant particular commodities and toward the more indeterminate realities of Creolization, the informal and illegal qualities of commerce, the shifting forced and free labor systems, or the negotiation of racial and cultural authority in the "world of goods." Emerging work on the relationship of Africa to the Western Hemisphere and the French, Dutch, and Spanish empires will continue to be woven more intricately into the fabric of the British Empire's development. Generally, scholars have not yet seriously challenged our long-standing views of the earlier rise, and then more definitive fading, of the Dutch empire in the Western Hemisphere; France's slower and more limited commercial rise as compared to England's emergence as the premier Western empire and first maturing industrial nation; and Spain's radically different (and much earlier) imperial character. Nor have we done enough to integrate interimperial commercial and cultural connections among the Atlantic-world empires. A rising generation of economic historians is only beginning to understand how the destinies of

---

20. Egnal, *New World Economies,* and his endnotes; Hancock, Chapter 2 in this volume; Thomas M. Doerflinger, *A Vigorous Spirit of Enterprise: Merchants and Economic Development in Revolutionary Philadelphia* (Chapel Hill: University of North Carolina Press, 1986); Cathy Matson, *Merchants and Empire: Trading in Colonial New York* (Baltimore: Johns Hopkins University Press, 1998); and Richard Buel Jr., *In Irons: Britain's Naval Supremacy and the American Revolutionary Economy* (New Haven: Yale University Press, 1998), chapter 1.

people in a broad hemispheric arena of interimperial commerce were intertwined. And as Chapter 2, David Hancock's "Rethinking *The Economy of British America*," explains, although the staples thesis can be claimed as part of the Atlantic-world studies enterprise, very few staples have in fact been studied, and almost never in the broader contexts of state-legislated *and* informal or illicit commerce. Hancock also urges closer attention to the ways we weave culture into our economic history; though essential to historical work, scholars' cultural perspectives are often inadequately grounded in class realities and the negotiation of conflict, and thereby actually ignore the economic experiences of Atlantic-world people, offering as hopelessly fuzzy a view of historical agency as some investigations of staples exporting do.[21]

Atlantic-world studies have also spurred new work about how colonists created investment capital, formed partnerships, lived with risk and debt, shared information, and initiated brokerage and insurance arrangements. Clearly, interregional, mutually reinforcing exchanges among families and local communities complicated North Americans' involvement in multidimensional and interimperial networks of commodities and credit throughout the Atlantic world. These networks thickened during the colonial era, especially after the 1720s, when consortia of colonial merchants, as well as the urban populations that supported commerce, became stronger and more independent of British merchants and manufacturers. New studies are looking at long-neglected connections among coastal traders in North America, West Indian merchants, and the markets of local populations that geared production toward exporting. Awaiting further—

21. The outpouring of Atlantic-world scholarship defies summary. Readers might start with the many resources available on the website of Harvard University's International Seminar on the History of the Atlantic World, www.fas.harvard.edu/~atlantic; David Armitage, "Three Concepts of Atlantic History," in *The British Atlantic World, 1500–1800*, ed. David Armitage and Michael J. Braddick, (New York: Palgrave, 2002), 11–30; Nicholas Canny, "Writing Atlantic History, or Reconfiguring the History of Colonial British America," *Journal of American History* 86 (December 1999), 1093–114; David Hancock, *Citizens of the World: London Merchants and the Integration of the British Atlantic Community, 1735–1785* (New York: Cambridge University Press, 1995); Egnal, *New World Economies;* the essays, in a forthcoming special issue of the *William and Mary Quarterly*, by Alec Dunn, Michelle Craig, Brooke Hunter, Sherry Johnson, and Evelyn Jennings; and Chapter 2 in this volume. For a recent study of the seventeenth-century Atlantic world, see April Lee Hatfield, *Atlantic Virginia: Intercolonial Relations in the Seventeenth Century* (Philadelphia: University of Pennsylvania Press, 2004), especially chapter 2; and for comparing empires, see e.g., Stanley L. Engerman, "France, Britain, and the Economic Growth of Colonial America," in McCusker and Morgan, *Early Modern Atlantic Economy*, chapter 9. Mary Douglas popularized the term "world of goods"; see citation above. Perhaps the most revisionist areas of work on the Atlantic world include transatlantic slavery and New World consumption; see, e.g., John Thornton, *Africa and Africans in the Making of the Atlantic World, 1400–1680* (New York: Cambridge University Press, 1998); John Thornton, "Teaching Africa in an Atlantic Perspective," *Radical History Review* (2000): 123–34; David Eltis, *The Rise of African Slavery in the Americas* (New York: Cambridge University Press, 2000); and David Eltis, Stephen D. Behrendt, David Richardson, and Herbert S. Klein, eds., *The Trans-Atlantic Slave Trade: A Database on CD-ROM* (Cambridge: Cambridge University Press, 1999). Compare to early work cited in notes 10 and 15 above, and other recent work cited in notes 24, 35, 41, 52, and 74 below.

and much needed—study are the ways that merchants diverted capital from trade to real estate development and manufacturing. At the PEAES conference in 2001, Peter Coclanis's paper also urged economic historians to go beyond reworking old issues and ask new questions with a range of fresh theoretical and method-ological models that could be applied to the painstakingly compiled data and inventories begun in earnest during the heyday of new economic history.[22]

The profoundly consequential impact of early West Indies and Latin American development on North American labor, commerce, technology, and business relations is becoming ever more important to economic historians in recent years, especially in comparative perspective. More particularly, we have new studies on the mutual interdependencies of the British Empire's twenty-three colonies in the Western Hemisphere, and scholars have shifted focus dramatically toward crosscurrents of exchange, Creolization, and blended economic cultures.[23] A few researchers have extended and modified the work of Eric Williams, which aroused heated discussion about the causal connections between Caribbean pros-perity, slavery and the slave trade, and the English Industrial Revolution. New work linking competitive North American merchants in the sugar trade to con-tinental and British commercial crises widens the sphere of analysis and offers fresh perspectives on the long-standing Williams thesis, as does work on other commodities. Another exciting vein involves the reexamination of slavery in transatlantic perspective in light of concerted efforts to compare slave experi-ences in various parts of the Western Hemisphere, as well as new databases of transatlantic slave voyages and landed migrations.[24]

22. Ibid., and Coclanis, "In Retrospect," and the reviews of important contributions in Daniel Vickers, "The Northern Colonies: Economy and Society, 1600–1775," *CEHUS,* 231, 235, 238.

23. See, e.g., the summary of this scholarship in *The Oxford History of the British Empire,* gen. ed. William Roger Lewis, especially vol. 1, *The Origins of Empire, British Overseas Enterprise to the Close of the Seventeenth Century,* ed. Nicholas Canny (New York: Oxford University Press, 1998), and vol. 2, *The Eighteenth Century,* ed. P. J. Marshall (New York: Oxford University Press, 1999); John Coatsworth, "Notes on the Comparative Economic History of Latin America and the United States," in *Development and Underdevelopment in America,* ed. Walther L. Bernecker and Hans Werner Tobler (Berlin: Walter de Gruyter, 1993), 10–30; Barry W. Higman, "Economic and Social Development of the British West Indies, from Settlement to ca. 1850," in *CEHUS,* chapter 7, and a comprehensive bib-liography down to 1994 in *CEHUS,* 433–37; and, for an example of the scholarship, John J. McCusker, "The Business of Distilling in the Old World and the New World During the Seventeenth and Eigh-teenth Centuries: The Rise of a New Enterprise and Its Connection with Colonial America," in McCusker and Morgan, *Early Modern Atlantic Economy,* chapter 8. McCusker notes that this early in-dustry might benefit from further analysis of its labor relations, refining processes, capital inputs, and business strategies. For a recent collection that places the commodity of sugar in Atlantic-world perspective, see Stuart B. Schwartz, ed., *Tropical Babylons: Sugar and the Making of the Atlantic World, 1450–1680* (Chapel Hill, University of North Carolina Press, 2004).

24. Eric Williams, *Capitalism and Slavery* (Chapel Hill: University of North Carolina Press, 1944); Walter Minchinton, "Abolition and Emancipation: Williams, Drescher, and the Continuing Debate," in *West Indies Accounts,* ed. Roderick A. McDonald (Barbados: University Press of the West Indies, 1996), chapter 13; Francois Crouzet, "America and the Crisis of the British Imperial Economy," in McCusker and Morgan, *Early Modern Atlantic Economy,* chapter 11; articles by Peter Kolchin and

The estimates of aggregate colonial per capita income and wealth derived by new economic historians during the 1960s and 1970s suggested a steady
upward slope in colonial economic growth after the earliest years of settlement,
and often included generalizations about the quickening pace of this growth in
the final colonial decades. Although by no means as rapid as the growth beginning in the 1820s to 1840s, colonial income and wealth rose appreciably. Percentages of growth by decade or generation varied from scholar to scholar, but
together figures bolstered the inescapable generalization that as agricultural
and craft productivity expanded, and as market and information networks grew,
colonial North Americans could boast of the most rapidly growing internal
economy in the Anglophone world by the 1750s, if not earlier. Contemporary
observations added colorful ratification of unfolding material improvement and
the relative absence of scarcities and endemic poverty in North America. After
years of debate among economic historians about the effects of mercantile legislation on colonial growth, few scholars after the 1970s disputed that colonial
trade with foreign islands and countries, expanding agricultural production, or
experiments with manufactures had been stymied very much by official imperial regulations. Most scholars would now readily admit that the Navigation
Acts were virtually unnecessary to limit colonial manufacturing (aside from the
ideological goal of asserting colonial subordination to imperial goals), since the
abundance of land, and the scarcity of capital and labor, steered colonists into
agricultural production anyway. But beyond generalizations about relatively
healthy rising per capita incomes, which implied a gathering momentum of more
goods for more people, could this work explain how colonists marshaled existing resources and overcame economic limitations to development, and could it
illuminate the nature of colonial growth more particularly?

Recent investigations have proceeded along two lines. One research
strategy involves refining and revising some of the boldest estimates of colonial
income and welfare, while affirming the importance of knowing something
about general trends in economic growth. These refinements often come from
economists who previously helped build the foundation of incomes and wealth
analysis, labor productivity, and estimates of colonial living standards. Starting

---

Michael J. Jarvis in a special issue of the *William and Mary Quarterly* on "Slaveries in the Atlantic World,"
vol. 59 (July 2002): 551–54, 585–622, and their citations to important new work concerning slavery in
Atlantic-world perspective; S. Max Edelson, "Planting the Lowcountry: Agricultural Enterprise and
Economic Experience in the Lower South, 1695–1785" (Ph.D. diss., Johns Hopkins University, 1998);
and Ira Berlin and Philip D. Morgan, *Cultivation and Culture: Labor and the Shaping of Slave Life in the
Americas* (Charlottesville: University Press of Virginia, 1993). See also Eltis, *Rise of African Slavery in the
Americas;* Eltis et al., *Trans-Atlantic Slave Trade,* a machine-readable database on CD of about 27,000
slaving voyages compiled at Harvard University; Joseph E. Inikori and Stanley L. Engerman, eds., *The
Atlantic Slave Trade: Effects on Economies, Societies, and Peoples in Africa, the Americas, and Europe* (Durham:
Duke University Press, 1992); and Robert E. Desrochers Jr., "Slave-For-Sale Advertisements and Slav-
ery in Massachusetts, 1704–1781," *William and Mary Quarterly* 59 (July 2002), 623–64.

with the admission that information about prices, household incomes, population, and capital investment is skimpy at best before the 1820s, these scholars nevertheless believe that cautious estimates of a gross domestic product (GDP) can tell us much about the contours of colonial growth. In the face of mounting evidence that standards of living rose during the colonial era, we still do not know much about who enjoyed the benefits of economic maturation or how the rates of growth compared from place to place. But refinements continue. For example, new work shows that the maturing mid-Atlantic coastal towns and frontier settlements, where land values rose rapidly, seem to have experienced the most rapid rate of growth, but that the "starting point" of development for frontier families was starkly lower than for well-endowed families moving into commercial centers. In addition, the proceedings of a 1995 conference organized by John McCusker, "The Economy of Early British America: The Domestic Sector," suggest that we should consider whether we have incorporated the shifting influences of economic culture, demography, epidemiology, and geography into our portraits of growth. The conference participants called on us to be more modest in our claims and to include consequential modifying variables in our work. An essay by Lance Davis and Stanley Engerman concluded that economic growth was "slow, but positive," probably slower than the previous optimistic estimates, but nevertheless at a rate faster than the mother country's during most of the eighteenth century. Other long-range studies, such as those on nutrition and its effects on height, longevity, and relationship to living standards, are just beginning. Elsewhere, Marc Egnal argues that we can allow for frequent moments of economic uncertainty even as we also discern patterns in overall per capita growth, and at a quickening pace after 1740. Still other researchers believe that there is hope for using probate records wisely. Although these records are not reliable guides to income, savings, or investment trends over large populations, they contain valuable information about the wealth of certain kinds of colonists late in their lives, and can be used to compare similar places at different times or different places at the same time. If one allows that portions of property are hidden from view, or bequeathed "silently" without stated rationales, we can still create valuable snapshots of colonial wealth, as Alice Hanson Jones did for the single year 1774.[25]

25. Some of the essays for this 1995 conference at the Huntington Library were revised for "The Economy of British North America," a special issue of the *William and Mary Quarterly,* 3d ser., 56 (January 1999); in the issue, see, Lance Davis and Stanley L. Engerman, "The Economy of British North America: Miles Traveled, Miles Still to Go," 9–22, quote at 21; Robert E. Gallman, "Can We Build National Accounts for the Colonial Period of American History?" 23–30. Also see Carole Shammas, *The Pre-Industrial Consumer in England and America* (New York: Oxford University Press, 1990); Robert E. Gallman and John J. Wallis, eds., *American Economic Growth and Standards of Living Before the Civil War* (Chicago: University of Chicago Press, 1992); McCusker and Menard, *Economy of British America,* 52–57; Egnal, *New World Economies,* introduction. On probate inventories, see Carole Shammas, "A New Look at Long-Term Wealth Inequality in the United States," *American Historical*

A second approach challenges the usefulness—and even the validity—of income and wealth estimates. Starting with the findings of community studies done during the 1960s and 1970s, which discovered a Malthusian crisis of population growth in numerous coastal colonial settlements that in turn delayed or stymied the economic advancement of young people by the fourth and fifth generations of settlement, econometricians' estimates of a relatively steady rise in colonial growth seem overly optimistic. Some social historians emphasized the dire consequences of demographic "crowding" for economic expectations and opportunities, while others found a noticeable rise in landlessness in New England and mid-Atlantic regions, stark inequalities of land ownership in southern and frontier regions, and a deepening chasm between the rich and poor in urban centers. These uneven results of colonization were reinforced by studies showing the variety of colonists' experiences within families or at various points in their individual life cycles, which in turn militated against reliable estimates of a GDP or per capita income. These latter were, in any case, often based on insufficient census or tax data, or on individual account books, correspondence, and probate inventories, which yielded little more than local snapshots of involvement in international trade or the domestic economy. Still other economic historians began to doubt whether wealth and income estimates could ever illuminate important dimensions of consumption, production, diet, foreign demand, life expectancy, family size, or gender roles. Nor can estimates of total domestic production tell us what we want to know about the ways that exchange and commodities affect political stability, elite formation, cultural distinctions, and family dynamics.[26]

Critical economic historians increasingly viewed these estimates as murky statistical averages that obscured the varieties of colonial economic experience, including time people spent on activities that produced no income, shared neighborhood labor and housework, smuggling, or informal market activities that added substantially to family incomes. Moreover, wealth and income estimates could not account for those whose wealth was so insignificant that it was unassessed, untaxed, or unnoticed, or whose condition put them outside British

---

Review 98 (April 1993): 412–32; Galenson, "Settlement and Growth of the Colonies," 189–93, 421–22. On wealth, see Alice Hanson Jones, *Wealth of a Nation to Be: The American Colonies on the Eve of the Revolution* (New York: Columbia University Press, 1980); Gloria L. Main and Jackson T. Main, "The Red Queen in New England?" *William and Mary Quarterly,* 3d ser., 56 (January 1999): 121–50; and on stature, Richard H. Steckel, "Nutritional Status in the Colonial American Economy," *William and Mary Quarterly,* 3d ser., 56 (January 1999): 31–53. For an especially creative use of recalcitrant source materials, and sensitive attention to the reservations pointed out in this paragraph, see Lorena Walsh, "Summing the Parts: Implications for Estimating Chesapeake Output and Income Subregionally," *William and Mary Quarterly,* 3d ser., 56 (January 1999): 53–95, and Walsh, Chapter 4 in this volume.

26. Reviews of this work may be found in Kulikoff, *From British Peasants to Colonial American Farmers,* 236–37, 350–51; and Stuart Bruchey, *Enterprise: The Dynamic Economy of a Free People,* (Cambridge: Harvard University Press, 1990), 64–65, 96–104.

definitions of "citizenship." Even when economic historians try to include slaves and Native Americans as part of their overall income estimates, they often are undecided about whether unfree labor or noncitizens should be taken into account in measuring per capita income. Disagreements arise about whether slaves should be included in per capita income measures or as part of the total capital of the colonies and reckoned as capital costs. When writing about another large North American population—farmers—economic historians have made only slight advances since the 1970s in understanding how farmers divided their productive time between field work, craft production and repair, neighborhood by-employments, and market travel. Yet, since slaves and small farmers (including small planters) made up the overwhelming majority of producing people in colonial America, our lack of understanding is consequential indeed. For example, anywhere in North America that slavery excluded large numbers of forcibly laboring people—sometimes the majority—from earning, saving, or investing, the concept of economic "growth" becomes problematic. Or, in the case of the free farming population, economic historians now concede that growing per capita incomes are not necessarily linked to increasing market participation, for many—some would argue, most—farm families strove for individual and collective "improvement" or "competence." In short, the scholarship of the past two decades confirms that the economic lives of early Americans were far more richly textured and qualified than measurements of the total domestic production or per capita wealth can illuminate.[27]

Economic historians' healthy self-critical regard for the limitations of sweeping wealth and income studies has spurred new interest in smaller units of analysis, including *regions* in North America, and especially in comparative perspective. Regional studies tend to give us a more nuanced appreciation of differences across social strata, interest groups, rural and urban settings, or frontier and coastal places than imperial or national ones have. Some studies remain highly synthetic analyses of large geographic regions in the British Western Hemisphere, while others look at more particular parts of economies—for example, the pace of livestock accumulation, the amounts of consumable goods available in regional markets, the activities of retailers, or trends in real estate ownership and transfer. The most revisionist new work involving colonial regions is beginning to redraw traditional geographical boundaries. Even analyses of probate, population, and land records that follow old methodologies show important new patterns of human choices and economic opportunities when put in comparative regional

27. Ibid. Although there is extensive fruitful work on the economic history of North American Native Americans, the British and European Caribbean, and the transatlantic slave trade, space constraints make it impossible to include much of this work in the present volume. For reviews of these topics with respect to economic issues, see, e.g., Neal Salisbury, "The History of Native Americans from Before the Arrival of the Europeans and Africans Until the American Civil War," in *CEHUS*, 1–52, 403–7; Higman, "Economic and Social Development of the British West Indies," 297–336, 432–37.

perspective.[28] Finally, economic historians reexamining long-standing general-izations about colonial regions have offered startling alternative explanations of economic conditions in them. For example, new social historians' advocacy of "declension" in New England—a prolonged phase of agricultural difficulties, rising landlessness and poverty, and "crowding" in the oldest settlement areas—is giving way to findings about adaptive and sometimes vibrant shipbuilding, coastal and West Indies carrying trade, profitable fisheries, creative mixed farm-ing, and innovative accommodations to labor shortages in a larger region en-compassing coastal and frontier areas. In comparative perspective, New England's regional economy no longer seems to be the unmitigated agricultural failure that scholars formerly posited.[29]

Analyses that encompass even more territory—from Maine to north-ern Delaware—show that economic development can be even more dynamic and diverse, especially when compared to the equally large territory of southern colonies. Mixed farming produced a variety of raw materials and semifinished commodities. Diversifying agriculture created a demand for a variety of services and skills from artisans, shopkeepers, boatmen, auctioneers, brokers, and many others. Farming blended with craft manufacturing in households and small shops, which in turn supported a rising number of merchants who mobilized local capital, family connections, and long-distance credit relations for colonial commerce. Regional shopkeepers kept accounts and acted as intermediaries for farmers who visited nearby towns to exchange goods in public markets or trav-eled to more distant cities to deal directly with merchants' agents. Even where rural produce was consumed primarily at home and neighbors shared labor and tools, markets drew small producers into a diversified economy of commerce and manufactures. Far from accepting older arguments about the waste and chaos of colonial northern farms, recent work shows ambitious farm families choosing to expand and develop landholdings and to produce import substitutes. Textiles production, furniture making, dairying, and a host of other by-employments rose steadily in southeastern Pennsylvania, northern Delaware, lowland New Jersey, and parts of the Hudson River valley, where there was substantial grazing and

28. E.g., Marc Egnal, *Divergent Paths: How Culture and Institutions Have Shaped North American Growth* (New York: Oxford University Press, 1996); and articles by Lorena S. Walsh, Gloria L. Main, and Jackson T. Main, in the forum "Toward a History of the Standard of Living in British North America," in *William and Mary Quarterly* 45 (January 1988): 116–70.

29. Phyllis Whitman Hunter, *Purchasing Identity in the Atlantic World: Massachusetts Merchants, 1670–1780* (Ithaca: Cornell University Press, 2001); David Meyer, *The Roots of American Industrialization* (Baltimore: Johns Hopkins University Press, 2003); Margaret E. Newell, "The Birth of New England in the Atlantic Economy: From Its Beginning to 1770," in *Engines of Enterprise: An Economic History of New England*. ed. Peter Temin (Cambridge: Harvard University Press, 2000), chapter 1; Gloria L. Main and Jackson T. Main, "Economic Growth and the Standard of Living in Southern New England, 1640–1774," *Journal of Economic History* 48 (March 1988): 27–46; Main and Main, "Red Queen in New England?" 121–50; and Innes, *Creating the Commonwealth,* which, however, exaggerates the role of rural "industries" and fails to distinguish different parts of New England.

dairying, saw and grist milling, potash and pearl ash production, coopering and shingle making, and other farm by-production.[30]

These formidable recent accomplishments complicate our view of northern regional development before the Revolution. But more remains to be done. We still do not know, for example, whether rising land values in most northern areas originated in higher agricultural yields, deliberate farm improvement strategies, the growing density of social relations and marketplaces, or some combination of these endeavors. Moreover, we continue to lump many discrete areas into one "North," and we have not yet fully compared New England's development to the mid-Atlantic colonies of New Jersey and nonurbanized parts of New York and Pennsylvania. We know little in comparative perspective about extractive and processing industries emerging by the eighteenth century; ties to English capital and manufactured goods; dependence on the West Indies for trade and credit; or the rates of diversified agricultural production resulting in larger exportable surpluses. Some work, for example, emphasizes that the mid-Atlantic region experienced not rising freehold occupancy of the land but increased tenancy and landlessness; even then, annual rents were relatively modest and credit relatively easy to obtain compared to Europe, and a large number of commercial farmers were able to diversify farm production by hiring occasional labor and relying on family members to work, much as New Englanders did.[31]

Many of the distinctions marking different parts of the colonial "North" were present in the "South" as well, although scholars are only beginning to understand their extent and social consequences. Divisions within the South such as the Chesapeake, the lower South, the southern backcountry, and the far southern frontier may have been as different from each other as from the North overall. For generations, scholars have emphasized the distinctions between the North's nurturing of indigenous northern mercantile elites (and their middling commercial peers), who controlled the trade of diverse commodities in coastal, West Indies, and transatlantic networks and who commanded ready access

---

30. In addition to sources in note 31 below, see the extensive summary of literature and bibliography in Allan Kulikoff, *The Agrarian Origins of American Capitalism* (Charlottesville: University Press of Virginia, 1992); see also Mary M. Schweitzer, *Custom and Contract: Household, Government, and the Economy in Colonial Pennsylvania* (New York: Columbia University Press, 1987); and Daniel Vickers, "Northern Colonies," 209–48, which argues less enthusiastically for the elasticity of New England farming strategies. For comparison with nineteenth-century analyses, see the market revolution discussion below.

31. E.g., Paul G. E. Clemens, *The Atlantic Economy and Colonial Maryland's Eastern Shore: From Tobacco to Grain* (Ithaca: Cornell University Press, 1980), and Richard Dunn, "After Tobacco: The Slave Labour Pattern on a Large Chesapeake Grain-and-Livestock Plantation in the Early Nineteenth Century," in McCusker and Morgan, *Early Modern Atlantic Economy,* chapter 12; Philip D. Morgan, *Slave Counterpoint: Black Culture in the Eighteenth-Century Chesapeake and Lowcountry* (Chapel Hill: University of North Carolina Press, 1998); Lorena S. Walsh, "Plantation Management in the Chesapeake, 1620–1820," *Journal of Economic History* 49 (June 1989): 393–406; and Ronald Hoffman, *Princes of Ireland, Planters of Maryland: A Carroll Saga, 1500–1782* (Chapel Hill: University of North Carolina Press, 2000), 122–24, 263–65.

to plenty of British capital and credit by the end of the seventeenth century, on the one hand, and the South's staples and plantation dependencies of growing British debt, increasing Scottish factoring, and heavy reliance on importation, on the other. Although certain Chesapeake and Carolina families certainly grew wealthier—their West Indies peers even more so—the commission and rural stores systems prevented the maturation of urban life and larger, more diverse commercial communities. But new work, including that presented in Russell Menard's and Lorena Walsh's essays in this volume, demonstrates an increasingly productive countryside, the rise of resident trading communities, and profitable independent southern maritime activity. The Chesapeake, studied at first as a classic staples exporting region, where tobacco production dominated the regional economy during the seventeenth century, now presents itself as a more diversified area. First in Maryland and then in Virginia, the transition from tobacco to cultivation of cereals was accomplished through the aggressive reorganization of slave labor, while investment in shipbuilding and shipping may have grown as rapidly there as it did in New England.[32]

The lower South, including colonial South Carolina and Georgia, was more clearly set apart from the colonial North than the Chesapeake was. It abutted large Spanish and French settlements as well as fiercely resistant Native American populations, and its slave-labor system became a defining characteristic of economic life more rapidly after initial settlement than in the Chesapeake. Nevertheless, scholars have begun asking how much and how quickly this region's economy truly developed. An older argument, offered most notably by James Shepherd and Gary Walton, established that declining shipping costs—the result of larger ships, smaller crews, shorter turnaround times, and more efficient management of direct trading routes—accounted for much of the rising wealth of southern planters; at the same time, closer ties of dependence on foreign markets for both imports and exports marked the "Carolina country." R. C. Nash's recent studies confirm parts of this picture of a staples-dominated region of rice and indigo production propped up by contrasts between the legendary wealth in the hands of a few and intensive slavery for the black majority, and in which the region's exports to Britain rose to triple the per capita export values of northern colonies during the eighteenth century.[33] David Carlton and Peter Coclanis's

32. Ibid., and the discussion and notes in Walsh, Chapter 4, and Menard, Chapter 3, in this volume.

33. In addition to sources in note 31 above, see James F. Shepherd and Gary M. Walton, *Shipping, Maritime Trade, and the Economic Development of Colonial North America* (New York: Cambridge University Press, 1972); R. C. Nash, "The Organization of Trade and Finance in the Atlantic Economy: Britain and South Carolina, 1670–1775," in *Money, Trade, and Power: The Evolution of Colonial South Carolina's Plantation Society,* ed. Jack P. Greene, Rosemary Brana-Shute, and Randy J. Sparks (Columbia: University of South Carolina Press, 2001), 74–107; R. C. Nash, "The South Carolina Indigo Industry, the Atlantic Economy, and the Slave Plantation System, 1745–1782," paper given at PEAES Conference, Philadelphia, 2001; Jack P. Greene, "Colonial South Carolina: An Introduction," in Greene et al.,

model of "path dependence" also shows that after an initial phase of profitable investment and export, the southern rice country became locked into dependence on foreign markets and inflexible investment in land and slaves rather than new technologies, transportation improvement, and urbanization.[34]

This argument for the lower South's distinctiveness is weakening as new studies document how small farmers and planters expanded southern agriculture, as planters responded to growing West Indies demand for cheap foodstuffs and tried to meet the expanding European demand for rice. Moreover, many studies demonstrate that periods of success and failure were unevenly experienced depending on whether we look at the tobacco area around Charles Town, an indigo plantation further south, or networks of rice fields. The picture of staples exporting grows more complicated as we learn more about regional production for household consumption; local exchange between small farms and plantations may have accounted for as much as 80 percent of all value exchanged, a figure comparable to many other British colonies. New work is also discovering that although international prices and demand for commodities continued to be important, local elites also could play a commanding role in shaping economic opportunities, depending on the outcomes of agricultural expansion, regional exchange of goods, currency, and internal improvements. Moreover, many planters "crossed over" into the commercial activities of exporting, organizing shipping services, and shipbuilding.[35]

Economic life at the geographical margins of colonial North America, from the most northerly to the most southerly frontiers, has come under more intense scrutiny of late. Although many studies confirm the conclusions of older works, which saw frontiers as the province of specialized fur trappers, aggressive investors, trains of packhorses, and sparse settlement that served as the advance

Money, Trade, and Power, vii–xiii; Coclanis, "In Retrospect"; and McCusker and Morgan, *Early Modern Atlantic Economy,* introduction.

34. David L. Carlton and Peter A. Coclanis, *The South, the Nation, and the World: Perspectives on Southern Economic Development* (Charlottesville: University of Virginia Press, 2003).

35. For a review of important work on the tobacco, rice, and indigo economies, in addition to notes 33 and 34 above, see Bruchey, *Enterprise,* 74–86; Stephen G. Hardy, "Colonial South Carolina's Rice Industry and the Atlantic Economy: Patterns of Trade, Shipping, and Growth, 1715–1775," in Greene, et al., *Money, Trade, and Power,* 108–40; Russell Menard, "Slavery, Economic Growth, and Revolutionary Ideology in the South Carolina Lowcountry," in *The Economy of Early America: The Revolutionary Period, 1763–1790,* ed. Ronald Hoffman, John J. McCusker, Russell R. Menard, and Peter Albert (Charlottesville: University Press of Virginia, 1988), 244–74; Peter A. Coclanis, *The Shadow of a Dream: Economic Life and Death in the South Carolina Low Country, 1670–1920* (New York: Oxford University Press, 1989); Russell R. Menard, "Financing the Lowcountry Export Boom: Capital and Growth in Early South Carolina," *William and Mary Quarterly* 51 (1994): 659–76; Joyce E. Chaplin, *An Anxious Pursuit: Agricultural Innovation and Modernity in the Lower South, 1730–1815* (Chapel Hill: University of North Carolina Press, 1993); and the ongoing work of another PEAES conference presenter, Laura Kamoie, "Three Generations of Planter-Businessmen: The Tayloes, Slave Labor, and Entrepreneurialism in Virginia, 1710–1830" (Ph.D. diss., College of William and Mary, 1999). Compare to work cited in notes 20 and 24 above.

guard of risk taking, new work also demonstrates that frontier people quickly formed communities and became dependent on outside forms of credit and necessities. As migrants cleared farms, their land values rose slowly, and initial poverty was mitigated by the successful marketing of small surpluses of cereals or timber products to eastern areas, confirming that the self-sufficient family farm, if it ever existed, was not a reality of frontier development. In many southern backcountry areas, stretching from western Maryland into Virginia, through the Carolina piedmont and small farming areas of western South Carolina and Georgia, slavery was at least initially less important to the economy than family farming on relatively small landholdings. Subsisting on livestock and grain production, farmers also sometimes produced hemp, tobacco, flax, and timber products to market to the East. The informalities of exchange and credit developed where institutions did not yet reach and populations were thin; and although European imperial expectations were attenuated by pragmatic local concerns, the economic efforts of settlers at the outposts of empire were often tied to coastal ports and the Atlantic world's commerce.[36]

Most scholars agree that given scarce labor and shortages of capital, the abundance of *land* became colonists' most important economic resource. Certainly this important difference from European economies has bolstered arguments for American exceptionalism. But the pre-1960s assessment of colonial agriculture as wasteful no longer finds such wide acceptance. Although colonists were not remarkably efficient and their technology changed very little before 1800, there is ample evidence that colonists grew or extracted from the land the commodities that yielded about 80 percent of their overall productivity. Indeed, colonists enjoyed a relatively wider distribution of landholdings, which were rising in value at faster rates, than did England or Europe. The hiving off of new townships and counties, and speculative investments in land to the west of original settlements, have been investigated in great detail and found in every colonial region. Whatever ideological or econometric arguments we employ, the most important source of capital for land and farm investment was generated by small farmers and local craft producers. Indeed, probably two-thirds of colonial householders owned and worked their own land in fee simple by 1750, and land ownership remained high even where tenancy grew. In short, recent work has affirmed the vital importance of land and agriculture to all colonial regions and refined our reasons for believing this was so. The most recent work is taking these findings a step further by showing how agriculture was also inextricably

36. Representative works include Vickers, "Northern Colonies," 214–18, and his bibliography; Martin Bruegel, *Farm, Shop, Landing: The Rise of a Market Society in the Hudson Valley, 1780–1860* (Durham: Duke University Press, 2002); Daniel H. Usner Jr., *Indians, Settlers, and Slaves in a Frontier Exchange Economy: The Lower Mississippi Valley Before 1783* (Chapel Hill: University of North Carolina Press, 1992); Wilma A. Dunaway, *The First American Frontier: The Transition to Capitalism in Southern Appalachia, 1700–1860* (Chapel Hill: University of North Carolina Press, 1996).

tied to commerce, labor systems, market networking, demography, technology, and shifting cultural boundaries.

For many years, Russell Menard has provided some of the most deftly crafted analyses of colonial agriculture, combining elements of the best kind of new economic history with sensitivity to historical argument. His chapter in this volume, "Colonial America's Mestizo Agriculture," reminds us that North Americans' close engagement with agriculture and its related services accounts for most gains in colonial wealth—however we measure it—and that surpluses often became available for exchange once family needs were met. In the past two decades we have learned much more about colonists' strategies for expanding this surplus when possible, including crop diversification, agricultural improvements, higher yields, and varying degrees of integration with commerce and processing industries before the Revolution. Using the rubric of a "mestizo" agricultural economy that blended Native American, European, and African techniques, skills, and responses to the environment, Menard paints a sophisticated portrait of agricultural maturation and offers a conceptual framework for the coming generation's research. Menard's work may be seen as part of a larger creative enterprise undertaken by numerous scholars to produce a more nuanced and sophisticated portrait of agriculture, including work on the Creolization of farming and frontier agriculture in numerous North American quarters, the "frontier exchange economy" presented in Daniel Usner's study of the lower Mississippi Valley, and the tasking and provision grounds in southern and Caribbean economies. This scholarship confirms that in every region, farmers and planters were innovative, hard working, increasingly savvy about soil and weather conditions, and open to growing new crops and raising new animals—whether because they put more land under the plow, worked harder, expanded their available labor, or had good market and meteorological luck. It demonstrates, as well, that agricultural productivity in turn generated demand for more ships and shipping services in every region, albeit unevenly over time and place, as well as more tools, containers, credit, storage, and hired hands. Studies suggesting relatively little innovation have been largely replaced with others showing productivity gains and highly motivated agricultural producers in thickening markets.[37]

Despite these important recent contributions, economic historians' view of land and agriculture from Maine to Georgia is still hazy. We still do not know

37. For this and the previous paragraph see reviews of literature in Menard, Chapter 3 in this volume; Vickers, "Northern Colonies"; Galenson, " Settlement and Growth of the Colonies," 135–52; and Bruchey, *Enterprise,* 98–101, 560–61, 160, 573. On the related theme of land investment, see Winifred B. Rothenberg, "The Market and Massachusetts Farmers, 1750–1855," *Journal of Economic History* 41 (June 1981): 283–314; and Gloria L. Main, "The Standard of Living in Southern New England, 1640–1773," *William and Mary Quarterly* 45 (January 1988) : 124–34. On land ownership, see Stephen Innes, "Review of *Inequality in Early America,* ed. Carla Gardina Pestana and Sharon V. Salinger," *Journal of Interdisciplinary History* 31 (Winter 2001): 468–69; Egnal, *New World Economies.* Compare to work cited in notes 47 and 48 below.

much about how families saved for farm investment, improved existing farms, or started up new businesses adjacent to farming communities. Numerous histories narrate rapid population increases that offset productivity gains, falling foreign prices for staples and disruptive wars, and the ill fortune of families that became prosperous over two generations and then sank into poverty—all of which challenge generalizations about rising per capita income and wealth based on huge aggregates of people and fragile data. But we know relatively little about the strategies agriculturalists used to expand production to meet new demand for their commodities during economic upswings—whether it was mainly by using more land, having larger families and more slaves to work the land, striving to increase yields, distributing economic burdens within communities, or a host of other possible strategies. Although we know something about rising productivity in some quarters, we know very little about what proportion of these goods stayed in local economies compared to the proportion being exported to meet rising foreign demand. Where was agriculture becoming more commercialized, and how might it have been facilitated by shifting strategies of exchange, credit, and payment? Were shifting proportions of land, labor, and capital used in farming? If so, did these inputs outstrip population growth, and thus create the basic conditions for a rising standard of living?

Answers to some of these questions may come from deeper understanding of colonial *labor*. Allan Kulikoff's recent work on rural North America summarizes much of what we know about family and community strategies for acquiring and transforming land holdings. A wealth of research demonstrates that, compared to conditions in Europe, colonists enjoyed relatively favorable environmental conditions and relatively unfettered access to abundant land. But the path toward becoming "yeomen" was bumpy, and farming was largely a "mixed enterprise." Independent landholders produced for distant sale as well as for home use and local exchange; a neighborhood borrowing system, through which farm households became mutually interdependent and leaned on strong community traditions, persisted for generations. As Kulikoff explains, separation of North Americans into free, servant, and slave populations obscures the considerably more complicated configurations of labor in every region. In the South, indentured servitude did not uniformly disappear as slavery took root, and small planters spread westward under various agricultural arrangements; in the mid-Atlantic, servants and cottagers were often as numerous as free laborers, while slavery flourished in particular areas; and in New England, poor landless people formed a pool of marginalized labor that could be hired on family farms and in craft shops. As Daniel Vickers has found, although tenancy rose, it benefited not only northern landowners who wished to develop their holdings but also renters, who gained a "measurable if qualified degree of independence." In all regions, thickening population led to out-migration, greater transiency, and diversification of tasks; but as Lucy Simler demonstrates for Chester County,

Pennsylvania, tenancy "was, in general, a rational, efficient response to economic conditions." Scholars are also finding that despite rising economic inequality, conflicts were stemmed by widespread land use and varied labor accommodations. Middling householders, argues Kulikoff, were not merely an ideal; they were the norm.[38]

In the case of New England, economic historians' revisionist insights into the competitive and accommodating strategies of farmers and craftsmen (see above at n. 29) often rely on the insights of labor historians. The region's farmers and small traders often worked together to trade and transport goods from the interior to external markets, and to channel imports through intricate networks of local exchange. Shipbuilding and ship sales, processing externally produced goods, supplying intermediate markets with timber and farm products, providing insurance and loans to far-flung networks of colonists—these and other activities brought together urban and rural labor and spurred the creation of many new arenas of economic negotiation. Successful family farming and fishing in New England made it possible to experiment boldly with paper money, land banks, new finishing crafts, and simple manufactures—in short, to develop an internal economy of significant flexibility and sophistication. We are just beginning to learn just how pervasive temporary labor was, what variety of family strategies of production existed, how the requirements of work determined many gender and age roles, and how individual family members came and went from households according to opportunities for work. Studies of Maine and Massachusetts argue convincingly that freeholders with modest amounts of land broke with the English tradition of sending children to work as contract servant labor on great estates or in towns, and instead held them longer on the family farm to work, or set women to work for long years of their early lives.[39]

These are tantalizing beginnings, but we still do not know how New England family labor strategies coexisted with the growing incidence of wage-earning day and seasonal labor of both unmarried males and small farmers. But

38. Kulikoff, *From British Peasants to Colonial Farmers,* chapter 5, and the endnotes, which provide an extensive bibliography supporting these generalizations.

39. For new views of the New England economy, see, e.g., Daniel Vickers, *Farmers and Fishermen: Two Centuries of Work in Essex County, Massachusetts, 1630–1850* (Chapel Hill: University of North Carolina Press, 1994); John Frederick Martin, *Profits in the Wilderness: Entrepreneurship and the Founding of New England Towns in the Seventeenth Century* (Chapel Hill: University of North Carolina Press, 1991); Main and Main, "Economic Growth and the Standard of Living," 27–46. On family farming, see Daniel Vickers, "Working the Fields in a Developing Economy: Essex County, Massachusetts, 1630–1675," in *Work and Labor in Early America,* ed. Stephen Innes (Chapel Hill: University of North Carolina Press, 1988), 49–69; Vickers, "Merchant Credit and Labour Strategies in the Cod Fishery of Colonial Massachusetts," in *Merchant Credit and Labour Strategies in Historical Perspective,* ed. Rosmary E. Ommer (Fredericton, New Brunswick: Goose Lane Editions, 1990), 36–48; Laurel Thatcher Ulrich, "Martha Ballard and Her Girls: Women's Work in Eighteenth-Century Maine," in Innes, *Work and Labor in Early America,* 70–105; and Christopher L. Tomlins, *Law, Labor, and Ideology in the Early Republic* (New York: Cambridge University Press, 1993). For general patterns of New England's adaptations and maturation, as opposed to its declension, see note 29 above as well.

the ways that family and paid labor intersected in neighborhoods and households is vital for understanding how families reconciled their advocacy of personal independence and relative self-sufficiency with the requirements of earning a "competency" by hiring neighbors and itinerant strangers. As McCusker and Menard signaled in 1985, we know very little about the extent of laboring people's capital investments in small businesses, stores, manufactures, and other property unrelated or indirectly related to farm ownership or shipping. Some more recent work offers glimpses of how jacks-of-all-trades and farmers contributed significantly to making and processing colonial commodities (especially timber, grain, and hides), as well as extending credit for building farms and local mills, or "sharing works" to meet the needs of local communities. But they are only glimpses, and we know next to nothing about how mixed partnerships of merchants, storekeepers, and farmers—sometimes formally constructed, sometimes informally sustained for years—expanded the economic potential of many neighborhoods.

John Murray and Ruth Herndon remind us that most labor in colonial America was unfree to some degree, and that poor children were especially vulnerable to forcible indenture and shoddy treatment by masters. Unlike voluntary indentures and free craft apprentices, who were able to negotiate certain living and labor conditions for temporary periods of time, pauper apprentices were comparatively powerless to negotiate the terms of their work and payment. In a nuanced and heavily researched essay, Christopher Tomlins, in Chapter 5 of this volume, "Indentured Servitude in Perspective," argues that fewer servants migrated to the colonies in the first generations than previous analyses claimed, and greater numbers of "free" workers (though not necessarily working for wages) in later colonial years. Tomlins's revisions go deeper than numbers, to two far-reaching conclusions. One is that formal indentured servitude may have been less important to the colonial economy than previously assumed, and the informal negotiations of free laborers and household workers more important— though possibly no less exploited than bound labor. "The ideal-typical migrant servant," Tomlins argues, "was not a gang laborer in waiting but a youth who substituted for scarcities in family labor in a mode of production largely organized through households." The other is that the transition from bound to free labor was probably murkier and longer-lived than previously proposed, and that the Revolution's celebration of a future "free-labor republic," premised on the transition from home-based and small-shop work to work outside homes and under employers' authority, was mostly inspirational rhetoric.[40]

40. John E. Murray and Ruth Wallis Herndon, "Markets for Children in Early America: A Political Economy of Pauper Apprenticeship," *Journal of Economic History* 62 (June 2002): 356–82, and their appended bibliography of recent work; Christopher Tomlins, Chapter 5 in this volume; and, for a prominent earlier view, Galenson, "Settlement and Growth of the Colonies," 135–208, especially 141–50 and 415–16.

Lorena Walsh's essay, "Peopling, Producing, and Consuming in Early British America," Chapter 4 of this volume, offers an expansive discussion of how various forms of unfree labor fit into our perspectives of population and household economy in colonial America. She points to our need for much more work comparing free and bound labor, families and individuals, women and men and children, and Africans and African Americans from region to region and within groups of laboring colonists. Methodologically, she argues, a fruitful approach to understanding the concrete life experiences of early North Americans will look at the records showing migration patterns, levels of mortality, and consumer preferences. Walsh makes the critical observation that recent demographic studies (following work in colonial labor studies generally) tend to abandon the chores of counting women, men, and children, and then linking available records to calculate longevity, birth rates, or mortality. Instead, they are more likely to pursue the social relations of coercion or failed opportunity, or to examine the effects of unfree labor on life experiences.

In some respects, the recent economic history about slavery moves in the opposite direction by reconsidering the cultural or "slave community" views prominent during the 1960s and 1970s. The efforts among slaves, especially in the plantation South and West Indies, to forge identities separate from plantation economies now seem to have emerged less autonomously from the social relations intersecting with slave lives. Economic historians have been taking a closer look at the subtle negotiations and adaptations of slave skills to production on plantations and in cities. In the interstices of these work experiences, it is becoming clearer that the lives of indentured servants, slaves, former bound laborers, and white farmers intersected time and time again. Much of this work focuses on the domestic households and local economies of slaves during the years following initial colonial instability; extending their questions and methodologies into the earlier years of Chesapeake, as well as upper and lower South, settlement will be important for understanding interracial and interclass economies over time. Until this happens, arguments about the origins of slavery remain much the same as they were in the early 1970s. The other major direction of recent work has been to put the lives of colonial North American slaves in transatlantic perspective, or in comparative perspective with West Indies and Brazilian forced labor. Even in the absence of substantially more documentary evidence about North American slaves, an Atlantic comparative perspective has promoted stimulating new perspectives about slavery.[41]

A number of other topics intermittently draw the attention of economic historians but deserve fuller systematic treatment. One closely related to our understanding of both colonial standards of living and labor conditions is the

41. In addition to notes 10, 20, 23, 24, and 35 above, see Galenson, "Settlement and Growth of the Colonies," 160–66, 416–19.

study of health and mortality rates, local and regional life expectancies, fertility, and age at marriage. The full import of accumulating evidence from this new work has not yet emerged. To give one example, however, we have generalized for many years about the distinctions between seventeenth-century northern colonists' long and healthy lives and relatively shorter lives and less stable family structure in the South. Many researchers now suggest that such generalizations about large-scale regional patterns of immigration, fertility, or diet and health conditions fail to do justice to the varieties of migration and settlement in a rapidly growing population.[42] A second topic involves the economic activities of peddlers, chapmen, commercial agents, inventors, advertisers, and retailers—the sinews of economic relations across large distances and into households. Rural storekeeping, for example, which was the site of many kinds of negotiated economic relationships, has been largely ignored. Third, recent scholars are more likely to acknowledge that household production (other than textiles) played a significant role in maturing colonial economic relations, as did experiments with small-scale manufacturing at household and local levels. We have begun to glimpse the consequences of these productive activities in work on both North Americans' transatlantic commerce and their internal "consumer revolution" (treated elsewhere in this chapter), but little systematic study of prerevolutionary innovation and manufacturing has appeared yet.[43]

A fourth area, colonial wars—abroad and on North American frontiers—also merits further integration into our views of the colonial economy. Despite the fact of continual warfare in the colonies, few studies have looked at the uneven, shifting effects on colonists of wartime scarcities or investments, especially the numerous wars with Native Americans and foreign imperial powers. The result has been unjustifiable overgeneralization about the beneficial or

42. See the summary of literature, ibid., 181–89.

43. Starting points include Jeanne M. Boydston, *Home and Work: Housework, Wages, and the Ideology of Labor in the Early Republic* (New York: Oxford University Press, 1990), chapter 1; Adrienne D. Hood, "The Material World of Cloth: Production and Use in Eighteenth-Century Rural Pennsylvania," *William and Mary Quarterly* 53 (January 1996): 43–66; Adrienne D. Hood, *The Weaver's Craft: Cloth, Commerce, and Industry in Early Pennsylvania* (Philadelphia: University of Pennsylvania Press, 2003); Laurel Thatcher Ulrich, "Wheels, Looms, and the Gender Division of Labor in Eighteenth-Century New England," *William and Mary Quarterly* 55 (January 1998): 3–38; Laurel Thatcher Ulrich, "Sheep in the Parlor, Wheels on the Common: Pastoralism and Poverty in Eighteenth-Century Boston," in *Inequality in Early America,* ed. Carla Gardina Pestana and Sharon V. Salinger (Hanover: University Press of New England, 1999), 182–200; Sarah F. McMahon, "Laying Foods By: Gender, Dietary Decisions, and the Technology of Food Preservation in New England Households, 1750–1850," in *Early American Technology: Making and Doing Things from the Colonial Era to 1850,* ed. Judith A. McGaw (Chapel Hill: University of North Carolina Press, 1994), 164–96; Kulikoff, *From British Peasants to Colonial American Farmers,* 222–24, 346n48. For early colonial manufactures, see Lawrence A. Peskin, *Manufacturing Revolution: The Intellectual Origins of Early American Industry* (Baltimore: Johns Hopkins University Press, 2003), chapters 1–2, and notes on scholarship; Matson, *Merchants and Empire,* chapters 5–6, and notes; and citations about labor and production during the revolutionary period in the next section of this chapter. For women's economies and colonial consumption, see notes 45–51 below.

detrimental economic effects of war. Fifth, study of the policies and institutional framework underlying "currency finance," the innovative colonial experiments with printing paper money, has unfortunately faded during recent years. But money and credit, whether officially legislated or informally negotiated, were persistently inadequate during the colonial period. Even with the growth of bills of exchange, paper money and land banks, promissory notes and private loans, colonists complained bitterly about their insufficient financial liquidity and conducted business without enough currency or adequate institutions to meet expanding economic needs, or with depreciated paper money that drew the wrath of imperial policymakers. We know that few colonists imagined the institutional and ideological support that would be necessary for significant financial changes, but that wars—especially the Seven Years' War—spurred commercial innovations, including expanded marine insurance, issues of bonds, personal banking, certificates of indebtedness, lines of guaranteed credit among international partnerships, and elaborated markets for bills of exchange. Information flowed more freely by the 1760s, though some international prices were no less volatile than in previous generations, and some scarce or overpriced commodities were no less the object of rural resistance and occasional urban consumer protests. Provincial legislatures and a vocal public discourse blamed periodic recessions on overextended credit and too much paper money without sufficient means to retire it from circulation, or on the rising prices imposed by farmers and small producers who needed a hedge against the declining value of their goods and money. But few foresaw the virtues of new financial institutions such as banks. Just how colonial thinking about all of these issues may have shifted over time, and how colonists responded informally and institutionally to these needs—and their integration into the economic lives of colonists more generally—bears much deeper scrutiny.[44]

Were European settlers in colonial North America already imbued with a capitalist ethos when they arrived, or did one emerge during the colonial era? Did they practice capitalist economic relations from the beginning of settlement, or did such relations take shape within the shifting contours of a wider Atlantic economy? The answers hinge on our definition of capitalism. Some views turn on historians' assessments of expanding landholding or rising consumption— what it meant that more than half of colonial Americans owned land, that middling households showed clear signs of attaining comfort—and, as such, lack the objectivity ever to be resolved. Other disagreements rely on a paucity of surviving evidence, limited local studies, and incautious comparisons of different

44. Initial efforts to complicate our view of financial aspects of the colonial economy are in Margaret Newell, *From Dependency to Independence: Economic Revolution in Colonial New England* (Ithaca: Cornell University Press, 1998); Bruce H. Mann, *Republic of Debtors: Bankruptcy in the Age of American Independence* (Cambridge: Harvard University Press, 2002), chapter 1.

places and times. Sometimes these disagreements hinge on scholars' divergent theoretical starting points or scholarly predilections about what kinds of lives colonial Americans enjoyed more generally. Often they derive from assumptions (usually unstated) about a particular, often innate and uniform, set of qualities that motivate economic activity, a disposition to believe that we are, at root, partners in either the pursuit of profit or the preservation of social relations evolved in a murky past. More recently, confusion has been added to the discussion through the deployment of terms such as "enterprise" and "markets" interchangeably with "economy" and "capitalism," though they are far from equivalent in meaning. In any event, scholars' definitions of capitalism are equally diverse. Some, following Max Weber, claim that capitalism exists when a few leading entrepreneurs and merchants exhibit regular and sustained efforts to earn profits. Capitalism, in this view, requires a set of values, including individualism, acquisitiveness, and the calculation of self-interest in either personal or group terms. Others insist that not merely entrepreneurial efforts but also sufficient accumulation of profits, normally through commerce in the early modern era (although possibly through savings in banks), which are then invested in new technologies and internal development, are prerequisites of capitalism. Still others identify capitalism as characterized by the transformation of markets from local places of exchange to webs of transactions in an intangible sphere of economic activity where prices matter more than people or social expectations. Finally, some scholars propose that capitalism could emerge only in the radical and thoroughgoing transformation of labor's relation to capitalists, often accompanied by the rise of free (or wage) labor and the separation of home from work. As the scores of articles and conference papers appearing in recent years attest, economic historians are deadlocked in hopeless disagreement over these conflicting definitions.[45]

During the 1950s and 1960s scholars probably came as close to a consensus about the capitalist nature of British colonial North America as they ever

45. For this paragraph and the next one, representative discussions of the issues include Allan Kulikoff, "The Transition to Capitalism in Rural America," *William and Mary Quarterly* 46 (January 1989): 120–44; Naomi R. Lamoreaux, "Rethinking the Transition to Capitalism in the Early American Northeast," *Journal of American History* 90 (September 2003): 437–61; and Douglas R. Egerton, "Markets Without a Market Revolution: Southern Planters and Capitalism," in *The Wages of Independence: Capitalism in the Early American Republic,* ed. Paul Gilje (Madison, Wis.: Madison House, 1997), 49–64. For problematic use of "exchange" and "markets," see, e.g., Joyce Appleby, *Inheriting the Revolution: The First Generation of Americans* (Cambridge: Harvard University Press, 2000), chapter 3; and Hunter, *Purchasing Identity in the Atlantic World,* and her discussion of Jurgen Habermas, A. O. Hirschman, and Benedict Anderson. For a discussion of markets as distinct from a capitalist economic system, see Stanley L. Engerman and Robert E. Gallman, "The Emergence of a Market Economy Before 1860," in *A Companion to Nineteenth-Century America,* ed. W. L. Barney (Malden, Mass.: Blackwell, 2001), 121–38. Compare Barney's argument to Joyce Appleby's call for a return to the "values" theorized by Max Weber, which, she argues in "The Vexed Story of Capitalism," are at the heart of the emergence of American capitalism.

would. Carl Degler's oft-repeated declaration, in 1959, that "capitalism came in the first ships" seemed to sum up the views of most historians of his generation. England, the original home of the great number of immigrants who ruled colonial institutions and dominated culture in the colonies, was itself commercializing and on the cusp of industrialization. British attitudes about landholding, business enterprise, and personal opportunities in markets were rapidly being shaken loose from a "traditional" economy, and when colonists came to North America (largely to New England, in this interpretation), the towns and farms they carved out of the howling wilderness were established on capitalist dreams of prosperity. Transatlantic commerce complemented settlers' goals by stimulating the pace of market development and the organization of merchants' capitalism. In 1972 the historical geographer James T. Lemon made his own argument for a liberal economic culture. Land-use records in Lancaster County, Pennsylvania, the geographer's methods of examining spatial population arrangements, and evidence of extensive commercial importation from abroad demonstrated, Lemon argued, that colonists "eagerly sought" the relations marking them as "agents of capitalism."[46]

By the early 1970s a rising tide of dissension challenged this view. Early critics were buoyed by the flourishing minor industry of community studies—especially those focused on the original New England towns—which seemed to prove that colonists had not embraced but rather had discarded or avoided the market individualism rising in England. Derived as they were from the methodologies of cultural anthropology, population studies, and enormous social-science databases, these community studies pointed economic historians toward a salutary corrective to the "always-capitalists" scholarship: initially prolific families that were healthy and long-lived experienced a declining abundance of land, which in turn spurred numerous social and economic strategies to hold modernization at bay. But however rich their source base seemed to be, few of these scholars examined household production or external market activity, which resulted in more speculation than demonstration of economic behavior in local communities. By the end of the 1970s Michael Merrill had shifted our focus by arguing that colonists may have been engaged in markets, but their "household mode of production" involved decentralized exchange and production for "need rather than price." Not cash relations but elaborate networks of indebtedness bound members of communities together. James Henretta added to this view by arguing that colonial farm families clearly sought economic gain, though

46. Carl Degler, *Out of Our Past: The Forces That Shaped Modern America* (New York: Harper and Row, 1959), introduction; James T. Lemon, *The Best Poor Man's Country: A Geographical Study of Southeastern Pennsylvania* (Baltimore: Johns Hopkins University Press, 1972); James T. Lemon, "Spatial Order: Households in Local Communities and Regions," in *Colonial British America: Essays in the New History of the Early Modern Era,* ed. Jack Greene and J. R. Pole (Baltimore: Johns Hopkins University Press, 1984), 102; Stephen Innes, *Labor in a New Land: Economy and Society in Seventeenth-Century Springfield* (Princeton: Princeton University Press, 1983), introduction; and Martin, *Profits in the Wilderness.*

not in a context of elevating the material well-being of many economic agents but rather in order to keep families secure along traditional lines (bequeathing land, saving what they could for children, sustaining customary agriculture, and shop-keeping) that valued relationships with neighbors and avoided risks in farming.[47]

After years of debate, most economic historians now concede that dramatically different economies developed in various places from Maine to the Leeward Islands, which makes any particular definition of colonial economic life—capitalist or otherwise—impossible. In addition, we have become more aware in recent years of the non-wage-labor, nonindustrial character of colonial economies, in which the household (and adjacent family land, improvements, and bound or slave labor) was the primary focus of production and the starting point of economic planning and investment for most colonists. Thoroughgoing changes in the size and complexity of communities, economic roles and marketing strategies, uses of time and tools, the division of labor and pace of production, institutional development, and much more altered colonial economies over time, and these factors stressed individual values and social relationships. Certainly wholesale merchants were practiced in taking commercial risks and calculating outcomes based on their knowledge about markets and consumer demand. Just as certainly, whole sectors of colonists were accustomed to mobile property relations and delighted in the world of goods created by energetic commerce, and a degree of refinement could be detected not only in genteel but also in the middling ranks of colonists. But these decisions and relations were not capitalist in nature. Possibly capitalism could be glimpsed on the largest sugar and indigo plantations, which required extensive investment in machinery and slaves and managerial and marketing relations that would later be replicated in nineteenth-century factories. But these enterprises were the exception to the rule of colonial development. Further, it is certainly true that colonial households were not self-sufficient miniature kingdoms of independent yeomen; colonists were connected deeply to the transatlantic economy and its relations of credit and exchange, at first by necessity and later by choice. But more often than not these connections stemmed more from long-established traditions than from a reorganization of the economy into capitalist forms.

Admirable efforts have been made to qualify points of the debate about colonial capitalism. Daniel Vickers's explanation of "competency" takes into account personal and family strategies for achieving material well-being by buying and selling in the best markets possible, while at the same time focusing

47. James Henretta, *The Origins of American Capitalism: Collected Essays* (Boston: Northeastern University Press, 1991); Michael Merrill, "Cash Is Good to Eat: Self-Sufficiency and Exchange in the Rural Economy of the United States," *Radical History Review* 3 (Winter 1977): 42–71; Christopher Clark, "Household Economy, Market Exchange, and the Rise of Capitalism in the Connecticut Valley, 1800–1860," *Journal of Social History* 13 (Winter 1979): 169–89.

efforts on sustaining households, cooperating with neighbors, and exchanging credit and work without recourse to coercive institutional intervention. Christopher Clark argues that colonists could exhibit liberal and customary behavior at the same time; they could orient their work toward international trade and household economies simultaneously. Richard Bushman has proposed a "composite" colonial farmer who blended the behaviors of seeking competence and eagerly entering competitive markets, and Kate Carte has proposed the concept of "moral capitalism" to explain the intertwined relationships of religious devotion and engagement in market exchanges.

Bushman and Carte argue that their historical agents did not live in a dual economy but rather in one in which an intertwined set of relationships struggled to achieve fairness and competition together. These and other recent efforts to address the economic nature of colonial America propose that a market orientation prevailed without involving capitalist social relations. Private property and commodification of land holdings were balanced with the need to regulate community markets and money prudently. But, as we shall see shortly, the problematic nature of a "transition to capitalism" arises in even bolder relief in studies of the revolutionary and early national eras.[48]

Inquiries about the pace and character of a possible "consumer revolution" reflect relatively new concerns of colonial economic historians. However, this work is closely related to studies of agricultural and small-craft productivity, household and farm division of labor, and importation of needed and desired goods. In addition, many of the sources for understanding consumption—account books, price series, import ledgers, advertisements, and commercial correspondence—are familiar. Most work on colonial consumption can also be divided along lines similar to those in other scholarship, in that it argues that colonists either strove to participate in markets to the extent of their ability, or clung to custom and "safety-first" strategies of buying and selling. In the first case, scholars tend to assume that colonists strove for less international or imperial dependency and more internal development, even progress toward some imagined degree of comfort or prosperity. Diversification, maturing institutions, and experiments with autonomous currency systems point toward economic development premised on such striving. Improving diet, life expectancy, and

---

48. Daniel Vickers, "Competency and Competition: Economic Culture in Early America," *William and Mary Quarterly*, 3d ser., 47 (January 1990): 1–33; Vickers, *Farmers and Fishermen;* Christopher Clark, *The Roots of Rural Capitalism: Western Massachusetts, 1780–1860* (Ithaca: Cornell University Press, 1990); Innes, *Creating the Commonwealth;* and Katherine Carté Engel, "The Strangers' Store: Moral Capitalism in Moravian Bethlehem, 1753–1775," *Early American Studies* 1 (Spring 2003): 90–126. For another effort to straddle the poles of debate, see Kulikoff, *From British Peasants to Colonial American Farmers.* For a recent study of the "social self" and the nonhomogeneous, indeterminate economic agent in a later era, see Jeffrey Sklansky, *The Soul's Economy: Market Society and Selfhood in American Thought, 1820–1920* (Chapel Hill: University of North Carolina Press, 2002). This subject merits scrutiny by early American economic historians as well.

types and quantities of household goods confirms this line of thought. This work finds evidence of colonists producing in order to buy goods made by others, eating well, dressing better, getting taller, and adorning their homes with more and more goods.[49]

Some of the most sophisticated recent work casts doubt on whether available evidence points so ineluctably toward abundant consumption and a uniform set of motivations to produce, exchange, and consume *more*. Recently, Lois Green Carr has brought together years of prodigious research on the Chesapeake region to suggest that within the context of what many scholars know to be an overall rise in the standard of living, there were important differences in how colonists consumed between the seventeenth and eighteenth centuries. By the early 1700s the standard of living had improved more rapidly for newly arriving immigrants and hard-working farm families than it had during previous generations; but because land was harder to acquire after the first years of settlement, it also became harder for immigrants and migrating families to continue getting ahead and become mature householders. Carr's conclusions are compatible with other findings that by the mid-1700s the wealthiest colonists were not qualitatively superior to others in the nature of their consumption, that differences between what the wealthy owned and what the middling owned were more a matter of degree than of kind—somewhat more furniture, bigger houses, more cattle. Even the wealthiest South Carolinian or Bostonian had little capital to invest or liquid medium of exchange until after 1750. Moreover, by then the gap between the wealthiest elite and middling colonists and a majority at the bottom of a consuming spectrum was well established, creating an equally wide chasm between a minority that aspired to even greater consumption and a majority grasping for modest comfort, sufficiency, or survival. Moreover, gentility can be learned and transmitted culturally, and what can be learned can also become the fuel for conflicts between different classes and interest groups outside the social relations of production, as happened when middling colonists began to appropriate meanings of expanding mobile wealth, and in turn to perceive their own

49. T. H. Breen, "Narrative of Commercial Life: Consumption, Ideology, and Community on the Eve of the American Revolution," *William and Mary Quarterly* 50 (July 1993): 471–501; Thomas M. Doerflinger, "Farmers and Dry Goods in the Philadelphia Market Area, 1750–1800," in Hoffman et al., *Economy of Early America,* 166–95; Cary Carson, Ronald Hoffman, and Peter J. Albert, eds., *Of Consuming Interests: The Style of Life in the Eighteenth Century* (Charlottesville: University Press of Virginia, 1994); Shammas, *The Pre-Industrial Consumer;* Ann Smart Martin, "Makers, Buyers, and Users: Consumerism as a Material Culture Framework," *Winterthur Portfolio* 28 (1993): 141–57; Hood, "The Material World of Cloth." Compare these works to Carole Shammas, "The Revolutionary Impact of European Demand for Tropical Goods," in McCusker and Morgan, *Early Modern Atlantic Economy,* 163–85; Lorena S. Walsh, "Consumer Behavior, Diet, and the Standard of Living in Late Colonial and Early Antebellum America, 1770–1840," in Gallman and Wallis, *American Economic Growth and Standards of Living,* 217–61, and its extensive review of the literature. See the uses of economic conditions to explain material culture in Linda Baumgarten, *What Clothes Reveal: The Language of Clothing in Colonial and Federal America* (New Haven: Yale University Press, 2002), chapter 3.

empowerment, in a series of struggles over food, prices, urban market regulation, exportation and consumer demand, and access to necessities.[50]

We are still undecided about whether consumption provided a creative impetus toward trade and craft production that leveled class distinctions over time, or whether it served primarily to mark status and reinforce differences among colonists, or both. Instead of asserting rising degrees of consumption across populations in particular periods of time, we need a better understanding of the relative degrees and character of consumption through the seventeenth, eighteenth, and early nineteenth centuries in order to appreciate the significance of consumption in any one place and time. We still need to ask: *more,* yes, but in relation to whom? When? Where? Did merchants and manufacturers, for example, control the quality, colors, and brand names of goods marketed in North America, or did consumer preferences make it imperative for colonial merchants to place specific orders according to customers' demands? Further, we need to separate more satisfactorily the undeniable improvement of personal comfort on a wide scale from the limitations imposed by imperial regulations. What motivated colonists' determination to pursue material goals outside the British Empire after the 1760s? At the end of the colonial era, some economic historians argue, nonimportation offered a significant moment for imagining how an old view of human frailties and minimal ability to produce goods could be overturned in favor of an era of manufacturing and plenty. But in all, despite having more and better measures of colonial goods in homes and ships, a better appreciation of demographic changes and the significance of rising land values from place to place, and other refinements, we have made few comparative studies of such aspirations and activities between regions, between colonies and British or continental experiences, or between the prerevolutionary era and later ones.

An even deeper problem arises for those who are looking not only at rising quantities of imported or home-produced goods, but also at the value these goods represented as a portion of colonists' incomes. The opening years of colonial economic development generated demand for necessities, most of them perishable or semidurable, and merchants imported large amounts of these. Colonists continued to import a great proportion of consumable items throughout the colonial era, but home, shop, and field production also grew, in a mutually reinforcing relationship to external commerce, overseas demand, and rising comfort in the colonies. For many years economic historians have recognized that early Americans were acquiring more goods for their immediate consumption and longer-term material rise, and at an accelerating rate. Imports increased steadily in all colonies; by 1770 a quarter of household budgets was allocated to

---

50. E.g., Lois Green Carr, "Emigration and the Standard of Living: The Eighteenth-Century Chesapeake," in McCusker and Morgan, *Early Modern Atlantic Economy,* chapter 12; Simon Midleton, "'How it came that the bakers bake no bread': A Struggle for Trade Privileges in Seventeenth-Century New Amsterdam," *William and Mary Quarterly* 58 (April 2001): 347–72.

consumer goods imported from abroad and coastal trading. But in recent years we have also puzzled over an apparent disparity between this increasing "world of goods" and the static or falling value of consumed goods in probate inventories. While colonists were buying more, there are few economic signs that they used larger portions of their total wealth to pay for goods. Possibly this surprising trend was due to falling prices for many goods, rising or steady wages, or the substitution of new goods for old ones of comparable value. Possibly, too, Americans experienced what Jan de Vries calls an "industrious revolution," a period in which households intensified and reorganized their labor, especially that of women and children, orienting it ever more toward earning the money needed to purchase imports and store-bought goods, with the result that as settlements became denser, mixed agriculture addressed the recurring problems of turbulent price swings for staples, surpluses of food and saleable by-products of farms that entered markets where craftsmen and retailers shopped for what they did not produce, and the intensification of milling, shipbuilding, and other activities—all fueling demand for more consumer goods, but not necessarily tied to expenditures of income. Moreover, these household strategies often focused on the purchase of goods that were easily replaced when they wore out and would not have been recorded in inventories or noted in private records.[51]

The Revolutionary Era

After a hiatus of comparative neglect, economic historians have recently returned to studying more intensively the revolutionary generation's efforts to reconstruct and further its economy from 1760 to 1815. Once examined primarily through the lens of business entrepreneurship, preindustrial technologies, the effects of British policies on colonial development, and leading transatlantic merchants, these efforts are now being viewed in the context of the complicated and negotiated economic culture and political economy of the era.[52]

51. A sample of the literature might include Carole Shammas, "How Self-Sufficient Was Early America?" *Journal of Interdisciplinary History* 13 (Autumn 1982): 247–72; Jan de Vries, "Between Purchasing Power and the World of Goods: Understanding the Household Economy in Early Modern Europe," in *Consumption and the World of Goods,* ed. John Brewer and Roy Porter (London: Routledge, 1993), 85–132; Walsh, Main, and Carr, "Toward a History of the Standard of Living," 116–66; and Ann Smart Martin, "Consumerism and the Retail Trade in the Eighteenth Century Backcountry," paper presented at the Rockefeller Library, Colonial Williamsburg, Williamsburg, Virginia, 1992. Knowledge of the rising standard of living at the end of the eighteenth century was not "news" in the 1980s and 1990s; already the work of Alice Hanson Jones had brought the issue to prominent attention; see note 25.

52. Progressive economic historians saw the Revolution as a clash of interests and forces but rarely set forth causes of the conflict with precision. See two examples in the work of Arthur M. Schlesinger Sr., *The Colonial Merchants and the American Revolution* (New York: Columbia University Press, 1918); and Louis Hacker, *The Triumph of American Capitalism* (New York: Simon and Schuster,

The scope of this new work has proceeded along two lines. One trajectory makes conceptual and causal links between the rising economic prosperity of the final colonial years and the economic opportunities presented by a long and gritty war. New work shows that although revolutionaries did not redistribute confiscated land wholesale, many did energetically speculate in newly acquired territories, marking a greater commodification of land and its uneven acquisition in the postrevolutionary years. Just how uneven land ownership became is still unclear, especially at the margins of farm-building frontiers, but despite widespread impoverishment (some of it temporary) by the war, many families founded on old liquid wealth, and great numbers of migrating new Americans, shared in the reshuffling of opportunities for entrepreneurship or commercial farming. In a slightly different vein, James Henretta and a few others have made a strong case that transcolonial supply movements during the war created new opportunities for economic experimentation by household producers, at first to sustain the war effort and then to expand with new manufacturing. Coastal merchants who before the war had few outlets for the profits they made in commerce and who had tended to reinvest in shipping, began to put capital from trade into local ironworks, distilleries, sugar refineries, milling, and other processing enterprises related to the goods they regularly transported. Contemporaries wrote prolifically about America's "infinite capacity" for expansion and production.[53]

The second direction of scholarship emphasizes not the opportunities but the hardships of warfare, the halting recovery of commerce and prices by war's end, and the extent of private and public indebtedness, all of which spurred social strife during a "critical period" and focused the political economy on post-1789 recovery. They challenge the notion that colonial productivity rose appreciably during the war and argue that, aside from anecdotal evidence about what the former colonists wished to produce and exchange, most studies provide little new information about the effects of the Revolutionary War on household

---

1940). Merrill Jensen kept alive the argument about economic causes for the Revolution in, e.g., *The New Nation: A History of the United States During the Confederation* (New York: Vintage Books, 1950). One of the most signal contributions of McCusker and Menard was their recapitulation and identification of areas for further work on the revolutionary economy; see chapter 17 of *The Economy of British America*. For recent summaries, with useful bibliographies, see Kulikoff, *From British Peasants to Colonial America Farmers*, 255–88, and notes; and Cathy Matson, "The Revolution, the Constitution, and the New Nation," in *CEHUS*, 363–402. For a series of recent studies on revolutions in the Atlantic world presented at the annual PEAES conference in November 2003, see www.librarycompany.org/economy. For a Marxist analysis of multiple revolutions over the entire early modern era of Atlantic-world development, with strong economic causal connections, see Peter Linebaugh and Marcus Rediker, *The Many-Headed Hydra: Sailors, Slaves, Commoners, and the Hidden History of the Revolutionary Atlantic* (Boston: Beacon Press, 2000).

53. E.g., James Henretta, "The War for Independence and American Economic Development," in Hoffman et al., *Economy of Early America*, 45–87; Peskin, *Manufacturing Revolution*, part 1 and its notes; and Buel, *In Irons*.

production, local exchange, and consumer tastes. Although the paucity of sources for the revolutionary era, as well as the truncated period of analysis, may partially account for these limitations, these critics may be correct that our research agendas and methodologies have been unnecessarily constricted. All too often we have narrated stories about the "rise" or "unfolding" of new enterprise, or we have discovered hopeful optimism amid the trauma of the war, but there is little work to date about how social relations may have changed, and how this early phase of a "transition to capitalism" was undoubtedly replete with social conflict and failure. For one thing, we know with certainty that external markets underwent traumatic dislocations during the war, that blockades and moving armies disrupted commerce deeply. A similar problem arises in many studies of the backcountry that illuminate economic issues: most adopt an argument favoring the presence of a moral economy or subsistence agriculture, or assert the swift arrival of market or capitalist relations in newly settled areas, but few have sorted through the varieties of agricultural activities and complicated social networks of the backcountry and frontier to add clarity to the debate about the character of the revolutionary period. As the debates about colonial wealth and incomes (see above) and the later market revolution (see below) inform us, both loosely narrated stories and generalization across great space and many peoples yield unsatisfying results; much work still needs to be done before we can draw a good balance sheet about the economic advances and setbacks of the Revolution.

And what of postwar recovery? Those who emphasize its halting and uneven nature offer two perspectives. Work that focuses on the international commerce of the new states tends to contrast the material prosperity and population growth of the colonial economy to the deep economic depression and extensive scarcities of the revolutionary years. Blockades seriously interrupted the flow of normal commerce through American ports during the Revolution, and commercial networks were disrupted or forced into alternative channels of communication and exchange, usually with poor results. But if commerce showed little or no profit at regional levels from the onset of the Revolution through much of the 1780s, Douglass North proposed it as a measuring rod for post-1789 recovery, when a sustained and significant commercial recovery was stimulated by the Napoleonic Wars: "the years 1793 through 1807 were extraordinarily prosperous for the American economy." Other economic historians, following North, typically reiterate that rapidly rising international demand for American foodstuffs during the 1790s spurred agriculture, shipping, and shipbuilding to qualitatively new levels.[54]

54. For this and the next paragraph, see Matson, "Revolution, Constitution, and New Nation"; and for the critical period's slow and fitful recovery, 372–82; Matson, "Risky Business: Winning and Losing in the Early American Economy, 1780–1850," (Philadelphia: Library Company of Philadelphia, 2003); Buel, *In Irons;* Douglass C. North, *Growth and Welfare in the American Past,* 2d ed.

A second view proposes that although recovery was certainly linked to commercial activity, internal farm production and exchange, as well as small businesses, took longer to achieve stability. The short-term costs of the Revolutionary War undoubtedly were steep: incomes fell sharply, citizens and soldiers endured scarcities, planting was disrupted when soldiers left home and armies marched through fields, and farmers' credit recovered only in fits and starts in the interior. Everywhere in North America it took time to meet the demands of a revived "consumer revolution" with domestic manufactures and commercial ties to old and new foreign markets. For many coastal retailers and craftsmen dependent on commerce, the discontinuities of international trade continued long after the war for American independence was over. Commercial farming revived quickly near reliable waterways, near large cities, and where large numbers of craftspeople lived, but very slowly where transportation was poor and capital scarce. The economy was dominated internally by local and regional, not nationally integrated, systems of transportation, information, finance, and exchange. Not until the first decade of the next century would per capita incomes—insofar as we can measure them—recover to prewar levels, and in many southern areas recovery was elusive or wildly uneven.

These arguments often emphasize that even in the early phases of postwar recovery, more goods and more people are not sufficient proof of economic recovery or a "transition to capitalism." Although the new states and their many energetic entrepreneurs had broken free of the restraints of the imperial system, scarcities of capital, labor, and technological knowledge continued to retard significant manufacturing and craft production. The clothing, household and small-craft tools, furniture, and processed foodstuffs Americans produced were capitalized with scant family funds and exchanged locally or to the moving army; networks of transportation, capital, and information were inadequate to Americans' expectations. For example, despite Oliver Evans's new technologies in the great three-story flour mills near Wilmington, Delaware, it took a generation for millers to adopt new flour-processing equipment widely and to replace their undershot water wheels with more efficient overshot wheels in the mid-Atlantic and upper South regions. Social distinctions, these historians conclude, could not have dissolved into the unifying discourses of republicanism and virtuous simplicity during the revolutionary crises, and the widespread liberal expectations for abundance and prosperity were often rudely checked in the first postwar decade.[55]

(Englewood Cliffs, N.J.: Prentice-Hall, 1974), 72–73. For reviews of this perspective, though they don't necessarily endorse it fully, see Wood, *Radicalism of the American Revolution;* Cathy Matson, "Capitalizing Hope: Economic Thought and the Early National Economy," in Gilje, *Wages of Independence,* chapter 7; and Kulikoff, *Agrarian Origins of American Capitalism,* 108.

55. In addition to note 54, see Thomas Weiss, "U.S. Labor Force Estimates and Economic Growth, 1800–1860," in Gallman and Wallis, *American Economic Growth and Standards of Living,* 26–35.

Recently Winifred Rothenberg has pressed the case for internal economic recovery that came well before the Napoleonic Wars' foreign demand. Far into the Massachusetts countryside after 1781, and increasingly so after 1789, "interest rates behaved more like prices, endorsed notes were more negotiable, credit networks were larger and more far-flung, and an entirely new menu of investment opportunities became available to rural residents." Rural Massachusetts people who once fretted over their local debts, perhaps six months past due, by the end of the eighteenth century were engaged in stocks and bonds markets; price convergence and active pursuit of the highest market prices for crops marked emergent integration of rural and urban, interior and coastal, farmer and merchant economic behavior during the generations straddling the American Revolution. Rothenberg and David Meyer, among others, assert that rural farmers and craft producers were not passive victims of markets and prices beyond their control; they sought efficiencies, invested to the extent of their abilities, and watched actively for price incentives. By extension, this argument establishes northeastern industrialization as a series of calculated risks undertaken willingly by men and women of various social strata, and not as a process of elite investment and wrenching reorganization of households and working people. Like others who look forward toward the nineteenth century, Rothenberg finds proof of a short but thoroughgoing "critical period" and a subsequent period of unprecedented private economic opportunity and institutional development, which neither colonial nor revolutionary-era Americans enjoyed.[56]

Although we are just beginning to incorporate our understanding of banks, insurance, securities markets, and brokerage into our portraits of the postwar economy, the recent revival of interest in early national finance reinforces a view of Americans unleashing unprecedented economic energy with the aid of bank securities and loans. Most early Americans pitted themselves against the supposed rapacious policies of the British public debt system that unfolded throughout the eighteenth century and believed that public and private debt posed a threat to republican liberty. But leading Americans of the era—in Congress and the army—took the view that political independence would bring economic freedom, including the elimination of customary legislation that stood in the way of new private enterprise, under the aegis of a federally funded public debt. Steep debts incurred from foreign and merchant loans, as well as hopelessly depreciated paper currencies, prompted leaders in the states and Congress to proclaim that debt was not, as Adam Smith put it, "dead stock," but, in Hamilton's

---

56. Winifred B. Rothenberg, "The Invention of American Capitalism: The Economy of New England in the Federal Period," in Temin, *Engines of Enterprise*, 81; Meyer, *Roots of American Industrialization;* Rockoff, "History and Economics," 48–76; Winifred B. Rothenberg, "The Emergence of a Capital Market in Rural Massachusetts, 1730–1838," *Journal of Economic History* 45 (December 1985): 806; and Gordon Wood, "The Enemy Is Us: Democratic Capitalism in the Early Republic," *Journal of the Early Republic* 16 (Summer 1996): 293–308.

famous paraphrase of Robert Walpole, "a national blessing." As Richard Sylla argues, the financial instruments and institutions created in the wake of revolution paved the way for market integration years before the transportation and market revolutions to follow. A flurry of recent work has recovered an important role for Hamilton's Bank of the United States (1791–1811). The bank was not only a large institution that could receive revenues and pay the debts of the states and nation; it also made private loans, guaranteed extensive regulatory functions, and opened its arms to foreign investors. Just as important, banks were becoming more appealing to large numbers of early Americans who believed they would have access to banking's benefits. In the mood of energetic business competition that was emerging by the early 1800s, loud calls were heard for more ready money and more extensive credit. Although, in mid-Atlantic and northeastern communities, middling entrepreneurs and established commercial interests offered competing interpretations of the benefits banks would bring and what kind of banks were best suited to the "genius of the Republic," the arguments had narrowed during the 1780s from those about the dangers of banking at all to those about what kind of banks to have. As state currencies became more unstable, confidence in the federal structure of government and finance may have been growing before Hamilton's First Bank of the United States expired in 1811.[57]

This picture of an early national rush into economic modernity may be challenged on a number of fronts. For one thing, the continuities of the early 1800s with colonial economic development—especially in light of the "catching up" many Americans did after the war years—are overlooked too frequently. Similarly, the shortcomings and failures of entrepreneurial efforts in the early part of the century contrast sharply with the developments of the 1830s to 1850s. More specifically, Michael Merrill delivers a telling critique of Rothenberg's case for an early and pervasive internal market society, and indirectly criticizes the notion of a financial revolution under the first federal government. Merrill insists, first, that deep economic change emanates from the conflicts of opposing worldviews and interests rather than from the ahistorical and universally similar character of a people who lived outside the authority of their cultures. His case study of early capitalist investment in the North paints a subtle portrait

57. E.g., Richard Sylla, "U.S. Securities Markets and the Banking System, 1790–1840," *Federal Reserve Bank of St. Louis Review* 80 (May–June 1998): 83–98; Richard Sylla, "Experimental Federalism: The Economics of American Government, 1789–1914," in *CEHUS*, vol. 2, chapter 12; Robert E. Wright, *The Wealth of Nations Rediscovered: Integration and Expansion in American Financial Markets, 1780–1850* (New York: Cambridge University Press, 2002); and Robert E. Wright, *Origins of Commercial Banking in America, 1750–1800* (Lanham, Md.: Rowman and Littlefield, 2001). The National Bureau of Economic Research and the *Journal of Economic History* have separately been publishing many historical interpretations of early finance in recent years. For a valuable case study, see A. Glenn Crothers, "Banks and Economic Development in Post-Revolutionary Northern Virginia, 1790–1812," *Business History Review* 73 (Spring 1999): 1–39.

of the historical moment when bankers, manufacturers, and merchants in a northern urban area probably accumulated enough capital to invest in enterprise and reorganize labor according to their individual investment strategies. In the early American "economic culture" of business investment, people made bad choices, information was imperfect, and competition was a messy affair. Kinship and community were essential in relations of debt and credit; reputation could weigh more heavily in the "court of community" than could contracts in courts of law; and the informal agreements of insurance, brokerage, and commercial partnerships assumed priority over formal institutions and systems of information.[58]

Chapters about the revolutionary era in this volume further complicate the character of the era's economic changes. David Waldstreicher's essay "Capitalism, Slavery, and Benjamin Franklin's American Revolution," Chapter 6, explicates one of the most important new directions in revolutionary-era work, that of the intimate connection between slavery and independence. Through the lens of Benjamin Franklin's shifting thought about slavery, Waldstreicher takes issue with scholars who have sustained the equation between the American Revolution, ideological arguments for constitutional freedom and a free economy, and the presumed link between postrevolutionary independence and emerging free labor. Instead, Waldstreicher argues, capitalism's rise was premised as much on the forced dependencies of slavery in a global labor market that existed throughout the early modern era as it was on the prospects for a national identity and the "freedom" of wage labor. In Chapter 7, "Moneyless in Pennsylvania: Privatization and the Depression of the 1780s," Terry Bouton's case study of postrevolutionary banking in Pennsylvania explicates the widespread opposition to the state's transition from a colonial legacy of widespread and plentiful public paper money to private finance under the aegis of state-chartered banks. Far from enabling the new Federalist regime and the new state government to fund energetic entrepreneurship, Pennsylvania's banks had the ill effects of contracting the money supply and putting most of the new currency into the hands of elite creditors. Bouton's work complements that of other scholars who insist that the nationalists did not represent, and did not win over, the majority of Americans during the 1780s and 1790s. Most citizens believed that money ought to be kept in a safe place and that it was not real capital but rather a marker of personal wealth; few believed that banks might be linked to investment, economic development, or democratic economic relations more widely. Indeed,

---

58. Michael Merrill, "Putting 'Capitalism' in Its Place: A Review of Recent Literature," *William and Mary Quarterly* 52 (April 1995): 315–26; and for comments on these early national themes, also Daniel M. G. Raff and Peter Temin, "Business History and Recent Economic Theory: Imperfect Information, Incentives, and the Internal Organization of Firms," in *Inside the Business Enterprise: Historical Perspectives on the Use of Information,* ed. Peter Temin (Chicago: University of Chicago Press, 1991), 7–35; and Lamoreaux, "Rethinking the Transition to Capitalism."

although depositors in the state-chartered banks came from many walks of life (as did speculators in the revolutionary-era paper debt of the states and nation), fears and antipathies persisted, especially outside larger population centers and the mid-Atlantic region. Popular resentment against "monopolistic" merchants who controlled supplies of necessary commodities and money, widespread belief that rights should be vested in specific written charters and not in the machinations of personal privilege, and persistent resentment of rising taxes associated with governments run by "greedy bankers" all filled the newspapers and pamphlet literature of the era. As popular fears persisted, serious social and political challenges arose against banking, especially central banking, after the War of 1812.[59]

Brooke Hunter's contribution to this volume, Chapter 8, "Creative Destruction: The Forgotten Legacy of the Hessian Fly," invites us to consider the power of environmental disruptions on postrevolutionary agricultural recovery in the mid-Atlantic and the vagaries of regional and world markets for foodstuffs. At a moment when many Americans looked forward to the Revolution's promise of economic abundance, and farmers and millers in the Delaware River valley produced unprecedented surpluses of grain and flour, devastating infestations of the Hessian fly spurred unprecedented agricultural diversification and improvement societies that helped salvage the most important economic activity in the region—at least until rising wheat production in Maryland and Virginia competed effectively with the surpluses of northern Delaware and southeastern Pennsylvania. Other scholars are also beginning to turn attention to the economic adaptations planters and farmers made during the postrevolutionary generation in the face of pestilence, storms, drought, erosion, and other environmental traumas that dislocated otherwise promising postwar agricultural recovery and international commerce.[60]

59. On slavery and capitalism in the revolutionary era, see David Waldstreicher, Chapter 6 in this volume, and representative discussions in Merrill, "Putting 'Capitalism' in Its Place"; David Eltis, "Slavery and Freedom in the Early Modern World," in *Terms of Labor: Slavery, Serfdom, and Free Labor*, ed. Stanley Engerman (Stanford: Stanford University Press, 1999), 25–49; and John Bezís-Selfa, *Forging America: Ironworkers, Adventurers, and the Industrious Revolution, 1640–1830* (Ithaca: Cornell University Press, 2004). For finance, see Terry Bouton, Chapter 7 in this volume; Richard Vernier, "The Fortunes of Orthodoxy: The Political Economy of Public Debt in England and America During the 1780s," in *Articulating America: Fashioning a National Political Culture in Early America, Essays in Honor of J. R. Pole*, ed. Rebecca Starr (Madison, Wis.: Madison House, 2000), 93–130; Cathy Matson and Peter Onuf, *A Union of Interests: Political and Economic Thought in Revolutionary America* (Lawrence: University Press of Kansas, 1990); and the older but still authoritative Drew R. McCoy, *The Elusive Republic: Political Economy in Jeffersonian America* (Chapel Hill: University of North Carolina Press, 1980). Compare Bouton's chapter in this volume to work by Richard Sylla and Robert Wright cited in note 57. Matson, "Risky Business," 4–7, addresses this scholarship further, as does Edwin J. Perkins, *American Public Finance and Financial Services, 1700–1815* (Columbus: Ohio State University Press, 1994).

60. Brooke Hunter, Chapter 8 in this volume; Matthew Mulcahy, "Weathering the Storms: Hurricanes and Risk in the British Greater Caribbean," *Business History Review* (Winter 2004): 635–64; Alan Taylor, "'The Hungry Year': 1789 on the Northern Border of Revolutionary America," in *Dreadful Visitations: Confronting Natural Catastrophe in the Age of Enlightenment*, ed. Alessa Johns (New York:

In sum, new views of the revolutionary economy start with many different subjects and suggest indeterminate and varied findings about opportunity and failure. As Bruce Mann's recent work reminds us, economic thought and policy unfolded unevenly over time, with unequal results for citizens of the Republic. Credit and debt were flip sides of the same American aspirations and opportunities in the early Republic; they were ubiquitous, and could cause people to slip into insolvency or bankruptcy quickly. Credit represented a partnership's opportunities, personal independence, the sinews of trade; yet the debts incurred by extending credit, as necessary risks in an era of money shortages and the vagaries of finance, when unpaid, could easily lead to overextended personal finance and besmirched reputations, the source of insolvency or imprisonment for debt. Without stable financial institutions, failures became a regular feature of commerce and internal business relations, rising to frightening proportions in the 1790s. Even though the stigma of debt faded—it was, after all, the basis for creative pursuit of economic opportunities—fears of dependency lingered and personal reputation still had great social currency. With the exception of a short-lived bankruptcy act in 1803, imprisonment for debt lasted in most states until after 1830, and each economic crisis prompted a flurry of pamphlets, sermons, and treatises expressing fears about debt as the source of damaging personal dependency. Disagreement has persisted among economic historians over whether these years held significant new opportunities for Americans or unprecedented disruptions from which Americans emerged only at some later point during the early Republic.[61]

The Economy of the Early Republic

The research agenda of economic history in the past generation has changed more dramatically for the years 1815 to 1850 than for the colonial or revolutionary eras. True, economic historians are only incrementally closer to resolving some long-standing scholarly disputes, including those about when and why economic growth may have become sustained before the Civil War. Moreover, a few scholars have incorporated elements of new research into established explanations of economic change after 1815. Typically this view insists that despite its ups and downs, the North American economy enjoyed a remarkable long-range transformation following the Revolution (or following the "critical period"), amounting to nothing short of an "economic miracle." Robert Gallman, for example, was for years in the vanguard of new economic historians who not

Routledge, 1999), 145–81; Joyce Appleby, "Commercial Farming and the 'Agrarian Myth' in the Early Republic," *Journal of American History* 68 (March 1982): 833–49; and Kulikoff, *Agrarian Origins of American Capitalism.*

61. Mann, *Republic of Debtors.*

only bequeathed numerous influential quantitative studies but also made important strides toward incorporating a historian's sensitivity to causation, chronology, and human choice into their work. His introductory chapter in volume 2 of the *Cambridge Economic History of the United States* provides an invaluable overview of economic change using the work of scores of economic historians. Deep within the amassed numbers is a familiar portrait of a prospering people, indeed of a people whose per capita income remained the highest in the world in the antebellum era—some would say until the end of the "long nineteenth century" marked by World War I.[62]

Most recent work on the early Republic, following the example of work on the colonial era, questions the metanarrative of steadily unfolding economic growth. It argues for introducing new historical subjects, new methodologies from sister disciplines, and more self-critical regard for the specific nature of what occurred, where, for whom, why, and how fast. Protracted inquires about a "transition to capitalism" and a "market revolution," while they have led in creative directions in scholarly discourse, have not yet stimulated more satisfying analyses of the economy. More fruitful work accepts the economic indeterminacy of these years and examines, for example, exceptional circumstances, the decisions of individuals or groups of Americans, the imperfections of information flows and credit, the divergent effects of markets on their participants, and entrepreneurial failures. Some of the most pathbreaking work also insists that local, regional, and sectional differences prevent us from theorizing an "American" economy or a "national" economic identity. If anything, the differences between a slave South and an industrializing North were exacerbated after 1815; certainly the proliferating strategies of production, exchange, and consumption

---

62. Robert Gallman, "Economic Growth and Structural Change in the Long Nineteenth Century," in *CEHUS*, 2:1–55, and his bibliographic essay on the literature of the 1960s and 1970s, 865–89, on short- and long-term growth, output, productivity, per capita income and its distribution, and other issues of concern to economists of early American history. An especially good recent compilation of essays by economists is Gallman and Wallis, *American Economic Growth and Standards of Living*. Optimism about relatively unimpeded economic development is echoed in Wood, *Radicalism of the American Revolution*, and in much of the literature during the 1980s and 1990s about the market revolution. For work on price series, which tend to show upward momentum in the economy when they encompass large areas and populations—but which need to be studied more in their local and short-term contexts—see the Warren-Pearson wholesale price index in U.S. Bureau of the Census, *Historical Statistics of the United States, Colonial Times to 1970*, 2 vols., bicentennial ed. (Washington, D.C.: U.S. Government Printing Office, 1975); the David-Solar index, in Paul David and Peter Solar, "A Bicentenary Contribution to the History of the Cost of Living in America," *Research in Economic History* 2 (1977): 1–80; Donald R. Adams Jr., "Prices and Wages in Maryland, 1750–1850," *Journal of Economic History* 46 (September 1986): 625–45; Donald R. Adams Jr., "Prices and Wages in Antebellum America: The West Virginia Experience," *Journal of Economic History* 52 (March 1992): 206–16; Anne Bezanson, et al., *Wholesale Prices in Philadelphia, 1784–1861* (Philadelphia: University of Pennsylvania Press, 1936); Winifred B. Rothenberg, "A Price Index for Rural Massachusetts, 1750–1855," *Journal of Economic History* 39 (December 1979): 975–1001; and G. R. Taylor, "Wholesale Commodity Prices at Charleston, South Carolina, 1796–1861," *Journal of Business and Economic History* 4 (February 1932): 356–77 (part 1) and (August 1932): 848–68 (part 2).

in countless localities defy econometric measurements that purport to illuminate sweeping patterns of large areas and populations.

Measurements of overall income or wealth—which have been at the center of narratives on long-term growth—have become frustratingly problematic, especially in the face of mounting evidence that wealth and income distribution became more, not less, unequal over time. Using a number of different measures, recent scholarship is refining our view of the poorest half of Americans, who owned virtually no wealth except household necessities by the 1850s. Households with people of foreign birth, female breadwinners, free African Americans, or long-term economic disadvantages were exceedingly likely to be poor at any time during the nineteenth century by any measurement available to economists. Farm and urban labor had considerably better, though mixed, economic prospects; the migration of farm families, the splitting off of growing children who left home for opportunities in the uncharted West or factory East, and the opportunity for some semiskilled and skilled labor for upward mobility, offset the ill fortune of those who did not fare well during economic crises or who could not find economic opportunities. Despite unprecedented immigration, westward migration, the dramatic transformation of towns and crossroads, and the maturation of cities and infant factories—as well as an unmistakably rising standard of living—the strains of growth were relentless. For one thing, although it has been customary to emphasize how a rapidly growing population of large families and steady immigration fanned out quickly into an expanding frontier, economic historians have helped to check this distorted perspective of the continent's social geography. We know from recent work that Americans in fact peopled the land only thinly in the first postrevolutionary generation; towns often were isolated from one another, which brought a train of consequences for market development and local exchange relations. Households may have been beehives of productivity, but they were not, contrary to many textbook portraits, centers of rapid material transformation. Moreover, political struggles over how to divide economic resources did not abate, regional quarrels over tariffs and banking continued strong, arguments about slavery and land distribution often became matters of economic interest, and support or condemnation of agricultural or manufacturing enterprise brought legislators to blows with each other.

Since the mid-1980s scholars have added theoretical nuance, incorporated new places and subjects of study, and widened their source base; they are adding views of the hinterlands to their coastal perspective, and many now work outward from the interior, toward stores, marketplaces and market networks, long-distance exchange, and into coastal and transatlantic areas—not only including the interior's production and exchange in their portraits of the early nation's economy but integrating the networks of peoples' economies in new geographical and vertical spaces. They are also examining farm men and women, storekeepers, crossroads craftsmen, sailors, trappers, brokers, boatmen, and many others whose collective weight qualifies simplistic portraits significantly. Many recent economic historians' numbers, dollar signs, peaks and troughs, and measured trends have provided concrete verification—even if imperfectly—of the impressions we gain from newspapers, diaries, legislative records, and account books that economic dislocation and failure were regular features of the era. The emerging picture confirms that many poor Americans prospered in new enterprises, while many wealthy Americans fell on hard times. In any event, economic historians have ceased to see unmitigated rising economic opportunity from the prerevolutionary to the Civil War years.[63]

Many economic historians have entered the thickets of debate about the pace and character of a "transition to capitalism," or an antebellum market revolution. Thus far, their work points in many directions, with uneven conclusions about when the acceleration of economic development became discernable (to contemporaries and to us), made a qualitative impact (and on whom, in what ways), and at what pace this happened. Some scholars argue that colonial limitations on the economy persisted well into the nineteenth century, making the emergence of capitalism problematic until a market society, capital accumulation, and the transformation toward free labor had become more certain. Most writers agree that there was indisputably an expanding market economy in the first two postrevolutionary generations, but few believe that there was an ineluctable accretion of change over time or widespread development of capitalism before 1850. Conflict, setback, failure, bankruptcy, and bad luck appeared with alarming frequency—the focus of many important new studies—and there was no flood of technological change or sudden appearance of economies of scale. America was still very much a commercial nation in the 1820s and 1830s; large numbers of merchants and planters were dependent on foreign markets and prices for their prosperity or failure, and myriad small producers, insurers, and transporters relied on commercial networks with the Far East, the Caribbean, and Latin America for their livelihood.[64]

The indeterminate and negotiable parameters of change are brought into even bolder relief in work that examines the political economies of early

63. For insights about this uneven and unequal development, see Temin, *Inside Business Enterprise;* Jeremy Atack, Fred Bateman, and William N. Parker, "Northern Agriculture and the Westward Movement," in *CEHUS*, 2:285–328; literature reviewed in Clayne Pope, "Inequality in the Nineteenth Century," *CEHUS*, 2:109–42; Charles Sellers, *The Market Revolution: Jacksonian America, 1815–1846* (New York: Oxford University Press, 1991); and essays in Melvyn Stokes and Stephen Conway, eds., *The Market Revolution in America: Social, Political, and Religious Expressions, 1800–1880* (Charlottesville: University Press of Virginia, 1996).

64. For a summary of scholarship before 1990, see Bruchey, *Enterprise,* 144–48, 160–61, and endnotes. New work on early national commerce has been scanty, and not tied closely enough to arguments about capitalism, the market revolution, consumption patterns, and household production. See Robert Lipsey's survey of the state of our knowledge in "U.S. Foreign Trade and the Balance of Payments, 1800–1913," *CEHUS*, 2:685–727.

Americans. Policymaking (itself a congeries of individuals and interests), changing public perceptions about the role of government in the economy, and the function of interest group politics in evoking economic change—all of these had a profound effect on the economy. Earlier emphasis on the role of federal, state, and local governments in furthering improvements such as roads and canals has been enriched by recent scholarship investigating the very consequential role of private investors teamed with local political authorities. Despite difficulties in securing reliable labor and profits for the investing proprietors, thousands of interest groups, clustered around local capitalists, laid the groundwork for more extensive state aid that was forthcoming only by the end of the 1820s. As John Larson argues, this era of rapid transformation drew on a deep public commitment, welling up from thousands of local sources, to working out how transportation and other improvements should be created to best serve multiple interests. There could be no linear progression of deepening government involvement; the Erie Canal's spectacular success rose up like a phoenix from scores of failed canal projects elsewhere in the Republic. Congressional battles over whether—and how—to implement an "American System" were persistently fought by advocates and opponents of government intervention in the economy. The views of earlier economic historians such as George Rogers Taylor, and perhaps Carter Goodrich, seem inadequate in the face of current work: in the long era after the Revolution, when the mantra of republican virtue fell easily from so many lips, a vision of public works for public welfare and the rise of a middling layer of entrepreneurs was obscured by the celebration of private interests and protection of wealth under policy and law. A republican consensus about shaping the West, and about binding the Republic together with a national infrastructure, gave way to contentious battles at local and state levels, where competing interests vied for the benefits of improvement or simply offering doomsday prophesies about the evil consequences of overweening power. A widening participatory political culture gave rise to internal changes that linked markets and migrations with half-finished and ill-conceived projects. Ideological fears, born of republicanism, undermined many of the best-conceived plans for economic development in the early Republic.[65]

Revisions to our views of credit, banking, and finance in the early Republic also reveal the gap between Federalist visions of the 1780s and the political economies Americans shaped through at least the 1830s. Strong central banking and federal regulation of commerce, though indisputably key to the nation's growth, were not accepted uncritically. As in the past, a wide swath of Americans—in state governments and in vocal interest groups—expressed considerable

65. See, e.g., Daniel B. Klein and John Majewski, "Economy, Community, and Law: The Turnpike Movement in New York, 1797–1845," *Law and Society Review* 26, no. 3 (1992): 469–512; John Lauritz Larson, *Internal Improvement: National Public Works and the Promise of Popular Government in the Early United States* (Chapel Hill: University of North Carolina Press, 2001).

opposition to new federal financial institutions. Popular demands for institutions accountable to local and state constituencies and available to a rapidly growing layer of middling investors and savers held central banking at bay for many years. This much we know from the public discourse and legislative battles of the era. But arguments for unregulated capital markets and extensive rural investment in paper instruments are also being qualified by studies of banking and financial crises during the early national years, work that often falls at the intersection of political economy and a more broadly conceptualized economic culture. Moreover, scholars are still unclear whether local and state banks contributed to early economic growth by stimulating credit and exchange, or whether their inadequate reserves of specie undermined business stability because credit and loans were vulnerable to the vagaries of markets. For example, it is still unclear whether states helped or hindered the creation of bankruptcy legislation in the antebellum era—laws varied from state to state—although we can agree that state laws probably did little to soften the blows of periodic recessions and panics, and limited liability law had a scruffy career during the market revolution. In Chapter 10, "Toward a Social History of the Corporation: Shareholding in Pennsylvania, 1800–1840," John Majewski's close look at Pennsylvania corporate (bank and canal) shareholders during the first three decades of the nineteenth century demonstrates that while citizens sometimes rioted in order to buy shares and sometimes virtually ignored investment opportunities until they were promoted loudly, laborers and artisans nevertheless widely owned stock and used it as liquid capital even in the early 1800s. The "mania" for bank stock that seized upper-class citizens in the 1790s was clearly present, argues Majewski, among the state's working people as well; and when access was limited, workers demanded greater participation in banking and lower prices for stock shares.[66]

Economic crises between 1815 and the 1850s deserve more concerted examination. As Majewski argues, following important new work, the Panic of 1819 forced many rural and small-town banks to close permanently. But, in an interesting reversal of our typical view of political economies in the 1820s and 1830s, he insists that the recoil from banking following the panic was fueled not by popular fears of "monster banks" but rather by elitist concerns about "excessive democracy." In a crafty rhetorical move, Jacksonians reversed the antibanking elitism of the 1820s and incorporated strong ideological arguments about banking into their crusade for economic democracy.

66. For this paragraph and the next three, see note 65; John Majewski, Chapter 10 in this volume; Daniel S. Dupre, Chapter 9 in this volume, including his citations to current and older work; Howard Bodenhorn, *State Banking in Early America: A New Economic History* (New York: Oxford University Press, 2002), which returns us to an econometric view that calls for testable hypotheses and measures of government and private debt; Edward J. Balleisen, *Navigating Failure: Bankruptcy and Commercial Society in Antebellum America* (Chapel Hill: University of North Carolina Press, 2001); and Matson, "Capitalizing Hope."

And as Daniel Dupre explains in Chapter 9, "The Panic of 1819 and the Political Economy of Sectionalism," the Panic of 1819 was the first truly national depression Americans experienced, the first long-term financial crisis to prompt Americans to examine deeply their ideological moorings and reassess their still-fragile economic institutions. The background to the panic is familiar: caught in the freefall of Europe's commodity prices in 1818, small farmers, southern planters, and rising entrepreneurs who had borrowed extensively— too extensively—against bank reserves entered a frightening period of business failures, unemployment, and creditor dunning. Foreclosures devastated hundreds of farm families. By early 1819 easy credit had come to a halt, and banks began to call in their loans, many of them demanding that borrowers from the eastern coastline to Cincinnati repay in specie. The devastation was deepest where expansion had been the greatest. Dupre argues that Americans understood this dark period in deeply sectional terms. Proliferating banks, currency legislation, tariffs, bankruptcy and stay laws, and commercial policies fit closely together in citizens' minds—and became associated with mid-Atlantic and northern economic goals—while free trade, independence from European prices and credit, and less circulating bank credit suited southern expansionists. But, as Dupre and others insist, the promotion of national economic interests could coexist comfortably with sectional difference; by the mid-1820s a few strong voices garnered increasing support from many state and local interests for "American" improvements and exchange over expanses of the interior, which eventually became associated with Henry Clay's "American System of Manufactures." A more widely enfranchised population demanded more democratic tariff and public land policies, general bankruptcy laws to aid small businesses and indebted entrepreneurs, and new credit and banking institutions less likely to suspend specie payments and terminate loans. Belief in the individual's moral responsibility for failure gave way to arguments about the responsibility of legislators to ease economic trauma. By the late 1820s Jacksonians had enlisted large numbers of these dissenters in a campaign against central banking—though not all banking in principle—which soon became an all-out "bank war." Supporters of the Second Bank of the United States (chartered in 1819) argued that the national bank had checked the tendency of state banks to issue excessive amounts of paper money on flimsy specie reserves, and that "easy banking" had promoted rampant land and credit speculation. But Jacksonians were in no mood to grant an early recharter to the national bank in 1832 and cheered the president's veto and subsequent dispersal of federal bank specie into regional "pet banks."

We are only beginning to understand and repackage the economic culture and political economy of the 1820s and 1830s. The linkages between the Panic of 1819, labor radicals who demanded wage increases and improvements in working conditions, and agrarian radicals who demanded land redistribution deserve closer investigation by economic historians. The economic circumstances

of Americans during the decade preceding another panic and depression, from
1837 to at least 1842, are hardly known at all, despite many good studies of the
structural banking and political conditions. Certainly excessive loans from state
banks were part of the problem, but recent work also emphasizes that tightening
credit in the northeast, the long-term decline of British credit to cotton planters
in the South, and Jackson's efforts to put Americans on a specie-payment basis
propelled the country into a depression that put an end to numerous internal
improvements; shifted focus from state sponsorship in many places to private
funding of manufactures and transportation; and provoked a new round of foreclosures, high food prices, and bankruptcies. Ironically, a large number of Jacksonians wished to return economic control to local and state authority, *including*
regulated financial institutions. Many scholars have shifted their focus on the
political development of the antebellum era from ethnocultural determinants to
economic ones; and party battles seem more closely linked to differences of economic perspective and interest, including the tariff and bank war. But there are
no major new monographs on the era's panics or the central role of economic
crises in shaping ideological and institutional remedies.

Scholars looking away from the coastline, away from new central institutions, and deeply into the social structure, are also finding that within rural
communities and households, the transition to capitalism was messy, irregular,
and largely incomplete during the antebellum era. Economic and social historians increasingly agree that many traditional ways of pricing goods, granting
credit and carrying debts, and exchanging labor and sharing resources persisted
in the early Republic; but the relatively simple material lives and insular community economies resulting from these practices did not necessarily deter hard
work or stifle widespread desire for gain. Indeed, the ideological tenets of frugality, restraint, and delayed gratification were resurrected repeatedly in heavily
populated areas and on the frontier fringe during the antebellum era, but great
numbers of Americans *also* demonstrated economic ambition according to the
needs of their families and locales, though they did not yet live in a world of unlimited acquisition. Many studies tracing economic change during the antebellum era echo the findings of colonial scholars who have made a strong case for
emphasizing "competency," "mixed farming," "moral capitalism," and "composite farms."

Martin Bruegel's recent study of the Hudson River valley demonstrates
that there was neither a timeless market in which buyers and sellers calculated
the best prices nor a three-way class struggle between capitalist exporters, landlords, and tradition-bound tenants. Moreover, while many mechanisms of a
market economy developed in the hinterlands before the War of Independence,
no market revolution had been completed a generation later. Farmers produced
surpluses for sale in markets beyond their family and community networks,
used cash, became ever more aware of market time, which was dissociated from

natural farming rhythms, and paid wages to farm laborers. But the valley's people were tied by the bonds of reciprocity and production for local exchange long into the 1800s as well. Similarly, Thomas Wermuth finds that the bonds of community endured long after the Revolution in Ulster County, New York, perhaps even longer than scholars have found for New England and parts of the Delaware Valley and upper Chesapeake. But the market revolution reached the area's residents incrementally, not because there were increases of crop yields, purchases of new farm equipment, or a more aggressive marketing mentality but largely because of external factors such as western migration, transportation innovations, credit from distant storekeepers and merchants, and outwork arrangements established in New York City. But, in addition to Wermuth's external causes for change, Breugel adds the local community's decision to introduce wage payments and manufactures as further rationale for a market revolution by the late 1820s in rural New York. Bigger mills supplanted outwork for many householders, even as artisan shops remained a feature of the countryside. Together, Bruegel and Wermuth invite us to see a more complicated countryside in which women worked and consumed, slaves and hired hands labored in homes and fields, and sloop landings became arenas in which to publicly negotiate economic relations. Family production, neighborhood sharing and exchange, and local markets became shields against the adversity facing most farmers periodically in the postrevolutionary decades; farmers strove to improve their land and produce more for exchange at a distance before they fully accepted the cash nexus and price convergence. Neighborhood exchange, in which goods were bought and sold according to need or rough calculations of value, coexisted comfortably with longer-distance markets that set more regularized prices for goods until the late 1820s.[67]

Although Christopher Clark found elements of farm wage labor and marketing of goods in regional markets in early national western Massachusetts, he insists that customary relations of agricultural production and a traditional household economy still prevailed. As others have added, the market relations Winifred Rothenberg posits for western Massachusetts after the 1780s did not yet include the capitalist labor and production relations of the later industrial era. Indeed, the rapid-fire economic changes often associated with a "market revolution" certainly involved commercialization, the extension of trading and marketing into the interior, and the thickening of crossroads, retailing, and urban networks during the entire antebellum era; but adding them all together does not amount to the discovery of capitalism. Even the capitalist values apparent in the early national mid-Atlantic region, which were closely related to the liberal political upheaval of the postwar generation, do not prove the existence of

67. See notes 36–39 above and Thomas S. Wermuth, *Rip Van Winkle's Neighbors: The Transformation of Rural Society in the Hudson River Valley, 1720–1850* (Ithaca: Cornell University Press, 2002).

a capitalist economic system. America's capitalism emerged in fits and starts and became a dominant economic system only when labor was commodified; wages became the dominant (though not universal) reward for work; entrepreneurs made capital investments in a generalized system of production associated with households losing autonomy over the labor of their members; infant factories absorbed people who had worked in small shops; and wage workers were separated from the products of their labor. Capitalism took decades to displace traditional forms of work, customary expectations of producers and consumers, and paternalistic authority. Finally, whether we use the term "takeoff" or "market revolution," each implying a different set of scholarly tools and methodologies, one of the most important consequences of the recent outpouring of studies has been a newfound appreciation of the interconnectedness of households, manufactures, transportation and information networks, banking, commerce, and policymaking. Although few scholars would argue for a universal desire for a capitalist Republic, it is still unclear how the connections among different economic activities in different places affected the pace and nature of capitalism's emergence.[68]

Rural and small-town Americans would have been acutely aware of the quickening pace of economic change, especially where settlement was thicker and internal improvements linked older and newer, countryside and town. Already in the late colonial era, the western portions of Massachusetts, large areas of Connecticut and New Jersey, and the comparatively densely populated region of southeastern Pennsylvania were filled with savvy farmers and craftsmen who welcomed market opportunities. Gradually, newly settled areas of the postrevolutionary period adopted price convergence and regularized patterns of production and exchange in place of customary pricing and local reciprocity. Transport costs fell with the building of roads and canals, as it became feasible to get products from the old Northwest to crowded cities of the East. Manufactured items filled the shelves of merchants along the Ohio River, carted there by mule trains

68. For the arguments and bibliography about early national capitalism, readers can start with Christopher Clark, "The Consequences of the Market Revolution in the American North," in Stokes and Conway, *Market Revolution,* 23–42; Clark, "Economics and Culture: Opening up the Rural History of the Early American Northeast," *American Quarterly* 43 (June 1991): 279–301; Winifred B. Rothenberg, *From Market-Places to a Market Society: The Transformation of Rural Massachusetts, 1750–1850* (Chicago: University of Chicago Press, 1992), especially chapter 1; Appleby, *Inheriting the Revolution,* especially chapter 3; Kulikoff, "Transition to Capitalism"; McCoy, *Elusive Republic;* Bruegel, *Farm, Shop, Landing,* introduction; Sellers, *Market Revolution;* special forum in the *Journal of the Early Republic* 12 (Winter 1992); Gilje *Wages of Independence;* Gregory Nobles, "The Rise of Merchants in Rural Market Towns: A Case Study of Eighteenth-Century Northampton, Massachusetts," *Journal of Social History* 24 (1990): 5–23; Lamoreaux, "Rethinking the Transition to Capitalism"; and Seth Rockman, Chapter 12 in this volume. Kulikoff offers a nuanced reading of the early countryside that incorporates hundreds of microhistories and recent economic findings in *From British Peasant to Colonial American Farmers.* On families, see Lee Craig, "The Value of Household Labor in Antebellum Northern Agriculture," *Journal of Economic History* 51 (March 1991): 67–82. On rural artisans, see Kulikoff, *From British Peasants to Colonial American Farmers,* 221–22, 346nn44–45; and Johanna Miller Lewis, *Artisans in the North Carolina Backcountry* (Lexington: University Press of Kentucky, 1995), especially chapters 2–6.

and flatboats. The time it took information to reach St. Louis and Pittsburgh about events hundreds of miles away diminished rapidly. Distinctive regions of agricultural specialization at once separated clusters of settled areas from older regions and tied them into elongating markets. Forges, mills, and banks became a regular feature of hundreds of new towns serving the surrounding country-side. Grain and livestock flowed from the newly developing breadbaskets beyond the Appalachian ridge, while older farming areas of New England turned either to mixing grain agriculture with vegetables, fruits, and some livestock, or to part-time, itinerant, and day laboring, as they could. Ironically, although new land was being settled and cultivated rapidly, productivity (as measured in the amount of work it took to produce marketable surpluses) remained the same in most regions, or fell, until greater mechanization took effect—largely after the 1840s. The result was constant high demand for working hands. Families adapted by putting more children to work in gardens, clearing projects, feeding and tend-ing chickens and livestock, weeding and harvesting crops, and other chores. Dairying became a prominent form of agricultural production in the mid-Atlantic region, first in the fringe neighborhoods around cities and then further into the countryside. Diversification became not only a hedge against the risks of uncertain markets but a clear indication of adaptive response to market oppor-tunities. Most people probably did not produce more per acre, but they plowed more acres and sent more food to market; they did not yet eat canned goods or travel by rail, but they made fewer products at home and accepted a greater degree of anonymity and distance between themselves and the ultimate markets for their surpluses. Still, although farmers welcomed market development, their participation in a capitalist system of agricultural production and exchange emerged unevenly over the course of the long nineteenth century.[69]

Capitalism's arrival was delayed in other ways as well. The putting-out system was still freshly extending itself into newly settled areas of the country-side for decades after some coastal New England and mid-Atlantic regions had made important strides toward capitalist relations of production, banking, and sophisticated information and market development. New frontier studies illumi-nate another process from which both research on older communities and econo-metric analysis might benefit. Case studies of the Ohio Valley and Louisiana demonstrate that alongside the apparent quickening and diversification of eco-nomic activity—including rapid town growth and land clearing—traditional economic relations among producers, middlemen, and merchants persisted rela-tively undisturbed. Diversification and population growth gave rise to numerous success stories (though certainly just as many failures), but they do not necessar-ily indicate higher crop yields, falling costs of production and transportation, or

---

69. On uses of the land, see Peter O. Wacker and Paul G. E. Clemens, *Land Use in Early New Jersey: A Historical Geography* (Newark: New Jersey Historical Society, 1995).

reliable markets. Moreover, frontier dependency on the North or South for goods and credit persisted for years in many new towns despite the rise of maturing cities along frontier riverways. Indeed, many recent studies reinforce the dominant view of scholars in the 1970s, in showing that many backcountry and frontier farm families believed their long-term goals were to avoid capitalist economic relations, or at least some of its presumed worst consequences, and to preserve the arrangements of local and family production at the same time.[70]

Our understanding of the lives of working people in the early national period has undergone a seismic shift in recent years, with profound consequences for studying the economy more broadly. While still committed to studying new technologies, land use, natural resource extraction, patterns of savings and investment, and improvement and invention, many scholars nevertheless now realize that changes in the size, ethnic and racial character, skills, and other characteristics of the workforce had a tremendous impact on antebellum economic development. As a previous generation of labor historians argued, the picture of labor's development in this era is complicated. In the aggregate, real wages grew over the course of the nineteenth century, especially for clerks and retailers; agricultural labor opportunities grew alongside urban ones, though not everywhere; and many new occupations arose in the Northeast and mid-Atlantic region, reinforcing the magnetic draw of their ports for immigrants.

Work in cities was intricately blended with general economic conditions, skill, race, gender, and ethnicity. Although about 15 percent of artisans attained somewhat prestigious positions as shop owners, small manufacturers, mill managers, or importing partners, fully 50 to 70 percent of city residents could barely make ends meet. Lately scholars have been giving most attention to the moderately successful shopkeepers, craftsmen, and retailers who showed signs of aggressive involvement in banking, real estate investment, and wage labor. In Chapter 11, "Small-Producer Capitalism in Early National Philadelphia," Donna Rilling finds ample evidence that Philadelphia house carpenters often were strategically placed during the 1820s and 1830s to secure capital to purchase labor and materials. Despite formidable risks, these urban entrepreneurs were in the forefront of ambitious manufacturing achievements in the city. Joyce Appleby's portraits of middling early Americans and Naomi Lamoreaux's look at "insider lending" suggest complementary views of significant economic success in the young nation. Older labor histories focused on the early nineteenth century's relatively dismal prospects for working-class individuals, while studies of business elites rarely investigated their intersection with the rising middle class or the incidence of devastating failure among the rich. At present, many studies are tipping the balance toward research about the rise of "innovation," "entrepreneurship,"

70. E.g., Kim M. Gruenwald, *River of Enterprise: The Commercial Origins of Regional Identity in the Ohio Valley, 1790–1850* (Bloomington: University of Indiana Press, 2002); Carol Sheriff, *The Artificial River: The Erie Canal and the Paradox of Progress, 1817–1862* (New York: Hill and Wang, 1996).

and "ambitious risk-taking," conceptual categories that often ignore the sharper edges of adversity or the peaks and troughs of economic opportunity from year to year. It bears remembering, however, that poverty became endemic in certain neighborhoods or whole towns; that skills were degraded or lost altogether in certain occupations; and that class and ethnic conflicts erupted periodically, putting a damper on the claims for a "capitalist miracle." Although few scholars are currently exploring working people's roles in forging industrial capitalism in the early nineteenth century, this would require rethinking the relationship between owners and workers, whose partially conflicting goals, mutual dependency, but unequal power demanded alterations in class relations. Workers would have to do more than generate capital alone, or build fortunes and make way for increasingly wealthy families, or become inured to class inequalities. These components of the "spirit of capitalism" were perhaps necessary preconditions for a capitalist economic system, but without the systematic control of free and slave labor, as well as restructured relations of production, they were insufficient for a transition to a capitalist economy.[71]

Views about the extent to which Americans had become a manufacturing—though not yet an industrializing—people by the 1850s parallel those about other issues during the period. For some scholars, a general increase in manufacturing accompanied the deepening transportation, market, and consumer "revolutions" of the early Republic, which were attached closely to conditions of international trade and war. In the northeastern and mid-Atlantic regions, according to this argument, merchants were spurred by expectations of economic independence from Europeans to invest capital from commercial profits in manufacturing, especially during the disruptive Napoleonic War years and Jefferson's embargoes of 1807–9. Partnerships and kinship networks pooled capital for coastal processing industries or factories. New England's Cabots and Lowells and Delaware's "Quaker Oligarchy," among others, used family savings and reputation to spread risks in commercial partnerships, build trustworthy linkages to retailers, and invest in a few manufacturing economies of scale. And although some narratives are more anecdotal than rigorously investigated, it seems clear that the prosperous merchants who initiated trade with China and Latin America generated profits that were often invested in shipbuilding, ginseng and other agricultural production, and mid-Atlantic manufactures.[72]

71. Donna J. Rilling, Chapter 11 in this volume; Appleby, "Vexed Story of Capitalism," sources cited in n. 72; and work reviewed in Robert Margo, "The Labor Force in the Nineteenth Century," *CEHUS*, vol. 2, chapter 5, and his bibliography. Compare these views to those of Seth Rockman, Chapter 12 in this volume; Jonathan A. Glickstein, *Concepts of Free Labor in Antebellum America* (New Haven: Yale University Press, 1991); Bruce Laurie, *Artisans into Workers: Labor in Nineteenth-Century America* (New York: Hill and Wang, 1989); Janet Siskind, *Rum and Axes: The Rise of a Connecticut Merchant Family, 1795–1850* (Ithaca: Cornell University Press, 2001); and the many bibliographical comments about labor and economy in Stokes and Conway, *Market Revolution in America*.

72. For work since 1985 assessed in this paragraph and the next five, see Bruchey, *Enterprise,*

Although the most extensive merchant involvement in reorganizing production and investing capital in new equipment occurred in textiles, other merchants teamed up with mine and forge operators or lumber and flour millers to more deeply finance existing enterprises and coordinate efforts to distribute their finished goods, such as iron, paper, and furniture. Still others turned from trade and invested in the boot and shoe industry, where—with skilled craftsmen, some of whom benefited from the new social and financial arrangements—they created central shops from which cut leather was put out for finishing in homes throughout eastern New England. From northern New England down through northern Delaware, merchants helped finance mill construction, purchased machines and raw materials, went into credit and debt with planters and foreign markets, and distributed the finished cotton and woolen cloth. Larger and more efficient mill works gradually displaced home manufactures and the putting-out system in woolen cloth, and cotton became more popular, especially as southern planters expanded their exploitation of land and slave labor in cotton agriculture. These investments had wide ramifications: transportation costs gradually declined, farm and urban markets were increasingly integrated, incomes and household consumption rose, and Americans glimpsed a profound transformation of work. The modernization of banking and financial services, as well as government tariffs, bounties, patents, land laws, and bank charters encouraged would-be manufacturers.

Critics believe that this rosy picture of manufacturing obscures as much as it illuminates. Some caution us against generalizing that all "Americans" in a roughly "middling" condition prospered in tandem across regional, ethnic, environmental, class, and other lines. Further, although these studies tend to give the worm's-eye view of specific communities, where local conditions cannot easily be generalized to other places and times, they have the virtue of placing manufacturing in its proper place between the colonial and industrial eras. Hamilton's

149–64, 570–72; Naomi Lamoreaux, "Entrepreneurship, Business Organization, and Economic Concentration," in *CEHUS*, 2:403–34, 914–19; Rothenberg, *From Market-Places to a Market Economy*; Atack, Bateman, and Parker, "The Farm, The Farmer, and the Market," *CEHUS*, 2:245–84; and Kenneth L. Sokoloff and B. Zorina Khan, "The Democratization of Invention During Early Industrialization: Evidence from the United States, 1790–1846," *Journal of Economic History* 50 (June 1990): 363–78. For the limitations of business accounting and difficulties of business prediction, see especially Judith A. McGaw, *Most Wonderful Machine: Mechanization and Social Change in Berkshire Paper Making, 1801–1885* (Princeton: Princeton University Press, 1987). For general assessments see the recent work on manufacturing, with excellent endnotes leading to other economic history, in Peskin, *Manufacturing Revolution;* Jonathan Prude, "Capitalism, Industrialization, and the Factory in Post-Revolutionary America," *Journal of the Early Republic* 16 (Summer 1996); and Bezís-Selfa, *Forging America*. For earlier work, see Philip Scranton, *Proprietary Capitalism: The Textile Manufacture at Philadelphia, 1800–1885* (New York: Cambridge University Press, 1983); and Thomas Dublin, *Women at Work: The Transformation of Work and Community in Lowell, Massachusetts, 1826–1860* (New York: Columbia University Press, 1979). For an example of manufacturing rising first in small towns but funded by elites, see Siskind, *Rum and Axes*. In general, compare the perspectives of essays in *CEHUS*, vol. 2; Sellers, *Market Revolution;* and the special forum in the *Journal of the Early Republic* 12 (Winter 1992).

Report on Manufactures, to take just one example, did not win government approval in the early 1790s, and would-be manufacturers resisted the kind of central government regulation it entailed for many years thereafter. At the center of Henry Clay's address to Congress in 1810, in which he previewed his "American System of Manufactures" plan, was a vision of an expanding, hard-working people of rising means, producing and consuming an ever-expanding variety of goods. "Comfort and convenience," Clay assured Congress and the public, not "excess and luxury," would accompany energetic government promotion of private and mixed enterprise. New studies suggest that these hopeful plans met with popular resistance, ethnic and labor conflict, piecemeal government policies, and competition between special interests that complicated the emergence of manufacturing. Moreover, if one believes that industrialization depended on the availability of capital and credit, new technologies that displaced human and animal power and used steam and water power, and significant economies of scale, then surely the early Republic's manufacturing was in its infant phase.

Coastal towns and cities may not have advanced as far along these lines as previous work suggested, even where textile production and milling were most advanced. The life stories of individual entrepreneurs, among them some of the era's leading merchants and bankers, often ignore how merchants used their financial resources in local and regional economies, how middlemen functioned between farmers or craftsmen and coastal wholesalers, and the extent of mutual reliance on brokers, bankers, and family fortunes. How did merchants come to think of commercial profits as capital for factory investment? How did they begin to think of customers as potential workers in new establishments organized on different terms? How did investors arrive at their decisions to create and use new financial institutions and business arrangements, and how did they weigh their hopes of investing successfully against the well-known risks? The stories of Lowell and Slater mills aside, many of the early manufacturing efforts initiated by coastal merchants did not survive the vagaries of international markets or the economic panics of the early Republic.

Before the 1850s small "manufactories" produced shoes, flour, furniture, metal tools, barrels, paper, and rope using hand tools and traditional water power along fast streams, as well as the coalmining that would spur the creation of forges and furnaces in the mid-Atlantic and upper South. Small proprietorships and partnerships—much more widespread than corporations during this era—were often short-lived or endured for the lifetime of one owner, were barely solvent or steeped in debt, remained vulnerable to impatient creditors, and frequently were "silent" participants in the economy because they did not advertise or trade with well-documented businesses. Also, despite the outpouring of studies during the 1970s and 1980s about the transition from artisan shop to factory production, current scholarship points toward the much slower adaptation of workers to new tools, technologies, and forms of production. At present, we are not able to argue cogently about what fundamental breakthroughs occurred in nontextile manufacturing technologies, and few have studied the incremental refinements in how work got done at the micro level. Such studies could tie manufacturing processes to changes in banking and bookkeeping, political discussions about the economy, and restructured family life. They could also address the long-standing debate about the causes of qualitative changes in productivity and standards of living—i.e., whether these came about because of new institutions, new technologies, and efficiencies in factory and labor organization, or whether they emerged because capitalists turned to more intensive employment of immigrant and rural labor, spearheaded the restructuring of artisans' work. Were Connecticut's and Rhode Island's wage-earning profiles—nearly half of employed mill and factory workers being women and children by 1820— typical of other areas? Was Baltimore's rise—dependent, as Seth Rockman's chapter reminds us, on the proving grounds of race and gender—duplicated in other cities?

Nor do we know enough yet about the ways that manufactures were started and sustained, or how support for them grew beyond the networks of capitalists who owned them. From the revolutionary generation until at least the Civil War, entrepreneurs generally followed simple forms of bookkeeping and calculations of their general profit or loss that had been practiced for generations; there is little evidence that manufacturers' thinking about "capital" had advanced beyond that of earlier family-run or partnership-based businesses, in which accounts were manipulated freely to take advantage of commercial opportunities and available assets were used freely to sustain households and creditors in retailing and wholesaling. Early manufacturers often measured their success by paying bills when they could, keeping inventories of goods flowing in and out of a store or warehouse, and purchasing household comforts and real estate. The popular view still held that special charters of incorporation for banks and manufacturing enterprises bred "monopolistic tendencies" that shut out democratic competition. It seems that state legislatures and courts began to push aside old privileges and responded to public demand for general incorporation acts, more democratic access to banking and stockholding, and modest protection of debtors only during the 1830s. However, it would take still another generation before a sizeable number of Americans owned many shares of manufacturing, development, and banking stock. In the meantime, much of the stock issued by manufacturing corporations seems to have been held by the very people who created the enterprises, who often used local banks on whose boards they sat to mobilize the capital they required. Clearly there are rich opportunities for work on manufacturing and the rise of American capitalism.

This picture of Americans' mixed and halting advances in manufacturing is put in bolder relief when scholars turn from the "American" or "national" economy to local, regional, and sectional geographies. Sectionalism, which is so firmly embedded in the political and cultural histories of the era, remains fundamental to much recent economic history as well. Few scholars dispute that the North consistently had a higher standard of living than the South, experienced the benefits of the market revolution earlier, and, especially in the mid-Atlantic states and coastal cities, accumulated more capital earlier and invested more extensively in developing the infrastructure and institutions that furthered economic development. The corollary argument often shows that the South remained dependent on staples exporting and slave labor. In cotton-producing areas, in fact, by the 1820s slave labor and planters' agricultural investment choices shaped the economic character of the South more than ever before.

Without disputing these very consequential sectional differences, new work has targeted important unresolved questions. Was the South possibly a more flexible economic region with more capitalist features than many analyses have allowed, albeit less so than the North? Were planters and merchants in the South as unable (compared to the North) to muster capital for investment, and as resistant to efficiencies of production, as we have argued? Could there have been a market revolution in the South, and if so, what was its character? New work suggests that exaggerated claims of sectional difference overlook the North's dependence on the vagaries of far-reaching commerce and credit that often left its merchants bereft of fluid funds, and underestimate the South's maturing infrastructure of mills, forges, roads, stores, and banks. Moreover, both regions experienced rising and falling commodities prices determined far from American soil; certainly, all parts of the country felt the blows of European recession after the War of 1812 and the Panic of 1819. To cite just one example highlighted by recent work, Virginia was the nation's leading producer of tobacco and a major exporter of wheat during the early Republic, and its ability to export these crops determined the economic well-being of its citizens to a very great extent. But much of the mid-Atlantic was just as reliant on exports of wheat and flour, and New England on carrying the foodstuffs and cotton of other regions. More intensive study comparing the *relative* significance of exporting, in the context of all economic activities, in each region could possibly erase some of the difference between these sections.[73]

73. For a lively debate about the argument that yeomen farmers were averse to market involvement in southern frontier areas, which was advanced by Steven Hahn in *Roots of Southern Populism: Yeoman Farmers and the Transformation of the Georgia Upcountry, 1850–1890* (New York: Oxford University Press, 1983), see Shawn Kantor and J. Morgan Kousser's exchange with Hahn in the *Journal of Southern History* 59 (May 1993). For continuing debates about whether the South was capitalist or precapitalist, see, e.g., Robert W. Fogel, *Without Consent or Contract: The Rise and Fall of American Slavery* (New York: W. W. Norton, 1989); sources cited in Bruchey, *Enterprise*, 237–52; and Chaplin, *An Anxious Pursuit*. Comparisons of major geographical sections are eloquently stated in Gallman, "Economic Growth and Structural Change in the Long Nineteenth Century," 1–56. For foreign markets and prices, see Weiss, "U.S. Labor Force Estimates," 21–23.

Indisputably, slavery set the South apart from the North economically. Rice, sugar, and cotton production required heavy capital investment in slaves and land, and sometimes ships and processing machinery; the domination of these crops over southern lives (and over northern lives in shipping) is clearest in the statistic that cotton represented nearly 60 percent of the value of all American exports on the eve of the Civil War. At that time the South also had only about 30 percent of the country's railroads and no more than 15 percent of its factories. Recent work has added nuance to older investigations of the cultural contours of "slave communities" by examining the modes of production, exchange, and deployment of distinctive material styles and forms within the larger societies of North America. This scholarship is almost invariably based on the starting premise that antebellum southern life was varied and changing, a mosaic of negotiable and mutually interdependent relations, shifting world markets, and spaces for the economic autonomy of slaves. Slaves were not only participants in Atlantic-world commerce but also objects of the domestic slave trade; they participated actively in the internal economy of plantations and in the marketplace by selling food from their gardens, entered a thriving black market, and occasionally became hired labor from which masters usually benefited. They labored largely outside the cash nexus, but at times crossed over into market society. New work on small farmers in the South adds important dimensions as well. Although, as numerous economic historians have argued, many small southern farmers produced goods that would best serve their family and neighborhood needs because staples production lay outside their financial means, they also entered local exchange with planters. Less market oriented than middling and great planters—sometimes less so than slaves whose skills were deployed as rivermen, blacksmiths, or miners—small farmers nevertheless sold food and family labor to planters and in turn purchased certain finished goods from importers. Indeed, because the great planters imported many manufactured goods and used skilled slaves to produce and repair a wide variety of farming equipment, buildings, and clothing, their relationship to small farmers was a more specialized one—premised on the exchange of food—than the one existed between merchants and the mixed economies in the northeast and mid-Atlantic. We may never know how extensively upland and interior yeomen families aspired to enter the market-oriented world of planters in the valleys and lowlands, or how readily they would have adapted certain farming strategies to staple crop agriculture with slave labor, had they been able to do so; but evidence points to pragmatic—as opposed to moral or cultural—decisions to avoid the route of larger planters. More commercially oriented farmers, who occupied a place between the successful planter and the yeoman practicing "safety-first" agriculture, tended to support measures to enhance market conditions, including more banks and roads in the South, and willingly took the risks of investing their small savings in internal improvements projects. The result for southern economic history is doubly ironic: on the one hand, many ambitious commercial agriculturalists were more vocal advocates of territorial expansion, banks, and transportation improvements than were some great slaveholding planters, and they were equally vocal critics of small farmers' deliberate strategy to produce for local exchange and avoid the calculating, self-interested route toward southern prosperity that cotton and slaves so clearly demonstrated. On the other hand, the large slave-holders, who were themselves involved in international markets, often limited their own involvement in the advance of southern industrialization.[74]

Recent studies of women's participation in the early American econ-omy centers on the three postrevolutionary decades, when urban, craft-based artisan work was increasingly displaced by wage labor in the northeast and mid-Atlantic regions, and when the differences between free-labor householders and plantation labor deepened in the economies and ideology of Americans. With and without large databases, many scholars are developing sophisticated views of northern and southern households; at a time when northern men increasingly left their homes to work in shops and small factories, and independent landown-ing yeomen became a critical feature of the national identity, women's activi-ties were being relegated to nonwage, nurturing, and spiritual roles, and, as Jeanne Boydston eloquently argues, women's household production and public exchanges began to disappear from view, ideologically speaking. Paradoxically, optimism about a free-labor republic in which homes would become a "repub-lican haven" went hand in hand with two contrary developments. One was that large numbers of women—whether as heads of poor households or in their capacity as supplemental providers for families—often were forced to rely on intricate informal negotiations and cooperative exchanges of goods and services with neighbors and storekeepers, or to resort to charity and poor relief. The other is that despite republican ideology, in reality women expanded their house-hold production, grew more dependent on external markets, and were thus ever more integrated into an expansive economic network. Some studies have begun to link these findings to women's economic roles as the proprietors of busi-nesses, whether owned by their husbands or run independently, confirming that

---

74. For new literature on slavery, see Stanley L. Engerman, "Bibliographic Essay," *CEHUS*, 2:905–9; Ira Berlin and Philip D. Morgan, eds., *The Slaves' Economy: Independent Production by Slaves in the Americas* (London: Frank Cass, 1991); Roderick A. McDonald, *The Economy and Material Culture of Slaves: Goods and Chattels on the Sugar Plantations of Jamaica and Louisiana* (Baton Rouge: Louisiana State University Press, 1993); Joseph P. Reidy, *From Slavery to Agrarian Capitalism in the Cotton Planta-tion South: Central Georgia, 1800–1890* (Chapel Hill: University of North Carolina Press, 1992); Harry L. Watson, "Slavery and Development in a Dual Economy: The South and the Market Revolution," in Stokes and Conway, *Market Revolution,* 43–73, especially 44–50; and Egerton, "Markets Without a Mar-ket Revolution." In addition, there has been an outpouring of new work on the place of slaves in the transatlantic networks of the eighteenth and early nineteenth centuries, not only from the standpoint of the slave trade but also including slaves as agents in shaping the nature of the Atlantic-world econ-omy's labor markets, consumption, and adaptations to material goods and their uses; see notes 20, 24, 35, and 41 above.

women often labored in a "hidden market" where they made important contributions to the survival or prosperity of a family. Women did not become
secluded in a moral economy; rather, they met customers, paid debts, signed for
loans from banks, paid workers, boarded and fed strangers, collected rent, and
shopped freely in public markets. In fact, women's paid and unpaid labor became
crucial to sustaining urban northern households and the economy overall. It was
the very extent and vitality of women's informal economic participation that
threatened customary economic roles for women and drew the wrath of pater-
nalists who wished for their "public absence."[75]

Most of these changes cannot be traced through legal records, business
papers, probate inventories, or other documents; interpretations require extrap-
olation about what, precisely, women did in household economies and cannot
be quantified to suit traditional economic historians' wishes. Of course, women
and men who wrote about prospering, or sometimes just getting by, suffused
their reflections about economic choice with assumptions about how work and
exchange differed according to gender. But beyond recovering such thoughts
about economic activities, we still have very few concrete studies about the division of labor within households, the degree to which women participated in
markets or made decisions about what to produce, and what significant differences may have existed between middling urban and rural consumer farmers'
households. Susan Branson has found that despite changing ideology, Philadelphia's middle-class Elizabeth Meredith was consistently involved in the family
business and the household economy through all of its changing fortunes. We
need comparative work on other times and places—for example, frontier communities and commercial farming areas of the South—to understand more fully
the meaning of Meredith's and other women's economic lives.[76]

75. For a sampling of this work, see Claudia Goldin and Kenneth L. Sokoloff, "Women,
Children, and Industrialization in the Early Republic: Evidence from the Manufacturing Censuses,"
Journal of Economic History 42 (December 1982): 741–74; Marla Miller, "The Accounts of Tryphena
Newton Cooke: Work, Family, and Community in Hadley, Massachusetts, 1780–1805," *Annual Proceed-
ings of the Dublin Seminar for New England Folklife* (1999); Seth Rockman, "Women's Labor, Gender
Ideology, and Working-Class Households in Early Republic Baltimore," *Explorations in Early American
Culture* 66 (1999): 174–200; Mary P. Ryan, *Cradle of the Middle Class: The Family in Oneida County, New
York, 1790–1865* (New York: Cambridge University Press, 1981); Kulikoff, *Agrarian Origins of American
Capitalism;* Claudia Goldin, "The Economic Status of Women in the Early Republic: Quantitative
Evidence," *Journal of Interdisciplinary History* 16 (Winter 1986); Boydston, *Home and Work;* Jeanne M.
Boydston, "The Woman Who Wasn't There: Women's Market Labor and the Transition to Capitalism in
the United States," in Gilje, *Wages of Independence,* 23–48. Also see Laurel Ulrich, *The Age of Homespun*
(New York: Knopf, 2001), for corroboration of women's expanding productive contributions to households and wider markets. Work on farming, the transition to capitalism, labor, and material culture
often contains important insights on women's economies; see discussions above. For material culture,
see, e.g., Cary Carson's essay about theory and research, "Consumption," in *A Companion to Colonial
America,* ed. Daniel Vickers (Malden, Mass.: Blackwell, 2003), 334–65, and his fine bibliography.

76. Susan Branson, "Women and the Family Economy in the Early Republic: The Case
of Elizabeth Meredith," in *Family and Society in American History,"* ed. Joseph Hawes and Elizabeth

In the final chapter of this volume, "The Unfree Origins of American Capitalism," Seth Rockman returns our focus to the welcome urgings of Tomlins and Waldstreicher to research more deeply the racial and gendered constructions of unfree labor, especially as we consider the capitalist nature of the early American economy. As many contributors to this volume demonstrate, the personal failure, social dislocation, and intensifying racism accompanying early national economic change may have affected African American and female workers more deeply than they did white urban workers. The emergence of capitalism was premised on more than commercial farmers willingly joining market society and self-made artisans-turned-owners availing themselves of ready credit; it was just as thoroughly based on legislated unequal economic benefits, the use of force and the law to circumscribe opportunities for large numbers of people, and securing the profits to northern capitalists from economic activities dependent on southern slavery. As numerous new studies show, American economic development relied as much, if not more, on various forms of coercion as on the liberal ideal of free opportunity and minimal government interference. But we need to know more about the shadings of meaning and real-life consequences of coercion for these huge numbers of Americans, and to historically construct a spectrum of distinctive and overlapping economies, including free and unfree, skilled and unskilled, rural and urban, native-born and immigrant working people.

The essays in this collection, and the conference for which they were produced, aimed to initiate a dialogue about an expansive conceptualization of what is "economic" in early American life, to incorporate both economic and historical studies, and to blend the voices of deeply divided interpretations of the past. Many of the authors in this volume attempt to incorporate particular lives and historical moments into work undertaken by generations of past economic historians, while others invite us to consider new methodological directions and new kinds of sources. Since 1985 work in economic history has also brought us closer to understanding the limitations of previous studies. We may never pin down the extent and character of economic growth before the 1850s to our satisfaction, or develop the correct balance of economic characteristics in commerce or agriculture across times and places, or understand sufficiently the onset of industrialization or origins of capitalism, or give our readers the best economic portraits of changing households, shops, and stores. Economists and historians

Nybakken (Urbana: University of Illinois Press, 2001), 72–94; Amy Dru Stanley, "Home Life and the Morality of the Market," in Stokes and Conway, *Market Revolution in America,* 74–96; Christine Stansell, *City of Women: Sex and Class in New York, 1789–1860* (New York: Knopf, 1986); and sources in note 75 above. For work on men's economies and their gendered participation in the market revolution, see Brian P. Luskey, "The Marginal Men: Merchants' Clerks and Society in the Northeastern United States, 1790–1860" (Ph.D. diss., Emory University, 2004).

may never agree, for example, about whether North American agricultural production in its many forms was driven primarily by external demand or by cultural choice, or both. We may never agree about whether output (as yields of crops, shipbuilding, small manufacturers, or any other economic activity) was rising because Americans were economically rational agents or because they followed available opportunities within the constraints of custom, local policies, or the environment. Nevertheless, economists and historians have learned much from each other. Economists have made profound contributions to our understanding of the past that involve much more than the manipulation of empirical data, and their analyses have permeated historians' thinking—often unwittingly—about many unresolved social, labor, and cultural issues. The essays published in this collection show that many economic historians have now joined context, narrative, and cultural interpretation to economic models and counterfactual propositions, and that only the most resolute scholars still insist that there is an overarching *homo economicus*. For their part, historians not only of business, banking, transportation, and commerce, but also of migrating peoples, slavery, agriculture, industry, urban and rural environments, technology, gender and family construction, and social inequality and opportunity have been deeply influenced by the findings and the provocative, if not always correct, assertions of economic historians in recent years.

Together, the authors in this volume add their research to the tremendous outpouring of new work—as the citations in this volume demonstrate—about issues and trends lying outside traditional economic models, in areas addressing risk, chance, contingency, and irrationality, which are undoubtedly economic in character and yield important insights about the people who lived during different eras of the country's economic past. The present generation is foraging unabashedly in other disciplines and adapting itself to the wave of culture studies washing over the profession, but it is also rediscovering political economy, "creative destruction" in economic development, the role of governments in facilitating or blocking economic change, the importance of statistics and data for understanding workers and consumers, and more. New questions are crowding under the capacious umbrella of "economic history" about race, labor relations, gender, intellectual climates of opinion, entrepreneurship, finance, commerce, manufacturing, war and revolution, and other themes. New work redefines old physical and social boundaries as well; in addition to colonial (or imperial) and national arenas of investigation, they are putting local, regional, sectional, and Atlantic-world contexts under close scrutiny, and employing comparative and interdisciplinary methodologies to do so.

In recent years the search for greater empirical accuracy and precise models—which in the first decades of the past century might have brought economists and historians closer together—has often been frustrated by competing methods and objectives in studying the past. As economists became more committed to mathematics, historians fell under the influences of culture studies, postmodernism, and postcolonial theories that insist on the indeterminacy of human experience.[77] To their credit, many historians of early American economic issues have, since the mid-1980s, used quantifiable evidence more, and more judiciously. They also tend to subject their work to closer self-criticism about economic assumptions, and to make their methodologies more explicit, as new economic history taught us to do. And as with any disciplinary or theoretical cross-fertilization, economic historians are beginning to link manufactures to household spending; banking to popular ideology; rises in agricultural productivity to the role of the state; merchants' international trade to the environment; community economies to Atlantic-world and global events; urban shop keeping to prices and demand during foreign revolutions; the relationship of empire and nation making to the economics of fashion. We are beginning to know more about the relationship of international prices or rising standards of living, on the one hand, even as we peer more deeply into the productive relations of households, follow Americans to work, and trace entrepreneurial failures. Between the top and bottom layers of the American economy, scholars are focusing intently on the "middling" artisan layer, the ambitious entrepreneurs, the small manufacturers, and others who have rarely been direct subjects of analysis in economic history. Slowly, too, we are making connections between owning and using objects, how they were produced or exchanged, and the wider economic consequences of these activities. Is it sufficient that economic historians are more self-conscious about the limitations of their methodologies and data, and bolder about entering the thickets of debate about ideologically charged questions? Certainly not. But if the field of economic history still suffers from the conceptual and professional sequestering of "economics" and "history"—and in this writer's opinion it assuredly does—it has nevertheless begun to refashion itself along more expansive lines, and that suggests that the dialogue in this volume will continue.

77. Arif Dirlik, *Postmodernity's Histories: The Past as Legacy and Project* (New York: Oxford University Press, 2000), chapter 6; roundtable on postcolonial studies in *Journal of American History* 88 (December 2001); Robert Blair St. George, ed., *Possible Pasts: Becoming Colonial in Early America* (Ithaca: Cornell University Press, 2000); and Patrick Joyce, "The End of Social History?" *Social History* 20 (Fall 1995): 81–91.

Chapter Two

Rethinking *The Economy of British America*

DAVID HANCOCK

In 1985, John McCusker and Russell Menard's *The Economy of British America, 1607–1789* captured the field as few books have. The authors rather blithely called their tome "a simple summary of the known" or, rather, "a survey of the state of the art, an assessment of where we stand, where we would like to be, and how we can get there from here." It was at once a plea for understanding economic life as "the interaction between the pull of external markets and the push of internal population pressures" (although it generally favored the explanatory power of the former over the latter), a survey of different regions within the British colonial economy, a discussion of economic topics like population and manufacturing, and a rather extensive bibliography—all packed into fewer than five hundred pages! They wrote it "both to provoke the exploration of the unknown and to offer the explorer guidance along the way." Provocation—guidance—roadmap: These were ambitious claims. Some twenty years on, it is worth looking anew at this *vade mecum*. How have students of the British American economy answered its call or followed its lead in the past fifteen years? What is left for us to do?[1]

McCusker and Menard posed a number of questions for further research and stated a number of hypotheses for future testing. They were not shy about this: "where the state of the art" was "somewhat deficient," they indicated what they "perceive[d] to be an opportunity for further work . . . and often venture[d] a guess about what" they "expect[ed] such further work will reveal."[2] Among the questions that they found

Special thanks for help with this essay go to Jerry Bannister, Jason Barrett, Stephen Behrendt, Rosalind Beiler, Michelle Craig, Ellen Hartigan-O'Connor, Eric Hinderaker, Alexander Kelso, Cathy Matson, John McCusker, Kenneth Morgan, Norris Nash, Mark Peterson, Donna Rilling, John Shy, and Ian Steele.

1. John J. McCusker and Russell R. Menard, *The Economy of British America, 1607–1789* (Chapel Hill: University of North Carolina Press, 1985), xix, 5, 10.

2. Ibid., 11.

inadequately answered, consider three that they considered fundamental. First, *how did British America grow?* For many of the features of the colonial economies that we most want to explain, we do not have adequate outlines of what happened and when. This is true, among other things, of standards of living and per capita measures of income and wealth, relative prices of factors of production and profitability rates, even the overall size and growth rates of the economies themselves. Second, *what were the effects of British mercantilism on Britain's American colonies?* For that matter, what were the effects of British mercantilism on Britain? Last, *what were the driving forces behind North American economic development?* McCusker and Menard pose this question as a contrast between the staples approach and the Malthusian approach to explaining the nature of the colonial economies and their development.

This essay offers some thoughts on the agenda McCusker and Menard set for economists and historians of early America, compared to what we have achieved in the past twenty years, which in general reflects a different set of concerns from the one they posed. It concludes with some hortatory comments about the road ahead—not so much a topical agenda as a call to create a more integrated picture of the past. While not a comprehensive review of all relevant work, it refers to many examples.

How Did British America Grow?

With respect to the "course of economic growth," in 1985 the authors overwhelmed the reader with a tsunami of research opportunities. Economic history needed "a satisfactory set of estimates of the gross national product for the colonies." Little was known about "the rate of return individuals earned on various enterprises, how this varied over time, how it differed among regions and societal groups." There was no colonial price index before the 1720s and there were few "carefully done price histories" in any of the colonies before the 1720s; close analysis and ancillary use of colonial prices were accordingly impoverished. On a larger scale, there was no "fully adequate index" of the terms of trade, though that might be excused by the unavailability of data. No one knew even imprecisely "the relative costs of the factors of production"—land, labor, capital, and managerial skills. With respect to overseas trade—one of the most heavily studied areas of colonial growth—we were still lacking, we were told, an accurate estimate of the balance of payments. Part of this would entail a better analysis of exported commercial services like the carrying trade, as well as of exported commodities in general, especially the wheat, corn, and rice that went in increasing volumes to southern Europe, and the wine, fruit, salt, bullion, and India goods that returned. Furthermore, "a detailed study of the sources of capital employed by the more independent colonial merchants" was required. The capital resources of arriving immigrants awaited their expositor. McCusker and Menard praised James Shepherd and Gary Walton for their work in estimating the balance of payments for 1768–72, but ended by noting that someone needed to extend their findings into the past and to the rest of British America.[3]

Heeding his own advice, in 1995 McCusker convened a conference at the Huntington Library—"The Economy of Early British America: The Domestic Sector," to review what we had learned about colonial gross domestic product and compare colonial output and standards of living to the examples of twentieth-century countries, about which much more is known. A variety of approaches were suggested, and some attempted, but few were more than tentative, and at the conference the economists and historians divided over the relative strengths of arguments from data versus story line. Some of the papers presented at the conference—by Lance Davis, Stanley Engerman, Robert Gallman, Richard Steckel, Lorena Walsh, Lois Carr, Russell Menard, Gloria and Jackson Main, and Frank Lewis—were published in 1999 as an issue of the *William and Mary Quarterly*. They reveal greater agreement than there was at the conference about the feasibility of measuring colonial gross domestic product. Still, in summing up, McCusker noted that "there is much yet to learn, many more passes at the data yet to be attempted, additional data to be collected, compiled, and analyzed, new estimates concocted, old estimates scrutinized and perfected."[4]

It is unclear whether scholars can overcome data constraints on the questions about prices that McCusker and Menard raised. Price series for most individual commodities are still lacking, although since 1985 a few have been brought together in dissertations and published work. Marc Egnal presents price indices culled from account books for dry goods in Montreal, textiles in Philadelphia, insurance in Philadelphia, and flour in Antigua. Frank Lewis and Ann Carlos have dissected fur prices of the Hudson's Bay Company trade. Alfred M. Pereira made new additions to the Chesapeake tobacco series for the period 1676–1713, and Lorena Walsh presented a very impressive series, the by-product of her Huntington conference essay, of farm prices for tobacco in three growing regions in the Chesapeake (Oronoco, Sweet-Scented, and Peripheral). The prices paid for indentured servants leaving from Liverpool have been reconstructed for 1697–1707. The greatest advance in our knowledge is about the prices of humans; a comprehensive price series for slaves is now accessible in Cambridge University Press's "Atlantic Slave Trade" CD-ROM. One important result of this project is an expanded awareness of the volatility as well as the levels of prices in the colonial era. Most of the price series we have are eighteenth-century prices; those for the seventeenth century for any commodity—human

3. Ibid., 53, 59n10, 64, 68, 72n2, 79, 80n15, 83, 84.
4. John J. McCusker, "Measuring Colonial Gross Domestic Product: An Introduction," 5–7, *William and Mary Quarterly*, 3d ser., 56 (January 1999).

or nonhuman—remain unknown. In addition, there are still few general indices of price levels.[5]

The story is much the same regarding rates of return on commercial voyages and domestic investment. Richard Grassby, in his compendium of seventeenth-century English business behavior, brought together all known studies of such rates, and I attempted to construct rates of return on various enterprises for a group of eighteenth-century slave traders and general merchants. This may only mean that we have a better understanding of how little we know about the profitability of early modern business.[6] Furthermore, there is still no adequate

5. Marc Egnal, *New World Economies: The Growth of the Thirteen Colonies and Early Canada* (New York: Oxford University Press, 1998), appendices A–E, 171–88; Ann M. Carlos and Frank D. Lewis, "Strategic Pricing in the Fur Trade: The Hudson's Bay Company, 1700–1763," in *Wildlife in the Marketplace*, ed. Terry Anderson and Peter Hill (Lanham, Md.: Rowman and Littlefield, 1995), 61–87; Alfredo M. Pereira, "Boom and Bust Hypothesis in the Colonial Chesapeake Economy: Empirical Evidence for the Period 1676–1713," Working Paper 91, UCSD Department of Economics, April 18, 1991; Alfredo M. Pereira and Rafael Flores de Frutos, "Export Growth and Economic Development in Colonial British America," *Review of International Economics* 6 (November 1998): 638–48; Lorena S. Walsh, "Summing the Parts: Implications for Estimating Chesapeake Output and Income Subregionally," *William and Mary Quarterly*, 3d ser., 56 (January 1999): 53–94; Farley Grubb and Tony Stitt, "The Liverpool Emigrant Servant Trade and the Transition to Slave Labor in the Chesapeake, 1697–1707: Market Adjustments to War," *Explorations in Economic History* 31 (July 1994): 376–405; for the most recent summation, see David Eltis, *The Rise of African Slavery in the Americas* (New York: Cambridge University Press, 2000), appendix B, 293–97. See also Daniel Vickers, "'A knowen and staple commoditie': Codfish Prices in Essex County, Massachusetts, 1640–1775," *Essex Institute Historical Collections* 124 (Salem, Mass.: Essex Institute, 1988), 186–203; Heinz W. Pyszczyk, "Economic and Social Factors in the Consumption of Material Goods in the Fur Trade of Western Canada," *Historical Archaeology* 6 (1988). On money and prices generally, see Bennett T. McCallum, "Money and Prices in Colonial America: A New Test of Competing Theories," *Journal of Political Economy* 100 (February 1992): 143–61; Bruce D. Smith, "Some Colonial Evidence on Two Theories of Money: Maryland and the Carolinas," in *Major Inflations in History*, ed. Forrest Capie (Brookfield, Vt.: E. Elgar, 1991), 217–50; Ron Michener, "Backing Theories and the Currencies of Eighteenth-Century America: A Comment," *Journal of Economic History* 48 (September 1988): 682–92, and "Fixed Exchange Rates and the Quantity Theory in Colonial America," *Carnegie-Rochester Conference Series on Public Policy* 37 (Fall 1987): 233–308. Anyone interested in specific prices should start by examining David Eltis, Stephen S. Behrendt, David Richardson, and Herbert S. Klein, eds., *The Trans-Atlantic Slave Trade: A Database on CD-ROM* (Cambridge: Cambridge University Press, 1999), which contains the records of more than 27,000 transatlantic slaving voyages from the end of the sixteenth century to the middle of the nineteenth century. It allows a scholar to compile data by region and period. Additional information includes materials on the slaves, sailors, and captains, plus the route of each voyage.

6. Richard Grassby, *The Business Community of Seventeenth-Century England* (New York: Cambridge University Press, 1995), 234–68; David Hancock, *Citizens of the World: London Merchants and the Integration of the British Atlantic Community, 1735–1785* (New York: Cambridge University Press, 1995); William J. Darity Jr., "Profitability of the British Trade in Slaves Once Again: Comment," *Explorations in Economic History* 26 (July 1989): 380–84; Philip Mirowski, "Adam Smith, Empiricism, and the Rate of Profit in Eighteenth-Century England," in his *Against Mechanism: Protecting Economics from Science* (Lanham, Md.: Rowman and Littlefield, 1988), 191–209, which gives typical rates of profit for British enterprises; Harley C. Knick, "Ocean Freight Rates and Productivity, 1740–1913: The Primacy of Mechanical Invention Reaffirmed," *Journal of Economic History* 48 (December 1988): 851–76; David Richardson, "The Costs of Survival," *Explorations in Economic History*, 2d ser., 24 (April 1987): 178–96; Christopher J. French, "Productivity in the Atlantic Shipping Industry: A Quantitative Study," *Journal of Interdisciplinary History* 17 (Winter 1986–87): 613–38.

index of the terms of trade (the ratio between the prices paid for imports and the prices received for exports), although, in this direction, Simon Smith has gone a considerable distance in his analysis of British wool textile exports to the colonies, finding that "augmented export revenue stimulated productivity in textiles" and that "the growth of exports reflected improving international competitiveness."[7] Nor have the colonies' sizeable trade with southern Europe, the colonial carrying trade, the costs of the factors of production, and the balance of payments for the colonies been looked at systematically since 1985, although recent work on the British balance of payments accounts in the period 1772–1820 might serve as a model for revisiting the British American side.[8] Capital resources of new settlers and transient merchants have received some attention by migration scholars such as Alison Games, and a consensus appears to be emerging that few people came with ready money. Instead, most free voyagers arrived with bills of exchange and letters of credit. Would-be planters traveling to the Chesapeake, for instance, made arrangements with merchants in England for orders and payments. If they purchased their plantations in advance, they did so on credit; they bought supplies by liquidating their assets at home, converting them into subsistence supplies or trade goods that they then used themselves or sold to others in the New World. The matter awaits a fuller investigation for regions other than New England and the Chesapeake. Not surprisingly, given the absence of complete statistics, no one has attempted to estimate the balance of payments for the pre-1768 period in a fashion even remotely approximating what Shepherd and Walton offered us for 1768–72.[9]

On the growth of manufacturing in America, the study of iron has led the charge. Robert B. Gordon's *American Iron* provides a sweeping three-century overview of early iron making, and corrects the view that the industry was late to develop. Although there has been some discussion of emergent technologies, much scholarship focuses on labor arrangements and relations. John Bezís-Selfa has recently compared two ironworks—one in southern New Jersey and another

7. Simon D. Smith, "British Exports to Colonial North America and the Mercantilist Fallacy," *Business History* 37 (January 1995): 45–63.

8. Javier Cuenca Esteban, "The British Balance of Payments, 1772–1820: India Transfers and War Finance," *Economic History Review* 54 (February 2001): 58–86. Cuenca constructs new estimates of net exports from Britain, carrying earnings, and merchant profits, and combines these with other figures to conclude that "without the accumulated credits from India transfers since 1757, Britain's financing of land warfare during the French wars could have been compromised" (58). Cf. R. C. Nash, "The Balance of Payments and Foreign Capital Flows in Eighteenth-Century England: A Comment," *Economic History Review* 50 (February 1997): 110–28; D. W. Jones, *War and Economy in the Age of William III and Marlborough* (Oxford: Oxford University Press, 1988), which makes annual estimates for 1686–1711.

9. James F. Shepherd and Gary M. Walton, *The Economic Rise of Early America* (Cambridge: Cambridge University Press, 1979); Alison F. Games, *Migration and the Origins of the English Atlantic World* (Cambridge: Harvard University Press, 1999), 64–65; cf. Jeanne Chase, ed., *Géographie du Capital Marchand aux Amériques, 1760–1860* (Paris: Editions de l'Ecole des hautes études en sciences sociales, 1987).

in the Virginia Tidewater—-and explored the benefits and costs of slave labor. The works in Virginia employed black slaves, which allowed more flexible staffing in response to demand but also made collective resistance of blacks a possibility. The more ethnically diverse all-white workforce in New Jersey that Bezís-Selfa examined militated against collective opposition, although it created other problems of promoting its productivity and retaining their service, which the owners could minimize to a certain extent by separate contracts. In looking at the account books of the Pennsylvania iron industry, Michael Kennedy found that rural craft workers played a significant role in eighteenth-century iron making; contrary to previous assumptions, many exhibited no aversion to industrial work, wage labor, or capital markets—in fact, they embraced them. Surprisingly complex labor arrangements existed early in the eighteenth century; subcontracting in particular flourished and was viewed as a system that benefited all.[10] The use of American products in Europe has not been subjected to the same scrutiny as American manufacturing; the processing of snuff and sugar in Britain has been investigated, but pig iron, lumber, indigo, coffee, and cocoa deserve attention.[11]

Scholars have begun to examine the evolution of economic institutions by looking at how agricultural and artisanal producers moved into trade, whether Carolina earthenware or Baltimore grain. Glass, furniture, rope, textiles, and gunpowder have been the subjects of recent study, although in only a few cases, such as glass, have their connections to overseas markets and their competition with

10. In the history of processing and manufacture of colonial products in America, iron is the best studied. See John Bezís-Selfa, "A Tale of Two Ironworks: Slavery, Free Labor, Work, and Resistance in the Early Republic," *William and Mary Quarterly* 3d ser., 56 (October 1999): 677–700; Michael V. Kennedy, "Working Agreements: The Use of Subcontracting in the Pennsylvania Iron Industry, 1725–1789," *Pennsylvania History* 65 (Autumn 1998): 492–508; Michael V. Kennedy, "An Alternate Independence: Craft Workers in the Pennsylvania Iron Industry, 1725–1775," *Essays in Economic and Business History* 16 (1998): 113–25; John Bezís-Selfa, "Slavery and the Disciplining of Free Labor in the Colonial Mid-Atlantic Iron Industry," *Pennsylvania History* 64, supplement (Summer 1997): 270–86; Michael V. Kennedy, "Furnace to Farm: Capital, Labor, and Markets in the Pennsylvania Iron Industry, 1716–1789" (Ph.D. diss., Lehigh University, 1996); Robert B. Gordon, *American Iron, 1607–1900* (Baltimore: Johns Hopkins University Press 1996); John Bezís-Selfa, "Forging a New Order: Slavery, Free Labor, and Sectional Differentiation in the Mid-Atlantic Charcoal Iron Industry, 1715–1840" (Ph.D. diss., University of Pennsylvania, 1995); Robert B. Gordon, "Material Evidence of Ironmaking Techniques," *Industrial Archaeology* 2 (1995): 69–80; Robert B. Gordon and David J. Killick, "Adaptation of Technology to Culture and Environment: Bloomery Iron Smelting in America and Africa," *Technology and Culture* 34 (July 1993): 243–70; Thomas Cowan, "William Hill and the Aera Ironworks," *Journal of Early Southern Decorative Arts* 13 (November 1987): 1–31; John S. Salmon, *The Washington Iron Works of Franklin County, Virginia, 1733–1850* (Richmond: Virginia State Library, 1986); John S. Salmon, "Ironworks on the Frontier: Virginia's Iron Industry, 1607–1783," *Virginia Cavalcade* 35 (Autumn 1986): 184–91; Basil Crapster, "Hampton Furnace in Colonial Frederick County," *Maryland Historical Magazine* 80 (Spring 1985): 1–8. Nothing has been done on the leather industry of early America since 1985, and little before that date.

11. Kenneth Morgan, "Sugar Refining in Bristol," in *From Family Farms to Corporate Capitalism: Essays in Business and Industrial History in Honour of Peter Mathias,* ed. Kristine Bruland and Patrick O'Brien (New York: Oxford University Press, 1998), 139–69; on snuff, see Jan Rogozinski, *Smokeless Tobacco in the Western World, 1550–1950* (New York: Praeger, 1990).

foreign alternatives been explored.[12] Despite the promise of protoindustrialization as a model in the early 1980s, cottage industry has been little scrutinized. Picking up on the work of early nineteenth-century scholars, Jeanne Boydston suggests a longer lineage for outwork than previous historians have allowed.[13]

12. On the manufacture of other goods, see Adrienne D. Hood, *The Weaver's Craft: Cloth, Commerce, and Industry in Early Pennsylvania* (Philadelphia: University of Pennsylvania Press, 2003); Rosalind J. Beiler, "Peterstal and Wistarburg: The Transfer and Adaptation of Business Strategies in Eighteenth-Century American Glassmaking," *Business and Economic History* 26 (October 1997): 343–53; Paul W. Schopp and Carter Litchfield, "The Burlington Windmill: An Unusual Colonial Manufactory," *New Jersey History* 114 (Spring 1996): 2–17; Edward S. Cooke Jr., *Making Furniture in Pre-Industrial America: The Social Economy of Newtown and Woodbury, Connecticut* (Baltimore: Johns Hopkins University Press, 1996); Allen G. Noble, "The Last Ropewalk in America," *Pioneer America Society Transactions* 16 (1993): 13–23; Gary A. O'Dell, "The Trotter Family, Gunpowder, and Early Kentucky Entrepreneurship, 1784–1833," *Register of the Kentucky Historical Society* 88 (Autumn 1990): 394–430. For a discussion of the connections between the domestic American production of earthenware and internal trade, see Carl Steen, "Pottery, Intercolonial Trade, and Revolution: Domestic Earthenwares and the Development of an American Social Identity," *Historical Archaeology* 33 (Fall 1999): 62–72. Similarly, the move from grain trading to manufacturing is explored by Tina H. Sheller, "Artisans, Manufacturing, and the Rise of a Manufacturing Interest in Revolutionary Baltimore Town," *Maryland Historical Magazine* 83 (March 1988): 3–17. For general collections, see Robert B. Gordon and Patrick M. Malone, *The Texture of Industry: An Archaeological View of the Industrialization of North America* (New York: Oxford University Press, 1994); Judith A. McGaw, ed., *Early American Technology: Making and Doing Things from the Colonial Era to 1850* (Chapel Hill: University of North Carolina Press, 1994).

13. Cottage industry and the processing of farm products are discussed in Jeanne M. Boydston, *Home and Work: Housework, Wages, and the Ideology of Labor in the Early Republic* (New York: Oxford University Press, 1990); Paul G. E. Clemens and Lucy Simler, "Rural Labor and the Farm Household in Chester County, Pennsylvania, 1750–1820," in *Work and Labor in Early America*, ed. Stephen Innes (Chapel Hill: University of North Carolina Press, 1988), 106–43; Joan M. Jensen, "Butter Making and Economic Development in Mid-Atlantic America from 1750 to 1850," *Signs* 13 (October 1988): 813–29; Joan M. Jensen, *Loosening the Bonds: Mid-Atlantic Farm Women, 1750–1850* (New Haven: Yale University Press, 1986). Their insights are compatible with those historians who focus most intensely on the early nineteenth century: Thomas Dublin, *Transforming Women's Work: New England Lives in the Industrial Revolution* (Ithaca: Cornell University Press, 1994); Mary H. Blewett, *Men, Women, and Work: Class, Gender, and Protest in the New England Shoe Industry, 1780–1910* (Urbana: University of Illinois Press, 1988); Christopher Clark, *The Roots of Rural Capitalism: Western Massachusetts, 1780–1860* (Ithaca: Cornell University Press, 1990).

Protoindustrialization is less a model for North Americans than it is for Latin Americans. Douglas C. Libby, "Reconsidering Textile Production in Late Colonial Brazil: New Evidence from Minas Gerais," *Latin American Research Review* 32 (Spring 1997): 88–108; and Manuel Miño Grijalva, "Proto-Industria Colonial?" *Historia Mexicana* 39 (October–December 1989): 793–818, which looks at the early modern Mexican industrial sector. The study of Europe continued in the 1990s. Elizabeth Musgrave, "Pottery Production and Proto-Industrialisation: Continuity and Change in the Rural Ceramics Industries of the Saintonge Region, France, 1250 to 1800," *Rural History* 9 (April 1998): 1–18; John Theibault, "Town, Countryside, and Proto-Industrialization in Early Modern Europe," *Journal of Interdisciplinary History* 29 (September 1998): 263–72; Cor Trompetter, *Agriculture, Proto-Industry and Mennonite Entrepreneurship: A History of the Textile Industries in Twente, 1600–1815* (Amsterdam: Nederlands Economisch Historisch Archiet, 1997); Sheilagh Ogilvie, *State Corporatism and Proto-Industry: The Württemberg Black Forest, 1580–1797* (New York: Cambridge University Press, 1997); Peter Kriedte et al., "Proto-Industrialization Revisited: Demography, Social Structure, and Modern Domestic Industry," *Continuity and Change* 8 (August 1993): 217–52; John Seed, "Capital and Class Formation in Early Industrial England," *Social History* 18 (1993): 17–30; Christine Hallas, "Cottage and Mill: The Textile Industry in Wensleydale and Swaledale," *Textile History* 21 (1990): 203–21; Chris Johnson, "A Proto-Industrial

What Were the Effects of British Mercantilism on Britain's American Colonies?

McCusker and Menard saw a similar wealth of opportunities for research in the study of mercantilism and the British imperial navigation system. There was in 1985 and there is still no study of "the movement of gold and silver in bars or in coins" through British America, although specie in the empire's bullion account goes to the heart of early mercantilism. As a driving force in mercantilist thinking and policymaking, *bullionism* enjoyed fewer adherents as the seventeenth century waned. Yet statesmen and enterprisers, led by the Bank of England, continued their pursuit of silver and gold, and the trade in precious metals continued unabated; both items were openly listed in markets. Despite the importance of understanding the bullion account and a plenitude of sources on this subject, no one has yet undertaken the work of gauging the flows of gold, silver, and foreign coin through North America. Global perspectives on the production and trade of monetary substances before 1800 are increasingly common, but they do not take into account North America, where, as elsewhere, gold and silver flows acted as powerful forces in economic integration.[14]

With respect to the importance of the colonies to Britain—as sources of raw materials and as markets for finished goods—much remained to be understood. Drawing on the suggestions of Jacob Price, McCusker and Menard called for investigation of "three areas of special significance": the processing and manufacturing of colonial goods, industrial innovation, and institutional change such as capital mobilization and financial sophistication.[15]

When they turned to the Navigation Acts[16]—the generally accepted backbone of British mercantile policy enacted between 1651 and 1696—the authors also found an array of questions still unanswered. Somewhat surprisingly, "the origins and effects of each of the Navigation Acts" had never been studied,

---

Community Study: Coggeshall in Essex, c. 1500–c. 1750" (Ph.D. diss., University of Essex, 1989); Chris Husbands, "Regional Change in a Pre-Industrial Economy: Wealth and Population in England in the Sixteenth and Seventeenth Centuries," *Journal of Historical Geography* 13 (October 1987): 345–59.

14. But cf. Stephen Quinn, "Gold, Silver, and the Glorious Revolution: Arbitrage Between Bills of Exchange and Bullion," *Economic History Review* 49 (August 1996): 473–90; Dennis O. Flynn and Arturo Giraldez, eds., *Metals and Monies in an Emerging Global Economy* (Aldershot, Eng.: Variorum, 1997).

15. McCusker and Menard, *Economy of British America*, 37, 44.

16. There were four principal acts. Parliament passed the first statute in 1651 and reenacted it in 1660. Among other things, the first act stipulated that all goods brought into England be imported only in English bottoms and that certain "enumerated commodities" be exported only to England or her colonies. The second act, passed in 1663, commanded that European commodities be exported to England's American colonies only via approved English ports. A third law, passed in 1673, set customs duties for the colonies and established a cadre of officers to collect them. A fourth law, in 1696, strengthened the machinery of metropolitan control with the institution of admiralty courts in the colonies. These acts promoted trade with the colonies and handicapped the trade of Scotland (before 1707), Ireland, and the Channel Islands by excluding them from the system. The target of criticism during the American revolutionary period, they were eventually discarded.

despite the monumental analysis of all the acts in Laurence Harper's and Oliver Dickerson's polemical works on the acts' contribution to the Revolution.[17] On the other side of the ocean, "the participation of colonial governments in the protection and promotion of the economy" was only dimly understood; and, if the enforcement of the acts was to be properly gauged, "detailed comparative studies of merchants' records and the colonial naval officers' shipping lists" would have to be made. In their discussion of the Navigation Acts, McCusker and Menard made a number of highly provocative assertions that cried out for evidence. "The laws created a closed system." "By 1713, colonial trade conformed in almost every particular to the navigation system" and "it continued to do so until the Revolution." The implementation of imperial policy "grew more efficient." The effects of smuggling were "insignificant except for one or two specific minor items" like sugar, molasses, rum, brandy, and sailcloth. Each assertion is still open to investigation.[18]

American historians have preferred to focus on whether the acts helped or hurt the Americans. Taking their cues from Harper and Dickerson, several authors have measured "the costs" of the laws. Jon Kepler has estimated the direct shipments of tobacco and sugar, both of which were important enumerated goods, from English America to continental Europe in the period before the acts had much influence. Larry Sawers has looked again at the acts as a trigger of the Revolution and concluded that they were more important than traditional scholarship allowed: conventional interpretations focused on the wrong period (before 1776 rather than after), minimized the distribution of the burdens, and ignored the losses imposed by the competition of British manufacturers and merchants. But in the drive to examine the burden of the acts on American manufacturing, historians have missed opportunities. No one has reexamined the origins of mercantilist legislation. While this may seem a daunting task, given the seeming comprehensiveness of Harper's contribution, we could learn much about why particular commodities were favored or frustrated, how lobbies and politics shaped legislation, and what alignments in government, nation, and empire shaped the results. Nor has anyone examined how the effects of the acts interacted with capital, technology, and information.[19]

Mercantilism more generally has fared better, as the perennial favorite of students of state building and economic ideology and an obvious "hook" for

17. Oliver M. Dickerson, *The Navigation Acts and the American Revolution* (Philadelphia: University of Pennsylvania Press, 1951); Lawrence A. Harper, *The English Navigation Laws: A Seventeenth-Century Experiment in Social Engineering* (New York: Columbia University Press, 1939).

18. McCusker and Menard, *Economy of British America*, 49n18, 48n17, 49n19; cf. 77–78, 47, 49, 50n20, 288.

19. Jon Kepler, "Estimates of the Volumes of Direct Shipments of Tobacco and Sugar from the Chief English Plantations to European Markets, 1620–1669," *Journal of European Economic History* 28 (Autumn 1999): 115–36; Larry Sawers, "The Navigation Acts Revisited," *Economic History Review* 45 (May 1992): 262–84.

those interested in economic, mercantile, or labor ideology.[20] In comparison, there is less on the role of colonial governments in ordering colonial economies. Allan Kulikoff has contributed a powerful, detailed analysis of Maryland and Virginia governments' regulation of tobacco, and Cathy Matson has done much the same for New York's attempts to control its fur and grain trades, but how pervasive such activity was or how these attempts related to other colonies' policies is still unclear.[21]

20. The most recent summary is by McCusker, "British Mercantilist Policies and the American Colonies," in *The Cambridge Economic History of the United States,* 3 vols., ed. Stanley L. Engerman and Robert E. Gallman (New York: Cambridge University Press, 1996), 1:337–62. On the workings of mercantilism in British America, see Joseph A. Ernst, "In the 'Age of Mercantilism,' Revolutionaries Were Not Economic Liberals After All," *Reviews in American History* 24 (September 1994): 400–405; John E. Crowley, *The Privileges of Independence: Neomercantilism and the American Revolution* (Baltimore: Johns Hopkins University Press, 1993); Sean T. Cadigan, "Artisans in a Merchant Town: St. John's, New-foundland, 1775–1816," *Journal of the Canadian Historical Association* 4 (1993): 95–119; Richard S. Keating, "From Conflict to Culture: A Literary Study of Colonial South Carolina's Economic Societies, 1670–1750" (Ph.D. diss., University of North Carolina, 1993); Joseph J. Persky, *The Burden of Dependency: Colonial Themes in Southern Economic Thought* (Baltimore: Johns Hopkins University Press, 1992); Neil A. Hamilton, "Connecticut Order, Mercantilistic Economics: The Life of Oliver Wolcott, Jr." (Ph.D. diss., University of Tennessee, 1988); Michael N. Hayes, "Mercantile Incentives: State-Sanctioned Market Power and Economic Development in the Atlantic Economy, 1553–1776" (Ph.D. diss., University of California, Davis, 1986).

On mercantilist ideas and programs in England and Britain, see Steven Pincus, "The Making of a Great Power: Universal Monarchy, Political Economy, and the Transformation of English Political Culture," *European Legacy* 5 (August 1990): 531–45; John Dunn, ed., *The Economic Limits to Modern Politics* (New York: Cambridge University Press, 1990); Terence W. Hutchison, *Before Adam Smith: The Emergence of Political Economy, 1662–1776* (New York: Basil Blackwell, 1988). On continental powers' mercantilist machinations, both in Europe and America, see Patrick O'Brien, "Mercantilism and Imperialism in the Rise and Decline of the Dutch and British Economies, 1585–1815," *De Economist* (Netherlands) 148 (2000): 469–501; Paul Cheney, "Mercantilism and *Moeurs*: Comparative History and Sociology in the Analysis of France's Overseas Trade, 1713–1748," working paper 99-02, "International Seminar on the History of the Atlantic World, 1500–1800," Harvard University, 1999; and Andrew Hamilton, "Atlantic Cosmopolitanism and Nationalism: Anglo-American Theories of Trade and Empire in the 1780s," working paper 99-27, "International Seminar on the History of the Atlantic World, 1500–1800," Harvard University, 1999; David La Vere, "Between Kinship and Capitalism: French and Spanish Rivalry in the Colonial Louisiana-Texas Indian Trade," *Journal of Southern History* 64 (Spring 1998): 197–218. Lars Magnusson has edited nine papers on the variety of interpretations and definitions connected with the concept of mercantilism. See his *Mercantilistic Economics* (Boston: Kluwer Academic Publishers, 1993), especially the essays by Cosimo Perrotta on Spanish mercantilism and the essays by William Grampp, Lars Herlitz, Salim Rashid, Keith Tribe, and Donald Walker on Virginia tobacco.

21. Allan Kulikoff, *Tobacco and Slaves: The Development of Southern Cultures in the Chesapeake, 1680–1800* (Chapel Hill: University of North Carolina Press, 1986), 104–16; Bruce A. Ragsdale, "George Washington, the British Tobacco Trade, and Economic Opportunity in Pre-Revolutionary Virginia," *Virginia Magazine of History and Biography* 97 (April 1989): 133–62; Cathy Matson, "'Damned Scoundrels' and 'Libertisme of Trade': Freedom and Regulation in Colonial New York's Fur and Grain Trades," *William and Mary Quarterly,* 3d ser., 51 (July 1994): 394–418; Cathy Matson, *Merchants and Empire: Trading in Colonial New York* (Baltimore: Johns Hopkins University Press, 1998). Some clues to a wider practice are found in Sydney V. James, *The Colonial Metamorphoses in Rhode Island: A Study of Institutions in Change,* ed. Bruce Daniels and Sheila Skemp (Hanover: University Press of New England, 2000). Certainly throughout America the poor combined to encourage or discourage governmental regulation and policymaking on a wide range of issues, like taxes, debt, and landownership, in the period 1760–90.

One aspect that continues to fascinate historians but receives nowhere near the serious attention it deserves, is smuggling. Outright smuggling crowned an extremely porous Atlantic trading system. Although it is difficult to document, for the arts of evasion depended on communicating face to face and destroying or not keeping records, much incidental evidence and comment suggests that smuggling was pervasive. Again and again, shippers and traders in British America were hauled into vice-admiralty courts for evasion of import duties and prohibitions, and these prosecutions were only the tip of the iceberg. McCusker and Menard admit the extent of sugar, molasses, and rum smuggling, yet they balk at regarding the behavior as widespread or disruptive. Other commodities were also smuggled—bullion, wine, foodstuffs, and fur, among others. The case of wine is a good example. Not just in war but also in peace, the varieties and amounts of wine available in British America were greater than those allowed by law and recorded at the customs house. The same was true in Portugal's empire for all kinds of goods, and the Americans were involved as well: a "lively contraband trade [was] carried on by the English, the Spaniards (via the Canaries), the French (through La Rochelle) and finally the Dutch, who . . . had the lion's share of the illegal traffic" before 1750. The Portuguese, for instance, with the British as their assistants, smuggled Spanish silver out of the Rio de la Plata, using the Colônia do Sacramento or Buenos Aires as their base; and the British, with the Brazilians at their command, smuggled Portuguese gold with the knowledge, if not the approval, of governmental authorities. Smuggling was part and parcel of American and transatlantic trade and life.[22]

Ruth Bogin, "Petitioning and the New Moral Economy of Post-Revolutionary America," *William and Mary Quarterly*, 3d ser., 45 (July 1988): 395–425. An obvious logical contrast to local American regulation is local English regulation, of which Tim Keirn's fine study of cloth regulations is an excellent example: "Parliament, Legislation, and the Regulation of English Textile Industries, 1689–1714," in *Stilling the Grumbling Hive: The Response to Social and Economic Problems in England, 1689–1750*, ed. Lee Davison et al. (Stroud, Eng.: Sutton, 1992), 1–24.

On responses to British regulation, and on attempts by the states to regulate after the war, see the work of Lawrence A. Peskin, who has written on the encouragement and protection of American manufactures: "To 'Encourage and Protect' American Manufactures: The Intellectual Origins of Industrialization, 1763–1830" (Ph.D. diss., University of Maryland, College Park, 1998); "From Protection to Encouragement: Manufacturing and Mercantilism in New York City's Public Sphere, 1783–1795," *Journal of the Early Republic* 18 (Winter 1998): 489–615; "'No More 'British Agents Among Us': Economic Independence and the Discourse of Manufacturing, 1768–1809," *Maryland Historian* 25 (Fall–Winter 1994): 22–29.

22. For some discussion of smuggling in the British Atlantic world, a topic that—given the extent of the phenomenon—has been woefully understudied since Richard Pares stopped writing in the late 1950s, see Samuel G. Margolin, "Guardships on the Virginia Station, 1667–1767," *American Neptune* 55 (Winter 1995): 19–41; Jan Grabowski, "Les Amérindiens domicilies et la 'contrabande' des fourrures en Nouvelle France," *Recherches Amérindiennes au Québec* 24 (1994): 45–52, on Indian intermediaries in the illegal fur trade between British and French merchants in the Montreal region; Nuala Zahedieh, "The Merchants of Port Royal, Jamaica, and the Spanish Contraband Trade, 1655–1692," *William and Mary Quarterly*, 3d ser., 43 (October 1986): 570–93, on English contraband trade with the

What Were the Driving Forces Behind North American Economic Development?

Nowhere were McCusker and Menard bolder in identifying areas where "the state of the art" was "deficient" than in Part I, "Points of Departure," where they supported "the staples approach" to the economy of British America. "The distinguishing feature of the staples approach," they argued, "is the contention that the size and the structure of the domestic sector in an export-led economy are shaped by the particular characteristics of the dominant staple. Some staples have powerful 'spread effects' and encourage development in the domestic economy. Others do not." This approach to the development of an economy, also known as the vent-for-surplus or export-led approach, stands in marked contrast to a Malthusian, or frontier, approach, that argues for the primacy of population growth and agricultural expansion, not overseas trade, in driving economic development. In understanding the effects of staples, "two interrelated aspects" were central to McCusker and Menard's schema: "the production function, that is, the proportions of land, labor, capital, and entrepreneurial skill required to produce a staple; and the propensity of the product to create 'linkages' by inducing investment in other parts of the economy."[23]

The problem facing McCusker and Menard was that the bulk of the work that would prove the thesis had yet to be undertaken. "The list of studies that, even implicitly, test the propositions of staples theory against evidence for British America" was "short."[24] The principal support for the thesis came from groundbreaking studies of the Canadian fish and fur industries by William Mackintosh in the 1920s and 1930s, Harold Innis in the 1930s and 1940s, and Melville Watkins in 1963. They argued that resources and trade underpinned the expansion and growth of Canada and ultimately of society and the state. But by

---

Spanish; John W. Tyler, *Smugglers and Patriots: Boston Merchants and the Advent of the American Revolution* (Boston: Northeastern University Press, 1986), 13–22, 90, 105, 115, 197–98, 249–50.

Compare studies of smuggling and contraband in non-British America: Wim Klooster, *Illicit Riches: Dutch Trade in the Caribbean, 1648–1795* (Leiden: KITLV Press, 1998), 124–72; Lance Grahn, *The Political Economy of Smuggling: Regional Informal Economies in Early Bourbon New Granada* (Boulder: Westview Press, 1997); Ramón Aizpurua Aguirre, *Curazao y la costa de Caracas: Introducción al estudio del contrabando en la provincia de Venezuela en tiempos de la Compañía Guipuzcoana, 1730–1780* (Caracas: Academia Nacional de Historia, 1993); A. J. R. Russell-Wood, *A World on the Move: The Portuguese in Africa, Asia, and America, 1415–1808* (Manchester: Carcanet in association with the Calouste Gulbenkian Foundation, 1992), 94, 135, 138, 140, 145; Héctor R. Feliciano Ramos, *El contrabando inglés en el Caribe y el Golfo de México (1748–1778)* (Seville: Excma. Diputación Provincial de Sevilla, 1990); Zacarías Moutoukias, "Power, Corruption, and Commerce: The Making of the Local Administrative Structure in Seventeenth-century Buenos Aires," *Hispanic American Historical Review* 68 (November 1988): 771–801; John R. McNeill, *Atlantic Empires of France and Spain: Louisburg and Havana, 1700–1763* (Chapel Hill: University of North Carolina Press, 1985), 155–58, 196–202.

23. McCusker and Menard, *Economy of British America*, 23–24.
24. Ibid., 29.

1980 doubts were being raised about the precision of the thesis and its ability to explain economic growth, although McCusker and Menard gave them short shrift. Bit by bit the staples thesis eroded, although it still has adherents for the pre-1850 period in Canadian history, with the caveat that the economy was far more differentiated and diversified than Innis and Watkins recognized.[25] Further research was needed, and not just on Canada. McCusker and Menard suggested commodities such as timber, wheat, corn, rice, and indigo as test studies. One could compile contemporary colonial observations on the impact of specific staples, they noted, but they dismissed these as insufficient by themselves. Alternatively, one could estimate the regional effects of a dominant commodity in one of three ways: "by studying the impact of an individual staple on a regional economy; by comparing regions producing different staple exports; and by examining the impact of a change in staple exports within a specific region." Almost in passing, McCusker and Menard also called for a testing of the Malthusian model, for "the identification of a homeostatic mechanism that kept income constant and wealth distribution stable, with migration ensuring regular extension of the agricultural frontier, thus permitting a rapid growth of population without producing a crisis of subsistence."[26]

Not surprisingly, given its origin in Canada, students of the Canadian fur and fish trades have continued to grapple with the viability of the staples thesis. Essays in *Merchant Credit and Labour Strategies* furthered work on the fish trade using the staples model. The conference that spawned this volume brought together a cadre of scholars who would continue to shape the field. Rosemary Ommer, who edited the book, had previously analyzed the Jersey-Gaspé cod fishery at the end of the eighteenth century; her recent *Fishing Places, Fishing*

25. Kenneth Buckley, *Capital Formation in Canada, 1896–1930* (Toronto: University of Toronto Press, 1955), and "The Role of Staples Industries in Canada's Development," *Journal of Economic History* 18 (December 1958): 439–50; G. W. Bertram, "Economic Growth and Canadian Industry, 1870–1915: The Staple Model and Take-Off Hypothesis," *Canadian Journal of Economics and Political Science* 29 (May 1963): 162–84; E. J. Chambers and D. F. Gordon, "Primary Products and Economic Growth: An Empirical Measurement," *Journal of Political Economy* 75 (December 1967): 881–85; Richard Pomfret, *The Economic Development of Canada* (Toronto: University of Toronto Press, 1981); Ann M. Carlos, "The Birth and Death of Predatory Competition in the North American Fur Trade, 1810–1821," *Explorations in Economic History* 19 (April 1982): 156–83; M. Brook Taylor, ed., *Canadian History: A Reader's Guide*, vol. 1, *Beginnings to Confederation* (Toronto: University of Toronto Press, 1994), 122–23, 190–91. A theoretical critique was offered by David McNally, "Staple Theory as Commodity Fetishism: Marx, Innis, and Canadian Political Economy," *Studies in Political Economy* 6 (Spring 1981): 35–63, but none of the critics has posed a viable alternative synthesis to replace it. Ronald Findlay and Mats Lundhal, "Natural Resources, 'Vent for Surplus,' and the Staples Theory: Trade and Growth with an Endogenous Land Frontier," Columbia University Economics Department, discussion paper 585 (1992); John Fogarty, "Staples, Super-Staples and the Limits of Staple Theory: The Experiences of Argentina, Australia and Canada Compared," in *Argentina, Australia and Canada: Studies in Comparative Development, 1870–1965*, ed. D. C. M. Platt and Guido di Tella (London: Macmillan, 1985), 19–36. Harold Innis's writings on the role of staples have been republished as *Staples, Markets, and Cultural Change: Selected Essays*, ed. Daniel Drache (Montreal: McGill-Queen's University Press, 1995), 438–42.

26. McCusker and Menard, *Economy of British America*, 31, 33.

People explores her thesis further. Perhaps more than anyone else, Sean Cadigan has reworked the staples thesis into a more historically accurate concept in an impressive study of the economic and social conditions affecting Newfoundland fisheries and fishermen between 1785 and 1855. His "revised" thesis solidly dismisses the idea that merchant conservatism contributed to underdevelopment; in its place, from painstaking archival research, he reconstructs the dynamic class relationships between the region's merchants and fishermen.[27] Scholars studying the American Indian experience and the Euro-Indian trade have also examined fur and fish trading in North America, but they tend to focus on labor relations and gender roles, paying less attention to economic development. In all, the debate seems to have stalled in the past few years and the issues are no longer as sharp as before.[28]

27. On the staples thesis, see Rosemary E. Ommer, ed., *Merchant Credit and Labour Strategies in Historical Perspective* (Fredericton, New Brunswick: Goose Lane Editions, 1990), 12, 14, 360–73; Sean T. Cadigan, "The Staple Model Reconsidered: The Case of Agricultural Policy in Northeast Newfoundland, 1785–1855," *Acadiensis* 21 (Autumn 1992): 52–60; Graham D. Taylor, "Restructuring Canadian Business History: A Review Essay," *Journal of Canadian Studies* 26 (Winter 1991): 169–78. With respect to fur, not all scholars have adhered to or repudiated the staples thesis, although it hovers in the background of most work. Because of the rekindling of interest in Indian history, fur studies have burgeoned. Edith I. Burley, *Servants of the Honourable Company: Work, Discipline, and Conflict in the Hudson's Bay Company, 1770–1870* (Toronto: Oxford University Press, 1997); José António Brandão, *"Your Fyre Shall Burn No More": Iroquois Policy Toward New France and Its Native Allies to 1701* (Lincoln: University of Nebraska Press, 1997); Carolyn F. Podruchny, "'Sons of the Wilderness': Work, Culture and Identity Among Voyageurs in the Montreal Fur Trade, 1780–1821" (Ph.D. diss., University of Toronto, 1999); Jo-Anne Fiske, Susan Sleeper-Smith, and William Wicken, eds., *New Faces of the Fur Trade: Selected Papers of the Seventh North American Fur Trade Conference, Halifax, Nova Scotia, 1995* (East Lansing: Michigan State University Press, 1995); Carolyn F. Podruchny, "Unfair Masters and Rascally Servants? Labour Relations Among Bourgeois Clerks and Voyageurs in the Montreal Fur Trade, 1780–1821," *Labour* (Canada) 43 (Spring 1999): 43–70; Bruce M. White, "The Woman Who Married a Beaver: Trade Patterns and Gender Roles in the Ojibwa Fur Trade," *Ethnohistory* 46 (Winter 1999): 109–47; Laurier Turgeon, "French Fishers, Fur Traders, and Amerindians During the Sixteenth Century: History and Archaeology," *William and Mary Quarterly*, 3d ser., 55 (October 1998): 585–610; Ann M. Carlos and Frank D. Lewis, "Indians, the Beaver, and the Bay: The Economics of Depletion in the Lands of the Hudson's Bay Company, 1700–1763," *Journal of Economic History* 53 (September 1993): 465–94; and, in *"Le Castor Fait Tout": Selected Papers of the Fifth North American Fur Trade Conference, 1985,* ed. Bruce Trigger et al. (Montreal: The Society, 1987), John A. Dickinson, "Old Routes and New Wares: The Advent of European Goods in the St. Lawrence Valley," 25–41; J. Frederick Fausz, "'To Draw Hither the Trade of Beavers': The Strategic Significance of the English Fur Trade in the Chesapeake, 1620–1660," 42–71; and Peter Marshall, "The Government of the Quebec Fur Trade: An Imperial Dilemma, 1761–1775," 122–43. On fish, see Rosemary E. Ommer and Dianne Newell, eds., *Fishing Places, Fishing People: Traditions and Issues in Canadian Small-Scale Fisheries* (Toronto: University of Toronto Press, 1999); Sean T. Cadigan, *Hope and Deception in Conception Bay: Merchant-Settler Relations in Newfoundland, 1785–1855* (Toronto: University of Toronto Press, 1995), 5–13, 79–83; Rosemary E. Ommer, *From Outpost to Outport: A Structural Analysis of the Jersey-Gaspé Cod Fishery, 1767–1886* (Montreal: McGill-Queen's University Press, 1991), 7–8, 107–10, 136–40, 166–75, 190–99; and Keith Matthews, *Lectures on the History of Newfoundland, 1500–1830* (St. Johns: Breakwater Books, 1988), which adheres closely to the Innis staples theory.

28. For fur trading in the thirteen colonies and lands to the west, which has been less affected by staples thinking, see Briton C. Busch and Barry M. Gough, eds., *Fur Traders from New England: The Boston Men in the North Pacific, 1787–1800: The Narratives of William Dane Phelps, William*

Few commodities have received this much attention, and the discussion is rarely framed within the staples/Malthusian debate. Sugar has been the subject of at least two major narratives; and, even after the publication of Allan Kulikoff's *magnum opus,* tobacco continues to engage colonial scholars well past the point of diminishing returns.[29] Rice has been at the center of two major interpretive works on the social and economic development of South Carolina—Joyce Chaplin's *An Anxious Pursuit* and Peter Coclanis's *The Shadow of a Dream*—but the scale and scope of the rice trade itself is still understood only in outline. Coclanis's next book will put American rice flows in global perspective.[30] Indigo has been examined in passing, but the rise of the dyestuff as South Carolina's second-most valuable export has been explained unsatisfactorily as the product

Sturgis, and James Gilchrist Swan, Northwest Historical Series 18 (Spokane: Arthur H. Clark, 1997); Oliver A. Rink, "1629: A Year of Decision for New Netherland," *De Halve Maen* 72 (1999): 84–90; Susan Sleeper-Smith, "Women, Kin, and Catholicism: New Perspectives on the Fur Trade," *Ethnohistory* 47 (Spring 2000): 423–52; S. Dale Standen, "François Chalet and the French Trade at the Posts of Niagara and Frontenac, 1742–1747," *Proceedings of the Annual Meeting of the French Colonial Historical Society* 22 (1996), 225–40; Walter S. Dunn Jr., *Frontier Profit and Loss: The British Army and the Fur Traders, 1760–1764* (Westport, Conn.: Greenwood Press, 1998); Marty O'Shea, "Springfield's Puritans and Indians, 1636–1655," *Historical Journal of Massachusetts* 26 (Winter 1998), 46–72. For fishing, the best study is Daniel Vickers, *Farmers and Fishermen: Two Centuries of Work in Essex County, Massachusetts, 1630–1850* (Chapel Hill: University of North Carolina Press, 1994).

29. The story of the Caribbean sugar industry is retold by in J. H. Galloway, *The Sugar Cane Industry: An Historical Geography from Its Origins to 1914* (New York: Cambridge University Press, 1989). A far more interesting attempt is Sidney W. Mintz's *Sweetness and Power: The Place of Sugar in Modern History* (New York: Viking, 1985). Although Mintz ignores distribution, his linkage of production and consumption provides a useful model for future commodity studies. New data on sugar exports is to be found in David Eltis, "New Estimates of Exports from Barbados and Jamaica, 1665–1701," *William and Mary Quarterly,* 3d ser., 52 (October 1995): 631–48. On the French sugar industry, see Robert L. Stein, *The French Sugar Business in the Eighteenth Century* (Baton Rouge: Louisiana State University Press, 1988). A world-systems analysis of the sugar complex is offered by Jason W. Moore, "Sugar and the Expansion of the Early Modern World-Economy: Commodity Frontiers, Ecological Transformation, and Industrialization," in *Review of the Fernand Braudel Center* 23 (October 2000): 409–34.

On tobacco, see Ragsdale, "George Washington, the British Tobacco Trade"; Kulikoff, *Tobacco and Slaves.* The exception to oversaturation is, of course, the work by Lorena S. Walsh; see her "Summing the Parts" for an excellent example of what can still be done on the subject. Unfortunately few seasoned veterans have her stamina.

30. Christopher Gould, "The South Carolina and Continental Associations: Prelude to Revolution," *South Carolina Historical Magazine* 87 (January 1986): 30–40; Peter A. Coclanis, *The Shadow of a Dream: Economic Life and Death in the South Carolina Low Country, 1670–1920* (New York: Oxford University Press, 1989); Peter A. Coclanis, "Distant Thunder: The Creation of a World Market in Rice and the Transformations It Wrought," *American Historical Review* 98 (October 1993): 1050–78; Joyce E. Chaplin, *An Anxious Pursuit: Agricultural Innovation and Modernity in the Lower South, 1730–1815* (Chapel Hill: University of North Carolina Press, 1993); Kenneth Morgan, "The Organization of the Colonial American Rice Trade," *William and Mary Quarterly* 52 (July 1995): 433–52. Only R. C. Nash has fully engaged with the Innis staples thesis: "Urbanization in the Colonial South: Charleston South Carolina as a Case Study," *Journal of Urban History* 19 (July 1992): 3–29, and "South Carolina and the Atlantic Economy in the Late Seventeenth and Eighteenth Centuries," *Economic History Review* 45 (November 1992): 677–702.

of either midcentury British bounty or wartime dislocations.[31] Little research has appeared on timber or coffee until the recent reports of James McWilliams and Michelle Craig.[32] No work has been published on wheat or corn, although Brooke Hunter's soon-to-be-published dissertation at the University of Delaware will fill a gap in our understanding of the Brandywine grain trade and the flour-milling industry.[33] Moreover, except perhaps for Lorena Walsh's regional analyses of tobacco varieties, none of the aforementioned studies methodically covers an entire American region or explicitly tests the staples thesis in quite the way that McCusker and Menard advocated. Indeed, the only professional historian to

31. Chaplin, *Anxious Pursuit,* 190–208, discusses indigo, yet her explication of its trade is thin. Although he is mainly concerned with commodities, S. Max Edelson provides a fuller, richer depiction of trade patterns in "Planting the Lowcountry: Agricultural Enterprise and Economic Experience in the Lower South, 1695–1785" (Ph.D. diss., Johns Hopkins University, 1998). See also Philip D. Morgan, *Slave Counterpoint: Black Culture in the Eighteenth-Century Chesapeake and Low Country* (Chapel Hill: University of North Carolina Press, 1998); Gould, "South Carolina and Continental Associations."

32. James E. McWilliams, "New England's First Depression: Beyond an Export-Led Interpretation," *Journal of Interdisciplinary History* 33 (Summer 2002): 1–20, and "From the Ground Up: Internal Economic Development and Local Commercial Exchange in the Massachusetts Bay Region, 1630–1705" (Ph.D. diss., Johns Hopkins University, 2001); James W. Hunter III, "Leaden Logs and Broken Ships: Pensacola's First Timber Industry, 1695–1712," *Gulf South Historical Review* 15 (Spring 2000): 6–20; William B. Leavenworth, "The Ship in the Forest: New England Maritime Industries and Coastal Environment, 1630–1850" (Ph.D. diss., University of New Hampshire, 1999); Michael Williams, *Americans and Their Forests: A Historical Geography* (New York: Cambridge University Press, 1989); Geoffrey L. Rossano, "Down to the Bay: New York Shippers and the Central American Logwood Trade, 1748–1761," *New York History* 70 (October 1989): 229–50; Julian Gwyn, "Shipbuilding for the Royal Navy in Colonial New England," *American Neptune* 48 (October 1988): 22–30; R. Richard L. Knight, "New England Forests and British Seapower: Albion Revisited," *American Neptune* 46 (October 1986): 221–29. On coffee, see Mark Pendergrast, *Uncommon Grounds: The History of Coffee and How It Transformed the World* (New York: Basic Books, 1999); James A. Delle, *An Archaeology of Social Space: Analyzing Coffee Plantations in Jamaica's Blue Mountains* (New York: Plenum Press, 1998); S. D. Smith, "Sugar's Poor Relation: Coffee Planting in the British West Indies, 1720–1833," *Slavery and Abolition* 19 (December 1998): 68–89; and, in *Cultivation and Culture: Labor and the Shaping of Slave Life in the Americas,* ed. Ira Berlin and Philip D. Morgan (Charlottesville: University Press of Virginia, 1993), David Geggus, "Sugar and Coffee Cultivation in Saint Domingue and the Shaping of the Slave Labor Force," 73–98, and Michel-Rolph Trouillot, "Coffee Planters and Coffee Slaves in the Antilles: The Impact of a Secondary Crop," 124–37; Barry W. Higman, "The Internal Economy of Jamaican Pens, 1760–1890," *Social and Economic Studies* 38 (January 1989): 61–86; Michel-Rolph Trouillot, "Motion in the System: Coffee, Color, and Slavery in Eighteenth-Century Saint-Domingue," *Review of the Fernand Braudel Center* 5 (Winter 1982): 331–88. See also Michelle L. Craig, "From Cultivation to Cup: A History of Coffee in the Atlantic World, 1765–1805" (Ph.D. diss., University of Michigan, 2005).

33. Brooke Hunter, "Rage for Grain: Flour Milling in the Mid-Atlantic, 1750–1815" (Ph.D. diss., University of Delaware, 2001); William H. Siener, "Charles Yates, the Grain Trade, and Economic Development in Fredericksburg, Virginia, 1750–1810," *Virginia Magazine of History and Biography* 93 (October 1985): 409–26, based on his dissertation, "Economic Development in Revolutionary Virginia: Fredericksburg, 1750–1810" (Ph.D. diss., College of William and Mary, 1982), which is primarily a study of southern urbanization. The prohibition of grain exports to the French West Indies from Louisiana's "German Coast" was one of the causes of revolt against Spanish rule in Louisiana in 1768. Reinhart Kondert, "The German Involvement in the Rebellion of 1768," *Louisiana History* 26 (Autumn 1985): 385–97. A recent sketch of the world grain commodity chain appears in Sheila Pelizzon, "Grain Flour, 1590–1790," *Review of the Fernand Braudel Center* 23 (January 2000): 87–196.

engage it directly is Marc Egnal, whose *New World Economies: The Growth of the Thirteen Colonies and Early Canada* finds little to recommend the idea. The "export-led" explanation, he avers, "rests on broad generalizations rather than measurable norms," "focuses on one aspect of the economy, and ignores other important reasons for growth," "ignores the impact of culture and long-lived institutions on growth," and "has an odd-static quality, and does not shed light on the rate of growth." Instead, Egnal proffers a study of sectoral developments and argues that British North America grew in two long economic waves, the first slow and the second expansive.[34]

It is striking how little of the agenda set forth in *The Economy of British America* has been pursued, how few of its questions have been answered. Historians interested in the economy of the British Atlantic world have largely chosen to address questions other than those posed by McCusker and Menard, and many (perhaps most) studies, while not incompatible or inconsistent with *The Economy of British America,* are simply different. For example, what fascinates one group of scholars is the integrated nature of the early modern Atlantic world: the connections agents forged in building the foundational information, distribution, and financial institutions. What intrigues these scholars is the decentralized nature of the emerging Atlantic economies, and the coordination of agent-based, nonhierarchical production, distribution, and consumption activities. One of the most insightful books in the field carefully reconstructs the trading routes that served as the principal communications channels and thus as the integument that held the empire together between 1675 and 1740. These trading routes served as the infrastructure for building a transoceanic community; the routinization, frequency, predictability, and profitability of transatlantic communication and movement turned the ocean, by 1740, into "just" another bridge to cross, presenting far fewer fears of harm or delay compared to a century earlier. Jacob Price sketched the widening credit net that London and Glasgow enterprisers cast between 1607 and 1789, while Thomas Doerflinger studied the agency of Philadelphia merchants as their business reached most of the globe in the second half of the eighteenth century.[35] Other scholars, too, have extended McCusker

---

34. Egnal, *New World Economies,* 5–6.

35. On decentralization, integration, and coordination, see David Hancock, "Self-Organized Complexity and the Emergence of an Atlantic Market Economy, 1651–1815: The Case of Wine," in *The Emergence of the Atlantic Economy,* ed. Peter A. Coclanis and Jack P. Greene (Columbia: University of South Carolina Press, 2005), 1–50; David Hancock, "Décentralisation et auto-organisation dans une économie de réseau émergente, 1640–1815," *Annales, histoire, sciences sociales* 58 (July–August 2003); David Hancock, ed., *Letters of William Freeman, London Merchant, 1678–1685* (London: London Record Society, 2002); Hancock, *Citizens of the World.* Cf. Ian K. Steele, *The English Atlantic, 1675–1740: An Exploration of Communication and Community* (New York: Oxford University Press, 1986); Thomas M. Doerflinger, *A Vigorous Spirit of Enterprise: Merchants and Economic Development in Revolutionary Philadelphia* (Chapel Hill: University of North Carolina Press, 1986); Jacob M. Price, "The Last Phase of the Virginia-London Consignment Trade: James Buchanan & Co. 1758–1768," *William and Mary Quarterly,* 3d ser., 43 (January 1986): 64–98, and "Sheffeild v. Starke: Institutional Experimentation in the

and Menard in directions they did not foresee, focusing on noncountable economies—smuggling and piracy—and agents previously regarded as marginal—
sailors, women, and Indians.[36]

London-Maryland Trade, c. 1696–1706," *Business History* 28 (July 1986): 19–39; Jacob M. Price and Paul
G. E. Clemens, "A Revolution of Scale in Overseas Trade: British Firms in the Chesapeake, 1675–1775,"
Journal of Economic History 47 (March 1987): 1–43.

    36. On smugglers, pirates and sailors, see Peter Linebaugh and Marcus Rediker, *The Many-
Headed Hydra: Sailors, Slavers, Commoners, and the Hidden History of the Revolutionary Atlantic* (Boston:
Beacon Press, 2000); W. Jeffrey Bolster, *Black Jacks: African American Seamen in the Age of Sail* (Cambridge: Harvard University Press, 1997); Grabowski, "Les Amérindiens domicilies et la 'contrabande'
des fourrures"; Marcus Rediker, "The Anglo-American Seaman as Collective Worker, 1700–1750," in
Work and Labor in Early America, ed. Stephen Innes, (Chapel Hill: University of North Carolina Press,
1988), 252–86, and *Between the Devil and the Deep Blue Sea: Merchant Seamen, Pirates, and the Anglo-American Maritime World, 1700–1750* (New York: Cambridge University Press, 1987); Zahedieh, "Merchants
of Port Royal." Legal piracy, in the form of privateering (the private business of cruising against the
warships or commerce of the enemy, taking their ships and goods, and profiting on resale), has been
the subject of several studies since 1985. James Farley, "The Ill-Fated Voyage of the *Providentia:* Richard
Vaux, Loyalist Merchant, and the Trans-Atlantic Mercantile World in the Late Eighteenth Century,"
Pennsylvania History 62 (October 1995): 364–75; Carl E. Swanson, *Predators and Prizes: American Privateering and Imperial Warfare, 1739–48* (Columbia: University of South Carolina Press, 1991); J. H. Betty,
"The Capture of the *Baltick Merchant* 1740," *Mariner's Mirror* 76 (January 1990): 36–39; David J. Starkey
et al., "Eighteenth-Century Privateering Enterprise," *International Journal of Maritime History* 1 (April
1989): 279–86; Gilbert M. Joseph, "John Coxon and the Role of Buccaneering in the Settlement of the
Yucatán Colonial Frontier," *Terrae Incognitae* 12 (January 1980): 65–84; Patrick Crowhurst, *The French
War on Trade: Privateering, 1793–1815* (Aldershot, Eng.: Scholar, 1989). On women, see Patricia A. Cleary,
Elizabeth Murray: A Woman's Pursuit of Independence in Eighteenth-Century America (Amherst: University
of Massachusetts Press, 2000); Elaine F. Crane, *Ebb Tide in New England: Women, Seaports, and Social
Change, 1630–1800* (Boston: Northeastern University Press, 1998); Sheila Skemp, *Judith Sargent Murray:
A Brief Biography with Documents* (Boston: Northeastern University Press, 1998); Patricia A. Cleary, "'She
Will Be in the Shop': Women's Sphere of Trade in Eighteenth-Century Philadelphia and New York,"
Pennsylvania Magazine of History and Biography 119 (July 1995): 181–202; Patricia A. Cleary, "'She Mer-
chants' of Colonial America: Women and Commerce on the Eve of the Revolution" (Ph.D. diss.,
Northwestern University, 1989). Cf. Ellen Hartigan-O'Connor, "Gender and the Early American
Urban Economies of Charleston and Newport" (Ph.D. diss., University of Michigan, forthcoming).
Taken together, work on women's work and gendered behavior suggests in one important dimension
a division of colonial life that had not been noted before; the analysis of gender gives us intersexual,
interracial, intercolonial, transatlantic, and even interimperial ways of reading the world. Particularly
instructive is what has been learned about the place and work of women in other cultures. See Amanda
Vickery, *The Gentleman's Daughter: Women's Lives in Georgian England* (New Haven: Yale University
Press, 1998); Elizabeth Kowaleski-Wallace, *Consuming Subjects: Women, Shopping, and Business in the
Eighteenth Century* (New York: Columbia University Press, 1997); Ramon Gutierrez, *When Jesus Came,
the Corn Mothers Went Away: Marriage, Sexuality, and Power in New Mexico* (Stanford: Stanford Univer-
sity Press, 1991); Karen Anderson, *Chain Her by One Foot: Women in Seventeenth-Century New France*
(London: Routledge, 1991); Barbara Bush, *Slave Women in Caribbean Society, 1650–1838* (Bloomington:
Indiana University Press, 1990); Marietta Morrissey, *Slave Women in the New World: Gender Stratification
in the Caribbean* (Lawrence: University Press of Kansas, 1989). On Indians, see Colin G. Calloway, *New
Worlds for All: Indians, Europeans, and the Remaking of Early America* (Baltimore: Johns Hopkins University
Press, 1997); Alan Gallay, "The Search for an Alternate Source of Trade: The Creek Indians and Jona-
than Bryan," *Georgia Historical Quarterly* 73 (Summer 1989): 209–30; Christopher L. Miller and George
R. Hamell, "A New Perspective on Indian-White Contact: Cultural Symbols and Colonial Trade," *Jour-
nal of American History* 73 (September 1986): 311–28.

Now, there is no question that our ability to follow these new research programs presupposes *The Economy of British America,* but even the scholars most sympathetic to McCusker and Menard's approach have focused their research on questions that are tangential to those they identified. Why is this? Three answers strike me as plausible: to readers, the book may seem to close more doors than it opens, to be too "economic" in its orientation, and to be insufficiently connected to historians' emerging interest in cultural studies.

The Economy of British America is a deft, comprehensive summation of years of scholarship and many points of view on traditional and emerging topics, a compendium of the best economic-historical practice. Few colonial historians seriously rejected the picture the authors painted, whether of overall economic growth and development or of the role of staple commodities.[37] Oh, the neo-Malthusians quibbled at the short shrift given to population and land, and they have gone to work since then to show that these things mattered more than McCusker and Menard appeared to allow.[38] Even so, the bold, broad outlines of the narrative, both chronological and regional, were generally accepted; certainly the topical and regional analyses were hard to dismiss or counter. But the book's acceptance may have dissuaded younger scholars from answering its call by leaving the impression that its kind of early modern economic history of North America leaves few interesting questions open. To some, the issues McCusker and Menard suggested for further research seem like gaps, not open questions, and the chore of filling gaps did not endear itself to a generation of ambitious colonial scholars. In addition, *The Economy of British America* may simply intimidate young scholars. Its virtues—comprehensive scope and magisterial synthesis—make measuring up to it seem a formidable task. It is far easier to sidestep direct comparison with McCusker and Menard by focusing on other issues.

Second, although McCusker and Menard are historians, and not themselves wedded to the new economic history of the 1960s and 1970s—in fact, they were open to many kinds of evidence about the colonial economy—their project has been tainted by the history profession's distrust of economics and

---

37. On the "general agreement," see McCusker, "Measuring Colonial Gross Domestic Product," 5. Apparently accepted are the conjectures that the "economy grew over time between 1607 to 1775"; "growth was not steady"; the "driving force of the economy was its foreign sector"; "the long-term rate of growth exceeded, perhaps even doubled, the rate of growth of Great Britain"; and, about 1775, per capita GDP was higher "than it had been a century or a century and a half earlier," higher than that of "any other nation in the world," and higher "than it would be again in the United States for some time to come."

38. On the diversification of domestic economy, increasing landlessness and tenancy, and the importance of population growth and the pressure it placed on land, see Allan Kulikoff, *From British Peasants to Colonial American Farmers* (Chapel Hill: University of North Carolina Press, 2000), 129; Peter C. Mancall and Thomas Weiss, "Was Economic Growth Likely in Colonial British North America?" *Journal of Economic History* 59 (March 1999): 17–40; Allan Kulikoff, *The Agrarian Origins of American Capitalism* (Charlottesville: University Press of Virginia, 1992); James Henretta, *The Origins of American Capitalism: Collected Essays* (Boston: Northeastern University Press, 1991), 189–90, 199–294.

disappointment in econometric and statistical methods. To many historians, the economic approach to economic history seems limiting; while economic theory is valuable and insightful, its subject matter seems constricted; it appears to leave much of economic life out of the picture. In addition, historians have not found "the explicit application of theory to the past and the testing of intractable hypotheses through statistical analysis" an attractive methodology. Such an exercise requires a turn of mind and mathematical skills most historians have never had. Economic approaches are more difficult and less revealing than usual about statistically dark periods such as the American world before the federal census, a situation McCusker and Menard appreciated when they noted that the surviving data leave "much to be desired." Still, the authors were optimistic: "early American history resembles a laboratory, containing sufficient diversity to encourage analysis but enough similarity to allow control of at least some variables." American "conditions offer abundant opportunities to test the [staples] model and hold out the possibility of some theoretical benefits, as empirical studies clarify relationships between staples and economic development."[39] The profession as a whole has not shared their optimism.

A third reason the profession has not thoroughly taken up McCusker and Menard's call is that the focus of historians' interest has turned from economic history toward cultural studies, with a heavy dollop of law, environment, and Atlantic specificity thrown in. Of those who have persisted in working on recognizably economic subjects, some (as the aforementioned pages suggest) have plowed familiar terrain, while others have relocated in microhistorical investigation.[40]

39. McCusker and Menard, *Economy of British America,* 5–6, 31–32.

40. The study of cultural, social and economic relationships on the microscopic level, reflecting the variety of the colonists' lived experiences, frees the historian from the structures of a not-always-applicable theory and unnecessary abstraction; it allows him or her to bridge several disciplines and fields; it encourages focus on common people, on agency (rather than structure and hierarchy); it allows the writer/reader to participate in ideas and feelings seldom laid bare by econometric number crunching; perhaps, more to the point of this essay, it provides the highly detailed work from which larger themes and conclusions—cultural and otherwise—emerge. Pat Hudson, "Industrialization in Britain: The Challenge of Micro-History," *Family and Community History* 2 (January 1999): 5–16; Brad S. Gregory, "Is Small Beautiful? Microhistory and the History of Everyday Life," *History and Theory* 38 (February 1999): 100–110; Peter Burke, "The *Annales* in Global Context," *International Review of Social History* 35 (December 1990): 421–32. Taking their inspiration from early modern European and Asian scholars are Carlo Ginzburg, *The Night Battles: Witchcraft and Agrarian Cults in the Sixteenth and Seventeenth Centuries* (1966; reprint, Baltimore: Johns Hopkins University Press, 1992), and its sequel, *The Cheese and the Worms: The Cosmos of a Sixteenth-Century Miller* (1976; reprint, Baltimore: Johns Hopkins University Press, 1980); Natalie Zemon Davis, *The Return of Martin Guerre* (Cambridge: Harvard University Press, 1983), and *Fiction in the Archives: Pardon Tales and Their Tellers in Sixteenth-Century France* (Stanford: Stanford University Press, 1987); Jonathan Spence, *The Question of Hu* (New York: Knopf, 1988). A few early American historians have blazed the trail: Laurel Ulrich, *A Midwife's Tale: The Life of Martha Ballard, Based on Her Diary, 1785–1812* (New York: Knopf, 1990); John Demos, *The Unredeemed Captive* (New York: Knopf, 1994); Alan Taylor, *William Cooper's Town: Power and Persuasion on the Frontier of the Early American Republic* (New York: Knopf, 1995); Donna Merwick, *Death of a Notary: Conquest and Change in Colonial New York* (Ithaca: Cornell University Press, 1999). In October 1999 the Omohundro Institute dedicated an entire conference (held in Storrs, Connecticut) to the subject.

Far more, however, have simply ignored it. Cultural history; the histories of marginal peoples, imagined communities and identities and private pursuits; studies of the Atlantic world; environmental and legal systems—these have been the ruling gods of the historical house since the 1980s, and they have been on steroids ever since, gaining mass as well as strength. Professional historians as a group have not been interested in investigating economies, organizations, and systems. As a group that comes from diverse backgrounds, American historians have found themselves attracted to porousness, hybridity, context, and multivalence. If theory is invoked, it is inspired by Derrida and Foucault, perhaps Wallerstein, but not Coase and Williamson, much less Harold Innis. Economic history and, by extension, the issues concerning growth raised by *The Economy of British America* seem far removed from current issues of interest. From this point of view, there are few problems to be solved with economic history, and a lot of new and exciting things to examine in other ways.[41]

Cultural history is not at cross-purposes with economic and social history *a priori*. As "the distinctive attitudes and actions that differentiate groups of people," culture is "the result of and expressed through religion, language, institutions, and history." This is suitably historical, for, while its attributes evolve incrementally, sometimes glacially, "they can and do change over time."[42] But for many cultural and culturally minded social historians, culture and economics do not intersect. Simply put, this is weird. The material substrate is the precondition for culture, whether of the kind that leaves archaeological, material evidence or the kind that leaves records, texts, and systems of signs to be interpreted. Some

41. Even the interest of publishers is waning. Consider the record of the Institute of Early American History and Culture. Of some fifty-four books published after 1985, only fourteen explicitly touched on economic life, although another seven did so indirectly. In short, this is not bad, but then the institute has always been one of the most supportive patrons of economically grounded history. Even so, of the twenty-two books published since 1995, only four dealt with the economy in some fashion or another. Change is afoot. Consider also the articles published by the institute's *William and Mary Quarterly*: of the 325 articles published in the journal between January 1985 and January 2001, 65 were on economic subjects and another 59 touched indirectly on economic subjects; more than half (201) covered totally unrelated topics. The share devoted to the economy is significant, and, again, the institute has championed the study more than most organizations, but the relevant point is the dwindling interest since 1985, down from a quarter of articles to roughly an eighth. Before 1950 political history and institutional history were the reigning paradigmatic interests; after 1950 social history, religious history, and intellectual history seized the imagination. Bridging the divide was economic history, and for a time in the 1970s it seemed likely that economic history would emerge in America much as it emerged in England, independent and influential. But it has not emerged as a third pillar of the field and does not appear to be doing so. "The field as a whole," not just in England but also in America, appears "marked by a loss of self-confidence and a contraction of interest." "Apparently unwilling or unable to redefine itself," it is "marginalized . . . within the history of the early modern period as a whole." Keith Wrightson, *Earthly Necessities: Economic Lives in Early Modern Britain* (New Haven: Yale University Press, 2000), 21.

42. Peter Temin, "Is It Kosher to Talk About Culture?" *Journal of Economic History* 57 (June 1997): 268. Cf. Lynn Hunt and Victoria Bonnell, eds., *Beyond the Cultural Turn: New Directions in the Study of Society and Culture* (Berkeley and Los Angeles: University of California Press, 1999), and Lynn Hunt, ed., *The New Cultural History* (Berkeley and Los Angeles: University of California Press, 1989).

of the principal arenas for culture are fundamentally economic, such as the organization and meaning of work and consumption, and the division of labor and
its relation to gender, class, race, and other cultural and sociocultural constructs.
Human lives are not neatly compartmentalized: culture cannot be separated from
economy. A problem therefore arises, as sometimes happens in current scholarship, when meaning is richer than experience, when ideas about the culture of
class, race, and gender drift in a sea of discourse that only vaguely washes over
the bodies, lives, and labors of actual people who created that culture.

Consider four examples of recent work that engage economic topics.
They trace a spectrum from curious to commendable and point us toward ways
to combine disparate fields and approaches. Jean-Christophe Agnew's popular
book, *Worlds Apart,* is an intensive semiological analysis that purports to show
how Elizabethan, Stuart, and Hanoverian theater became a venue in which to
explore the emerging social relationships of an increasingly capitalistic Anglo-
American world. Theater "furnished its urban audience with a laboratory and
an idiom within which these difficulties and contradictions could be acted out."
For Agnew, the metaphor of the theater was transformed "into a complex, sec-
ular commentary on the commodity world." If he had stayed with that idea, he
might have made an interesting point about mimicry and representation, and the
encroachment of commercialization on certain walks of life. But, in addition,
Agnew believes his analysis explicates developments in the market economy over
those three hundred years. He argues that market processes, characterized by
misrepresentation, antagonism, and the use of money, converted what had been
transparent exchange and moral accountability into an impersonal and essentially
theatrical world. This is a grand contention, a variant on what Deirdre McCloskey
has labeled the "conceived in sin" argument about capitalism. It would be an
important argument if Agnew were persuasive. But he fails to ground his discussion in evidence about the actual economic development of England, or
even in the voluminous contemporary discourse about that development. He
deservedly criticizes economic historians for ignoring "the complexity of feel-
ing and meaning associated with commodity and exchange," but then proceeds
to ignore the subtlety and intricacy with which ingenious people put commodities and exchange opportunities to work for themselves. As a result, he does
not seem to notice that an exchange-based commodity economy was not fully
formed until the eighteenth century. Even in his chosen literary realm, he does
not seem much fussed that his sources are almost solely critics of the theater, not
patrons, playwrights, producers, actors, or audiences. Yet in some historical circles, this least economic of books now defines current understanding of the early
modern Anglo-American market.[43]

43. Jean-Christophe Agnew, *Worlds Apart: The Market and the Theater in Anglo-American
Thought, 1550–1750* (New York: Cambridge University Press, 1986), especially 12.

Scholars who deal more directly with colonial America and economic agents have also fallen into the "non-intersection fallacy."[44] In *Forced Founders,* Woody Holton wants to understand why Virginia's elite became patriotic revolutionaries, and his answer is class conflict within the colony. He repudiates Bernard Bailyn's now canonical argument that the separation was a political, constitutional, and ideological struggle, and in doing so revives the Progressive historians' line that it was a controversy among social groups. In his particular view, Virginia's gentry sought independence in order to maintain their place at the top of colonial society. While intriguing as an argument, Holton sadly presents class conflict in revolutionary Virginia as cultural contest shorn of economic moorings. He has little knowledge of colonial money, for instance, and the ways it flowed through society. More critical to his thesis, he has little appreciation for colonial debt, its role in the colony and the ways it affected the minds and actions of Virginians. In particular, he has no sense of the benefits and costs of indebtedness, an ignorance that would have shocked the planters he writes about. The effect is to hollow out his thesis, emptying it of its connections to the lives and concerns of the people he is trying to understand.

Text-, class-, race-, and gender-based analysis of American culture has produced striking examples not only of catastrophic misunderstanding but also of possible alternative courses, methods for combining economy and culture in important, revealing ways. The course is neither always clear nor always easy. Yet serious scholars are working in this vein.[45] Kathleen Brown's *Good Wives, Nasty Wenches, and Anxious Patriarchs* notes the effects of worker dislocation in England on the eve of colonization and population trends and demographic imbalances in Virginia, for instance; she tries to connect material behavior and economic activity to a system of beliefs ordered by attitudes about gender and race. Each of the book's three sections begins with an anecdote about gender or race, weaves a story of its economic dimensions, and uses the narrative to initiate a discussion about belief systems generally. In the end, however, the book's

44. Woody Holton, *Forced Founders: Indians, Debtors, Slaves and the Making of the American Revolution in Virginia* (Chapel Hill: University of North Carolina Press, 1999). Similar instances of the non-intersection fallacy appear in Jill Lepore, *The Name of War: King Philip's War and the Origins of American Identity* (New York: Knopf, 1999); David S. Shields, *Civil Tongues and Polite Letters in British America* (Chapel Hill: University of North Carolina Press, 1997). Economic examples are endless. Writing the history of a trade with little or no reference to business practices and economic matters is not peculiar to the colonial period. For a recent example, see Malcolm Goldstein, *Landscape with Figures: A History of Art Dealing in the United States* (New York: Oxford University Press, 2000).

45. Kathleen M. Brown, *Good Wives, Nasty Wenches, and Anxious Patriarchs: Gender, Race, and Power in Colonial Virginia* (Chapel Hill: University of North Carolina Press, 1996); Cornelia Dayton, *Women Before the Bar: Gender, Law, and Society in Connecticut, 1639–1789* (Chapel Hill: University of North Carolina Press, 1995). Equally good at grounding the story is Michael Warner's impressive *Letters of the Republic,* in which one finds an excellent model examination of the socioeconomic background of readers and writers, and the role of trade in the diffusion of ideas. Warner, *The Letters of the Republic: Publication and the Public Sphere in Eighteenth-Century America* (Cambridge: Harvard University Press, 1990).

interpretative direction veers toward reification of gender and race as free-floating constructs, and therefore fails to sustain its analysis of gender and racial politics embedded in economic life. This leads Brown to some puzzling conclusions. She concludes that Elizabethan men funded voyages and backed settlements *not* to make money but to address problems of sexual identity (the need for "elite male self definition and validation"). We should applaud Brown for bringing the "search for conquest" to our attention; economic and business historians have been generally unwilling to factor gender concerns into their study of enterprise. But the social construction of voyages as conquest and of conquest as masculine did not occur in a vacuum. The perceived profitability of such ventures relative to the adventurers' other alternatives almost certainly had something to do with it. These are questions about which economic and business perspectives have something to contribute.

More successfully, Cornelia Dayton's *Women Before the Bar* links law, gender, and economics to show what women experienced in the colonial Connecticut judicial system. Perhaps she is fortunate in her subject and sources: the process of dispute, proceedings, and decision bridges abstract encoded legal meaning with material life. Whatever the reason, Dayton convinces us that women's legal position shifted from central to marginal between 1639 and 1789. *Women Before the Bar* has many virtues: Dayton is persistent and even-handed in linking Puritan theology, social ideals concerning patriarchy and status, and commercial ethics to workaday peoples and their businesses; she is receptive to quantitative data modulated by personal stories; she presents a close, unforced reading of the records, readable prose, and a clear narrative; and she emphasizes the complexities and ongoing interactions of the personalities and principles that shaped the construction of gender and the transition toward legal marginality. Her subjects are real people who made daily decisions and thought specific thoughts that sprang naturally from their activities. Dayton's agent-based approach allows her to integrate topics and ideas that are often treated separately and to plead her case persuasively.[46]

---

46. Equally good are cultural biographies and the studies of material culture written from a cultural history perspective. Taylor, *William Cooper's Town,* for instance, carefully ties ideas to activities, interweaving the possibilities and disappointments of business on the frontier to a quest for gentility; it focuses on commercial practices, political ambitions, *and* the identity construction of grasping enterprisers. More historians should follow this model. Likewise, many material culture studies are well grounded in the economic substrate. See, for example, Laurel Thatcher Ulrich, "Hannah Barnard's Cupboard," in *Through A Glass Darkly: Reflections on Personal Identity in America,* ed. Ronald Hoffman et al. (Chapel Hill: University of North Carolina Press, 1997); Robert St. George, *Conversing by Signs: Poetics of Implication in Colonial New England Culture* (Chapel Hill: University of North Carolina Press, 1998). Such studies, however, can all too easily veer toward an isolationistic view of life in the Atlantic world. Historians of material culture, usually so sensitive to economic matters, have been too quick to slight the processes of production or distribution in their examination of consumption or the drivers of consumer demand. Tim Breen's influential articles on American consumption are probably the best known on the subject, but in his desire to explicate class representation and attraction, Breen ignores

The challenge does not fall on only one side, of course, for many economists and economic historians also seem to think that culture and economics do not intersect. As good as they are, one looks in vain into David Galenson's and Farley Grubb's technically impressive analyses of indentured servitude and the slave trade for the play of cultural influence. Marc Egnal's provocative attempt to upend McCusker and Menard's staples thesis identifies no cultural influences on the cycles of economic growth. Two recent presidents of the American Economic History Association in the late 1990s, both trained as economists, have argued in favor of factoring cultural explanations into economic history. "To explain how markets live, to explain where technology and tastes originate, to explain what symbolic system supported or discouraged the people living in the economies of olden days," Deirdre McCloskey suggests, "we need culture, in both the anthropologist's and the aesthete's sense." "Something happened between Adam Smith and now. Somehow a view of Economic Man that placed him in a system of virtues and made him out to be a complete character got mislaid." But, she argues, it is "a scientific mistake to set the other virtues aside even when you wish to deal mainly with Prudential," that is, profit-maximal, consequences. The intensity of their argument is indicative of the void they hope to fill. Economic historians and economists, too, "need to become more aware of the concerns of [cultural] historians"—and not just of those of us who share their outlooks and priorities.[47]

So, what is to be done? We could start by adopting the habits of mind that informed McCusker and Menard in the late 1970s at the launch of their project: openness to many disciplines, topics, and areas, and ingenuity and flexibility in combining them. The authors, along with Jack Greene, were some of the first Americanists to include in a serious manner British Canada and the British West Indies in a narrative of early American economic and social

---

the production, labor, financial, and entrepreneurial structures that facilitated access to consumer goods. See T. H. Breen, "An Empire of Goods: The Anglicization of Colonial America, 1690–1776," *Journal of British Studies* 25 (October 1986): 467–99; T. H. Breen, "'Baubles of Britain': The American and British Consumer Revolutions of the Eighteenth Century," *Past and Present* 119 (May 1988): 73–104.

47. David W. Galenson, *Traders, Planters, and Slaves: Market Behavior in Early English America* (New York: Cambridge University Press, 1986); Farley Grubb, "The Market for Indentured Immigrants: Evidence on the Efficiency of Forward-Labor Contracting in Philadelphia, 1745–1773," *Journal of Economic History* 45 (December 1985): 855–68, and "The Auction of Redemptioner Servants, Philadelphia, 1771–1804: An Economic Analysis," *Journal of Economic History* 48 (September 1988): 583–603; Egnal, *New World Economies*, which is perplexing given the *cri de coeur* for culture he issued two years before in *Divergent Paths: How Culture and Institutions Have Shaped North American Growth* (New York: Oxford University Press, 1996); Deirdre N. McCloskey, "Bourgeois Virtue and the History of P and S," *Journal of Economic History* 58 (June 1998): 300, 305, 306; Temin, "Is It Kosher to Talk About Culture?" 282–83. A good model set by an economist is John E. Murray, "Fates of Orphans: Poor Children in Antebellum Charleston," *Journal of Interdisciplinary History* 33 (Autumn 2003): 519–45, which compares to the most recent historical work on the subject by Ruth W. Herndon, *Unwelcome Americans: Living on the Margin in Early New England* (Philadelphia: University of Pennsylvania Press, 2001).

history.[48] Similarly, they were some of the first to weave studies of material culture and historical archaeology into their syntheses. Such forays into uncharted waters should give us courage.

In the same spirit, we can enrich our field of inquiry by realizing the limits of the methods generally adopted by economic historians. McCusker and Menard did the profession an inestimable service in summarizing the state of knowledge—and the state of ignorance—of the economy of British America after thirty-plus years of dedicated research using economic data and econometric analysis. They showed how substantial the achievements of this effort were. But there are many questions that cannot be answered, and some that cannot even be framed, using the economic techniques of the second half of the twentieth century. We can enrich the field by returning to the more inclusive economic history championed by late nineteenth- and early twentieth-century scholars, a history not defined solely by the somewhat Whiggish preoccupation with economic growth, as important as that is, and not answered primarily by statistical analysis.[49]

History is all of a piece, because lives are lived all of a piece. As historians, we have not finished our task until we have reintegrated the pieces. This is why integrating economic history and cultural history is so important. Economic events are embedded in cultural contexts that affect what they mean, how people view and react to them, and, ultimately, how people make economic decisions and act to provision themselves. The only way for us to understand *homo economicus* is to understand ourselves as cultural creatures.[50] Likewise, cultures, including discourses, are embedded in economic contexts that affect how, and how well, people are able to make their livings, how they organize themselves to compete or cooperate—opposing or affiliating with others—and, ultimately, what resources they have for creating cultures. The only way for us to

48. The "imperial school of early American history" as established by Charles Andrews, George Beer, and Lawrence Gipson, had long pursued this tack. See also Jack P. Greene, *Pursuits of Happiness: The Social Development of Early Modern British Colonies and the Formation of American Culture* (Chapel Hill: University of North Carolina Press, 1988).

49. William Cunningham, Thorold Rogers, and William Ashley, three Britons, led the way in this regard. As Wrightson notes in *Earthly Necessities,* they were interested in "past economic cultures in the round, with their institutional frameworks, characteristic relationships and central ideas. They were acutely aware that economic change involved a myriad of factors other than the strictly economic" (14).

50. Temin, "Is It Kosher to Talk About Culture?" 280. Temin is primarily interested in the "culture of Protestantism," its presence or absence, and the motives for individual industry or saving. That is, he is interested in individualism, in both its constructive and destructive forms. The fusion is prefigured by some historians who have attempted to combine business history and material culture and sketch the complete material lives of merchants. See Hancock, *Citizens of the World;* Peter Earle, *The Making of the English Middle Class: Business, Society, and Family Life in London, 1660–1730* (Berkeley and Los Angeles: University of California Press, 1989); Tamara Thornton, *Cultivating Gentlemen: The Meaning of Country Life Among the Boston Elite, 1785–1860* (New Haven: Yale University Press, 1989); Doerflinger, *Vigorous Spirit of Enterprise.*

understand ourselves as cultural animals is to understand ourselves as economic creatures. Integration will generate new questions, some of them connected to the intellectual discourse about gender, race, and class. It will deploy a greater variety of disciplinary techniques from anthropology, sociology, geography, industrial archaeology, law, political science, religion, science, and art, as well as economics. It should produce "a vastly enriched sense of the context of economic change."[51]

The power of integrating economic and cultural history shows in two areas where integrative work is being done today: Atlantic linkage and political economy.[52] First of all, there has been a considerable move toward viewing the early modern Atlantic basin as a dynamic, syncretic region in which the rules of governance, management, exchange, and interaction built upon, but differed from, the rules within countries or regions. McCusker and Menard knew this; British America, they asserted, could "not be understood apart from the larger [Atlantic] process." "Developments in Europe, Africa, and elsewhere in the Americas formed the arena within which colonists lived, constantly creating, restricting, and channeling their opportunities." Research and writing that highlight the themes of transoceanic flow, mutuality, and decentralization help us correct the view of America as a fortress or as exceptional.[53] This perspective has gained force from the histories published in the past fifteen years that argue that the Atlantic was a "single functional unit" and "the scene of a vast interaction" between two old worlds and one new one, as well as from the studies that describe the interdependence of regions around the oceanic rim.[54]

51. Wrightson, *Earthly Necessities,* 22.

52. McCusker and Menard acknowledged the existence and relevance of some of these areas in 1985, and tried "to remain sensitive to issues in economic history that are difficult to quantify, to questions of political economy" and the creative role of entrepreneurs, as well as to interactions between the "economic," "social," and "cultural" dimensions of colonial life. But their interest and argument lay elsewhere. *Economy of British America,* 7.

53. Ibid., 7–8.

54. Ibid., 86–87; Donald Meinig, *The Shaping of America: A Geographical Perspective on 500 Years of History* (New Haven: Yale University Press, 1986), 1:65; Hancock, *Citizens of the World;* Bernard Bailyn, "The Idea of Atlantic History," *Itinerario* 20 (1996): 12–14, 33; John Thornton, *Africa and Africans in the Making of the Atlantic World, 1400–1800,* 2d ed. (New York: Cambridge University Press, 1998). Other intriguing works that take this particular perspective include Franklin W. Knight and Peggy K. Liss, eds., *Atlantic Port Cities: Economy, Culture, and Society in the Atlantic World, 1650–1850* (Knoxville: University of Tennessee Press, 1991); Nicholas Canny, *Kingdom and Colony: Ireland in the Atlantic World, 1560–1800* (Baltimore: Johns Hopkins University Press, 1988). The most recent comprehensive collection attempts, a la Wallerstein, to invoke the idea of a system; it is Horst Pietschmann, ed., *Atlantic History: History of the Atlantic System, 1580–1830* (Göttingen: Vanderhoeck & Ruprecht, 2002). Cf. "L'Atlantique," *Dix-Huitième Siècle* 33, special issue (2001), which is less willing to impose unity. Cultural historians have not been shy about filling the arena. In *Cities of the Dead: Circum-Atlantic Performance* (New York: Columbia University Press, 1996), Joseph Roach (heavily influenced by Paul Gilroy's "Black Atlantic") struggles to recreate the flow of information around the Atlantic in his analysis of the relationship of memory, performance, and substitution, and to locate "the peoples of the Caribbean rim at the heart of an oceanic interculture embodied through performance." In the end Roach succeeds merely in comparing theatrical performance in London and New Orleans. Laura Brown, in *Ends of Empire* (Ithaca: Cornell University Press, 1993), makes a more successful attempt to write a history of one aspect of

For example, an Atlantic perspective forces historians to consider the foreignness of British America. The non-Englishness of Anglo-American life is only beginning to be glimpsed. Studies of the lives, movements, and labors of migrants and the persistence of the communities they erected in America have flourished in the past twer.ty years: the Scottish, Welsh and Irish;[55] the French who settled in New France, Louisiana, and the Illinois Country;[56] the Spanish;[57] and the Dutch.[58] About the only group to escape close scholarly scrutiny—yet—

"oceanic interculture" in feminist readings of colonialist ideology, especially in the way the image of the female shaped capitalist commodification in early eighteenth-century English literature; it is, though, only a community of the mind.

55. Games, *Migration and Origins;* Marianne S. Wokeck, *Trade in Strangers: The Beginnings of Mass Migration to North America* (University Park: Pennsylvania State University Press, 1999); Ned C. Landsman, "Nation, Migration, and the Province in the First British Empire: Scotland and the Americas, 1600–1800," *American Historical Review* 104 (April 1999): 463–75; Bernard Bailyn and Philip D. Morgan, *Strangers Within the Realm: Cultural Margins of the First British Empire* (Chapel Hill: University of North Carolina Press, 1991); Angus J. L. Winchester, "Ministers, Merchants, and Migrants: Cumberland Friends and North America in the Eighteenth Century," *Quaker History* 80 (Fall 1991): 85–99; Todd Gray, "Devon's Coastal and Overseas Fisheries and New England Migration, 1597–1642" (Ph.D. diss., University of Exeter, 1988); Audrey Lockhart, "The Quakers and Emigration from Ireland to the North American Colonies," *Quaker History* 77 (Fall 1988): 67–92; Bernard Bailyn, *The Peopling of British North America: An Introduction* (New York: Knopf, 1986); Bernard Bailyn, *Voyagers to the West: A Passage in the Peopling of America on the Eve of the Revolution* (New York: Knopf, 1986).

56. Leslie P. Choquette, *Frenchmen into Peasants: Modernity and Tradition in the Peopling of French Canada* (Cambridge: Harvard University Press, 1997); Leslie P. Choquette, "Le Sud-Ouest et le Canada au XVIIIème Siècles: Analyse d'un Mouvement Migratoire," *Proceedings of the Annual Meeting of the French Colonial Historical Society* 22 (1996): 65–72; M. Brook Taylor, ed., *Canadian History: A Reader's Guide* (Toronto: University of Toronto Press, 1994), 1:33–111; Gwendolyn M. Hall, *Africans in Colonial Louisiana: The Development of Afro-Creole Culture in the Eighteenth Century* (Baton Rouge: Louisiana State University Press, 1992); Daniel H. Usner Jr., *Indians, Settlers, and Slaves in a Frontier Exchange Economy: The Lower Mississippi Valley Before 1783* (Chapel Hill: University of North Carolina Press, 1992); Winstanley Briggs, "Le Pays des Illinois," *William and Mary Quarterly,* 3d ser., 48 (January 1990): 30–56; Peter N. Moogk, "Reluctant Exiles: Emigrants from France in Canada Before 1760," *William and Mary Quarterly,* 3d ser., 46 (October 1989): 463–505; Béatrice Craig, "Immigrants in a Frontier Community: Madawaska, 1785–1850," *Social History* (Canada) 19 (November 1986): 277–97; Carl Ekberg, *Colonial Ste. Geneviéve: An Adventure on the Mississippi Frontier* (Gerald, Mo.: Patrice Press, 1985).

57. The literature on Spanish migrations to and possessions in Florida, the American Southwest, Mexico, and the Caribbean Sea is extensive. For example, see Doyce B. Nunis Jr., "Alta California's Trojan Horse: Foreign Immigration," *California History* 76 (Summer–Fall 1997): 299–330; Patricia Seed, *Ceremonies of Possession in Europe's Conquest of the New World, 1492–1640* (New York: Cambridge University Press, 1995); Juan Ignacio Arnaud Rabinal et al., "Estructura de la Poblacion de Una Sociedad de Frontera: La Florida Española, 1600–1763," *Revista Complutense de Historia de América* (Spain) 17 (1991): 93–120; Abel Poitrineau, "Demography and the Political Destiny of Florida During the Second Spanish Period," *Florida Historical Quarterly* 66 (April 1988): 420–43. See also Magnus Mörner, "Spanish Historians on Spanish Migration to America During the Colonial Period," *Latin American Research Review* 30 (October 1995): 251–67; David J. Robinson, ed., *Migration in Colonial Spanish America* (New York: Cambridge University Press, 1990).

58. Joyce Goodfriend, *Before the Melting Pot: Society and Culture in Colonial New York City, 1664–1730* (Princeton: Princeton University Press, 1992); Donna Merwick, *Possessing Albany, 1630–1710* (New York: Cambridge University Press, 1990); Thomas E. Burke Jr., *Mohawk Frontier: The Dutch Community of Schenectady, New York, 1661–1710* (Ithaca: Cornell University Press, 1991); Oliver A. Rink, *Holland on the Hudson* (Ithaca: Cornell University Press, 1986).

are the Portuguese, even though Portuguese merchants, factors, apprentices, and exiles formed communities in all the major British-American port towns.[59] Four recent books on German voyagers show how prospective immigrants— pushed by "conditions in southwestern Germany encouraging emigration," aided by "recruiting and transportation networks that facilitated and channeled the migration flows," and pulled by "opportunities that settlement in America offered"—broke ranks with fellow Germans on the move and turned their eyes westward. Some hundred thousand of them, according to the most reliable esti- mates, poured into British North America between 1683 and 1783: families led by mature men who could pay their way in advance, and others who were un- able to pay but willing to sign contracts of servitude to pay for their transport. Once settled, they persisted in speaking German and German dialects, printing German newspapers, keeping German accounts, drinking German wines, and marrying into other German immigrant families. The significance of the large portions of the population who owed no ethnic allegiance to England has yet to be fully appreciated. This is an astonishing story, and forty years ago we knew little more than that they had come! It is a major achievement of our profession in the past twenty years, and economic history was central to it.[60]

Commerce was the great site for Atlantic interaction, and merchants have come in for detailed investigation as the agents who spread commodities to the far ends of the ocean.[61] With respect to markets that encompassed the Atlantic basin, new scholarship reveals how producers,[62] distributors,[63] and con- sumers[64] linked the Atlantic world together, in ways that were both innovative

59. Steven R. Pendery, "Portuguese Tin-Glazed Earthenware in Seventeenth-Century New England: A Preliminary Study," *Historical Archaeology* 33 (December 1999): 58–77.

60. Wokeck, *Trade in Strangers;* Aaron S. Fogleman, *Hopeful Journeys: German Immigration, Settlement, and Political Culture in Colonial America, 1717–1775* (Philadelphia: University of Pennsylvania Press, 1996); A. G. Roeber, *Palatines, Liberty, and Property: German Lutherans in Colonial British America* (Baltimore: Johns Hopkins University Press, 1993); Mack Walker, *The Salzburg Transaction: Expulsion and Redemption in Eighteenth-Century Germany* (Ithaca: Cornell University Press, 1992).

61. Louis M. Cullen, *The Brandy Trade Under the Ancien Régime: Regional Specialisation in the Charente* (New York: Cambridge University Press, 1998); Hancock, *Citizens of the World;* Kenneth Mor- gan, *Bristol and the Atlantic Trade in the Eighteenth Century* (New York: Cambridge University Press, 1993); Jacob M. Price, *Perry of London* (Cambridge: Harvard University Press, 1992); David H. Sacks, *The Widening Gate: Bristol and the Atlantic Economy, 1450–1700* (Berkeley and Los Angeles: University of California Press, 1991); John G. Clark, *La Rochelle and the Atlantic Economy During the Eighteenth Cen- tury* (Baltimore: Johns Hopkins University Press, 1981).

62. Morgan, *Slave Counterpoint;* Lois Green Carr, Russell R. Menard and Lorena S. Walsh, *Robert Cole's World: Agriculture and Society in Early Colonial Maryland* (Chapel Hill: University of North Carolina Press, 1991); Mintz, *Sweetness and Power.* Ronald Hoffman's new book is squarely in this tra- dition, retelling the tale of one family's mercurial experience with American planting in Maryland. He fails, however, to situate the work of the Carrolls in an Atlantic emerging market context as fully as the Carrolls probably would have.

63. Hancock, *Citizens of the World;* Morgan, *Bristol and the Atlantic Trade;* Price, *Perry of Lon- don;* Sacks, *Widening Gate.*

64. Breen, "Empire of Goods"; Breen, "'Baubles of Britain'"; Lorna Weatherill, *Consumer Behavior and Material Culture in Britain, 1660–1770* (London: Routledge, 1988); Carole Shammas, *The*

and imitative, shaped by opportunism as well as inheritance, face-to-face and distant. Europeans were the most active commercial players, but they did not dominate everywhere. Africans and Native Americans were aggressive in setting the courses of the African (not just slave) and Indian trades. Colin Calloway, for instance, has shown that North American Indians were quite skillful at adopting aspects of European culture that enhanced their lives, despite the devastations wrought upon them. Indians were consumers tied to a growing global market; they were fussy buyers and shrewd bargainers, whose demand, in fact, gave rise to factories in Europe that tailored their output to their needs. They were not passive recipients of European goods. They used European goods to elaborate traditional objects and complicate traditional crafts; unbound by European custom, they devised new meanings and uses for them.[65]

These phenomena show what porous and decentralized constructs the European empires were, despite metropolitan efforts to restrict communication and exchange. This view of empire considerably complicates and enriches our view of Atlantic life. It avoids American Anglocentrism and, when properly executed, Eurocentrism, weaving the experiences of Africans, islanders, and Indians into the fabric of the narrative.[66] It shows Atlantic-rim agents developing extra-imperial ties, negotiating multiple national imperatives, and interacting with local environments and Creole creations—in the process building syncretic economies and cultures.

A second example of how integrating economic history and cultural history enriches our understanding comes from the study of economic ideas and political economy. Their considerable political economic discourse shows that early modern people recognized the "close relationship between government, or the polity, and the social and economic order."[67] Studying this discourse demands partnerships between cultural and economic history. Attention to the role of women and gendered language has helped us think differently about political

Pre-Industrial Consumer in England and America (New York: Oxford University Press, 1990); Cary Carson, Ronald Hoffman, and Peter J. Albert, eds., *Of Consuming Interests: The Style of Life in the Eighteenth Century* (Charlottesville: University Press of Virginia, 1994).

65. David Eltis, "The Volume and Structure of the Trans-Atlantic Slave Trade: A Reassessment," *William and Mary Quarterly*, 3d ser., 58 (January 2001): 17–46; Eltis, *Rise of African Slavery;* Calloway, *New Worlds for All;* Usner, *Indians, Settlers, and Slaves.* Commercial information and ideas flowed, too, whether by word of mouth or by imported printed publications. See Robin Myers and Michael Harris, eds., *Spreading the Word: The Distribution Networks of Print, 1550–1850* (Winchester, N.H.: St. Paul's Bibliographies, 1990); John J. McCusker and Cora Gravesteijn, *The Beginnings of Commercial and Financial Journalism: The Commodity Price Currents, Exchange Rate Currents, and Money Currents of Early Modern Europe* (Amsterdam: NEHA, 1991); Julius Scott III, "A Common Wind: Currents of Afro-American Communication in the Age of the Haitian Revolution" (Ph.D. diss., Duke University, 1986).

66. For a cautionary note on the writing of Atlantic History, see Peter A. Coclanis, "*Drang Nach Osten:* Bernard Bailyn, the World-Island, and the Idea of Atlantic History," *Journal of World History* 13 (Spring 2002): 169–82.

67. Drew R. McCoy, *The Elusive Republic: Political Economy in Jeffersonian America* (Chapel Hill: University of North Carolina Press, 1980), 6.

economy, the percolation of its precepts throughout society, and their manifestations in the minds and manners of everyday folk.[68] Two recent examinations of Puritanism show how religion and commerce reinforced each other in New England. Stephen Innes has revived Max Weber's Protestant ethic in *Creating the Commonwealth*. A powerful religious ethic, Innes argues, informed New Englanders' construction of economic institutions such as safeguarding land titles, affirming free labor, and supporting individual enterprise with governmental assistance. Puritanism's ascetic insistence on diligence, direction, and discipline, and its approval of profit as long as it was not deleterious to the cohesion of the community, legitimated and encouraged prodevelopmental behavior in immigrants, whatever their national origin. In *The Price of Redemption,* Mark Peterson compares the trajectories of two Massachusetts churches (Edward Taylor's in Westfield and Boston's Old South Church), and argues that trade supported piety, at least up to the Great Awakening, where his account ends. Peterson carefully integrates the reality of commercial development into the story of religious development. He "reveals how New England's spiritual economy was sustained by commercial growth, by the dispersion of the population across the countryside, and by the lasting commitment of its members to replicate their culture in new places among future generations." These books show how intertwined economic and religious discourse, as well as practice, was.[69]

Margaret Newell's *From Dependency to Independence* pays close attention to the ways that money affected politics, ideology, and class. Much like Innes, Newell argues that a spirit of frugality and industriousness nurtured economic diversification, increased productivity and entrepreneurial innovation, and created wide support for protectionism. The strength of her work is that she moves beyond ideology and shows how political-economic thinking induced economic change. Her dissections of the lobbies for and against paper money and

---

68. On gender, see Susan Juster, *Disorderly Women: Sexual Politics and Evangelicalism in Revolutionary New England* (Ithaca: Cornell University Press, 1994), 137–41; Linda Kerber, "'History Can Do It No Justice': Women and the Reinterpretation of the American Revolution," and Laurel Thatcher Ulrich, "Daughters of Liberty: Religious Women in Revolutionary New England," both in *Women in the Age of the American Revolution,* ed. Ronald Hoffman and Peter Albert (Charlottesville: University Press of Virginia, 1989), 3–42 and 211–43, respectively; Carol Smith-Rosenberg, "Beyond Roles, Beyond Spheres: Thinking About Gender in the Early Republic," *William and Mary Quarterly,* 3d ser., 46 (July 1989): 573; Carol Smith-Rosenberg, "Domesticating 'Virtue': Coquettes and Revolutionaries in Young America" in *Literature and the Body: Essays on Populations and Persons,* ed. Elaine Scarry (Baltimore: Johns Hopkins University Press, 1988), 166; Ruth Bloch, "The Gendered Meaning of Virtue in Revolutionary America," *Signs* 13 (Autumn 1987): 37–58.

69. Stephen Innes, *Creating the Commonwealth: The Economic Culture of Puritan New England* (New York: W. W. Norton, 1995); Mark A. Peterson, *The Price of Redemption: The Spiritual Economy of Puritan New England* (Stanford: Stanford University Press, 1997), especially 22. Cf. John Frederick Martin, *Profits in the Wilderness: Entrepreneurship and the Founding of New England Towns in the Seventeenth Century* (Chapel Hill: University of North Carolina Press, 1991). For a recent rumination on the Weber thesis and its applicability to early American history, see Joyce Appleby, "The Vexed Story of Capitalism Told by American Historians," *Journal of the Early Republic* 21 (Spring 2001): 1–18.

the land bank in 1714–21, the vexatious land bank imbroglio of 1740, and New Englanders' political responses to the 1751 Currency Act show colonists' economic thinking at work. Their thinking was transformed after 1760, as ideas of economic independence fostered by the earlier money debates collided with parliamentary attempts to reform the American imperial system, ultimately producing an economy of resistance and revolution. Her attention to ideas, culture, and identity broadens our understanding of the monetary system beyond its purely economic aspects to its role in society.[70]

One final model of the power of political-economic ideas to integrate cultural and economic narratives concerns the course of the Revolution. This work builds on the strides taken during the 1960s, 1970s, and early 1980s toward understanding revolutionary ideology. At least with respect to the 1754–1815 period, one of the great unknowns has been the political and economic thought of colonial traders, especially outside of their responses to the milestone imperial reforms. By digging deeply into records left by New York City's wholesalers and focusing on the relationships among activities, status, and patterns of economic thought, Cathy Matson has moved us toward an understanding of what colonial New York merchants thought about the economy before the Revolution. She believes colonial merchants distinguished mercantile regulation from economic freedom. They understood the Navigation Acts and attendant imperial, provincial, and urban rules governing trade and manufacturing as regulatory and restrictive, and freedom as thwarting or overturning such constraints. Merchants' reasoning about economic issues was closely correlated with where they traded, what goods they carried, and their connections to credit and family. Matson's work will almost certainly not be the last word on this subject, but her example provides a valuable model for the additional work that needs to be done.[71]

The boundaries of political-economic history are still waiting to be pushed back in a number of directions. We still have a one-sided view of mercantilism as a uniform, quasi-official "strategy" for enhancing state power in an increasingly commercial world, embodied in the English navigation system, the British national debt, and the Bank of England, and articulated by political leaders, chartered companies, and powerful metropolitan transoceanic merchants. We

70. Margaret E. Newell, *From Dependency to Independence: Economic Revolution in Colonial New England* (Ithaca: Cornell University Press, 1998). To be more convincing, her portrait should have engaged the agrarian political economy as well, given the thriving agricultural sector in New England. Cf. the more recent work by Phyllis Hunter, who is less Weberian than Newell: *Purchasing Identity in the Atlantic World: Massachusetts Merchants, 1670–1780* (Ithaca: Cornell University Press, 2001).

71. Cathy Matson, *Merchants and Empire: Trading in Colonial New York* (Baltimore: Johns Hopkins University Press, 1998); Newell, *From Dependency to Independence*. Cf. Newell, "Robert Child and the Entrepreneurial Vision: Economy and Ideology in Early New England," *New England Quarterly* 68 (June 1995): 223–56; Gerhard Ens, "The Political Economy of the 'Private Trade' on the Hudson's Bay: The Example of Moose Factory, 1741–1744," in Trigger, *"Le Castor Fait Tout,"* 382–410.

need a greater sense of the to-and-fro in the evolution of mercantilist thought, of the debates over political and economic policies in the metropolis and the colonies. Divisions abounded in the commercial world as they did in the political. None of the great chartered companies and London firms maintained the same stances with regard to mercantile policy over the course of their histories. Why not study the shifting contours of economic policymaking at the center of the empires and provincial governments? Or the effects of the divisions on the colonists? Nor do we yet adequately understand the Revolution's economic ideology.[72] We need to re-create the sense of contingency and accident that was central to the war's outcome and aftermath.[73] The economic success, widespread

72. Studies of the political-economic writings of the empire and the Revolution include David Armitage, *The Ideological Origins of the British Empire* (New York: Cambridge University Press, 2000), 146–69; Nancy Koehn, *The Power of Commerce: Economy and Governance in the First British Empire* (Ithaca: Cornell University Press, 1994); David Raynor and Andrew Skinner, "Sir James Steuart: Nine Letters on the American Conflict, 1775–1778," *William and Mary Quarterly*, 3d ser., 51 (October 1994): 755–76; Crowley, *The Privileges of Independence;* Ann Fairfax Withington, "Republican Bees: The Political Economy of the Beehive in Eighteenth-Century America," *Studies in Eighteenth-Century Culture* 18 (January 1988): 39–77; Joseph A. Ernst, "The Political Economy of the Chesapeake Colonies, 1760–1775: A Study in Comparative History," in *The Economy of Early America: The Revolutionary Period, 1763–1790*, ed. Ronald Hoffman, John J. McCusker, Russell R. Menard, and Peter Albert (Charlottesville: University Press of Virginia, 1988), 196–243. For a later period, see John R. Nelson Jr., *Liberty and Property: Political Economy and Policymaking in the New Nation, 1789–1812* (Baltimore: Johns Hopkins University Press, 1987). For a more general picture, see Michael Merrill, "The Political Economy of Agrarian America" (Ph.D. diss., Columbia University, 1985).

73. The transformation of the study of war has strengthened our understanding of the Revolution's political economy. Historians are increasingly viewing the wars that affected colonial and early American life as full-bodied organisms, the economic aspects of which, while an important part of the narrative, extended far beyond general British-American overseas exchange. John Brewer's *Sinews of Power* embedded the story of the buildup of the British war machine in a larger economic, social, and cultural context; he tied eighteenth-century wars to state building, raising revenue, and the rise of bureaucracies and the public political sphere. In exploring what at times seem essentially cultural phenomena, he provided the material context for war. Fred Anderson's *Crucible of War* is probably the best example of this approach as applied to American warfare. In an expansive "total history" of the Seven Years' War, Anderson weaves analyses of the financing of the war, postwar recession and depression, debt, rates of exchange, colonial currency matters, and of course British taxes, among other things, into a narrative that includes subjects not always covered in traditional histories, among them social unrest, the cultural effects of war, allegorical representations of imperialism, ideological resistance to imperial authority, French society and economy, and intercultural relations. Something similar should be done, on large and small scale alike, to the other transatlantic wars. Economic historians adopting just such an approach would allow themselves and their readers to gauge more clearly than they have in the past war's effects on black, red, and white men and women, effects that have been generally ignored in favor of commercial origins, trade policy, and the costs of war. See John Brewer, *The Sinews of Power: War, Money, and the English State, 1688–1783* (Boston: Unwin Hyman, 1989); Lawrence Stone, ed., *An Imperial State at War: Britain from 1689 to 1815* (London: Routledge, 1994); Fred Anderson, *Crucible of War: The Seven Years' War and the Fate of Empire in British North America, 1754–1766* (New York: Knopf, 2000). Colin Calloway's *The American Revolution in Indian Country* (New York: Cambridge University Press, 1995), and Ian Steele's *Warpaths: Invasions of North America* (New York: Oxford University Press, 1994), move in similar directions, toward a richer, fuller (though more ethnographic) contextualization of American warfare. Several new studies rely heavily on economic and social history to broaden the questions under investigation: John Resch, *Suffering Soldiers: Revolutionary War Veterans, Moral Sentiment, and*

prosperity, and rapid growth that McCusker and Menard ascribe to the colonial period should be balanced with a closer look at the ups and downs of the period, as well as the moral dimensions of economic life.[74] At the very least, we should clarify a paradox we have unfortunately accepted—on the one hand, Americans deeply resented the economic dislocations of the 1760s and 1770s, and these resentments conditioned a rejection of British trade; but on the other hand, their beliefs (or sensibilities) were reworked in the course of winning the war and gaining independence so that, by the 1780s, British merchants and commerce had been accepted again and Americans were once again actively pursuing participation in the British mercantile system. How and why that happened has never been fully explained.[75]

This essay makes no pretence to being comprehensive, especially about a subject as large as the potential for integrating economic history and cultural history. Showing the connectedness of the Atlantic world and its vibrant political economy are two directions now proving fruitful, but they are two among many. But whatever the subject, for history to become more integrated, and so truer to lived experience, it is important that we keep human agency in the forefront of our analyses. "Human agency" is a phrase that cultural anthropologists and historians use to remind themselves that concepts boil down, in the end, to the initiatives and actions of individuals, people who could have acted differently. Keeping agency at the center of the economic history narrative helps ward off reification by focusing on the task of connecting our concepts and analytical apparatus to the ultimate carriers of the economy and culture.[76] These carriers include the Schumpeterian entrepreneurs and Hughesian innovators who affected material and economic action and influenced economic allocations and

Political Culture in the Early Republic (Amherst: University of Massachusetts Press, 1999); Paul Koistinen, *Beating Plowshares into Swords,* vol. 1 (Lawrence: University Press of Kansas, 1996); Holly A. Mayer, *Belonging to the Army: Camp Followers and Community During the American Revolution* (Columbia: University of South Carolina Press, 1996); and Harold E. Selesky, *War and Society in Colonial Connecticut* (New Haven: Yale University Press, 1990). Still provocative as a suggestion of what constitutes a comprehensive historical approach to war is Arthur Marwick, "The Impact of the First World War on British Society," *Journal of Contemporary History* 3 (January 1968): 51–63.

74. McCusker and Menard, *Economy of British America,* 354; McCoy, *Elusive Republic,* 6.

75. Here we might want to follow the lead of John E. Crowley, who argues that, in the debate over the Constitution, both Federalists and Anti-Federalists agreed on the desirability of a stronger regulatory role over commerce for the central government: Federalists presented their case "in thoroughly mercantilist terms," arguing that American commerce could not grow except through vigorous government support; more forward-looking than previously supposed, Anti-Federalists looked to market forces to redress the foreign trade imbalance. Whether or not he is correct in his assessment, Crowley is persuasive in turning to political economy and individual human thought for a solution to the puzzle over the *volte-face* in commercial affairs. "Commerce and the Philadelphia Constitution: Neo-Mercantilism in Federalist and Anti-Federalist Economy," *History of Political Thought* 13 (January 1992): 73–97.

76. Joan Scott, "Experience," in *Feminists Theorize the Political,* ed. Judith Butler and Joan Scott (New York: Routledge, 1992), 28.

outcomes.[77] But they also include marginal men and women. Joy and Richard Buel and Laurel Ulrich have written narratives of Connecticut matriarchs and Maine midwives that highlight the personal aspects of the Revolution and the relationships of individual women to the economy and politics. David Eltis has painted, on a very broad canvas, the stories of slave trading in Africa, shipboard insurrections, and the like—of men and women who generally did not possess the good fortune to be able to record their thoughts. As with all really profound uncoverings of earlier lives, these individual stories show "how individuals usually stacked several loyalties together quite comfortably; different aspects of life simply evoked different mental boundaries," not just in conflict with others but also in collaboration. By viewing history through the lens of human agency, we elucidate how "colonial denizens sought to make sense of their world in ways that affected both their thought and behavior."[78]

Work on the marginal people of the sea—merchant-captains, privateers, sailors, smugglers and pirates, black, red, and white, female and male, Muslim and Christian—has also moved in this direction. People on the sea could be at least partially free of the economic, social, cultural, and political boundaries of the lands they sailed from; and freedom created possibilities ripe for investigation by traditionally minded economic historians as well as avant-garde cultural historians. These folk re-created ideas, behaviors, and institutions from their disparate traditions of origin and craft. The recombinations produced "in-betweenness" and hybridity, and also replicated ethnocentrism and racism. Economic tools alone cannot make complete sense of this potent, influential mixture.[79]

About the time that John McCusker and Russell Menard were wrestling with *The Economy of British America,* Albert Hirschman noted the importance of breadth in economics:

77. Joseph A. Schumpeter, *Essays: On Entrepreneurs, Innovations, Business Cycles, and the Evolution of Capitalism,* ed. Richard Clemence (New Brunswick, N.J.: Transaction Publishers, 1989); Jonathan Hughes, *The Vital Few: American Economic Progress and Its Protagonists* (New York: Oxford University Press, 1973).

78. Joy Day Buel and Richard Buel Jr., *The Way of Duty: A Woman and Her Family in Revolutionary America* (New York: W. W. Norton, 1984); Ulrich, *Midwife's Tale;* Eltis, *Rise of African Slavery;* Paul E. Lovejoy and David Richardson, "Trust, Pawnship, and Atlantic History: The Institutional Foundations of the Old Calabar Slave Trade," *American Historical Review* 104 (April 1999): 332–55; Ian Steele, "Exploding Colonial American History: American Indian, Atlantic, and Global Perspectives," *Reviews in American History* 26 (January 1998): 78.

79. Bolster, *Black Jacks;* David Voorhees, "The 'Fervent Zeale' of Jacob Leisler," *William and Mary Quarterly,* 3d ser., 51 (July 1994); Anne Perotin Dumon, "The Pirate and the Emperor: Power and Law on the Seas, 1450–1850," in *The Political Economy of Merchant Empires: State Power and World Trade, 1350–1750,* ed. James D. Tracy (Cambridge: Harvard University Press, 1991); Julius S. Scott III, "Afro-American Sailors and the International Communication Network: The Case of Newport Bowers," in *Jack Tar in History,* ed. Colin Howell and Richard Twomey (Fredericton, New Brunswick: Goose Lane Editions, 1995); Rediker, *Between the Devil and the Deep Blue Sea;* Scott, "Common Wind"; Robert C. Ritchie, *Captain Kidd and the War Against the Pirates* (Cambridge: Harvard University Press, 1986).

What is needed [is] for economists to incorporate into their analysis, whenever it is pertinent, such basic traits and emotions as the desire for power or sacrifice, the fear of boredom, pleasure in both commitment and unpredictability, the search for meaning and community, and so on. . . . When one has been groomed as a "scientist" it just takes a great deal of wrestling with oneself before one will admit that moral considerations of human solidarity can effectively interfere with those hieratic, impersonal forces of supply and demand.[80]

Hirschman's comment is as pertinent to the work of a historian of the economy as to any economist. Only by paying attention to colonists' thinking and the extent to which their lives, ideas, and emotions were conditioned by confusion, struggle, vacillation, and doubt can we appreciate the delicate task of explaining economic development. Perhaps this is just another way of saying that as students of the economy we need to become fully engaged with the people we are writing about.

80. Albert O. Hirschman, *Essays in Trespassing: Economics to Politics and Beyond* (New York: Cambridge University Press, 1981), 303–4.

Chapter Three

Colonial America's Mestizo Agriculture

RUSSELL R. MENARD

In the early 1980s, when John McCusker and I were writing *The Economy of British America,* there was a broad consensus among scholars, which we endorsed, that the early American economy grew on a per capita basis at a rate of between 0.3 and 0.6 percent per year.[1] Despite some additional empirical work supporting that proposition,[2] Peter Mancall and Tom Weiss have recently challenged that consensus, arguing instead that the rate of growth was probably closer to zero.[3] When writing our book, McCusker and I did more with the notion of growth than simply report an existing consensus. Indeed, we used growth as an organizing theme, looking for evidence of growth as we surveyed the literature on the several sectors and regions of the colonial economy. The literature was full of such evidence, for we were not the first to be struck by the liveliness of the colonial economy or of the creativity of early Americans. In those cases where the literature failed to yield such evidence, we knew we had identified an opportunity for additional research. Mancall and Weiss, although they are to be commended for forcing a reexamination of the question, seem unlikely to persuade many economic historians. They offer no new empirical evidence but instead proceed with a

Earlier versions of this paper were presented at the annual meeting of the Social Science History Association, Chicago, November 1998, and at the Early American History Workshop at the University of Minnesota in 1995. I would like to thank participants in both meetings for helpful comments.

1. John J. McCusker and Russell R. Menard, *The Economy of British America, 1607–1789* (Chapel Hill: University of North Carolina Press, 1985), 52–57.

2. This is a large body of literature, much of it discussed below, but, for examples, see Marc Egnal, *New World Economies: The Growth of the Thirteen Colonies and Early Canada* (New York: Oxford University Press, 1998), and the 1999 special issue of the *William and Mary Quarterly,* on the domestic sector of the early American economy.

3. Peter C. Mancall and Thomas Weiss, "Was Economic Growth Likely in Colonial British North America?" *Journal of Economic History* 59 (March 1999): 17–40.

few heroic assumptions, assumptions at odds with the literature, and some "back-of-the-envelope" calculations. For example, they assume that the per capita value of American food consumption was constant over the colonial period, despite considerable empirical work reporting improvements in diet.[4] They make a similar, and equally questionable, assumption about the value of colonial housing. Dwellings and structures are assumed to have constituted a constant share of wealth across the period. As anyone with even a passing familiarity with the subject knows, this is a complex question, and there is a large body of literature showing that the share of their income colonials invested in housing varied by region, class, and time.[5] Those who work in the field are more likely to be persuaded by Lance Davis and Stan Engerman, who, after surveying recent contributions to the field, seemed to conclude that the 1985 consensus still prevailed. Although they did not give a number, they concluded that "there was probably some slow and positive growth in per capita income and wealth in most parts of the colonies between original settlement and the time of the American Revolution. Slow as it was, growth was probably higher than in most parts of the world at that time."[6] This certainly seems consistent with the old consensus.

While Mancall and Weiss seem sorely mistaken in their evaluation of the performance of the early American economy, they do make one point that students of the early American economy ought to take very seriously. Early American economic historians have paid little attention to the indigenous inhabitants of the colonies, and our field would be richer if we took them seriously as economic actors and participants in the economic life of the colonies. Unfortunately, having identified a weakness in the field and a major research opportunity, Mancall and Weiss then pursue a tactic that seems more a step backward than an advance. Their tactic for bringing the Indians in is to strip the tribes of North America of their independence and autonomy by creating a sort of generalized statistical Indian; in effect they assume that if you have measured one Indian, you have measured them all. As even passing familiarity with the now booming field of Native American history shows, this is inadequate.[7] Serious

4. See, in addition to work cited in note 43, Sarah F. McMahon, "Laying Foods By: Gender, Dietary Decisions, and the Technology of Food Preservation in New England Households, 1750–1850," in *Early American Technology: Making and Doing Things from the Colonial Era to 1850*, ed. Judith A. McGaw (Chapel Hill: University of North Carolina Press, 1994), 164–96.

5. This large body of literature is ably introduced by Edward A. Chapell, "Housing a Nation: The Transformation of Living Standards in Early America," in *Of Consuming Interests: The Style of Life in the Eighteenth Century*, ed. Cary Carson, Ronald Hoffman, and Peter J. Albert (Charlottesville: University Press of Virginia, 1994), 167–232; and by Richard L. Bushman, *The Refinement of America: Persons, Houses, Cities* (New York: Knopf, 1992).

6. Lance Davis and Stanley L. Engerman, "The Economy of British North America: Miles Traveled, Miles Still To Go," *William and Mary Quarterly*, 3d ser., 56 (January 1999): 21.

7. This is not the place to provide a comprehensive guide to work on Native Americans in British North America. Economic historians interested in the subject might wish to begin with Neal Salisbury, "The History of Native Americans from Before the Arrival of Europeans and Africans Until

study of Native Americans will require more splitting than lumping, and it will require careful attention to regional variation, a task that will take economic historians into subjects (material culture) and methods (archaeology) with which they have seldom dealt.

Given the structure of the colonial economy, it is necessary to pay careful attention to agriculture, which was key to the overall performance of the colonial economy.[8] With roughly 80 percent of the workforce in agriculture, performance in that sector dictated performance in the economy as a whole.[9] If the old consensus is correct and the colonial economy showed moderate gains in income per head, there ought to be some evidence of productivity gains in the recent literature on colonial agriculture.[10] If a careful review of recent literature fails to uncover evidence of productivity gains in colonial agriculture, then this would be a substantial piece of evidence in favor of the Mancall and Weiss position that the early American economy failed to grow. With the exception of work in what might be called the "moral economy" tradition, which pays little attention to what farmers actually did and thus provides a blunt instrument for understanding agricultural history, recent scholarship provides little comfort for Mancall and Weiss.[11] By contrast, work in what can be called the "new agricultural history," which uses quantitative methods to describe the behavior of farmers and is often informed by economic theory, yields a good deal of evidence of productivity gains in colonial agriculture.

For nearly two centuries, beginning with late eighteenth-century critics, colonial farmers have been portrayed as predators rather than careful husbandmen, as slovenly abusers of the land who cared poorly for their livestock, accepted small yields and low incomes, used primitive tools, and resisted useful innovations, instead clinging to custom and following the dead hand of tradition. "Farmers do many things," Samuel Deane noted in 1790, "for which they can assign no other reason than custom." "They usually give themselves no trouble

---

the Civil War," which includes a brief bibliographical note, in *The Cambridge Economic History of the United States,* 3 vols., ed. Stanley L. Engerman and Robert E. Gallman (New York: Cambridge University Press, 1996), 1:1–52. Other work of particular interest to economic historians includes Jean M. O'Brien, *Dispossession by Degrees: Indian Land and Identity in Natick, Massachusetts, 1650–1790* (New York: Cambridge University Press, 1997).

    8. A strong caveat is needed on this point. In our book, McCusker and I attempted a comprehensive survey of the literature. This essay makes no such claim, although it does identify some of the major developments in the field of early American agricultural history over the past fifteen years.

    9. For the share of the workforce in agriculture, see McCusker and Menard, *Economy of British America,* 248.

    10. The essays by Menard, Vickers, and Higman, in Engerman and Gallman, *Cambridge Economic History of the United States,* vol. 1, provide recent overviews of early American agriculture. Allan Kulikoff, *From British Peasants to Colonial American Farmers* (Chapel Hill: University of North Carolina Press, 2000), takes a much different perspective on the field from that offered here, but offers a useful and fairly comprehensive bibliography of recent work.

    11. The literature on the moral economy tradition is cited below, in notes 49–51.

in thinking, or in examining their methods of agriculture, which have been handed down from father to son, from time immemorial."[12] Such charges, once made, stuck, and they dominated the interpretation of colonial agriculture for the next two centuries. Approaching the issue from this eighteenth-century perspective, one can understand how Mancall and Weiss might have failed to consider the possibility that farmers achieved significant gains in productivity over the colonial period. Recent scholarship, however, suggests that we may be about to break free from this outmoded understanding.

The challenge to the traditional viewpoint rests on several insights that emerge from recent scholarship. First, contemporary denigration of early American agriculture often rested on the testimony of frustrated agricultural reformers annoyed with farmers who rejected their advice, or on inappropriate comparisons with European farmers, who faced a much different set of constraints.[13] In early America, where land was cheap and labor dear, it seldom made sense to follow the "best" European practices. Behavior that seemed slovenly and wasteful to many observers often reflected efforts to save labor costs in an area where wages were high.

Second, contemporaries and historians who have held colonial farmers in contempt underestimated their impressive accomplishments, most evident in the creation of what might be called a new, mestizo agricultural tradition that blended Native American, African, and European farming techniques with newly developed methods to create an American system of husbandry consistent with the requirements of the environment.[14]

The term *mestizo* (*mestisage* in French), from the Spanish for mixture, derived from the Latin *miscere* (to mix), initially referred to the biological offspring of a European and an Indian. More recently, however, Latin Americanists have broadened the concept to encompass cultural products created by the interaction of Europeans, Africans, and Indians, and it is in this sense that the term is used here.[15]

Finally, those who accused colonial farmers of laziness also ignored the hard work of farm building and its major contributions to the colonial

---

12. Samuel Deane, *The New England Farmer, or Geographical Dictionary* (Worcester, Mass.: Isaiah Thomas, 1790), 64.

13. For a sampling of contemporary opinion, see Percy Wells Bidwell and John I. Falconer, *History of Agriculture in the Northern United States, 1820–1860* (Washington, D.C.: Carnegie Institution, 1929), 84–87.

14. I am of course using the notion of mestizo to refer to a cultural phenomenon, rather than in its biological sense. For an argument that America's history is mestizo in the biological sense of the term, see Gary B. Nash, "The Hidden History of Mestizo America," *Journal of American History* 82 (December 1995): 941–63.

15. My understanding of the notion of mestizo has been shaped by Colin L. MacLachlan and Jaime E. Rodriguez O., *The Forging of the Cosmic Race: A Reinterpretation of Colonial Mexico* (Berkeley and Los Angeles: University of California Press, 1990).

economy.[16] Colonial farmers and their families, servants, and slaves carved work-ing farms out of the dense forests of eastern North America, clearing fields, building fences, barns, and houses, planting orchards, and building livestock herds, thereby providing a capital-starved economy with a scarce resource while at the same time providing much of the impetus for the impressive increases in wealth per capita achieved in the early colonial period.

Surprisingly, the most thoroughgoing assaults on the traditional view of colonial agriculture have come from students of the southern colonies, home, one might have thought, to the most backward of early American farmers. In the upper South, for example, recent scholarship has identified the gradual elaboration of "the Chesapeake system of husbandry," a method of farming that blended European, African, and Native American farming techniques with new methods worked out locally, as farmers "learned by doing."[17] Chesapeake planters thus created a highly productive system of agriculture, a labor-saving long-fallow farming style with a twenty-year field rotation using simple tools to grow tobacco and corn, while cattle and hogs were allowed to range freely in the still sparsely settled colonies.

Further south, in the coastal rice-growing districts, one finds a markedly different but equally innovative style of farming, this one blending African and European techniques to create a unique system of agriculture that provided the economic base for the richest region in North America. Planters in the lower South seem to have been especially experimental and innovative. "The culture of rice in South Carolina," David Ramsey noted, "was in a state of constant improvement," as planters developed new methods of irrigation and new vari-eties better suited to the local environment, and steadily improved the cleaning process.[18] It is likely that this creativity reflected the mestizo character of low-country agriculture and rested on the skills of slaves. Indeed, it has been argued that Africans introduced the technology of rice cultivation to the low country and that planters sought (and paid premium prices for) slaves from ethnic groups

16. On farm building and its importance to the colonial economy, see Russell R. Menard, "Economic and Social Development of the South," in Engerman and Gallman, *Cambridge Economic History of the United States*, 1:249–95.

17. The details of the Chesapeake system of husbandry are elaborated in Lois Green Carr, Lorena S. Walsh, and Russell R. Menard, *Robert Cole's World: Agriculture and Society in Early Colonial Maryland* (Chapel Hill: University of North Carolina Press., 1991), and in Lois Green Carr and Rus-sell R. Menard, "Land, Labor, and Economies of Scale in Early Colonial Maryland: Some Limits to Growth in the Chesapeake System of Husbandry," *Journal of Economic History* 49 (June 1989): 407–18.

18. David Ramsey, *The History of South Carolina from its First Settlement in 1670 to the year 1808* (Charleston, S.C.: David Longworth, 1809), 206. Joyce Chaplin stresses the experimental, innova-tive character of South Carolina agriculture in *An Anxious Pursuit: Agricultural Innovation and Modernity in the Lower South, 1730–1815* (Chapel Hill: University of North Carolina Press, 1993). For a less bullish interpretation of the region, see Peter A. Coclanis, *The Shadow of a Dream: Economic Life and Death in the Carolina Low Country, 1670–1920* (New York: Oxford University Press, 1989).

familiar with the crop.[19] While the notion that the arrival of Africans is the key to understanding the rise of the rice industry strikes me as insufficiently attentive to the role of European demand, Africans did bring important technical skills across the Atlantic, and the skills and knowledge of slaves were crucial to the success of plantation colonies. This may have been particularly true with rice. The crop was grown in West Africa under a variety of conditions and by different techniques. Further, the low-country tasking system placed major responsibilities for the organization of work in the hands of slaves, while offering them incentives to work more efficiently.[20]

Even British east Florida, long dismissed as a "small and insignificant colony whose growth was slow and whose return to Spain after twenty years was a confession of failure,"[21] has recently found some defenders. Many historians are now persuaded that east Florida's story is that of a colony prevented by political turmoil from realizing the potential evident in its innovative and creative agriculture.[22] Recent work on Florida makes it clear that blended farming systems were not created exclusively by Europeans. As Brent Wiseman has demonstrated, the Seminole created their own unique and highly successful plantation system by blending African, European, and Native American farming styles to create a distinctive system of husbandry in eighteenth-century Florida.[23] Wiseman's work suggests that there may be opportunities for new research on the ways that other Indian peoples created blended farming techniques out of the several traditions available to them. The notion of a "frontier exchange economy," as developed by Daniel Usner, provides a useful framework for understanding the creation of blended traditions, which seem to have been especially common on the frontier.[24]

19. The most recent, and most persuasive, version of this argument is Judith A. Carney, *Black Rice: The African Origins of Rice Cultivation in the Americas* (Cambridge: Harvard University Press, 2001).

20. On the tasking system, see Philip D. Morgan," Task and Gang Systems: The Organization of Labor on New World Plantations," in *Work and Labor in Early America,* ed. Stephen Innes (Chapel Hill: University of North Carolina Press, 1988), 189–220.

21. The judgment is Charles Loch Mowat's. See his *East Florida as a British Province, 1763–1784* (Berkeley and Los Angeles: University of California Press, 1943), 149.

22. See Donald L. Shafer, "Plantation Development in British East Florida: A Case Study of the Earl of Egmont," *Florida Historical Quarterly* 63 (October 1984): 172–83, and the essays in Jane G. Landers, ed., *Colonial Plantations and Economy in Florida* (Gainesville: University Press of Florida, 2000). Not all of the recent literature on East Florida is so positive, however. At least two prominent historians are closer to Mowat than to the revisionists. See David Hancock, *Citizens of the World: London Merchants and the Integration of the British Atlantic Community, 1735–1785* (New York: Cambridge University Press, 1995); and Bernard Bailyn, *Voyages to the West: A Passage in the Peopling of America on the Eve of the Revolution* (New York: Knopf, 1986).

23. Brent R. Wiseman, "The Plantation System of the Florida Seminole Indians and Black Seminoles During the Colonial Era," in Landers, *Colonial Plantations and Economy in Florida,* 136–50.

24. Daniel H. Usner Jr., *Indians, Settlers, and Slaves in a Frontier Exchange Economy: The Lower Mississippi Valley Before 1783* (Chapel Hill: University of North Carolina Press, 1992).

One of the distinguishing characteristics of early American agriculture, especially in the southern colonies, is that slaves did much of the work. Early Americanists continue to show a lively interest in slavery.[25] One of the major developments has been the release of a new data set on the slave trade by David Eltis and his collaborators. This data set includes information on more than twenty-seven thousand slave voyages and may, the compilers estimate, include two-thirds of the voyages conducted between 1527 and 1866.[26] Already this data set has had a substantial impact on our understanding of the slave trade. Its appearance and impact suggest a major opportunity for additional scholarship.[27] Many of the slaves who came to the mainland colonies arrived by way of the British West Indies. This route developed not, as much of the literature assumes, because sugar planters sold seasoned and partly acculturated slaves to the mainland, but rather because North American ship captains who delivered provisions and wood products to the islands bought small cargoes of slaves at the great auctions at Bridgetown and Port Royal to fill their ships for the return voyage and sell at home. Thus the distinction one often encounters in the literature between slaves who arrived directly from Africa and those who came by way of the islands is largely meaningless. Still, studying those who came by way of the islands could prove rewarding. Compiling a voyage-based data set of the slave trade between the sugar islands and the mainland would provide a major new resource for understanding that important trade and the impact of slavery on mainland agriculture during its crucial early years.

One major theme in the recent literature of particular importance to economic history has been the relationship of skills acquired in Africa to the work done by slaves in the Americas. This subject has been most thoroughly developed in the rice industry, but it has also been studied in to the areas of livestock husbandry and tobacco.[28] It seems likely, as the impact of this work spreads, that references to newly arrived enslaved Africans as unskilled workers will disappear from the literature. Another area of recent scholarship on early American slavery of particular interest to economic historians has concerned the organization of labor, particularly the distinction between the task and gang systems. While there has been some discussion of the origins of tasking, the history of the

25. Ira Berlin's *Many Thousands Gone: The First Two Centuries of Slavery in North America* (Cambridge: Harvard University Press, 1998), surveys the field and provides a fairly comprehensive guide to the literature. Another recent survey is Kenneth Morgan, *Slavery and Servitude in Colonial North America: A Short History* (New York: New York University Press, 2001)

26. David Eltis, Stephen S. Behrendt, David Richardson, and Herbert S. Klein, eds. *The Trans-Atlantic Slave Trade: A Database on CD-ROM* (Cambridge: Cambridge University Press, 1999).

27. See the essays in the January 2001 special issue of the *William and Mary Quarterly.*

28. Recent work on the importance of African skills and technology in early American agriculture includes Carney, *Black Rice,* and Lorena S. Walsh, *From Calabar to Carter's Grove: The History of a Virginia Slave Community* (Charlottesville: University Press of Virginia, 1997).

gang system has been virtually ignored.[29] Given its importance, both as a source of the high productivity of slave-based agriculture and as a source of so much misery, the origin of the gang system is a major opportunity for further research.[30]

Traditionally, the literature on the comparative history of slavery has emphasized the differences between the institution in West Africa and in the Americas. More recent work by Judith Carney indicates that it might be helpful to think about the similarities. Many of the people enslaved in the Americas had been slaves in Africa before being sold into the Atlantic slave trade. It would not be surprising, Carney suggests, to find that these slaves tried to make the institution in the Americas conform to their African experience. Thus Carney thinks that the task system may have been a West African way of organizing slave labor that was brought to the Carolinas by slaves familiar with it. The provision ground system, in which slaves were allotted small plots on which they could grow much of their food, common throughout the West Indies, may have had similar origins.[31] The examples of tasking and provision grounds suggest that it is time to rethink the comparative history of slavery in Africa and the Americas, to review the evidence and look for similarities as well as differences.

While much of the scholarship on what might be called the new agricultural history of early America has focused on the southern mainland colonies, other regions have not been neglected. We clearly need more work on the agriculture of the sugar islands. In a recent reevaluation of Eric Williams's decline thesis, David Ryden makes a strong case that planters there captured significant productivity gains when faced with falling sugar prices and rising prices for slaves and provisions.[32] Further, Matt Mulcahy has recently shown that planters exhibited considerable inventiveness in learning to live with the extreme environmental conditions they faced.[33] When combined with John McCusker's recent sweeping interpretation of the West Indian economy, the work of Ryden and Mulcahy indicates that there is a major opportunity in a new look at West Indian agriculture, one that challenges the traditional view of planters as hidebound conservatives unwilling to innovate or take risks, and that pays close attention to the major productivity gains achieved in the West Indian sugar industry during the colonial era.[34]

29. Morgan's "Task and Gang Systems" summarizes what we know about the origins of tasking.

30. On gang labor and productivity, see Robert W. Fogel, *Without Consent or Contract: The Rise and Fall of American Slavery* (New York: W. W. Norton, 1989), chapter 2. David Eltis opens the question of the history of the gang system in *The Rise of African Slavery in the Americas* (New York: Cambridge University Press, 2000).

31. Carney, *Black Rice*, 98–101.

32. David B. Ryden, "Producing a Peculiar Commodity: Sugar Manufacturing, Slave Life, and Planter's Profits in Jamaica, 1750–1807," (Ph.D. diss., University of Minnesota, 1999).

33. Matthew Mulcahy, "Melancholy and Fatal Calamities: Natural Disasters and Society in the Greater British Caribbean," (Ph.D. diss., University of Minnesota, 1999).

34. For the traditional view, see Lowell Joseph Ragatz, *The Fall of the Planter Class in the British Caribbean, 1750–1833: A Study in Social and Economic History* (New York: Century Company,

Moreover, we are just beginning to understand the importance of and the creativity behind the reorganization of the sugar industry that occurred on Barbados in the middle of the seventeenth century, despite its dreadful consequences for Africans. For nearly a century we have explained the rise of the Barbadian sugar industry by means of the idea of a sugar revolution. Recent research has identified some difficulties with that concept, suggesting that we very much need a fresh look at the rise of sugar in the English Caribbean.[35]

Given the persistent image of colonial farmers as technological primitives who showed little interest in new tools, it might be expected that work on the history of technology would support the position of Mancall and Weiss and those who cling to the "slovenly farmer" model. If we define technology narrowly as concerned chiefly with men, metals, and machines, it does. If we adopt the broader view now favored by those who work in the field, however, and think of technology as the way things were made or done, then early American agriculture becomes a site of considerable technological innovation.[36] Plantations, often thought to be especially resistant to new technologies, furnish numerous examples of technological creativity. All of the plantation colonies in British America probably achieved a major boost in productivity by shifting from a labor force dominated by English indentured servants to one dominated by African slaves. As Lorena S. Walsh has noted in a Chesapeake context, this transition permitted planters to ignore the conventions that had protected English servants from overwork and other forms of abuse. Along the Chesapeake, these conventions included a rest period in the heat of the day, many traditional holidays, and Saturday afternoons off.[37] Another major innovation was the emergence of the integrated plantation on Barbados in the second half of the seventeenth century. Previously, sugar had typically been grown by small farmers, who brought their crop to a big man's mill for processing. Barbadians, who had close connections to the London merchant community and thus access to the capital needed to finance the increase in scale, discovered that there were efficiencies to be gained in integrating the growing and processing of the crop under one planter's control.[38]

1928). John McCusker challenges Ragatz in "Growth, Stagnation, or Decline? The Economy of the British West Indies, 1763–1790," in *The Economy of Early America: The Revolutionary Period, 1763–1790,* ed. Ronald Hoffman, John J. McCusker, Russell R. Menard, and Peter J. Albert (Charlottesville: University Press of Virginia, 1988), 275–302.

35. John McCusker and I have begun that task in "The Sugar Industry in the Seventeenth Century: A New Perspective on the Barbadian Sugar Revolution," in *Tropical Babylons: Sugar and the Making of the Atlantic World, 1450–1680,* ed. Stuart B. Schwartz (Chapel Hill: University of North Carolina Press, 2004), 289–330.

36. On these issues, see the introduction to McGaw, *Early American Technology.*

37. Lorena S. Walsh," Slave Society and Tobacco Production in the Tidewater Chesapeake, 1620–1780," in *Cultivation and Culture: Labor and the Shaping of Slave Life in the Americas,* ed. Ira Berlin and Philip D. Morgan (Charlottesville: University Press of Virginia, 1993), 170–203.

38. This issue is discussed in Russell R. Menard, "Law, Credit, the Supply of Labour, and the Organization of Sugar Production in the Colonial Greater Caribbean: A Comparison of Barbados

Even if we stick to the older, narrow vision of technology, the West Indian sugar industry was not without productivity gains driven by technological innovation. Over the colonial era, Barbadian planters gradually shifted from animal-driven mills to mills powered by wind and water, which not only saved feed and labor costs but also made the windmills turn more forcefully and thus extracted more juice from the cane.[39]

Technological innovation was not confined to plantations but also occurred on farms. As Virginia DeJohn Anderson has recently pointed out, building up livestock herds in the colonies, a task essential to successful agriculture, was more complicated than simply shipping a few animals across the Atlantic and watching them increase. In the Chesapeake region, at least, it involved developing the new technology of "free-range husbandry," a technology to which Africans doubtless contributed.[40] Finally, there were some important technological gains in processing agricultural products, particularly in brewing, distilling, and preserving.[41]

Some recent work on agriculture in the middle colonies has no place for the "slovenly farmer" of traditional accounts.[42] Instead of farmers so bound by tradition that they refused to experiment with new methods, Judith McGaw found farmers in Pennsylvania and New Jersey "a distinctly innovative lot."[43] Given that the vast majority of early Americans lived in the countryside and earned their incomes from agriculture, it is appropriate to discuss recent work on population history within the context of the agricultural sector. Early drafts of this essay included a short discussion of recent work on colonial population history, but Lorena Walsh's essay in this volume allowed me to cut that part of the essay. I would, however, like to add a brief note to Walsh's discussion.

---

and Brazil in the Seventeenth Century," in *The Early Modern Atlantic Economy,* ed. John J. McCusker and Kenneth Morgan (New York: Cambridge University Press, 2000), 154–62.

39. The conversion to vindmills is documented in Richard B. Sheridan, *Sugar and Slavery: The Economic History of the West Indies, 1623–1775* (Baltimore: Johns Hopkins University Press, 1974).

40. Virginia DeJohn Anderson, "Animals into the Wilderness: The Development of Livestock Husbandry in the Seventeenth-Century Chesapeake," *William and Mary Quarterly* 59 (April 2002): 377–408.

41. On brewing, see Patrick W. O'Brannon, "Inconsiderable Progress: Commercial Brewing in Philadelphia Before 1840," in McGaw, *Early American Technology,* 148–63. On distilling, see John J. McCusker, "The Business of Distilling in the Old World and the New World During the Seventeenth and Eighteenth Centuries: The Rise of a New Enterprise and Its Connection with Colonial America," in McCusker and Morgan, *Early Modern Atlantic Economy,* 186–224. On food preservation, see Sarah McMahon, "Laying Foods By."

42. Peter O. Wacker and Paul G. E. Clemens, *Land Use in Early New Jersey: A Historical Geography* (Newark: New Jersey Historical Society, 1995); Paul Clemens and Lucy Simler, "Rural Labor and the Farm Household in Chester County, Pennsylvania, 1750–1820," in *Work and Labor in Early America,* ed. Stephen Innes (Chapel Hill: University of North Carolina Press, 1988), 70–105.

43. Judith A. McGaw, "So Much Depends on a Red Wheelbarrow: Agricultural Tool ownership in the Eighteenth-Century Mid-Atlantic," in McGaw, *Early American Technology,* 348.

It seems to me that the field of early American historical demography is in serious crisis. Steve Ruggles recently launched a devastating critique of family reconstitution showing that, because it fails to control the impact of migration, family reconstitution often misestimates age at marriage, life expectancy, and fertility, and that much of what has long been accepted as established fact in the field is probably incorrect. Almost simultaneously with Ruggles's paper, Jean Russo issued a powerful critique of the Turnerian, Malthusian model that had informed much of early American demographic history, in a careful, detailed reconstruction of population dynamics and economic development in Somerset County, Maryland. Jackson and Gloria Main constructed a similar critique out of New England materials.[44] Historians of New England families and communities have usually operated within an economic framework that assumed a looming Malthusian crisis that could be alleviated only by migration.[45] The Mains, however, show rather conclusively that there was no Malthusian crisis looming in colonial New England but that the New England economy grew at a fairly healthy rate over the colonial period. This crisis yields a major opportunity. We desperately need an assessment of where we stand in early American population history in light of the work of Ruggles, Russo, and the Mains.

Given the enduring power of a narrative based on "declension" and the persistent image of New England as a "struggling immiserating region in which long winters, rocky soils and rugged uplands condemned those poor but prolific Yankee farmers to a life of perpetual struggle," it would seem that New England agriculture would offer but cold comfort to those in search of evidence of a growing colonial economy.[46] But evidence recently assembled by Jackson and Gloria Main shows, to the contrary, that by a variety of different measures—wages, land prices, and wealth in probate inventories—New England's economy "grew at a healthy long-term rate that showed little sign of slowing as the American Revolution approached."[47] Further, as the work of Winifred Rothenberg makes clear,

44. Steven Ruggles, "Migration, Marriage, and Mortality: Correcting Sources of Bias in English Family Reconstitutions," *Population Studies* 56 (November 1992): 507–22; Jean E. Russo, "The Interest of the County: Population, Economy, and Society in Somerset County, Maryland" (Ph.D. diss., University of Minnesota, 1999); Gloria L. Main and Jackson T. Main, "The Red Queen in New England?" *William and Mary Quarterly* 56 (January 1999): 121–50.

45. This view finds what is perhaps its most forceful expression in Paul Boyer and Stephen Nissenbaum, *Salem Possessed: The Social Origins of Witchcraft* (Cambridge: Harvard University Press, 1974), although it also appears in classic New England community studies such as Kenneth A. Lockridge, *A New England Town: The First Hundred Years: Dedham, Massachusetts, 1636–1736* (New York: W. W. Norton, 1974); and Philip J. Greven Jr., *Four Generations: Population, Land, and Family in Colonial Andover, Massachusetts* (Ithaca: Cornell University Press, 1970).

46. On declension as a narrative style in New England historiography, see Jack P. Greene, *Pursuits of Happiness: The Social Development of the Early Modern British Colonies and the Formation of American Culture* (Chapel Hill: University of North Carolina Press, 1988), 55–80. The quotations are from Main and Main, "Red Queen in New England?" 141.

47. Main and Main, "Red Queen in New England?" 141. For a more recent statement, see Gloria L. Main, *Peoples of a Spacious Land: Families and Cultures in Colonial New England* (Cambridge: Harvard University Press, 2001).

much of that growth was fueled by productivity gains in agriculture.[48] Rothenberg's important study furthermore challenges the conventional wisdom that industrialization began in cities and was imported from England, by pointing to the domestic origins of America's Industrial Revolution and by showing that agriculture provided the labor force, capital, and much of the expertise that made industrialization possible. A similar story emerged from Lucy Simler's work on the middle colonies.[49] Exploring the rural origins of American industrialization and completing the work begun by Rothenberg and Simler is a major need and a promising opportunity for students of early American economic history.

Jack P. Greene's 1988 survey of colonial social and economic history is particularly attentive to agriculture and rural life. Greene reports no trace of the slovenly farmer but finds, on the contrary, colonial farmers committed to the pursuit of familial and individual happiness, "a commitment that led them to acquire a preparedness for novelty, a psychology of accommodation, a receptivity to change, and a tolerance for diversity," habits that produced an agriculture of extraordinary productivity.[50] In sum, we seem to be on the verge of reclaiming colonial agriculture for what it was, a lively, creative engagement of diverse farming traditions with the American environment, and the gradual elaboration of blended farming traditions that generated high incomes for colonial farmers,[51] especially in the eighteenth century, when living standards rose as the terms of trade shifted in favor of agriculture.[52] This high productivity had several sources, including the creativity of colonial farmers evident in the blended systems they created; the abundance and fertility of American land; and the hard work of farm families, including farm wives, who often helped in the fields, did dairying, and kept gardens, in addition to performing all the indoor work traditionally associated with women.[53]

48. Winifred B. Rothenberg, *From Market-Places to a Market Economy: The Transformation of Rural Massachusetts, 1750–1850* (Chicago: University of Chicago Press, 1992).

49. Simler published several articles on various aspects of this issue and was just beginning work on a book, which illness, unfortunately, kept her from completing. Her essays include "The Township: The Community of the Rural Pennsylvanian," *Pennsylvania Magazine of History and Biography* 106 (Spring 1982): 41–68; "Tenancy in Colonial Pennsylvania: The Case of Chester County," *William and Mary Quarterly 33* (January 1986): 142–69.

50. Greene, *Pursuits of Happiness*, 141.

51. For the wealth and incomes of colonial farmers, see the work discussed in McCusker and Menard, *Economy of British America*, 262–69, and, more recently, Lois Greene Carr and Russell R. Menard, "Wealth and Welfare in Early Maryland: Evidence from St. Mary's County," *William and Mary Quarterly,* 3d ser., 46 (January 1999): 95–120.

52. In the eighteenth century, the terms of trade shifted in favor of agriculture as population growth drove food prices up, while the early stages of industrialization brought prices for manufactured goods down. P. M. G. Harris, "Inflation and Deflation in Colonial America, 1634–1860: Patterns of Change in the British American Economy," *Social Science History* 20 (Winter 1996): 469–506.

53. There is a large and growing literature on the work of women in early America. It has yet to be pulled together into a synthesis. Joan M. Jensen, *Loosening the Bonds: Mid-Atlantic Farm Women, 1650–1750* (New Haven: Yale University Press, 1986); and Laurel Thatcher Ulrich, *Good Wives: Image*

The high productivity and high incomes generated by colonial agriculture meant that the free population in rural areas lived well by early modern standards, as is evident in their improving diets,[54] in their rich material culture,[55] and in the new anthropometric evidence[56] now being collected on rural early Americans.

Now that recent work on early American agriculture has liberated us from the dead hand of the slovenly-farmer tradition, we are on the verge of being able to claim American agricultural history for what it should have been all along. For English migrants reared in an agricultural tradition in which farmers learned to experiment and borrow widely to cope with the prolonged decline in grain and wool prices after 1640, the colonial blended style would have seemed quite familiar.[57] An emphasis on the blended characteristics of early American agriculture answers the Mancall-Weiss challenge of bringing the Indians in by highlighting their contributions to economic development, but it does so without destroying their individuality and autonomy. In order to understand the development of a blended tradition, we have to first understand the particular traditions from which it was created.

It would be premature, however, to celebrate the passing of the slovenly farmer from colonial agricultural history, for just as he was being chased off center stage by new empirical work, he was being snuck back in, stage left, disguised as a stalwart defender of the moral economy against capitalism and the encroachments of the market by historians who work in what has been called the "moral economy" tradition of early American agricultural history.[58] Although traditional critics of colonial agriculture and historians in the moral economy tradition have

---

and Reality in the Lives of Women of Northern New England, 1650–1750 (New York: Knopf, 1991) are good places to start. Lorena Walsh's contribution to this volume provides a comprehensive set of references.

54. On diets, see the work discussed in McCusker and Menard, *Economy of British America,* 104, 249, and, more recently, Henry M. Miller, "An Archaeological Perspective on the Evolution of Diet in the Colonial Chesapeake, 1620–1745," in *Colonial Chesapeake Society,* ed. Lois Greene Carr, Philip D. Morgan, and Jean B. Russo (Chapel Hill: University of North Carolina Press 1988), 176–99.

55. For the growing literature on material culture, see Carson, Hoffman, and Albert, *Of Consuming Interests.*

56. For recent anthropometric work, see Richard H. Steckel, "Stature and the Standard of Living," *Journal of Economic Literature* 33 (December 1995): 1903–40.

57. Joan Thirsk, "Patterns of Agriculture in Seventeenth-Century England," in *Seventeenth-Century New England,* ed. David Hall and David Grayson Allen (Boston: Colonial Society of Massachusetts, 1984), 39–54.

58. On this tradition, see the critiques in Rothenberg, *From Market-Places to a Market Economy,* 24–55; and Richard M. Bushman, "Markets and Composite Farms in Early America," *William and Mary Quarterly,* 3d ser., 55 (July 1998): 351–74, and the more sympathetic assessment provided by Allan Kulikoff, "Households and Markets: Toward a New Synthesis of American Agrarian history," *William and Mary Quarterly,* 3d ser., 50 (1993): 342–55. Gordon Wood attempts a balanced view in "Inventing American Capitalism," *New York Review of Books* (June 2002). For more recent contributions to the debate, see Wilma A. Dunaway, *The First American Frontier: The Transition to Capitalism in Southern Appalachia, 1700–1860* (Chapel Hill: University of North Carolina Press, 1996), 1–22, and Robert E. Mutch, "The Debate About the Transition to Capitalism," *Theory and Society* 9 (November 1980): 847–64.

quite different visions of life in rural America, their views of the early American farmer have much in common. Both traditions characterize that farmer as running a low-productivity operation and avoiding innovation and risk, even when risk taking seemed warranted. That is, the central figure in both views of early American agriculture is inconsistent with recent empirical work stressing the colonial farmer's creativity and high productivity. If such empirical work continues, perhaps the stouthearted defender of the moral economy will join his dimwitted cousin offstage and we will be able to get on with the task of trying to understand the behavior of early American farmers.

But such a quick dismissal of the moral economy tradition will not do, for there are some important issues at stake in what is sometimes called "the New England debate."[59] Historians working in the moral economy tradition raised important questions that students of early American agriculture ought to take seriously, starting with the assumption that the slovenly farmer working a low-productivity farm captures the essence of early American agriculture. First of all, they maintain that the farmer's limited aspirations, his satisfaction with a "competency," and his embeddedness in a moral economy explain his behavior. Colonial farmers, moral economy historians argue, put community, family, and neighborliness ahead of improving their financial condition.[60] Further, such attitudes acted as a significant obstacle to economic growth and development and had to be changed before the American economy could achieve the rapid growth rates of the nineteenth century. Expansion of aspirations and a willingness to sacrifice community ties for the higher income that came from market participation seem to constitute what historians working in the moral economy tradition mean by the transition to capitalism. What exactly drove that transition, however, is not entirely clear in work on the moral economy. For some it seems to be the destruction of patriarchy and the general liberating impact of the American Revolution. For others, the "consumer revolution" of the late eighteenth century spurred the transition.[61]

While the consumer revolution may seem to skeptics to be one revolution too many, the empirical literature supporting it perhaps constitutes the final nail in the coffin of the slovenly farmer. If early American agriculture was so unproductive, how did farm families pay for all those consumer goods?

One way to evaluate competing interpretations of early American agriculture is to ask if they help us understand the cotton boom in the lower South

59. What is at stake seems often to have gotten lost in more recent contributions, but the issues are laid out clearly in the seminal essay by James Henretta, "Families and Farms: Mentalité in Pre-Industrial America," *William and Mary Quarterly,* 3d ser., 35 (January 1978): 1–32.

60. On the notion of competency, see Daniel Vickers, "Competency and Competition: Economic Culture in Early America," *William and Mary Quarterly,* 3d ser., 47 (January 1990): 3–29.

61. The best introduction to the idea of the consumer revolution is Cary Carson, "The Consumer Revolution in Colonial British America: Why Demand?" in Carson, Hoffman, and Albert, *Of Consuming Interests,* 444–82.

in the early nineteenth century, certainly one of the major turning points of American agricultural history. If we view the early American farmer as a slovenly husbandman, reluctant to innovate, or as a stalwart defender of the moral economy against the encroachments of the market, the cotton boom must remain a mystery.

While one cannot claim that the cotton boom was a clear example of a the blending of agricultural techniques, aspects of the boom become clear when we remember that farmers reared in a blended tradition, in which borrowing and the creative combination of different traditions to develop a technology appropriate to a new environment, were common. The development of both sea island and upland cotton involved considerable experimentation with different varieties grown in different parts of the world, in a conscious search for types that would flourish in the particular environments of the lower South. Once they found the appropriate variety, upland farmers applied to the new crop the methods they used to grow tobacco and grain. Thus cotton was topped, suckered, cured, and initially planted in hills, pre-Columbian style, while tobacco presses were used to create compact bales, and farmers asked the legislature to adapt the inspection systems developed for tobacco to ensure the quality and reputation of their new crop.[62] Eli Whitney's cotton gin is itself a good example of a blended technology, as it combined an East India charka with English hackles.[63]

Recently Carole Shammas, building on a point Eric Williams made long ago with regard to the English Empire in America,[64] has reminded us of the central role plantation crops played in the creation of the European empires of the early modern era. While her point is an important one, Shammas focuses on European demand for tropical products as the driving force behind this process, to the neglect of the important contribution made by productivity gains in plantation agriculture.[65] During the seventeenth century, both the sugar and tobacco industries were characterized by an inverse relationship between prices and output, as prices, both at the farm and in the major European markets, plummeted, while output grew rapidly. Planters blamed the falling prices on overproduction and the taxes and restrictions of a restrictive mercantilist system,

62. The ways in which upland cotton planters drew on techniques applied to tobacco and grain is stressed in Chaplin, *Anxious Pursuit*, 298–99. On the business of experimenting with different varieties, see Lewis Cecil Gray, *The History of Agriculture in the Southern United States to 1860* (Washington, D.C.: Carnegie Institution, 1933), 673–89; and Ulrich B. Phillips, *American Negro Slavery* (Baton Rouge: Louisiana State University Press, 1966), 150–59.

63. On the cotton gin as blended technology, see Angela Lakwete, "Cotton Ginning in America" (Ph.D. diss., University of Delaware, 1996).

64. Eric Williams, *Capitalism and Slavery* (Chapel Hill: University of North Carolina Press, 1944). Williams has of course provoked a long debate, which is reviewed in Russell R. Menard, "Reckoning with Williams: Capitalism and Slavery and the Reconstruction of Early American History," *Callalo* 20 (1997): 791–99.

65. Carole Shammas, "The Revolutionary Impact of European Demand for Tropical Goods," in McCusker and Morgan, *Early Modern Atlantic Economy*, 163–85.

and complained loudly of hard times. While historians have often accepted the planters' analysis, recent research makes clear that the price of the staples fell because planters improved the efficiency of the operations and passed on the savings to consumers in an effort to expand their markets.[66] The effort was successful. Falling prices put tobacco and sugar within the budgets of larger numbers of potential consumers. Over the course of the seventeenth century, European consumption of tobacco and sugar both widened, spreading from the major ports to the countryside, and deepened, moving from a luxury for the rich to become commodities that the working poor regarded as necessities.[67]

The success of tobacco and sugar planters in improving the productivity of their operations has implications for that hearty perennial question concerning the character of the planter class. As Michael Mullin has recently put it, "Were planters capitalists or medieval seigneurs, that is, forward or backward looking?"[68] However hidebound or conservative they may have later become, the men who built the great plantation economies in the seventeenth century were clearly willing to take risks and experiment if they thought it might improve their bottom line. In this context, it is worth noting that the planters of seventeenth-century Brazil, often described as the most atavistic plantocracy in the Americas, who were subjected to the same pressures to reduce costs as their counterparts in the English Caribbean, exhibited the same risk-taking and innovative approach to making sugar.[69] Not all the productivity gains associated with early American agriculture were achieved on the plantations and farms. There were also improvements in shipping, transactions, and capital markets (which lowered interest rates), all of which combined to help lower commodity prices in Europe and thus increased consumption of American plantation commodities.[70]

66. We know much more about this process in the tobacco industry than in sugar. On tobacco, see, in addition to the work cited above in note 18, Russell R. Menard, "The Tobacco Industry in the Chesapeake Colonies, 1630–1730: An Interpretation," *Research in Economic History* 5 (1980): 109–77. I address the issue with respect to the sugar industry in *Sweet Negotiations: Sugar, Slavery, and Plantation Agriculture in Early Barbados* (Charlottesville: University of Virginia Press, forthcoming).

67. For sugar, this process is described in detail in Sidney W. Mintz, *Sweetness and Power: The Place of Sugar in Modern History* (New York: Viking, 1985) For tobacco, see Jordan Goodman, *Tobacco in History: The Cultures of Dependence* (London: Routledge, 1993).

68. Michael Mullin, *Africa in America: Slave Acculturation and Resistance in the American South and the British Caribbean, 1736–1831* (Urbana: University of Illinois Press, 1992), 115. This is an old debate, and there is, of course a large body of literature, which is ably introduced in Peter Kolchin, *American Slavery, 1618–1877* (New York: Hill and Wang, 1993), 278–382.

69. Stuart B. Schwartz, *Sugar Plantations in the Formation of Brazilian Society: Bahaia, 1550–1835* (New York: Cambridge University Press, 1985), 431–34. Anyone interested in early American plantation agriculture should know Schwartz's fine book.

70. On shipping costs, see Russell R. Menard, "Transport Costs and Long-Range Trade: Was There a European Transport Revolution in the Early Modern Era? in *The Political Economy of Merchant Empires: State Power and World Trade, 1350–1750*, ed. James D. Tracy (New York: Cambridge University Press, 1991), 228–75. On transaction costs, see the essays by Douglass North and Jacob Price in the same volume. On interest rates, see McCusker and Menard, *Economy of British America,* 59n, 60n, and 69n.

This essay has reviewed recent scholarship in early American agricultural history, finding that, with the exception of an essay by Mancall and Weiss and work in the moral economy tradition, neither of which pays much attention to what farmers actually did, recent studies describe an agriculture marked by persistent experimentation and innovation, as colonial farmers built a new mestizo agricultural regime that blended the several farming traditions available to them. That new regime produced some remarkable advances in productivity over the colonial era, advances sufficient to keep the colonial economy growing on a per capita basis at a slow but not unimpressive rate by the standards of the early modern era, a growth that made Americans of European descent one of the wealthiest groups in the world by the eve of the American Revolution.

Chapter Four

Peopling, Producing, and Consuming in Early British America

LORENA S. WALSH

This essay reviews work undertaken over the past fifteen years in three areas, the growth of population, the colonial labor force, and consumption and the domestic economy. These are all topics to which McCusker and Menard devoted considerable attention in *The Economy of British America*. It first asks to what extent scholars have addressed the issues identified in their synthesis as most in need of further work. Second, it assesses the impact of McCusker's and Menard's synthesis.[1] This strategy is adopted because the answer to the question "Are we answering the call?" is "Sometimes yes, and sometimes no." A partially negative answer, however, does not mean either that scholars have paid little attention to McCusker's and Menard's summary or that their ambitious agenda was flawed or incomplete. It means, rather, that they have apparently done too good a job. In his introduction to the special January 1999 issue of the *William and Mary Quarterly*, which featured articles on the domestic economy of British North America, McCusker lamented, "The authors presumed that . . . [this now] twenty-year-old synthesis of what was then the state of the art . . . would stir others either to challenge or to refine these and related notions . . . [but] this has not yet happened."[2]

In a recent essay that assessed the matter of economic growth in the colonies, Lance Davis and Stanley Engerman concluded that "there is far too much work to be done to permit the task to be completed within our lifetime."[3] Many

1. The task of surveying fifteen years of literature on these three issues is daunting, and this brief assessment is necessarily selective in the works chosen for discussion. The primary emphasis is on the upper South, the region that I know best. Suggestions for future research agendas also emphasize issues and approaches that I consider most interesting and most critical for addressing long-standing historical problems.

2. John J. McCusker, "Measuring Colonial Gross Domestic Product: An Introduction," *William and Mary Quarterly*, 3d ser., 56 (January 1999): 5.

3. Lance Davis and Stanley L. Engerman, "The Economy of British North America: Miles Traveled, Miles Still to Go," ibid., 22.

scholars of early American economic history seem indeed to have reserved much of the collecting and analyzing of additional economic data, not to mention the challenging and refining of McCusker and Menard's synthesis, for some future generation. Part of the reason lies in the changing interests of early American historians, especially their widespread disenchantment with quantitative approaches to early American history and a decline in the kind of large-scale collaborative research projects common in the 1970s and early 1980s. Although these joint efforts have tended not to yield the ambitious summarizing tomes the participants initially envisioned, they did generate many of the data on which McCusker and Menard drew, served as a catalyst for other scholars working on related topics, and encouraged a degree of coherence in approaches to big questions that has subsequently been lacking, as scholars have largely opted each to go their own ways. Prosopographical studies of county populations, studies of comparative urban history, and projects exploring economic development through probate documents, for example, have yielded databases that individual scholars continue, some twenty years later, to mine intensively. In some instances, detailed summarizing volumes have been abandoned, owing to the dispersal of the initial research teams or the inability of the collaborators to find adequate support for writing up the results. In other cases, partial results have eventually been published in more modest and scattered form.

The components of colonial population growth have generated scant interest in recent years. In a 1993 *William and Mary Quarterly* symposium on the future of early American history, Russell Menard asked, "Whatever happened to early American population history?"[4] That matters of sex and death, at least as demographers study them, still remain unfashionable is amply documented in the new Cambridge *Population History of North America*.[5] In the bibliography accompanying Henry Gemery's summation of the current state of knowledge of the white population of North America to 1790, only fourteen of the 110 publications cited were published in the 1990s. Evarts B. Green and Virginia D. Harrington, and Stella H. Sutherland, who published most of their work in the 1930s, remain the standard sources for early American population estimates, along with Gemery's work on emigration, completed in the 1980s, and, yes, revisions made by McCusker and Menard's volume.[6] A somewhat more encouraging

4. Menard, "Whatever Happened to Early American Population History?" *William and Mary Quarterly*, 3d ser., 50 (April 1993): 356–66.

5. Michael R. Haines and Richard H. Steckel, eds., *A Population History of North America* (New York: Cambridge University Press, 2000). See also David W. Galenson, "The Settlement and Growth of the Colonies: Population, Labor, and Economic Development," in *The Cambridge Economic History of the United States*, 3 vols., ed. Stanley L. Engerman and Robert E. Gallman, (New York: Cambridge University Press, 1996), 1:135–208.

6. Henry A. Gemery, "The White Population of the Colonial United States, 1607–1790," in Haines and Steckel, *Population History of North America*, 143–90. Gloria Main, "Rocking the Cradle: Marital Fertility in New England," paper presented at the annual meeting of the Social Science History Association, 2000, discusses one of the few early American demographic studies currently in progress.

twenty-seven of the seventy-eight references cited in my chapter on the African American colonial population date to the past decade, but nonetheless I concluded that "models and methods developed some 20 years ago still dominate.... Without the stimulus of new work in the field, thinking about ... demographic insights ... has ossified."[7] Historians and anthropologists have continued to work on better establishing the parameters of the pre- and postcontact Native American populations. But lack of agreement still characterizes this literature, and Native American population history remains poorly integrated with mainstream North American economic history.[8]

While our understanding of marriage, fertility, and death in early America and of the "dynamic interaction between demographic and economic processes" has not advanced much beyond the materials synthesized by McCusker and Menard, scholars have responded to their characterization of demographers' other staple, migration, as a neglected topic. In *The Peopling of British North America,* a project under way before 1985, Bernard Bailyn sketched out the beginnings of a survey of the population of British North America in the years before the Revolution, and posed a big question: How did the movement of so many thousands of people shape eighteenth-century American society and culture? Bailyn's areas of interest extended beyond economic history, but his emphasis on the international context of migration, on viewing Old and New World labor markets as an integrated unit, and on assessing the fortunes of migrants in varying regional contexts paralleled McCusker and Menard's recommendations.[9]

Bailyn's study advanced four propositions about population movements in the preindustrial era, and Bailyn further developed them in *Voyagers to the West: A Passage in the Peopling of America on the Eve of the Revolution.* These works merit review, since Bailyn's propositions have informed most subsequent research on prerevolutionary North American immigration. First, the flow to North America can be understood as an extension of domestic Old World mobility patterns, but it was also a "new and dynamic force in European population history, which

---

7. Lorena S. Walsh, "The African-American Population of the Colonial United States," in Haines and Steckel, *Population History of North America,* 191–240, quotation at 222. An important exception to this dismal overview is Susan E. Klepp, "Seasoning and Society: Racial Differences in Mortality in Eighteenth-Century Philadelphia," *William and Mary Quarterly,* 3d ser., 51 (July 1994): 473–506.

8. Russell Thornton, "Population History of Native North Americans," in Haines and Steckel, *Population History of North America,* 9–50; Douglas H. Ubelaker, "Patterns of Disease in Early North America," ibid., 51–98; and Neal Salisbury, "The History of Native Americans from Before the Arrival of the Europeans and Africans Until the American Civil War," in Engerman and Gallman, *Cambridge Economic History of the United States,* 1:209–24. Peter H. Wood, "The Changing Population of the Colonial South: An Overview by Race and Region, 1685–1790," in *Powhatan's Mantle: Indians in the Colonial Southeast,* ed. Peter H. Wood, Gregory A. Waselkov, and M. Thomas Hatley (Lincoln: University of Nebraska Press, 1989), 35–103, provides an exceptional integrated interpretation.

9. Bernard Bailyn, *The Peopling of British North America: An Introduction* (New York: Knopf, 1986).

permanently altered the traditional configuration."[10] Second, settlement and development in the North American colonies were highly differentiated processes. The experiences of immigrants must be evaluated in the context of the multiple and diverse localities into which they moved. Third, the major stimuli to population recruitment and settlement were labor markets and land speculation. These resulted in two distinctly different migration streams and processes, drawing on different socioeconomic groups and leading to different modes of integration into the host society. One stream was composed primarily of young, single males from southern and central England, many of them artisans, who indentured themselves to pay for their passage, and the other was composed primarily of mature family groups from northern England and Scotland, often from rural backgrounds, who had sufficient resources to pay transportation costs. A fourth proposition, that early American culture "becomes most fully comprehensible when seen as the exotic far western periphery, a marchland, of the metropolitan European culture system," was explored in part in *Voyagers to the West* and further developed by others in *Strangers Within the Realm: Cultural Margins of the First British Empire,* which Bailyn co-edited with Philip Morgan.[11]

The great English migration of the early seventeenth century has also continued to command attention, both quantitative and qualitative. New England, the Chesapeake, and the West Indies have all been studied recently in transatlantic perspective by David Cressy, Virginia DeJohn Anderson, James Horn, and Alison Games. Other volumes of essays on transatlantic migration have concentrated primarily on filling in the picture for peoples (Germans, Irish, Scotch-Irish, Dutch, French, and Spanish) and places (the West Indies, Spanish North America, and French Canada) that figured less prominently or had been omitted in Bailyn's survey. The editors and authors of these volumes emphasize the increasing ethnic and cultural diversity of eighteenth-century America, as migrants, coerced and voluntary, from Africa, non-English Britain, and continental Europe largely replaced the English in the transatlantic flow in the first two-thirds of the eighteenth century.[12] David Hackett Fischer's work stands virtually alone in

10. Ibid., 20; Bernard Bailyn, *Voyagers to the West: A Passage in the Peopling of America on the Eve of the Revolution* (New York: Knopf, 1986).

11. Bailyn, *Peopling of British North America,* 112; Bernard Bailyn and Philip D. Morgan, eds., *Strangers Within the Realm: Cultural Margins of the First British Empire* (Chapel Hill: University of North Carolina Press, 1991).

12. David Cressy, *Coming Over: Migration and Communication Between England and New England in the Seventeenth Century* (New York: Cambridge University Press, 1987); Virginia DeJohn Anderson, *New England's Generation: The Great Migration and the Formation of Society and Culture in the Seventeenth Century* (New York: Cambridge University Press, 1991); James Horn, *Adapting to a New World: English Society in the Seventeenth-Century Chesapeake* (Chapel Hill: University of North Carolina Press, 1994); Alison F. Games, *Migration and the Origins of the English Atlantic World* (Cambridge: Harvard University Press, 1999); Ida Altman and James Horn, eds., *"To Make America": European Emigration in the Early Modern Period* (Berkeley and Los Angeles: University of California Press, 1991); and Nicholas Canny, ed., *Europeans on the Move: Studies on European Migration, 1500–1800* (New York: Oxford

arguing for the continuing hegemony of English cultures,[13] while Aaron Fogle-man's tackles German migration, and Marianne S. Wokeck's deals with both Germans and Irish. Wokeck identifies similar dual indentured and free migra-tions from the north and south of Ireland, and changes over time in the sorts of German-speaking peoples who chose transatlantic migration instead of move-ment within Europe.[14]

A number of scholars objected to the concentration, in *Voyagers to the West,* on English and Scottish migration to the neglect of other groups and peoples, and some have argued that Bailyn's estimate of European migration in the eighteenth century before the 1770s overstates the number of free migrants. So, not surprisingly, bound and involuntary European migrants have subsequently received much compensatory attention in, for example, the work of A. Roger Ekirch and Peter Coldham and in Kenneth Morgan's essays on convict labor in Maryland. These authors have emphasized the continued addition of substantial numbers of involuntary European migrants to the eighteenth-century North American labor force. But the fact that convicts who survived their terms of service, unlike enslaved Africans and their descendants, did eventually gain their freedom and then left scant trace of their subsequent lives makes their contri-bution to eighteenth-century economic and demographic growth difficult to evaluate.[15] In addition, Farley Grubb's many articles on the labor market for and characteristics of indentured servants, convicts, and redemptioners in the middle colonies, Sharon V. Salinger's *"To Serve Well and Faithfully": Labor and Inden-tured Servants in Pennsylvania, 1682–1800,* and my own study of mercantile strate-gies and the Chesapeake labor supply in the eighteenth century have helped to

---

University Press, 1994). For a recent summary of the literature see James Horn, "British Diaspora: Emigration from Britain, 1680–1815," in *The Eighteenth Century,* vol. 2 of *The Oxford History of the British Empire,* ed. P. J. Marshall (New York: Oxford University Press, 1998), 28–52.

13. David Hackett Fischer, *Albion's Seed: Four British Folkways in America* (New York: Oxford University Press, 1989).

14. Aaron S. Fogleman, *Hopeful Journeys: German Immigration, Settlement, and Political Cul-ture in Colonial America, 1717–1775* (Philadelphia: University of Pennsylvania Press, 1996); Marianne S. Wokeck, *Trade in Strangers: The Beginnings of Mass Migration to North America* (University Park: Penn-sylvania State University Press, 1999).

15. A. Roger Ekirch, *Bound for America: The Transportation of British Convicts to the Colonies, 1718–1775* (New York: Oxford University Press, 1987); Peter W. Coldham, *Emigrants in Chains: A Social History of Forced Emigration to the Americas of Felons, Destitute Children, Political and Religious Non-Conformists, Vagabonds, Beggars, and Other Undesirables, 1607–1776* (Baltimore: Johns Hopkins University Press, 1992); Kenneth Morgan, "The Organization of the Convict Trade to Maryland: Stevenson, Ran-dolph and Cheston, 1768–1775," *William and Mary Quarterly,* 3d ser., 42 (April 1985): 201–27; Kenneth Morgan, "English and American Attitudes Towards Convict Transportation 1718–1775," *History,* n.s., 72 (October 1987): 416–31; Kenneth Morgan, "Convict Runaways in Maryland, 1745–1775," *Journal of American Studies* 23 (August 1989): 253–68. Susan E. Klepp and Billy G. Smith, eds., *The Infortunate: The Voyage and Adventures of William Moraley, an Indentured Servant* (University Park: Pennsylvania State University Press, 1992) offers a rare glimpse into the world of obscure and less successful eighteenth-century bound migrants.

clarify the relationships between the supply of and demand for short-term bound labor.[16]

In addition to studying groups and regions that did not take center stage in Bailyn's narrative, historians have taken up another of the major themes of *Voyagers to the West,* the relationship between immigration and the American Revolution. Some of the most thought-provoking work is asking how eighteenth-century European migration was similar to or different from the great migrations of the nineteenth century, and why. Wokeck, for example, argues that the systems that European and American merchants developed for transporting Germans and Irish in the eighteenth century became the model for the nineteenth-century "trade in strangers." Marilyn C. Baseler, in *"Asylum for Mankind": America, 1607–1800,* explores the impact of the Revolution on immigration policies and naturalization procedures. She finds that as former colonists gained control over who could migrate, and made decisions about what sorts of migrants would be judged worthy of naturalization and citizenship, "the 'mankind' that revolutionary Americans served was selective and remained European," and the preferred immigrants were precisely "the propertied, industrious, committed republican[s]," on whom Bailyn had focused attention.[17] The theme of the Revolution as a turning point in the peopling of British America is most

---

16. See the following articles by Farley Grubb: "The Incidence of Servitude in Trans-Atlantic Migration, 1771–1804," *Explorations in Economic History* 22 (July 1985): 316–39; "The Market for Indentured Immigrants: Evidence on the Efficiency of Forward-Labor Contracting in Philadelphia, 1745–1773," *Journal of Economic History* 45 (December 1985): 855–68; "Immigrant Servant Labor: Their Occupational and Geographic Distribution in the Late Eighteenth-Century Mid-Atlantic Economy," *Social Science History* 9 (Summer 1985): 249–75; "Redemptioner Immigration to Pennsylvania: Evidence on Contract Choice and Profitability," *Journal of Economic History* 46 (June 1986): 407–18; "Colonial Labor Markets and the Length of Indenture: Further Evidence," *Explorations in Economic History* 24 (January 1987): 101–6; "British Immigration to Philadelphia: The Reconstruction of Ship Passenger Lists from May 1772 to October 1773," *Pennsylvania History* 55 (July 1988): 118–41; "The Auction of Redemptioner Servants, Philadelphia, 1771–1804: An Economic Analysis," *Journal of Economic History* 48 (September 1988): 583–603; "Servant Auction Records and Immigration into the Delaware Valley, 1745–1831: The Proportion of Females Among Immigrant Servants," *Proceedings of the American Philosophical Society* 133 (June 1989): 154–69; "The Long-run Trend in the Value of European Immigrant Servants, 1654–1831: New Measurements and Interpretations," *Research in Economic History* 14 (1992): 167–240; "Fatherless and Friendless: Factors Influencing the Flow of English Emigrant Servants," *Journal of Economic History* 52 (March 1992): 85–108; "Lilliputians and Brobdingnagians, Stature in Early America: Evidence from Servants, Convicts, and Apprentices," *Research in Economic History* 19 (1999): 139–203; "The Transatlantic Market for British Convict Labor," *Journal of Economic History* 60 (March 2000): 94–122; and see Farley Grubb and Tony Stitt, "The Liverpool Emigrant Servant Trade and the Transition to Slave Labor in the Chesapeake, 1697–1707: Market Adjustments to War," *Explorations in Economic History* 31 (July 1994): 376–405; Sharon V. Salinger, *"To Serve Well and Faithfully": Labor and Indentured Servants in Pennsylvania, 1682–1800* (New York: Cambridge University Press, 1987); Lorena S. Walsh, "Mercantile Strategies, Credit Networks, and Labor Supply in the Colonial Chesapeake in Trans-Atlantic Perspective," in *Slavery in the Development of the Americas,* ed. David Eltis, Frank D. Lewis, and Kenneth L. Sokoloff (New York: Cambridge University Press, 2004), 89–119.

17. Marilyn C. Baseler, *"Asylum for Mankind": America, 1607–1800* (Ithaca: Cornell University Press, 1998), 331.

cogently addressed by Aaron S. Fogleman in "From Slaves, Convicts, and Servants to Free Passengers: The Transformation of Immigration in the Era of the American Revolution."[18] Fogleman's estimates of total immigration reveal the stark divide between predominantly unfree migration throughout the colonial era and the almost entirely free migration of the nineteenth century, a topic earlier explored by Menard in an essay on the "re-peopling" of British America between 1600 and 1790, which was published in a volume on nineteenth-century immigration that largely escaped the attention of early Americanists.[19]

Major opportunities remain to better identify how specific local Old World circumstances, particular information flows, and specialized trade and transport connections induced particular sorts of people from particular kinds of places to migrate to British America rather than to move elsewhere or to stay put. As Menard noted in 1993, while labor markets account for much of the transatlantic migration of Europeans, the movement of free people in family groups has been portrayed as "at most tied only indirectly to the process that brought servants." This literature, "focused for the most part on particular migrant groups and much concerned with their uniqueness, leaves the impression that the transatlantic migration of families consisted of a series of discrete, unrelated bursts" to which the concept of a migration field supplies little help.[20] Early Americanists need to turn to the recent literature on other transatlantic European migrations to gain fresh perspectives. For example, Jose C. Moya has supplied a powerful model for connecting migration structures with individual agency in his investigation of Spanish immigrants to Buenos Aires, which scholars of British America could fruitfully borrow from and adapt. On the sending side, Moya explores the connections between rural impoverishment and emigration and the role of transportation, information, and kinship networks in facilitating emigration and in shaping the timing, volume, and composition of outflows from particular towns and regions within Spain. On the receiving side he demonstrates how the interaction of kinship links, social class, and ecological factors determined residential patterns in Argentina, how migrants' Old World experience and New World social networks affected their choice of occupation and their success or failure in improving their economic status, and how the social and economic composition of emigrant streams affected the institutions and social life of different groups in their new homes.[21]

18. Aaron S. Fogleman, "From Slaves, Convicts, and Servants to Free Passengers: The Transformation of Immigration in the Era of the American Revolution," *Journal of American History* 85 (June 1998): 43–76.

19. Russell R. Menard, "Migration, Ethnicity, and the Rise of an Atlantic Economy: The Re-Peopling of British America, 1600–1790," in *A Century of European Migrations, 1830–1930*, ed. Rudolph J. Vecoli and Suzanne M. Sinke (Urbana: University of Illinois Press, 1991), 58–77.

20. Menard, "Whatever Happened to Early American Population History?" 360–61.

21. Jose C. Moya, *Cousins and Strangers: Spanish Immigrants in Buenos Aires, 1850–1930* (Berkeley and Los Angeles: University of California Press, 1998).

In addition, much work remains to be done on the differing impacts of the bound and free migration streams on the economic and social development of receiving localities. The oft-criticized preoccupation with the better-documented minority of free immigrants may be justified when the focus is on issues of economic and social development. That the free migrant minority had a disproportionate influence on the economic, social, political, and cultural development of the places to which they moved has never been doubted. Free family migrants did contribute more to natural population increase than did single bound laborers; they transferred some nonhuman capital of their own and were able to borrow more through the transatlantic connections they maintained, and they could begin almost immediately contributing to economic development both as farm builders and as consumers.

In the context of receiving localities, to borrow a concept from Steve Hochstadt's study of migration within nineteenth-century Germany, family migrants had higher rates of "migration efficiency" than did single female and especially single male migrants, a pattern also identified, but not so clearly elucidated, for parts of British America. In the colonies former servants, free single migrants, and those who came in family groups were all prone to move on to new localities in search of better opportunities, but whole families were less likely to relocate than the other two migrant groups. More "efficient" free family migrants thus contributed most to the demographic and social reproduction of the communities in which they settled. Regions capable of attracting significant numbers of immigrant servants—primarily young single men—enjoyed higher levels of per capita productivity than did regions receiving more demographically balanced migration streams. But such areas also suffered from the destabilizing effects of high levels of demographically and socially "inefficient" in- and out-migration, although the least "efficient" migrants almost invariably paid the heaviest price in terms of early death and in restricted chances for marrying and reproducing and for improving their economic and social status. We still have much to learn about how differences in immigration shaped the overall growth process.[22]

22. On free immigrants, see Altman and Horn, "Introduction," and James Horn, "'To Parts Beyond the Seas': Free Emigration to the Chesapeake in the Seventeenth Century," in Altman and Horn, *To Make America,* 1–29, 85–130; Horn, *Adapting to a New World;* Wokeck, *Trade in Strangers;* and Bailyn, *Peopling of British North America,* 12–15. Among studies that suggest greater migration efficiency for family migrants are Darrett B. Rutman and Anita H. Rutman, "'More True and Perfect Lists': The Reconstruction of Censuses for Middlesex County, Virginia, 1668–1704," *Virginia Magazine of History and Biography* 88 (January 1980): 37–74; Lorena S. Walsh, "Staying Put or Getting Out: Findings for Charles County, Maryland, 1650–1720," *William and Mary Quarterly,* 3d ser., 44 (January 1987): 89–103; and Richard Archer, "New England Mosaic: A Demographic Analysis for the Seventeenth Century," *William and Mary Quarterly,* 3d ser., 47 (October 1990): 477–502. For the concept of migration efficiency, see Steve Hochstadt, *Mobility and Modernity: Migration in Germany, 1820–1989* (Ann Arbor: University of Michigan Press, 1999), 92–106.

The forced migration of millions of Africans westward and, to a lesser extent, eastward, is now emerging as a more dynamic area of study. Overwhelmingly, historians have written about the transfers of people from Europe and sub-Saharan Africa to various American destinations during the sixteenth through eighteenth centuries in total isolation from one another. As a result of intensive study in the past three decades of the transatlantic slave trade, we have better information about the forced migration from Africa than we do for many voluntary migrations from Europe and perhaps ever will. But, long bogged down in esoteric numbers games, and intensely focused on that most accessible aspect of this anomalous migration, the Middle Passage, the bulk of slave-trade studies can scarcely be characterized as "immigration history" as most scholars understand it.[23]

The publication of *The Trans-Atlantic Slave Trade: A Database on CD-ROM*, an outstanding example of collaborative effort, affords a major breakthrough in immigration history in ways that we can only dimly glimpse at present. Ostensibly about voyages and numbers in the slave trade rather than the life histories of the millions of men, women, and children who were its victims, this database is nonetheless a powerful tool for uncovering and linking critical information about the cultural and technological resources these coerced migrants brought with them, and about some of the spatial and demographic constraints that affected later social and cultural adaptations. Already it is becoming clear that the forced African migration to the Americas was as strongly patterned as were voluntary European flows. American destinations for the enslaved were determined by complex transatlantic trade connections between Europe, Africa, and the American colonies. Some of the mechanisms of the trades in slaves, indentured servants, and free migrants were strikingly similar, the marked difference being that the elements of choice and opportunity that are so central to European immigration history played no role in the African Diaspora.[24]

Important parts of the history of the coerced African migration can be recovered from the refined numbers on the ports from which the captives were shipped, the ethnic groups to which they probably belonged, the differing sex and age composition of captive populations, and the destinations to which they were sent. The transatlantic slave trade database (and the additions to it now in progress) will permit this kind of research. But historians have yet to devise alternative techniques for reconstituting the particular experiences of these transported

---

23. The bibliography in David Eltis, *The Rise of African Slavery in the Americas* (New York: Cambridge University Press, 2000) provides a comprehensive listing of prior studies.

24. David Eltis, Stephen D. Behrendt, David Richardson, and Herbert S. Klein, *The Trans-Atlantic Slave Trade: A Database on CD-ROM* (Cambridge: Cambridge University Press, 1999); Lorena S. Walsh, "The Chesapeake Slave Trade: Regional Patterns, African Origins, and Some Implications," *William and Mary Quarterly*, 3d ser., 58 (January 2001): 139–70; Lorena S. Walsh, "The Differential Cultural Impact of Free and Coerced Migration to Colonial America," in *Coerced and Free Migration: Global Perspectives*, ed. David Eltis (Stanford: Stanford University Press, 2002), 117–51.

captives after they disembarked. The conventional methodology for tracing voluntary migrants in the New World—the linking of named individuals—is unavailable for enslaved peoples. This seemingly insurmountable obstacle poses one of the major challenges that early American historians must now address. Moreover, while "more precise descriptions of migration patterns" have been forthcoming, our understanding of how these migration flows translated into regional demographic regimes unfortunately still awaits the "better estimates of the size and composition of colonial populations, additional work on the demography of slavery," and further local studies of the demographics of European migrants and their descendants that McCusker and Menard called for.[25]

By way of illustrating this point, let me outline the problems of evidence that I continue to grapple with in my ongoing research on the composition of eighteenth-century African and African American populations in the colonial Chesapeake. The base population estimates from which other measures are derived remain those published in *Historical Statistics of the United States,* a series that McCusker and Menard characterized as not "wildly inaccurate or likely to mislead those interested in rough estimates of the relative size of the colonies or in the general pattern of growth, even if [the] guesses are sometimes off the mark by a factor of two." To these estimates scholars have made minor adjustments, sometimes specifying the reasoning or alternate sources employed, sometimes alluding only to the author's best estimates or educated guesses and thus known only to him or her, to the detriment of readers who need to know how these estimates were derived in order to judge their merit. Deaths are then estimated using a study of mortality rates that is now twenty-four years old and that continues to represent a significant advance over no evidence at all but summarizes the life experiences of only thirty-two Africans (for which full information exists for only seventeen) brought to a single Virginia estate situated in a notoriously unhealthy microenvironment. Lack of evidence also necessitates the unlikely assumption that females and males shared identical chances for survival across their adult lives. Rates of natural increase, selected by "judgment" in the absence of any direct evidence, are used to estimate births, with the remainder, after subtracting estimated deaths from estimated births, attributed to estimated net immigration.[26]

25. John J. McCusker and Russell R. Menard, *The Economy of British America, 1607–1789* (Chapel Hill: University of North Carolina Press, 1985), 234–35.

26. Ibid., 214. For the estimating procedure, see Henry A. Gemery, "Emigration from the British Isles to the New World, 1630–1700: Inferences from Colonial Populations," *Research in Economic History* 5 (1980): 179–231, and, also by Gemery, "European Emigration to North America, 1700–1820: Numbers and Quasi-Numbers," *Perspectives in American History,* n.s., 1 (1984): 283–342. Estimates of black immigration employing growth models include David W. Galenson, *White Servitude in Colonial America: An Economic Analysis* (New York: Cambridge University Press, 1981), appendix H; Robert W. Fogel, "Revised Estimates of the U.S. Slave Trade and of the Native-Born Share of the Black Population," in *Without Consent or Contract: The Rise and Fall of American Slavery; Evidence and Methods,* ed.

To compound the problems of evidence and methodologies, it is not at all certain that careful estimates now under way of the numbers of Africans imported into various North American destinations, calculated from extant shipping records (and making allowance for missing records), are going to add up to totals approaching the number of immigrants projected from population-growth models. In addition, at least in the Chesapeake, estimates of the proportions of Africans and creoles calculated from growth models do not always fit well with evidence about sex and child-woman ratios derived from probate inventories, which suggest somewhat different chronologies for the shift from an immigrant to a native-born population. Virginia probate records do not unambiguously replicate the clear and plausible progression that Menard identified for Maryland. The differences may be due to problems of evidence reflecting differing probate recording practices in the two colonies. But it seems equally possible that variations in the volume, in the sex, or in adult-child ratios, or in the ethnic composition of forced African migrants brought to different parts of the Chesapeake, produced different subregional demographic outcomes.[27]

Rates of natural increase were almost certainly strongly affected by the proportion of women of childbearing age in local populations, and also by the proportion of recent arrivals, who suffered higher mortality and had fewer children than did more seasoned captives. A great imbalance between women and men continues to be posited as the main factor that prevented natural increase among forcibly transplanted Africans. But the severity of that imbalance in North American localities is usually inferred from averages for the entire transatlantic trade or from merchants' oft-stated ideal goal of shipping two men for every woman. Information on the actual sex and age composition of slave

Robert W. Fogel, Ralph A. Galatine, and Richard L. Manning (New York: W. W. Norton, 1992), 53–58; and Philip D. Morgan, *Slave Counterpoint: Black Culture in the Eighteenth-Century Chesapeake and Low-country* (Chapel Hill: University of North Carolina, 1998), 58–61. For a preliminary estimation from shipping records, see David Eltis, "The British Transatlantic Slave Trade Before 1714: Annual Estimates of Volume and Direction," in *The Lesser Antilles in the Age of European Expansion,* ed. Robert L. Paquette and Stanley L. Engerman (Gainesville: University Press of Florida, 1996), 182–205. For slightly revised population estimates building on the series in U.S. Bureau of the Census, *Historical Statistics of the United States, Colonial Times to 1970,* 2 vols., bicentennial ed. (Washington, D.C.: U.S. Government Printing Office, 1975); see Ira Berlin, *Many Thousands Gone: The First Two Centuries of Slavery in North America* (Cambridge: Harvard University Press, 1998), 369–71. Mortality estimates are found in Allan Kulikoff, "A 'Prolifick' People: Black Population Growth in the Chesapeake Colonies, 1700–1790," *Southern Studies* 16 (Winter 1977): 391–428.

27. Russell R. Menard, "The Maryland Slave Population, 1658 to 1730: A Demographic Profile of Blacks in Four Counties," *William and Mary Quarterly,* 3d ser., 32 (January 1975): 29–54; Philip D. Morgan, "The Development of Slave Culture in 18th-Century Plantation America" (Ph.D. diss., University College London, 1977), 291–300; Philip D. Morgan and Michael L. Nicholls, "Slaves in Piedmont Virginia, 1720–1796," *William and Mary Quarterly,* 3d ser., 46 (April 1989): 211–51; Lorena S. Walsh, *From Calabar to Carter's Grove: The History of a Virginia Slave Community* (Charlottesville: University Press of Virginia, 1977), 30, 141–44; Walsh "Chesapeake Slave Trade," and "Differential Cultural Impact of Free and Coerced Migration."

cargoes sent to various North American ports demonstrates that adult sex ratios were less skewed than is commonly supposed. Thus alternative explanations for low birthrates among Africans, including cultural ones, merit further study.[28] Nonetheless, improved demographic measures remain the first priority, even for the comparatively well studied Chesapeake.

Historians have responded rather more strongly to the call for additional work on the colonial labor force, albeit in rather fragmented fashion. Fine studies of particular occupational groups such as sailors, fishermen, and ironworkers address important but often overlooked components of the workforce.[29] Recent works on communities or colonies in New England have supplied much new information on family labor, hired agricultural workers, early factory labor, and the role of outwork in supplementing incomes in rural areas.[30] In the middle colonies, Billy Smith's survey of the work, incomes, and living standards of Philadelphia's laboring poor stands out, as do Paul Clemens and Lucy Simler's studies of cottagers, inmates, and other part-time rural laborers, and Joan Jensen's work on mid-Atlantic farm women. Less attention has been given to New York and New Jersey, although Peter Wacker and Paul Clemens summarize an impressive array of data on land distribution, agriculture, and the makeup of the workforce in New Jersey.[31] Further south, Christine Daniels's and Jean Russo's work on artisans and other wage workers has added much to our knowledge of the little-studied Chesapeake free workforce, and others are now researching

28. Fogel, "Revised Estimates of the U.S. Slave Trade"; David Eltis and Stanley L. Engerman, "Fluctuations in Sex and Age Ratios in the Transatlantic Slave Trade, 1663–1864," *Economic History Review* 46 (May 1993): 308–23; Walsh, "Differential Cultural Impact of Free and Coerced Migration." Jennifer Lyle Morgan, "This Is 'Mines': Slavery and Reproduction in Colonial Barbados and South Carolina," in *Money, Trade, and Power: The Evolution of Colonial South Carolina's Plantation Society,* ed. Jack P. Greene, Rosemary Brana-Shute, and Randy J. Sparks (Columbia: University of South Carolina Press, 2001), 187–216, addresses the issue of reproduction from a gendered and ideological perspective.

29. For example, Daniel Vickers, *Farmers and Fishermen: Two Centuries of Work in Essex County, Massachusetts, 1630–1850* (Chapel Hill: University of North Carolina Press, 1994); W. Jeffrey Bolster, *Black Jacks: African American Seamen in the Age of Sail* (Cambridge: Harvard University Press, 1997); John Bezís-Selfa, "A Tale of Two Ironworks: Slavery, Free Labor, Work, and Resistance in the Early Republic," *William and Mary Quarterly,* 3d ser., 56 (October 1999): 677–700; John Bezís-Selfa, *Forging America: Adventurers, Ironworkers, and America's Industrious Revolution* (Ithaca: Cornell University Press, 2004).

30. Citations to the more significant studies can be found in the bibliographical essay accompanying Daniel Vickers, "The Northern Colonies: Economy and Society, 1600–1775," in Engerman and Gallman, *Cambridge Economic History of the United States,* 1:209–48.

31. Billy G. Smith, *The "Lower Sort": Philadelphia's Laboring People, 1750–1800* (Ithaca: Cornell University Press, 1990); Paul G. E. Clemens and Lucy Simler, "Rural Labor and the Farm Household in Chester County, Pennsylvania, 1750–1820," in *Work and Labor in Early America,* ed. Stephen Innes (Chapel Hill: University of North Carolina Press, 1988), 106–43; Lucy Simler, "Tenancy in Colonial Pennsylvania: The Case of Chester County," *William and Mary Quarterly,* 3d ser., 43 (October 1986): 542–69; Lucy Simler, "The Landless Worker: An Index of Economic and Social Change in Chester County, Pennsylvania, 1750–1820," *Pennsylvania Magazine of History and Biography* 114 (April 1990): 163–99; Joan M. Jensen, *Loosening the Bonds: Mid-Atlantic Farm Women, 1750–1850* (New Haven: Yale University Press, 1986); Peter O. Wacker and Paul G. E. Clemens, *Land Use in Early New Jersey: A Historical Geography* (Newark: New Jersey Historical Society, 1995).

urban workers in southern cities.[32] Since 1985 a number of scholars have turned their attention to the economies of South Carolina and Georgia, beginning, as did historians of the Chesapeake, with studies of the staple crops of indigo and rice, international trade, land distribution, and the development of a plantation economy. A good sampling of this recent work appears in *Money, Trade, and Power: The Evolution of Colonial South Carolina's Plantation Society*, as well as in this volume,[33] and a number of new studies deal with the predominantly black labor force of the lower South.[34]

Scholars have also created more precise data on wage rates, poring over thousands of pages of account books for New England, the middle colonies, and the upper South. As a result, it is now possible to identify periods of increasing or decreasing labor productivity in agriculture in the late colonial and early national years, and some progress has been made in identifying gender and age differentials, changes in levels of workforce participation among women, and duration of employment in agriculture among men.[35]

32. Christine Daniels, "Alternative Workers in a Slave Economy: Kent County, Maryland, 1675–1810," (Ph.D. diss., Johns Hopkins University, 1990); see also the following articles by Christine Daniels: "'Wanted: A Blacksmith who understands Plantation Work': Artisans in Maryland, 1700–1800," *William and Mary Quarterly*, 3d ser., 50 (October 1993): 743–67; "Gresham's Laws: Labor Management on an Early-Eighteenth-Century Chesapeake Plantation," *Journal of Southern History* 62 (May 1996): 205–38; "'Getting his [or her] Livelihood': Free Workers in Slave Anglo-America, 1675–1810," *Agricultural History* 71 (Spring 1997): 125–62; and Jean B. Russo, "Self-sufficiency and Local Exchange: Free Craftsmen in the Rural Chesapeake Economy," in *Colonial Chesapeake Society*, ed. Lois Green Carr, Philip D. Morgan, and Jean B. Russo (Chapel Hill: University of North Carolina Press, 1988), 389–432; Jean B. Russo, *Free Workers in a Plantation Economy: Talbot County, Maryland, 1690–1759* (New York: Garland, 1989); Tina H. Sheller, "Freemen, Servants, and Slaves: Artisans and the Craft Structure of Revolutionary Baltimore Town," in *American Artisans: Crafting Social Identity, 1750–1850*, ed. Howard B. Rock, Paul A. Gilje, and Robert Asher (Baltimore: Johns Hopkins University Press, 1995), 17–32; T. Stephen Whitman, *The Price of Freedom: Slavery and Manumission in Baltimore and Early National Maryland* (Lexington: University Press of Kentucky, 1997); Christopher Phillips, *Freedom's Port: The African American Community of Baltimore, 1790–1860* (Urbana: University of Illinois Press, 1997); Seth Rockman, "Laboring Under the Market Revolution: Wage-Workers in Baltimore, 1790–1820," (Ph.D. diss., University of California, Davis, 1999).

33. Greene et al., *Money, Trade, and Power*. See also R. C. Nash, "South Carolina and the Atlantic Economy in the Late Seventeenth and Eighteenth Centuries," *Economic History Review* 45 (November 1992): 677–702.

34. Betty Wood, *Women's Work, Men's Work: The Informal Slave Economies of Lowcountry Georgia* (Athens: University of Georgia Press, 1995); Robert Olwell, *Masters, Slaves, and Subjects: The Culture of Power in the South Carolina Low Country, 1740–1790* (Ithaca: Cornell University Press, 1998); Judith A. Carney, *Black Rice: The African Origins of Rice Cultivation in the Americas* (Cambridge: Harvard University Press, 2001).

35. Donald R. Adams Jr., "Prices and Wages in Maryland, 1750–1850," *Journal of Economic History* 46 (September 1986): 625–45; Wacker and Clemens, *Land Use in Early New Jersey;* Daniels, "'Getting his [or her] Livelihood'"; Gloria L. Main, "Gender, Work, and Wages in Colonial New England," *William and Mary Quarterly*, 3d ser., 51 (January 1994): 39–66; Winifred B. Rothenberg, "The Emergence of Farm Labor Markets and the Transformation of the Rural Economy: Massachusetts, 1750–1855," *Journal of Economic History* 48 (September 1988): 537–66; Winifred B. Rothenberg, *From Market-Places to a Market Economy: The Transformation of Rural Massachusetts, 1750–1850* (Chicago: University of Chicago Press, 1992); Smith, *"Lower Sort."* Output per worker, an alternative measure of labor

Allocation of tasks by gender has also received considerable attention. Varied approaches have added significantly to our understanding of women's work within the household and to a lesser extent in the wage and market economies. Changes in local economies during and after the Revolution, which appear to have enticed or forced more free women into wage work in New England and the middle colonies, curtailed the kinds of work available to women in the upper South. Few women, and especially few rural women, worked primarily for wages, however, and although rural women's production of goods for market undoubtedly increased in the eighteenth century, the volume and value of such labor continue to elude any systematic measurement.[36] McCusker and Menard concluded that "modern notions of the labor force or of the participation rate—the share of the population in the work force—cannot be applied usefully to the colonial economy." This is especially true for free women, and so long as the measurements most economists use exclude women's domestic work from the "domestic economy," the chances of integrating women's work into broader economic history remain slim.[37]

Until quite recently little new research was done on child labor. This is in part because of the continued scarcity of good evidence about children's work roles as either family, wage, or bound laborers, and in part because the proportion of children among unfree migrants has usually been considered quite low and thus of little importance. Concentration on adult males, the majority among all migrant groups, and on servants who arrived with indentures has long tended to obscure the extent to which immigrant child workers were employed in colonial British America. On lists of indentured servants leaving England in the seventeenth and early eighteenth centuries, for example, males and females under age fifteen are usually no more than 3 to 7 percent. These, however, were servants who had obtained written indentures in England before embarking for the New World, and they were a minority by no means representative of all migrating servants. In the seventeenth century many more left Britain without indentures and served according to the less advantageous customs of the colony in which their labor was eventually sold. Among servants without indentures

productivity, is used in Lorena S. Walsh, "Slave Life, Slave Society, and Tobacco Production in the Tidewater Chesapeake, 1620–1820," in *Cultivation and Culture: Labor and the Shaping of Slave Life in the Americas,* ed. Ira Berlin and Philip D. Morgan (Charlottesville: University Press of Virginia, 1993), 170–99.

36. Kathleen M. Brown, *Good Wives, Nasty Wenches, and Anxious Patriarchs: Gender, Race, and Power in Colonial Virginia* (Chapel Hill: University of North Carolina Press, 1996); Judith Carney, "Rice Milling, Gender, and Slave Labour in Colonial South Carolina," *Past and Present* 153 (November 1996): 108–34; Main, "Gender, Work, and Wages"; Daniels, "'Getting his [or her] Livelihood.'"

37. McCusker and Menard, *Economy of British America,* 237. Carole Shammas, "Defining and Measuring Output and the Workforce in Early America," paper presented at a conference on "The Economy of Early British America: The Domestic Sector, 1995" California Institute of Technology, Huntington Library, San Marino, California, October 27–29, 1995; Nancy Folbre and Barnet Wagman, "Counting Housework: New Estimates of Real Product in the United States, 1800–1860," *Journal of Economic History* 53 (June 1993): 275–88.

coming to the Chesapeake, a range of between 15 to 20 percent below age fifteen seems likely throughout the seventeenth century.[38]

By the early eighteenth century the transportation of European child laborers was largely abandoned. But enslaved Africans brought to the Chesapeake included a higher proportion of children than is commonly supposed, and this proportion grew steadily. Between a fifth and a quarter of the new Africans for whom sale records survive were youths.[39] In addition to immigrant African and European children, native-born youths, especially orphaned and illegitimate children and children of mixed race, were also part of the bound child workforce. Their neglect is now being remedied. The publication of John E. Murray and Ruth Wallis Herndon's "Markets for Children in Early America: A Political Economy for Pauper Apprenticeship," was quickly followed up with a conference organized by Murray and Herndon on children bound to labor in early America. A planned conference volume will address issues of bound child labor throughout North America in the eighteenth and early nineteenth centuries.[40] This research is supplemented by a number of additional works on the apprenticing of black children during the long transition from slavery to freedom in New England and the middle colonies.[41] Research into the economics of British American slavery has now culminated in an outpouring of significant new publications in which labor has an equal or more prominent role than the more traditional issues of master-slave relationships and the evolution of slave codes. (Demographics also have a prominent explanatory role in much of this work, but, as noted above, most of the measures employed are far from new.) Two essay collections edited by Ira Berlin and Philip Morgan, as well as their individual monographs, are the most comprehensive.[42]

38. Walsh, "Differential Cultural Impact of Free and Coerced Migration"; James Horn, "Tobacco Colonies: The Shaping of English Society in the Seventeenth-Century Chesapeake," in *The Origins of Empire: British Overseas Enterprise to the Close of the Seventeenth Century,* vol. 1 of *The Oxford History of the British Empire,* ed. Nicholas Canny (New York: Oxford University Press, 1998), 177–78.

39. Douglas Brent Chambers, "'He Gwine Sing He Country': Africans, Afro-Virginians, and the Development of Slave Culture in Virginia, 1690–1810," (Ph.D. diss., University of Virginia, 1996), chapter 4; Douglas Brent Chambers, "The Transatlantic Slave Trade to Virginia in Comparative Historical Perspective, 1698–1778," in *Afro-Virginian History and Culture,* ed. John Saillant (New York: Garland, 1999), 3–28; Morgan and Nicholls, "Slaves in Piedmont Virginia"; Walsh, "Differential Cultural Impact of Free and Coerced Migration."

40. John E. Murray and Ruth Wallis Herndon, "Markets for Children in Early America: A Political Economy for Pauper Apprenticeship," *Journal of Economic History* 62 (June 2002): 356–82; and, by the same authors, "'Proper and Instructive Education': Children Bound to Labor in Early America," paper given at a conference at the University of Pennsylvania, sponsored by the McNeil Center for Early American Studies, November 1–2, 2002.

41. For example, Gary B. Nash and Jean R. Soderlund, *Freedom by Degrees: Emancipation in Pennsylvania and Its Aftermath* (New York: Oxford University Press, 1991); and Joanne Pope Melish, *Disowning Slavery: Gradual Emancipation and "Race" in New England, 1780–1860* (Ithaca: Cornell University Press, 1998).

42. Ira Berlin and Philip D. Morgan, eds., *The Slaves' Economy: Independent Production by Slaves in the Americas* (London: Frank Cass, 1991); Berlin and Morgan, *Cultivation and Culture;* Morgan,

The task now remaining is to put all the parts together and to analyze afresh the interactions of demand for and supplies of various kinds of labor in British America. Direct comparisons of coerced and free migrations are beginning to yield important insights. For example, all studies of slavery in the Americas have put great emphasis on the deleterious consequences of unbalanced sex ratios among the enslaved. But David Eltis and Stanley Engerman have shown that the sexual imbalance among enslaved migrants was in fact significantly smaller than that among indentured Europeans, and similar to or smaller than the imbalance among free migrants. Had all been equal, forced African migrants should have stood greater chances than Europeans of marrying, having children, and reproducing Old World cultures. That this was not the outcome suggests that even greater emphasis should be placed on the inhibiting effects of slave regimes on biological and cultural reproduction. Absence of freedom rather than relative scarcity of women made the crucial difference.[43]

Integrating the history of all migration streams may also help researchers see more of the dark underside of the peopling of the Americas and to revise the emphasis on freedom and opportunity that now tends to dominate the story. The more intellectually dynamic field of forced African migration provides us with a few starting points. For example, in *The Rise of African Slavery in the Americas,* David Eltis has begun to explore how both cultural preconceptions and differing conceptions of identity among Africans and Europeans determined what sorts of peoples moved freely or were forcibly moved. James Horn and Philip D. Morgan, in "Settlers and Slaves: European and African Migrations to Early Modern British America," compare the migration experiences of Europeans and Africans destined for the North American colonies. *The British Atlantic World, 1500–1800,* edited by David Armitage and Michael J. Braddick, includes essays on migration and economic development that analyze these issues from a transatlantic perspective. More comparative work on migration flows within the Portuguese, Spanish, French, and Dutch overseas empires, as well as the British, should enlarge our understanding of both generally shared patterns and critical differences.[44]

Slave Counterpoint: Black Culture in the Eighteenth-Century Chesapeake and Lowcountry (Chapel Hill: University of North Carolina Press, 1998); and Berlin, *Many Thousands Gone,* the notes of which are an excellent guide to additional recent, more localized studies too numerous to mention here. In *Generations of Captivity: A History of African-American Slaves* (Cambridge: Harvard University Press, 2003), Berlin summarizes the interpretation he presented in *Many Thousands Gone,* revising some of the points that were criticized in the original but not altering his basic arguments. David Eltis, Frank D. Lewis, and Kenneth L. Sokoloff, eds., *Slavery in the Development of the Americas* (Cambridge: Cambridge University Press, 2004) presents more recent work of economic historians on slave systems in the Americas.

43. David Eltis and Stanley L. Engerman, "Was the Slave Trade Dominated by Men?" *Journal of Interdisciplinary History* 23 (Autumn 1992): 237–57; Eltis and Engerman, "Fluctuations in Sex and Age Ratios"; Walsh, "Differential Cultural Impact of Free and Coerced Migration."

44. Eltis, *Rise of African Slavery;* James Horn and Philip D. Morgan, "Settlers and Slaves: European and African Migrations to Early Modern British America," in *The Creation of the British*

David Eltis's recent edited volume treats early modern migrations in a global context, asking, "What did the fact that most early modern transatlantic migrations were unfree mean for the patterns and character of the migration, for migration's impact on societies at either end of the migrant route, and perhaps also for conceptions of freedom?" It explores as well the similarities and differences between transatlantic and contemporaneous transcontinental coerced migrations of Europeans eastward and the role of identity in first facilitating and then ending forms of coerced migration. In *The History of Human Populations,* a significant work summarizing decades of research and analysis, P. M. G. Harris delineates recurring patterns in the growth of populations throughout the world. Most pertinent to the issues considered here, volume 2 of this work teases out similar recurring patterns in the timing, volume, and character of migration flows and relates them to the pace of economic growth or decline in sending and receiving areas. Previous estimates of European emigration to the British American colonies are rigorously scrutinized, and revisions, especially for eighteenth-century British emigration, presented.[45]

Most of us, however, tend to think in less than global terms. For British America, the transatlantic slave trade database (and the additions now under way) supply figures on annual imports of Africans to individual colonies, and also additional information on the prices of new slaves. In combination with the materials surveyed above on European migration, and with respectable price series for sugar, tobacco, rice, and indigo already at hand, scholars now have a grand opportunity to test the explanatory power of alternative models about demand for and changes in supply of labor about which they could previously do little more than speculate. For example, did the supply of slaves as well as of European servants mirror cycles in staple prices? What factors influenced marked shifts in the annual supply of slaves between the various West Indian islands, the Chesapeake, and South Carolina? What was the effect of international wars on labor supply?[46]

Atlantic World, ed. Elizabeth Mancke and Carole Shammas (Baltimore: Johns Hopkins University Press, 2005); David Armitage and Michael J. Braddick, eds., *The British Atlantic World, 1500–1800* (London: Palgrave Macmillan, 2002). Christine Daniels and Michael V. Kennedy, eds., *Negotiated Empires: Centers and Peripheries in the Americas, 1500–1820* (New York: Routledge, 2002) presents comparative work on the development of the Spanish, Portuguese, French, and Dutch as well as of British colonial empires.

45. Eltis, *Coerced and Free Migration,* especially Eltis, "Introduction: Migration and Agency in Global History," and "Free and Coerced Migrations from the Old World to the New," 1–32 and 33–74, respectively. See also P. M. G. Harris, *The History of Human Populations,* vol. 1, *Forms of Growth and Decline* (Westport, Conn.: Praeger, 2001), and vol. 2, *Migration, Urbanization, and Structural Change* (Westport, Conn.: Praeger, 2003).

46. For tobacco prices, see McCusker and Menard, *Economy of British America,* and Lorena S. Walsh, "Summing the Parts: Implications for Estimating Chesapeake Output and Income Subregionally," *William and Mary Quarterly,* 3d ser., 56 (January 1999): 53–94. Sugar prices can be found in John J. McCusker, *Rum and the American Revolution: The Rum Trade and the Balance of Payments of the Thirteen Continental Colonies* (New York: Garland, 1989), 1143. For rice and indigo prices, see Peter A.

The expanded evidence on the slave trade also needs to be compared with the supply of European bound labor. It is often supposed, for example, that the transition from temporarily bound to enslaved labor in the Chesapeake was basically complete by the early years of the eighteenth century. Yet Ekirch estimates that about forty thousand convicts were shipped to the Chesapeake between 1718 and 1775. This estimate is fully half of the eighty thousand blacks who can be documented or inferred from shipping records to have been imported during these years, and even when slave imports are adjusted upward for missing records, the proportion of convicts is unlikely to drop below 40 percent, with smaller numbers of indentured servants still to be accounted for. Servants and slaves thus continued to represent viable alternative forms of labor in this region across the eighteenth century. Who was choosing which form, and why?[47]

Analysis of prices alone will go a long way toward providing answers, but additional research is also needed on mercantile and credit networks. Highly specialized international trade and credit networks connected particular British, continental European, African, and colonial ports, and organized the transportation of willing and unwilling migrants in highly patterned flows. Credit, whether extended directly to purchasing planters or indirectly in the form of security to local agents who sold slaves on behalf of European merchants, forged invisible connections between ostensibly separate trades. Varying terms on which imported bound labor was offered, ranging from immediate payment in bills of exchange or specie at one extreme, to promises to pay in some staple product at a future date, at the other, surely influenced who could and would buy slaves and servants. Such mercantile and credit networks are best studied, at least initially, at the level of individual agents and individual localities, carefully placed in the context of transatlantic trade and migration.[48]

Coclanis, *The Shadow of a Dream: Economic Life and Death in the South Carolina Low Country, 1670–1920* (New York: Oxford University Press, 1989), 106–7; and Nash, "South Carolina and the Atlantic Economy." For new African slave prices, see David Eltis and David Richardson, "Prices of African Slaves Newly Arrived in the Americas, 1673–1865: New Evidence on Long-Run Trends and Regional Differentials," in Eltis et al., *Slavery in the Development of the Americas*, 181–218.

47. Ekirch, *Bound for America*, 115–16. Chesapeake slave imports were compiled from the databases described in Walsh, "Chesapeake Slave Trade."

48. Jacob M. Price, "Credit in the Slave Trade and Plantation Economies," in *Slavery and the Rise of the Atlantic System,* ed. Barbara L. Solow (New York: Cambridge University Press, 1991), 293–339; Walsh, "Mercantile Strategies, Credit Networks, and Labor Supply"; David Hancock, *Citizens of the World: London Merchants and the Integration of the British Atlantic Community, 1735–1785* (New York: Cambridge University Press, 1995). See also David Hancock, "'A World of Business to Do,': William Freeman and the Foundations of England's Commercial Empire, 1645–1707," *William and Mary Quarterly,* 3d ser., 57 (January 2000): 3–34; and Kenneth Morgan, "Business Networks in the British Export Trade to North America, 1750–1800, in *The Early Modern Atlantic Economy,* ed. John J. McCusker and Kenneth Morgan (New York: Cambridge University Press, 2000), 36–62.

Finally, as McCusker and Menard noted, economic models that have "to ignore the existing stocks of labor and deal only with the flow of new workers entering the labor force" have decided limitations. For example, the natural increase of the enslaved population in parts of the Chesapeake Tidewater was sufficient by the mid-1740s to reduce demand for new Africans to a mere trickle. The primary way established planters acquired slaves shifted dramatically from purchase of new Africans to inheritance or to acquisition of creole slaves by a variety of means. Small and middling planters became slave owners or slave users either by buying seasoned or native-born slaves locally or by hiring rather than buying surplus bondspeople from others. Here, as in areas where family labor was the predominant form, the literature of economics continues to offer "only limited guidance."[49]

Patterns of consumption and demand are closely related to issues of demography and migration and have attracted considerable interest in the past fifteen years, not just from social historians but also from architectural historians, art historians, archaeologists, and museum curators. Cary Carson, in a book-length essay entitled "The Consumer Revolution in Colonial British America: Why Demand?" that appeared in a volume he co-edited with Ronald Hoffman and Peter Albert, argues that the answer lies in changed ways of thinking in the first half of the eighteenth century "that deployed personal possessions in support of social hierarchies built not upon precedence but on manners." In a world increasingly in motion, upper-class northern Europeans needed "standardized architectural spaces equipped with fashionable furnishings," which "became universally recognized settings for social performances that were governed by internationally accepted rules of etiquette." Social relationships came to require the intercession of household goods and personal possessions, leading to "a demand-driven consumer revolution" in the late seventeenth century that subsequently required "power-driven industrialization" to supply it. Other essays in the volume survey rising colonial demand from multiple angles, as measured by probate inventories and tax lists, surveys of surviving household furnishings, houses, and works of art, and studies of retailing, reading, and leisure. Bushman advances a similar argument about the instrumental role of gentility in reshaping the material lives of the upper middle classes, and the adoption of some of its components by a majority of the population. Extending the story later into the middle of the nineteenth century, Bushman argues that it was the interaction of gentility with domesticity and religion, the capture of aristocratic culture for use in republican society, that produced "a dilute gentility associated with respectability," which "turned [the vast middle of] producers into consumers." More recently John E. Crowley has added physical comfort to the list of evolving rationales

49. McCusker and Menard, *Economy of British America*, 240, 246.

that prompted redefinition of what constituted "necessities" and "luxuries" and hence encouraged rising levels of consumption.[50]

These are sweeping, sophisticated arguments to which it is impossible to do justice in summary form, as are the recently published results of a number of long-term, large-scale quantitative studies on the nature and distribution of consumer durables, quality of housing, and diet.[51] Material culture has emerged as a dynamic field that encourages lively interdisciplinary dialogue between economic and social historians, historians of technology, architecture, art, and sport, historical archaeologists, anthropologists, and museum curators.[52] The dialogue across disciplines has encouraged interdisciplinary research into other aspects of welfare, including height as a measure of net nutrition, health through analysis of human remains, and rural and urban food-provisioning systems approached

50. Cary Carson, "The Consumer Revolution in Colonial British America: Why Demand?" in *Of Consuming Interests: The Style of Life in the Eighteenth Century*, ed. Cary Carson, Ronald Hoffman, and Peter J. Albert (Charlottesville: University Press of Virginia, 1994), 483–697, quotations at 487, 523, 558. See also Richard L. Bushman, *The Refinement of America: Persons, Houses, Cities* (New York: Knopf, 1992), xv, xvii–xviii; John E. Crowley, "The Sensibility of Comfort," *American Historical Review* 104 (June 1999): 749–82.

51. On consumer durables, see chapters by Kevin M. Sweeney, Lois Green Carr and Lorena S. Walsh, and T. H. Breen, in Carson, Hoffman, and Albert, *Of Consuming Interests;* Carole Shammas, *The Pre-Industrial Consumer in England and America* (New York: Oxford University Press, 1990); Carole Shammas, "Changes in English and Anglo-American Consumption from 1550 to 1800," in *Consumption and the World of Goods,* ed. John Brewer and Roy Porter (London: Routledge, 1993), 177–205; and "Forum: Toward A History of the Standard of Living in British North America," *William and Mary Quarterly,* 3d ser., 45 (January 1988): 116–70. Recent works that include new research on consumer durables include Shammas's article, just cited; Deborah A. Rosen, *Courts and Commerce: Gender, Law and the Market Economy in Colonial New York* (Columbus: Ohio State University Press, 1997); and Gloria L. Main, *Peoples of a Spacious Land: Families and Cultures in Colonial New England* (Cambridge: Harvard University Press, 2001). For housing stock see the chapter by Edward A. Chappell in Carson, Hoffman, and Albert, *Of Consuming Interests;* Lee Soltow, *The Distribution of Wealth and Income in the United States in 1798* (Pittsburgh: University of Pittsburgh Press, 1989); and Carole Shammas, "The Space Problem in Early United States Cities," *William and Mary Quarterly,* 3d ser., 57 (July 2000): 505–42, which reports on a portion of a long-term research project on housing in the early Republic. For diet, see the following articles by Sarah F. McMahon: "A Comfortable Subsistence: The Changing Composition of Diet in Rural New England, 1620–1840," *William and Mary Quarterly,* 3d ser., 42 (January 1985), 26–65; "'All Things in Their Proper Season': Seasonal Rhythms of Diet in Nineteenth-Century New England," *Agricultural History* 63 (Spring 1989): 130–51; and "Laying Foods By: Gender, Dietary Decisions and Technology of Food Preservation," in *Early American Technology: Making and Doing Things from the Colonial Era to 1850,* ed. Judith A. McGaw (Chapel Hill: University of North Carolina Press, 1994); Joanne V. Bowen, "A Study of Seasonality and Subsistence: Eighteenth-Century Suffield, Connecticut" (Ph.D. diss., Brown University, 1990); Henry M. Miller, "An Archaeological Perspective on the Evolution of Diet in the Colonial Chesapeake, 1620–1745," in Carr, Morgan, and Russo, *Colonial Chesapeake Society,* 176–99.

52. In 1996 material culture studies were recognized in a special issue of the *William and Mary Quarterly.* Ann Smart Martin, "Material Things and Cultural Meanings: Notes on the Study of Early American Material Culture," *William and Mary Quarterly* 53 (January 1996); and Ann Smart Martin and J. Ritchie Garrison, eds., *American Material Culture: The Shape of the Field* (Winterthur, Del.: Henry Francis du Pont Winterthur Museum; Knoxville, Tenn., 1996) provide overviews of the state of the field. A technologically oriented approach is McGaw, *Early American Technology.*

from a combination of archaeological and documentary evidence.[53] As a result, we have a much greater understanding, both qualitative and quantitative, not just of lifestyles but of living standards among varying wealth groups throughout most of British America. Thanks in part to McCusker and Menard's volume, most students of material culture recognize that issues of economic choice, process, and constraints are as critical to analysis as are cultural dimensions. And economists are beginning to acknowledge that it is time to include demand and consumption among the variables in analyses of economic growth and development. Carole Shammas's studies of rising demand for imported groceries and David Hancock's and John McCusker's work on the burgeoning international trades in wine and distilled spirits are good examples.[54]

Despite these encouraging trends and substantive achievements, however, a number of the issues have simply failed to capture the hearts and minds of many historians of early America. Probably few would disagree in theory, for example, with McCusker's call to "think more systematically about how to gauge the performance of the economy of the United States of America during its colonial period." But in practice, despite McCusker's enthusiastic prodding, and even despite burgeoning interest in transatlantic interconnections, developing estimates of historical gross domestic product (GDP) is just not a high priority on most scholars' research agendas. Although there are recurring criticisms of its applicability to developing economies, GDP remains the most commonly

53. Studies of height are surveyed in Richard H. Steckel, "Nutritional Status in the Colonial American Economy," *William and Mary Quarterly*, 3d ser., 56 (January 1999): 31–52. The results of a major interdisciplinary collaborative project "A History of Health and Nutrition in the Western Hemisphere," nine years in the making, is reported in Richard H. Steckel, ed., *The Backbone of History* (New York: Cambridge University Press, 2002). A preliminary report on the urban provisioning project is Lorena S. Walsh, "Provisioning Tidewater Towns," *Explorations in Early American Culture* 4 (2000): 46–80.

54. Robert E. Gallman and John J. Wallis, eds., *American Economic Growth and Standards of Living Before the Civil War* (Chicago: University of Chicago Press, 1992), reflected this new awareness by including chapters on consumer behavior and diet and on stature and living standards, in addition to the more traditional topics of labor force size, capital stock, wealth distribution, wages and prices, market integration, and productivity growth. Lois Green Carr, "Emigration and the Standard of Living: The Eighteenth-Century Chesapeake," in McCusker and Morgan, *Early Modern Atlantic Economy*, 319–43, pulls together a number of these issues. Economists are now also recognizing that they need to pay attention to consumption by both the rich and the poor when assessing trends in inequality of income or wealth. The purchasing power of different income classes changes with shifts in relative prices of luxury goods and staple food and fuels, and these need to be taken into account in measurements of "real inequality." See, for example, Philip T. Hoffman, David Jacks, Patricia A. Levin, and Peter H. Lindert, "Prices and Real Inequality in Europe Since 1500," paper presented at the Washington Area Economic History Seminar, September 2000. Studies of increased consumption of consumer perishables include Carole Shammas, "The Revolutionary Impact of European Demand for Tropical Goods"; John J. McCusker, "The Business of Distilling in the Old World and the New World During the Seventeenth and Eighteenth Centuries: The Rise of a New Enterprise and Its Connection with Colonial America"; and David Hancock, "'A Revolution in the Trade': Wine Distribution and the Development of the Infrastructure of the Atlantic Market Economy, 1703–1807," all three in McCusker and Morgan, *Early Modern Atlantic Economy*, 163–85, 186–224, and 105–53, respectively.

used measure of the economic performance of nation-states today. Historians of earlier periods are constantly challenged to answer the question: How well was the colonial American economy performing? As Davis and Engerman, two economic historians sympathetic to the endeavor, concluded, "the time is not right, many never be right, to meet . . . [this] challenge."[55] Unresolved theoretical and technical problems that raise well-founded doubts about whether payoffs would justify the strenuous efforts required, and widespread reluctance to enter into long-term, collaborative efforts that could well fizzle out, explain part of the failure to answer this and other calls. So too does justifiable impatience with the testing of models that force us to discard what appear to be the most interesting, but apparently nonquantifiable, variables. Less justifiably, but understandably, given human nature, is the simple unwillingness to think as big and to toil as hard in the vineyards of a statistical dark age as McCusker and Menard have.

McCusker and Menard trod the landscape of British colonial America wearing Brobdingnagian boots. Many of their readers, for better or worse, have remained content to recast their volume's carefully crafted but often tentative syntheses of the state of the art in 1985 into far more concrete and enduring generalizations than the authors ever intended. Doubtless, since then, they have experienced alternating moments of gratification and bouts of aggrieved frustration over their readers' failure to heed their call or to follow only in Lilliputian footgear. Davis and Engerman subtitled their essay in the *William and Mary Quarterly* special issue on the economy of British North America "Miles Traveled, Miles Still to Go." Scholars of my generation applaud McCusker and Menard for personally traversing so many of those miles, acknowledge the continuing inspiration of fellow travelers, now departed, who shared in that journey, and still hope in some measure to live up to their high expectations, or at the least to persuade younger scholars to roll up their sleeves and get on with the important tasks remaining.

55. McCusker, "Measuring Colonial Gross Domestic Product," 3; Davis and Engerman, "Economy of British North America," 9. An exception is Stanley L. Engerman, "France, Britain and the Economic Growth of Colonial North America," in McCusker and Morgan, *Early Modern Atlantic Economy*, 227–49.

Chapter Five

Indentured Servitude in Perspective: European Migration into North America and the Composition of the Early American Labor Force, 1600–1775

CHRISTOPHER TOMLINS

The history of European migration to early mainland America, and particularly of the recruitment and deployment of European labor, has been dominated by the phenomenon of indentured servitude. David Galenson, long a leading scholar in the field, has designated the practice "an important early solution to the labor problem in many parts of English America" that was "widely adopted," becoming "a central institution in the economy and society of many parts of colonial British America." In the southern colonies, Jacqueline Jones argues, indentured servitude furnished "the bulk of labor until slavery began to predominate."[1] Such observations have led

I would like to thank Cathy Matson, Douglas Deal, Farley Grubb, and the members of the Washington Area Economic History seminar for their comments on earlier drafts of this essay, and Carole Shammas and Kevin Kelly for permission to use their unpublished work. This essay is a revised and updated version of "Reconsidering Indentured Servitude: European Migration and the Early American Labor Force, 1600–1775," *Labor History* 42 (February 2001): 5–44. It is accompanied by one research appendix, here revised and updated, that originally appeared with that article. Three other (unrevised) research appendices could not be included with this essay for reasons of space. They can be found accompanying "Reconsidering Indentured Servitude" and are cited as such in the notes to this essay.

1. David W. Galenson, "The Settlement and Growth of the Colonies: Population, Labor, and Economic Development," in *The Cambridge Economic History of the United States,* 3 vols., ed. Stanley L. Engerman and Robert E. Gallman (New York: Cambridge University Press, 1996), 1:158; David W. Galenson, "The Rise and Fall of Indentured Servitude in the Americas: An Economic Analysis," *Journal of Economic History* 44 (March 1984): 1; Jacqueline Jones, *American Work: Four Centuries of Black and White Labor* (New York: W. W. Norton, 1998), 31. Aaron Fogleman's is the most recent general statement: "For the first two centuries of the history of British North America, one word best characterizes the status of the vast majority of immigrants—servitude." Aaron S. Fogleman, "From Slaves, Convicts, and Servants to Free Passengers: The Transformation of Immigration in the Era of the American Revolution," *Journal of American History* 85 (June 1998): 43. The linkage of servitude to immigration accurately reflects social reality, for there is little evidence that servitude

scholars to conclude that only in the revolutionary era does one begin to encounter anything other than a predominantly unfree workforce. The transition to a largely free workforce during the early Republic thus stands as a major vindication of the revolutionary era's discourse of egalitarianism, and powerfully signifies republican America's self-differentiation from the old regime.[2]

Analysis of the available evidence suggests, however, that other conclusions are at least as plausible. This essay offers an intensive examination of migration to the three regions of mainland North America that received the vast majority of English and other European migrants during the seventeenth and eighteenth centuries—New England, the Chesapeake, and the Delaware Valley. My goal is to refine our understanding of just how prevalent migrant indentured servitude was during the colonial era.[3] Through decade-by-decade estimates of servant incidence in migrant population, servant mortality and contract length measures, and overall population growth, I conclude that the incidence of migrant servitude in the early American population and labor force was substantially lower than scholars have assumed. Though an important source of labor power, migrant indentured servitude was rather less significant in establishing a foundational character for labor in the colonial era than we have thought.

To help explain the structure of migration and the composition of the working population that emerged in early America, I propose that we refract colonial demand for labor through the cultures of work centered on the household that prevailed on both sides of the Atlantic. The reason is simple. Household production furnished the organizational backbone for the performance of work throughout much of the mainland both before and after the Revolution. This continuity, however, suggests that the American political economy's overall trajectory toward a "free" workforce (market-driven allocation of individual capacities to labor through wage contracts) in the late eighteenth and nineteenth centuries is rather more complicated than existing historiography supposes.[4]

---

as such was a significant condition of working life among the non-African native-born. Bound labor certainly existed among white Creoles—apprenticeship, pauper servitude, debt servitude, compensatory servitude by those convicted of crimes—but, apart from apprenticeship, formal binding was incidental in Creole work relations. See, for example, Farley W. Grubb, "Immigration and Servitude in the Colony and Commonwealth of Pennsylvania: A Quantitative and Economic Analysis" (Ph.D. diss., University of Chicago, 1984), 163–65.

2. For Fogleman, the American Revolution was a transformative event in the history of freedom in North America. "Slaves, Convicts, and Servants," 45, 65–66. David Montgomery also sees the half-century after the Revolution as one of decisive repudiation of "traditional" social hierarchies, affirming "the durable legacy of egalitarian practice" left by the Revolution. See his *Citizen Worker: The Experience of Workers in the United States with Democracy and the Free Market During the Nineteenth Century* (New York: Cambridge University Press, 1993), 5, 13–51.

3. Migration to the British West Indies does not feature in this analysis.

4. I canvass the issue in Christopher Tomlins, "Why Wait for Industrialism? Work, Legal Culture, and the Example of Early America—An Historiographical Argument," and "Not Just Another Brick in the Wall: A Response to Rock, Nelson, and Montgomery," *Labor History* 40, no. 1 (1999): 5–34

The legal-transactional basis of early American indentured servitude was a written agreement committing one party to make a series of payments benefiting the other—settlement of transport debt, provision of subsistence over the (negotiable) contractual term, a one-time payment in kind, or, less commonly, cash at the conclusion of the term—in exchange for which the beneficiary agreed to be completely at the disposal of the payer, or the payer's assigns, for performance of work, during the negotiated term.[5] All aspects of the transaction were secured by law.[6]

Immigrant Europeans working under indenture can be found in all regions of mainland North America during the seventeenth and eighteenth (and well into the nineteenth) centuries.[7] As a decisive contributor to labor supply,

---

and 45–52. Chris Tilly and Charles Tilly have recently emphasized the crucial importance of recognizing how a range of differentiated relational settings supply meanings for work as social action. Free labor markets "embody an unusual, historically specific organization of work." Chris Tilly and Charles Tilly, *Work Under Capitalism* (Boulder: Westview Press, 1998).

5. During the seventeenth century, commercial migrant servitude was founded on deeds of indenture that committed migrants to labor for a negotiated period on terms agreed with a shipper prior to embarking. The shipper would recover transportation costs and margin by selling the servant's indenture on arrival. Costs of migrants who neither paid their own passage nor negotiated indentures prior to departure would be recovered from planters who retained the servants on standard terms and conditions of servitude ("the custom of the country") prescribed in local legislation and administered through the courts. These proceedings largely involved children (on which see below, this essay, and Tomlins, "Reconsidering Indentured Servitude," 41–43 (appendix 4, servants' ages).

During the eighteenth century, a variation on seventeenth-century practice developed in the Delaware Valley labor market in which the migrant did not commit to a future service agreement prior to embarking but instead indemnified the shipper by agreeing to enter a service contract on terms sufficient to liquidate the transportation debt within a specified period after arrival, should other means to satisfy the debt (such as advances or gifts from family, friends, or former neighbors) fail to materialize. This so-called "redemptioner" system, which might also be viewed as a variation on debt servitude, dates from the 1720s and was dominant in the migrant servant trade by the 1750s. See David W. Galenson, *White Servitude in Colonial America: An Economic Analysis* (New York: Cambridge University Press, 1981), 3–4; Farley Grubb, "The Auction of Redemptioner Servants, Philadelphia, 1771–1804: An Economic Analysis," *Journal of Economic History* 47 (September 1988): 583–602; Robert J. Steinfeld, *The Invention of Free Labor: The Employment Relation in English and American Law and Culture, 1350–1870* (Chapel Hill: University of North Carolina Press, 1991), 198; Aaron S. Fogleman, *Hopeful Journeys: German Immigration, Settlement, and Political Culture in Colonial America, 1717–1775* (Philadelphia: University of Pennsylvania Press, 1996), 73–79; Georg Fertig, "Eighteenth-Century Transatlantic Migration and Early German Anti-Migration Ideology," in *Migration, Migration History, History: Old Paradigms and New Perspectives*, ed. Jan Lucassen and Leo Lucassen (Bern: Peter Lang, 1997), 271–90. A further innovation appearing in the 1770s was the "indenture of redemption," an assignable prenegotiated agreement to serve that could be voided by the migrant if better terms or unexpected resources were available on arrival. See Farley Grubb, "Labor, Markets, and Opportunity: Indentured Servitude in Early America, a Rejoinder to Salinger," *Labor History* 39, no. 2 (1998): 237n14.

6. On the efficacy of legal oversight, see Christine Daniels, "'Liberty to Complaine': Servant Petitions in Colonial Anglo-America," in *The Many Legalities of Early America*, ed. Christopher Tomlins and Bruce H. Mann (Chapel Hill: University of North Carolina Press, 2001), 219–49.

7. Farley Grubb, "The Disappearance of Organized Markets for European Immigrant Servants in the United States: Five Popular Explanations Reexamined," *Social Science History* 18 (Spring 1994): 1. See also Steinfeld, *Invention of Free Labor*, 122–46.

however, immigrant indentured servitude is primarily associated with two periods of substantial migration into two mainland regions: the Chesapeake (Virginia and Maryland) between 1630 and the early 1700s, and the Delaware Valley (primarily Pennsylvania, Delaware, and New Jersey, but with continuing inflow also to Maryland) between the late 1670s and the early 1770s. Migrant indentured servitude was far less significant in other regions of European settlement. In New England, servant migration was of modest incidence in a population movement that was itself confined primarily to one convulsive spasm between 1630 and 1640. Migration into the Appalachian backcountry was more sustained, but few migrants entered as indentured servants and the institution did not develop any lasting presence.[8]

8. In the case of the eighteenth century's Appalachian backcountry migrant stream, "remarkably few came in bondage." David Hackett Fischer, *Albion's Seed: Four British Folkways in America* (New York: Oxford University Press, 1989), 614. The New England case is more complicated and has stimulated heightened levels of inquiry. Servants were present among the roughly 21,000 migrants who entered Massachusetts Bay during the decade after 1630, but their incidence was much lower than in migrant streams going to other regions of mainland settlement. Scholars' estimates of the numbers of servants in the New England migrant stream have concentrated on the male population, varying in incidence from one in three to one in six of male migrants. Given that roughly 60 percent of migrants were males and (again roughly) that male servants outnumbered female by three to one, this suggests that servants constituted no fewer than 12.5 percent and no more than 25 percent of the Great Migration. Fischer, *Albion's Seed,* 16, 27, 28; Richard Archer, "New England Mosaic: A Demographic Analysis for the Seventeenth Century," *William and Mary Quarterly,* 3d ser., 47 (October 1990): 480, 486–87; Roger Thompson, *Mobility and Migration: East Anglian Founders of New England, 1629–1640* (Amherst: University of Massachusetts Press, 1994), 122–23. Scholars have favored the lower end of this range. Richard S. Dunn argues that 15 percent of migrants to New England in the 1630s were servants. See his "Servants and Slaves: The Recruitment and Employment of Labor," in *Colonial British America: Essays in the New History of the Early Modern Era,* ed. Jack P. Greene and J. R. Pole (Baltimore: Johns Hopkins University Press, 1984), 160. Daniel Vickers concludes that "almost 17 percent" of 1630s migrants were servants. See his *Farmers and Fishermen: Two Centuries of Work in Essex County, Massachusetts, 1630–1850* (Chapel Hill: University of North Carolina Press, 1994), 37. Aaron Fogleman offers "about 16 percent" ("Slaves, Convicts, and Servants," 46). Based on analysis of eleven passenger lists from ships embarking from a variety of English ports in 1635, 1637, and 1638, David Cressy identifies a somewhat higher 20.7 percent of migrants as servants. See his *Coming Over: Migration and Communication Between England and New England in the Seventeenth Century* (New York: Oxford University Press, 1987), 52–53, 66. Based on analysis of embarkations from one port (London) in one year (1635), Alison Games argues for 33.8 percent. See her *Migration and the Origins of the English Atlantic World* (Cambridge: Harvard University Press, 1999), 27–30, 52. Games's figures, however, are biased upward by her concentration on London. Both Thompson and Archer report a very low ratio of servants in total migrants among those migrating from greater East Anglia, who embarked from North Sea and channel ports as well as from London ports. Thompson positively identifies only 5 percent of migrant East Anglians as servants. See, generally, Thompson, *Mobility and Migration,* 26, 114–25; Archer, "New England Mosaic," 486–88.

In the matter of persistence, Cressy proposes that servants formed about 25 percent of New England's landed migrant population (*Coming Over,* 53), while Games suggests that the nearly 34 percent incidence of servants among all migrants leaving London in 1635 translates directly into a similar incidence of servants in the landed population (*Migration and Origins,* 72, 74). It is not plausible, however, to maintain that servants persisted in population at migrant ratios after the flow of migration slowed virtually to nothing after 1640. Even assuming that Games's 34 percent rate was accurate and persisted throughout the 1630s, assuming a total migration during this period of 21,000, with peaks in

Historians have offered varying accounts of the total numbers of Europeans migrating to America during the seventeenth and eighteenth centuries and of the likely incidence of servants in those migrant populations. Richard S. Dunn estimates that roughly 350,000 servants entered all of British America (mainland and island) between 1580 and 1775.[9] Philip Morgan suggests that a figure of 500,000 servants in a total European migration of 750,000, or two-thirds of all migrants, is more appropriate.[10] Such disparities in outcomes produced by experienced historians indicate the degree to which global migration and population portraits remain unavoidably tentative and dependent on approximations. Nevertheless, as specialists have refined their methods, a somewhat narrower range of numbers has begun to emerge. For the mainland alone, through 1780, current estimates indicate a likely total European migration of between 470,000 and 515,000. Of these, approximately 54,500 were involuntary migrants (convicts or prisoners of war), the vast majority of whom (50,000–52,200) entered North America during the eighteenth century. Of the 415,500 to 466,500

1634–35 and 1637–38, allowing moderate mortality (25 per 1,000) after initial "seasoning" (75 per 1,000) and an average term of service of five years, it is still highly unlikely that there were more than 2,500 migrant servants in New England at the end of 1640 (that is, no more than 18.5 percent of the white population at that time). Allowing Cressy's 21 percent rate to persist throughout the decade with all other conditions held constant, the servant population would be closer to 1,500, or about 11 percent of white population at the end of 1640. Thereafter, in the absence of further significant migration, servant numbers would have decreased rapidly. On the scarcity of servants after 1640, see Vickers, *Farmers and Fishermen,* 55–58. Vickers offers 5 percent of population as an absolute upper bound for servants in the later seventeenth century and sets his lower bound at less than 2 percent.

For the mortality assumptions made above, see Games, *Migration and Origins,* 86; Fischer, *Albion's Seed,* 112. Games cites impressionistic contemporary evidence that suggests an early mortality rate among landed migrants of up to 1 in 10; I have chosen a lower early rate of 75 in 1,000. This is applied to each year's entry cohort of servants, followed by reversion to the "normal" regional mortality rate of 25 in 1,000 reported by Fischer. But see also Robert P. Thomas and Terry L. Anderson, "White Population, Labor Force, and Extensive Growth of the New England Economy in the Seventeenth Century," *Journal of Economic History* 33 (September 1973): 647 (reporting a mortality rate of 22 per 1,000). I am not aware of any available per-annum influx breakdown, so I have assumed an annual "base" of 1,000 per annum throughout the period 1630–40, with peaks of 2,000 in 1630, 3,000 in 1634, 5,000 in 1635, 2,000 in 1637, and 3,000 in 1638. For a rough guide to this influx distribution, see Thompson, *Mobility and Migration,* 22. On contract term, Lawrence W. Towner reports a New England average of three to five years, with variations. I have adopted the top of the average range. See Lawrence W. Towner's 1955 dissertation, finally published as *A Good Master Well Served: Masters and Servants in Colonial Massachusetts, 1620–1750* (New York: Garland, 1998), 39. (Both my initial mortality and my contract-length assumptions will bias the incidence of servants in population upward.) New England population at the end of the 1630s (13,500) is taken from John J. McCusker and Russell R. Menard, *The Economy of British America, 1607–1789* (Chapel Hill: University of North Carolina Press, 1985), 103. Given a migration of 21,000 over the previous decade into a relatively benign disease environment, this figure reflects significant return and onward migration, on which see Games, *Migration and Origins,* 193–203; Cressy, *Coming Over,* 121–212.

9. Dunn, "Servants and Slaves," 159. Dunn estimates that 315,000, including 50,000 convicts, came from the British Isles and Ireland, and 35,000 from Germany.

10. Philip D. Morgan, "Bound Labor," in *Encyclopedia of the North American Colonies,* ed. Jacob E. Cooke et al. (New York: Charles Scribner's Sons, 1993), 2:18.

"voluntary" migrants, the analysis undertaken in this essay suggests that some 48 to 50 percent were committed to an initial period of servitude by indenture or similar arrangement. This status was more common during the seventeenth century, when it applied to some 60 to 65 percent of voluntary migrants, than during the eighteenth, when it applied on average to 40 to 42 percent.[11] In addition to these indentured Europeans, between 285,000 and 310,000 enslaved Africans entered the mainland colonies, the vast majority during the century after 1680.[12]

The central purpose of this essay is to refine aggregate numbers by examining the migration and population history of the major regions and periods of intake. In the Chesapeake case, the sole contemporary measure of servant incidence in settler population is a 1625 Virginia census that counted servants somewhat in excess of 40 percent of total population,[13] but for other times we can infer incidence indirectly from overall immigration and population estimates. Russell R. Menard's decadal series for immigration to the Chesapeake, together with compatible population estimates, permits development of decadal servant migrant estimates that allow us to chart shifts in the proportion of servants in the total population over time.[14] Among early American historians the default assumption has been that throughout the colonial period between half and two-thirds of all European migrants to mainland North America were indentured servants, with fluctuations up to and even beyond 80 percent not unimaginable for particular places at particular moments. In light of the overall results already mentioned (48 to 50 percent), "half to two-thirds" is clearly too broad a range with too high an upper bound, certainly as a percentage of voluntary migrants. The lower third of the range is feasible (through 55 percent) but only if all convict migrants are included.[15] In the seventeenth-century Chesapeake, however,

11. On involuntary European migration (transported convicts and other prisoners), see A. Roger Ekirch, *Bound for America: The Transportation of British Convicts to the Colonies, 1718–1775* (New York: Oxford University Press, 1987), 26–27, 70–132; Fogleman, "Slaves, Convicts, and Servants." Ekirch suggests 50,000 convicts transported during the eighteenth century, Fogleman 2,300 during the seventeenth century and 52,200 during the eighteenth. The global figures summarized in the text have emerged from a synthesis of a number of sources. For full details, see the appendix to this essay.

12. On Africans, see Bernard Bailyn, *Voyagers to the West: A Passage in the Peopling of America on the Eve of the Revolution* (New York: Knopf, 1986), 25–26; Aaron S. Fogleman, "Migration to the Thirteen British North American Colonies, 1700–1775: New Estimates," *Journal of Interdisciplinary History* 22 (Spring 1992): 697–99; Philip D. Curtin, *The Atlantic Slave Trade: A Census* (Madison: University of Wisconsin Press, 1969), 137.

13. Dunn, "Servants and Slaves," 159. Two eighteenth-century Maryland censuses are treated in Tomlins, "Reconsidering Indentured Servitude," 40 (table A3).

14. Russell R. Menard, "British Migration to the Chesapeake Colonies in the Seventeenth Century," in *Colonial Chesapeake Society,* ed. Lois Green Carr, Philip D. Morgan, and Jean B. Russo (Chapel Hill: University of North Carolina Press, 1988), 104–5 (tables 2 and 3); McCusker and Menard, *Economy of British America,* 136 (table 6.4).

15. Ekirch concludes that although a majority of transported convicts were probably indentured to labor on arrival, certainly not all were. *Bound for America,* 119–20. Hence even the lower end of the default range is a little shaky. See also Farley Grubb, "The Transatlantic Market for British Convict Labor," *Journal of Economic History* 60 (March 2000): 94–122.

the incidence of servants in total migration did indeed approach 80 percent. In the estimates that follow I have therefore assumed that a consistent 80 percent of all Chesapeake migrants were indentured servants (see Table 1).[16]

Over the course of the century, these figures suggest, slightly more than 86,000 servants migrated into the Chesapeake. But how many were there in the region at any given moment, and what was their incidence in population? To answer these questions we must produce an annual average from the estimated number of landed migrants for each decade, allowing for term of service[17] and for attrition—that is, both "seasoning" (adverse reaction to an alien disease environment) and general mortality. As Table 2 indicates, the outcome is a more or less continuous decline in the incidence of indentured servitude in population, from near majority at the beginning of sustained migration in the late 1620s, to somewhere in the range of 4 to 8 percent by the end of the century.

Table 1   European Migration, Servant Migration, and Population Estimates: Maryland and Virginia, 1600–1700 (in thousands)

Decade ending	Maryland		Virginia		Total Chesapeake servant migr.	Total white pop.
	All migr.	Servant migr.	All migr.	Servant migr.		
1610*	—	—	1.5	1.20	1.20	0.3
1620*	—	—	3.0	2.40	2.40	0.9
1630*	—	—	4.0	3.20	3.20	2.4
1640	0.7	0.56	8.2	6.56	7.12	8.0
1650	1.8	1.44	6.0	4.80	6.24	12.4
1660	4.6	3.68	11.6	9.28	12.96	24.0
1670	12.2	9.76	6.5	5.20	14.96	38.5
1680	12.4	9.92	8.1	6.48	16.40	55.6
1690	—	—	—	—	10.64	68.2
1700	—	—	—	—	11.12	85.2

* Approximation.

16. Data for Table 1 is derived from sources detailed in note 14 above. Menard suggests that "at least 70 percent" of Chesapeake migrants were indentured servants. "British Migration to the Chesapeake Colonies," 105–6. Other estimates of seventeenth-century migration to the Chesapeake range from 100,000 to 150,000 and place the incidence of servants in the range of 70 to 85 percent. See the appendix to this essay; also Lois Green Carr, "Emigration and the Standard of Living: The Seventeenth-Century Chesapeake, *Journal of Economic History* 52 (June 1992): 272.

17. On term of service, see James Horn, *Adapting to a New World: English Society in the Seventeenth-Century Chesapeake* (Chapel Hill: University of North Carolina Press, 1994), 66–67; Galenson, *White Servitude,* 102; Gloria L. Main, *Tobacco Colony: Life in Early Maryland, 1650–1720* (Princeton: Princeton University Press, 1982), 98–99; David Eltis, "Seventeenth-Century Migration and the Slave Trade: The English Case in Comparative Perspective," in Lucassen and Lucassen, *Migration, Migration History, History,* 102. The average length of contracts concluded prior to embarkation appears to be 4.5 years. Because the servant population contained significant numbers of minor children migrating without indentures and serving on arrival by "custom of the country," this average length should be revised upward. See Tomlins, "Reconsidering Indentured Servitude," 39 (appendix 3, supplementary estimates: table A2), and 41–43 (appendix 4, servants' ages).

The declining incidence of migrant servants in population over the course of the seventeenth century is less surprising than the implication that at no time after the 1620s did indentured servants even approach a majority of the colonizing population, and that by midcentury they made up less than one-fifth of population, and by the end of the century less than 5 percent. Even the most generous alternative estimate indicates that migrant servants made up no more than one-third of population at midcentury and no more than 8 percent by the end.[18] This outcome, particularly the rapid decrease after midcentury despite strong migration rates, is explained by the development of a local reproducing population, and eventually of absolute population growth through natural increase.[19]

Further adjustments to population figures allow the development of an estimate of labor force participation (numbers of individuals contributing directly to production), using the proportions suggested in 1978 by Terry Anderson and Robert Thomas.[20] These tell us that in 1640 indentured servants made up less

Table 2   European Servant Migration and Persistence in Population: Maryland and Virginia, 1600–1700 (in thousands)

Decade ending	N of servants migrating[1]	Landed servant population[2]	Servant pop. after attrition[3]	White pop. at end of decade	% Servant
1610*	1.20	0.60	0.40	0.3	**
1620*	2.40	1.20	0.80	0.9	**
1630*	3.20	1.60	1.07	2.4	44.5
1640	7.12	3.56	1.79	8.0	22.4
1650	6.24	3.12	2.09	12.4	16.8
1660	12.96	6.48	4.35	24.0	18.1
1670	14.96	7.48	5.02	38.5	13.0
1680	16.40	8.20	5.51	55.6	9.2
1690	10.64	5.32	3.57	68.2	5.2
1700	11.12	5.56	3.77	85.2	4.4

* Approximation.

** Insufficient data for meaningful computation.

1. From Table 1.

2. Column 1 adjusted to show servant population for any one year within the decade, allowing for persistence through an average contract length of five years (N migrating ? ÷ 10)(5).

3. For attrition (seasoning and mortality) estimates, see Christopher Tomlins, "Reconsidering Indentured Servitude: European Migration and the Early American Labor Force, 1600–1775," *Labor History* 42 (February 2001): 38–39 (appendix 2).

18. For alternative estimates reflecting variation in seasoning/mortality patterns, contract terms, and migration rates, see Tomlins, "Reconsidering Indentured Servitude," 39 (table A2).

19. Migrant indentured servants persist as a significant component of population somewhat longer in seventeenth-century Maryland than in Virginia, and they remain more numerous in the eighteenth century. See ibid., 40 (table A3).

20. Terry L. Anderson and Robert P. Thomas, "The Growth of Population and Labor Force in the Seventeenth-Century Chesapeake," *Explorations in Economic History* 15 (July 1978): 304–5 and tables A-1 and A-2.

than one-third of the labor force, in 1670 less than a quarter, and by 1700 just 9.7 percent (see Table 3).

The actual incidence of servants in working population was probably lower than this. Anderson and Thomas's calculations of labor force participation employ a concept of labor force "as found in modern developed countries."[21] In such environments, work is seen "as a discrete activity in a distinct economic realm."[22] Work in early America, however, was not thus compartmentalized—virtually everyone worked in some capacity.[23] Applying modern definitions of

Table 3 Indentured Servants in the Chesapeake Labor Force, 1630–1700 (in thousands)

Decade ending	White population	% Population in labor force	White labor	White servant population	Servant as % of labor force
1640	8.0	75.6	6.05	1.79	29.58
1650	12.4	71.4	8.85	2.09	23.62
1660	24.0	66.5	15.97	4.35	27.23
1670	38.5	57.7	22.22	5.02	22.59
1680	55.6	58.1	32.3	5.51	17.06
1690	68.2	51.5	35.12	3.57	10.16
1700	85.2	45.7	38.93	3.77	9.68

21. Ibid., 304. Anderson and Thomas hypothesize that the proportion of population in labor force is equivalent to all adult males plus 10 percent of adult females. Restating this hypothesis in terms of an actual population of men, women, and children, they estimate that the components of the labor force at any given moment will be all single males under age sixty plus a proportion (declining over time from 44 percent to 31 percent) of "reproducibles" (that is, paired males and females, and children). Applied to the census figures of Virginia in 1625, their calculation yields a labor force that includes 85 percent of all adult males present in the colony, 44 percent of adult females, and 44 percent of the children. Others have argued that total adult population is a better measure of labor force equivalence for the early American economy. See Alice Hanson Jones, *Wealth of a Nation to Be: The American Colonies on the Eve of the Revolution* (New York: Columbia University Press, 1980), 56. In recent work offering estimates of workforce for the eighteenth century, Carole Shammas estimates workforce equivalents on the basis of differential participation rates of a population disaggregated by age and race (whites aged sixteen and older, 90 percent; whites aged ten to fifteen, 45 percent; blacks aged ten and older, 85 percent). Shammas also offers lower bound estimates based on uniform white adult participation rates of 85 percent and blacks ten years and older of 80 percent. See Carole Shammas, "Defining and Measuring Output and the Workforce in Early America" (unpublished manuscript). Her results show average workforce participation rates declining over the eighteenth century from around 56 percent to around 52.5 percent for the mainland as a whole, but with pronounced regional variation. Shammas hypothesizes that seventeenth-century rates were substantially higher. There is also credible seventeenth-century evidence from both New England and the Chesapeake, and from the late seventeenth-century Delaware Valley, that migrant and settler children were considered fully capable of productive work by age ten, and thus that the participation rate of children aged fifteen and under is probably higher during the first century of settlement than the 44–45 percent suggested by Anderson and Thomas.

22. Patrick Joyce, ed., *The Historical Meanings of Work* (New York: Cambridge University Press, 1987), 2.

23. As McCusker and Menard put it, "the conventional definition of the labor force as 'all persons producing marketable goods and services' seems inappropriate to economies in which people's productive energies were focused in large part on subsistence rather than on the market." *Economy of British America*, 236.

"labor force" to the seventeenth century will understate general population participation rates and hence overstate the importance of servants.[24]

By adding estimates of the Chesapeake's slave population we can measure the overall size of the explicitly bound component of the regional population. As Table 4 indicates, immigrant servants accounted for a majority of the Chesapeake's unfree population until the 1680s, the same decade in which the combined population of servants and slaves reached its lowest level ever of less than 15 percent of total population. Thereafter, while servant numbers continued to decline, rising slave imports and natural increase saw rapid growth in the African population.

By expressing the combined count of servants and slaves as a proportion of "labor force" (setting aside the latter's conceptual problems), we see that bound labor accounts fairly consistently for between 25 and 35 percent of the Chesapeake labor force during the seventeenth century, the rise in the African American population in the last quarter of the century partly substituting for the declining numbers of servants during that period (see Table 5).[25]

Table 4   Slaves and Servants in the Chesapeake Colonies, 1610-1780 (in thousands)

Year	Chesapeake African pop.[1]	Servant pop.[2]	Sum of 1 and 2	Total population	% Slave and servant
1610		.40	.40	0.3	★★
1620		.80	.80	0.9	★★
1630	0.1	1.07	1.17	2.5	46.8
1640	0.1	1.79	1.89	8.1	23.3
1650	0.3	2.09	2.39	12.7	18.8
1660	0.9	4.35	5.25	24.9	21.1
1670	2.5	5.02	7.52	41.0	18.3
1680	4.3	5.51	9.81	59.9	16.4
1690	7.3	3.57	10.87	75.5	14.4
1700	12.9	3.77	16.67	98.1	17.0
1710	22.4	—	—	123.7	18.1
1720	30.6	—	—	158.6	19.3
1730	53.2	—	—	224.6	23.7
1740	84.0	—	—	296.5	28.3
1750	150.6	—	—	377.8	39.7
1760	189.6	—	—	502.0	37.7
1770	251.4	—	—	649.6	38.7
1780	303.6	—	—	786.0	38.6

1. John J. McCusker and Russell R. Menard, *The Economy of British America: 1607–1789* (Chapel Hill: University of North Carolina Press, 1985), 136, table 6.4. This table assumes African population is wholly enslaved.
2. From Table 2, column 4.
★★ Insufficient data for meaningful computation.

24. Simply put, the higher the labor force participation rate in the general population, the lower the proportionate contribution of indentured migrants to the labor force.
25. On substitution, see Farley Grubb and Tony Stitt, "The Liverpool Emigrant Servant Trade and the Transition to Slave Labor in the Chesapeake, 1697–1707: Market Adjustments to War,"

All these figures are, by their nature, necessarily approximations. Their utility lies in their refinement of the simple magnitudes, such as total numbers of servant immigrants over the entire colonial period, that scholars tend to rely on to substantiate the importance of indentured servitude. The results are not one-sided: for much of the seventeenth century migrant indentured servitude was clearly a significant enough presence in the Chesapeake to influence the social and legal relations of Europeans at work. On the other hand, we can see that by midcentury substantially more work was being performed outside indentured relations than within them.

Migrant servitude was not "crowded out" by resort to slavery. The turn to slavery did not come decisively until the end of the century, as a solution to increasing labor scarcity, not as an additional bound labor force. The declining demographic importance of migrant indentured servitude instead reflects the general expansion of regional population, increasingly Creole (native-born) in origin, among whom unfree migrant servants formed a decreasing minority.

During the eighteenth century the major site of indentured labor importation was the Delaware Valley. Table 6 presents estimates of immigration to the Delaware ports of Newcastle and Philadelphia. It shows the initial English and Welsh migration of the late seventeenth and early eighteenth centuries, followed by an overwhelmingly German and Irish migration in full swing by the

Table 5 Slaves and Servants in the Chesapeake Labor Force, 1630–1700 (in thousands)

Decade ending	White labor force	Total labor force 1[1]	Total labor force 2[1]	Slave/srvt pop.	%[1]	%
1640	6.05	6.1	6.15	1.89	31.0	30.7
1650	8.85	9.0	9.15	2.39	26.5	26.1
1660	15.97	16.4	16.87	5.25	32.0	31.1
1670	22.22	23.4	24.52	7.52	32.1	30.7
1680	32.3	34.2	36.6	9.81	28.7	26.8
1690	35.12	38.2	42.4	10.87	28.5	25.6
1700	38.93	44.5	51.8	16.67	37.4	32.2

1. Two estimates are presented. The first (column 3) uses Anderson and Thomas's estimates of black population participation in labor force (Terry L. Anderson and Robert P. Thomas, "The Growth of Population and Labor Force in the Seventeenth-Century Chesapeake," *Explorations in Economic History* 15 [July 1978]: 304–5, and tables A-1 and A-2). The second (column 4) assumes that the entire black population should be included in labor force. The alternative percentages of bound labor in total labor force that they generate are given in columns 6 and 7.

Explorations in Economic History 31 (July 1994): 376–405; Gloria L. Main, "Maryland in the Chesapeake Economy, 1670–1720," in *Law, Society, and Politics in Early Maryland,* ed. Aubrey C. Land, Lois Green Carr, and Edward C. Papenfuse (Baltimore: Johns Hopkins University Press, 1977), 134–52; Russell R. Menard, "From Servants to Slaves: The Transformation of the Chesapeake Labor System," *Southern Studies* 16 (Winter 1977): 355–90; Eltis, "Seventeenth-Century Migration and the Slave Trade"; David Eltis, "Labor and Coercion in the English Atlantic World from the Seventeenth to the Early Twentieth Century," *Slavery And Abolition* 14 (April 1993): 207–26.

late 1720s, and finally the resumption of British (predominantly English, some Scottish) migration after 1760.[26]

As in the Chesapeake estimates, general migration figures become the basis for estimates of the numbers of migrants arriving as servants (see Table 7).[27]

Finally, we can proceed to a rough measure of the servant population and of its incidence in general population (see Table 8).[28]

Table 6 Immigration to the Delaware Valley, 1670–1780 (in round numbers)

Decade	British	German	S. Irish	N. Irish	Total arrivals	Arrivals in Phila.
1670–79	1,500	—	—	—	1,500	—
1680–89	11,000	77	—	—	11,077	—
1690–99	3,000	76	—	—	3,076	—
1700–09	2,500	—	—	—	2,500	—
1710–19	5,000	646	—	—	5,646	—
1720–29	—	2,956	723	296	3,975	3,000
1730–39	—	13,006	3,362	2,476	18,844	17,000
1740–49	—	20,850	4,047	5,284	30,181	24,000
1750–59	—	30,374	3,547	8,191	42,112	36,000
1760–69	4,215	8,058	3,737	12,141	28,151	21,000
1770–79	2,830	4,926	1,741	7,150	16,347	13,000

26. Sources for Table 6: for the British column, 1670–1720, Fischer, *Albion's Seed,* 421; 1760–76, Bailyn, *Voyagers to the West,* 206–7, 230–31 (my estimate assumes that the totals Bailyn reports for the period 1773–76 represent constant flows for the previous ten years as well). For the German and Irish columns, Marianne S. Wokeck, *Trade in Strangers: The Beginnings of Mass Migration to North America* (University Park: Pennsylvania State University Press, 1999), 45–46, 172–73. Wokeck's estimates of Irish migration include residuals to account for vessels whose ports of embarkation could not be determined. I have allocated these to the northern and southern columns according to the annual ratio of identified northern and southern migrants. For Philadelphia arrivals, see Susan Klepp, "Demography in Early Philadelphia, 1690–1860," *Proceedings of the American Philosophical Society* 133, no. 2 (1989): 111. See also the appendix to this essay.

27. In contrast to the seventeenth-century Chesapeake, where the estimates presented assumed that a uniform 80 percent of European migrants entered as servants, the better-developed secondary literature on Philadelphia's intake allows somewhat better estimates. See discussion in the appendix to this essay.

28. Table 8 assumes that servants served an average four-year term. This is an upper bound. Most scholars agree that contract lengths dropped well below four years as the century progressed. See, for example, Grubb, "Labor, Markets, and Opportunity," 239; Fertig, "Eighteenth Century Transatlantic Migration," 282; Wokeck, *Trade in Strangers,* 162. Table 8 also applies an attrition rate of 14.3 percent, calculated to reflect an early mortality rate (seasoning) among new migrants reported to be about 1.7 times higher than the general Philadelphia-region mortality rate of 47 per 1,000 (i.e., recent migrants died off at a rate approaching double the Creole rate). This calculation reflects an overall survival rate over a four-year contract term of almost 80 percent; i.e., where N^1 is the size of the entry cohort, the percentage of survivors (N^2) is calculated as $[(N^1 -8 \text{ percent})(-4.7 \text{ percent})(-4.7 \text{ percent})(-4.7 \text{ percent})]$, which is 79.6 percent. For further details, see the explanation of the similar Chesapeake calculation in Tomlins, "Reconsidering Indentured Servitude," 39 (appendix 2). On death rates in the Philadelphia region during the eighteenth century, see Klepp, "Demography in Early Philadelphia," 94, 96, 103–5, table 2.

Table 7   Servant Immigration to the Delaware Valley, 1670–1780 (in round numbers)

Decade	British approx. 35%[1] approx. 66%[2]	German approx. 35%[3] approx. 58%[4]	S. Irish approx. 66%	N. Irish approx. 25%	Total servant imports
1670–79	525	—	—	—	525
1680–89	3,850	—	—	—	3,850
1690–99	1,050	—	—	—	1,050
1700–09	875	—	—	—	875
1710–19	1,750	226	—	—	1,976
1720–29	—	1,034	477	74	1,585
1730–39	—	4,552	2,219	619	7,390
1740–49	—	7,297	2,671	1,321	11,289
1750–59	—	10,630	2,341	2,048	15,019
1760–69	2,781	4,673	2,466	3,035	12,955
1770–79	1,868	2,857	1,149	1,787	7,661

1. 1670–1720
2. 1760–1776
3. 1720–1760
4. 1760–1776

Table 8   Delaware Valley Servant Population and Pennsylvania European Population Based on Immigration Estimates, 1670–1780 (in round numbers)

Decade	Servant imports	Landed servant population[1]	Servant pop. after attrition	Pa. white population[2]	% Servant
1670–79	525	210	180	647	27.82
1680–89	3,850	1,540	1,320	10,545	12.51
1690–99	1,050	420	360	16,650	2.16
1700–09	875	350	300	22,570	1.33
1710–19	1,976	790	677	28,675	2.36
1720–29	1,585	634	543	47,822	1.14
1730–39	7,390	2,956	2,533	79,180	3.20
1740–49	11,289	4,516	3,870	110,722	3.50
1750–59	15,019	6,007	5,148	169,922	3.03
1760–69	12,955	5,182	4,441	222,092	2.00
1770–79	7,661	3,064	2,626	302,752	0.87

1. Column 1 adjusted to show servant population for any one year within the decade, allowing for persistence through average contract length (N migrating ÷ 10)(4).
2. This series is produced from the Pennsylvania population series reported by McCusker and Menard, deflated by 7.5 percent, which is the average proportion of the African-originating component of population in all middle-colony population, as reported in the same source. *The Economy of British America: 1607–1789* (Chapel Hill: University of North Carolina Press, 1985), 203.

Estimates specific to the city of Philadelphia may be gleaned from the work of Sharon Salinger.[29] Salinger has calculated figures for a servant workforce that, when combined with her figures for population and workforce for the city as a whole, suggest that servant numbers never pushed above 10 percent of the city's population or 21 percent of its workforce, and that even these magnitudes were approached for only a short period, during the 1750s (see Table 9).[30]

Salinger's figures also suggest that over the same period (1720–75) Philadelphia absorbed more than 15 percent of all Delaware Valley servant imports (9,500 of 56,000). If Philadelphia indeed represented a concentration of servant labor, the remainder would have been dispersed widely through the rural population, rendering it highly unlikely that the servant population of nonurban areas would approach even the comparatively modest levels observable in the city.[31]

Table 9 Servants in Philadelphia Population and Workforce (adapted from Salinger estimates) (in round numbers)

Decade ending	Servant pop.[1]	Philadelphia pop.[2]	% Servants in pop.	Philadelphia workforce[3]	% Servants in workforce
1730	285	5,808	4.9	3,177	9.0
1740	575	8,017	7.2	4,249	13.5
1750	635	10,720	5.9	4,996	12.7
1760	1,305	13,413	9.7	6,266	20.8
1770	396	15,718	2.5	6,438	6.1
(1775)	457	18,692	2.4	7,526	6.1

1. Decadal averages derived from data reported in Sharon V. Salinger, *"To Serve Well and Faithfully": Labor and Indentured Servants in Pennsylvania, 1682–1800* (New York: Cambridge University Press, 1987), table A3, column 3 ("Servant Immigration—Total") and 4 ("Servant Work Force"). See Christopher Tomlins, "Reconsidering Indentured Servitude: European Migration and the Early American Labor Force, 1600–1775," *Labor History* 42 (February 2001): 17n33.
2. Decadal averages derived from data in Salinger, *"To Serve Well and Faithfully,"* table A3, column 8 ("Philadelphia Population").
3. Decadal averages derived from data ibid., table A3, columns 7 ("Total Unfree Work Force") and 9 ("Philadelphia Work Force").

29. Sharon Salinger, *"To Serve Well and Faithfully": Labor and Indentured Servants in Pennsylvania, 1682–1800* (New York: Cambridge University Press, 1987), 172–84, tables A.1–A.3.

30. In producing my figures I have added together Salinger's columns 7 and 9 to achieve a total Philadelphia workforce estimate. Where there are data gaps in Salinger's table I have estimated workforce on the basis of the proportion of population in workforce in adjoining periods for which data is available. Salinger's figures for city population are substantially lower than other more recent estimates. See, for example, Klepp, "Demography in Early Philadelphia," 103–5, table 2. Klepp's city population figures deflate estimates of the incidence of servants in city population and workforce by 20 to 25 percent before 1760 and 40 percent after. The concept "workforce" used here poses some of the same conceptual difficulties as "labor force" discussed earlier in the Chesapeake context. Salinger's data indicate that "total workforce" varies from 40 to 54 percent of population over the period in question (1729–75).

31. See, for example, the "Town Book" for Goshen, Chester County, 1718–1870, Historical Society of Pennsylvania, Philadelphia. Sixty servants are listed as "Imported into this Province and purchased by the Inhabitants of this Township" covering the period 1736–72. The twenty-eight purchasers constituted only one-third of Goshen's farmers. Moreover, eleven of the twenty-eight only ever bought

Moreover, numbers of servants imported through Delaware Valley ports traveled on to New Jersey, New York, Maryland, and beyond. Maryland, by contrast, remained a site of servant importation during the eighteenth century, and numbers of these servants may have entered the Delaware Valley region, perhaps offsetting those who left.

Overall, estimates of the incidence of servants in general population for Philadelphia and for Pennsylvania suggest that, even more than in the seventeenth-century Chesapeake, the influence of migrant indentured servitude in defining the social and legal relations of work in the eighteenth-century Delaware Valley was substantially overshadowed by the rapid growth of the region's free white population. Certainly the institution was of importance in shaping the performance of work. Just as certainly, the great bulk of work was performed within a much wider range of productive relations.

As in the Chesapeake, the picture is incomplete without a consideration of slavery. Mary Schweitzer argues that slavery "simply was not common" in Pennsylvania, "particularly in the countryside."[32] Salinger's figures indicate that in Philadelphia slavery had a presence of some significance, outweighing the incidence of European migrant servitude both in population and "work force." Servants appear to have outnumbered slaves only at midcentury, and then only briefly (see Table 10).

In Pennsylvania, unlike the Chesapeake, slaves did not substitute for servants. "Rather, servants and slaves were used interchangeably throughout the history of the colony, and when unfree labor disappeared it was replaced by free

Table 10   Servants and Slaves in Philadelphia Population (adapted from Salinger estimates) (in round numbers)

Decade ending	Srvt. pop.	Slave pop.[1]	Phila. pop.	% Srvts in Phila. pop.	% Slaves in Phila. pop.	Srvt:Slave ratio
1730	285	880	5,808	4.9	15.2	1:3
1740	575	1,209	8,017	7.2	15.1	1:2
1750	635	1,131	10,720	5.9	10.6	1:2
1760	1,305	1,136	13,413	9.7	8.5	1:1
1770	396	1,682	15,718	2.5	10.7	1:4
(1775)	457	1,394	18,692	2.4	7.5	1:3

1. Decadal averages derived from data in Salinger, *"To Serve Well and Faithfully": Labor and Indentured Servants in Pennsylvania, 1682–1800* (New York: Cambridge University Press, 1987), table A3, column 5 ("Slave Population").

one servant; ten only ever bought two. One family alone accounted for nearly 30 percent of all purchases; three families accounted for 50 percent. Servants would thus be encountered routinely only in a small minority of households. See also Barry Levy, *Quakers and the American Family: British Settlement in the Delaware Valley* (New York: Oxford University Press, 1988), 240.

32. Mary M. Schweitzer, *Custom and Contract: Household, Government, and the Economy in Colonial Pennsylvania* (New York: Columbia University Press, 1987), 45.

labor."[33] That replacement appears to have been under way from quite early on in the eighteenth century. Considered as a percentage of Pennsylvania population, imported servants never exceeded 6 percent at any point during the century and, as we have seen, appear to have been concentrated in Philadelphia. Together, servants and slaves reached approximately 20 percent of Philadelphia's population in the 1730s, but from that point onward the trend for all bound labor was downward. Slaves, like servants, were less common outside Philadelphia than within.

Workforce estimates tell the same story. Slaves peaked at slightly over 20 percent of the Philadelphia workforce in the 1730s, falling thereafter to 12–15 percent in the next three decades, and 7.5 percent in the 1770s. Although the number of slaves in the city continued to increase, the rate did not keep pace with the general expansion of the population.[34] Together, slaves and servants constituted about one-third of Philadelphia's workforce throughout most of the first half of the eighteenth century, but declined quite rapidly from those levels in the fifteen years before the Revolution (see Table 11).

According to Bernard Bailyn's examination of the dimensions and structure of migration from Britain to North America in the years immediately before the American Revolution, what took place was a "dual emigration."[35] Substantial numbers of young unmarried males, traveling alone, migrated from south, central, and western England. Dubbed, misleadingly, a "metropolitan" migration because final departures were from London, this movement included

Table 11 Servants and Slaves in Philadelphia Population and Workforce (adapted from Salinger estimates)

Decade ending[1]	S/S pop.	S/S workforce	Philadelphia population	% S/S in population	Philadelphia workforce	% S/S in workforce
1730	1,165	901	5,808	20.0	3,177	28.4
1740	1,784	1,457	8,017	22.3	4,249	34.3
1750	1,766	1,427	10,720	16.5	4,996	28.6
1760	2,441	2,100	13,413	18.2	6,266	33.5
1770	2,078	1,354	15,718	13.2	6,438	21.0
(1775)	1,851	1,031	18,692	9.9	7,526	13.7

1. Decadal averages derived from data in Salinger, *"To Serve Well and Faithfully": Labor and Indentured Servants in Pennsylvania, 1682–1800* (New York: Cambridge University Press, 1987), table A3.

33. Salinger, *"To Serve Well and Faithfully,"* 17.

34. Derived from ibid., table A3, column 6 ("slave work force"). Where data are unavailable I have assumed that the slave workforce constituted 70 percent of the slave population. This figure is consistent with those that Salinger reports through 1757. We should note that applying Klepp's population figures (cited in note 30 above) to Tables 10 and 11 will have a similar deflationary effect on the general incidence of bound labor in population and workforce reported here.

35. Bailyn, *Voyagers to the West,* 126–203.

few women or families and a high incidence of indentured servants. Simultaneously, a distinct "provincial" migration took place from northern and western ports, involving migrants from Yorkshire, the north of England, and Scotland. This stream included substantial numbers of women and children, a high incidence of family groups, and a low incidence of indentured servants. Collectively, metropolitan migrants' principal resource was their labor power. The ideal-typical metropolitan migrant was "an isolated male artisan in his early twenties, a bondsman for several years of unlimited servitude."[36] The ideal-typical provincial migrant, by contrast, was a family member. Collectively, provincial migrants represented "the transfer of farming families, whose heads were men of some small substance, or at least to some extent economically autonomous."[37] Different people from different places, metropolitan and provincial migrants had different destinations. Metropolitan migrants went to Pennsylvania, Virginia, and, overwhelmingly, Maryland, where labor was in demand. Provincial migrants went to North Carolina, New York, and Nova Scotia, where they hoped to find relief from the hardships (but not destitution) that they had left behind. Not a "general milling and thronging of people," Bailyn's migration was patterned and purposeful: "a work force to the central colonies; a social movement of substantial families to New York, North Carolina, and Nova Scotia."[38]

Though based on intensive analysis of one short paroxysm of transatlantic movement, Bailyn's conclusions describe tendencies readily detectable in 150 years of prior migrations. First came a seventeenth-century sequence, in which an almost exclusively English migration transferred some 137,000 people to New England (1630–40) and the Chesapeake (1625–1700), with about 15,000 to the Delaware Valley after 1675 and a small number of others to the lower South. Second came an eighteenth-century sequence, in which a more varied European migration transferred a further 307,000–350,000 people to a variety of destinations along the Atlantic seaboard from Georgia to New York, most of them to the Delaware Valley and Maryland.

Each sequence exhibits the distinctive "dual" pattern that Bailyn describes. The initial phase of seventeenth-century migration, involving some 35,000 people between 1625 and 1640, was a dual movement of families and of single young males headed for different destinations. Families were in the majority among those going to New England. Migration to Virginia, by contrast, was completely dominated by unattached youthful males. After migration to New

36. Ibid., 203, 188–89. The validity of the label "metropolitan" is questionable because migrants leaving from London were in no sense exclusively from the metropolis but came from all over the country. See note 59 below and accompanying text.

37. Ibid., 203.

38. Ibid., 228, and generally 204–28. See also Nicholas Canny, "English Migration into and Across the Atlantic During the Seventeenth and Eighteenth Centuries," in *Europeans on the Move: Studies on European Migration, 1500–1800*, ed. Nicholas Canny (New York: Oxford University Press, 1994), 52.

England tapered off dramatically early in the 1640s, seventeenth-century migration temporarily lost its dual quality, becoming until the late 1670s almost exclusively a movement to the Chesapeake of some 50,000 people largely single, young, and male.[39] After 1675 migration reverted to the earlier dual pattern as continuing Chesapeake migration was supplemented by a flow of families from the northwest Midlands into the Delaware Valley. All told, some 15,000 migrants moved into the Delaware Valley between 1675 and 1700 (23,000 between 1675 and 1715). Both families and single male servants participated.[40]

For the eighteenth century, studies of migrants entering the port of Philadelphia after 1725 contrast the family-oriented migration originating in Germany and Ulster—by far the largest groups of migrants—with the continuing youthful, single, and male character of flows from England (considerably diminished for most of the period from 1720 to 1760) and southern Ireland. The incidence of families in German migration declined over the course of the eighteenth century, relative to migration of younger single persons. David Hackett Fischer argues, however, that during the same period migration from "North Britain" (Yorkshire, the border counties, Scotland, and Ulster) into the Appalachian backcountry was consistently one of families.[41]

The dual migration model refines our assessments of migrant population structure. Bailyn's division of that population into "family" (relatively intact households) and "labor force" streams, however, wrongly implies that colonial work relations assigned exclusive, or at least predominant, participation in labor to single youthful male migrants restrained in conditions of bonded servitude. Certainly such persons were involved in legally distinct categories of work. But, as we have seen, they did not represent anywhere near the sum of the colonies'

---

39. See, generally, Horn, *Adapting to a New World,* 30–38; Games, *Migration and Origins,* 27, 47.

40. Fischer suggests that somewhere between 40 and 60 percent of the Delaware Valley's initial migrants migrated in family groups (*Albion's Seed,* 434). In *Quakers and Politics: Pennsylvania, 1681–1726* (Princeton: Princeton University Press, 1968), 50, Gary Nash suggests that approximately 66 percent of early Delaware Valley migrants (and a bare majority of adult male migrants—51 percent) arrived free of indenture.

41. On the character of German and Irish migration, see Wokeck, *Trade in Strangers;* Marianne S. Wokeck, "German and Irish Immigration to Colonial Philadelphia," *Proceedings of the American Philosophical Society,* 133, no. 2 (1989): 128–43; and Marianne Wokeck, "The Flow and the Composition of German Immigration to Philadelphia, 1727–1775," *Pennsylvania Magazine of History and Biography* 105 (July 1981): 249–78. On trends in German family migration, see Wokeck, "Flow and Composition," 266–73, and Grubb, "Immigration and Servitude," 104–5. Both Wokeck and Grubb date the relative decline in family migration to the resumption of emigration flows following the interruption of the Seven Years' War (1755–62). Even then, however, Grubb finds that "German immigrants had over four times the proportion of dependent movers" as English ("Immigration and Servitude," 105). On migration into Appalachia, Fischer reports that at its peak in the 1770s, 61 percent of northern English emigrants, 73 percent of Scottish emigrants, and 91 percent of Ulster emigrants traveled in family groups (*Albion's Seed,* 610). See also Bailyn, *Voyagers to the West,* 134–47. See, generally, the discussion in the appendix to this essay.

labor force, nor even its largest collectively identifiable component.[42] Given the clear evidence of extensive engagement of women and children in agricultural and protoindustrial work in seventeenth- and eighteenth-century Europe, given the ubiquity of household relations of production and family reproduction throughout the mainland colonies, to include only youthful males in a description of an eighteenth-century migratory labor force is highly misleading. "Labor force" and "family" or "household" all represent forms of work relations rather than distinct spheres of work and nonwork.[43] With this firmly in mind, let us now consider in detail the characteristics of the population that seventeenth- and eighteenth-century emigration brought to the various recipient regions.

From 1630 through 1640 some twenty-one thousand people emigrated from England to Massachusetts Bay. After 1640 migration tailed off sharply to an average of only a few hundred people per decade.[44] Commonly identified as a religiously motivated exodus of Puritans,[45] the migration drew a plurality (38 percent) of its participants from the Puritan stronghold of East Anglia (Norfolk, Suffolk, and Essex) and Kent. These people traveled in cohesive household groups with few unattached single males.[46] A further 17 percent of the migrants came from London and the remaining home counties, and 16 percent from the southwest. The rest were a scattering from virtually every other region of England.[47]

42. That distinction belongs, of course, to enslaved Africans.

43. Maxine Berg, "Women's Work, Mechanisation and the Early Phases of Industrialisation in England," in Joyce, *Historical Meanings of Work,* 64–98; David Levine, "Production, Reproduction, and the Proletarian Family in England, 1500–1851," in *Proletarianization and Family History,* ed. David Levine (Orlando, Fla.: Academic Press, 1984), 87–127; R. E. Pahl, *Divisions of Labor* (Oxford: Blackwell, 1984), 17–62; Keith Snell, *Annals of the Labouring Poor: Social Change and Agrarian England, 1660–1900* (Cambridge: Cambridge University Press, 1985), 270–373; Laurel Thatcher Ulrich, *Good Wives: Image and Reality in the Lives of Women in Northern New England, 1650–1750* (New York: Knopf, 1982), 13–50, and, also by Ulrich, "Martha Ballard and Her Girls: Women's Work in Eighteenth-Century Maine," in *Work and Labor in Early America,* ed. Stephen Innes (Chapel Hill: University of North Carolina Press, 1988), 70–105; Christopher Clark, "Social Structure and Manufacturing Before the Factory: Rural New England, 1750–1850," in *The Workplace Before the Factory: Artisans and Proletarians, 1500–1800,* ed. Thomas Max Safley and Leonard N. Rosenband (Ithaca: Cornell University Press, 1993), 11–36, particularly 19–23; Eric G. Nellis, "The Working Lives of the Rural Middle Class in Provincial Massachusetts," *Labor History* 36 (Fall 1995): 505–29; Gloria L. Main, "Gender, Work, and Wages in Colonial New England," *William and Mary Quarterly,* 3d ser., 51 (January 1994): 39–66; Joan M. Jensen, *Loosening the Bonds: Mid-Atlantic Farm Women, 1750–1850* (New Haven: Yale University Press, 1986), 36–113; Allan Kulikoff, *The Agrarian Origins of American Capitalism* (Charlottesville: University Press of Virginia, 1992), 24–33; Jeanne M. Boydston, *Home and Work: Housework, Wages, and the Ideology of Labor in the Early Republic* (New York: Oxford University Press, 1990), 1–29; Schweitzer, *Custom and Contract,* 34–35; Vickers, *Farmers and Fishermen,* 60–77.

44. Thomas and Anderson, "White Population, Labor Force and Extensive Growth," 641–42.

45. Fischer, *Albion's Seed,* 18.

46. Thompson, *Mobility and Migration,* 14; Archer, "New England Mosaic," 483. Compare Fischer, *Albion's Seed,* 16–17, 31–36. See also Fischer, "*Albion* and the Critics: Further Evidence and Reflection," part of "*Albion's Seed: Four British Folkways in America*–A Symposium," *William and Mary Quarterly,* 3d ser., 47 (April 1991): 264–74.

47. Archer, "New England Mosaic," 483.

The proportion of youthful unattached males was much higher among migrants from outside East Anglia than from within. In all, approximately 60 percent of all migrants were under age twenty-four; about half of these (or roughly one-third of the original settler population) were single unattached males.[48] Although few can be identified explicitly as servants, it has been suggested that up to 34 percent of the emigrant population might have been destined for service in New England. However, even this extreme upper estimate of incidence produces a servant population falling well below 20 percent of total population by the end of the Great Migration.[49] Thereafter, the migrant servant population would have dwindled very rapidly indeed, exacerbating major labor shortages.[50]

As elsewhere in areas of mainland settlement, the surplus of single males among the original settlers meant delayed marriage for men and early marriage for women. In combination with healthy diets and high fertility rates, early marriage for women meant a much higher rate of childbearing than in England. Unlike other mainland regions, the healthy environment and relatively even distribution of wealth promoted family stability and personal longevity. As sex ratios stabilized with the maturing of the first Creole generation, male age at marriage began to drop. These conditions enhanced the demographic trends already in place: for the remainder of the colonial period "New Englanders had low infant mortality, large families, and long lives."[51] Hence "the population grew without the need for new colonists or an imported labor force."[52] Already by the early

48. Ibid., 479, 481. See also Cressy, *Coming Over,* 52–63. Fischer faults Archer for inaccurate age and sex ratios, preferring those of Virginia DeJohn Anderson ("*Albion* and the Critics," 268). The difference in age ratios is slight, in sex ratios more substantial although not wildly so. Archer argues that 60 to 67 percent of the migrants were males ("New England Mosaic," 480, 482), Anderson slightly under 57 percent. See her *New England's Generation: The Great Migration and the Formation of Society and Culture in the Seventeenth Century* (New York: Cambridge University Press, 1991), 222, 223. Games, *Migration and Origins,* 47, finds New England migrants leaving via London in 1635 to have been 61 percent male. Both Thompson and Archer report a very low ratio of servants in total migrants among those migrating from Greater East Anglia. Of those that could be determined to be servants, Thompson shows that most were adolescents or younger and migrated as part of a household in which they were already living. The substantially greater numbers of non–East Anglian young males in the migration were largely unattached. See, generally, Thompson, *Mobility and Migration,* 114–25; Archer, "New England Mosaic," 486–88.

49. See discussion in note 8 above. At an incidence of 16.5 percent (the preponderance of opinion) but holding all other assumptions stable, the servant population by the end of 1640 would have been slightly under twelve hundred, or 9 percent.

50. References to the scarcity of labor in New England are common in local records and become more pronounced during the 1640s. See, for example, Vickers, *Farmers and Fishermen,* 45–64; Thompson, *Mobility and Migration,* 230; Stephen Innes, *Creating the Commonwealth: The Economic Culture of Puritan New England* (New York: W. W. Norton, 1995), 101–5.

51. Archer, "New England Mosaic," 499, 486 488–92, 494–95. See also Robert V. Wells, "The Population of England's Colonies in America: Old English or New Americans," *Population Studies* 46 (March 1992): 90–99; Daniel Scott Smith, "American Family and Demographic Patterns and the Northwest European Model," *Continuity and Change* 8, no. 3 (1993): 395–96; Jim Potter, "Demographic Development and Family Structure," in Pole and Greene, *Colonial British America,* 139–41.

52. Archer, "New England Mosaic," 499.

1650s, the emergence of self-sustaining population growth had established local natural increase as the principal source of new labor, and family-centered households as the principal institutional structure through which work would be organized and workers procured. Near-universal participation in marriage and family formation confirmed the pattern.

Labor supply and labor control hence followed an explicitly generational and intrafamilial dynamic. Age was the crucial line demarcating the legal difference between master and servant.[53] In itself, this was no different from other areas of colonial settlement, or indeed from Britain;[54] in all areas of British mainland settlement, servitude and youth were closely associated (at least among Europeans). In New England, however, the availability of local sources—one's own children, local adolescents[55]—meant there was no need for continuous renewal of the region's labor supply through regular influxes of youthful migrant servants. Hence migrant servitude had little impact on the legal relations of work. This gave work and its legal culture a distinctive character compared to the seventeenth-century Chesapeake.[56]

Organized emigration to the Chesapeake began in 1607 with the founding of Jamestown and continued erratically through the 1620s, then strengthened substantially in the decades after 1630. Emigration had peaked by the early 1670s but continued strong until flows were disrupted by European warfare between 1688 and 1713.[57] Chesapeake migrants came from roughly the same general areas as the majority of those to New England: at first mostly from the southeast—London, the home counties, Kent, and Essex; later from southwest

53. Vickers, *Farmers and Fishermen*, 52–77; Christopher L. Tomlins, *Law, Labor, and Ideology in the Early American Republic* (New York: Cambridge University Press, 1993), 244–47.

54. On the close identity of youth and servitude in Britain, see Paul Griffiths, *Youth and Authority: Formative Experiences in England, 1560–1640* (Oxford: Oxford University Press, 1996), particularly 290–350; Ann Kussmaul, *Servants in Husbandry in Early Modern England* (New York: Cambridge University Press, 1981); M. F. Roberts, "Wages and Wage-Earners in England, 1563–1725: The Evidence of the Wage Assessments" (D.Phil., Oxford University, 1981), 133–63. See also D. C. Coleman, "Labour in the English Economy of the Seventeenth Century," *Economic History Review* 2d ser., 8 (April 1956): 284–86; Keith Thomas, "Age and Authority in Early Modern England," *Proceedings of the British Academy* 62 (1976): 205–48.

55. Vickers, *Farmers and Fishermen*, 52–77. See also Main, "Gender, Work and Wages," 56–57. See generally *Diary of Joshua Hempstead of New London, Connecticut* (New London: New London County Historical Society, 1901).

56. Winifred Rothenberg speculates that "an agricultural labor force, unconstrained and free to move, may well be a New England innovation." *From Market-Places to a Market Economy: The Transformation of Rural Massachusetts, 1750–1850* (Chicago: University of Chicago Press, 1992), 181, 182–83. Seventeenth-century evidence suggests that the institutional conditions of that innovation were established early. See Vickers, *Farmers and Fishermen*, 56–57nn51–52.

57. On the earliest decades, see, generally, Edmund S. Morgan, *American Slavery, American Freedom: The Ordeal of Colonial Virginia* (New York: W. W. Norton, 1975), 71–130; Virginia Bernhard, "'Men, Women, and Children' at Jamestown: Population and Gender in Early Virginia, 1607–1610," *Journal of Southern History* 58 (November 1992): 599–618. On later migration, see Menard, "British Migration to the Chesapeake Colonies"; Horn, *Adapting to a New World*, 24–25.

England, south Wales and the west Midlands, through Bristol, and the north, through Liverpool.[58] London served both as a regional center and as a magnet that drew eventual transatlantic emigrants from all over the country.[59] Bristol's hinterland was more concentrated. The very substantial East Anglian influence that imprinted a lasting familial character on migration to New England was, however, absent from the Chesapeake migration. Family migration to the Chesapeake was largely restricted to the small minority of wealthy migrants.[60]

Chesapeake's migrants, like New England's, were strikingly young. Unlike New England, however, single males were absolutely predominant (the male to female sex ratio among indentured migrants was 6:1 in the 1630s, dropping to 3:1–2:1 during the second half of the century). Males also predominated among the 15 to 25 percent of migrants who paid their own way (roughly 2.5:1). Self-supporting migrants tended to be single, like the indentured, but somewhat older: 75 percent were below age thirty-five but they clustered in the twenty-to-thirty-four age range. Indentured migrants were considerably more youthful, 30 percent under nineteen (increasing to 50 percent by the end of the century) and 80 percent under twenty-four.[61] In fact, the servant migration was substantially more youthful than even these figures indicate. Age ranges are calculated from records of terms of service agreed before departure. But many who would become servants in the Chesapeake arrived without indentures, destined to serve according to terms and conditions specified in local statute law. The characteristics of servants in this group can be learned only from the records of the local Chesapeake courts responsible for determining the new arrivals' ages and terms of service. Although no comprehensive survey of those records has been undertaken with this specific issue in mind, piecemeal research has established that servants retained according to local statute were consistently younger than those negotiating indentures in England. One may conclude that throughout the seventeenth century male servant migrants clustered in the lower rather than the

58. Horn, *Adapting to a New World,* 39–48.

59. On migration to London and eventual transatlantic migration from London, see James P. Horn, "Servant Emigration to the Chesapeake in the Seventeenth Century," in *The Chesapeake in the Seventeenth Century: Essays on Anglo-American Society,* ed. Thad W. Tate and David L. Ammerman (Chapel Hill: University of North Carolina Press, 1979), 70–74; Games, *Migration and Origins,* 13–41. On the pull of London and migration patterns in general in sixteenth- and seventeenth-century England, see Peter Clark and David Souden, "Introduction," in *Migration and Society in Early Modern England,* ed. Peter Clark and David Souden (Totowa, N.J.: Barnes and Noble, 1988), 11–48.

60. Fischer, *Albion's Seed,* 212–46; Horn, *Adapting to a New World,* 19–77; Horn, "Servant Emigration to the Chesapeake," 51–95. Horn and Fischer debate the interpretation of regional migration patterns in James Horn, "Cavalier Culture? The Social Development of Colonial Virginia," and Fischer, "*Albion* and the Critics," both in "*Albion's Seed*–A Symposium," 238–45 and 277–89.

61. On sex ratios, see Horn, *Adapting to a New World,* 37; Games, *Migration and Origins,* 47. On age at embarkation, see Horn, *Adapting to a New World,* 36. Thomas ("Age and Authority," 216), states that of 5,000 migrants leaving for American plantations in 1635, well over half were under age twenty-four. Among them were unattached children of age ten to eleven. Games (*Migration and Origins,* 25) finds 70 percent of this group under age twenty-four.

upper half of the "typical" fifteen to twenty-four age range. On this evidence, male servant migrants on the whole are far more appropriately considered boys and youths than young adults.[62]

The Chesapeake colonies attracted few formed families. Nor did the region prove particularly conducive to local family formation. Disease routinely claimed a significant proportion of the entering population; those who survived enjoyed much shorter life expectancy than northern colonists. Indentured servitude delayed entry into marriage for both men and women, and the persistent male-biased sex ratios in the migrant population further hindered the extent of family formation. Foreshortened life expectancy for parents limited the size of families. Poorer general health and greater inequalities in resource distribution than in New England dampened fertility. All told, the Chesapeake population was not self-sustaining until late in the seventeenth century.[63]

Nevertheless, local reproduction took place from the outset. Although not sufficient to replace population lost through death and out-migration until late in the century, accelerating local reproduction meant that reliance on immigration to maintain and increase population declined, at least in relative terms.[64] Until the last quarter of the century, migrant servants completing their terms had greater opportunity to acquire or at least rent land and enter into independent production than they could expect in England.[65] Families were formed, children were born, and a Creole population was established that "married sooner and lived a little longer" than its migrant parents, "acquiring time to have more children." Creoles' longer life spans meant that children could grow to maturity unimpeded by early parental death.[66] The social effects are obvious. Immigration meant a constant supply of new youthful labor, but migrant servants increasingly became only one part, rather than the main component, of local population.[67]

62. See Tomlins, "Reconsidering Indentured Servitude," 41–43 (appendix 4, servants' ages).

63. Horn, *Adapting to a New World,* 136–39; Anderson and Thomas, "Growth of Population and Labor Force," 295–305, especially 303; Carr, "Emigration and the Standard of Living," 271–87; Russell R. Menard, "Immigrants and Their Increase: The Process of Population Growth in Early Colonial Maryland," in Land et al., *Law, Society, and Politics in Early Maryland,* 88–110.

64. Carr, "Emigration and the Standard of Living," 273.

65. Ibid., 282–86. Horn, *Adapting to a New World,* 151–59, 292, argues for a rather more constrained range of opportunity, particularly in Virginia and particularly after 1670, but does not in the end dispute the comparative advantage of migration.

66. Carr, "Emigration and the Standard of Living," 273. See, generally, Lois Green Carr and Lorena S. Walsh, "The Standard of Living in the Colonial Chesapeake," in "Forum: Toward a History of the Standard of Living in British North America," *William and Mary Quarterly,* 3d ser., 45 (January 1988): 135–59.

67. Horn argues that by the 1660s the population was divided into two roughly equal segments. One segment was "dependents"—that is, "servants, slaves, and recently freed men and women." The other was the free Creole population, mostly (around 40 percent) "small and middling planters, including tenant farmers, who used their own family labor to work their holding or who possessed a few servants," the rest (around 10 percent) "wealthy planters, merchants, gentry, and a small group of

The distribution of servants in the third quarter of the century rein-forces an image of a society not starkly divided between a small free and a large bound population. Most plantations were small, worked by families or male part-ners; many had no bound laborers at all. Most servants were scattered among small plantations, not concentrated on large units. Most plantation masters relied on a mixture of servants, family members, and hired hands.[68] Indeed, to the extent that youthful migrant servants substituted for scarcities in local family labor, one can conclude that immigrant servitude in the Chesapeake sustained a local society that shared certain structural characteristics with New England. In both regions, settlers set up production in household units; in both, they relied upon the young to supply most of the dependent labor. The relational form that youthful dependency took differed, but not the fact of it.

As the century progressed, however, Chesapeake settlers increasingly divided and used the land differently from those of New England. "A steady upward drift in mean plantation size" began after midcentury, when a minority of established planters began adding considerable new investments in land and labor to their existing holdings. Concentration of landholding squeezed poorer planters and comprehensively undermined opportunities for recently freed immigrant servants to acquire land. The effects of both developments—the drive to expand production and to improve the rate of return from land, and the dete-rioration of opportunity for freed servants—were accentuated by poor tobacco prices, which placed a premium on ready access to capital and credit networks.[69] By the 1690s, the result was accelerating stratification within Creole society and rates of out-migration among freedmen reaching "epidemic" proportions.[70] Meanwhile, European warfare after 1688 disrupted what had already become a dwindling supply of youthful migrant labor. Under these circumstances, Chesa-peake planters expanded their reliance on slavery.[71] Servant immigrants con-tinued to enter the region, particularly Maryland, but their presence in the

artisans." *Adapting to a New World,* 160. My own estimates (assuming that five years is a reasonable demarcation of "recently freed") suggest that the "dependent" segment of the population was rather closer to one-third than one-half, and that this segment was itself divided 60-40 between bound work-ers and the recently freed.

68. Lois Green Carr and Lorena S. Walsh, "Economic Diversification and Labor Organi-zation in the Chesapeake, 1650–1820," in Innes, *Work and Labor in Early America,* 153, 148–57; Horn, *Adapting to a New World,* 281–83.

69. Russell R. Menard, "From Servant to Freeholder: Status Mobility and Property Accu-mulation in Seventeenth-Century Maryland," *William and Mary Quarterly,* 3d ser., 30 (January 1973): 37–64, at 57–59, 60; Lorena S. Walsh, "Servitude and Opportunity in Charles County, Maryland," in Land et al., *Law, Society, and Politics in Early Maryland,* 127.

70. Lois Green Carr and Russell R. Menard, "Immigration and Opportunity: The Freed-man in Early Colonial Maryland," in Tate and Ammerman, *Chesapeake in the Seventeenth Century,* 236, 230–40.

71. Menard, "From Servants to Slaves," 373–74, 385–88; Grubb and Stitt, "Liverpool Emi-grant Servant Trade," 5–7. Allan Kulikoff, *Tobacco and Slaves: The Development of Southern Cultures in the Chesapeake, 1680–1800* (Chapel Hill: University of North Carolina Press, 1986), 38.

labor force was overshadowed by the importation (and natural increase) of enslaved Africans. Henceforth, slavery would determine the dynamics of work relations in the Chesapeake, not only between whites and blacks but also among whites.[72]

Seventeenth-century British emigrants to New England and the Chesapeake came largely from southern and western England. As movement from these areas slowed toward the end of the century, however, emigration from the Midlands and the north of England increased—at first from the north Midlands (Cheshire, Nottinghamshire, Derbyshire) and the Pennine counties (Lancashire and Yorkshire), but increasingly supplemented by movement from the border counties (Cumberland and Westmoreland), Scotland, and Ulster. Some movement from these areas had already occurred through the staging areas of London and Bristol, but by 1680 Liverpool provided a rival, more convenient, point of embarkation.[73]

Some of these "north British" emigrants continued to land in the Chesapeake.[74] Beginning in the 1680s, however, substantial numbers headed for the Delaware Valley, a region already thinly settled by a scattering of European migrants.[75] After 1713 this movement widened to encompass the first non-British mass immigration, that of ethnic Germans from the southern Rhineland (southwest Germany and Switzerland).[76]

In several respects the first phase of migration into the Delaware Valley (1675–1715) resembled the Great Migration to New England a half-century before. Approximately the same number of people was involved. Each movement had a strong ideological and institutional core inspired by dissenting religion—Quakerism in the Delaware Valley case. Each had a strong regional core—the trans-Pennine north and north Midlands in the Delaware Valley case.[77] Finally, each had a pronounced "family" character: approximately 50 percent of the migrants arriving during the first half of the 1680s traveled in family groups.[78]

72. The classic account of this dynamic is Edmund Morgan's. See his *American Slavery, American Freedom*, 295–387.

73. See Horn, *Adapting to a New World*, 43, 39–41.

74. Grubb and Stitt, "Liverpool Emigrant Servant Trade," 385–88.

75. Fischer, *Albion's Seed*, 420–24, 445–51. One should assume that after 1688 wartime interruptions also caused lengthy pauses in the flow of North British emigrants into the Delaware Valley.

76. By midcentury Germans were the largest single ethnic group in the Pennsylvania region, at some 42 percent of population. Settlers of English and Welsh origin accounted for approximately 28 percent, as did Ulster and southern Irish. See Fischer, *Albion's Seed*, 431n7. On German migration, see, generally, A. G. Roeber, *Palatines, Liberty, and Property: German Lutherans in Colonial British America* (Baltimore: Johns Hopkins University Press, 1993), 27–61; Grubb, "Immigration and Servitude," 1–12; Wokeck, *Trade in Strangers*; Fogleman, *Hopeful Journeys*.

77. The Delaware Valley's ethnic Germans also shared a core regional point of origin, as Fogleman makes clear in *Hopeful Journeys*, 15–65.

78. Fischer, *Albion's Seed*, 434.

The familial imprint on the early Delaware Valley migrant stream attests to the likelihood of a migrant population somewhat younger than the contemporaneous English population, and thus suggests an age profile similar to other seventeenth-century English migrations to North America. The earliest immigrants also included numbers of servants.[79] Higher than in the earlier migration to New England, the incidence of servants in the Delaware migration did not approach the levels witnessed in the Chesapeake.[80] Socially, however, they were similar. First, migrants traveling apart from family groups were much more likely to be male than female. Second, they were also much more likely to be adolescents than adults. Local court records suggest that, as in the Chesapeake migration, a substantial proportion of imported servants were boys in early to midadolescence.[81] Servants traveling with family groups in intact households were also likely (as in the East Anglian migration to Massachusetts) to be children.[82] Overall, service and youth were as closely related in the early Delaware Valley as elsewhere on the North American mainland.

After 1713 migrants from the Palatinate and from Ulster became prominent in the Delaware Valley migrant stream. Migrants' characteristics, however, remained relatively constant. Both the German and the Ulster (although not the southern Irish) migrants came largely in family groups with considerable numbers of dependent children. Given that almost 44 percent of adult male migrants and 37.5 percent of females were in the sixteen-to-twenty-five age bracket, and that they were accompanied by large numbers of dependent children, one may be certain that at least 60 percent of ethnic German migrants were under age twenty-five and that at least 47 percent were under the age of twenty.[83] Among

79. Ibid., 437.

80. Gary Nash suggests that approximately 35 percent of all early settlers and 50 percent of adult males were indentured. *Quakers and Politics,* 279. David Galenson concludes that although Pennsylvania began appearing as a recorded destination for indentured servants in the 1680s, it did not become a major importer of servants until the eighteenth century. *White Servitude,* 85.

81. In the eight years following October 1683, 83 persons appeared before the Chester County court of quarter sessions to have terms of service set in "custom of country" hearings. Of these, three were adults and the remaining eighty were minors. The mean age of the minors (as judged) was 13 years, 2 months. Sixty-seven were boys (mean age 13) and 13 were girls (mean age 13 and a half), a ratio of 5:1. See Chester County, Pennsylvania, *Docket and Proceedings of the County Court,* vol. 1–2 (1681–97), transcribed as *Records of the Courts of Chester County, Pennsylvania,* 2 vols. (1910; Philadelphia: Colonial Society of Pennsylvania, 1972). Galenson reports a similar male to female ratio of 5:1 among servants destined for Pennsylvania in the 1680s and 1690s. *White Servitude,* 84–85.

82. Gary B. Nash, *The Urban Crucible: Social Change, Political Consciousness, and the Origins of the American Revolution* (Cambridge: Harvard University Press, 1979), 15; Levy, *Quakers and the American Family,* 138.

83. During the period 1730–38, for example, 10,670 Germans were recorded as taking passage for Philadelphia. Of these, 3,997 were men over sixteen and the remainder were women and children. The latter group breaks down at approximately 1.176 children per woman, suggesting that there were 3,607 children and 3,066 women. Given that 44 percent of the men, 37.6 percent of the women, and all of the children were twenty-five or younger, we can conclude that 61 percent of the migrant stream was below that age. Given that 19 percent of the men, 20.3 percent of the women, and

the Germans, the numbers of independent single males migrating rose over time; hence the composition of the German migration became relatively less family-oriented. But there was little change in its age distribution.[84]

Migrant numbers rose as the century progressed, but immigration was a secondary factor in sustaining Delaware Valley population growth. Virtually from the beginning of English settlement, local population growth rates consistently exceeded those of New England and the Chesapeake.[85] Fertility rates across the region were high, reflecting the youthfulness of the population, early marriage ages for women, and the comparatively healthy environment. Early birth rates were retarded by male-female gender imbalance, which capped family-formation, and by servitude's imposition of a delay of entry into marriage, mostly affecting men. Nevertheless, by the early eighteenth century the region's population was growing primarily by natural increase.[86] The young family orientation of the German migrant stream furthered the process.[87] By the 1720s even Philadelphia—described as a "demographic disaster" during its early years—was moving toward self-sustaining growth.[88]

Immigration continued to supply bound labor. Overall, about 40 percent of all voluntary immigrants entering the Delaware Valley after 1720 underwent a period of servitude.[89] Yet the rapid growth of the Creole population underscores that, as elsewhere, immigrants were only one of a number of sources of labor for the region. Bound immigrant labor substituted for shortages of family labor in the households—rural and urban—that, as elsewhere, were the key units of production. We have seen that over time the servant population became concentrated in Philadelphia and other regional urban centers, but initially servants were as likely to be found in rural and agricultural pursuits as in urban.

---

all the children were twenty or younger, we can conclude that 47 percent of the migrant stream was below that age. Estimates calculated from figures supplied in Wokeck, "German Immigration to Philadelphia," 260, adjusted for age and social composition by the estimates presented in Farley Grubb, "German Immigration to Pennsylvania, 1709 to 1820," *Journal of Interdisciplinary History* 20 (Winter 1990): 421, 427.

84. Grubb, "German Immigration to Pennsylvania," 427.

85. Russell R. Menard, "Was There a 'Middle Colonies Demographic Regime'?" *Proceedings of the American Philosophical Society* 133, no. 2 (1989): 216.

86. Susan E. Klepp, "Fragmented Knowledge: Questions in Regional Demographic History," ibid., 223–33.

87. Grubb, "German Immigration to Pennsylvania," 435–36.

88. Klepp, "Demography in Early Philadelphia," 92, 91–96. As Klepp shows, Philadelphia did not enjoy a sustained positive rate of natural increase until midcentury, when death rates began to fall consistently. By the 1720s, however, birth rates had risen to the point where they at least offset high death rates.

89. Between 1720 and 1770 the incidence of servants in overall migration appears to vary narrowly around 40 percent between 1720 and 1750 and around 46 percent between 1760 and 1775, with an intervening fall to about 36 percent in the 1750s. These figures reflect the varying incidence of servitude among different ethnic migrant groups. For a detailed breakdown, see Tables 6 and 7, and the appendix to this essay.

More to the point, however, in no area did their percentage incidence in population exceed single digits.[90]

Migrant indentured servitude was an important source of labor power for many of the mainland colonies of British North America in their crucial opening phases of establishment and early growth. But have historians been sensitive to its diminished importance thereafter? Are historians correct in seeing the early Republic as a moment of transition to a predominantly free laboring population from a colonial-era workforce predominantly unfree, debased, and continuously refreshed in that character by successive waves of bound immigrants? Was this indeed the crucial moment that proved the reality of revolutionary-era egalitarianism, the cultural achievement of historic proportions that "alter[ed] the outlook for 'freedom' for most Americans"?[91]

The analysis presented here suggests that migrant indentured servitude was not as significant, either in supplying labor or in determining the structure and culture of colonial-era work relations, as historians have assumed.[92] The ideal-typical migrant servant was not a gang laborer in waiting but a youth who substituted for scarcities in family labor in a mode of production largely organized through households. As settler populations achieved self-sustaining growth, labor supply became more homegrown, migrant servitude less important. The result was a working population in the colonial era segmented by age, gender, and race, working under highly differentiated legal conditions. Legal relations of work clearly approximating "free" labor existed among white Creole males long before the Revolution. Legal relations reproducing unfree labor for others clearly existed long afterward.[93] In this light, the contention that the revolutionary era marked a sharp point of demarcation between bound and free labor as the prototypical condition of working life requires reexamination. In light of the composition of the colonial-era working population, trends outlined by scholars in support of the contention may turn out to be rather less momentous,

90. See Tables 8 and 9. See also Farley Grubb, "Immigrant Servant Labor: Their Occupational and Geographic Distribution in the Late Eighteenth-Century Mid-Atlantic Economy," *Social Science History* 9 (Summer 1985): 249–76, at 251–55.

91. Fogleman, "Slaves, Convicts, and Servants," 45, 65–66.

92. For similar conclusions regarding the incidence of indentured servitude, see Smith, *Colonists in Bondage,* 336 (by the 1670s, throughout the British American colonies, "about one white person in every ten was under indenture"); Farley Grubb, "The End of European Immigrant Servitude in the United States: An Economic Analysis of Market Collapse, 1772–1835," *Journal of Economic History* 54 (December 1994): 796n5 (servants made up less than 10 percent of the mainland colonial population by 1700); Alice Hanson Jones, *American Colonial Wealth: Documents and Methods,* 2d ed. (New York: Arno Press, 1978), 3:1787, table 4.21 (servants were 2.3 percent of the population by the 1770s.)

93. Christopher Tomlins, "Early British America, 1585–1830: Freedom Bound," in *Masters, Servants, and Magistrates in Britain and the Empire, 1562–1955,* ed. Paul Craven and Douglas Hay (Chapel Hill: University of North Carolina Press, 2004), 150–52; Tomlins, *Law, Labor, and Ideology,* 223–92. See also Robert J. Steinfeld, *Coercion, Contract, and Free Labor in the Nineteenth Century* (New York: Cambridge University Press, 2001); Amy Dru Stanley, *From Bondage to Contract: Wage Labor, Marriage, and the Market in the Age of Slave Emancipation* (New York: Cambridge University Press, 1998).

and certainly less linear in their illustration of a general "freedom," than has been supposed.

To assess fully the significance of the portrait of migration, servitude, and labor force composition detailed here, it is now necessary to move beyond the exploration of population per se. "Peopling" is not an autonomous self-directing social process that occurs outside cultural or political contexts. Neither migration nor servitude creates its own meaning. Historians must study institutions and ideologies on both sides of the Atlantic—social and cultural, governmental, legal—to discover the meaning of movements of population and their significance for colonial social and economic life in general and for the performance of work in particular. To assess properly the extent to which a transformation in civic identity—"freedom"—was on offer at the end of the colonial era, we need to map the persistent segmentation of the working population and its legal expression. We need to understand the differentiated legal culture of work and its governance prevailing throughout the colonial era if we are to understand properly the extent and limits, the conditions and relativities, of the freedom apparently available at its end.

APPENDIX
European Migration to Mainland America, 1600–1780, and the Incidence of Indentured Servitude: Estimates and Sources

For the mainland alone, through 1780, current estimates suggest a total European migration of between 470,000 and 515,000, including 54,500 involuntary migrants (convicts or prisoners). Of voluntary migrants, I estimate that 48–50 percent were committed to an initial period of servitude by indenture or other arrangement. This status described on average 60–65 percent of voluntary migrants in the seventeenth century and 40–42 percent in the eighteenth.

My estimates suggest a total migration to the Chesapeake of 108,000, of which 80 percent (86,400) were servants; to New England of 24,000, of which 16.5 percent (4,000) were servants; to the Delaware Valley of 15,000, of which 35 percent (5,250) were servants; to the lower South of 8,000, of which 40 percent (3,200) were servants; and to New Netherlands of 6,000, of which 3,300 (55 percent) were servants. The key sources (full citations of which are in the footnotes to this article) are as follows:

(1) *For the century as a whole:* Henry Gemery, "Emigration from the British Isles to the New World, 1630–1700: Inferences from Colonial Populations," *Research in Economic History: A Research Annual* 5 (1980): 179–231, and "Markets for Migrants: English Indentured Servitude and Emigration in the Seventeenth and Eighteenth Centuries," in *Colonialism and Migration: Indentured Labor Before and After Slavery,* ed. P.C. Emmer (Dordrecht: M. Nijhoff, 1986), 33–54, at 40.

(2) *For the Chesapeake:* Menard, "British Migration to the Chesapeake Colonies," 105 (table 3) for 1630–1700, and 102 for 1600–1630; Horn, *Adapting to a New World,* 25.

(3) *For New England:* Gemery, "Emigration from the British Isles," and sources cited in note 7 to this essay.

(4) *For the Delaware Valley:* Fischer, *Albion's Seed,* 421; Nash, *Quakers and Politics,* 50.

(5) *For the lower South:* McCusker and Menard, *Economy of British America,* 171–72; Galenson, *White Servitude,* 154–55, 217; Warren B. Smith, *White Servitude in Colonial South Carolina* (Columbia: University of South Carolina Press, 1961).

(6) *For New Netherlands:* Ernst van den Boogaart, "The Servant Migration to New Netherland, 1624–1664," in Emmer, *Colonialism and Migration,* 55–81.

Gemery suggests a total British migration during 1630–1700 of 155,000, of which 116,000 was to the Chesapeake and lower South and 39,000 to the middle colonies and New England. For New England I use the common estimate of 21,000 for the 1631–40 period, plus a nominal 500 per decade for the remainder of the century. Servant numbers, at 16.5 percent, are based on the preponderance of the estimated percentages reported in note 7 to this essay. For the middle colonies I use Fischer's estimate of 15,000 for migration to the Delaware Valley and Nash's estimate of 35 percent for the proportion of servants in that migration. Together, these figures fit Gemery's overall estimate very well. For the Chesapeake I use Menard's decadal migration figures for 1630–1700, supplemented by adjustments he makes to cover the period from 1607 to 1630. It is worth noting that this figure is lower than Menard's own "best guess" of approximately 123,000 for the entire seventeenth century, but that figure is simply the middle of the range of possibilities (99,000—146,000) that he offers and does not fit well with other estimates of overall seventeenth-century migration. Nor does it fit with the total produced by his decadal series. Disaggregated decadal figures are more useful to my project in this essay, so I have chosen to stick with the overall figure they produce. I have deliberately set my estimate of the proportion of servants in Chesapeake migration (80 percent) at the top of the range of conjectural estimates offered by experts (see, e.g., Horn, *Adapting to a New World,* 25): indentured migrants 70 to 85 percent of total and probably "nearer the upper bound"; Games, *Migration and Origins,* 74: 77 percent of total. For the lower South I can offer no more than a guess, based in part on the residual of round numbers left from the other, more reliable, estimates. The figure is clearly an upper bound. To the extent that it is inflated, the Chesapeake numbers could be raised by 2,000 to 3,000.

My seventeenth-century totals are highly compatible with those of Aaron Fogleman, whose estimates are based on ethnicities rather than regions of reception. Fogleman proposes a slightly larger total European migration of

165,000 (compared with my 161,000) but suggests a somewhat lower percentage (60 percent, compared with my 64 percent) of immigrants committed to an initial term of servitude. Fogleman's figures include 2,300 involuntary European (mostly Scottish) immigrants in the category "convicts and prisoners," as well as some 1,500 miscellaneous (mostly Swedish and German) migrants. It is unlikely that these are counted in the sources I have used. If they are not, then our overall migrant numbers become very close indeed. See his "Slaves, Convicts, and Servants," 68.

For the eighteenth century (through 1780), the range of numbers offered in the literature is substantially wider. An additional hazard for the "regions" approach used here is that the literature also tends to differentiate migrant numbers and population characteristics by ethnicity rather than region of reception. Recent research by Aaron Fogleman, however, has synthesized much of the existing literature and has produced a set of estimates that has been greeted as the best currently available for eighteenth-century transatlantic migration. See his "Slaves, Convicts, and Servants." For a complete explanation of his estimates, see Aaron Fogleman, "Migrations to the Thirteen British North American Colonies, 1700–1775: New Estimates," *Journal of Interdisciplinary History* 22 (Spring 1992): 691–709. For comments on Fogleman's figures, see John M. Murrin, "In the Land of the Free and the Home of the Slave, Maybe There Was Room Even for Deference," *Journal of American History* 85 (June 1998): 86; Georg Fertig, "Transatlantic Migration from the German-Speaking Parts of Central Europe, 1600–1800: Proportions, Structures, and Explanations," in Canny, *Europeans on the Move,* 199, 201; James Horn, "British Diaspora: Emigration from Britain, 1680–1815," in *The Oxford History of the British Empire,* vol. 2, *The Eighteenth Century,* ed. P. J. Marshall (Oxford: Oxford University Press, 1998), 28–52.

Calculating eighteenth-century migration according to ethnic group and time period, Fogleman arrives at a total of 307,400 European migrants, voluntary and involuntary (convict) as shown in Table A-1.

Table A-1 Eighteenth-Century Migration to the Thirteen Mainland Colonies by European Ethnic Group (in thousands)

Decade ending	German	N. Irish	S. Irish	Scottish	English	Welsh	Other	Total
1709	0.1	0.6	0.8	0.2	0.4	0.3	0.1	2.5
1719	3.7	1.2	1.7	0.5	1.3	0.9	0.2	9.5
1729	2.3	2.1	3.0	0.8	2.2	1.5	0.2	12.1
1739	13.0	4.4	7.4	2.0	4.9	3.2	0.8	35.7
1749	16.6	9.2	9.1	3.1	7.5	4.9	1.1	51.5
1759	29.1	14.2	8.1	3.7	8.8	5.8	1.2	70.9
1769	14.5	21.2	8.5	10.0	11.9	7.8	1.6	75.5
1779	5.2	13.2	3.9	15.0	7.1	4.6	0.7	49.7
Total	84.5	66.1	42.5	35.3	44.1	29.0	5.9	307.4

Fogleman's total is low (although not unacceptably so) when compared with global estimates in the range of 340,000–370,000 offered by several scholars for this period. See Potter, "Demographic Development and Family Structure," 135–36 (summarizing work of Henry Gemery, David Galenson, and Potter himself); Henry Gemery, "Disarray in the Historical Record: Estimates of Immigration to the United States, 1700–1860," *Proceedings of the American Philosophical Society* 133, no. 2 (1989): 123–27, and "European Emigration to North America, 1700–1820: Numbers and Quasi-Numbers," *Perspectives in American History,* new ser., 1 (1984): 283–342.

Fogleman's disaggregated ethnic group figures tend in most cases to inhabit the low end of ranges suggested by the work of other scholars. In the German case, for example, the work of other scholars suggests a range of 90,000–120,000. See Wokeck, "German and Irish Immigration," 128–33, and "Flow and Composition," 260–61. Wokeck has refined and restated her estimates in *Trade in Strangers,* 45–53, where she suggests an overall German migration to all of North America of 111,000 and to Philadelphia alone of 80,000. The literature on German migration (excluding Wokeck's most recent work) is discussed in Fertig, "Transatlantic Migration." See also Grubb, "Immigration and Servitude," 15–16, 175, and "German Immigration to Pennsylvania," 417–36; Gunter Moltmann, "The Migration of German Redemptioners to North America, 1720–1820," in Emmer, *Colonialism and Migration,* 105–22, at 115; Bailyn, *Voyagers to the West,* 25–26. Wokeck's refined figure of 111,000 clearly establishes the upper bound in a range of 84,500–111,000, and should be treated as authoritative.

In the Irish case the range of estimates is substantially wider, tending from 65,000 to more than 200,000. The upper bound is supplied largely by Bailyn's claim of 100,000–150,000 "Scotch-Irish" for 1720–60, which may, however, include other Celtic migrants, and by William J. Smyth's proposed average of 5,000 per annum "to colonial America" between 1700 and 1776. Patrick Griffin follows Bailyn, arguing for "more than 100,000." Based on projections of migrant numbers from a surname-sensitive analysis of their descendants (the U.S. population in 1790), Thomas Purvis suggests 114,000 Ulster migrants before 1775.

James Horn states that the number for all Irish migrants is "at least 115,000." Marianne Wokeck's study of German and Irish immigration to Philadelphia finds that at the peak (1763–73) of Irish entries to Philadelphia in excess of two-thirds of all Irish entering the Delaware Valley were from Ulster ports, which, if a constant, would suggest (on Bailyn's and Purvis's figures) an all-Ireland total of 150,000–250,000. But Wokeck's counts of actual arrivals at Philadelphia provide much lower overall totals and have been accepted as the more accurate by L. M. Cullen. Cullen suggests that the Delaware Valley total should be inflated by 50 percent to allow for aggregate Irish migration to all North American ports. Wokeck's recent restatement of her research on Irish immigration in *Trade in Strangers*, 172–73, gives further support to the lower figure, arguing for a total Irish immigration to the Delaware Valley of 51,676. Invoking Cullen's multiplier produces an aggregate of 77,500. Wokeck's restatement also reaffirms the two-thirds preponderance of northern Irish migrants and dates the beginnings of that preponderance from the mid-1740s. For Irish migration, see Wokeck, "German and Irish Immigration," 135–43, revised and refined in *Trade in Strangers*, 172–73; William J. Smith, "Irish Emigration, 1700–1920," in P. C. Emmer and M. Mörner, *European Expansion and Migration: Essays on the Intercontinental Migration from Africa, Asia, and Europe* (New York: Berg, 1992), 49–78; Bailyn, *Voyagers to the West*, 25–26; Patrick Griffin, *The People with No Name: Ireland's Ulster Scots, America's Scots Irish and the Creation of a British Atlantic World, 1689–1764* (Princeton: Princeton University Press, 2001), 1, 67; Thomas L. Purvis, "The European Ancestry of the United States Population, 1790," *William and Mary Quarterly*, 3d ser., 41 (Jan. 1984): 95–96; Horn, "British Diaspora," 31; L. M. Cullen, "The Irish Diaspora of the Seventeenth and Eighteenth Centuries," in Canny, *Europeans on the Move*, 113–49, especially 115–16. Fogleman's aggregate of 108,600 (including involuntary migrants, whom Ekirch advises "were often disguised by merchants as indentured servants," *Bound for America*, 114) is extrapolated from Wokeck's earlier calculations and from research on shipping destinations, the effect of which is to suggest that Cullen's multiplier should be doubled. In light of Wokeck's and Cullen's work, Fogleman's aggregate might best be seen as a well-documented upper bound, establishing the range for Irish immigration at 77,500–108,600.

The German and Irish cases are the best documented in current scholarship on eighteenth-century migration to the mainland. Estimates for other ethnicities are more conjectural. Take Scottish migration. Fogleman's figure for Scottish migration, 35,300, is lower for the whole period through 1775 than Bailyn's estimate of 40,000 for the period 1760–75 alone. The total is also substantially lower than the 62,500 Purvis suggests, a figure concurred in by Smout, Landsman, and Devine. See Bailyn, *Voyagers to the West*, 25–26, 170–71, 175, 243; Purvis, "European Ancestry," 95–96; T. C. Smout, N. C. Landsman, and T. M. Devine, "Scottish Emigration in the Seventeenth and Eighteenth Centuries," in Canny, *Europeans on the Move*, 97, 98, 104. Hence we can set a notional range at 35,000–62,500.

Fogleman's figures for English and Welsh migration are also (as he notes himself) somewhat conjectural. As in the Scottish case, reliable data are sparse. Fischer suggests that 7,500 migrants (mostly from northern England and the Welsh border) arrived in the Delaware Valley in the first two decades of the eighteenth century. Bailyn proposes "over 30,000" English migrants for the period after 1760. Galenson offers evidence of only a modest rate of influx for the intervening period. For English migration, see Fischer, *Albion's Seed*, 421; Bailyn, *Voyagers to the West*, 25–26, 170–71, 175, 243; Galenson, *White Servitude*, 51–56,

93. In this light Fogleman's suggested overall figure of 44,100 for the English component of the English/Welsh aggregate (which, if Fischer and Bailyn are correct, would imply an average English migration of only 1,600 persons per decade between 1718 and 1760) is not on the face of it unreasonable. Galenson, however, was not taking involuntary (convict) importation into account in his assessment of the modesty of rates of English migration in the period intervening between the end of early eighteenth-century Delaware Valley migration and the post-1760 revival. On Ekirch's figures, between 1718 and 1775 some 36,000 convicts could be included in the category of English/Welsh migrants entering the thirteen colonies (overwhelmingly the Chesapeake). See *Bound for America*, 114–16, 116. Allowing for these in the overall total requires that we assume a higher average migration rate for English/Welsh migrants (voluntary and involuntary) for the 1718–60 period. Horn's suggestion of 80,000 English/Welsh migrants, 1701–80, reinforces the case for this adjustment. It is likely that, as in the Irish case, convict migrants may have become compounded with the voluntary migrant category because the processes of their transportation did not readily render them an administratively distinct migrant stream (*Bound for America*, 111–19). Hence some convicts probably figure in Galenson's and Bailyn's estimates of post-1718 migration rates. But a substantial proportion should be considered additional to the figures already mentioned, and thus should increase the estimated English/Welsh totals. Thus, discussing English migration alone, Canny suggests that a figure of 50,000, including convicts, is appropriate for the period 1700–1775. See Canny, "English Migration," in Canny, *Europeans on the Move*, 58. As an additional consideration, Fogleman's figure of 29,000 for the Welsh component of the English/Welsh amalgam is based on Purvis, but the ratio of migrants to descendant population suggested by Purvis's other estimates (that is, suggested by his analyses of the relationships between Ulster and Scottish migration and Ulster- and Scottish-descended population segments) would argue for a larger estimate, one on the order of 45,000. It is necessary, of course, to adjust any addition to the Welsh component to try to avoid double-counting convict importations. A notional range in the English/Welsh case is thus established as 73,000–95,000.

The overall effect of Marianne Wokeck's recent research in the German and Irish cases and of allowing some upward flexibility in the areas of least reliable data (that is, Scottish, English, and Welsh migration) is to push Fogleman's total modestly upward, to 350,500 (this total accepts Fogleman's figure of 6,000 "other European"). This sits comfortably in the range of scholarship discussed by Potter (see above). Treating Fogleman's original grand total as an aggregate lower bound, we can argue that the appropriate range for European migration to the mainland, 1700–1780, is on the order of 307,000–350,000.

In estimating the incidence of servants in eighteenth-century migration, all scholars note considerable fluctuation in the proportion of servants to total numbers of migrants, varying primarily according to factors of ethnic origin and chronology of migration. In the German case, Moltmann suggests a range of 50–66 percent servants in total migration. Grubb offers "roughly half" as an approximation of incidence over the whole period 1709–1820. His much more detailed studies of red mptioner migration to Philadelphia produce a more exact proportion of 58 percent for the period 1771–73, which also has the virtue of occurring at the midpoint of Moltmann's range. Relying on Wokeck, how-ever, Fogleman arrives at a substantially lower 35 percent overall (this comprises a tripartite periodization of none before 1720, about one-third, 1720–60; and about one-half, 1760–75. See his "Slaves, Convicts and Servants," 72). Wokeck herself puts the incidence of servants in total migration at "at least half" after the 1750s, implying a lower rate than this for the preceding period of heaviest German migration through 1760. (See *Trade in Strangers*, 233). Collectively, the available evidence and opinion suggests that Moltmann's range is too high, except for the years after 1760, where it is best represented by the 58 percent midpoint that Grubb calculated for Philadelphia. For purposes of arriving at a very rough estimate of the incidence of servitude in German migration for the entire period, one might choose the midpoint between the 35 percent of the earlier period and the 58 percent of the later, arriving at 46 percent, which is certainly within the range of Grubb's "roughly half." Given that the bulk of German migration occurred prior to 1760 (that is, during the "low-incidence" period), 46 percent is a generous estimate.

In the Irish case, Wokeck, "German and Irish Immigration," estimates the incidence of servants at the peak of entries to Philadelphia at 20–25 percent among Ulster migrants and 50–66 percent among southern Irish migrants. Applying these proportions to the overall Irish migrant stream, and adjusting to reflect the relative contribution of southern and northern Irish migrants), one arrives at an overall figure of approximately 36 percent. This agrees with Fogleman's figure based on the same sources: the addition of convicts to the cal-culation elevates the proportion of bound Irish migrants (whether voluntary or involuntary) to a bare majority of 51 percent. Once Wokeck's revised and refined figures (*Trade in Strangers*, 172–73) for Irish Delaware Valley migration are fully absorbed into the calculation, however, it seems inevitable that the incidence of servitude in Irish migration will fall, for, as already indicated, Wokeck's figures suggest that the preponderance of northern Irish in overall Irish migration, clear in the 1760s, was actually well established by the mid-1740s.

In the Scottish case, Bailyn argues that for the period 1774–76 fewer than one in five migrants was indentured. Can one, however, assume the con-stancy of the 1770s rate (which reflects the high proportion of family migrants in total movement)? Fogleman applies a rate of 50 percent for the period through 1760, producing an overall proportion of servants in total migration of 21 per-cent. Including convicts and prisoners, the incidence of bound (voluntarily and involuntarily) migrants on his figures increases to 27 percent of all Scottish migrants.

In the English/Welsh case the incidence of indentured servants among the early eighteenth-century Delaware Valley migrants is likely to have continued at approximately 35 percent (the rate of the late seventeenth century to that area). We know, however, that earlier seventeenth-century rates were much higher, and Bailyn shows that by the 1770s the rate had returned to better than two-thirds voluntarily bound among all voluntary migrants. Fogleman assumes that the two-thirds rate holds for all voluntary English/Welsh migrants during the eighteenth century. Most of the century's transported convicts and prisoners also came from these sources, which results in a total bound English/Welsh migration (voluntary and involuntary) on his figures approaching 80 percent.

To arrive at an overall proportion of indentured servants in voluntary migrants, we must adjust the ranges of migrant numbers to allow for involuntary convict migrants. Fogleman suggests that of 52,500 convicts transported, 32,500 (62 percent) were English/Welsh, 17,500 (33.5 percent) Irish, and 2,200

Table A-2   Eighteenth-Century Migration to the Thirteen Mainland Colonies, by European Ethnic Group and Status (in thousands)

(a) Results derived from Fogleman[1]					
	All migrants	Involuntary	Voluntary	# Servant	% Servant
Irish	108.6	17.5	91.1	39.0	42.8
English/Welsh	73.1	32.5	40.6	27.2	67.0
Scottish	35.3	2.2	33.1	7.4	22.3
German	84.5	—	84.5	30.0	35.5
Other	5.9	—	5.9	—	—
Total	307.4	52.2	255.2	103.6	40.6

(b) Tomlins Alternative					
	All migrants	Involuntary	Voluntary	# Servant	% Servant
Irish	77.5	17.5	60.0	21.6	36.0
English/Welsh	95.0	32.5	62.5	41.9	67.0
Scottish	62.5	2.2	60.3	12.7	21.0
German	111.0	—	111.0	51.1	46.0
Other	5.9	—	5.9	—	—
Total	351.9	52.2	299.7	127.3	42.4

1. Aaron S. Fogleman, "From Slaves, Convicts, and Servants to Free Passengers: The Transformation of Immigration in the Era of the American Revolution," *Journal of American History* 85 (June 1998): 44 (tables 1 and 2), 71 (table A3).

(4.2 percent) Scottish. There is some departure here from Ekirch's figures, un-explained in the English/Welsh case, but for the sake of consistency I will adopt Fogleman's numbers. Applied to the range of 307,000–350,000 voluntary migrants, we can express the results in two tables, the first restating Fogleman's results, the second offering my own variation (see Table A-2).

Although calculated differently, the two outcomes are very close. In each scenario, just over 40 percent of all voluntary migrants, 1700–1775, appear committed to an initial period of servitude. Reinclusion of all transported convicts as similarly committed to an initial period of servitude (in fact Ekirch's work would caution against this; see *Bound for America,* 119–20), raises the percentage of migrants committed to an initial period of servitude, 1700–1775, to slightly in excess of 50 percent.

Treating finally the entire seventeenth- and eighteenth-century period through 1775 as a whole, we find that using Fogleman's figures, some 48 percent of all voluntary migrants into mainland British America were committed to an initial period of servitude; if we include all convicts, as above, the percentage rises to 54 percent. On my adjusted figures the result is 50 percent and 55 percent, respectively. Thus in each case, notwithstanding the adjustments in proportions and in particular ethnic contributions that I have suggested, the overall conclusion agrees very closely with Fogleman's.

Chapter Six

Capitalism, Slavery, and Benjamin Franklin's American Revolution

DAVID WALDSTREICHER

In *Capitalism and Slavery* (1944), Eric Williams described the rise of the American North, and ultimately the American Revolution itself, as an outgrowth of the rise of the West Indian sugar colonies. The origin of capitalism and the conditions for the American Revolution lay with and within, not outside or against, slavery.[1] Perhaps the neglect of Williams's work by scholars of early America and the Revolution derives from his focus on the British colonies that did not rebel, and his argument, later in the book, that the Revolution did encourage industrial capitalism and led to the end of slavery. The emphasis shifts from causes to consequences, from slavery to antislavery; the Revolution becomes mainly a pivot in explaining how, in Williams's later much-debated terms, slavery declined because British capitalism no longer had use for the institution. Williams's transition from the Revolution to the economic causes for slavery's decline turns on a quotation from Adam Smith, for whom English colonial policy amounted to "a manifest violation of the most sacred rights of mankind . . . impertinent badges of slavery imposed upon [colonists], without any sufficient reason, by the groundless jealousy of the merchants and manufacturers of the mother country." In 1776, according to Williams, Smith had captured a fundamental meaning and ultimate effect of the American Revolution: its rejection of one form of capitalism

I would like to thank John Bezís-Selfa, Joanne P. Melish, Cathy Matson, and the incomparable and unconvinced Michael Zuckerman for their extremely helpful comments on drafts of this essay.

1. Russell R. Menard argues that Williams provides a more realistic picture of American colonial development than we get from recent syntheses. Menard, "Epilogue: Capitalism and Slavery; Personal Reflections on Eric Williams and Reconstruction of Early American History," in *The World Turned Upside Down: The State of Eighteenth-Century American Studies at the Beginning of the Twenty-First Century,* ed. William G. Shade and Michael V. Kennedy (Bethlehem: Lehigh University Press, 2001), 321–31.

(mercantilist–colonial–slave-based) and its embrace of another (free trade–industrial–free-labor). But slavery also created the conditions that Smith and the American revolutionaries wanted to credit to freedom.[2]

Smith's adoption of the rhetoric of British enslavement of the colonists is especially striking in light of his evasion of the subject of slave-produced wealth in the British nation. Where did this argument come from?[3] Why did the quintessential exponent of free-market capitalism denigrate the value of slaves and equate mercantilist regulation with slavery? The American Revolution discredited slavery ideologically. It did so, however, by neglecting its economic importance to the very people who had depended upon its fruits to catapult them into a position where they could even imagine national self-sufficiency.

Like historians of British capitalism, Caribbean slavery, and abolition, Americanists have devoted far more attention of late to the aftermath of the American Revolution and its admittedly paradoxical effects. Only recently have they focused on the ways in which slaves and slavery came to be implicated in

2. Eric Williams, *Capitalism and Slavery* (Chapel Hill: University of North Carolina Press, 1944), 107, 120; see also Eric Williams, *From Columbus to Castro: The History of the Caribbean* (1970; reprint, New York: Vintage Books, 1984), 217. Smith's involvement in these debates has been noted and elaborated on elsewhere. See Richard B. Sheridan, *Sugar and Slavery: An Economic History of the British West Indies, 1623–1775* (Baltimore: Johns Hopkins University Press, 1974), 5–11; David Brion Davis, *The Problem of Slavery in the Age of Revolution, 1770–1823* (Ithaca: Cornell University Press, 1975), 351–54; Seymour Drescher, *The Mighty Experiment: Free Labor Versus Slavery in British Emancipation* (New York: Oxford University Press, 2002), 19–33, 247n41.

3. Students of Adam Smith and Franklin have weighed the evidence for their meeting of the minds and the latter's particular influence, evidence for which includes their common attraction to physiocracy, their similarly "provincial cosmopolitanism," Smith's possession of copies of Franklin's *Observations on the Increase of Mankind* (printed in 1755, 1760, and 1769), their meeting in Scotland in 1759, and a remembrance of the two conferring, and even by one account passing drafts, during the years Franklin resided in London. Most recently, Michael Perelman has argued that Smith derived his rose-colored view of the North American economy, including his limited ability to factor in slavery or unfree labor generally, from Franklin. Smith agreed with Franklin on the folly of coercion, and much of *The Wealth of Nations* can be seen as a brief against British policy vis-à-vis the colonies in the years leading up to 1776. But by the time Smith was ready to publish, Franklin was anathema in England and could not be cited, much less credited as an authority. Lewis J. Carey, *Franklin's Economic Views* (New York: Doubleday, Doran, 1928), 36, 59, 106–31; Thomas D. Eliot, "The Relations Between Adam Smith and Benjamin Franklin Before 1776," *Political Science Quarterly* 39 (1924): 67–96; J. Bennett Nolan, *Benjamin Franklin in Scotland and Ireland, 1759 and 1771* (Philadelphia: University of Pennsylvania Press, 1938), 200; Joseph Dorfman, "Benjamin Franklin: Economic Statesman" in *Essays on General Politics, Commerce, and Political Economy, Being Volume II, Part II, of The Works of Benjamin Franklin*, ed. Jared Sparks (1836; reprint, New York, 1971), 6n2, 9, 18–19n41; Esmond Wright, "This Fine and Noble China Vase, the British Empire: Benjamin Franklin's Love-Hate View of England," *Pennsylvania Magazine of History and Biography* 111 (October 1987): 449; Jerry Z. Muller, *Adam Smith in His Time and Ours: Designing the Decent Society* (New York: Macmillan, 1993), 22; Donald Winch, *Riches and Poverty: An Intellectual History of Political Economy in Britain, 1750–1834* (New York: Cambridge University Press, 1996), 3; Ian Simpson Ross, *The Life of Adam Smith* (New York: Oxford University Press, 1995), 186, 255–56; Michael Perelman, *The Invention of Capitalism: Classical Political Economy and the Secret History of Primitive Accumulation* (Durham: Duke University Press, 2000), 237–47, 254–79.

the imperial controversies before 1776.[4] Recent synthetic accounts, however, emphasize the sunny side: the Revolution's antislavery effects rather than its slave-owning roots. Gordon S. Wood describes conditions of freedom and entre- preneurship already present before the Revolution and credits the Revolution for further unleashing free enterprise. The founders are responsible "for all our current egalitarian thinking" and it is nothing short of perverse to suggest that they could have done more than they did to address the matter of slavery. For Joyce Appleby, the persistence of slavery in the new nation is a function of southern backwardness and resistance to the rise of capitalism. For both schol- ars, Benjamin Franklin epitomizes the capitalist, democratic, and antislavery thrust of the Revolution. Franklin's America was hardworking, independent, proudly middle-class, and ultimately antislavery.[5]

Such interpretations surely have something to do with the popularity of Franklin in recent years. To call Franklin "the first American" is to identify America and its colonial origins with freedom rather than slavery.[6] The identi- fication of Franklin in particular with freedom, and with opposition to slavery, has been reinforced during the past decade by our leading historians. For Joseph J. Ellis and others, Franklin's antislavery credentials, ratified by his prominent sig- nature on an antislavery petition presented to the first federal Congress, stands as a jewel in the founders' crown, particularly at a time when other revolutionary

---

4. See David Brion Davis, *The Problem of Slavery in Western Culture* (Ithaca: Cornell Uni- versity Press, 1966), 440–42; Davis, *Problem of Slavery in the Age of Revolution;* Christopher L. Brown, "An Empire Without Slaves: British Concepts of Emancipation in the Era of the American Revolu- tion," *William and Mary Quarterly,* 3d ser., 56 (April 1999): 273–306; Christopher L. Brown, "Politics and Slavery," in *The British Atlantic World, 1500–1800,* ed. David Armitage and Michael J. Braddick (Lon- don: Palgrave Macmillan, 2002), 214–32. For the Revolution as a struggle to save a slave South that led slaves to take matters into their own hands, see Robert Olwell, *Masters, Subjects, and Slaves: The Culture of Power in the South Carolina Low Country, 1740–1790* (Ithaca: Cornell University Press, 1998); Woody Holton, *Forced Founders: Indians, Debtors, Slaves, and the Making of the American Revolution in Virginia* (Chapel Hill: University of North Carolina Press, 1999). These works build on Benjamin Quarles, *The Negro in the American Revolution* (Chapel Hill: University of North Carolina Press, 1961), and Sylvia Frey, *Water from the Rock: Black Resistance in a Revolutionary Age* (Princeton: Princeton University Press, 1991). See also Davis, *Problem of Slavery in the Age of Revolution,* 256. Some of the best works of the 1960s and 1970s emphasized the "paradox" of the Republic's attack on "slavery" and its dependence on slavery but also emphasized the striking rise of antislavery and racism in the early Republic. Winthrop Jordan, *White Over Black: American Attitudes Toward the Negro, 1550–1812* (Chapel Hill: University of North Carolina Press, 1967); Duncan McLeod, *Slavery, Race, and the American Revolution* (Cambridge: Cambridge University Press, 1974).

5. Gordon S. Wood, *The Radicalism of the American Revolution* (New York: Knopf, 1992), 7; Joyce Appleby, *Inheriting the Revolution: The First Generation of Americans* (Cambridge: Harvard Univer- sity Press, 2000); Gordon S. Wood, "The Enemy Is Us: Democratic Capitalism in the Early Republic," *Journal of the Early Republic* 16 (Summer 1996): 293–308; Joyce Appleby, "The Vexed Story of Capital- ism Told by American Historians," *Journal of the Early Republic* 21 (Spring 2001): 1–18.

6. Alan Taylor, "The Good Father," *New Republic,* January 19, 2003, 38–42; H. W. Brands, *The First American: The Life and Times of Benjamin Franklin* (New York: Doubleday, 2000).

leaders are coming under renewed scrutiny for their slaveholding.[7] Even those who believe that the founding of the Republic solidified, rather than undermined, the institution of slavery find Franklin's antislavery useful. Building the case for Thomas Jefferson's hypocrisy, Paul Finkelman contrasts him with Franklin, "who, unlike Jefferson, believed in racial equality."[8]

Like Jefferson, Franklin had an extremely long career in public life, which tempts us to take his late statements and actions as the most significant, authentic, and wise positions of the founders. In part because he retired from business early, in part because he went to Europe and escaped his own Pennsylvania house, which continued to be home to slaves, he evaded the gaps between principle, policy, and practice that seem to condemn other founders. Franklin even lived long enough for his household slaves to run away or die off. Yet only when antislavery beliefs became politically safe in his home state, after he returned from France, did he make fighting slavery part of his public identity. A longer view must confront the belated nature of Franklin's public criticism of American slavery, despite his earlier private and anonymously published statements against the institution.[9] The accepted view of an enlightened Franklin moving from a proslavery (or indifferent) position to active antislavery in his later years underestimates Franklin's tacit and active support of slavery during

7. Joseph J. Ellis, *Founding Brothers: The Revolutionary Generation* (New York: Knopf, 2000), 108–13; Thomas G. West, *Vindicating the Founders: Race, Class, Sex, and Justice in the Origins of the United States* (Lanham, Md.: Rowman and Littlefield, 1998), 5, 8; Edmund S. Morgan, "Secrets of Benjamin Franklin," *New York Review of Books* 38 (January 3, 1991): 46.

8. Paul Finkelman, *Slavery and the Founders: Race and Liberty in the Age of Jefferson*, 2d ed. (Armonk, N.Y.: M. E. Sharpe, 2001), 174; Mary Frances Berry, "Ashamed of George Washington?" *New York Times*, November 29, 1997.

9. For the currently accepted trajectory of Franklin's change of heart, see Claude-Anne Lopez's groundbreaking work, first in *The Private Franklin*, ed. Claude-Anne Lopez and Eugenia W. Herbert (New Haven: Yale University Press, 1975), 291–302, and more recently in "Franklin and Slavery: A Sea Change" in *My Life with Benjamin Franklin*, ed. Claude-Anne Lopez (New Haven: Yale University Press, 2000), 196–205. Franklin himself first purchased slaves for his own use in the early 1730s. In his will of 1757, two slaves, Peter and Jemima, were to be freed after his death, but he took Peter and another slave, King, to England with him that year. King ran away in 1760. Another slave, George, served Deborah Franklin until her death in 1774. Bills from E. E. [H. S] Warner and Charles Moore, vol. 66, folios 46a and 71a, Benjamin Franklin Papers, American Philosophical Society; Franklin, Last Will and Testament [1757] in *The Papers of Benjamin Franklin*, 37 vols., ed. Leonard W. Labaree et al (New Haven: Yale University Press, 1959–) (hereafter *PBF*), 7:203; Franklin to Abiah Franklin, April 12, 1750, *PBF* 3:474; Franklin to Deborah Franklin, February 19, 1758, June 27, 1760, *PBF* 7:10, 174; Deborah Franklin to Franklin, February 10, 1765, February 5–8, 1766, June 30, 1772, *PBF* 12:45, 13:117–18, 19:192. On Franklin and antislavery, see also Gary B. Nash and Jean R. Soderlund, *Freedom by Degrees: Emancipation in Pennsylvania and Its Aftermath* (New York: Oxford University Press, 1991), ix–xiv; Carey, *Franklin's Economic Views*, 61–99; John C. Van Horne, "Collective Benevolence and the Common Good in Franklin's Philanthropy," in *Reappraising Benjamin Franklin: A Bicentennial Perspective*, ed. J. A. Leo LeMay (Newark: University of Delaware Press, 1993), 433–37. I develop the argument about Franklin's early exposure to antislavery in "Benjamin Franklin, Religion, and Early Antislavery," in *The Problem of Evil*, ed. Steven Mintz and John Stauffer (Amherst: University of Massachusetts Press, forthcoming).

more than fifty years as a printer, writer, and statesman. In this light, Jefferson's postrevolutionary trimming might be considered no more important than that of Franklin before 1776 (or 1787, when he signed on as president of the Pennsylvania Abolition Society). Franklin's careful rhetoric and diplomacy helped Jefferson and other slaveholders resolve the contradiction between their fight against English tyranny and their ownership of slaves. He played a crucial mediating role between those who came to believe that the Revolution should end slavery and those who hoped the Revolution would do away with disturbing *threats* to slavery.

Celebrants of Franklin as our capitalist antislavery founder are correct, however, to assume that Franklin's perspective on slavery reflected his understanding and experience of the early American economy. His disillusionment with imperial political economy turned first and repeatedly on the colonists' investments in labor as commodity and as capital. For this reason Franklin's interest in slavery also provides a useful window on the labor question, and capitalism more generally, in the making of the American Revolution.[10] While the intensification of market relations in early eighteenth-century New England and mid-eighteenth-century Philadelphia and its environs may have led Franklin to become the very incarnation of the spirit of capitalism, as Max Weber argued, the same relations spelled the rise of unfree labor markets. The freedom of some white men in a booming Atlantic economy depended on the bondage of others, some distant and some quite near.[11]

10. Recent work has stressed that capitalism was more a result than a cause of, or issue in, the Revolution. See Michael Merrill, "Putting 'Capitalism' in Its Place: A Review of Recent Literature," *William and Mary Quarterly* 52 (April 1995): 315–26; Allan Kulikoff, *The Agrarian Origins of American Capitalism* (Charlottesville: University Press of Virginia, 1992), 99–150; James Henretta, *The Origins of American Capitalism: Collected Essays* (Boston: Northeastern University Press, 1991), 203–94; Edward Countryman, "'To Secure the Blessings of Liberty': Language, the Revolution, and American Capitalism," in *Beyond the American Revolution: Explorations in the History of American Radicalism*, ed. Alfred F. Young (DeKalb: Northern Illinois University Press, 1993), 123–48; Edward Countryman, "The Uses of Capital in Revolutionary America: The Case of the New York Loyalist Merchants," *William and Mary Quarterly* 49 (January 1992): 3–28; Joyce Appleby, "The Popular Sources of American Capitalism," *Studies in American Political Development* 9, no. 2 (1995): 437–57, and Appleby, *Inheriting the Revolution*.

11. Barbara L. Solow, "Capitalism and Slavery in the Exceedingly Long Run," in *British Capitalism and Caribbean Slavery: The Legacy of Eric Williams*, ed. Barbara L. Solow and Stanley L. Engerman (New York: Cambridge University Press, 1987), 51–77; Barbara L. Solow, "Slavery and Colonization," and David Richardson, "Slavery, Trade, and Economic Growth in Eighteenth-Century New England," both in *Slavery and the Rise of the Atlantic System*, ed. Barbara L. Solow (New York: Cambridge University Press, 1991), 21–42 and 237–64, respectively; David Eltis, "Slavery and Freedom in the Early Modern World" in *Terms of Labor: Slavery, Serfdom, and Free Labor*, ed. Stanley L. Engerman (Stanford: Stanford University Press, 1999), 25–49; Bernard Bailyn, "Slavery and Population Growth in Colonial New England," in *Engines of Enterprise: An Economic History of New England*, ed. Peter Temin (Cambridge: Harvard University Press, 2000), 253–60; Peter Linebaugh and Marcus Rediker, *The Many-Headed Hydra: Sailors, Slaves, Commoners, and the Hidden History of the Revolutionary Atlantic* (Boston: Beacon Press, 2000); John Bezís-Selfa, *American Crucible: Adventurers, Ironworkers, and the Struggle to Forge an Industrious Revolution, 1640–1830* (Ithaca: Cornell University Press, 2004), introduction; Joseph E. Inikori, *Africans and the Industrial Revolution in England* (Cambridge: Cambridge University Press, 2002).

During the eighteenth century capitalism broke down many of the constraints of family and tradition, and did so with a particularly poignant if not tragic unevenness in regions on the periphery of both the economy and traditional institutions. The peripheral nature of the New World is precisely what led the old institution of slavery to become central to empire's new economic enterprises.[12] Therefore it is especially important to define capitalism, as I will do here, not only in terms of its freedoms but also in terms of its constraints. As recent Marxian accounts emphasize, capitalism coerced more and more people into dependence on the international labor market during the eighteenth century. Capitalism began to commodify everything, beginning with the colonies' most scarce commodity: people.[13]

Franklin puzzled over the changes involved in turning intimate relationships with reciprocal obligations—such as the apprenticeship to his brother that he escaped by running away—into something else. Starting with the American scarcity of labor, in his popular early writings Franklin experimented with *people as capital,* a rhetoric that could address the freeing of some and the enslavement of others in the marketplace. He championed personal freedom within the bounds of one's station in life, while finessing the fact that rising men in colonial America had to prevent others from seizing their freedom. His role as a printer and proponent of paper money during the 1730s and 1740s inspired him to craft playful but revealing commentaries on the simultaneous rise of capitalism and unfree labor. The ironic distance he kept from his middling personae, such as Poor Richard Saunders, attests to their nature as marketed products. Paper money, and other products of his press, not only reflected but also helped regulate the conditions of freedom and unfreedom during capitalism's mid-Atlantic takeoff. Franklin's experience and his writings tell the optimistic side of

On capitalism and slavery in the early modern period, see also Fernand Braudel, *The Wheels of Commerce: Civilization and Capitalism, 15ᵗʰ–18ᵗʰ Centuries,* vol. 2, trans. Sian Reynolds (New York: Cambridge University Press, 1979), 272, 280, 372, 383; Eugene D. Genovese and Elizabeth Fox-Genovese, *Fruits of Merchant Capital: Slavery and Bourgeois Property in the Rise and Expansion of Capitalism* (New York: Oxford University Press, 1983); James Oakes, *Slavery and Freedom: An Interpretation of the Old South* (New York: Knopf, 1990), 40–79; Robin Blackburn, *The Making of New World Slavery: From the Baroque to the Modern, 1492–1800* (London: Verso, 1997), especially 6–13, 351–55. The importance of placing slavery in the context of the "labor question" as part of a broader "big-picture" approach to New World slavery has recently been asserted by Peter Kolchin in "The Big Picture: A Comment on David Brion Davis's 'Looking at Slavery from Broader Perspectives,'" *American Historical Review* 105 (April 2000): 468.

12. David Eltis, *The Rise of African Slavery in the Americas* (New York: Cambridge University Press, 1999); Blackburn, *Making of New World Slavery.*

13. While neo-Marxian scholars disagree about the relative importance of agrarian change and overseas trade, and the nature of the relationship between the two, they seem to me to converge on this crucial point. See especially Immanuel Wallerstein, *Historical Capitalism, with Capitalist Civilization* (London: Verso, 1995); David McNally, *Political Economy and the Rise of Capitalism: A Reinterpretation* (Berkeley and Los Angeles: University of California Press, 1988); Perelman, *Invention of Capitalism;* Ellen Meiksins Wood, *The Origin of Capitalism: A Longer View* (New York: Verso, 2002); Linebaugh and Rediker, *Many-Headed Hydra.*

the story, in which there seemed to be little difference between the coercion of servants and slaves and the other healthy workings of the expanding market. If it produced wealth and stability, the regulation of persons and laborers by the press could even stand as a model form of public service.

Only later, from the late 1740s until the early 1760s, did Franklin develop a merchant capitalist critique of slavery, arguing that slavery was inefficient compared to free labor. He explicitly distanced white colonists from their slaves, from the Indians, and from racialized European immigrants, all of whom threatened to dilute Anglo-American equality and the profits of property-owning colonists. But because his analysis was so patently unpersuasive in the age of staple-driven colonization, he began to experiment with racism to supplement his attack on the institutions of slavery and convict labor. When this strategy proved ineffective, Franklin began to compare the unwillingness of the English to allow Americans to regulate their own trade—especially the trade in labor—to a kind of enslavement of the white colonists, an enslavement that left British Americans awash in a sea of undesirable nonwhites. Eventually, the critique of metaphorical or political "slavery" (and real or African slavery, blamed on the British) became a critique of the empire itself, as Franklin helped to forge a historically crucial combination of revolutionary American nationalism, capitalism, antislavery, and racism.

In the process, Franklin projected criticisms of colonial slavery back across the ocean, turning them into the very mark or essence of anti-Americanism. It was in this geopolitical context, during the 1770s, that Franklin developed the myth of northern colonial America as the land of the free, a myth into which he literally wrote his own life in the famous first part of the *Autobiography*. This politically useful myth of early American freedom required Franklin to mislead his readers about the economic impact of unfree labor on his life and his world. It still prevents us from seeing the extent to which Franklin's and America's independence depended first upon slavery and later on the denial of slavery's importance to a nascent American capitalism.[14]

In 1723 Benjamin Franklin broke the terms of his apprenticeship to his brother and ran away from Boston to New York. Failing to find freeman's wages there, he proceeded to Philadelphia. Writing his autobiography some forty-eight years later, Franklin took special pleasure in narrating that moment when, after various nautical mishaps, he finally strolled off the Philadelphia wharf in his dirty, sodden clothes. Twice, he informs us, he was "suspected to be some runaway Servant, and in danger of being taken up on that Suspicion." Such scenes, narrated with humor and not a little irony, have the remarkable effect of drawing our

---

14. Seth Rockman makes a persuasive case for the unfree origins of American capitalism in Chapter 12 of this volume.

attention to Franklin's rise from obscure origins and away from the fact that he in fact *was* a runaway servant and could well have been arrested. That he faced such a potential diversion from his eventual rise was due to a structuring fact of life in Franklin's mid-Atlantic world: the trade in laborers.[15]

Production for export, the settlement of new lands, and the "consumer revolution" created a huge demand for labor in the mid-Atlantic colonies that was filled alternately, depending largely on supply and price, by indentured immigrant servants from the margins of the newly named "Great Britain," and by slaves from Africa, the West Indies, and other mainland colonies.[16] While in the long term slave labor may have been less efficient for the mixed needs of mid-Atlantic property owners, in the meantime a remarkably flexible labor system emerged, wherein slaves and servants were regularly rented as well as sold. Pennsylvanians "regarded black labor as just another commodity," to be bought or sold as profit dictated. In Pennsylvania as elsewhere this workforce was clearly multiracial—white and black and mixed blood; foreign, Creole, and native—as well as free, indentured, and slave.[17] It was not at all clear that either slavery or

15. Benjamin Franklin, *The Autobiography*, ed. J. A. Leo LeMay (New York: Library of America, 1990), 23, 26. On the demand for labor as helpful to Franklin as a printer, see Ralph Frasca, "From Apprentice to Journeyman to Partner: Benjamin Franklin's Workers and the Growth of the Early American Printing Trade," *Pennsylvania Magazine of History and Biography* 104 (April 1990): 229–41.

16. Recent scholarship on the "consumer revolution" of the eighteenth century depicts Anglo-American colonists as integrated further into the British "empire of goods," and thus as more likely to develop a common language of protest. There was more, though, to the Anglicization, or "Atlanticization," of the colonial economy than the consumption of goods and the ensuing possibility of politicizing them. The literature has had the perhaps unintended effect of drawing attention away from labor. See T. H. Breen, "An Empire of Goods: The Anglicization of Colonial America, 1690–1776," *Journal of British Studies* 25 (October 1986): 467–99; T. H. Breen, "'Baubles of Britain': The American and British Consumer Revolutions of the Eighteenth Century," *Past and Present* 119 (May 1988): 73–104; T. H. Breen, "Narrative of Commercial Life: Consumption, Ideology, and Community on the Eve of the American Revolution," *William and Mary Quarterly* 50 (October 1993): 471–501; Cary Carson, Ronald Hoffman, and Peter J. Albert, eds., *Of Consuming Interests: The Style of Life in the Eighteenth Century* (Charlottesville: University Press of Virginia, 1994); Richard L. Bushman, *The Refinement of America: Persons, Houses, Cities* (New York: Knopf, 1992); Jon Butler, *Becoming America: The Revolution Before 1776* (Cambridge: Harvard University Press, 2000), 137–84.

17. Darold D. Wax, "The Demand for Slave Labor in Colonial Pennsylvania," *Pennsylvania History* 34 (October 1967): 331–45; Darold D. Wax, "Negro Imports into Pennsylvania, 1720–1766," *Pennsylvania History* 32 (July 1965): 254–87; Darold D. Wax, "Negro Import Duties in Colonial Pennsylvania," *Pennsylvania Magazine of History and Biography* 87 (January 1973): 26–44; James G. Lydon, "New York and the Slave Trade, 1700 to 1774," *William and Mary Quarterly*, 3d ser., 35 (April 1978): 375–96; James A. Rawley, *The Transatlantic Slave Trade: A History* (New York: W. W. Norton, 1981), 385–418; Jean R. Soderlund, *Quakers and Slavery: A Divided Spirit* (Princeton: Princeton University Press, 1985), 54–86; A. J. Williams-Myers, "Hands That Picked No Cotton: An Exploratory Examination of African Slave Labor in the Colonial Economy of the Hudson River Valley to 1800," *Afro-Americans in New York Life and History* 11 (January 1987): 25–51; Thelma Wills Foote, "Black Life in Colonial Manhattan, 1664–1786" (Ph.D. diss., Harvard University, 1991), 23, 41–52; Sharon V. Salinger, *'To Serve Well and Faithfully': Labor and Indentured Servants in Pennsylvania, 1682–1800* (New York: Cambridge University Press, 1987), 81; Edgar J. McManus, *Black Bondage in the North* (Syracuse: Syracuse University Press, 1973), 13–14, 47–51; Richard Shannon Moss, *Slavery on Long Island: A Study in Local*

servitude was on the decline at any time before the Revolution. If anything, the profusion of both sorts of alienated "others" warranted concern, but not enough to elicit any consistent official action, such as import duties, because the availability of both servants and slaves depressed the prices of both, thereby alleviating the "problem" (for employers) of high wages for freemen.[18]

This mixed labor market spelled the contradictory extremes of freedom and bondage, extremes captured in the term "picaresque unfree," which Marcus Rediker has used to describe the empire's mobile workers. On the one hand, there were occasional opportunities to earn freedom, choose one's master, or steal oneself by running away, as Franklin did. On the other hand, the risks to masters involved in this flexible labor market encouraged them to invest more heavily in bound labor and to look for ways to promote security in their labor investments, to reduce "turnover cost." This was particularly true in the mid-Atlantic hinterlands of New York and Philadelphia, areas that, not surprisingly, saw the most creative and extensive use of new methods for importing, selling, renting, and recapturing bound labor, such as the advertisements that underwrote Franklin's newspaper.[19]

Institutional and Early African-American Communal Life (New York: Garland, 1993), 79–81, 97; Graham Russell Hodges, *Slavery and Freedom in the Rural North: Monmouth County, New Jersey, 1665–1865* (Madison, Wis.: Madison House, 1997).

18. Compare Richard S. Dunn, "Servants and Slaves: The Recruitment and Employment of Labor" in *Colonial British America: Essays in the New History of the Early Modern Era*, ed. Jack P. Greene and J. R. Pole (Baltimore: Johns Hopkins University Press, 1984), 180–83, and James T. Lemon, *The Best Poor Man's Country: A Geographical Study of Early Southeastern Pennsylvania* (Baltimore: Johns Hopkins University Press, 1972), with Marilyn C. Baseler, *"Asylum for Mankind": America, 1607–1800* (Ithaca: Cornell University Press, 1998); Marianne S. Wokeck, *Trade in Strangers: The Beginnings of Mass Migration to North America* (University Park: Pennsylvania State University Press, 1999); O. Nigel Bolland, "Proto-Proletarians? Slaves Wages in the Americas," in *From Chattel Slaves to Wage Slaves: The Dynamics of Labour Bargaining in the Americas*, ed. Mary Turner (London: James Currey, 1995), 123–47; John Bezís-Selfa, "Slavery and the Disciplining of Free Labor in the Colonial Mid-Atlantic Iron Industry," *Pennsylvania History* 64, supplement (Summer 1997): 270–86; Christine Daniels, "Shadowlands: Freedom and Unfreedom in Anglo-America," paper presented at the American Historical Association annual meeting, Washington, D.C., January 1999; Jacqueline Jones, *American Work: Four Centuries of Black and White Labor* (New York: W. W. Norton, 1998), 125–68; Kathleen M. Brown, "Antiauthoritarianism and Freedom in Early America," *Journal of American History* 85 (June 1998): 77–85. For the general efficiency of colonial labor markets, especially in the mid-Atlantic, see David W. Galenson, "Labor Market Behavior in Colonial America: Servitude, Slavery, and Free Labor" in *Markets in History: Economic Studies of the Past*, ed. David W. Galenson (New York: Cambridge University Press, 1989), 51–96; David W. Galenson, "The Settlement and Growth of the Colonies: Population, Labor, and Economic Development," in *The Cambridge Economic History of the United States*, 3 vols., ed. Stanley L. Engerman and Robert E. Gallman (New York: Cambridge University Press, 1996), 1:176, 207.

19. Marcus Rediker, "Good Hands, Stout Heart, and Fast Feet: The History and Culture of Working People in Early America," in *Reviving the English Revolution: Reflections and Elaborations on the Work of Christopher Hill*, ed. Geoff Eley and William Hunt (London: Verso, 1988), 236; Marcus Rediker, *Between the Devil and the Deep Blue Sea: Merchant Seamen, Pirates, and the Anglo-American Maritime World, 1700–1750* (New York: Cambridge University Press, 1987); Peter Linebaugh, *The London Hanged: Crime and Civil Society in Eighteenth-Century England* (New York: Cambridge University Press, 1992), 119–52, 169–70; Ira Berlin, "From Creole to African: Atlantic Creoles and the Origins of African

In the world of Benjamin Franklin, slavery, servitude, and freedom worked together and provided a flexible basis for American expansion. In a set of queries written for the Junto, the club he founded in 1727, Franklin revealed this open-endedness by asking, "Does the importation of Servants increase or Advance the Wealth of our Country?" Franklin was thinking of the wealth *in* servants as well as the wealth servants produced. The importation of not-yet-free people would certainly increase their own and the polity's wealth if all servants were destined to become wealth-producing freemen, but even when Franklin asked this question in 1732, he knew this proposition to be uncertain and that his own experience was as much an exception as the rule. Nor, on the other hand, could servants always be counted on as a good investment for their masters, especially if they ran away as Franklin had. Consequently, Franklin's next question for the Junto was, "Would not an Office of Insurance for Servants be of Service, and what Methods are proper for erecting such an Office?"[20] Masters might, in other words, leverage the capital invested in servants to share the risks associated with buying potential runaways. Since masters also often acted individualistically, in an entrepreneurial fashion, by hiring for wages men who might turn out to be runaway servants, an insurance scheme could save employers from each other as well as from the expropriations of their self-stealing bondsmen.[21]

Franklin identified the wealth of masters with that of "our Country," a logical extension of Franklin's daily practice as printer of the *Pennsylvania Gazette,* for the newspaper had emerged as an important institution for the sale and recovery of unfree laborers. When Samuel Keimer started the paper in 1728, he offered each subscriber a free advertisement every six months. The first three ads to appear in the paper were for land, a runaway servant, and the sale of a Negro man: "enquire of the Printer, and know further." During the twenty years that followed, Franklin became the paper's owner and a wealthy man from its

American Society in Mainland North America," *William and Mary Quarterly,* 3d ser., 53 (April 1996): 251–88; W. Jeffrey Bolster, *Black Jacks: African American Seamen in the Age of Sail* (Cambridge: Harvard University Press, 1997); Christopher Hanes, "Turnover Cost and the Distribution of Slave Labor in Anglo-America," *Journal of Economic History* 56 (September 1996): 307–30; Steven Deyle, "'By farr the most profitable trade': Slave Trading in British Colonial North America," *Slavery and Abolition* 12 (1989): 116–17; David Waldstreicher, "Reading the Runaways: Self-fashioning, Print Culture, and Confidence in Slavery in the Eighteenth Century Mid-Atlantic," *William and Mary Quarterly* 3d ser., 56 (April 1999): 243–72. For the ways in which mobility has structured new mixes of seemingly archaic and modern labor relations, I am indebted to Gunther Peck, *Reinventing Free Labor: Padrones and Workers in Industrial America, 1880–1925* (New York: Cambridge University Press, 2000).

20. "Proposals and Queries to Be Asked the Junto" (1732), in *Benjamin Franklin: Writings,* ed. J. A. Leo LeMay (New York: Library of America, 1987) (hereafter *Writings*), 209.

21. The implications are rather surprising when we consider that Franklin was later considered a champion of artisans' interests, but things become clearer when we recall that the artisans Franklin would later champion were masters who got ahead by combining their own hard work with that of journeymen, apprentices, servants, and/or slaves. Shane White pointed out the extent of artisan slaveholding in *Somewhat More Independent: The End of Slavery in New York City, 1770–1810* (Athens: University of Georgia Press, 1991).

profits. The *Gazette* carried runaway and servant and slave-for-sale ads in every issue until, by the 1750s, when he received a silent partner's share averaging 467 pounds a year, each issue carried more than a dozen fugitive and sale ads.[22]

Franklin not only ran local ads, he also participated in the local slave and servant trade by selling goods and persons and acting as an agent for their sale. In 1732 he offered sugar, soap, goose feathers, coffee, servants, and slaves, sometimes in the same ad: "To BE SOLD, A Dutch Servant Man and his Wife, for Two Years and Eight Months, a genteel riding Chair, almost new, a Ten Cord Flat with new Sails and Rigging, a Fishing Boat, and sundry sorts of Household Goods." The language of the ads was the same whether the commodity was sundry or genteel, indentured like the German couple or enslaved like the "Two likely Young Negroes, one a Lad about 19. The other a Girl of 15, to be sold. Inquire of the printer." Clothes, tea, servants, or slaves: all were advertised as "parcels," as a divisible number of mutually exchangeable commodities. Franklin also acted as an agent for masters seeking to recapture their absconded property. The material ramifications of print, despite its creation of disembodied community, were nowhere more evident than when masters arrived at Franklin's shop to get more information about a worker who had been put on sale, or to pick up fugitives who had been caught and delivered. And the reach of print was nowhere more telling than in its creation of a network of printers and readers who bought and sold workers or garnered cash rewards for information about them. This network, which Franklin extended and developed more effectively than any other contemporary printer, stood in direct opposition to the attempts of the indentured and enslaved to use their mobility to their own advantage.[23]

How can we square such facts with the venerable interpretive tradition that stresses Franklin's almost single-handed invention of the market-oriented free individual? Or with the more recent literature on Franklin as an innovator of a particularly republican print culture?[24] Republican print culture embodied

22. *Pennsylvania Gazette,* October 1 (prospectus), November 2, 1728; Billy G. Smith and Richard Wojtowicz eds., *Blacks Who Stole Themselves: Advertisements from the Pennsylvania Gazette, 1728–1790* (Philadelphia: University of Pennsylvania Press, 1989); Daniel E. Meaders, ed., *Eighteenth-Century White Slaves: Runaway Notices,* vol. 1, *Pennsylvania, 1729–1760* (Westport, Conn.: Greenwood Press, 1993); Carl Van Doren, *Benjamin Franklin* (New York: Viking, 1939), 123, 129. For the number of ads, see the table in Waldstreicher, "Reading the Runaways," 250.

23. Benjamin Franklin, "Accounts Posted or Ledger" (ledgers A and B), American Philosophical Society, Philadelphia, copy in Benjamin Franklin Papers, Yale University, Sterling Library; *Pennsylvania Gazette,* September 12, 1732; June 20, 1734; October 2, 1735; September 8, 1738; August 9, 1739; September 4 and December 4, 1740; September 3, 1741; January 6, July 22, December 2, 1742; December 6, 1745; September 4, 1746; May 7, 1747; May 3, 1733; May 22, 1734; June 12, 1740, *PBF* 1:345, 378, 2:287; Waldstreicher, "Reading the Runaways," 268–72.

24. For the republican Franklin, see Ormond Seavey, *Becoming Benjamin Franklin: The Autobiography and the Life* (University Park: Pennsylvania State University Press, 1988); Michael Warner, *The Letters of the Republic: Publication and the Public Sphere in Eighteenth-Century America* (Cambridge: Harvard University Press, 1990), 72–96; Larzer Ziff, *Writing in the New Nation: Prose, Print, and Politics in the Early*

communal good while easing the path of commerce; newspapers were, after all, a "metacommodity," a commodity about commodities. In this context, especially early in the century, the worthy editor straddled a delicate position between old and new understandings of individuality and the common good in market culture. The printer as public servant performed a balancing act between promoting trade and curbing its excesses. In a 1731 "Petition to the Pennsylvania Assembly regarding Fairs," Franklin complained that fairs were not real or serious commerce, but rather were run for "a Concourse of Rude people." At fairs, youths found themselves "in mix'd Companies of vicious Servants and Negroes. That Servants who by Custom think they have a Right to Liberty of going out at those Times, commonly disorder themselves so as to be unfit for Business in some Time after; and what is worse, having perhaps done some Mischief in their liquor, and afraid of Correction, or getting among ill Companions, they combine to run away more than at any other Time." One of the excesses of the colonial American marketplace was the uncontrolled circulation of human commodities (including fugitives), which if unchecked could undermine the wealth and improvement it was supposed to create.[25]

Another, related excess, quickly emerging as a central theme in Franklin's public writing, was improper, counterproductive consumption, especially by the lower orders. In the first *Poor Richard's Almanack* (1733) Franklin invented the persona of the sensible if eccentric Richard Saunders, whose "excessive proud" wife threatened to keep him "excessive poor." The next year, public patronage of the *Almanack* created an embarrassment of riches explicitly addressed in the *Almanack*'s own introduction: while Richard bought only a secondhand coat, his wife purchased shoes, two new shifts, and a petticoat. In part by constructing women as the hyperconsuming Other, Franklin invented a virtuous yet poor male persona, and claimed print culture (via the almanac) and

United States (New Haven: Yale University Press, 1992), 83–106. For the liberal or capitalist Franklin, see Max Weber, *The Protestant Ethic and the Spirit of Capitalism,* trans. Talcott Parsons (1930; reprint, New York: Routledge, 1992); Mitchell R. Breitwieser, *Cotton Mather and Benjamin Franklin: The Price of Representative Personality* (New York: Cambridge University Press, 1984), 171–305; Mark R. Patterson, *Authority, Autonomy, and Representation in American Literature, 1776–1865* (Princeton: Princeton University Press, 1988), 3–33; R. Jackson Wilson, *Figures of Speech: American Writers and the Literary Marketplace* (New York: Knopf, 1989), 21–65; Michael Zuckerman, "The Selling of the Self: From Franklin to Barnum," in *Benjamin Franklin, Jonathan Edwards, and the Representation of American Culture,* ed. Barbara B. Oberg and Harry S. Stout (New York: Oxford University Press, 1993), 152–70; Grantland S. Rice, *The Transformation of Authorship in America* (Chicago: University of Chicago Press, 1997), 3–6, 45–69.

25. Benedict Anderson, *Imagined Communities: Reflections on the Origins and Spread of Nationalism,* 2d ed. (New York: Verso, 1991), chapter 2; *PBF* 1:211–12. For debates over the marketplace, see Jean-Christophe Agnew, *Worlds Apart: The Market and the Theater in Anglo-American Thought, 1550–1750* (New York: Cambridge University Press, 1986). On the need to situate the origins of the public sphere in the market, see also Colin Jones, "The Great Chain of Buying: Medical Advertisement, the Bourgeois Public Sphere, and the Origins of the French Revolution," *American Historical Review* 101 (February 1996): 13–40, especially 39.

the marketplace (via the virtues of thrift) for ordinary free men.[26] Gender differences symbolize the order of class here, an order that participation in the market (and print) could and did sometimes obscure. Franklin celebrated the market's ability to reduce everything to relative value, to enable people to pretend theatrically to be other than what they are, only to shore up, in statements that could be read either as parodies of the lower orders or as satires on elite pretensions, the need for a rational, calculating approach to behavior in order to conserve the opportunities the marketplace offered.

Franklin's populism was real enough, but it was tempered by political realism, a counting of the cost of drawing large numbers into the marketplace without excessively offending the wealthy or overexciting the indigent and unfree. His first published writing on the subject of race, a short essay signed "Blackamore" that appeared in the *Pennsylvania Gazette* just before the first *Poor Richard's Almanack,* also diminished a social distinction in the service of an ambivalent market ethics. In the voice of a self-described "mechanick," Franklin anonymously satirized a "molatto gentleman," but not for the purpose of decrying racial intermixture—a phenomenon he revealingly took for granted as a social reality. Franklin's target, instead, was again the irrational, self-destructive would-be gentleman. Mulattoes are a metaphor for those of intermediate or mutating social status: people putting on airs, or missing their cues.[27] They are no exception but rather the rule about modesty and the proper limitations of self-fashioning in a world of two classes—the ordinary and the gentle.

> Their Approach towards Whiteness, makes them look back with some kind of Scorn upon the Colour they seem to have left, while the Negroes, who do not think them better than themselves, return their Contempt with Interest: And the Whites, who respect them no Whit the more for the nearer Affinity in Colour, are apt to regard their Behaviour as too bold and assuming, and bordering upon Impudence. As they are next to Negroes, and but just above 'em, they are terribly afraid of being thought Negroes, and therefore avoid as much as possible their Company or Commerce: and Whitefolks are as little fond of the company of *Molattoes.*

Where association is conceived of as "commerce," reputation is a competitive marketplace, and resentment can be likened to social capital, ironically

26. Franklin, *Poor Richard's Almanack* (1733, 1734), *PBF* 1:288, 311, 349. On Franklin's early populism, see William Pencak, "Politics and Ideology in *Poor Richard's Almanack," Pennsylvania Magazine of History and Biography* 116 (April 1992): 183–211.

27. Franklin, *Writings,* 218–20; *Pennsylvania Gazette,* August 30, 1733. This essay was only recently identified by J. A. Leo LeMay as Franklin's. See LeMay, *The Canon of Benjamin Franklin, 1722–1776: New Attributions and Reconsiderations* (Newark: University of Delaware Press, 1990), 78–79.

let out with "interest."[28] As the rest of the essay is devoted to the social (not racial) "Mungrel" (one of whom is compared to "a Monkey that climbs a Tree, the higher he goes, the more he shows his Arse"), the overall effect is to relativize race as another form of social distinction, perhaps no less but certainly no more real than gentility. Indeed, by suggesting that "there are perhaps *Molattoes* in religion, in Politicks, in Love, and in several other Things," and that "none appear to me so monstrously ridiculous as the *Molatto Gentleman*," Franklin leaves open the possibility that racial prejudice is wholly arbitrary, at least compared to the real yardstick of class. Race is only a version of class—a cheap substitute in fact. In this view, blacks, though lowest on the social scale, can contribute to the social good, and in fact might do so by providing a lesson of humility to their upwardly mobile betters. The "mechanick" author (Franklin) suggests as much by making his own racial status ambiguous in signing himself "BLACKAMORE"—possibly a black man, possibly a white man passing, theatrically, as black.

Franklin's combination of sympathy for and ridicule of those who strove for wealth and distinction is as striking as his willingness to employ racial categories to relativize racial difference. The "mulatto gentleman" essay provides important clues as to Franklin's perspective at the defining moment of his emergence as a social commentator. Together with his other early writings and what we know of his personal history, it suggests that the Benjamin Franklin of the early 1730s, a promising young artisan and former runaway, found himself suspended experientially and ideologically between gentility and the multiracial "Atlantic working class" so eloquently recovered by Marcus Rediker and Peter Linebaugh. To describe him as middle-class would be anachronistic for an age when the "middling sorts" were only just emerging; to emphasize solely his attack on undeserving elites, or his seizure of gentility on behalf of artisans, would be to tell only parts of his story, to account for only fractions of his complex process of reinvention and appropriation.[29] He resolved, or rather worked with, the contradictions of this position through astounding uses of irony, in fictive criticisms of the high and the low, through the successive invention of imaginary selves (Silence Dogood, Richard Saunders) who were then deconstructed in turn.

There is reason to believe that many people were working through these ambiguities in an expanding marketplace. And yet Franklin's position was already a privileged one. We cannot ignore the distances created by his printing and his personae or the fact that he began to profit so handsomely from them.

28. For the relationships between print, commercial exchange, and character in England at this time, see James Thompson, *Forms of Value: Eighteenth-Century Political Economy and the Novel* (Durham: Duke University Press, 1996); Deidre Shauna Lynch, *The Economy of Character: Novels, Market Culture, and the Business of Inner Meaning* (Chicago: University of Chicago Press, 1998), 1–79.

29. Linebaugh and Rediker, *Many-Headed Hydra*; Stuart M. Blumin, *The Emergence of the Middle Class: Social Experience in the American City, 1760–1900* (New York: Cambridge University Press, 1989). For emphasis on Franklin's adaptation of gentility, see Daniel Walker Howe, *Making the American Self: Jonathan Edwards to Abraham Lincoln* (Cambridge: Harvard University Press, 1997), 8.

His invention of imaginary people, disembodied abstractions of the self who worked in the marketplace and on the page for him and the "public," reflected efforts at mastery more than they told about the lives of the unfree. However picaresque and creative many of the unfree were, they represented themselves, in the flesh. The successful practice of anonymous authorship and the deft editorial hand, by contrast, were lessons in surrogacy: they showed that it is possible to invent or project other persons who act, under one's own control, in one's stead.[30] It was a lesson Franklin learned early, when, as he tells us in his autobiography, his first broadside poems and serious essays moved people more when they did not know the actual identity of the person who wrote them. He learned it again when his brother, James Franklin, slapped with a special edict that he *"should no longer print the Paper called the New England Courant,"* came up with the idea that it could be printed under the name of his apprentice brother Benjamin, whose unfreedom would be renounced—temporarily, for the occasion. Under pressure from his betters, James Franklin's freedom, his ability to act, increased greatly insofar as he could manipulate the terms of his brother's obligation. This incident, however, enabled young Ben to do him one better, claiming to be a freeman because his new, secret indentures could not be publicly acknowledged. The logics of property and "representative personality" freed the owned Franklin to become an owner.[31]

For Franklin, then, there were compelling parallels between writing for print, the printing trade, and the actions of the people and property one owned in the marketplace. His attitude toward paper money, a very controversial subject at the time, typifies this emerging set of relationships. Franklin took many occasions to sing the praises of paper currency, even as it arguably sped the process of turning labor, and laborers, into commodities. The money problem provided the first occasion for Franklin's expression of a labor theory of value—but from the perspective not just of laborers, as Ronald Schultz has argued, but of the consumers, the owners, of labor. "The riches of a country are to be valued by

30. On surrogation as a process of inventing and repressing "the other" in the context of Anglo-American colonialism and its aftermath, see Joseph Roach, *Cities of the Dead: Circum-Atlantic Performance* (New York: Columbia University Press, 1996). Grantland Rice stresses the commodification of the self-inherent in the new, Franklinian modes of authorship in his *Transformation of Authorship in America.* For Franklin's creation of a generalized authority stripped of interiority, see Warner, *Letters of the Republic,* 72–96, and Warner, "Savage Franklin," in *Benjamin Franklin: An American Genius,* ed. Gianfranca Balestra and Luigi Sanpietro (Rome, 1993), 75–87.

31. Franklin, *Autobiography,* 20; Van Doren, *Benjamin Franklin,* 31. For Franklin as technologist of representative personality, see especially Breitwieser, *Cotton Mather and Benjamin Franklin.* Timothy Hall and T. H. Breen describe the "homology" between paper money and itinerancy ca. 1740 in "Structuring Provincial Imagination: The Rhetoric and Experience of Social Change in Eighteenth-Century New England," *American Historical Review* 103 (December 1998): 1411–38. For the depersonalization that accompanied the advent of paper money at this time, see Bruce H. Mann, *Neighbors and Strangers: Law and Community in Colonial Connecticut* (Chapel Hill: University of North Carolina Press, 1987), 12–42.

the quantity of labor its inhabitants are able to purchase, and not by the quantity of silver and gold they possess," he wrote in *A Modest Enquiry into the Nature and Necessity of a Paper-Currency* (1729). The particularities of American economy required paper money, to encourage free men to hope to see the results of their labor, to decrease the consumption of European goods, and ultimately to spur the immigration of "labouring men." Thus, for Franklin, not only can money be seen as "Coined Land," as the land bankers of the era had begun to describe it: money is also coined labor. Since labor is nothing if not human time, if the circulation of a currency saves money, it actually creates real—not just paper—wealth.[32]

Of course, Franklin did not believe that people were literally equivalent to money. Rather, he demonstrated, and would continue to demonstrate in his widely distributed writings, that paper and people were usefully analogous. What people were like money? What kind of people performed labor that saved more money than investment in their time and tools cost? To say that paper money would solve the particular American problem of scarce labor was actually to say more than that money facilitated exchange by turning "labor value" into "exchange value" (as Karl Marx put it in his critical gloss on Franklin). Money was not just coined labor: in its ideal form it was coined unfree labor—implicitly and innovatively in the form of the servant or slave, but metaphorically in the unpaid work of women and children.[33] In *Advice to a Young Tradesman, Written by an Old One* (1748), a compendium and elaboration of the maxims in the *Poor Richard's Almanack* series, we find not only "Time is Money" and "Credit is Money," but "Money is of a prolifick generating Nature. Money can beget Money, and its offspring can beget more, and so on." If the creation of capital is a blessing on the order of human reproduction, its destruction can be a metaphor for true evil: "He that murders a Crown, destroys all it might have produc'd, even Scores of Pounds." This understanding of people and money, and people *as* money, could even, in the famous "Speech of Miss Polly Baker" (1747), get an unwed mother off the juridical hook, because she produced wealth in

---

32. Franklin, *Writings*, 119–35; Van Doren, *Benjamin Franklin*, 102. For Franklin as a champion of artisans' economic interests, see Ronald Schultz, *The Republic of Labor: Philadelphia Artisans and the Politics of Class, 1720–1830* (New York: Oxford University Press, 1993), 25. On the land bank and money debates, see Margaret E. Newell, *From Dependency to Independence: Economic Revolution in Colonial New England* (Ithaca: Cornell University Press, 1998), chapters 7–11.

33. Karl Marx simultaneously celebrated and denigrated Franklin for offering "the first conscious, clear and almost trite analysis of exchange value into labor value," stressing that he did so in a fundamentally bourgeois vein that "abstracted" and "alienated" labor. Marx, *On America and the Civil War*, ed. Saul K. Padover (New York: Oxford University Press, 1972), 18–19; Marx, *Capital*, trans. Ben Fowkes (New York: Vintage Books, 1977), 1:142n18; Carey, *Franklin's Economic Views*, 16–44. I would like to thank John Bezís-Selfa for helping me clarify and extend these points; I owe to him the formulation of the term "unfree labor." I am also indebted to the analysis of slavery, racism, and misogyny in Kathleen M. Brown, *Good Wives, Nasty Wenches, and Anxious Patriarchs: Gender, Race and Power in Colonial Virginia* (Chapel Hill: University of North Carolina Press, 1996).

persons, thus adding to the commonwealth. The radical potential of Franklin's sexual politics relied on the logic of the production and commodification of persons as capital. Debates about women and their children might even be resolved by considering people as the ultimate form of capital.[34]

In this context, the famous prefaces and sayings in *Poor Richard's Almanack* (written by Franklin annually from 1733 to 1756) addressed free men with and without servants, urging them, ultimately, to come to grips with and naturalize a cash economy dependent on unfree as well as wage labor. As Poor Richard Saunders, Franklin gave low-priced lessons about the relationship between labor, property, and money—even while conducting an intermittent monologue over whether he (Richard) or the printer (Franklin) actually made a profit in doing so. Franklin even played with the idea that he, the printer, exploited Richard, apprenticing him to the public. By splitting himself in this manner, Franklin made it possible to speak simultaneously to various constituencies of freemen, a task his maxims, taken in aggregate, repeatedly accomplished. For every encomium to simple self-reliance—without servants—in the almanacs ("If you'd have a Servant that you like, serve your self"), there is a suggestion that people, especially those who work with their hands, should not "forget their proper Station," a directive about keeping servants in their place ("Never intreat a servant to dwell with thee"), and advice on how to recognize, and generalize, good surrogates ("There are three faithful friends, an old wife, an old dog, and ready money").[35]

In a context in which bound servitude was a structure for the repayment of what immigrants, bankrupts, and those without capital owed for their maintenance, Poor Richard glorified the independent farmer or artisan and urged him not to fall into debt. Where freedom was literally the absence of debt, and servitude its presence, it made all the more sense to equate capital with freedom and with command over others' labor. Thus the advice Richard Saunders gave, for all his protestations of poverty, applied to masters and those who aspired to be masters, artisans and small farmers who could ill afford to offend elite patrons and ordinary customers.[36] Its delightful theatricalities should not obscure

34. Franklin, *Writings*, 320–22; "The Speech of Miss Polly Baker" (1747), ibid., 305–8. For Franklin's reliance on women as surrogates and an interpretation of Polly Baker in this light, see Jan Lewis, "Sex and the Married Man: Benjamin Franklin's Families," in *Benjamin Franklin and Women*, ed. Larry Tise (University Park: University of Pennsylvania Press, 2000), 67–82, especially 77–78.

35. *Poor Richard's Almanack* (1735, 1736, 1737, 1738), *PBF* 2:5, 165, 261; 3:170, 192, 196.

36. While Poor Richard continued to trumpet the labor theory of value, and thus the claims of artisans, in the 1740s, the almanacs staked out a precarious middle ground between the advocacy of wealth and warnings against the dangers of wealth seeking by working people. This middle ground is the only way, it seems to me, to account for the old tradesman's serious advice, its comic overabundance, and the final ridicule of the old tradesman by the people in the marketplace, who ignore him and go about their (commercial) business. Pencak observes that, while "a key function of almanacs was to spread populist ideology up the social ladder," Franklin was simultaneously closing this new public sphere "to the vast majority of the population of North America." Pencak, "Politics and Ideology," 196, 203.

its meanings for labor, which can be summarized as: work hard—and make sure your servants do the same. The ambivalences, even contradictions about work in the almanacs—who does it and under what circumstances—reflect the mixed labor system of Franklin's America, his strategy of attempting to rationalize the system through the trope of people as capital. These were the ambivalences of the master classes in early America who were driven simultaneously to value their dearly bought laborers and insist that the same unskilled menials were undeserving of freedom. For example, in 1748, Poor Richard entreated husbandmen to keep working, "Tho' his collected Rent his Bags supply, / Or honest, careful Slaves scarce need his eye." Three years later he wrote, "Not to oversee Workmen, is to leave them your Purse open."[37] Franklin addressed the kind of masters who had to work and who also worried about whether their surrogates were working just as hard and who needed to squeeze the most out of their sometimes recalcitrant subordinates.

Franklin continued to devote significant intellectual energy to the problem of surrogates, especially as he himself amassed enough capital to retire from his Philadelphia print shop in 1748 but remained invested in several printing establishments up and down the Atlantic coast, from Newport to Antigua.[38] Because others recognized the potential of treating circulating labor like capital, and because servants themselves learned how to take advantage of such a situation, Franklin became quite interested in the problem of runaway servants—especially those who enlisted in the British service or were impressed during wartime.[39] The tendency for slaves and servants to run away seems to have led Franklin to think about what sorts of servants were more valuable because they did not so quickly take their value into their own hands. The trade in slaves and contract labor seemed, at midcentury, to undermine security in that labor. Much

---

37. *Poor Richard's Almanack* (1739, 1745, 1748, 1754, 1755), *PBF* 2:218; 3:260; 4:85–86, 94, 97; 5:181, 473, 475. This contradiction appears repeatedly in runaway advertisements, where servants' many skills are enumerated even as the servant in question is declared to be untrustworthy. See the analysis in Waldstreicher, "Reading the Runaways," 255–56, 260–68. For the lack of deference in eighteenth-century America, see Michael Zuckerman, "Tocqueville, Turner, and Turds: Four Stories of Manners in Early America," *Journal of American History* 85 (June 1998): 13–42; for a view closer to my own, see Brown, "Antiauthoritarianism and Freedom," especially 78.

38. Articles of Agreement with Louis Timothee, *PBF* 1:339; Articles of Agreement with David Hall, *PBF* 3:263; Franklin to William Strahan, October 19, 1748, *PBF* 3:321–22; Van Doren, *Benjamin Franklin*, 116–22.

39. *Pennsylvania Gazette,* April 22, August 14, 1742, *PBF* 2:288–89, 360; "Record of Service in the Assembly, 1751–64," *PBF* 4:165; Franklin, "A Plan for Settling Four Western Colonies," *PBF* 5:458; "Militia Act" (1755), Pennsylvania Assembly: Address to the Governor (1756), *PBF* 6:272, 396–400; Pennsylvania Assembly Committee: Report on Grievances (1757), *PBF* 7:141; Franklin to Earl of Loudon, May 21, 1757, Franklin to Isaac Norris, May 30, 1757, *PBF* 7:214–15, 225–26; Franklin to Thomas Leeds and Assembly Committee of Correspondence, June 10, 1758, Franklin to Joseph Galloway, April 7, 1759, Franklin to the printer of the London Chronicle, May 9, 1759, *PBF* 8:90, 311–12, 350–51; James A. Sappenfield, *A Sweet Instruction: Franklin's Journalism as a Literary Apprenticeship* (Carbondale: Southern Illinois University Press, 1973), 109.

as there were limits to the ability of paper money to stimulate labor and thus wealth, there were limits to the circulation of labor itself. The roots of Franklin's antislavery, then, lay in the same place as his acceptance of slavery: his understanding of labor and capital. This fundamental contradiction became manifest in the context of increasing slave importation, slave resistance, and imperial regulation, and soon led him to articulate a form of racism previously absent in his writing and practice.

Colonial growth led directly to imperial wars that joined metropolitans and colonists in a common enterprise but also put special strains on colonial societies, exposing the fault lines of race and bondage as well as differing assumptions about economic regulation and governance.[40] In *Plain Truth* (1747), Franklin advocated the need for wartime defenses as Quaker-dominated Philadelphia faced a possible French raid in 1747, insisting that if the people did not take up arms against this possible raid, "your Persons, Fortunes, Wives and Daughters, shall be subject to the wanton and unbridled Rage, Rapine, and Lust of *Negroes, Molattoes,* and others, the vilest and most abandoned of mankind." People of color are again a metaphor, as in the "Blackamore" essay, but here with a much surer sense of the whiteness of a community of "we, the middling People." For the ordinary "Tradesmen, Shopkeepers, and farmers of this Province and City," mulatto seamen symbolize all the disorders of a world turned upside down, literally embodying (while racializing and sexualizing) the problem itself. Having divided the city rhetorically between rich and "midling" sorts, Franklin rested his call to arms upon the common, cross-class characteristics of the "BRITISH RACE . . . BRITONS, tho' a Hundred Years transplanted, and to the remotest part of the Earth, may yet retain . . . that *Zeal* for the *Publick Good,* that *military Prowess,* and that *undaunted Spirit,* which has in every Age distinguished their Nation." Adding some praise for the "Brave Irish protestants" and "brave and steady Germans," Franklin, writing anonymously as "a Tradesman of Philadelphia," sought a racial and imperial nationhood that would counter domestic divisions and the risks to profits, safety, and the interdependence of ranks brought on by the wars of the trading empire.[41]

Three years later Franklin penned his "Observations on the Increase of Mankind," a calculated effort to reimagine the political economy of the mid-Atlantic, and the American future generally, without slaves or a permanent class of servants. The essay is often pointed to as an early formulation of the

40. For the imperial wars and their settlements as a watershed in the empire, beginning in 1748, see Lawrence Henry Gipson, *The British Empire Before the American Revolution,* 15 vols. (New York: Knopf, 1936–70), 13:181–84; Jack P. Greene, "An Uneasy Connection: An Analysis of the Preconditions of the American Revolution," in *Essays on the American Revolution,* ed. Stephen Kurtz and James Huston (Chapel Hill: University of North Carolina Press, 1973), 132–80.

41. Franklin, *Plain Truth: or, Serious Considerations on the Present State of the City of Philadelphia, and Province of Pennsylvania* (1747), *PBF* 3:198–99, 202–4.

safety-valve or frontier thesis of American history, whereby the lower classes shake the dust off and move to unclaimed land rather than remaining where they are and becoming a depressed and exploited urban proletariat. Upward mobility and earlier marriage would spur a rapid rise in the population: "our People must at least be doubled every 20 Years." The population boom would in turn create a market for consumer goods made in England. Both colony and metropolis would thrive in these circumstances, so that even if industrious colonists began to manufacture, the high cost of labor would make it impossible for colonial manufactures to compete with British imports in any way harmful to the empire.[42]

The main threat to this prosperous empire, besides conquerable Indians, ill-advised imperial taxation, and the overconsumption of luxuries, was the mistaken idea that "by the Labour of Slaves, *America* may possibly vie in Cheapness of Manufactures with *Britain.*" It was mistaken because slavery was a bad investment when interest rates were high in the colonies, wages for manufacturing work were low in England, and "every Slave being *by Nature* a *thief.*"[43] Only the tendency of whites to graduate or run away from servitude lured strapped masters to buy slaves, a strategy that in the long run only stunted the economy and, Franklin implied, could easily be regulated out of existence. The number of whites in a nation, whose labor is equivalent to true wealth, actually diminished in proportion to the number of slaves. Counterintuitively (as far as the view from London was concerned), Franklin argued that the slave societies cultivating the Caribbean and the South did not represent the future of the empire and America, because their white populations remained stagnant. Slaves and their owners did not exhibit "frugality and Industry": they were wasteful, unlike the infinitely compounding free people-commodities of Pennsylvania.

In "Observations," Franklinian "Industry and Frugality" required racism to bring the seemingly divergent interests of the colonists and the metropolis back together, despite the well-known fact that so much wealth continued to be expropriated from enslaved bodies. Dismissing the wealth-producing capacities of slaves while bringing the topics of policy and peopling together enabled Franklin boldly to address the slavery question, which, the wars of the 1740s had taught him and other colonists, was also a question of imperial policy. This was even more the case in 1750, when a treaty with Spain awarded the *asiento*, or right to supply slaves, to the British.[44] He turned slavery, understandably, into a question of the trade in people, in which it looked like a bad bargain.

42. *PBF* 4:225–34.

43. Eighteen years later Franklin altered the phrase "every slave being by nature a thief" to "every slave being by the nature of slavery a thief," a change that has encouraged scholars to stress his rethinking of the matter and his final stand against racism as well as slavery. *PBF* 4:229n9; 19:113n1.

44. For the report of the treaty, see James Parker's *New York Gazette and Weekly Post Boy,* May 27, 1751.

Slaves were taking up spaces that could be occupied by white immigrants, who would in the long run add more wealth to an expanding empire. If the English thought correctly about their common interest with their fellow Britons across the water, they would actually free the trade in people from a narrowly conceived mercantilist-nationalist policy, which posed the rights and interests of Englishmen over colonists and everyone else, and instead use race as a benchmark for imperial economic policy. Colonists and Englishmen were white Britons; they deserved preferment over all darker races. This is why "Observations" concluded with its now-famous passage pleading not only for the whitening of America but also for the Americanization of whiteness:

> . . . the Number of purely white People in the World is proportionably very small. All *Africa* is black or tawny; *Asia* chiefly tawny; *America* (exclusive of the new Comers) wholly so. And in *Europe*, the *Spaniards, Italians, French, Russians,* and *Swedes,* are generally of what we call a swarthy Complexion; as are the *Germans* also, the *Saxons* only excepted, who with the *English,* make the principal Body of White People on the Face of the Earth. I could wish their Numbers were increased. And while we are, as I may call it, *Scouring* our Planet, by clearing *America* of Woods, and so making this Side of our Globe reflect a brighter Light to the Eyes of Inhabitants in *Mars* or *Venus,* why should we in the Sight of Superior Beings, darken its People? Why increase the Sons of *Africa,* by planting them in *America,* where we have so fair an Opportunity, by excluding all Blacks and Tawneys, of increasing the lovely White and Red?

From an extraterrestrial height, substituting scientific perspective for God's watch, Franklin ratified the solidarity of white Anglo-Americans, at the expense of blacks, Indians, and Europeans not (yet) considered white. Whiteness was nothing less than enlightenment: "a brighter *light.*" The problem was that to anyone still on the ground, it was obvious that "America" still belonged to the black, the tawny (Indians), the swarthy.[45] But not for long. He concluded by turning the looking glass on himself, and in doing so depicted the real Anglo-American as white with the turn of a phrase: "But perhaps I am partial to the Complexion of my Country, for such Kind of Partiality is natural to Mankind." If "race" prejudice is irrational, it is a "natural" irrationality. Even if the darker races are

45. Franklin's identification of Native Americans as "tawney" rather than "red," which is an adjunct of white, follows much eighteenth-century usage. See Alden Vaughan, "From White Man to Redskin," *Roots of American Racism: Essays on the Colonial Experience* (New York: Oxford University Press, 1996), 3–32; Nancy Shoemaker, "How Indians Got to Be Red," *American Historical Review* 102 (June 1997): 625–44.

not, after all, inferior, *racism* can be naturalized and identified with industrious America—Europe's enlightened future.[46]

Franklin's "Observations" repressed more than the very conditions of the mid-Atlantic economic development he celebrated. The essay linked virtue and whiteness and secured that linkage with a final gesture of preemptive self-criticism that justified racism by equating it with both nationality and universal human psychology. Franklin was quite up to date in pairing enlightenment with racism but against slavery. During the late 1740s David Hume began to argue that slavery had spoiled the republics of the ancient world, while also maintaining that Africa, innately inferior, had produced neither poets nor scientists.[47] Like the thinkers of the Scottish Enlightenment, Franklin had special reason to attempt to write the provinces into the history of British imperial progress. He had more reason, though, to keep slaves and their economic contributions out of the picture of "my Country." And he had still more reason to promulgate racial distinctions, if this would advance white colonists' claims to equality in an empire its theorists associated with commerce and progress.

During the 1750s Franklin became the foremost provincial theorist of British colonialism and nationalism, in an era in which colonists and other Britons repeatedly disagreed about how they should view and treat each other.[48] Far more than historians have acknowledged, these controversies included debates about the supply of labor, especially in the wake of King George's War and the Seven Years' War, when disrupted trading patterns had forced colonial masters to compete with imperial armies for the bodies of free and unfree men. In light

46. For a pathbreaking early analysis of "Observations" that grasped the "white liberal" outlook in Franklin's essay, see Paul W. Conner, *Poor Richard's Politicks: Benjamin Franklin and the New American Order* (New York: Oxford University Press, 1965), 75–84. Douglas Anderson has objected that Franklin is being ironic about racism in the service of a true pluralism. He is right about the irony but neglects the nationalism that the self-critical gesture implies. Anderson, *The Radical Enlightenments of Benjamin Franklin* (Baltimore: Johns Hopkins University Press, 1997), 158–67. For an interpretation of the essay similar to my own, one that stresses the support race gave to an imperial British nationalism, see Timothy Shannon, *Indians and Colonists at the Crossroads of Empire: The Albany Congress of 1754* (Ithaca: Cornell University Press, 2000), 98–101. For the Pennsylvania context of Franklin's ethnic and racial politics, see Francis Jennings, *Benjamin Franklin, Politician: The Mask and the Man* (New York: W. W. Norton, 1996).

47. David Hume, "Of National Characters" (1748) and "Of Money" (1752), in Hume, *Political Essays*, ed. Knud Haakonsen (Cambridge: Cambridge University Press, 1994), 86, 123; Roy Porter, *The Creation of the Modern World: The Untold Story of the British Enlightenment* (New York: W. W. Norton, 2000), 200. Hume and Franklin later became good friends; eventually Hume singled out Franklin as the first genius of the New World, precisely the kind he contrasted to Africans. Van Doren, *Benjamin Franklin*, 290.

48. Verner W. Crane, *Benjamin Franklin—Englishman and American* (Baltimore: Johns Hopkins University Press, 1936); Gerald Stourzh, *Benjamin Franklin and American Foreign Policy*, 2d ed. (Chicago: University of Chicago Press, 1969), 33–112; Ormond Seavey, "Benjamin Franklin as Imperialist and Provincial" in Balestra and Sampietro, *Benjamin Franklin: An American Genius*, 19–37; Wright, "'Fine and Noble China Vase,'" 435–64; Gordon S. Wood, "Not So Poor Richard," *New York Review of Books* 43 (June 6, 1996): 47–51.

of subsequent developments, it is striking how early and consistently Franklin employed his adept vocabulary of people, labor, and capital to improve upon what became the patriots' most consistent and internally unifying protest rhetoric: their complaint against being treated like "slaves."

Franklin's earliest complaints concerned the sale of British convicts in America as indentured servants, which the administration in London forbade colonial assemblies to regulate. The forced transportation of convicts put into practice the idea of the colonies as a satellite for inferiors, turned into, at best, half-citizens and, at worst, objects laboring for the benefit of the home country.[49] If the premise of convict labor dumping was that the colonies were inferior to the metropole, the subject forced Franklin to engage in a different rhetorical strategy from the unifying British nationalism of *Plain Truth* and the "Observations on the Increase of Mankind." Indeed, in articulating his opposition to the flood of English, Scots, and Irish reprobates he saw arriving in the colonies, Franklin for the first time took on a distinctive American identity, signing a 1751 *Pennsylvania Gazette* essay "AMERICANUS."

In the editorial that set up "Americanus," Franklin had retailed news about the venal activities of convicts, the epitome of which was a Maryland servant who, poised to stab his mistress, cut off his hand instead, only to add, "*Now make me work, if you can.*" A work world in which "hands" not only ran away with their own limbs but cut off them off to spite their masters was a seriously deranged world, in which virtuous natural increase was replaced by sin, disease, and filth.

> . . . what good *Mother* ever sent *Thieves* and *Villains* to accompany her *Children;* to corrupt some with their infectious Vices, and murder the rest? What *Father* ever endeavour'd to spread the *Plague* in his *Family!*— We do not ask Fish, but thou givest us *Serpents,* and worse than Serpents!—In what can *Britain* show a more Sovereign Contempt for us, than by emptying their *Jails* into our Settlements; unless they would likewise empty their *Jakes* on our Tables?"

The "Americanus" essay developed the symbol of the snake as a figure for this unnatural, yet original and sexual, sin of empire. Franklin insisted that America's native rattlesnakes, "Felons-convict from the Beginning of the World," should be sentenced not to death but to transportation—to England! Perhaps the change in climate would change their nature, he remarked in a satirical reversal of both continental speculation about the effects of New World weather and English justifications for exporting their felons (to reform them). He further questioned

---

49. Franklin also saw the impressment of seamen as a contravention of the rights of Britons and compared it to slavery as early as 1762. "Franklin's Remarks on Judge Foster's Argument in Favor of the Right of Impressing Seamen," *PBF* 35:497.

where empire's original sins lay—in the garden or with the master planters?—by adding that some Parliament courtiers were already all too reptilian in their venal, seducing habits. Franklin had taken a symbol of British insult and colonial inferiority and thrown it back. The snakes came from England.[50]

Yet it was not long before the threat of Indian depredations, and the uneven integration of Americans into imperial priorities and strategies during wartime, inspired Franklin to make the snake the symbol of a possible American unity.[51] Protesting against being lumped with the dregs of empire (convicts, outlanders like the Irish and Scots, Indians, and Africans), Franklin and the colonial master classes could not but seek to invert the stereotypes. In the process they not only engaged with but also began to appropriate the charges of inequality and exploitation being leveled by, and on behalf of, the empire's truly oppressed peoples.[52] Writing to Governor Shirley of his plan of union in 1754, Franklin asked whether colonists had, "by hazarding their Lives and Fortunes in subduing and settling new Countries, extending the Dominion and encreasing the Commerce of their Mother Nation," "forfeited the native Rights of Britons, which they think ought rather to have been given them, as due to such Merit, if they had been before in a State of Slavery." Even if the colonists had once had more in common with American slaves than with Britons, they possessed natural rights, not least because of their labor. They should not be taxed like a conquered people.[53]

What did the "Rights of Britons" have to do with actual slaves and servants? Nothing and everything. The rights of the empire to impress labor into the navy would "intirely destroy the Trade of bringing servants to the Colonies," Franklin complained in a letter to another colonial official in 1756. Taking one servant from a household or business could make others useless, as he had found in his printing house. Even voluntary enlistment was the end of colonists' wealth rather than the glory of empire, for servants could multiply themselves and their

---

50. Franklin, *Writings,* 357–59, 359–61, 377.

51. Lester C. Olson, *Emblems of American Community in the Revolutionary Era: A Study in Rhetorical Iconology* (Washington, D.C.: Smithsonian Institution Press, 1990), 24–74; J. A. Leo LeMay, "The American Aesthetic of Franklin's Visual Creations," *Pennsylvania Magazine of History and Biography* 111 (October 1987): 465–99; Anne Norton, *Reflections on Political Identity* (Baltimore: Johns Hopkins University Press, 1988), 88–91.

52. On Creole identities in the wake of colonization, see Nicholas Canny and Anthony Pagden, eds., *Colonial Identity in the Atlantic World, 1500–1800* (Princeton: Princeton University Press, 1987); Anderson, *Imagined Communities,* 47–66. For the Irish and Scots as themselves both "subordinate and dominant" in the empire, see Martin Daunton and Rick Halpern, "Introduction: British Identities, Indigenous Peoples, and the Empire," in *Empire and Others: British Encounters with Indigenous Peoples, 1600–1850,* ed. Martin Daunton and Rick Halpern (Philadelphia: University of Pennsylvania Press, 1999), 5. In calling for colonial unity and invoking the example of the Iroquois league against the possibility of war with the Indians, Franklin appropriated (rather than simply took inspiration from) contemporary movements for intertribal unity. For a fine critique of the Iroquois influence thesis, which has centered on Franklin's plans for union, see Shannon, *Indians and Colonists at the Crossroads of Empire.*

53. Franklin to William Shirley, December 4, 1754, *PBF* 5:447.

own capital by collecting bounties and running away: "he may repeat the Frolick as often as he pleases." The American owning classes' loss of freedom to manipulate their property in persons was nothing less than a form of enslavement that would create more (black) enslavement and a decline in white freedom: "Upon the whole I see clearly, that the Consequence will be, the Introduction of slaves, and thereby weakening the Colonies, and preventing their Increase in White Inhabitants."[54]

It was Franklin's innovation, then, to tie the discourse of liberty and slavery not merely to abstract rights or to a demand for belonging in the materially thriving British empire but also to the specific problems of labor, population, and colonial profits, understood as questions of capital (and thus later, logically as well as viscerally, of taxation).[55] After traveling to England in 1757 as a colonial agent, he evinced what in retrospect appears a contradictory position on slavery itself, one explicable only when we accept that he was playing a representative role in which his own views on slavery were less relevant than the desire for the debate over "slavery" to strengthen rather than weaken the colonists' position. His "Observations" (reprinted, for example, in 1760 with his pamphlet on keeping Canada in the empire) certainly suggested that he opposed slave labor. He began to work with the Associates of Dr. Bray, early proponents of philanthropic antislavery, in setting up schools for young blacks. He engaged intermittently in a dialogue with a coterie of British thinkers who attempted to theorize empire without slavery during the 1760s. Yet at the same time Franklin, as the official agent of Georgia, pushed that colony's new charter, complete with a slave code, through Parliament.[56]

Did these contradictions disturb Franklin? He had already maintained publicly (and there is no evidence to suggest that he did not believe) that the slave and convict servant trade existed more for the benefit of British investors than for American colonists. Slavery's persistence and growth were the result of imperial policy, an example of what went wrong when the colonists' economic ventures were unfairly regulated. In this context, and with the imperial controversy heating up after the Seven Years' War ended, the critique of slavery could be aligned with a fight for America's British rights, not just because slavery was the opposite of liberty, or because chattel slavery was the particular "nightmare" of slaveholding American patriots, but also because of the special importance of the labor supply in the colonies. For Franklin, the inability of the

54. "Address to the Governor," Franklin to Sir Everard Fawkener, July 27, 1756, *PBF* 6:396–400, 472–75.

55. See in this regard "The Interests of Great Britain Considered," *PBF* 9:73–79. David Brion Davis has described Franklin as "perhaps the first modern man to subject the institution [of slavery] to a bookkeeping analysis." Davis, *Problem of Slavery in Western Culture,* 427.

56. Franklin to John Waring, December 17, 1763, *PBF* 10:395–96; Van Doren, *Franklin,* 288; I. Bernard Cohen, *Science and the Founding Fathers* (New York: Knopf, 1995), 191–92; Van Horne, "Collective Benevolence and the Common Good"; Brown, "Empire Without Slaves."

colonists to regulate their own labor supply contributed to Americans' rhetorical self-identification as slaves in the protest movement.[57]

Their lack of control over labor (for Franklin, the source of wealth; for masters, a crucial repository of capital) made colonists slaves of the metropole. The struggle against the changing conditions of labor recruitment—not just trade and taxes but also the trade in workers—lay at the precise overlap of economic and political concerns, as the inefficacy of colonial protest against new regulations quickly came to be seen as itself a form of political "slavery." Franklin pursued this theme for a transatlantic audience with characteristic humor and devastating clarity. In "Invectives Against the Americans" (1765), a typically pseudonymous piece for the English press, he adopted an English voice to observe that the Americans are called a *"republican race, a mixed rabble of Scotch, Irish and foreign vagabonds, descendants of convicts"*: "Our slaves they may be thought: But every master of slaves ought to know, that though all the slave possesses is the property of the master, his *goodwill* is his own, he bestows it where he pleases; and it is *some importance* to the master's *profit,* if he can obtain that *good-will* at the cheap rate of a few kind words, with fair and gentle usage." It is striking that here, almost for the first time in his voluminous writings, Franklin looked at exploitive labor relations from the point of view of the laborer. He returned to the theme of personality and representation as value, as commodities in the marketplace, but in an uncharacteristically sarcastic vein. It was as if talk, "the cheap rate of a few kind words," had been devalued now that Americans were the objects, not the subjects, of capitalist ventures. But not permanently. In truth, "These people [the colonists], however, are not, never were, nor ever will be our slaves." The world is still divided in two, but the real Americans are on the free, and property-owning, side: "The first settlers of New England particularly, were English gentlemen of fortune." English descent is the source of freedom, the justification for colonists' political agency.[58]

57. For a different interpretation of the origins of the "slavery" metaphor that stresses the "discovery of inequality" and "fear of exclusion" by colonists (but not the labor problem), see T. H. Breen, "Ideology and Nationalism on the Eve of the American Revolution: Revisions *Once More* in Need of Revising," *Journal of American History* 84 (June 1997): 13–39. For an account that ties the slavery issue to the rhetorical exigencies of the colonial protest, seeing the slavery issue as "a lever promoting revolutionary action," see Patricia Bradley, *Slavery, Propaganda, and the American Revolution* (Jackson: University Press of Mississippi, 1998), xii. See also F. Nwabueze Okoye, "Chattel Slavery as the Nightmare of the American Revolutionaries," *William and Mary Quarterly,* 3d ser., 37 (January 1980): 3–28; Bernard Bailyn, *The Ideological Origins of the American Revolution* (Cambridge: Harvard University Press, 1967), 232–46; David R. Roediger, *The Wages of Whiteness: Race and the Making of the American Working Class* (New York: Verso, 1991), 27–33.

58. Franklin, *Writings,* 562–64; Verner W. Crane, "Introduction," *Benjamin Franklin's Letters to the Press, 1757–1775,* ed. Verner W. Crane (Chapel Hill: University of North Carolina Press, 1950), xli–liii. For the colonists' use of history at this time, see H. Trevor Colbourn, *The Lamp of Experience: Whig History and the Intellectual Origins of the American Revolution* (Chapel Hill: University of North Carolina Press, 1965); Bailyn, *Ideological Origins of the American Revolution.*

How, then, might colonists account for such treatment from the English themselves? The "Mother Country," Franklin wrote in a song, might well act like an old woman who cannot accept that her children are grown, "But still an old Mother should have due Respect, / *which nobody can deny, &c.*" It was the "Abuse of [from] her Man" that was truly intolerable to the innocent young colonists and need not be borne, because as legitimate children the colonies were not to be subjected to corporal punishment. Unlike such children, "when Servants make mischief, they earn the Rattan."[59] Franklin chose to develop the trope of the colonies as children in order to object to the alternative: the colonies as servants and slaves. The familial discourse of British national politics allowed colonial protest to develop within recently revised, sentimentalized notions of monarchy in particular and patriarchy in general.[60] Questioning an inferior status as Britain's surrogate while implying, at the end of the song, that only time (the mother's death) would eventually solve the generational conundrum, Franklin was at the forefront of colonists' efforts to spin the familial language of politics in such a way as to wiggle the Creole sons out of a servile position.

Unfortunately for Franklin and the other patriot leaders, the objection to being treated like slaves could, in the absence of racism, all too easily be inverted in the name of the servants and slaves themselves. The English political context is of crucial importance here. The rhetoric of American innocence and enslavement moved some Britons at home—after all, it improved on some domestic struggles for liberty—but not enough of them, and not in sympathy with white colonists alone. Some abolitionists used the mounting protest of the colonies to amplify their arguments against slavery, but anti-Americanism proved just as useful to those who wanted to point to what they understandably saw as a more severe case of oppression. Opponents of American protest, in turn, did not hesitate to use antislavery rhetoric against the Americans. In the deft hands of a Samuel Johnson, anti-Americanism and antislavery reinforced each other.[61]

---

59. Franklin, *Writings*, 565–66.

60. Franklin had written in 1754 that "Instructions from the Crown to the Colonies. . . . Should be plainly just and reasonable, and rather savour of Fatherly Tenderness and Affection, than of Masterly harshness and Severity." Franklin to Peter Collinson, May 28, 1754, *PBF* 5:332. On the sentimentalized monarchy of the late eighteenth century, see Linda Colley, *Britons: Forging the Nation, 1707–1837* (New Haven: Yale University Press 1992), 195–236; Gordon S. Wood, *The Radicalism of the American Revolution* (New York: Knopf, 1992), 95–100; Jay Fliegelman, *Prodigals and Pilgrims: The American Revolution Against Patriarchal Authority, 1750–1800* (New York: Cambridge University Press, 1982); Richard L. Bushman, *King and People in Provincial Massachusetts* (Chapel Hill: University of North Carolina Press, 1985). For the sense of changed treatment on Franklin's part as a problem in the relationship of colonies to empire, see Jack P. Greene, "Pride, Prejudice, and Jealousy: Benjamin Franklin's Explanation for the American Revolution" in LeMay, *Reappraising Benjamin Franklin*, 119–42.

61. Elijah Gould, *The Persistence of Empire: British Political Culture in the Age of the American Revolution* (Chapel Hill: University of North Carolina Press, 2000), 106–47; Neill R. Joy, "Politics and Culture: The Dr. Franklin–Dr. Johnson Connection, with an Analogue," *Prospects* 23 (1998): 60–81. Johnson's famous quotation from *Taxation No Tyranny* (London, 1775) replied directly to Franklin, a fact not missed by writers for the opposition. Helen Louise McGuffie, "Dr. Johnson and the Little Dogs:

By 1770 it had become all too clear to antislavery agitators that the colonists cared much more about "slavery" when they—not their slaves—were seen as its victims. Franklin addressed the contradiction between antislavery theory and colonial protest that year in the form of "A Conversation between an Englishman, a Scotchman, and an American, on the subject of Slavery" (1770). That he had been backed into a corner is apparent from the beginning, for the Englishman gets the first, Johnsonian word, accusing the Americans of hypocrisy and recommending that they read "*Granville Sharpe's* Book upon Slavery." The American responds that it is indeed a good book, but that the hypocrisy lies with the English, since the larger effect of this attack on the Americans is "to render us odious, and to encourage those who would oppress us, by representing us as unworthy of the Liberty we are now contending for."[62]

The antislavery complaint against Americans, Franklin insists, is too "general" because the "Foundation" of slavery in America is not general. New England has few slaves, mostly "Footmen"; the same is true for New York, New Jersey, and Pennsylvania. Even in Virginia and South Carolina, slavery is a vestige of privilege for the few, the "old rich Inhabitants." The real Americans— ninety-nine out of one hundred families—do not own a slave. What is more, the poor in England, far more than in America, are regulated like slaves. England, in fact, began the slave trade, which continues only because "You bring the Slaves to us, and tempt us to purchase them."

When the English interlocutor cites the harshness of slave laws, the American responds by asserting that they are less harsh where there are fewer slaves. He chides the abolitionist for sentimentalism concerning blacks: "Perhaps you may imagine the Negroes to be a mild, tempered tractable Kind of People. Some of them indeed are so. But the Majority are of a plotting Disposition, dark, sullen, malicious, revengeful, and cruel in the highest Degree. . . . Indeed many of them, being mischievous Villains in their own Country, are sold off by their Princes by the Way of Punishment by Exile and Slavery, as you here ship off your Convicts." As in the "Observations" two decades earlier, Franklin undermines slavery only to ultimately confirm racial differences and black inferiority in the Americas. The blame for the evils of the unfree labor system can then be fixed on prior historical and natural factors. In this case, it also serves to buttress an argument about "the Villains you transport" and why they "must be ruled with a Rod of Iron." When the Scotsman objects that the Americans willingly buy both slaves and felons, the American refuses to budge. With low prices, "you force upon us the Convicts as well as the Slaves." Anticipating the arguments of later (southern) defenders of slavery, Franklin goes so far as to call up the image

The Reaction of the London Press to *Taxation No Tyranny,*" in *Newsletters to Newspapers: Eighteenth-Century Journalism; Papers Presented at a Symposium, at West Virginia University,* ed. Donovan H. Bond and W. Reynolds McLeod (Morgantown: West Virginia University, 1977), 196.

62. Franklin, *Writings,* 646–47.

of white slavery in the coalmines of Scotland. Finally the American, transformed into the defender of all liberties, redefines slavery as all unfree, bought labor, accusing the English of founding their great empire on the slavery of soldiers and sailors who not only experience social death but cause the deaths of others.[63]

By 1772 Franklin had explicitly placed himself on the side of antislavery in private letters to Anthony Benezet and Granville Sharp. Yet a close examination of his public writings and correspondence on the subject shows how carefully he exculpated the colonists from any responsibility for the institution. In April 1773 he wrote to the Dublin cleric Richard Woodward of hearing that "a Disposition to abolish Slavery prevails in North America, that many of the Pennsylvanians, have set their Slaves at liberty, that even the Virginia Assembly have petitioned the King to make a Law for preventing the Importation of more Slaves into that Colony." But he predicted (rightly) that the king would disallow this law, as with anti–convict importation measures: "the Interest of a few Merchants here [in London] has more Weight with Government than that of Thousands at a Distance." Antislavery proved the case for English corruption, which suggested the virtues of American self-government. Thus antislavery sentiment itself, for Franklin, needed to be recast as sympathy for colonists whenever it suggested the reverse. In response to the Somerset decision, which seemed to declare slavery illegal on British soil, Franklin ridiculed the liberation of one slave by a nation that still jealously guarded its slave trade. It did not help, doubtless, that Lord Mansfield, the presiding judge, was a consistent critic of colonial resistance.[64]

Soon the matter of Franklin's own loyalty, amid his blistering attacks on British man trading as the epitome of the government's oppressive tendencies, got intertwined with the slavery issue. Franklin's decisive alienation from Great Britain probably occurred in January 1774, when he was called on the carpet before the Privy Council's Committee on Plantation Affairs and called a thief by Solicitor General Alexander Wedderburn. The alienation, though, was deeper than psychological, and had been building for some time, for Wedderburn's otherwise inexplicably harsh denunciation of Franklin in the "cockpit" responded explicitly to Franklin's very public rhetorical projection of the theft of persons onto the British. In this context, it is rather less surprising that Wedderburn compared Franklin, "the wily American," so publicly to a "bloody African" slave trader, a character in a contemporary play. The experience only confirmed what Franklin had been warning against: arrogant Englishmen who could not tell the difference between a fellow Briton and a slave-trading African chieftain.[65]

63. Ibid., 648–53.

64. Anthony Benezet to Franklin, April 27, 1772, Franklin to Benezet, August 22, 1772, *PBF* 19:113–17, 269; Franklin, "The Sommersett Case and the Slave Trade," *PBF* 19:187–88; Franklin to Benezet, February 10, July, 14, 1773, Franklin to Richard Woodward, April 10, 1773, Benjamin Rush to Franklin, May 1, 1773, *PBF* 20:41, 193, 155–56, 296.

65. Carey, *Franklin's Economic Views,* 72–73; Jack P. Greene, "The Alienation of Benjamin Franklin, British American" in his *Understanding the American Revolution: Issues and Actors* (Charlottesville:

In response, Franklin wrote more letters for the press depicting the British as intentional man traders. At the height of the imperial controversy he did more than anyone else to develop and dramatize the notion of Great Britain's enslavement of the colonies. In letters both published and unpublished he depicted a British ruling class literally ready to sell the colonists "to the best Bidder." In ventriloquized English voices, he described Americans in these pieces as runaways, convicts, and chattel, to be ruled by "the method made use of by the Planters in the West Indies . . . who appoint what they call a Negro Driver, who is chosen from among the Slaves." He took on the voice of a "FREEHOLDER OF OLD SARUM" (the ultimate rotten borough and a symbol of aristocratic corruption) to propose castration as "the most feasible Method of humbling our rebellious Vassals of North America," lest they "slip their Necks out of the Collar, and from being Slaves set up for Masters." The same essay suggested that oppressing the Americans would prevent excess emigration to the colonies and an ensuing loss of English wealth. America was the land of opportunity and freedom, Britain the home of tyranny and oppression. In such a context, an attack on American mainland slavery would make little sense, except for those willing to celebrate British privileges of enslavement. Thus Franklin's rhetorical inflation of all colonial relations to forms of unfree labor—as in a fake bill disallowing Britons for emigrating for more than seven years—drew attention to the slave trade but away from the everyday aspects of labor in North America. At a time when the nascent British antislavery movement focused on the evils of the trade, this was a potent appropriation, to say the least.[66]

In a series of letters to British friends in late 1775 and 1776, Franklin depicted reconciliation as impossible because Britain had "burnt our defenceless Towns in the midst of Winter, excited the Savages to Massacre our Farmers, and our Slaves to murder their Masters." Returning to Philadelphia, he sat on the committee of the Continental Congress that drafted the Declaration of Independence, including the eventually excised paragraph condemning the king for both bringing Africans to America and inciting them to bloody rebellion. This passage may not have made much sense in light of many colonists' explicit defense of slavery; but it was utterly consistent with Franklin's rhetorical strategy as it had developed over the previous decade. The paragraph foundered not simply on southern resistance but also, in a wider sense, on the multiplicity of

---

University Press of Virginia, 1995), 248; Van Doren, *Benjamin Franklin,* 470, 519; Ronald Clark, *Benjamin Franklin: A Biography* (New York: Random House, 1983), 243–44; Franklin, "Rules by Which a Great Empire May Be Reduced to a Small One" (1773), *PBF* 20:390; "The Final Hearing Before the Privy Council Committee on Plantation Affairs" (1774), *PBF* 21:50.

66. Franklin, "An Open Letter to Lord North" (1774), "A Method of Humbling Rebellious American Vassals" (1774), "An Imaginary Speech" (1775), "Fragments of Two Letters to the Press" (1774–75), "Notes on Britain's Intention to Enslave America" (1774–75), *PBF* 21:183–86, 221–22, 485, 605, 608.

audiences for the Declaration, national and international. Its absence from the finished text, where slavery remains present in the form of "domestic insurrections," suggests the transitional moment the Declaration occupies in the politics of slavery, when American nationhood began to weaken the effectiveness of blaming the British, but war itself justified talking of slaves as enemies at home.[67]

In the imaginary but rhetorically effective conception of the antislavery founders Franklin and Jefferson, colonial contradictions were equated with slavery and foisted upon England. What remained American were the positive sides of merchant capitalism: free labor, imperial wealth, and neomercantilist economic independence.[68] While minister to France, Franklin followed the logic of the virtuous free labor of Americans to the level of myth. America was "a manufactory of men"—free men. Luxury goods, he insisted, were not a significant source of wealth or debt in America, though they were the source of England's corruption as a navigating, privateering nation.[69] In *Information to Those Who Would Remove to America* (1782, also printed on his own press in 1784), Franklin depicted the quintessential American as a freeholder who worked for himself, with his own hands: "America is the Land of Labour," where wages became property, as "Multitudes of poor People from England, Ireland, Scotland and Germany, have by this means in a few Years become wealthy Farmers."[70]

Where are the slaves, the multiracial unfree labor force, in Franklin's postrevolutionary vision? They are ventriloquized, in West Indian dialect, into commentators on the Americans' propensity to work.

> In Europe [high birth] has indeed its Value, but it is a Commodity that cannot be carried to a worse Market than to that of America, where People do not enquire concerning a Stranger, *What is he?* but *What can he DO?* . . . The People have a Saying, that God Almighty is himself a Mechanic, the greatest in the Universe; and he is respected and admired

67. Franklin to Jonathan Shipley, July 7 and September 13, 1775, Franklin to David Hartley, September 12, 1775, Franklin to Lord Howe, July 20, 1776, *PBF* 22:97, 196, 200, 519; Franklin, "Memoirs of the State of the Former Colonies," *PBF* 23:118; Franklin to Jan Ingenhousz, (February 12–March 6), 1777, *PBF* 23:310. Many works consider the antislavery passage in the Declaration an unrealistic flight of fancy on Jefferson's part; see, for example, Garry Wills, *Inventing America: Jefferson's Declaration of Independence* (Garden City, N.Y.: Doubleday, 1976), 146–47; Pauline Maier, *American Scripture: Making the Declaration of Independence* (New York: Knopf, 1997), 72–74. For slaves as an enemy nation, see Peter S. Onuf, "'To Declare Them a Free and Independent People': Jefferson, Race, and National Identity," *Journal of the Early Republic* 18 (Spring 1998): 1–47.

68. John E. Crowley, *The Privileges of Independence: Neomercantilism and the American Revolution* (Baltimore: Johns Hopkins University Press, 1993). On Franklin's political economy for the new Republic, see Drew R. McCoy, *The Elusive Republic: Political Economy in Jeffersonian America* (Chapel Hill: University of North Carolina Press, 1980), 51–69; Doron Ben-Atar, "Nationalism, Neo-Mercantilism, and Diplomacy: Rethinking the Franklin Mission," *Diplomatic History* 22 (April 1998): 108–12.

69. Franklin to Lord Howe, July 20, 1776, *Writings*, 992–94; Van Doren, *Franklin,* 711, 747–51, 770.

70. Franklin, *Writings,* 976–77.

more for the Variety, Ingenuity and Utility of his Handiworks, than for the Antiquity of his Family. They are pleas'd with the Observation of a Negro, and frequently mention it, that *Boccarorra* (meaning the White-man) make de Blackman workee, make de Horse workee, make de Ox workee, make ebery ting workee; only de Hog. He de Hog, no workee; he eat, he drink, he walk about, he go to sleep when he please, *he libb like a Gentleman*. According to these Opinions of the Americans, one of them would think himself more oblig'd to a Genealogist, who could prove for him that his Ancestors & Relations for ten Generations had been Ploughmen, Smiths, Carpenters, Turners, Weavers, Tanners, or even Shoemakers, & consequently that they were useful Members of Society; than if he could only prove that they were Gentlemen, doing nothing of Value, but living idly on the Labour of others, mere *fruges consumere nati,* and otherwise *good* for *nothing,* till be their Death, their Estates like the Carcase of the Negro's Gentleman-Hog, come to be *cut up.*

Like his earlier references to African Americans and to slavery, Franklin's ventriloquism here repays close attention. The embedded slave-trickster tale depicts whites as exceptional slave drivers who become hoglike in the process. But Franklin deflects this more obvious interpretation of white "American" character by implanting the black dialect story in a paragraph contrasting the hardy American citizenry with a European aristocracy that derives land and wealth from the accident of birth. In the process, New World slavery is actually projected onto Old World tyranny, and the American yeomanry emerges as the antithesis of both. Some white people may be gentlemen-hogs—maybe in the West Indies, as in Europe—but not in our America. The discourse of national comparison (Europeans versus Americans) abstracts America from the Americas, from the slave societies that the West Indian accent of the Negro otherwise signals. Americans are whites, but never slave drivers. The way they drive "de Blackman" reflects only their own greater national industry, rather than their historical, and continuing, implication in New World slavery.

Franklin's minstrelization did more than miss or deflect the point. It actually appropriated the slaves' story, and thus obscured even as it presented their very different understanding of whose labor had made America and their different prediction of who, in the end, might justly find themselves under the knife, "cut up" into pieces. The Negro's tale that Franklin retailed was at least a century old: one version was reported in a 1676 English pamphlet about a slave rebellion in Barbados.[71] Its presence in Franklin's defining portrait of the postcolonial

71. *Great Newes from Barbadoes, or a True and Faithful Account of the Grand Conspiracy of the Negroes Against the English* (London, 1676), quoted and cited in Linebaugh and Rediker, *Many Headed Hydra,* 125, 372n51. On minstrelsy as appropriation, see Eric Lott, *Love and Theft: Blackface Minstrelsy and the American Working Class* (New York: Oxford University Press, 1993). On slave trickster tales, see

United States suggests that, as Linebaugh and Rediker have argued, when we neglect the complex interrelation of working people's resistance and "bourgeois" political revolutions, we impoverish our understanding of early America and the Atlantic world. In the complex processes of appropriation and misrecognition that seem to have characterized colonial (and revolutionary) subcultures in the eighteenth century, it was not only slaves and other working people who pursued deep politics through tricksterlike storytelling and retelling. Franklin's own highly publicized stories, his pictures of the American colonies as a chopped-up snake, and his narratives of convict servants poised to stab innocent American women or, even worse, chopping off their own working hands, should be seen as countertrickster tales that took the rhetorical knife out of the hands of blacks and Britons. Parables of merchant capitalism gone mad, they made the fattened British Empire the agent of its own division and sale.[72]

In the late 1780s, scholars maintain, Franklin emerged as a true antislavery hero and even a believer "in racial equality," relatively speaking.[73] But it matters how he got there. Franklin's perceptions of emergent capitalism, his criticisms of slavery, and his skillful deployment of racism made him the perfect person to justify America—slavery and all—in the crucible of revolution. Combined with his other arguments about British national identity, the labor market, and imperial political economy, antislavery actually became integral to the Revolution once Franklin turned it on the British. But it was an antislavery compromised by its projection of blame for slavery onto the metropole and an antislavery that racialized the emerging American identity in such a way as to reinforce

---

Lawrence Levine, *Black Culture and Black Consciousness: Afro-American Folk Thought from Slavery to Freedom* (New York: Oxford University Press, 1977). For the ways in which vernacular stories from below can be lodged within and appropriated by the dominant class for its own purposes, see Edward E. Baptist, "Snell's Homecoming: Accidental Ethnography in an Antebellum Southern Newspaper," *Journal of American History* 84 (March 1998): 1355–83. On forgetting slavery, I am indebted to Joanne Pope Melish, *Disowning Slavery: Gradual Emancipation and "Race" in New England, 1780–1860* (Ithaca: Cornell University Press, 1998), and Michel-Rolph Trouillot, *Silencing the Past: Power and the Production of History* (Boston: Beacon Press, 1995).

72. In light of the sudden cultural valuation of ordinary (white) men's labor in the wake of the Revolution, Franklin's appropriation and forgetting of slavery makes the ideology of the Revolution look less like "democratic capitalism" than like "war propaganda" (although free-labor doctrine would have its antislavery uses). Compare Wood and Appleby (cited above, note 5) with Francis Jennings, *The Creation of America: Through Revolution to Empire* (New York: Cambridge University Press, 2000), 9, 193, 203–5. For Wood's own dismissal of Jennings as presentist, see Wood, "The Greatest Generation," *New York Review of Books* 48 (March 29, 2001): 18.

73. Finkelman, *Slavery and the Founders,* 174. In an earlier essay, not reprinted in *Slavery and the Founders,* Finkelman called Franklin's silence at the Constitutional Convention "curious," and noted that he played a particularly significant role in the compromise that resulted in the three-fifths clause and slavery's institutionalization in the new nation. Finkelman, "The Pennsylvania Delegation and the Peculiar Institution: The Two Faces of the Keystone State," *Pennsylvania Magazine of History and Biography* 112 (January 1988): 70–71.

the assumption that Africans were not and could not be members of the new national polity.

Capitalism has been given credit, by some, for the rise of antislavery; for others, antislavery helped legitimize wage labor, and thus industrial capitalism, in the same historical epoch.[74] In the North American case, the story of capitalism and slavery is longer than this, more complicated, and certainly more disturbing for those who would like to see capitalism as a harbinger of progress. The appropriation of antislavery by one of America's premier theorists of capitalism may have helped delegitimize slavery in the long run, but it first deflected attention from black slavery, while also advancing the racially exclusive dimensions of revolutionary nationalism. Only by disregarding the importance of slavery to the rise of Franklin and his North can we understand the Revolution as having had antislavery effects but no proslavery causes.

The Revolution did upset slavery, but so did earlier colonial wars, which—like the American Revolution—might well be seen, without reductionism, as driven by imperial rivalries for slave-grown profits.[75] We do not yet understand how the American Revolution both divided and united colonists who held slaves and others who held fewer or none but may still have had economic interests in the slave system; we do not have anything like an analysis of the era that puts international political economy—and thus slavery—center stage. Nevertheless, it seems safe to say that there were many roads to revolution and many of them did not lead, even indirectly, to the end of slavery. The equation of revolutionary ideology with antislavery and capitalism puts the ideological cart before the economic horse.

The metaphor of historical roads traveled and ignored may be extended further, for it helps us return to Eric Williams's insight and the missed opportunity provided by his economic approach to major historical changes. The political road North Americans traveled freed them from the empire and from their political—though not their economic—connections with the West Indies. This made it even easier to imagine America as a land of the free, as in effect noncolonial, even nonmerchant capitalist. In 1759, the year he met Franklin, Adam Smith attacked America—North and South, mainland and islands—as a moral world turned upside down, thanks in large measure to slavery. By 1776 and *The Wealth of Nations,* Smith accepted the Franklinian view that slavery neither

74. See the essays by David Brion Davis, Thomas Haskell, and John Ashworth in Thomas Bender ed., *The Antislavery Debate: Capitalism and Abolitionism as a Problem in Historical Interpretation* (Berkeley and Los Angeles: University of California Press, 1993).

75. Stanley Engerman has noted the role of wars and politics, as opposed to economics, in ending slavery. The economic causes of those wars suggest the need for an integrated approach to eighteenth-century political and economic history. See Engerman, "The Atlantic Economy of the Eighteenth Century: Some Speculations on Economic Development in Britain, America, Africa, and Elsewhere," *Journal of European Economic History* 24 (June 1995): 156.

amounted to much on the mainland nor accounted for capitalist wealth.[76] The change is fraught with implications for understanding the American Revolution. As elsewhere, reality was one thing, ideology another. Franklin and the revolutionary movement he led depended upon forgetting the roots of capitalist growth, most of all the economic role of New England and the middle colonies in the world economy. The American Revolution surely set in motion a chain of events that changed capitalism and undermined slavery in some places. But it also mystified the late colonial past. The tendency for Americans and their historians to take Franklin's ideological arguments, and even his autobiography, as a starting point for explaining the Revolution or capitalism practically guarantees that the role of slavery in the creation of the nation will be fundamentally understated if not completely ignored.

Freedom from the West Indies has also meant, for most historians of the Revolution, freedom from the economics and politics of slavery; but this is a luxury that the historiographies of the colonial and early Republic periods less often afford themselves of late, with good reason. Many of the early Republic's specific diplomatic and political struggles can be traced to the impossibility of rendering the United States not only independent but free of New World slavery.[77] "Atlantic" approaches have helped, but so would a willingness to expand the scope of analysis to include causes and consequences of the Revolution, rather than isolating them from each other or conflating either or both with the ideologies or justifications that admittedly made the event possible.[78] The Revolution is too important to be understood through the eyes of its foremost propagandist, not least because Americans and their historians remain in his debt.

76. Williams, *From Columbus to Castro*, 135; Adam Smith, *The Theory of the Moral Sentiments* (1759), ed. D. D. Raphael and A. L. Macfie (1976; reprint, Indianapolis: Liberty Fund, 1982), 206–7. Scholars of Smith seem to gloss over the change in emphasis and context as much as do scholars of Franklin. See, for example, Jerry Z. Muller, *The Mind and the Market: Capitalism in Modern European Thought* (New York: Knopf, 2002), 74. For correctives, see Perelman, *Invention of Capitalism*, 229–53; Drescher, *Mighty Experiment*, 19–33, 247n41.

77. William W. Freehling, *The Road to Disunion*, vol. 1, *Secessionists at Bay, 1776–1854* (New York: Oxford University Press, 1990); Robert P. Forbes, "Slavery and the Meaning of America, 1819–33" (Ph.D. diss., Yale University, 1993); Don E. Fehrenbacher, *The Slaveholding Republic: An Account of the United States Government's Relation to Slavery* (New York: Oxford University Press, 2001); Leonard Richards, *The Slave Power: The Free North and Southern Domination, 1790–1860* (Baton Rouge: Louisiana State University Press, 2000); Matthew Mason, "The Battle of the Slaveholding Liberators: Great Britain, the United States, and Slavery in the Early Nineteenth Century," *William and Mary Quarterly*, 3d ser., 59 (October 2002): 665–96.

78. For a recent paean to Atlantic and comparative approaches that surprisingly neglects matters of periodization, causation, and questions of economy, see Joyce E. Chaplin, "Expansion and Exceptionalism in Early American History," *Journal of American History* 89 (March 2003): 1431–55.

Chapter Seven

Moneyless in Pennsylvania: Privatization and the Depression of the 1780s

TERRY BOUTON

Nothing is more common than for men to pass from the abuse of a good thing to the disuse of it. Some persons disgusted by the depreciation of the money, are chimerical enough to imagine it would be beneficial to abolish all paper credit, annihilate the whole of what is now in circulation and depend altogether upon our specie both for commerce and finance. The scheme is altogether visionary and in the attempt would be fatal.

—ALEXANDER HAMILTON TO ROBERT MORRIS, APRIL 30, 1781

It may be considered as an incontrovertible Proposition, that all paper Money ought to be absorbed by Taxation or otherwise and destroyed before we can Expect our public Credit to be fully reestablished. For so long as there be any in Existence, the Holder will view it as a monument of national Perfidy.

—ROBERT MORRIS TO THE PRESIDENT OF CONGRESS, JULY 29, 1782
The Papers of Robert Morris, ED. E. JAMES FERGUSON ET AL., 8 VOLS.
(PITTSBURGH: UNIVERSITY OF PITTSBURGH PRESS, 1973 99), 1:43–44, 6:61

Economic historians have recently begun to talk about the 1780s as the start of the privatization of American finance. This "privatization of financial services," as one scholar calls the transformation, happened as the War of Independence drew to a close and state governments began ceding to newly created private banks the power to issue paper currency and to make loans. As these scholars note, the change was radical, especially in the colony/commonwealth of Pennsylvania. In the fifty years before independence, Pennsylvania's colonial government had compensated for perpetual specie shortages and inadequate credit reserves by printing paper money to serve as a medium of exchange. The government also provided direct loans to the public through a "land bank" that distributed the currency by means of long-term loans at low interest that could be obtained by nearly anyone who owned land. This money held its value because it was backed by land: if borrowers defaulted on their mortgage payments, the colonial government could foreclose on their estates. But foreclosures tended to be rare because, with sufficient currency available, most people were able to pay their mortgages as well as other internal debts and taxes. As an added benefit, the government-run land bank cut the tax burden: the colonial assembly used the interest collected on the land loans to build roads and bolster the colony's defenses.[1]

This public system came under attack during the Revolutionary War owing largely to the hardships faced by a specie-poor nation trying to fight a war with paper money. During the war, Congress and Pennsylvania's new state government issued paper money that was backed by taxation (ideally the currency held its value because citizens would need it to pay future taxes). But when the demands of war caused Congress and the state to print far more money than they could collect in taxes, the value of the currencies plummeted. Inspired by the depreciation of wartime currencies, beginning with Pennsylvania in 1781, states across the new nation began making a "general movement" to change "from public to private control of money and banking." This transition was solidified by the ratification of the federal Constitution of 1787, which banned states from printing paper money, a prohibition that effectively killed the land-bank system. With the public system dismantled by constitutional restrictions, states came to rely on chartering private banks as a way to meet the currency and credit needs of the citizenry.[2]

Although they acknowledge the dramatic—even "revolutionary"— nature of privatization, most economic historians suggest that the transition to

---

1. For scholarship noting the great utility of paper money and land banks, see E. James Ferguson, "Currency Finance: An Interpretation of Colonial Monetary Practices," *William and Mary Quarterly*, 3d ser., 10 (April 1953): 153–80, and *Power of the Purse: A History of American Public Finance, 1776–1790* (Chapel Hill: University of North Carolina Press, 1961), 3–24; Gary B. Nash, *The Urban Crucible: Social Change, Political Consciousness, and the Origins of the American Revolution* (Cambridge: Harvard University Press, 1979), 26–53, 76–101, 129–57, 198–232, 264–384; Joseph Ernst, *Money and Politics in America, 1755–1775: A Study in the Currency Act of 1764 and the Political Economy of Revolution* (Chapel Hill: University of North Carolina Press, 1973); Leslie Van Horne Brock, *The Currency of the American Colonies, 1700–1764* (New York: Arno Press, 1975); Richard A. Lester, "Currency Issues to Overcome Depressions in Pennsylvania, 1723 and 1729," *Journal of Political Economy* 46 (June 1938): 324–75, and *Monetary Experiments, Early American and Recent Scandinavian* (Princeton: Princeton University Press, 1939), 56–151; Paton Wesley Yoder, "Paper Currency in Colonial Pennsylvania" (Ph.D. diss, Indiana University, 1941); Mary M. Schweitzer, *Custom and Contract: Household, Government, and the Economy in Colonial Pennsylvania* (New York: Columbia University Press, 1987), 115–67; John J. McCusker and Russell R. Menard, *The Economy of British America, 1607–1789* (Chapel Hill: University of North Carolina Press, 1985), 338–39.

2. For quotes, see, Edwin J. Perkins, *American Public Finance and Financial Services, 1700–1815* (Columbus: Ohio State University Press, 1994), 123, 3. For others characterizing the postwar decades as a period of privatizing public functions, see Richard Sylla, John B. Legler, and John J. Wallis, "Banks and State Public Finance in the New Republic: The United States, 1790–1860," *Journal of Economic History* 47 (June 1987): 391–403; Richard Sylla, "Three Centuries of Finance and Monetary Control in America," *Journal of Economic History* 55 (December 1995): 902–7, and "Shaping the US Financial System, 1690–1913," in *The State, the Financial System, and Economic Modernization*, ed. Richard Sylla, Richard Tilly, and Gabriel Tortella (New York: Cambridge University Press, 1999), 249–70.

private banking was rather painless and unusually successful. According to Richard Sylla, the privatization movement capped off by Alexander Hamilton's financial program "happened so neatly, and became so engrained in the order of things, that many, forgetting how different was the previous financial order, failed to comprehend what he [Hamilton] and the Federalists had wrought." Edwin Perkins has declared the shift to private banking during the 1780s (in the three states that chartered banks—Pennsylvania, New York, and Massachusetts) an "immediate success." Robert Wright has argued that private banks met the nation's currency needs and made credit available to "a broad segment of the business community, including artisans, farmers, and women."[3]

Economic historians give especially high marks for the transformation in Pennsylvania, home to the nation's first private bank, the Bank of North America. According to Wright, "Pennsylvanians pretty readily accepted the notions that banks fueled economic growth and regularized, nay almost democratized, economic relations." Perkins reaches essentially the same conclusion: "The process of substituting private for government currency was accepted with little controversy or heated public debate in Pennsylvania in 1781." Perkins admits that the transition was not perfect, conceding that "the lending function of the bank was oriented toward only a small segment of the population" and that the state's farming majority had a hard time getting loans. He also acknowledges that bank notes fell short of the goal of providing a medium of exchange. "Given the growth in population," he notes, "bank note circulation on a per capita basis in Pennsylvania by the mid-1780s was about one-quarter the figure recorded for colonial paper money two decades earlier." But Perkins claims that the bank overcame these shortcomings and that the monetary system in Pennsylvania during the 1780s "functioned satisfactorily." According to Perkins, the level of credit was adequate because the bank lent money to merchants who in turn "extended more favorable terms to small shopkeepers and storekeepers, and they in turn could allow their farm and artisanal customers to purchase more goods by increasing the volume of outstanding book credit." Perkins argues that Pennsylvania farmers thought this arrangement sufficient. "The farm majority was willing, at least initially, to forego the opportunity for direct access to bank credit from urban financial institutions in return for reasonably strong assurances that bank notes would not only serve as a convenient medium of domestic exchange for every occupational group but as a reliable store of value as well." Besides, Perkins asserts, the Pennsylvania legislature made up the difference by printing new paper money and opening a new public loan office. He concludes that privatization was a decided success: after the wartime dislocations, "monetary

3. Sylla, "Shaping the US Financial System," 261; Perkins, *American Public Finance,* 350; Robert E. Wright, "Bank Ownership and Lending Patterns in New York and Pennsylvania, 1781–1831," *Business History Review* 73 (Spring 1999): 40–60.

conditions settled down and stayed on a fairly even keel for the rest of the con-federation period."[4]

This essay challenges the portrait of privatization as a smooth process that fostered economic growth during the 1780s by examining the transition in Pennsylvania. I argue that, rather than rescuing Pennsylvania's economy from wartime monetary problems, privatization made the crisis far worse. The poli-tics of privatization—the effort to eliminate government-issued paper currency, the creation of the Bank of North America, and the attempt of bankers and their political allies to put Pennsylvania on a specie standard—radically contracted the money supply and left the economy without a sufficient medium of exchange. Moreover, the currency and credit the commonwealth provided in 1785 to com-pensate for privatization's shortcomings were also deficient. The currency issued was scarcely sufficient to serve as an effective medium of exchange. At the same time, because the state distributed most of the money as a yearly interest pay-ment to war debt speculators living in Philadelphia, the new currency did not enter readily into general circulation.

The result of privatization during the 1780s is a textbook example of a painful deflationary spiral. Most farmers and artisans living beyond Philadelphia found that they could not obtain the bank credit and bank notes that had been substituted for government currency. New specie taxes drained the countryside of what little hard money remained in circulation. Stripped of purchasing power, ordinary citizens stopped ordering new goods, which caused trade to stagnate. Worse yet, most people had trouble acquiring funds to pay outstanding debts and taxes, leaving creditors dissatisfied, treasuries empty, and courts filled with bereft debtors and taxpayers. Those looking to sell their property to pay debts (either voluntarily or through forced sheriff's auctions) were crushed by falling prices: their land and livestock sold for a small fraction of their usual value, which made it increasingly difficult for them to pay their debts. This was the initial result of privatization: a profound scarcity of money that lasted until war in Europe brought hard money into the economy during the 1790s. Far from spurring eco-nomic development (or easing a "liquidity crisis"), privatization in Pennsylvania during the 1780s led to widespread insolvency and retarded economic growth for at least a decade.

The privatization movement in Pennsylvania began in 1781, as state currencies depreciated rapidly and the continental currency issued by Congress collapsed. In this desperate moment, both Pennsylvania and Congress placed the direction of fiscal and monetary policy in the hands of Robert Morris, a Phil-adelphia merchant whose wartime profiteering as head of the Congress's Secret Committee of Trade had made him perhaps the wealthiest man in America. It

---

4. Robert E. Wright, *Origins of Commercial Banking in America, 1750–1800* (Lanham, Md.: Rowman and Littlefield, 2001), 189; Perkins, *American Public Finance*, 119–23, 358–60.

was Morris's intention to use the powers entrusted to him to privatize the monetary system and to put the nation on a strict specie standard. His objective was to eliminate the government-issued currencies and replace them with specie-backed notes printed by the new, privately owned and operated Bank of North America. Morris thought the Philadelphia bank would fulfill the credit and currency needs of the nation, provide a nondepreciating medium of exchange, and make loans to merchants, artisans, and farmers alike. In his model, boards of directors elected by shareholders would, in effect, manage the money supply by deciding how many bank notes to print and to whom they should be lent. To fill the gap until the bank was up and running, Morris issued a currency backed by his personal wealth—the so-called "Morris Notes." Government also had a role in this privatization scheme, chartering the bank and levying new taxes in specie, bank notes, or Morris Notes.[5]

Although the Morris plan had the support of a majority in Congress and the Pennsylvania legislature, the transition was nevertheless controversial. In Pennsylvania, among the earliest doubters was state president Joseph Reed, a vocal opponent of Morris who foresaw that privatization would lead to a severe contraction of the money supply. In Reed's opinion, eliminating government-issued paper money and enacting specie taxes was a recipe for disaster because the economic needs of Pennsylvania and the nation—especially at a time of war—were simply "beyond the Reach of private Credit." Reed warned that unless Morris supplemented bank notes and Morris Notes with government-issued currency, privatization would bring widespread hardship by denying the public a medium of exchange.[6]

Reed was not alone. The same concern was raised during the spring of 1781 by a less hostile voice, Morris's friend Alexander Hamilton, the future secretary of the treasury and architect of Federalist financial policy. Hamilton warned Morris that the nation's supply of specie was insufficient to support an economy based on hard money. As Hamilton observed, "We have not a competent stock of specie in this country, either to answer the purposes of circulation in Trade, or to serve as a basis for revenue." He predicted devastating results for trade: "a stagnation of business would ensue" and the economic life of the nation would be reduced to trade "carried on by barter." What was more, Hamilton estimated that there was not enough money to allow the war effort to continue: "could the whole of our specie be drawn into the public treasury annually . . . it would be little more than one half of our annual expense." In short, he said,

5. For Morris's rise to power and his economic plan, see Ferguson, *Power of the Purse,* 70–145, and Clarence L. Ver Steeg, *Robert Morris: Revolutionary Financier* (Philadelphia: University of Pennsylvania Press, 1954).

6. Joseph Reed, president of Pennsylvania, to Robert Morris, July 27, 1781, *The Papers of Robert Morris,* ed. James E. Ferguson et al., 9 vols. (Pittsburgh: University of Pittsburgh Press, 1973–99), 1:405–9.

the idea that the nation could sustain an economy based on hard money was "a supposition that carries absurdity on the face of it."[7]

Despite his skepticism, Hamilton believed that Morris could pull off his plan, if—and only if—the bank had an enormous capital base with which to sustain a national currency. To avoid economic disaster, Hamilton suggested that the bank should contain capital of about $8 million. To put this figure in perspective, Hamilton estimated that there was no more than $6 million in the entire American economy, or "one fifth of the circulating medium before the war." This meant that to keep the country from economic peril, the bank would have to possess more hard money than Hamilton believed existed in the entire nation. While he thought that the bank could probably function "if one half the sum could be obtained," the amount of money his plan required was in his own judgment completely impractical.[8]

In practice, the Bank of North America began with far less startup capital than either Hamilton or Morris imagined—a woeful $400,000 in specie— and most of it came not from private investors but from Congress. Using his control of the national treasury, Morris diverted $254,000 of public money obtained by a French loan to buy the bank stock that private investors had failed to purchase. As Morris confessed to Hamilton, "The Capital proposed falls far Short of your Idea and indeed far Short of what it ought to be." In May 1781 he admitted that "four hundred thousand Dollars are not sufficient for [the purposes of government] nor those of private Commerce because no considerable Circulation of Paper can be founded on so narrow a Basis." As a result, there would be far fewer bank notes to replace the paper money Morris was working to eliminate.[9]

Despite the small circulation of bank notes, Morris and the Pennsylvania legislature pressed ahead with enacting new specie taxes, reasoning that the citizenry possessed enough hard money to pay. It quickly became apparent that their assumption was wrong. Part of the problem was that during the war most farmers and artisans had sold their crops and services for paper money that had depreciated. After the continental currency collapsed, Congress and state officials began issuing IOUs instead. These slips of paper represented promises by Congress and Pennsylvania to pay the holder their face value plus the interest that had accrued. By 1782 many Pennsylvanians—and especially those who had supplied the war effort—were holding government IOUs instead of specie. The problem, from the perspective of ordinary citizens, was that at Robert Morris's insistence neither Pennsylvania nor Congress would accept the IOUs for unpaid

7. Alexander Hamilton to Morris, April 30, 1781, ibid., 1:31–60.
8. Ibid.
9. Morris to Alexander Hamilton, May 26, 1781, ibid., 1:79; Robert Morris, "Plan for Establishing a National Bank with Observations," ibid., 1:70. For the Bank of North America's undercapitalization, see Ferguson's discussion, ibid., 1:647.

taxes—even for taxes that went to make the yearly interest payment on these same IOUs.[10]

This policy generated hardship and anger across Pennsylvania even before the new specie taxes were enacted. In 1781 tax commissioners in Philadelphia County explained that most farmers, having sold grain for IOUs, had no "other ways [to] command Cash" and as a result found it "very difficult to pay the many Taxes they are call'd upon for." Officials in Cumberland County reported that people were angry because they "had their property sold to pay their taxes tho' the public is largely indebted to them." York County revenue officials explained that most people were "willing to pay off" their taxes but could not acquire the funds owing to the "want of money." Unless the state accepted the IOUs or grain instead of specie, York officials said they would be forced to take "Severe Steps" and "put the Laws in force" against those who could not pay. In the western county of Westmoreland, farmers could not even afford to pay in crops because they had sold their grain to feed the army. Many families had sold so much that they no longer had "a sufficient quantity of grain for their support." Holding only government IOUs, these people did not have the "power to raise money sufficient to purchase necessaries for their Families."[11]

When the state legislature followed Morris's plan and enacted new specie taxes in 1782, many Pennsylvanians were both bewildered and incensed. Summarizing the situation, one Lancaster County resident explained that unless Pennsylvanians were allowed to use the IOUs to pay taxes, trouble would surely follow. "It is my opinion," he said, "that our State cannot pay the Taxes for the year 82 unless the Inhabitants receive their Pay from the Public or at least be permitted to discount their taxes with such public accounts." "If something of the kind is not done, I really dread the consequences," he concluded. "For it is very grievous to any man to have his property sold for taxes when at the same time the public is indebted to him a much larger sum."[12]

Spurred on by the IOU policy and the general lack of specie, in February and March 1782 thousands of people from nearly half the counties in

10. Morris encouraged state legislatures not to take certificates for specie taxes, arguing, "I must be of the opinion that a general Permission to receive them in Taxes will be very injurious, not only to the public revenue, but to the reputation of our measures." Morris to the president of Congress, November 5, 1781, ibid., 3:144.

11. Commissioners of taxes of Philadelphia County to President Reed, May 2, 1781, *Pennsylvania Archives,* ed. Samuel Hazard, 12 vols. (Harrisburg: 1852–56), ser. 1, 9:116; Robert Hoops, Cumberland County, to Ephraim Blaine, June 15, 1780, Papers of Ephraim Blaine, box 36, Cumberland County Historical Society, Carlisle, Pennsylvania; Commissioners of Taxes of York County to President Joseph Reed, April 1780, frame 1311, reel 15, Records of Pennsylvania's Revolutionary Government, Pennsylvania Historic and Museum Commission, Harrisburg; "Petition of the Inhabitants of the County of Westmoreland," 1779, reel 2, Records of the General Assembly, microfilm, Pennsylvania Historic and Museum Commission, Harrisburg.

12. Philip Marsteller, Lebanon, to George Bryan, Philadelphia, March 23, 1782, folder 6, box 1, George Bryan Papers, Historical Society of Pennsylvania, Philadelphia.

Pennsylvania (mostly those surrounding Philadelphia) drafted petitions against the specie taxes. Petitioners declared that the war had left most people's finances "greatly impaired" and that specie was extremely scarce. Given the circumstances, petitioners stated that the new taxes were "much more than can be raised on the Inhabitants" and would cause "great distress" for most and "the utter ruin of many individuals."[13]

The petition campaign—along with the deteriorating economic circumstances—caused Robert Morris to admit that his program had run into trouble. In March Morris confessed to being "Sensible of th[e] Truth" that "hard Money is scarce" and that it would be "as difficult to pay your [tax] Quota without Money as it was of old to *make Bricks without Straw.*" He lamented the "truly alarming. . . . Scene of private Distress" about him. Morris worried that people were being crushed by an even "greater Weight as the Collection of Taxes creates a general Demand for Money." His fears deepened when he considered that, owing to the cash scarcity and closed markets, "those who have Articles of Produce on Hand cannot possibly vend them" to raise funds. His worries deepened further in May when he was compelled to admit that the Bank of North America was overextended and would have to limit its loans. Morris even admitted that his personal notes were, "as is said, and as I really believe, deficient." He foresaw continued distress. "Few Persons even here are acquainted with the Extent of this Calamity which is now only in it's Commencement," he said in May 1782. "If not speedily checked," the cash scarcity would "produce the most fatal Consequences."[14]

In this moment of candor, Morris even made some concessions to alleviate the worst of the suffering. For one thing, he allowed impoverished farmers in western Pennsylvania to pay the specie taxes in flour rather than gold and silver. But backcountry Pennsylvanians had already sold "that little which they did raise" to feed soldiers stationed on the frontier. They wanted to pay their taxes with the IOUs they had received for provisioning the army, not surrender the remaining grain they needed to feed their families. Moreover, many western farmers were deeply skeptical about Morris's motives in demanding that they pay in crops instead of IOUs. As one observer put it in June, most westerners were convinced that this was merely another of Morris's schemes to enrich himself at the public expense: "Bob Morris knew his own Ends by so doing and meant only to serve himself." He would "receive the Flour at his own price and after supplying the Troops here, He would send the remainder to [New]

13. "Petition and Remonstrance of a Number of the Inhabitants of the County of Philadelphia," 1782, misc., reel 4, Records of the General Assembly, microfilm, Pennsylvania Historic and Museum Commission, Harrisburg. For remaining petitions, see the entries for February 25–March 2, 1782, *Minutes of the General Assembly* (Philadelphia: John Dunlap, 1782).

14. Robert Morris to John Wendell, March 25, 1782, *Papers of Robert Morris*, 4:453; Diary, May 23, 1782, ibid., 5:242; Morris to the governor of Rhode Island, January 4, 1782, ibid., 4:20; Morris to Comte de Grasse, May 16, 1782, ibid., 5:193.

Orleans, sell it to the best advantage & put the profits in his own pockett." Such fears were not far-fetched: Morris and other public officials had in fact used similar practices elsewhere for personal gain. Regardless, the episode did little to improve Morris's negative view of ordinary citizens, or their negative impression of him.[15]

If anything, this June report from the backcountry relieved Morris's conscience and convinced him that the money scarcity was not as serious as people made it out to be. In fact, by July 1782 he had begun saying that the country was not experiencing any kind of financial problem beyond the unwillingness of people to pay taxes. "As to the Complaint made by the People of a Want of Money to pay their taxes it is nothing new to me, nor indeed to any body," Morris wrote. "The Complaint is I believe quite as old as Taxation and will last as long. That Times are hard, that Money is scarce, that Taxes are heavy, and the like are Constant themes of Declamation in all Countries and will be so." To Morris, such declarations of scarcity were themselves evidence that the problem did not exist. "The very Generality of the Complaint shows it to be ill founded," he concluded. He insisted that the larger problem of the scarcity of money was nothing more than a "Delusion" of the country's collective imagination: "The several States and many of their public Officers have so long been in the Habit of boasting superior Exertions that what was at first Assumption has advanced along the Road to Belief to perfect Conviction." The more people complained of shortages, the more certain Morris became that the money supply was adequate and that only force would end the delusion about its scarcity. "If the People be put in the Necessity of procuring Specie they will procure it," he said. "They can, if they will." It was an extraordinary leap of faith: cause the public to need money, and money will appear.[16]

In time Morris became so wedded to this belief that he refused to change his policies even when presented with compelling evidence of their shortcomings from trusted sources. In September 1782 Hamilton informed him that the Morris Notes were printed in denominations too large for ordinary citizens to acquire. "Your Notes though in Credit with the Merchants by way of remittance do not enter far into ordinary circulation," Hamilton wrote, "and this principally on account of their size; which even makes them inconvenient for paying taxes." The smallest denomination Morris printed was a twenty-dollar bill, and as Hamilton pointed out, farmers would have to pool their resources to be able to use a note that large. "If the Notes were in considerable part of

15. Deposition of John Robinson, June 20, 1782, *Pennsylvania Archives*, ser. 1, 9:572. For personal profiteering by Morris and other officials during the war, see Ferguson, *Power of the Purse*, 70–105.

16. Morris to the governor of Connecticut, July 31, 1782, *Papers of Robert Morris*, 6:112; Morris to Alexander Hamilton, September 17, 1782, ibid., 6:385; Morris to the governor of Maryland, July 29, 1782, ibid., 6:84.

five, eight or ten dollars," Hamilton advised, "their circulation would be far more general."[17]

Likewise, General Timothy Pickering complained that the Morris Notes were hindering his attempts to supply the army because the denominations were too large for him to do business with individual farmers. "Only cash or such small notes for taxes will procure grain as without one or the other the farmers will not thresh," Pickering complained. Pickering advised scrapping Morris Notes for army procurement and instead issuing farmers "notes receivable for their hard money taxes." Such an "emission of bills" would satisfy the "universal cry That the people have not cash to pay their taxes" and allow the quartermaster department to "secure so much grain" that it would "insure the army from suffering the ensuing fall and winter." From Pickering's perspective, the result would be a win–win situation.[18]

Morris rejected both Hamilton's and Pickering's proposals. He was not surprised, he said, that his notes failed to find their way into the hands of most citizens; in fact, he was glad of it. "If my Notes circulate only among mercantile People," Morris wrote Hamilton, "I do not regret it, but rather wish that the Circulation may for the present be confined to them and to the wealthier Members of other Professions." He did not trust ordinary people to make good decisions with money or to preserve its worth. "Had a considerable Quantity been thrown into the Hands of that Class of the People whose Ideas on the Subject of Money are more the Offspring of Habit than of Reason," he said, "it must have depreciated." In particular Morris was suspicious of the country's farming majority: "For you must know that whatever fine plausible Speeches may be made on this Subject, the Farmers will not give full Credit to Money merely because it will pay Taxes, for it is an Object they are not very violently devoted to." Farmers were not sufficiently conditioned or educated to understand the value of money, and therefore it was better, in Morris's view, that they go without the new paper money than depreciate what little was in circulation. Needless to say, the public's subsequent inability to shoulder the burden of heavy taxation only reinforced Morris's assessment of the fiscal ignorance and irresponsibility of farmers.[19]

Besides, Morris reasoned, whatever problems his tight money policies generated were a small price to pay for a stable currency. "Confidence is a plant of very slow growth, and our political Situation is not too favorable to it," he wrote Hamilton in October 1782. "I am therefore very unwilling to hazard the Germ of a Credit which will in its great Maturity become very useful." If, in the effort to protect this "Germ of Credit," Morris enacted policies that

17. Alexander Hamilton to Morris, September 21, 1782, ibid., 6:413.

18. Hint on tax notes from the quartermaster general to Morris, July 24, 1782, ibid., 6:19; quartermaster general to Morris, September 19, 1782, ibid., 6:405.

19. Morris to Alexander Hamilton, October 5, 1782, ibid., 6:499–500.

caused widespread social and economic dislocation, this was only a "partial Evil." In his eyes, restraining currency depreciation was far more important than establishing policies designed to limit public suffering.[20]

In fact, as the war drew to a close, it was more important to him than ensuring that the army was properly supplied. When confronted by the conflicting goals of heavy wartime spending and the desire to limit inflation, Morris often opted to curtail inflation. Although he could not muster enough money to procure horses for one corps, he declared that he would prefer that the army "never moved than that they should distress or destroy the little Public Credit which I have established." His orders to the deputy quartermaster general for the southern army were more explicit: "It is better that any Part of the public Service remain unperformed than that you should pay these Notes away at the smallest degree of depreciation or by giving one farthing more for Articles or service than the same could be procured for with hard money in hand." Things were so bad that a British spy wrote encouragingly of Morris's policies: "Money is exceedingly scarce, so much so that they cannot comply with their Contracts, the consequence of which is that most of the Contractors for the Army have declined for the want of Cash, which they were to have been furnished with from the Bank." As this spy realized, Morris's whole supply effort rested on hard money, and there was not enough of this commodity in the American economy to equip the army sufficiently. Luckily for Morris, the major fighting had ended by 1782.[21]

But peace did not end the fiscal crisis, nor did a fully operational bank end the cash scarcity in Pennsylvania. By spring 1783 state legislators were forced to admit that the experiment with privatization was not working out very well. In March state leaders acknowledged that since with the beginning of privatization in 1781, money had "become more scarce and difficult to be procured," and that land values had plummeted well below their actual worth. Legislators acknowledged that many debtors and taxpayers were being foreclosed and that the resulting sheriffs' sales were not raising enough money to cover unpaid debts and taxes. Should money remain scarce, they admitted, "great numbers of honest debtors . . . will be ruined." The Bank of North America had done little to cure the shortage of a circulating medium.[22]

20. Ibid.; "Plan for Establishing a National Bank, with Observations," May 17, 1781, ibid., 1:7.

21. Diary, February 18, 1782, ibid., 4:249; Morris to Edward Carrington, April 25, 1782, ibid., 5:57; Pierre Guillaume De Peyster to Morris, May 1782, ibid., 5:377n5.

22. "An Act for Extending the Provision Made in the Seventh Section of the Act, Entitled 'An Act for the Repeal of so Much of the Laws of this Commonwealth as Make the Continental Bills of Credit and the Bills Emitted by the Resolves or Acts of Assemblies of the Said Commonwealth a Legal Tender, and for Other Purposes Therein Mentioned,'" March 12, 1783, in Statutes at Large of Pennsylvania from 1682 to 1801, 17 vols., ed. James T. Mitchel and Henry Flanders (Harrisburg: Clarence M. Busch, State Printer of Pennsylvania, 1896–1915), 11:36–38.

The bank did perhaps even less to ease the credit crunch. Although Morris and his supporters claimed that the bank lent money to a wide span of the population, the countryside was generally shut out of the loan system. In its first year of operation, 1782–1783, the bank made 1,806 loans to people living in Pennsylvania. Of that figure, 1,785 went to Philadelphians, primarily to wealthy merchants. Those living beyond Philadelphia were granted just twenty-one loans—a mere 1 percent of the credit issued to Pennsylvanians. More stunning was the lack of credit made available to farmers, the vast majority of the population in this agrarian economy. Bank loans to borrowers identified as farmers totaled just two![23]

Contrary to claims made by bank supporters (and by today's economic historians) that farmers benefited indirectly when they borrowed from merchants who had received bank loans, the narrow scope of lending tended to stifle the credit market. The clearest sign of the bank's shortcomings were the sky-high interest rates during the 1780s. If the bank had provided adequate credit, one would expect interest rates to have remained low—perhaps even approaching the traditional low rates Pennsylvanians had enjoyed during the colonial period under the public land-bank system: 5 to 6 percent per year. Instead, under the Bank of North America, private interest rates remained at the astoundingly high level of 5 to 12 percent *per month*. Moreover, they stayed at these shocking levels for the better part of the decade. Needless to say, such high rates suggested a crippled monetary system. Indeed, soaring interest only caused the economy to stagnate further and undermined the well-being of ordinary farmers and artisans.[24]

Thousands of Pennsylvanians began to demand an end to the privatization scheme and a return to the traditional public land-bank system. Beginning in 1783 and with increasing frequency during 1784 and 1785, ordinary folk flooded the General Assembly with petitions citing the "Sad and awful effects" and "fatal Calamities" of the cash scarcity that had "nearly reduced" both "Public Trade and Private transactions of Human Life" to a "total Stagnation." Such petitions arrived from across the state. Petitioners in Philadelphia County, just beyond the city limits, called for the creation of a public loan office "similar to those instituted by former Assemblies" to provide a "greater proportion of circulating cash, the better to enable the citizens of this state to discharge their debts." In Cumberland County, in the center of the state, petitioners explained how, "since the commencement of the war, they have labored under great disadvantages from the scarcity of a circulating currency." These people beseeched the legislature for "an emission of paper currency." From the backcountry county of Westmoreland came petitions declaring "the necessity of having some other

23. George David Rappaport, *Stability and Change in Revolutionary Pennsylvania: Banking, Politics, and Social Structure* (University Park: Pennsylvania State University Press, 1996), 235.

24. For interest rates, see Pennsylvania General Assembly, *Minutes of the General Assembly of Pennsylvania*, September 6, 1785 (Philadelphia: Francis Bailey, 1785); *Papers of Robert Morris*, 6:79n51.

Circulation medium for the purpose of Extending agriculture and commerce within this state" than bank notes and specie.[25]

Many petitioners emphasized that, in their opinion, the recent problems with paper money had been solely the product of wartime conditions. Indeed, even as paper money fell swiftly in value in 1781, many Pennsylvanians spoke glowingly of government currency despite their "losses by the said Depreciation." At the height of the wartime currency crisis in 1781, petitioners from Bucks County in Pennsylvania's southeast corner took "Consolation" from the fact that depreciation was "operating as a Tax" on everyone and that it was producing "a continual Sinking of the public Debt" rather than accumulating an onerous postwar tax burden (exactly what would soon happen under the Morris plan). Likewise, after the war, a series of petitions sent to the Pennsylvania legislature in February and March 1785 attested that many people still believed in the utility of a "paper currency emitted on the faith of the government." These petitioners reminded state leaders that government paper money had been responsible for "most of our improvements" in building farms and businesses "from the earliest settlement of America." Farm petitions insisted that, with the war now over, paper money could return to its usual steady value. "The State of Pennsylvania is now in a situation entirely different from any they have been in since the beginning of the late national contest," agreed Westmoreland County farmers in 1784. "Your petitioners are persuaded, that with proper management, now that we are relieved from the burdens and calamities of war, public faith might be restored." According to these petitioners, with the war now over, state-issued currency backed by land could once again resume its place as a safe and secure medium of exchange. "We now stand upon entire new ground, so firm, that nothing but an unwarrantable timidity can occasion distrust," petitioners declared. It was time to revive "the ancient system" of government-issued paper money for "the great ease of the inhabitants and emolument of the community." There was no better way to "save this State from inevitable ruin."[26]

Petitions made clear that, in calling for government currency, they did not want paper money backed by the kind of taxes that had led to massive

25. "Humble Petition of the Subscriber Inhabitants of the Said State," 1784, frame 186, reel 21, frames 501–5, reel 22, Records of Pennsylvania's Revolutionary Government, microfilm, Pennsylvania Historic and Museum Commission, Harrisburg; petition from Philadelphia County, December 5, 1783, and Petition of Cumberland County, Derry and Wayne Townships, January 31, 1784, both in *Minutes of the General Assembly* (Philadelphia: Holland Sellers, 1784); Petition from Westmoreland County, 1784, Records of the General Assembly, Petitions, reel 3 (Harrisburg: Pennsylvania Historic and Museum Commission Microfilms, 1784).

26. "The Petition of Sundry Inhabitants of the County of Bucks," March 1781, reel 2, Records of the General Assembly, Pennsylvania Historic and Museum Commission, Harrisburg. For the basic text of the petition signed by farmers from across Pennsylvania, see "The Petition of the Subscribers," *Pennsylvania Evening Herald*, February 26, 1785. For submissions of this petition to the state legislature, see February and March 1785 entries in *Minutes of the General Assembly of Pennsylvania* (Philadelphia: Francis Bailey, 1785). Petition from Westmoreland County, 1784, petitions, reel 3, Records of the General Assembly (Harrisburg: PHMC Microfilms).

wartime inflation, but rather a return to the land-bank system that had performed so well during the colonial period. "We do not want any kind of paper imposed on the people," explained one Pennsylvania farmer, "but such as will stand on its own foundation." Petitioners called for a currency "established on a permanent foundation" like mortgaged land. They declared that money backed by land would hold its value and would not "injure the interest of any private individual or that of any particular Corporation, nor . . . obstruct the Extension of trade." Rather, land-backed currency would promote trade by boosting the purchasing power of ordinary citizens just as it had done in the past. All petitioners were trying to do was return to "the ancient, safe and successful plan" for promoting economic growth.[27]

Many of these petitions—signed by thousands of Pennsylvanians across the state—called for the General Assembly to revoke the bank's charter, which was clearly not serving the public good. Unlike the land-bank system, which worked for "the promotion of agriculture, or for an enlargement of the export trade, and the general benefit of commerce," the new private bank worked solely for the benefit of its directors and stockholders. Petitioners noted that the bank's directors lent money to such a small circle of men that even those "who could furnish the best security are distressed for want of being able to find men willing to lend." For ordinary farmers and artisans, the chances of obtaining credit from the private bank were slim at best. And even if they could get credit, the short lending periods did not meet the needs of farmers who required long-term loans—as the land-bank system had done. As long as the private system remained in place of a public land bank, petitioners declared, "it will ever be impossible for the husbandman or mechanic to borrow on the former terms of legal interest and distant payments of the principal."[28]

In 1785 the state did temporarily reassert monetary control, but the results barely resembled the kind of system rural petitioners had called for. The state legislature printed $400,000 in new paper money, but only a third of the sum, $130,000, went into a new land bank. The remaining two-thirds, $270,000, was distributed to those who held war-debt certificates (mostly speculators) and was backed by future taxes—the kind of system that had operated during the Revolutionary War, which rural petitions had said they did not want to see

---

27. "A Letter from a respectable farmer in York County," *Pennsylvania Evening Herald,* March 5, 1785; Petition of Cumberland County, Derry and Wayne Townships, January 31, 1784, *Minutes of the General Assembly;* "The Petition of the Subscribers," *Pennsylvania Evening Herald,* February 26, 1785, and February–March 1785 petitions, in *Minutes of the General Assembly;* Petition from Westmoreland County, 1784, petitions, reel 3, Records of the General Assembly (Harrisburg: PHMC Microfilms); "Humble Petition of the Subscriber Inhabitants of the Said State," 1784, frame 186, reel 21, frames 501–5, reel 22, Records of Pennsylvania's Revolutionary Government, microfilm, Pennsylvania Historic and Museum Commission, Harrisburg.

28. "The Petition of the Subscribers," *Pennsylvania Evening Herald,* February 26, 1785, and petitions from February–March 1785 session of the General Assembly, *Minutes of the General Assembly.*

repeated. As a result, many farmers were enraged by the new law. Lancaster County citizens complained that the land bank was "too small . . . to give adequate relief to the several counties." A "respectable farmer" in York County declared that the land bank was "not about quarter enough" of what the state needed. Indeed, capitalized at only $130,000, the new public bank was three times smaller than the 1773 land bank established in Pennsylvania under British rule— a loan office that colonists had condemned for being underfunded. To make matters worse, this much smaller bank was supposed to serve a far larger population: about 150,000 more people lived in Pennsylvania than had in 1773. Moreover, the state spread the new land loans across Pennsylvania's fifteen counties, so that each county received only a small infusion of currency and credit. For example, the state allotted Cumberland County $8,000 to lend to its citizens. To put this figure in perspective, at the time the county owed the state treasury $59,000 in paper money back taxes and $140,000 in specie—not to mention outstanding private debts that one observer estimated to be approximately $65,000 worth of goods. Compared to these figures, the loans offered by the new land bank were a drop in the bucket.[29]

As inadequate as the new land bank was, many farmers were even more upset by the $270,000 issued to the holders of war-debt certificates. Aside from anger over what they saw as a state-sponsored windfall for speculators who had purchased war-debt certificates for pennies on the dollar, many people worried that by suddenly releasing several hundred thousand dollars in new paper money into Philadelphia (where most of those holding war-debt certificates lived), the value of the currency would depreciate rapidly. They feared that this dramatic flood of currency would merely tarnish the image of all paper money and undermine the land-backed currency from the new state loan office. "The country wants money bad enough," explained the York County farmer, "but this very funding bill will be a means of destroying the paper money." In his opinion, the new land bank had merely been a "trick to obtain consent to the taxes" that would go to pay speculators in the war debt. If the assembly had "designed in good earnest to help us," its representative would have put into the land bank "all the paper you propose making" instead of just a third. The plea to the assembly was unequivocal: "do not mix this paper money in your schemes of obtaining 60 per annum for your own speculations."[30]

29. Petition from Lancaster County, February 23, 1785, *Minutes of the General Assembly;* "A Letter from a respectable farmer in York County," March 5, 1785, *Pennsylvania Evening Herald.* For the Pennsylvania loan office of 1773, see Yoder, "Paper Currency in Colonial Pennsylvania," 317–18. For Cumberland County tax deficits, see "State of the Accounts of the Treasury . . . from 1782 . . . to 1785," in *Pennsylvania Archives,* 3d ser., 5:373. For estimate of private debt in Cumberland County, see John Armstrong to William Irvine, August 16, 1787, Irvine Family Papers, Historical Society of Pennsylvania, Philadelphia.

30. "A Letter from a respectable farmer in York County," March 5, 1785, *Pennsylvania Evening Herald.*

In practice, the fate of the $270,000 paid to war-debt speculators con-firmed what many farmers had feared. Soon after it was printed, the entire $270,000 was deposited in the Bank of North America. "It appears," Robert Morris reported in April 1786, "that the whole of the emission . . . has already passed through the bank." And, according to Morris, the new paper money was deposited in the accounts of just sixty-seven people. Such a concentration offered only scant relief to the cash-poor countryside. Moreover, just as rural critics had warned, the sudden flood of paper money into the city—paper sup-ported only by taxation—caused the new currency to depreciate.[31]

This scenario raises questions, to put it mildly, about the claims of some economic historians that the currency issued by the state government during the 1780s was sufficient to compensate for the limited circulation of bank notes. The records of the Bank of North America and complaints by farmers suggest that the amount of paper money was much too small to meet the needs of Penn-sylvania citizens and that the modes of currency distribution failed to get the paper into general circulation. Like bank notes, this new government currency tended to concentrate among affluent Philadelphians. Such a concentration may have provided an adequate medium of exchange for wealthy folk in the city, but it did not offer much relief for the countryside. As with the privatization movement, this brief shift back to public monetary control tended to perpetu-ate the crisis rather than relieve it because it was geared to war-debt speculators living in Philadelphia rather than the majority of the population who farmed the countryside.

For most Pennsylvanians, the end result of both privatization and the temporary return of public control under the direction of war-debt speculators was a decade-long depression that resulted in thousands of citizens losing their property for debts and taxes they could not pay. County court dockets from the period reveal the sad tale of property executions due to mass insolvency. In the eastern county of Berks, a decade of debt litigation between 1782 and 1792 produced 3,400 executions for a taxable population that averaged about 5,000 families—or enough to foreclose 68 percent of the taxable population. In neigh-boring Lancaster County, the court issued 3,900 writs of foreclosure between 1784 and 1789, enough to cover 66 percent of the county's 5,900 taxpayers. In Northumberland County on the northern frontier, between 1785 and 1790 the sheriff delivered more writs of foreclosure (2,180) than there were taxpayers (2,140). West of the Appalachian Mountains in Westmoreland County, between 1782 and 1792 judges issued a remarkable 6,100 separate orders to foreclose goods

31. For Morris's comments on deposits in the Bank of North America, see Matthew Carey, ed., *Debates and Proceedings of the General Assembly of Pennsylvania: On the Memorials Praying a Repeal or Suspension of the Law Annulling the Charter of the Bank* (Philadelphia, 1786). See also Janet Wilson, "The Bank of North America and Pennsylvania Politics, 1781–1787," *Pennsylvania Magazine of History and Biography* 66 (January 1942): 10.

and lands for a population of about 2,800 taxpayers. Tracing these writs to individual households, it becomes apparent that the county sheriff foreclosed at least 1,200 different families—or 43 percent of Westmoreland's taxable population. Such were the fruits of privatization in Pennsylvania during the 1780s.[32]

In the final analysis, the vast disparity between the portrait of privatization presented here and the picture of success painted by many economic historians is probably best explained by the blind spot financial historians have when it comes to farmers and the agrarian economy. The story of privatization's success is generally a tale of urban America and financial services geared toward merchants and nascent manufacturers. Scholars of banking have far less to say about what privatization meant for ordinary farmers. Indeed, farmers figure hardly at all in these studies. Nor does hard evidence that private banks offered loans to farmers. Robert Wright asserts throughout his book on the origins of commercial banking that private banks provided farmers with loans. But the only real evidence he supplies to support this claim is an analysis of customer lists from a bank in Utica, New York, for the period 1812–14, in which, as Wright admits, "few of the Bank's customers are described in sources as 'farmers.'"[33]

Reasoning like this has caused many economic historians to overstate the benefits of privatization and to understate what was lost with the displacement of the public land-bank system. Although it is difficult to tell from histories of banking, the United States was an agrarian nation in which most of the population farmed the land. The public land-bank system was geared to this reality, lending money to farmers, artisans, and merchants in rough correspondence to their proportion of the population. Farmers, being the majority, received the bulk of the loans.[34] And the nature of the loans fit the needs of farmers, providing long-term and low-interest credit in sync with the rhythms of the rural economy. By contrast, the new private banks lent largely to merchants and manufacturers, far in excess of their proportion of the population. Moreover, the new banks generally refused to make long-term loans or loans based on mortgaged land—the kinds of loans that were most useful for farmers, who usually had little of value beyond land or livestock to offer as collateral. In most banking

32. Berks County Execution Dockets (Berks County Government Services Building, Reading, Pennsylvania); Lancaster County Execution Dockets, Book 2 (Lancaster County Courthouse, Lancaster, Pennsylvania); Northumberland County Execution Dockets (Northumberland County Courthouse, Sunbury, Pennsylvania); Westmoreland County Execution Dockets, 1782–92 (Westmoreland County Courthouse, Greensburg, Pennsylvania). For more on the hardship generated by the cash scarcity, see Terry Bouton, "A Road Closed: Rural Insurgency in Post-Independence Pennsylvania," *Journal of American History* 87 (December 2000): 855–87, and "'No wonder the times were troublesome': The Origins of Fries' Rebellion, 1783–1799," *Pennsylvania History* 67 (Winter 2000): 21–42.

33. Wright, *Origins of Commercial Banking*, 190.

34. Evidence from the 1785 Pennsylvania loan office indicates that farmers received 66 percent of the loans, artisans 17 percent, gentlemen 13 percent, and merchants 3 percent. John Paul Kaminski, "Paper Politics: The Northern State Loan-Offices During the Confederation, 1783–1790," (Ph.D. diss., University of Wisconsin, 1972), 77–78.

histories, we never see the costs for farmers of this shift from a public to a private system of banking that all but shut its lending window to the farming majority. By failing to factor these dynamics into their analyses of privatization, students of banking have presented a skewed portrait of privatization's merits and the alleged ease of the transition from public land banks to private banking.

Finally, these same considerations raise questions about claims that privatization democratized the economy. If democratization means that banks in the 1820s lent to a wider circle of people than they did in the 1780s and 1790s (and it is not always clear that they did), then the term has some meaning, although it hardly supports the assertion that the banks democratized economic life to the extent claimed by both banking scholars and historians like Joyce Appleby and Gordon Wood.[35] But if we consider the changes from the standpoint of ordinary farmers and the transition from the land-bank system, claims of democratization are more difficult to sustain. Shifting from a financial system geared to the needs of the farming majority to one that failed to provide farmers with credit hardly seems a democratizing process. It is worth remembering that at the time many farmers in Pennsylvania and elsewhere did not think so. And if many farmers came to accept private banking as a way of life (and after the Constitution prevented states from printing paper money, what choice did they really have?), the support did not last long. This private system fostered speculative manias and wild boom-and-bust cycles that often had tragic consequences for farmers. It is no coincidence that by the 1820s and '30s, farmers emerged as perhaps the staunchest foes of private banks and the paper money they issued. Such opposition, like the opposition in Pennsylvania during the 1780s, suggests that privatization was a far more complex process, with far higher social and economic costs, than banking scholars have allowed.

35. For the continued limited circles of lending, see Naomi Lamoreaux, *Insider Lending: Banks, Personal Connections, and Economic Development in Industrial New England* (New York: Cambridge University Press, 1994). Robert Wright notes that over time the bank in Philadelphia made loans to fewer artisans. Wright, *Origins of Commercial Banking*, 150–52. Gordon S. Wood, *The Radicalism of the American Revolution* (New York: Knopf, 1992); Joyce Appleby, *Inheriting the Revolution: The First Generation of Americans* (Cambridge: Harvard University Press, 2000).

Chapter Eight

Creative Destruction: The Forgotten Legacy of the Hessian Fly

BROOKE HUNTER

Although old King George never knew it, he imposed upon the American colonists and their descendants a tax many times the tax on tea which
he tried to collect. This tax is paid every year. This tax was imposed
through the instrumentality of the most hated of King George's troops, his
hired Hessians. It is levied by a little insect.

—WESLEY PILLSBURY FLINT AND C. L. METCALF, *Insects: Man's Chief Competitors*
(BALTIMORE: WILLIAMS AND WILKINS, 1932), 106–8.

In September 1788 the *Pennsylvania Gazette* declared that "two
great evils or calamities" threatened to destroy the early
American Republic: the scarcity of cash and the Hessian fly.
While historians of early America have devoted much attention to postrevolutionary commercial crises,[1] they have almost

Many people contributed to the development of this essay, starting with the
PEAES Inaugural Conference presenters and audience who took such an interest in the Hessian fly. I would like to thank the staff of the Library Company
of Philadelphia, the staff of the Historical Society of Pennsylvania, the McNeil
Center for Early American Studies, and PEAES for their support. I am especially grateful to Paul G. E. Clemens, Laura Hyatt, Michelle Craig, and Cathy
Matson for their editorial comments.

1. Quoted in *Pennsylvania Gazette,* September 24, 1788, Library
Company of Philadelphia (hereafter LCP). During the 1960s a lively debate
surrounded the state of the postrevolutionary economy. Curtis P. Nettels and
Merrill Jensen emerged as the leading voices of the two sides. Nettels argued
for a depressed economy, while Jensen promoted the idea of rapid recovery and
development. See Nettels, *The Emergence of a National Economy, 1775–1815* (New
York: Harper and Row, 1962); Merrill Jensen, *The New Nation: A History of the
United States During the Confederation* (New York: Vintage Books, 1950). Gordon
Carl Bjork attempted to weave the disparate interpretations together in *Stagnation and Growth in the American Economy, 1784–1792* (New York: Garland, 1985).
Bjork argued that the economy recovered rapidly during the 1780s but that
long-term economic growth was not achieved. See also Bjork, "The Weaning
of the American Economy: Independence, Market Changes, and Economic
Development," *Journal of Economic History* 24 (December 1964): 541–60. By the
1970s the negative interpretation of the postrevolutionary economy had become
dominant and has continued to define the period. See James F. Shepherd and
Gary M. Walton, "Economic Change After the American Revolution: Pre- and
Post-war Comparisons of Maritime Shipping and Trade," *Explorations in Economic*

completely ignored the insect problem.[2] Yet the Hessian fly was no common housefly. It was a major player on the stage in the age of Revolution. It is time to give this winged avenger its due.

The Hessian fly had been around since the 1770s, but the first reports of widespread infestation appeared in the nation's leading newspapers during the spring of 1787. Over the course of the next few years the flies brought northern frontier farmers to the brink of starvation, while swarms in Pennsylvania, the heart of the mid-Atlantic wheat belt, incited panic as the insect threatened to "totally deprive" farmers, millers, and exporters of their "most precious grain."[3] A regional agricultural disaster turned into a national commercial crisis when England banned American wheat in the fall of 1788. Earlier in the spring, Phineas Bond, the English consul in Philadelphia, warned London of a severe insect infestation. "The ravages are beyond all conception ruinous," he declared, and "many farms have had the crops so completely cut off as to be left without bread, corn, or even seed." In June English officials responded with an Order in Council prohibiting the importation of wheat from America. Bond praised the English government for "the precautions [undertaken] to prevent the extension of so deadly a mischief."[4]

From Paris, Thomas Jefferson denounced the English government for "libel" and accused English authorities of maliciously committing "a mere assassination" of American character and the reputation of its grain by spreading "a groundless alarm in those countries of Europe where our wheat is constantly &

History 13 (December 1976): 399–401; John J. McCusker and Russell R. Menard, *The Economy of British America, 1607–1789* (Chapel Hill: University of North Carolina Press, 1985), 367–77, which reviews literature of the 1970s; and Lance Davis and Stanley L. Engerman, "The Economy of British North America: Miles Traveled, Miles Still to Go," *William and Mary Quarterly,* 3d ser., 56 (January 1999): 21, which reviews recent literature.

2. Exceptions include Philip J. Pauly, "Fighting the Hessian Fly: American and British Responses to Insect Invasion, 1776–1789," *Environmental History* 7 (July 2002): 377–400; Alan Taylor, "'The Hungry Year': 1789 on the Northern Border of Revolutionary America," in *Dreadful Visitations: Confronting Natural Catastrophe in the Age of Enlightenment,* ed. Alessa Johns (New York: Routledge, 1999), 145–81; William Cronon, *Changes in the Land: Indians, Colonists, and the Ecology of New England* (New York: Hill and Wang, 1983), 153–56. For a historical account of the Hessian fly, see Asa Fitch, *The Hessian Fly, Its History, Character, Transformation, and Habits* (Albany: Joel Munsell, 1846), available at LCP.

3. Quoted in "To the FARMERS of Pennsylvania, Signed a Countryman," *Pennsylvania Gazette,* July 23, 1788, LCP. On frontier famine, see Taylor, "'The Hungry Year,'" 146–47, 153–55, 164. More than twenty accounts of the Hessian fly appeared in the *Pennsylvania Gazette* alone from 1787 to 1790. The insect also headlined the "Rural Concerns" section of Mathew Carey's inaugural edition of the *American Museum* (January 1787): 529–31, LCP.

4. Quoted in Phineas Bond to Lord Carmarthen, October 1, 1788, in *American Historical Association Annual Report* 1 (1896): 576, 580–81. On Bond, see Joanne Loewe Neel, *Phineas Bond: A Study in Anglo-American Relations, 1786–1812* (Philadelphia: University of Pennsylvania Press, 1968), 63. Britain placed a ban on the importation of American wheat on June 25, 1788. An announcement of the ban's removal ran in the *Pennsylvania Gazette,* March 3, 1790. See Pauly, "Fighting the Hessian Fly," for an excellent investigation of the foreign-relations angle of the story.

kindly received."[5] This was Jefferson doing damage control. He knew that the fly was more than a political intrigue because his friend James Madison kept him updated on the insect and its progress in the middle states. From his vantage point across the Atlantic, however, Jefferson recognized better than most the danger England's policy posed to the new Republic's commercial stability and the American government's need to take a stand against it. The years between the Revolution and the ratification of the Constitution marked a critical period in American history, when the nation's future hung in the balance. Volatile political, social, and economic conditions threatened to destroy the republican experiment. At the height of the storm the grain trade kept America's commerce afloat as wheat and flour overtook tobacco as the nation's most valuable exports. In this climate, combating the destructive insect became a matter of economic necessity and national preservation.[6]

Within the context of this volume, restoring the Hessian fly to its rightful place in history gives us the chance to reflect on the strengths of an environmental approach to studies of early American economic life. Tracking the Hessian fly uncovers important insights about postrevolutionary farmers and the natural world, the relationship between politics and agricultural improvement, and the environmental impact of market agriculture. Production decisions and yields varied from year to year depending on market conditions, labor conditions, and, most important, environmental conditions. The Hessian fly represents one of the many natural factors that circumscribed the lives of farmers but that have seldom been discussed by historians. Weather conditions, a host of plant diseases, and swarms of insects injured crops annually, affecting farm families and markets alike. Yet the regular occurrence of natural disasters—from droughts to weevils—has been overshadowed in the historical record by political events and structural social changes, particularly during the early national period. The Hessian fly provides a new perspective from which to view the founding era. The insect invasion united farmers, millers, and merchants in a common cause at a time when politics, immigration, and warfare seemed to drive people apart.

Thinking about the Hessian fly in terms of "creative destruction" follows naturally from its species name, *Mayetiola destructor*.[7] The oxymoron signifies the tensions between man, markets, and environment, but it also suggests that the

5. Thomas Jefferson to Benjamin Vaughn, May 17, 1789, in *The Papers of Thomas Jefferson*, 34 vols., ed. Julian K. Boyd, Charles T. Cullen, and John Catanzariti (Princeton: Princeton University Press, 1950–2000) (hereafter *Papers of Thomas Jefferson*), 15:133–34. See also the editorial note on "The Northern Journey," ibid., 20:445–46.

6. For a classic statement on the critical period, see Gordon S. Wood, "The Significance of the Early Republic," *Journal of the Early Republic* 8 (Spring 1988): 1–20. For a fuller discussion of the rapid postwar recovery of the grain trade, see Brooke Hunter, "Rage for Grain: Flour Milling in the Mid-Atlantic, 1750–1815" (Ph.D. diss., University of Delaware, 2001), chapter 3.

7. The phrase was first coined in Joseph Schumpeter, *Capitalism, Socialism, and Democracy* (New York: Harper and Row, 1950).

insect had both positive and negative effects. Most important, "creative destruction" captures not only the significant role nonhuman actors played in shaping historical events but also the large part humans played in generating, and often worsening, those situations.[8] The Hessian fly helped to destroy an older grain culture in the mid-Atlantic region and to create a new, more complex one. First of all, the pest spurred agricultural improvement, especially experiments in diversification and cultivation of other grains. The fly also accelerated a shift in grain production toward the South that was already under way before the American Revolution in Maryland and Virginia.

Enemy Insect

The first European immigrants brought wheat to the mid-Atlantic region in the seventeenth century. They developed a brisk grain trade with both the southern and New England colonies as well as the West Indies by the early eighteenth century. While New Englanders imported grain because their rocky soil and shorter growing season could not support their growing urban population, southern planters—in Carolina and the Caribbean—relied on mid-Atlantic farmers for food so that they could concentrate on staple production. The mid-Atlantic grain trade expanded significantly during the 1740s in response to Atlantic-world conditions. Population growth, crop failures, war, and natural disasters increased demand for food in North America, the West Indies, and Europe. These conditions intensified during the final decades of the eighteenth century as populations boomed, cold and unsettled weather consistently ruined European grain harvests, revolutions erupted in America, France, and Saint Domingue, and, finally, the Napoleonic Wars engaged much of the world at the turn of the century.[9] Changing international markets form an important part of this story, but such forces should not be given too much weight. The Hessian fly reminds us that individual actions and local events were just as important and influential. It mattered not only that distant populations were starving, but also that farmers produced surplus grain that millers then manufactured into flour and merchants marketed overseas. The Hessian fly clearly complicated this process during the 1780s and 1790s.[10]

8. Here I am drawing on the ideas about the environment expressed in Taylor, "'The Hungry Year,'" 145–81; Cronon, *Changes in the Land,* 127–70; and Carville Earle, *Geographical Inquiry and American Historical Problems* (Stanford: Stanford University Press, 1992), 258–99.

9. Weather is becoming a popular historical subject. See Brian Fagan, *The Little Ice Age: How Climate Made History, 1300–1850* (New York: Basic Books, 2000), chapters 6–11.

10. I am complicating the staples approach taken by many historians writing commodity history. For discussions of the uses and abuses of an export-led framework, see McCusker and Menard, *Economy of British America,* 10–13, 18–32, 71–88, 189–208; and Marc Egnal, *New World Economies: The Growth of the Thirteen Colonies and Early Canada* (New York: Oxford University Press, 1998).

From the start, wheat farmers confronted a number of environmental hazards, often concurrently. Droughts withered plants, hailstorms battered crops, and floods washed away entire fields. Plant diseases such as scab, mildew, rust, and smut flourished in the mid-Atlantic region, where humidity produced the ideal conditions for fungal growth. For example, wet weather in 1747 mildewed wheat so badly that farmers reported that the crop was not worth the effort of reaping. Of these diseases smut was the most serious. Smut spores covered the ripening wheat with a black dust that either stunted its growth or killed the wheat stalks completely. Smutted wheat had little market value for milling or seed and was commonly referred to as "stinking smut" because of its powerful fishy odor. Before their encounter with the Hessian fly, farmers battled other pests, including weevils, chinch bugs, locusts, lice, moths, and worms. Weevils infested harvested grain and were a big problem for wheat cultivators, especially in Delaware, Maryland, and Virginia. The Hessian fly joined the ranks of this menacing insect army during the final quarter of the eighteenth century. The new invader quickly became the number-one pest of wheat.[11]

Certain characteristics make the Hessian fly a classic villain. First, it has long, dark whiskers, and second, it is almost invisible to the naked eye. It develops in four stages: egg, larva, pupa, and fly. After mating in the late summer, female flies deposit eggs in newly sown wheat fields. Adult flies do not feed, and die within a few days. A single fly can lay up to two hundred eggs, which hatch in only three to ten days. Larva feed on the young plant's juices, reaching the pupa stage at the beginning of winter and emerging the following spring as flies. The females of this second generation repeat the cycle by laying eggs on the leaves of maturing plants in the same or a nearby wheat field. Larvae enter the pupa stage before harvest and pass the summer in the wheat stubble. In late August or early September the cycle begins again with a new generation of flies.[12] The Hessian fly typically completes two generations per year in the

11. For a thorough discussion of insects and plant diseases injurious to wheat, see Peter Tracy Dondlinger, *The Book of Wheat: An Economic History and Practical Manual of the Wheat Industry* (reprint, Wilmington: Scholarly Resources, 1973), 155–69. Also see George Terry Sharrer, "Flour Milling and the Growth of Baltimore, 1783–1830" (Ph.D. diss., University of Maryland, 1975), 191–92. On crop damage in 1747, see Anne Bezanson, Robert D. Gray, and Miriam Hussey, *Prices in Colonial Pennsylvania* (Philadelphia: University of Pennsylvania Press, 1935), 35.

12. For discussions of the insect's lifecycle, see the following issues of the *Pennsylvania Gazette*: June 27, 1787; September 26, 1787; August 20, 1788; June 18, 1800, LCP. See also George Pennock to Humphry Marshall, September 12, 1788, Papers of Humphry Marshall, Series 10, Historical Manuscripts, U.S. Department of Agriculture History Papers, Washington D.C. See also various accounts in *Papers of Thomas Jefferson*, 20:434–61; 22:139–40, 244–52; 24:77–80–81, 446–47, 471. This information generally fits with modern science; see F. M. Webster, "The Hessian Fly," *United States Department of Agriculture Farmers' Bulletin* 640 (1915): 1–20; R. H. Ratcliffe and J. H. Hatchett, "Biology and Genetics of the Hessian Fly and Resistance in Wheat," in *New Developments in Entomology*, ed. Khorsand Bondari (Trivandrum, India: Research Signpost, 1997), 47–56; D. G. Buntin and J. W. Chapin, "Biology of the Hessian Fly in the Southeastern United States: Geographic Variation and Temperature-Dependent Phrenology," *Journal of Economic Entomology* 83 (July 1990): 1015–24.

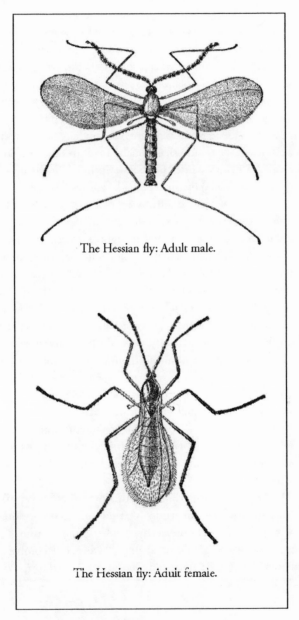

The Hessian fly: Adult male.

The Hessian fly: Adult female.

Figure 1   The Hessian Fly
Source: F. M. Webster, "The Hessian Fly," *United States Department of Agriculture Farmers' Bulletin* 640 (1915), 1-2.

mid-Atlantic region, although additional generations may appear if weather conditions permit. Climate greatly affects the rate of the insect's development, with warm temperatures and high humidity causing the fastest growth. Given the right environment—cool and dry—the Hessian fly can survive in the pupa stage for more than a year, an ability that makes the insect an even greater threat.[13]

Damage depended on the degree of infestation by the larvae. A single larva could suck the life out of a plant. The severest infestations wiped out entire crops, while serious ones made it impossible for farmers to reap as much as they sowed. A fall swarm was more catastrophic to a wheat crop than a spring swarm as early outbreaks often killed plants outright, while wheat attacked later was only stunted. Wheat attacked by a fall swarm usually froze to death because the feeding larvae decreased a plant's winter hardiness. Spring-infested wheat produced grain, but the plants, weakened by the feeding larvae, usually fell over before harvest. Farmers at the time described a badly infested wheat field in the spring as looking like "a herd of cattle had passed through it."[14]

A combination of factors in the late eighteenth century sped the insect's reproduction. First, the cultural practices of eighteenth-century American farmers created an ideal habitat for the Hessian fly. The wheat stubble farmers left in fields after harvest provided a cozy home for the pest, while the early sowing of a highly susceptible variety of wheat opened an all-you-can-eat buffet for flies. Moreover, the limited practice of crop rotation permitted the Hessian fly, a weak flyer, to find wheat plants easily. Second, the commercial economy intensified such conditions. By committing themselves to wheat as a staple crop, farmers increased the acreage of the Hessian fly's favorite food supply. As a last resort, the insect would infest other grains such as rye and barley, but in the mid-Atlantic region, market conditions ensured that wheat was almost always available, and the Hessian fly rarely had to compromise its tastes. High and steady demand for wheat and flour in regional, national, and international markets secured the devotion of farmers to growing the grain, which in turn assured the fly's future in America.[15]

The Hessian fly is not native to North America but was probably introduced around the time of the American Revolution. Common lore connected the fly's arrival with the Hessian mercenary soldiers from whom the insect received its name during the revolutionary era. "We could combat their other Hessian Auxiliaries," Richard Peters told George Washington in 1788, "but this

13. USDA, *Climate and Man* (Washington, D.C.: U.S. Government Printing Office, 1941), 49, 507; Charles V. Riley, "The Hessian Fly: An Imported Insect," *Canadian Entomologist* 20 (January 1888): 121–27.

14. Quoted in Sharrer, "Flour Milling and the Growth of Baltimore," 192–93. On damage, see Dondlinger, *Book of Wheat*, 170–74; Fitch, *Hessian Fly*, 43–44.

15. On cultural conditions, see Dondlinger, *Book of Wheat*, 170. On market conditions, see Taylor, "'The Hungry Year,'" 145–81, and Cronon, *Changes in the Land*, 153–56.

is unconquerable."[16] Contemporary theories about the insect ranged from the patriotic—the Hessian soldiers had "brought over thousands of little insects, on purpose to destroy" the United States—to the scientific—the Hessian fly arrived in America "by means of some straw made use of in package, or otherwise, landed on Long Island with the force of Sir William Howe at an early period of the late war."[17] Today the scientific consensus is that the Hessian fly evolved in western Asia along with wheat, migrated as far west as southern Europe by the eighteenth century, and crossed the Atlantic during the 1770s with the British.[18] Philip Pauly has recently offered a compelling new twist on the old theory, suggesting that rather than arriving in New York in 1776 in straw bedding used for horses, the insect came in the forage shipped from Europe to New York beginning in 1777. Because of the insect's life cycle, according to Pauly, it took "the peculiarly uneconomic transport of large quantities of wheatstraw" to feed military horses to introduce the Hessian fly to North America.[19] Yet even if the insect's migration was isolated from commercial affairs, its survival depended on the Atlantic-world economy. A new habitat sown with wheat was familiar and inviting rather than foreign and inhospitable to the arriving insect. It naturally took to the fields, spreading from New York to wherever farmers cultivated wheat.

In the spring of 1791 Thomas Jefferson and James Madison set out on a journey to chart the insect's destructive path. They traveled by carriage through New York and Connecticut, "where this animal has raged much." Jefferson's notes provide the most detailed account ever written of the Hessian fly's early migration patterns. He recorded that the Hessian fly first appeared on Long Island around 1776 and caused localized damage until 1779. The fly then simultaneously spread westward from Manhattan to Perth Amboy on the New Jersey side of the Hudson River, northward along the river to Poughkeepsie, and eastward along Long Island and across Long Island sound to Middletown, Connecticut, by 1786. The fly reached Saratoga, New York, in 1789, two hundred miles north of its point of origin, and soon buzzed into Canada.[20]

16. W. W. Abbot, ed., *The Papers of George Washington, Confederation Series* (1784–88), 6 vols. (Charlottesville: University Press of Virginia, 1997), 6:358.

17. The first quotation comes from a sermon, *The Prophet Nathan, or Plain Friend; Containing Some Observations Respecting the Late Insects Commonly called the Hessian Fly, Considering Them as a Judgment Upon the Land* . . . (Hudson, N.Y: Ashbel Stoddard, 1788), 10–18. The second is an entry from the *Encyclopedia Britannica,* probably taken from excerpts of letters from Phineas Bond; see Neel, *Phineas Bond,* 63. Bond clearly received most of his information about the fly from George Morgan, Jeremiah Wadsworth, Samuel L. Mitchill, and other American gentlemen farmers. On Bond and his information network, see also *Papers of Thomas Jefferson,* 20:445–46.

18. Riley, "Hessian Fly," 121–27; Pauly, "Fighting the Hessian Fly," 490–91.

19. Pauly, "Fighting the Hessian Fly," 500–501.

20. "Jefferson's Notes on the Hessian Fly," *Papers of Thomas Jefferson,* 20:445–47, 456–62. Despite the extensive modern research on the insect, very little work has gone into tracking the migration of the Hessian fly before or after its initial arrival in the United States.

It is impossible to re-create the fly's southern route as fully as Jefferson did for its northern migration. Still, scattered pieces of evidence make it possible to trace the fly's movement with fair accuracy. The fly appeared as far west as Princeton in 1786 and crossed over the Delaware River into Pennsylvania in 1787 or 1788. Between 1788 and 1790, the fly destroyed an immense quantity of wheat in New Jersey and Pennsylvania. The fly arrived in Delaware in 1791 and the following year vast multitudes of flies ate up farmers' wheat in Delaware, on Maryland's eastern shore, and as far south as Baltimore. In early November 1792 the overseer of Benjamin Chew's Delaware plantation wrote that the "wheat in ground is half destroyed by insect cauld the heashon fly." The following spring the fly appeared in several probate records. For instance, when New Castle County appraisers inventoried David Craven's estate near Cantwell's Bridge, they noted that his "wheat [had been] injured materially by [the] Hessian fly and not worth more than the expense of attending it."[21] The menace had infiltrated the mid-Atlantic region's supreme granary and reduced the crop by at least one-third in the first year of its infestation.[22]

The fly made inroads into Virginia by 1795 but did not inflict heavy crop losses there until the early 1800s. When William Strickland toured the state in 1794–95 he commented that Virginians "scarcely knew" the Hessian fly. James Madison first discovered the fly at his plantation in Virginia's piedmont region in 1798. Agricultural reformer and writer John Binns claimed that the fly did not infest his wheat in northwestern Virginia until 1800.[23] Residents in Richmond recorded the fly's arrival in 1801. The insect's ravages continued in Virginia until 1804, when the Hessian fly disappeared.[24] Damage by Hessian fly went unrecorded in the mid-Atlantic region between 1805 and 1817, probably because it was limited geographically and economically. Reports of ravages in New York, Pennsylvania, Maryland, and Virginia surged in 1817. Since then the Hessian fly has become omnipresent, spreading to all major wheat-growing areas in the United States. Although widespread outbreaks of the fly like those

21. George Ford to Benjamin Chew, November 9, 1792, Chew Family Papers, box 265, Historical Society of Pennsylvania (hereafter HSP), Philadelphia, Pennsylvania. See also David Craven, April 20, 1793, New Castle County Probate Inventory Records, Delaware State Archives, Dover, Delaware.

22. Henry Hollingsworth to Levi Hollingsworth (hereafter LH), May 20, 1793; Solomon Maxwell to LH, July 5, 1793; Herman Stump to LH, October 4, 1793, Hollingsworth Papers, HSP.

23. William Strickland, *Observations on the Agriculture of the United States of America* (reprint, New York: New-York Historical Society, 1971), 50–51; John Binns, *A Treatise on Practical Farming* (Frederick-town, Md.: John B. Colvin, 1803), 61–71, LCP.

24. William Hughlett to LH, May 14, 1800; Henry Hollingsworth to LH, August 18, 1801; McKinney Smack to LH, October 17, 1801; William Cooch to LH, December 27, 1802; Richard Bassett to LH, May 10, 1803; Zebulon Hollingsworth to LH, October 12, 1803; Thomas and Samuel Hollingsworth to LH, November 16, 1803; Thomas and Samuel Hollingsworth to LH, December 2, 1803, Hollingsworth Papers.

experienced by farmers in the late eighteenth century are rare, local outbreaks continue to cause extensive crop losses today.[25]

Almost immediately Americans searched for the deeper meaning of skies swarming with threatening insects. Many turned first to the familiar explanatory power of religion. "Nothing can more strongly exhibit the dependence or littleness of man," instructed the minister Timothy Dwight, "than the destruction of his valuable interests by such minute, helpless beings, nor can anything more forcibly display the ease with which his Maker punishes his transgressions." Dwight pointed out that the animals people learned to fear—the serpent, the tiger, and the lion—were more "solemn amusement and fireside affright than rational, or even real, anxiety." He reminded his readers that "cankerworms, caterpillars, and locusts" made up the "Great army God sent upon the Jews." And he warned them that "these and their compeers have in every age been the army of God which has humbled the pride, frustrated the designs, and annihilated the hopes of man." The Hessian fly was a wake-up call sent by "divine Providence," which Dwight believed would turn out to be a "great blessing."[26] Dwight was not alone. Between 1787 and 1800 a variety of Americans argued that for some the flies were a blessing, for others a curse, but for most they were both. Thus early Americans were the first to see the Hessian fly in terms of "creative destruction."

The insect's redemptive power began with its name. George Morgan, a gentleman farmer from Princeton, New Jersey, who had watched the flies devour his wheat fields in the mid-1780s, took credit for naming the fly. In a letter dated August 26, 1788, Morgan claimed that he and a friend referred to the insect as "Hessian" to reflect their sentiments of the "two Animals," and hoped that it would be passed down "with all possible Infamy as a useful National Prejudice."[27] Morgan's name reduced the enemy soldiers to the status of subhuman pests and conflated the human invaders with the insect threat.[28] The name would be "a useful national prejudice" because by identifying their enemies, Americans identified themselves. To Morgan it seemed that the losses caused by the insect invasion could be recouped in some measure through the creation of American nationalism. It is no accident that the name "Hessian fly" first appeared in print during the constitutional crisis of 1787. At that moment

25. H. Y. Hind, *Essay on the Insects and Diseases Injurious to the Wheat Crops* (Toronto: Lovell & Gibson, 1857), chapter 3.

26. Theodore Dwight, *Travels in America* (Glasgow: R. Griffin & Co., 1848), 211. See also *Pennsylvania Gazette*, September 24, 1788, LCP.

27. George Morgan to Sir John Temple, August 26, 1788, copy in Thomas Jefferson Manuscripts Division, Library of Congress, Washington, D.C. (http://memory.loc.gov/ammem/mtjhtml/mtjhome.html).

28. Historians of modern America have explored these connections more fully than early modern historians did. For example, see the work of Edmund Russell, *War and Nature: Fighting Humans and Insects with Chemicals from WWI to "Silent Spring"* (Cambridge: Cambridge University Press, 2001).

the need to forge a national identity could not have been more acute. As citizens divided over the design of government and the nature of the Republic, the Hessian fly united them against a common enemy. At the same time, it reminded them of the war and their struggle for independence. The insect was a foreign invader and, just like the Hessian mercenary soldiers, it engaged Americans in a struggle for survival that could be won only through the extermination of the enemy. To call the insect Hessian empowered Americans, for the name foretold the outcome of the struggle between man and bug. Since the patriots had defeated the Hessian soldiers in the War of Independence, they would triumph over the Hessian flies as well.[29]

That the insect feasted upon wheat in particular had significant political and symbolic meaning in the late eighteenth century because of the grain's republican connotations. Revolutionaries held up wheat as the ideal republican crop, especially in comparison to tobacco. In his *Notes on the State of Virginia*, Thomas Jefferson referred to tobacco as "a culture productive of infinite wretchedness," associated with royal government, debt, slavery, and poor agricultural practices. Jefferson believed that together wheat and the Revolution freed American farmers from colonial burdens and created conditions for national self-sufficiency. "Besides clothing the earth with herbage, and preserving its fertility," Jefferson claimed, "[wheat] feeds the laborers plentifully, requires from them only a moderate toil, except in the season of harvest, and diffuses plenty and happiness among the whole." As he saw it, since wheat cultivation required less attention than crops like tobacco, farmers would have more time for intellectual pursuits and civic participation. Jefferson's "chosen people of God" cultivated grain. Agricultural reformer John Beale Bordley seconded Jefferson's opinion, noting that "as the culture of wheat travelled southward into Maryland, and then Virginia, the people became more happy, and independent." Through the production of one of "the *necessary articles of life*," observed Bordley, grain cultivation created a new society of simple, virtuous, and uncorrupted farmers. Wheat exemplified American independence from political corruption and international dependence.[30]

Republicans read the fly invasion as a punishment for the loss of American virtue. "It behoves every good citizan," observed Joseph Kirkbride in 1788, "to guard against [the] approaching Evil of the Insect—the Fly—for the general good of the country." Without such vigilance the new Republic's future was in

29. Pauly also talks about the political links between the Hessian fly and the constitutional crisis. See "Fighting the Hessian Fly," 488–91.

30. Thomas Jefferson, *Notes on the State of Virginia* (reprint, Chapel Hill: University of North Carolina Press, 1982), 157, 166–68. John Beale Bordley, *Essays and Notes on Husbandry and Rural Affairs* (Philadelphia: Budd and Bartram, 1799), 371, LCP. The best discussion of the republican connotations of wheat remains T. H. Breen, *Tobacco Culture: The Mentality of the Great Tidewater Planters on the Eve of Revolution* (Princeton: Princeton University Press, 1985), xiii–xiv, 31, 55–56, 180–82, 204–7. See also John T. Schlotterbeck, "Plantation and Farm: Social and Economic Change in Orange and Greene Counties, Virginia, 1716 to 1860" (Ph.D. diss., Johns Hopkins University, 1980), 57.

jeopardy. The fly had been sent because the loss of the spirit of industry and frugality among farmers had been most dreadful. The writer observed that farmers
had become obsessed with luxury to the point that they mortgaged their land
and neglected their laborers' wages, creating a mountain of debt. Thus reduced,
farmers "were obliged to sacrifice all their FINERY and all their infatuated expectations, and sink into poverty and contempt." The writer urged farmers that
a change "must take place in [their] hearts; for unless [they] immediately cease
to live beyond [their] circumstances, [they] must become poor, needy, necessi-
tous and contemptibly wretched." It could only be hoped that the threat of the
Hessian fly would awaken farmers to their folly and return them to their fields.[31]

Still others used the fly as an opening for political discussions about
the course of American economic development, and in particular the need for
domestic manufacturing. In a report to the Philadelphia County Society for
Promoting Agriculture and Domestic Manufacturing, Samuel Jones encouraged
mid-Atlantic farmers to turn from grain cultivation to sheep raising because
grazing would be "much more favourable to our views of manufacturing, and
may prove the means of saving those immense sums of money that are now sent
abroad for woollens of all kinds." Jones worked out a national plan for textile
production. As "we depend on the southern states for cotton to furnish us with
summer wear," he reasoned, "it is to the middle states we must look for our
winter clothing." Mid-Atlantic farmers should turn to raising sheep "by the lure
of gain and the good of our country," Jones explained, for they would not only
profit individually but also help to develop domestic manufacturing and establish American economic independence. "The loss of our wheat may prove a
blessing to us," he concluded, if it pushed mid-Atlantic farmers into other enterprises. Like those who interpreted the fly as a divine punishment or a political
warning, Jones and other manufacturing boosters saw redemption in its wrath.[32]

Symbolism aside, for the farmers, millers, and merchants who depended
upon the grain trade for their livelihood, the Hessian fly was a practical problem
in need of a solution. As the center of America's grain trade, Philadelphia naturally emerged as the headquarters for the scientific operation against the Hessian
fly. The Pennsylvania Supreme Executive Council called upon the Philadelphia
Society for the Promotion of Agriculture (PSPA) in September 1788 to investigate the Hessian fly and find a way to stop the destructive insect from injuring
foreign markets for the state's staple crop. The PSPA had been created in 1785
with the aim of "exciting a spirit of improvement" among American farmers

31. Joseph Kirkbride to LH, August 24, 1788, Hollingsworth Papers. Also *Pennsylvania
Gazette,* "To the Farmers of Pennsylvania," July 23, 1788.
32. *Pennsylvania Gazette,* December 15, 1788. On the competing views of American economic development in the early Republic, see Joyce Appleby, "Commercial Farming and the 'Agrarian Myth' in the Early Republic," *Journal of American History* 68 (March 1982): 833–49; Drew R. McCoy,
The Elusive Republic: Political Economy in Jeffersonian America (Chapel Hill: University of North Carolina
Press, 1980), 76–105.

through meetings, publications, and annual prizes. To encourage experimentation and innovation, the society offered awards in a variety of categories every year, including the best experiment in crop rotation, the greatest quantity of manure collected in one year, and the best information for preventing damage to crops by insects. In early 1789 the PSPA revised the insect category, adding the Hessian fly to a list already including the "wheat-fly, pea-bug, and corn chinch-bug."[33]

A small group of agricultural reformers within the PSPA led the offensive against the Hessian fly. Among them was George Morgan, who had made his fortune in the Ohio River valley's fur trade following the Seven Years' War as a partner in a large Philadelphia commercial firm. During the American Revolution he retired to a farm in Princeton, New Jersey, eager to take on the "quiet rational life of an agriculturalist." But Morgan was anything but quiet. One of the twenty-three founding members of the PSPA, he frequently contributed ideas and shared experiments at its meetings. In 1786 he won the society's gold medal for his farmyard plan. When the Hessian fly attacked, Morgan was the first to call for government action, to seek information from European agricultural societies, and to conduct scientific experiments on the Hessian fly "pass[ing] through every stage in glass jars" in his library.[34]

John Beale Bordley stepped up to manage the southern front. Born in Maryland in 1727, Bordley grew up on the eastern shore and studied law in Annapolis during the 1740s, but gave it up to become a planter.[35] In 1770 he moved to a sixteen-hundred-acre plantation on Wye Island on the eastern shore, where he cultivated "the spirit for improvement." Bordley worked out a six-field system of crop rotation based on "replenishing" crops such as clover, beans, and turnips. He was the founder and first vice president of the PSPA. Bordley mobilized the planter community and synthesized information on the Hessian fly in his agricultural works published in the 1790s.[36]

---

33. The society's constitution was published in the *Pennsylvania Gazette,* April 27, 1785. For a general history of the PSPA, see Simon Baatz, *"Venerate the Plough": A History of the Philadelphia Society for the Promotion of Agriculture, 1785–1985* (Philadelphia: Philadelphia Society for Promoting Agriculture, 1985). For announcements of a prize for information on the Hessian fly, see *Pennsylvania Gazette,* February 18, 1789, March 31, 1790. On the national implications of these societies, see Jennifer Clark, "The American Image of Technology from the Revolution to 1840," *American Quarterly* 39 (Autumn 1987): 445–46. For an important investigation of one "expert," see Christopher Grasso, "The Experimental Philosophy of Farming: Jared Eliot and the Cultivation of Connecticut," *William and Mary Quarterly* 50 (July 1993): 527–28.

34. *Pennsylvania Gazette,* June 27, 1787, LCP. For a fuller discussion of Morgan's role, see Pauly, "Fighting the Hessian Fly," 487–91.

35. On Bordley's life, see a sketch by his daughter, Elizabeth Gibson, in *Biographical Sketches of the Bordley Family, of Maryland . . .* (Philadelphia, 1865), 62–159, LCP. See also O. M. Gambrill, "John Beale Bordley and the Early Years of the Philadelphia Agricultural Society," *Pennsylvania Magazine of History and Biography* 66 (October 1942): 410–39; David Hackett Fischer, "John Beale Bordley, Daniel Boorstin, and the American Enlightenment," *Journal of Southern History* 28 (August 1962): 330–42.

36. For example, see Bordley, *Essays and Notes on Husbandry,* 30–48 47, 98–99, 108–18, 244–59, 318, 482, 493–94.

The efforts of agricultural reformers to reach farmers had yielded disappointing results before the late 1780s. Farmers had shown little interest in changing their cultivation habits and were reluctant to follow advice about deep plowing and restorative crops. But remedies for the Hessian fly found an interested audience, and in that moment agricultural reformers reinvented themselves as experts on the fly.[37] Men such as Morgan and Bordley proposed both cultural and biological remedies for stopping the Hessian fly, including delaying seeding and planting fly-resistant wheat. Despite advances in modern science, farmers today control the pest in much the same way.

Studies of the Hessian fly's behavior indicated that the earlier a crop was sown, the more likely it was to be damaged. Accordingly, reformers advised farmers to sow their wheat later in order to interrupt the insect's lifecycle. Traditionally, mid-Atlantic farmers planted wheat in late August or early September. Morgan suggested that they sow their wheat between September 10 and September 20 in Pennsylvania and points north, and even later in more southern areas. Late-sown wheat may have escaped the Hessian fly, but it was often exposed to frost and to attacks of rust and other weather-related diseases before it ripened. Still, many farmers delayed seeding, thus changing the region's traditional agricultural rhythms. For example, Benjamin Chew ordered his overseer at Whitehall Plantation in Kent County, Delaware, not to sow the wheat "so soon as has been customary." A farmer's testimonial printed in the *Pennsylvania Gazette* in 1800 put the safe time for seeding wheat around Philadelphia during the last week of September and first week of October. Today late planting among wheat farmers has been formalized in the agricultural cycle by the annual publication of "fly-free date" calendars. Then as now, planting too soon could cost farmers their crops.[38]

But most of the self-styled experts agreed that the best means of thwarting the Hessian fly was the adoption of fly-resistant wheat. Wheat varieties were distinguished by the color of the chaff—red, white, or yellow—and by the texture of the head—bald or bearded. Millers preferred white grain to red or yellow, and all bald wheat to bearded varieties, because of eighteenth-century milling methods, which could not completely separate the bran from the flour. As a

37. Grasso, "Experimental Philosophy of Farming," 504–6, 516–18, 527–28. Grasso noted that Wadsworth received recognition from farmers only after he introduced a fly-resistant variety of wheat. Sharrer also argued that agricultural reform showed promise where advice coincided with market realities. See Sharrer, "Flour Milling and the Growth of Baltimore," 195. The Internet is full of advice for modern wheat farmers on the subject of managing the Hessian fly. For example, see New York State's Integrated Pest Management Program's website at http://www.nysipm.cornell.edu/lfc/fieldcrops/wheat/hes_guide_01.html.

38. Morgan's advice appears in the *Pennsylvania Gazette*, July 16, 1788; Benjamin Chew to James Raymond, July 19, 1793, Chew Family Papers, box 264; *Pennsylvania Gazette*, August 27, 1800. For an example of a fly-free date calendar, see Pennsylvania State University, College of Agricultural Sciences, Cooperative Extension, entomological notes from the Department of Entomology at http://www.ento.psu/extension/factsheets/hessian_fly_wheat.htm.

result, red bran naturally discolored the flour more than white bran did, and flour made from red wheat fetched a lower price. Accordingly, mid-Atlantic farmers traditionally cultivated white wheat to meet market demand.[39] This type of wheat happened to be highly susceptible to the Hessian fly, which explains the severity of the initial infestation. In 1780 or 1781 Isaac Underhill, a Long Island miller, discovered that yellow bearded wheat possessed "some peculiar quality" that resisted the fly. Reformers attributed its resistance to its small, hard stalk, which they believed prevented the fly from penetrating the plant. Scientists are still not certain how resistant varieties stop the fly, but it appears that the fly-resistant strains of wheat contain a biochemical compound that detects and blocks the enzymes secreted by larvae to degrade the cell wall and allow them to live off the plant's juices. Basically, resistant varieties starve the larvae to death. The important point here is that early republican farmers identified fly-resistant wheat varieties, even if they did not fully understand the mechanism of resistance.[40]

George Morgan was among the first to publicize the merits of yellow bearded wheat, telling farmers in 1787 "that their absolute reliance (under Providence) must be on the yellow bearded wheat, not the white, nor the red." Morgan sent samples to several individuals, including George Washington. "But if the march of the Hessian Fly, Southerly, cannot be arrested," Washington wrote, "White Wheat must yield the palm to the yellow bearded, which alone, it seems, is able to resist the depredations of that destructive insect." Convinced of the powers of the yellow bearded wheat, Washington helped spread the news that it alone resisted the "ravages of this, otherwise, all conquering foe." Levi Hollingsworth, one of Philadelphia's busiest flour merchants, began advertising the sale of yellow bearded wheat in 1788 at eleven shillings per bushel, or almost twice the value of the best white wheat.[41] The number of farmers adopting the yellow bearded wheat increased during the 1790s. In 1792 Charles Carroll purchased three hundred bushels of yellow bearded seed to use at his Maryland plantation after the Hessian fly ruined two of his wheat fields. As seeding time approached for the 1794 crop, Benjamin Chew ordered his overseer at Whitehall Plantation to see that "no wheat be sewed but the yellow bearded as the best securing against the Fly." Andrew Fisher, a miller near Newark, Delaware,

39. R. O. Bausman and J. A. Munroe, "James Tilton's Notes on the Agriculture of Delaware in 1788," *Agricultural History* 20 (Spring 1946): 180. Cronon suggests that the Hessian fly brought an end to the cultivation of white bald wheat in Connecticut (*Changes in the Land,* 153).

40. On Underhill, see *Pennsylvania Gazette,* August 20, 1788. The explanation of resistance can be found in Dwight, *Travels,* 211. For a modern scientific explanation of resistance, see Roger Ratcliffe, "Breeding for Hessian Fly Resistance in Wheat," in Radcliffe's IPM World Textbook at http://ipmworld.umn.edu.

41. For Morgan, see *Pennsylvania Gazette,* July 16, 1788, LCP. For Washington, see "The Hessian Fly" at http://www.mountvernon.org/pioneer/farms/hessian.html. For Hollingsworth, *Pennsylvania Gazette,* September 10, 1788, LCP.

defended the high quality of his flour in 1797 based on his use of only "yellow wheat." The evidence from Fisher provides a strong indication of how widely yellow bearded wheat had been adopted, because the wheat he milled came from farmers living across a large region. Moreover, millers—from Underhill to Fisher—played an integral role in educating farmers about Hessian fly prevention and distributing resistant varieties of wheat to their neighborhoods.[42]

Clearly, fighting the Hessian fly helped to develop a new spirit of experimentation in the region's grain culture based on the exchange of ideas and seeds. For one thing, farmers, millers, and merchants paid more attention to wheat varieties than they had before. When George Morgan first asked George Washington about yellow bearded wheat, Washington confessed, "I have paid too little attention to the growth of this particular kind hitherto, to inform you in what degree of cultivation it is in this State, I may venture, at a hazard, however, to add that it is *rare:* because it is unusual to see fields of bearded wheat of *any* kind growing with us."[43] The Hessian fly changed all that. By 1800 fields of yellow bearded wheat stretched from Long Island to the Appalachian ridge. In addition, farmers, millers, and merchants started to differentiate varieties commercially, listing separate prices for red, white, and yellow wheat. The Hessian fly forced them to take a closer look at their wheat.

Reformers did not stop at hooking farmers on late seeding and yellow bearded wheat. They also returned to promoting agricultural improvements such as crop rotation, deep plowing, fertilizing, and planting restorative crops, all of which they insisted combated the Hessian fly. Reformers encouraged farmers to prepare their fields more extensively and intensively by plowing the ground several times to mix the soil and to destroy all the remaining grass or weeds. They also suggested that crops planted on fertilized ground suffered less injury from the fly. Jefferson noted during his 1791 journey that farmers on Long Island had increased their use of manure as instructed by reformers, and remarked that "by the improvement of manure the country really has been benefited." John Binns claimed in his *Treatise on Practical Farming* that wheat yields in Virginia had been greatly increased through the use of manure, and "especially by the use of Plaster of Paris." Manure and plaster of paris improved plant vitality but could not stop the Hessian fly in its tracks. While farmers and reformers did not fully realize it at the time, the improvement that was actually most effective against the Hessian fly was the clearing of fields of volunteer wheat, grass, and weeds on which the insect could lay its eggs. Although it is impossible to determine

42. See entries on June 4, 18, and 23, 1792, Charles Carroll of Carrollton Journal, 1792–1802, Maryland Historical Society, Baltimore, Maryland. On Whitehall, see Benjamin Chew to James Raymond, July 19, 1793, Chew Family Papers, box 264. On milling, see Andrew Fisher to LH, October 23, 1797, Hollingsworth Papers.

43. George Washington to George Morgan, August 25, 1788, in Abbot, *Papers of George Washington,* 6:474–75.

exactly how many farmers changed their farming methods, evidence suggests that many did, and that some at least increased their wheat yields. Thus, according to Bordley, Jefferson, and other reformers, the Hessian fly "indirectly rendered a good service to wheat cultivation." The bug certainly did not bring about agricultural improvements all on its own, but the invasion encouraged widespread evaluation of agricultural practices and the adoption of some new cultivation techniques. The Hessian fly played an important role in early American agricultural history, and in no small measure laid the groundwork for the development of agricultural societies, newspapers, and fairs in the nineteenth century.[44]

While mid-Atlantic grain farmers faced the most menacing agricultural pest they had ever encountered, they also experienced the greatest demand for their produce they had ever known. Normal conditions in the West Indies combined with growing North American markets and a series of harvest failures in Europe during the late 1780s to increase demand for mid-Atlantic grain. Grain scarcity played a well-known role in bringing on the French Revolution. Across the channel, English officials removed the ban on American grain in December 1789, more owing to the failure of their own harvests and fear of the spread of revolution than to reports of a fly-free harvest in America.[45] The Napoleonic Wars made certain that European nations would not be able to feed their populations without American assistance between 1792 and 1815. The increased demand for breadstuffs during the Napoleonic Wars provided mid-Atlantic farmers with further incentives to plant alternative grains, and their actions had a ripple effect in the Atlantic-world marketplace and on the region's grain culture.

With their staple commodity under siege, many mid-Atlantic farmers looked for new opportunities. During the late 1780s and 1790s farmers increasingly plowed up their fly-infested wheat fields and sowed them over with other grain crops. In fact, farmers in parts of Connecticut, New York, and New Jersey never again cultivated as much wheat as they had before the Hessian fly invasion. By the mid-1790s many northern farmers had abandoned commercial wheat cultivation entirely. During a tour of the Hudson River valley, William Strickland observed that "much wheat used to be grown in this neighborhood, but the Hessian fly has stopped the cultivation." For Connecticut, Timothy

---

44. Binns, *Treatise on Practical Farming*, 2–17; "The Northern Journey," *Papers of Thomas Jefferson*, 20:459; Bordley, *Notes and Essays on Husbandry*, 30, 243. On agricultural improvement during this period, see Percy Wells Bidwell and John I. Falconer, *History of Agriculture in the Northern United States, 1820–1860* (New York: P. Smith, 1941), 239; Dondlinger, *Book of Wheat*, 10–11, 14, 173.

45. On France, see Judith Miller, *Mastering the Market* (Cambridge: Cambridge University Press, 1999); Cynthia Bouton, *The Flour War: Gender, Class, and Community in Late Ancien Regime France* (University Park: Pennsylvania State University Press, 1993); Steven Kaplan, *Provisioning Paris: Merchants and Millers in the Grain and Flour Trade During the Eighteenth Century* (Ithaca: Cornell University Press, 1984); and Fagan, *Little Ice Age*, 162–66. On England, see Pauly, "Fighting the Hessian Fly," 491–98; Charles R. Ritcheson, *Aftermath of Revolution: British Policy Toward the United States, 1783–1795* (Dallas: Southern Methodist University Press, 1969), 199–203.

Dwight estimated in the early nineteenth century that "the cultivation of wheat has for more than twenty years been in great measure discontinued." He pointed to the village of Greenwich as an example, noting that before the insect invasion farmers exported ten thousand bushels of wheat annually but that they had since become wheat importers. Export figures indicate that many Connecticut farmers turned their fields of wheat into acres of oats. Many New Jersey farmers switched over to growing rye to supply the state's growing distilling industry.[46]

But these states had never been the most productive wheat centers in North America. American wheat export totals did not drop significantly until 1795, after the Hessian fly arrived in the home of the region's most productive wheat farmers in Delaware and eastern Maryland. There the Hessian fly reduced yields from an average of twelve bushels to less than five bushels per acre, and in extreme cases to as low as one bushel per acre.[47] American wheat exports averaged more than 1 million bushels per year between 1789 and 1792. Wheat exports began dropping in 1792, the time of the fly's arrival in Delaware and Maryland. In 1795 American wheat exports plummeted from more than one hundred thousand bushels to around thirty thousand bushels. Wheat exports virtually ceased between 1796 and 1799, courtesy of the Hessian fly's appetite and American relations with Britain and France, falling to an all-time low of ten thousand bushels in 1798. The first years of the nineteenth century marked a modest rebound in American wheat exports.[48]

South of New Jersey, decisions to alter cultivation strategies were of greater consequence. Here farmers also plowed up injured fields in the 1790s, but they did not abandon wheat to the same degree northern farmers had. Instead of replacing wheat with another grain, they supplemented their staple with other cereals. The accounts of Benjamin Chew's Whitehall Plantation in Kent County, Delaware, document the damage done by the Hessian fly during the 1790s and one individual's strategy for coping with the insect. Whitehall Plantation bordered Little Duck Creek and contained nearly one thousand acres worked by approximately forty slaves, who produced large quantities of wheat for market each year. Chew often made contracts to sell his entire crop to a single merchant miller, usually on the Brandywine. Table 1 shows that wheat harvests at Whitehall were severely affected by the fly in 1793, 1794 and 1798.[49]

46. On the Hudson Valley, see William Strickland, *Journal of a Tour in the United States of America, 1794–1795* (New York: New York Historical Society, 1971), 90, 99. On Connecticut, see Dwight, *Travels,* 210–11.

47. For a discussion of the Hessian fly in America's wheat belt, see John Beale Bordley, *Sketches on the Rotation of Crops* (Philadelphia: printed by Charles Cist, 1792), 9. Damage reported in Richard Parkinson, *The Experienced Farmer's Tour of America,* 8 vols. (London: printed for John Stockdale, 1805), 1:201–2, both available at the LCP.

48. Thomas C. Cochran, ed., *The New American State Papers, Commerce and Navigation,* 47 vols. (Wilmington: Scholarly Resources, 1974), 1:31, 118, 315, 354, 374, 397, 417; 2:26, 57, 97, 129, 190, 279, 305; 3:24, 35, 109, 147, 164, 252, 283, 317.

49. See Whitehall records, Chew Family Papers, boxes 264–67.

The Hessian fly did not attack Chew's wheat until the fall of 1792, and the flies continued to wreak havoc through 1799. In November the overseer, George Ford, reported that the insect destroyed more than half of the newly sown wheat at Whitehall. Chew's wheat sales plunged from more than one thousand bushels in 1792 to fewer than two hundred bushels in 1793. Most of the farmers around Little Duck Creek produced one-half of their normal crop yields in 1793, whereas Chew harvested only 20 percent of his typical yield. Chew responded to the fly's damage by instructing Ford to follow to the letter the preventive measures advocated by agricultural reformers, from late seeding to planting only yellow bearded wheat. Fear of another attack also induced Chew to reduce the amount of seed used by one-third. That fall Ford sowed seventy bushels of yellow bearded wheat and five bushels of the white wheat prized by millers. Although the harvest was by no means bountiful, it was a marked improvement over the previous year. Chew sold his surplus white wheat to Philadelphia flour merchant John Wall for the high price of twenty shillings per bushel. For the harvest in 1794, Ford sowed eighty-nine bushels of yellow bearded and twenty-three bushels of white wheat. The yellow bearded wheat resisted the fly between 1794 and 1796. Although Ford notified Chew in November 1796 that the fly was in the wheat, the harvest yield in 1797 indicates that the damage was not as severe as in 1793.[50]

Table 1   Wheat Production at Whitehall Plantation, Kent County, Delaware, 1790–1802

Harvest Year★	Sown (bushels)	Yield (bushels)	Sold (bushels)	Price (shillings/pence)
1790		1,000		
1791		1,007	907	
1792	122	1,145	1,045	9
1793	114	205	189	9/3
1794	75	402	390	12
1795	111	666	569	15
1796	132	902.5	761.5	12
1797	113.5	840	770	
1798	112	532.5	326	
1799	127	858	596	14/3
1800	150	1,102	1,000	
1801	135	1,087	933	9
1802	121	1,382	1,140	

Source: Chew Family Papers, Kent County Lands, Whitehall Plantation, Historical Society of Pennsylvania, Philadelphia.
★Chew planted winter wheat, so the year indicates the date of the summer harvest, meaning the crop was sown the previous fall and sold the following winter or spring.

50. George Ford to Benjamin Chew, November 9, 1792; June 19, 1794; n.d. November 1794; April 26, 1795; November 9, 1796; November 6, 1797, Chew Family Papers, box 265. On agricultural reforms, see Benjamin Chew to James Raymond, July 19, 1793, ibid., box 264.

A recurrence in 1798 cost Chew half his crop. A possible reason for the reversal in fortune may be that although he cultivated yellow bearded wheat, he also sowed more of the defenseless white wheat each year between 1794 and 1798, thus setting himself up for a fall. The Hessian fly did not bring an end to white bald wheat production in the mid-Atlantic, largely because millers and consumers kept demand alive. The yellow bearded wheat may have been fly resistant, but it reportedly produced dirty-looking flour, and, when made into bread, dried out much faster than bread made from white bald wheat. As a result, farmers like Chew continued to plant select fields in white bald wheat despite the high risk of infestation. Washington sowed three types of wheat at Mount Vernon in the late-1790s—spring wheat, yellow bearded wheat, and "a very fine white wheat."[51]

As the situation declined on Chew's Delaware plantation, circumstances in Europe also took a turn for the worse. By 1795 many European nations faced both harvest failures and invading armies. As in 1789, England and France removed trade restrictions in order to prevent their people from starving. Crop shortages at home and abroad encouraged mid-Atlantic farmers to drive up the price of wheat. New wheat opened high in late July, at fourteen shillings per bushel. By fall, a miller exclaimed, "wheat has got beyond everything, one man told me he was offered eighteen shillings per bushel."[52] Chew sold his wheat surplus in 1795 to a Brandywine miller for fifteen shillings per bushel. So even with a small crop, Chew made a tidy profit. In some ways, a low yield was better than a bountiful harvest for a large commercial farmer like Chew. Good harvests meant that farmers sold more grain, but at a lower price and a higher cost for harvesting, threshing, and transporting the produce to market. By contrast, better harvests translated into higher incomes for smaller grain farmers, especially tenants, even at reduced prices. In a good year, a tenant farmer produced enough grain to feed his family, pay his landlord, provide for next year's seed, and leave enough for a surplus to sell on the market. In a bad year, tenant farmers struggled to make ends meet. Their priorities were to feed their families and maintain their leases, which at the time were typically paid in wheat rather than cash. Consecutive failed harvests, as experienced during the Hessian fly invasion, would have weighed heavily against the mid-Atlantic region's smaller and tenant farmers. Large grain farmers, especially landlords who reaped their tenants' harvests, gained at their expense. Short crops and high prices generally continued through 1799 to the advantage of Chew and the mid-Atlantic region's other large grain producers.

At the same time that Chew experimented with fly remedies, he also increased his corn production for market to make up for losses on wheat. As

51. George Washington to Richard Peters, July 23, 1797 in John C. Fitzpatrick, ed., *The Writings of George Washington* (Washington, D.C.: U.S. Government Printing Office, 1931–44), 35:509.
52. Samuel Carter to LH, October 1, 1795, Hollingsworth Papers.

many as 150 acres each year were planted with corn at Whitehall. Still, the majority of corn produced was used to feed slaves and livestock. On average, two thousand bushels of corn were harvested each year during the 1790s, of which Chew sold approximately eight hundred bushels. After 1798 corn production increased to three thousand bushels per year on average, and Chew's sales grew to around one thousand bushels annually. To support greater corn production Chew had a new corncrib built in 1798. Corn proved to be a reliable alternative for mid-Atlantic farmers; exports held at more than a million bushels per year except during the quasi war with France in 1798. Traditionally shipped to the West Indies as a cheap food for slaves, corn was also needed to feed soldiers stationed in the Caribbean during the Napoleonic Wars and Haitian Revolution. Corn also found ready markets in Europe, given the ruinous combination of harvest failures and war that decade.[53] Chew also turned to other grains. Following the disastrous harvest in 1793, he had Ford plant barley on the best field because "the fly is not so fond of it as it is of the wheat." Ford also sowed rye, sending 254 bushels for Chew to sell in Philadelphia in the spring of 1795.[54] The case study of Chew's Whitehall Plantation shows how crop diversification and farming practices changed as a result of the arrival of the Hessian fly.

The Hessian fly hurt the region's millers as much as it did farmers because their business depended on a plentiful supply of good grain. The insect not only reduced crop size but also damaged the grain that was harvested, so that fly-damaged wheat produced less flour. At the same time that millers struggled with fly-eaten wheat, they also labored to produce high-quality superfine flour out of the newly popular yellow bearded wheat.[55] Still, flour exports did not decline as sharply as wheat exports, especially between 1795 and 1799. Flour exports averaged around 750,000 barrels per year between 1789 and 1804, dropping to a low of 515,633 barrels in 1796–97 and peaking at 1.3 million barrels in 1802–3 with the resumption of war in Europe.[56] Several factors explain why flour remained more stable than wheat during the Hessian fly invasion. For one thing, flour had been the region's primary export commodity since the 1740s, when it overtook wheat. The fly only intensified the pattern by which millers channeled the bulk of the region's surplus wheat to their mills. For another thing,

53. Cochran, *New American State Papers*, 1:31, 118, 315, 354, 374, 397, 417; 2:26, 57, 97, 129, 190, 279, 305; 3:24, 35, 109, 147, 164, 252, 283, 317.

54. George Ford to Benjamin Chew, March 25, 1795. See also George Ford to Benjamin Chew, December 23, 1796; November 6, 1797; Joseph Porter to Benjamin Chew, January 7, 1798; August 29, 1799; June 8, 1799; November 28, 1800; April 9, 1801; n.d. October 1803, all in Chew Family Papers, box 264.

55. For millers' complaints, see Jeremiah Brown to LH, October 19, 1795; James Douglass to LH, August 16, 1792; Thomas and Samuel Hollingsworth to LH, November 16, 1803; James Douglass to LH, March 3, 1794; Adam Henchman to LH, October 13, 1795; Jonathan Booth to LH, October 30, 1795, Hollingsworth Papers. See also Dondlinger, *Book of Wheat*, 10–11, 14, 173.

56. Cochran, *New American State Papers*, 1:31, 118, 315, 354, 374, 397, 417; 2:26, 57, 97, 129, 190, 279, 305; 3:24, 35, 109, 147, 164, 252, 283, 317.

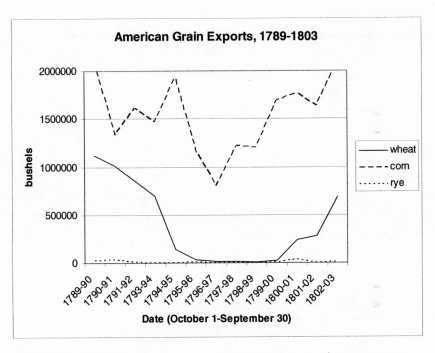

American Grain Exports, 1789-1803

bushels

2000000
1500000
1000000
500000
0

— wheat
- - - corn
······ rye

1789-90 1790-91 1791-92 1793-94 1794-95 1795-96 1796-97 1797-98 1798-99 1799-00 1800-01 1801-02 1802-03

Date (October 1-September 30)

Source: The New American State Papers, vol. 1, 31, 118, 315, 354, 374, 397, 417; vol. 2, 26, 57, 97, 129, 190, 279, 305; vol. 3, 24, 35, 109, 147, 164, 252, 283, 317.

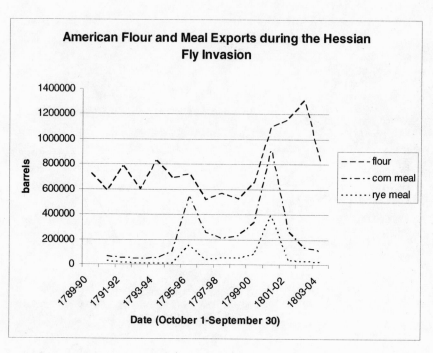

American Flour and Meal Exports during the Hessian Fly Invasion

barrels

1400000
1200000
1000000
800000
600000
400000
200000
0

1789-90 1791-92 1793-94 1795-96 1797-98 1799-00 1801-02 1803-04

Date (October 1-September 30)

- – – flour
- – · – corn meal
- · · · · · rye meal

Source: The New American State Papers, vol. 1, 31, 118, 315, 354, 374, 397, 417; vol. 2, 26, 57, 97, 129, 190, 279, 305; vol. 3, 24, 35, 109, 147, 164, 252, 283, 317.

poor harvests and war in Europe increased demand for ready foodstuffs to feed citizens and soldiers on the continent and in the Caribbean. It appears that millers manufactured into flour most of the surplus wheat mid-Atlantic farmers managed to harvest during the Hessian fly invasion.

Millers also followed farmers in the making of new market products. The Hessian fly encouraged many of the region's millers to expand their enterprises to include cornmeal. In the late 1780s Henry Hollingsworth started sending "kiln dryed indian meal" to market, which he found "answers better than grinding wheat." William Hughlett purchased the Spring Mills outside Dover in 1794 at the height of the Hessian fly's ravaging of the area, and not surprisingly he immediately put the custom mill to work manufacturing cornmeal for export. He hoped to take advantage of the productive cornfields in his neighborhood and in particular the crops of John Dickinson and his numerous tenants in Kent County, Delaware.[57]

Milling corn required different processes from wheat. Most important, corn had to be dried before it could be ground; otherwise the grain's moisture caused the meal to rot. As millers increased their cornmeal production, they sought better ways of drying it. Millers like William Cooch built elaborate corn kilns designed to maximize the amount of corn dried per cord of wood and prevent smoking, a common problem with older kilns. In addition, millers also ground corn with different stones to prevent corn oils from mixing with and tainting wheat flour. Despite the growth in corn milling, cornmeal exports never surpassed corn exports during this period.[58]

While many millers coped with the Hessian fly invasion by manufacturing cornmeal, others mixed corn with fly-damaged wheat in an attempt to produce a modified superfine flour. This practice adulterated the flour and raised fears about the reputation of American flour abroad. The Pennsylvania legislature responded to the threat by passing an act in 1795 that created fines for mixing wheat flour with cornmeal.[59] Maryland legislators followed suit with a similar law to stop "the horrid practice [of] grinding corn with wheat."[60]

The laws failed to prevent the mixing of grains. Several millers caused a commotion when they bought up several thousand bushels of damaged wheat from Virginia during the fall of 1803. Merchants in Baltimore and Philadelphia worried that "if it is manufactured it must eventually injure the credit of the

57. Henry Hollingsworth to LH, October 12, 1788; William Hughlett to LH, August 23, 1794, Hollingsworth Papers. On Dickinson, see William Huglett to John Dickinson, circular letter dated February 13, 1796, LCP.

58. William Cooch to LH, May 28, 1795, Hollingsworth Papers. On Baltimore, see Joseph Scott, A Geographical Description of the States of Maryland and Delaware (Philadelphia: Kimber and Conrad, 1807), 80–82, LCP.

59. James T. Mitchell and Henry Flanders, comp., The Statutes at Large of Pennsylvania from 1682 to 1801 (Harrisburg, 1896–1911), 15:482–85, HSP.

60. Zebulon Hollingsworth to LH, September 11, 1800, Hollingsworth Papers.

flour" of the port that exported it. Although one merchant confessed "only God knows what they do with fly eaten wheat," of course there was no great mystery. Millers were undoubtedly "well skilled in the art of mixing" and very capable of passing "deceptions unnoticed." This too might help to explain the greater stability of flour exports versus wheat exports during the Hessian fly invasion.[61]

Millers who were unwilling to build corn kilns or risk mixing wheat and corn could produce rye meal for export. Millers had previously turned to rye when wheat crops failed, but they usually found limited markets for rye meal apart from German bakers. Before the Revolution a merchant miller commented that rye made a ready sale only to Philadelphia's "Dutch bakers." During the early national era, however, demand for rye meal rose. Part of the reason for the growing taste for rye meal must have been the disruption of wheat harvests by the Hessian fly. Germans had long raised wheat for market and used rye for household consumption. During the Hessian fly invasion, many farmers in Pennsylvania, Maryland, and Virginia produced more rye. The large German population in Jeremiah Brown's neighborhood of Little Britain in Lancaster County gave Brown access to large rye surpluses. In 1795 he wrote to Philadelphia that he could make a great quantity of rye meal because of the abundant harvest. Not surprisingly, rye meal exports peaked following the worst years of the Hessian fly invasion.[62]

Official export reports started to include separate categories for "corn meal" and "rye meal" in 1790, an indication of their growing importance in trade. Further proof of the rising significance of corn and rye in international markets is provided by the passage of new laws regulating their export. Beginning in 1800 Pennsylvania established a separate inspection for rye and corn flour because "its exportation had risen in recent years, especially for fine rye flour."[63]

The fly magnified and accelerated an important geographical shift in grain cultivation toward the south already under way since the Revolution. Traffic at grain depots such as Baltimore, Alexandria, and Richmond increased rapidly.[64] Strong markets and high prices for wheat during the three decades following the American Revolution reversed the declining fortunes of many Chesapeake planters. "Our farmers have never experienced such prosperity,"

61. Thomas and Samuel Hollingsworth to LH, August 6, 1803, September 16, 1803, December 2, 1803, ibid.

62. Thomas May to LH, May 17, 1774; Jeremiah Brown to LH, July 29, 1795, ibid. See also Bidwell and Falconer, *History of Agriculture*, 92.

63. For requests to manufacture rye meal, see Henry Hollingsworth to LH, August 7 and 25, 1789; Hollingsworth Papers. On new regulations, see Mitchell and Flanders, *Statutes at Large of Pennsylvania*, 16:289–90.

64. Bjork, *Stagnation and Growth in the American Economy*, appendix 3, 94. For instance, Alexandria exported 37,891 bushels of corn and 102,268 bushels of wheat in 1788–89. Baltimore exported 143,174 barrels of flour, 249,310 bushels of corn, and 228,116 bushels of wheat. See appendix 3, 92.

James Madison told Albert Gallatin in 1810.[65] By the 1790s Maryland and Virginia were the nation's leading wheat producers and the main suppliers of wheat to the mid-Atlantic's commercial flourmills. Together they supplied more than half of American wheat exports. In addition, Virginia led the nation in corn exports, far outproducing the other states. Maryland and Virginia had become the new center of American grain production.[66]

Planters in the upper South switched to wheat as the Hessian fly moved into older wheat regions in the north. They produced good wheat crops during the demand peak in 1789 when their northern counterparts could not. They also benefited from the preventive measures developed during the 1780s. Ultimately, when the fly did arrive, southern planters adapted better because they were better prepared, chiefly thanks to the efforts of their northern peers. Large planters in Virginia and Maryland practiced diversified market agriculture, sending several crops to market at once or in alternation. Moreover, planters with large plantations and diversified agriculture were able to respond to changing market conditions such as rising and falling prices. Because they did not gamble their entire livelihood on one market crop—wheat—they could weather the ravages of the fly better.[67] In the end the Hessian fly contributed to the creation of a new grain culture marked by greater diversification, and in the process helped to redraw the map of the mid-Atlantic region by pushing grain cultivation deeper into the upper South.

The Hessian fly was alarming at first because it was unknown and arrived during a critical period in American history, but by the early nineteenth century the shock had subsided. The invader became a common pest, accepted by farmers as just another one of nature's constant challenges, alongside drought, mildew, and chinch bugs. While the grain community failed to exterminate the destructive insect, they found ways to live with it (just as Americans had resided side by side with the Hessian soldiers who settled in the United States after the

65. Quoted in Schlotterbeck, "Plantation and Farm," 55.

66. Warren R. Hofstra and Robert D. Mitchell, "Town and Country in Backcountry Virginia: Winchester and the Shenandoah Valley, 1730–1800," *Journal of Southern History* 59 (November 1993): 619–46; David Klingaman, "The Significance of Grain in the Development of the Tobacco Colonies," *Journal of Economic History* 29 (June 1969): 268–78; Paul G. E. Clemens, *The Atlantic Economy and Colonial Maryland's Eastern Shore: From Tobacco to Grain* (Ithaca: Cornell University Press, 1980), 82–83, 184; Lorena S. Walsh, "Plantation Management in the Chesapeake, 1620–1820," *Journal of Economic History* 39 (June 1989): 393–406.

67. On mixed-market agriculture in the Chesapeake, see Walsh, "Plantation Management in the Chesapeake," 393–406; Clemens, *From Tobacco to Grain,* chapter 6; Schlotterbeck, "Plantation and Farm," 57–58, 61–65. Richard Beeman touches on the subject in *The Evolution of the Southern Backcountry: A Case Study of Lunenburg County, Virginia, 1746–1832* (Philadelphia: University of Pennsylvania Press, 1984). The work of Allan Kulikoff is the most developed; see his *From British Peasants to Colonial American Farmers* (Chapel Hill: University of North Carolina Press, 2000); *The Agrarian Origins of American Capitalism* (Charlottesville: University Press of Virginia, 1992); *Tobacco and Slaves: The Development of Southern Cultures in the Chesapeake, 1680–1800* (Chapel Hill: University of North Carolina Press, 1986).

War of Independence). Tracking the Hessian fly has allowed us to see how the mid-Atlantic region's farmers, millers, and merchants confronted and managed an environmental and commercial crisis. At the same time, the insect invasion broadens our understanding of the workings of the transatlantic economy during the late eighteenth century. We need more studies that recover the lost connections between economic and environmental conditions.

Chapter Nine

The Panic of 1819 and the Political Economy of Sectionalism

The dialectical relationship between nationalism and sectionalism helped to shape the "Era of Good Feelings." Sectional interests might have stretched back to the particular settlement patterns and economic structures of the colonies, but there could be no deep-rooted *sectionalism,* a sense of sectional identity, until there was a nation to be a part of, and the process of nation building did not end with the ratification of the Constitution. A significant moment in that process occurred in 1815, when news of Andrew Jackson's remarkable victory against the British at New Orleans and the successful conclusion of America's second war of independence swept through the country, inspiring a wave of patriotic nationalist fervor. A new "Era of Good Feelings" had arrived, crowed one newspaper editor, eager to celebrate the collapse of a Federalist Party tainted by its opposition to the war. With the Republicans ascendant in national politics, the partisan rancor of the past could be put to rest.[1]

Historians who use the term "Era of Good Feelings" to describe the late 1810s and early 1820s understand its irony, for the superficial political unity of the age masked serious tensions. Congress, emboldened by postwar nationalism and confronted with very real problems, pursued an ambitious legislative agenda that thrust the federal government into the economic sphere in ways reminiscent of the early 1790s, when Alexander Hamilton had advanced his developmental policies. Congress created the Second Bank of the United States to bring stability to a shaky financial system, established a tariff to protect America's fledgling industries, and proposed but

I would like to thank John Larson, Donna Gabaccia, and Cathy Matson for comments on earlier drafts of this chapter.

1. Thomas P. Abernethy makes the point that there could be no sectionalism without nationalism; see *The South in the New Nation, 1789–1819* (Baton Rouge: Louisiana State University Press, 1961), 2.

failed to pass a program of extensive internal improvements to bind together an expanding nation. While politicians were promoting a nationalistic economic policy, John Marshall's Supreme Court was asserting the primacy of federal power and Congress was debating Missouri's bid for statehood. Each issue sparked controversy, provoking a backlash among those committed to limited government and strict constitutional construction and those looking after particular sectional interests. By the early 1820s the Republican consensus had fractured into democratic and national wings and sectional tensions had intensified. Those divisions would flower more fully in the coming decade, laying the foundation for the political conflicts of the Age of Jackson.[2]

Economic upheaval during the "Era of Good Feelings" sharpened those tensions and divisions. Peace brought the resumption of international trade, but it also created a speculative boom fueled by rising European demand for American agricultural exports, a flood of cheap imported manufactured goods, and a proliferation of banks and credit. That postwar bubble burst in 1818, as agricultural prices fell and as the Second Bank of the United States adopted a contractionary monetary policy, triggering a panic in 1819 that ushered in several years of hard times. The Panic of 1819 was the first major depression of the nineteenth century and it shattered the prosperity and confidence of the postwar years, shaking people up and pushing them to confront government policies in search of both the causes of and solutions to the crisis. Tariffs, specie, bank notes, bankruptcy, and stay laws all became fodder for popular debate, a discourse that often took sectional forms. William Hendricks, a member of the House from Indiana, wrote in 1821 that popular pressure on Congress had intensified because of the "pecuniary embarrassments of the times" and noted that *the interests and necessities of almost every section,* have found their way into the Hall, and have advocates

2. Countless works touch on various aspects of this period's history, but several are particularly effective in the totality of their coverage. See, for example, Frederick Jackson Turner, *Rise of the New West, 1819–1829* (1906; New York: Collier Books, 1962); George Dangerfield, *The Era of Good Feelings* (New York: Harcourt, Brace & World, 1952); and Robert H. Wiebe, *The Opening of American Society: From the Adoption of the Constitution to the Eve of Disunion* (New York: Knopf, 1984). On the connections between strict construction and southern sectionalism, see Norman K. Risjord, *The Old Republicans: Southern Conservatism in the Age of Jefferson* (New York: Columbia University Press, 1965); and Charles S. Sydnor, *The Development of Southern Sectionalism, 1819–1848* (Baton Rouge: Louisiana State University Press, 1948). On the controversies surrounding the Marshall Court, see Charles F. Hobson, *The Great Chief Justice: John Marshall and the Rule of Law* (Lawrence: University Press of Kansas, 1996); and Robert E. Shalhope, *John Taylor of Caroline: Pastoral Republican* (Columbia: University of South Carolina Press, 1980). On Missouri, see Don E. Fehrenbacher, *Sectional Crisis and Southern Constitutionalism* (Baton Rouge: Louisiana State University Press, 1995); William W. Freehling, *The Road to Disunion*, vol. 1, *Secessionists at Bay, 1776–1854* (New York: Oxford University Press, 1990); and Glover Moore, *The Missouri Controversy, 1819–1821* (Lexington: University Press of Kentucky, 1953). One of the best ways to get a feel for this period, albeit from a "high political" perspective, is to browse through James F. Hopkins, ed., *The Papers of Henry Clay* (Lexington: University Press of Kentucky, 1961) and Charles Francis Adams, ed., *Memoirs of John Quincy Adams, Comprising Portions of His Diary from 1795 to 1848* (1874–77; reprint, New York: AMS Press, 1970).

on the floor of the House of Representatives" (emphasis added).[3] Westerners railed against northeastern merchants and bankers as they watched specie drain from their region, while southerners in Virginia and the Carolinas cocked concerned ears northward at the increasing clamor for protective tariffs in the mid-Atlantic states. This heightened awareness of sectional interests and identities counterbalanced the nationalism of the age.

The sectional and political tensions of the "Era of Good Feelings" can only be understood within the context of the opportunities and hardships of the economic boom and bust, yet very little has been written about the Panic of 1819. The only monograph on the subject was published more than forty years ago.[4] Since then, scores of historians have explored the complex relationship between economic, social, and political change in the early Republic, but few have closely examined the central economic crisis of the period.[5] The speculative

3. William Hendrick, Indiana, February 28, 1821, in Nobel E. Cunningham Jr., *Circular Letters of Congressmen to Their Constituents, 1789–1829* (Chapel Hill: University of North Carolina Press, 1978), 3:1138.

4. Murray N. Rothbard, *The Panic of 1819: Reactions and Policies* (New York: AMS Press, 1962).

5. For older works on the panic, see Samuel Rezneck, "The Depression of 1819–1822: A Social History," *American Historical Review* 39 (October 1933): 28–47; Dorothy Dorsey, "The Panic of 1819 in Missouri," *Missouri Historical Review* 29 (January 1935): 79–91; Thomas Greer, "Economic and Social Effects of the Depression of 1819 in the Old Northwest," *Indiana Magazine of History* 44 (1948): 227–43; Thomas Bard Jones, "Legacy of Change: The Panic of 1819 and Debtor Relief Legislation in the Western States" (Ph.D. diss., Cornell University, 1968); and Vincent Francis Bonelli, "The Response of Public and Private Philanthropy to the Panic of 1819 in New York City" (Ph.D. diss., Fordham University, 1976). Several recent interpretations of the "market revolution" pay close attention to the panic. See Harry L. Watson, *Liberty and Power: The Politics of Jacksonian America* (New York: Noonday Press, 1990); Charles Sellers, *The Market Revolution: Jacksonian America, 1815–1846* (New York: Oxford University Press, 1991); Richard E. Ellis, "The Market Revolution and the Transformation of American Politics, 1801–1837," in *The Market Revolution in America: Social, Political, and Religious Expressions, 1800–1880,* ed. Melvyn Stokes and Stephen Conway (Charlottesville: University Press of Virginia, 1996); and Donald J. Ratcliffe, "The Crisis of Commercialization: National Political Alignments and the Market Revolution, 1819–1844," in Stokes and Conway, *Market Revolution in America.* For an examination of the economic culture of the panic, see Sarah A. Kidd, "The Search for Moral Order: The Panic of 1819 and the Culture of the Early American Republic," (Ph.D. diss., University of Missouri, Columbia, 2002). For studies of the impact of the panic on local and state economy and politics, see Daniel S. Dupre, *Transforming the Cotton Frontier: Madison County, Alabama, 1800–1840* (Baton Rouge: Louisiana State University Press, 1997); J. David Lehman, "Explaining Hard Times: Political Economy and the Panic of 1819 in Philadelphia," (Ph.D. diss., University of California, Los Angeles, 1992); Andrew R. L. Cayton, "The Fragmentation of 'A Great Family': The Panic of 1819 and the Rise of a Middling Interest in Boston, 1818–1822," in *New Perspectives on the Early Republic: Essays from the Journal of the Early Republic, 1981–1991,* ed. Ralph D. Gray and Michael A. Morrison (Urbana: University of Illinois Press, 1994); Gary L. Browne, "Baltimore and the Panic of 1819," in *Law, Society and Politics in Early Maryland,* ed. Aubrey C. Land (Baltimore: Johns Hopkins University Press, 1977); Janet A. Reisman, "Republican Revisions: Political Economy in New York After the Panic of 1819," in *New York and the Rise of American Capitalism,* ed. William Pencak and Conrad Wright (New York: New York Historical Society, 1988); Robert M. Blackson, "Pennsylvania Banks and the Panic of 1819: A Reinterpretation," *Journal of the Early Republic* 9 (Fall 1989): 335–58; Sandra F. VanBurkleo, "'The Paws of Banks': The Origins and Significance of Kentucky's Decision to Tax Federal Bankers, 1818–1820," *Journal of the Early Republic* 9 (Fall 1989): 457–87; Sandra F. VanBurkleo, "'That Our Pure Republican Principles Might Not

boom and the Panic of 1819 generated a voluminous discourse on the state of the nation's economy, including essays by political economists, newspaper editorials, congressional reports, government documents, politicians' speeches, polemical pamphlets, and memorials from citizens, each addressing in one way or another the intersection of the state and the economy. Through this largely informal literature of political economy one can view a people trying to make sense of the economic transformations of their age and, in the process, confronting the very debates over trade and banking that shaped the sectional animosities and political divisions of the "Era of Good Feelings."[6]

One congressman from Virginia, for example, applauded the personal sacrifice that had led to victory in the War of 1812 and looked to the future with optimism. Men had abandoned "their ploughs, shops, stores, and professions . . . [and] suddenly converted into soldiers, rushing to the field of battle," John Kerr wrote his constituents in February. But that sacrifice had been worthwhile, since America had "established a national character . . . and proved to the astonished world, that we are capable of self-government." Now peace would bring trade, and soldiers once again would become economic men. "Commerce will resume its wonted course; our cities and towns will swarm with merchandize; our flying canvass will whiten every sea, bearing the abundant productions of our prolific soil to every clime."[7] Here was the coupling of prosperity and patriotism so characteristic of the early postwar period; national honor won in the cypress swamps of Louisiana would be ratified and projected across the seas by the flow of imports and exports. Kerr looked ahead to future prosperity by harkening back to the glory days of prewar America, when international trade fueled national economic growth.

Economic prospects were gloomier six years later. Early in 1821 the House of Representatives' Committee on Manufactures issued a voluminous report examining what had gone wrong in a nation struck by a "burst of universal distress" following the Panic of 1819. After detailing the dire effects of the depression, the committee concluded that a free-trade policy that had flooded postwar America with cheap foreign merchandise was to blame. The problem

---

Wither': Kentucky's Relief Crisis and the Pursuit of 'Moral Justice,' 1818–1826," (Ph.D. diss., University of Minnesota, 1988); and Matthew Schoenbachler, "The Origins of Jacksonian Politics: Central Kentucky, 1790–1840," (Ph.D. diss., University of Kentucky, 1994). See also Edwin J. Perkins, "Langdon Cheves and the Panic of 1819: A Reassessment," *Journal of Economic History* 44 (June 1984): 455–61.

6. One recent work on popular economic thought, although primarily from a pre–War of 1812 perspective, is Cathy Matson, "Capitalizing Hope: Economic Thought and the Early National Economy," in *Wages of Independence: Capitalism in the Early American Republic*, ed. Paul A. Gilje (Madison, Wis.: Madison House, 1997), 117–36. An older work that is still useful is Joseph Dorfman, *The Economic Mind in American Civilization, 1606–1865* (New York: Viking, 1966). The best treatment of American political economists is Paul Conkin, *Prophets of Prosperity: America's First Political Economists* (Bloomington: Indiana University Press, 1980).

7. John Kerr, Virginia, February 22, 1815, in Cunningham, *Circular Letters,* 2:917–18.

was not just the damage done to the nation's fledgling manufactures but the financial consequences of an unequal balance of trade. Excessive British imports and diminished American exports during the depression led to a currency that "flows in a torrent-like stream beyond its jurisdiction never to return." Create a home market under a protective tariff, however, the committee argued, and both America's manufacturers and its banking system would benefit. Currency would become "a steady, gentle current, meandering through every occupation within the great circle of national industry, giving use and value to every production, [and] floating it to every market."[8] The committee rejected the trade relationships of the past, envisioning an "American System" that as yet did not exist.

Archibald D. Murphey, a North Carolina state legislator, also was concerned about the close relationship between trade and banking in the summer of 1821. The collapse of much of the nation's financial system in the Panic of 1819 left his state, along with most others outside New England, with rapidly depreciating bank notes at a time when many of North Carolina's citizens were struggling with debt. Farmers and merchants exchanged North Carolina's bank notes at a fraction of their value outside the state when purchasing supplies or paying debts. Those same notes could then be presented to the issuing banks to be redeemed in gold or silver coin, resulting in a drain of specie from the state. Murphey lobbied for inconvertible state notes that could not be redeemed in specie and thus would not travel to "distant markets," and for state funding of public works. The key to North Carolina's "permanent prosperity is to adopt a system of policy as will give us a home market. Our money will easily sustain its credit among its own citizens, and if we had markets at home it could not travel much abroad."[9] Stability, in trade and in finances, could come only by drawing close boundaries and generating an internal exchange of goods and notes bolstered by the confidence of local people.

The related issues of trade and banking were two of the most vital and contentious topics of postwar America. Those in search of scapegoats and remedies for the panic looked to the nation's trade relationship with Europe and to the instabilities of the financial system for answers, and argued about the relative merits of tariffs and free trade and about the nature of banking and money. Those debates, sharpened by the hard times of the depression, would come to define the political conflicts of the Jacksonian period.

These three examples deal with the possibilities and problems associated with exchange, which was intimately connected to questions of boundaries and identities. Kerr celebrated the establishment of "a national character" through warfare, but he clearly linked national honor and prosperity to the international flow of goods. The congressional committee, on the other hand, called for trade

---

8. "Protection to Manufactures," January 15, 1821, no. 609, 16th Cong., 2d sess., *American State Papers: Finance*, 3:595, 598.

9. Murphey to Colonel William Polk, July 24, 1821, cited in Rothbard, *Panic of 1819*, 64.

to travel the "great circle of national industry," binding occupations and sections together by sheltering them from the ill effects of trade with a hostile world. Murphey also sought to draw a protective boundary around "home," but to his mind danger lay not in England but in the state next door. Murphey offered a cautionary note to Kerr's eager anticipation of a resumption of America's place in the world of trade and the Committee on Manufactures' vision of a new American economy. From the perspective of North Carolina in the depths of the depression, "home" and "abroad" were defined by the state's borders. The flow of goods and bank notes or specie could reinforce an awareness of inter-dependence between sections or nations, blurring or extending boundary lines and softening narrow identities. But that same flow could accentuate differences or reinforce resentments, leading to a hardening of sectionalism or localism. A closer look at the causes of ·he Panic of 1819 and the discourse surrounding the crisis can help us better understand the relationship between trade and banking and the competing identities that defined the "Era of Good Feelings."

The conclusion of the War of 1812 sowed the seeds of future economic and cultural nationalism but also entangled the nation even deeper in interna-tional trade. For thirty years America had been oriented toward the Atlantic world in ways that brought both prosperity and political turmoil. The French Revolution and the Napoleonic Wars opened opportunities for American ship-ping and agricultural interests but also embroiled the nation in bitter conflicts, from the partisan warfare of the late 1790s to the embargo and war in 1812. That orientation began to shift in 1815. Popular reaction to the lopsided victory over the British in the Battle of New Orleans constituted a cultural version of that transition. Andrew Jackson's troops had blasted forth a second declaration of independence in January 1815 and, in the public's imagination, it was the very character of America itself that had defeated the most powerful army in the world. John William Ward's brilliant analysis of Jackson as a cultural symbol traces the ways in which the battle permeated national consciousness. He por-trays a society embracing traits once scorned, a society celebrating the skills and vigor of the crude "Hunters of Kentucky," frontiersmen at once of nature and conquerors of nature. After 1815, Ward argues, America was a nation that looked to the interior for its soul.[10]

Economic historians concerned with long-term trends reinforce Ward's portrait of postwar America and the significance of 1815 as at least the begin-ning of a turning point. The transition to an increasingly national economy reflected both new realities in America's trade relationship with Europe at the close of the Napoleonic Wars and new opportunities for economic development at home. The carrying trade and the repackaging of imports for reexport, which

10. John William Ward, *Andrew Jackson: Symbol for an Age* (New York: Oxford University Press, 1955).

had created tremendous profits before Jefferson's embargo and war, rose briefly but then fell as Europe settled into peace. Industrialization, transportation improvements, the opening of western lands to settlement, and the penetration of mercantile networks into the country's interior became increasingly important to American economic growth after 1815. The transition was not immediate, however. Manufacturing was slow to develop and limitations in transportation often left western settlers isolated, while agricultural exports, especially cotton, remained vitally important to American economic growth through the first half of the nineteenth century. But important changes in 1815 laid the groundwork for the eventual emergence of a national economy.[11]

The immediate effect of peace in 1815, however, was an even deeper entanglement in international trade. The transition to a peacetime economy in Europe took some time, and weather-related crop failures in 1815 and 1816 on the Continent intensified demands for American agricultural exports. As a consequence, prices paid for wheat and flour soared. Cotton, which made up 39 percent of the total value of exports between 1816 and 1820, was also in great demand once the pressures of war lifted. American farmers exported cotton valued at $17,529,000 in 1815 but reached new heights in 1818 with cotton exports worth $31,334,258, a jump that reflected rising prices far more than increased production.[12] As high-priced exports flowed out of America, imports flooded into the country, primarily British manufactured goods, cheap cotton fabrics from the East Indies, and tropical products from the West Indies. The value of imports, which had plummeted to a low of $12,967,659 in 1814, rose to $85,356,680 in 1815 and then jumped to a high of $151,448,644 the following year. Volume accounts for that astounding reversal, for import prices were actually falling— 15 percent from 1814 to 1815, 20 percent the following year, and another 15 percent from 1816 to 1817.[13]

Consumers prospering during the postwar trade boom appreciated the flood of cheap imports, but America's fledgling manufacturers struggled to stay afloat. The rate of factory incorporations makes clear the impact of the embargo, war, and peace on industrial development. In 1809 state legislatures incorporated 26 new factories, and the number of incorporations continued to rise each year, reaching 66 in 1813 and 128 in 1814. Most of these factories produced textiles,

11. Douglass C. North, *The Economic Growth of the United States, 1790–1860* (Englewood Cliffs, N.J.: Prentice-Hall, 1961), 66–67; Harold D. Woodman, "Economy from 1815 to 1895," in *Encyclopedia of American Economic History: Studies of the Principal Movement and Ideas,* ed. Glenn Porter (New York: Charles Scribner's Sons, 1980), 1:67; Jeremy Atack and Peter Passell, *A New Economic View of American History from Colonial Times to 1940,* 2d ed. (New York: W. W. Norton, 1994), 130; Wiebe, *Opening of American Society,* 147–51.

12. North, *Economic Growth of the United States,* 75, 233; Morton Rothstein, "Foreign Trade," in Porter, *Encyclopedia of American Economic History,* 252.

13. North, *Economic Growth of the United States,* 78–80, 228; Atack and Passell, *New Economic View of American History,* 130.

and they faced stiff competition as peacetime trade resumed. While 78 new factories were incorporated in 1815, that number dropped to 26 the following year, with only 28 starting up between 1817 and 1819.[14] John Kerr had eagerly awaited the day when "our cities and towns will swarm with merchandize" as evidence of the prosperity promised by peace. His Virginia constituents probably enjoyed the cheap and plentiful imports and almost certainly benefited from the soaring prices of agricultural commodities. But the manufacturers and workers of Massachusetts and especially of New York and Pennsylvania struggled amid the general prosperity. Playing upon the residual patriotism and Anglophobia of the war years, the manufacturing interest successfully lobbied Congress for the passage of a protective tariff in 1816.[15]

High export prices fueled prosperity after 1815, but so too did the proliferation of banks. The war years laid the groundwork for that expansion; in 1811 only eighty-eight banks had been chartered in the United States, but that figure had grown to 208 by the beginning of 1815. Many had issued notes far in excess of their gold and silver reserves, especially in the mid-Atlantic and southern states. New England's banks followed a more conservative policy of issuing notes, and that, coupled with government purchases of supplies from the region during the war, led to a draining of specie from the South and West to the Northeast. By 1814 most banks outside New England had suspended specie payments. Peace did not bring a solution to the problem; by the end of 1815, notes from 246 banks fluctuated wildly in value, complicating economic transactions.[16]

Congressional leaders, seeking a uniform and sound currency and a safe depository for government funds, turned in 1816 to the creation of a Second Bank of the United States. Seeking both financial stability and political unity, Congressman Lewis Williams of North Carolina supported the bank bill and predicted that it "will give us money of universal credit and circulation throughout the country" and "bind the states more closely together." Others agreed that the Bank of the United States could eradicate sectional inequities. Israel Pickens of North Carolina wrote that bank notes "vary in their value in different quarters from local and temporary causes: much depending on the relative balances of trade in between different sections," and contended that the Bank of the United States would solve that problem. Samuel Conner, a congressman from Massachusetts, identified his region as the principal victim of the postwar financial disorders. "While the middle and southern states paid their taxes in their

14. Atack and Passell, *New Economic View of American History,* 122.

15. George Dangerfield, *The Awakening of American Nationalism, 1815–1828* (New York: Harper and Row, 1965), 13–16; Atack and Passell, *New Economic View of American History,* 130–31.

16. Rothbard, *Panic of 1819,* 3–4, 7; Leon M. Schur, "The Second Bank of the United States and the Inflation After the War of 1812," *Journal of Political Economy* 68 (February 1960): 119. Bray Hammond, *Banks and Politics in America from the Revolution to the Civil War* (Princeton: Princeton University Press, 1957) remains the best comprehensive source on banking in early-Republic and antebellum America.

depreciated paper," he informed his constituents, "New England paid them in gold and silver, which is fifteen and twenty per cent. above the currency of Philadelphia or Baltimore." Even those who, like Isaac Thomas of Tennessee, believed banks to be "cancerous ulcers seated on the political body," turned to the Bank of the United States for relief. The chartered banks had "swallowed up the precious metals, [and] gorged the country with their notes," Thomas wrote, but a national bank, "by diffusing through the country an appreciated paper," would either "coerce the state banks to resume specie payments, or stifle the profits of their business."[17]

The Bank of the United States dashed those high hopes in its first years when it jumped on the inflationary bandwagon. Instead of demanding specie installments from stockholders to build its capital base, the national bank accepted promissory notes, especially from the directors and officers of the Philadelphia and Baltimore branches. By the beginning of 1818 the Bank of the United States had lent more than $41 million and had a total money issue of $23 million, with a specie reserve of only $2.5 million. Some of the state-chartered banks resumed specie redemption during this period, but their notes fluctuated in value and the national bank did not exert pressure to curtail the smaller banks' excessive note issue. Meanwhile the demand for credit and banking facilities grew, so that the 246 banks that had dotted the country at the end of 1815 had jumped to 392 by 1818.[18]

The rapid expansion of credit and overheated trade following the war sparked a speculative boom between 1816 and 1818. Settlers in the West borrowed heavily to purchase government land on credit, sure that either high crop prices would pay off their installments or newcomers would take it off their hands at a tidy profit. Merchants throughout the country overextended themselves in a rush to benefit from advantageous trade conditions and were aided in their efforts by the availability of bank credit. While manufacturers might have been struggling in 1817 and 1818, large numbers of Americans embraced the boom, driven by what one observer called "the almost universal ambition to get forward."[19]

But the prosperity of 1818 was built on fragile foundations that could not withstand increasing pressures in banking and trade. The flow of gold and silver abroad, both in payment for imports and to cover the Louisiana Purchase debt, was draining the specie reserves of the Bank of the United States. This problem, coupled with a congressional investigation into the corporation's

17. Lewis Williams, North Carolina, April 25, 1816, Israel Pickens, North Carolina, April 26, 1816, Samuel S. Conner, Massachusetts, April 22, 1816, and Isaac Thomas, Tennessee, April 30, 1816, in Cunningham, *Circular Letters,* 2:973–74, 976–78, 982, 995.

18. Hammond, *Banks and Politics in America,* 253–54; Rothbard, *Panic of 1819,* 8.

19. Quotation from *Niles' Weekly Register* cited in Gordon S. Wood, *The Radicalism of the American Revolution,* (New York: Knopf, 1992), 340.

fraudulent practices, persuaded the directorship to renounce profligacy and adopt a more conservative contractionary policy in the summer of 1818. Branches of the bank began redeeming their holdings of state bank notes to collect specie and also began to curtail demand liabilities, which declined from $22 million in the fall of 1818 to $12 million by January 1819. This policy saved the bank from ruin but put tremendous pressure on the smaller banks that were dangerously overextended, especially in the mid-Atlantic, southern, and western states. Many suspended specie payments over the next couple of years, leading to a depreciation of their notes.[20]

The collapse of the financial system came at a time when European demand for American agricultural products, especially wheat, flour, and cotton, was in a slump. Continental farmers had begun to recover from decades of war and several years of bad harvests, depressing demand for imported goods. Britain passed the Corn Laws, which imposed high tariffs on foreign grain and imposed restrictions on trade in the Caribbean, closing off other markets for American farmers. The total value of the nation's exports, which had been at a high of $93,281,133 in 1818, fell to $70,142,521 in 1819 and hit a low of $54,596,000 in 1821. Since production remained high, dramatic declines in prices account for the reduction in export values during the depression. Cotton, which had reached highs of 33 to 35 cents a pound in the Charleston market in 1818, fell to around 15 cents a pound in 1819.[21]

The monetary contraction and the fall in agricultural prices sent shock waves through the economy in the winter and spring of 1819, traveling from the seaboard to the interior along lines of credit. Merchants in the East and in the larger cities scrambled to liquidate their assets to cover debts owed to foreign creditors, and they in turn pressed smaller merchants and shopkeepers to the west and south for payment on merchandise sold on credit. Those small-scale merchants in the interior scrambled to stave off bankruptcy by pressuring their customers, usually farmers, to pay off their debts. But falling crop prices and the scarcity of specie or reputable bank notes made that difficult, forcing both merchants and farmers to face foreclosure and the sale of property. Frontier settlers were hit especially hard. Those who had purchased high-priced public land on credit during the boom time, when cotton and grain prices were high, were saddled with a tremendous debt and faced forfeiture of their land to the federal government. Manufacturers in New York and the mid-Atlantic states, already forced to compete with the heavy importation of foreign goods during the post-war boom, now had to contend with a tightened credit market and declining prices for their products. Many laid off workers, contributing to rising unemployment in the cities. Hard times persisted for several years. In some parts of

20. Rothbard, *Panic of 1819*, 11–13; Perkins, "Langdon Cheves and the Panic of 1819," 456–58.

21. North, *Economic Growth of the United States*, 233, 262; Rothstein, "Foreign Trade," 254.

the country, economic recovery began in 1821, but in others prosperity did not return until the mid-1820s.[22]

From an economic perspective, the Panic of 1819 appears relatively insignificant. Some historians believe that the disruptions of the postwar period led to a dramatic slowing of economic growth, perhaps even retrogression, compared to the prewar period, when shipping earnings stimulated the economy. Others suggest that the long-term impact of the panic on American economic growth was probably trivial, a momentary downturn in the fairly steady upward trend through the first half of the century. The crisis of 1819 seemed less severe than the depressions that followed the panics of 1837 and 1857. All three shared a pattern of speculative boom followed by financial bust, but economic production did not decline as much in the early 1820s as in later depressions, in part because such a large proportion of the labor force worked in agriculture.[23]

Placing the panic within that larger context helps us understand the fluctuations of economic development during the first half of the nineteenth century, but it obscures the impact of the financial crisis. Americans at the time did not live in a world of per capita real output, nor did they know that more severe and longer-lasting depressions lay ahead. What they understood was that the panic hurt every sector of the economy in virtually every region of the country and that its causes were complex and confusing. The panic mattered to Thomas Percy, a cotton planter in Alabama. He noted that on his last trip into the nearby town of Huntsville, "the great interests of the nation: the Spanish relations [and] the more momentous Missouri question . . . were not thought of or talked of by any one," because "every one had too much to occupy him in the deficiency of his own revenue." Percy concluded that it was best to stay away from town for a while, "for I shall be asked for money & it is what I have not got."[24] Those everyday efforts to scrape together financial resources, to dodge creditors, to find employment or to hold on to a farm all had political implications. John C. Calhoun worried about the "enormous numbers of persons utterly ruined" by the panic and feared that the "multitudes in deep distress" had created "a general mass of disaffection to the Government."[25] Exploring the point

22. For a description of the ways in which the panic filtered into a frontier community, see Dupre, *Transforming the Cotton Frontier*, 50–57. For employment figures in Philadelphia trades, see Lehman, "Explaining Hard Times," 286.

23. Two historians who emphasize the economic importance of the panic are George Rogers Taylor, *The Transportation Revolution, 1815–1860* (New York: Rinehart, 1951), and North, *Economic Growth of the United States*. On the debate over the pacing of economic growth in the first half of the nineteenth century, see Robert Gallman, "Economic Growth," in Porter, *Encyclopedia of American Economic History*, 1:133–50; and Thomas Weiss, "Economic Growth Before 1860: Revised Conjectures," in *American Economic Development in Historical Perspective*, ed. Thomas Weiss and Donald Schaefer (Stanford: Stanford University Press, 1994), 11–27.

24. Thomas Percy to John Williams Walker, February 8, 1820, cited in Dupre, *Transforming the Cotton Frontier*, 53.

25. Adams, *Memoirs of John Quincy Adams*, 5:128.

of view of those affected by the panic not only illuminates popular perceptions of economic change but also helps us understand the governmental policies that helped shape that change.

Historians have not ignored the panic, although it is understudied. A number of older historians, including Frederick Jackson Turner and George Dangerfield, recognized the importance of the panic as a pivotal point in American history that contributed to the fracturing of the Republican consensus along sectional and ideological lines. Murray Rothbard published the only monograph devoted to the Panic of 1819 back in 1962. The book is a useful resource because Rothbard closely examines, state by state, the wide range of debates in response to the panic, including those over monetary contraction or expansion, debtor relief and bankruptcy legislation, and protectionism. He captures the depth of the economic crisis and the ways in which it stirred up political ferment in the states, especially in the trans-Appalachian West, setting the stage for the emergence of the second party system.[26] Since the publication of his book, however, the early Republic has become a battleground, as historians argue about the relative strengths of republican and liberal ideology and the character of the "market revolution." While a number of recent historians place the panic within this broader context, few have focused much attention on the crisis itself. The discourse of both the postwar boom and the subsequent bust offer great opportunities for historians interested in understanding the broader political, cultural, and social impact of the economic transformations of the early nineteenth century.[27]

Two recent contributions to the debate offer opposing interpretations of the "market revolution" that closely parallel the boom-and-bust mentalities that characterized the "Era of Good Feelings," but each misreads the panic itself.

---

26. Turner, *Rise of the New West;* Dangerfield, *Era of Good Feelings;* Rothbard, *Panic of 1819.*

27. See note 5 for citations of works on the panic. The literature on republicanism, liberalism, and the "market revolution" is too voluminous to cite but some of the most important works are James Henretta, "Families and Farms: *Mentalité* in Pre-Industrial America," *William and Mary Quarterly,* 3d ser., 35 (January 1978): 3–32; Drew R. McCoy, *The Elusive Republic: Political Economy in Jeffersonian America* (Chapel Hill: University of North Carolina Press, 1980); Joyce Appleby, *Capitalism and a New Social Order: The Republican Vision of the 1790s* (New York: New York University Press, 1984); Christopher Clark, *The Roots of Rural Capitalism: Western Massachusetts, 1780–1860* (Ithaca: Cornell University Press, 1990); Winifred B. Rothenberg, *From Market-Places to a Market Economy: The Transformation of Rural Massachusetts, 1750–1850* (Chicago: University of Chicago Press, 1992); and James T. Kloppenberg, "The Virtues of Liberalism: Christianity, Republicanism, and Ethics in Early American Political Discourse," *Journal of American History* 74 (June 1987): 9–33. A number of historians have surveyed the field and attempted to summarize the debate in historiographical essays. See Daniel T. Rodgers, "Republicanism: The Career of a Concept," *Journal of American History* 79 (June 1992): 11–38; Michael Merrill, "Putting 'Capitalism' in Its Place: A Review of Recent Literature," *William and Mary Quarterly* 52 (April 1995): 315–26; Gordon S. Wood, "The Enemy Is Us: Democratic Capitalism in the Early Republic," *Journal of the Early Republic* 16 (Summer 1996): 294–340; and Paul A. Gilje, "The Rise of Capitalism in the Early Republic," *Journal of the Early Republic* 16 (Summer 1996): 159–81. For a useful overview and bibliography, see Paul E. Johnson, "The Market Revolution," in *Encyclopedia of American Social History,* ed. Mary Kupiec Cayton, Elliott J. Gorn, and Peter W. Williams (New York: Charles Scribner's Sons, 1993), 1:545–60.

Gordon Wood's depiction of the early Republic—a fluid and expansive society of entrepreneurial people emboldened by a sense of mastery—captures the exuberance of the postwar boom society. An older revolutionary generation still enamored of republican notions of civic virtue might lament the avarice that underlay the proliferation of banks and paper money, corporations and commerce, but ordinary Americans celebrated those keystones of capitalism as manifestations of opportunity, the foundation of democracy, according to Wood. Private passions, not the public sphere of government, generated that expansion, and it was a chaotic process. But a profound sense of optimism tempered that chaos, Wood argues, a belief that somehow the private pursuit of self-interest, magnified across the whole society, would create a kind of order in the midst of liberation.[28]

If Wood's capitalism was the brash optimism and opportunism of the boom, then the suffering and sharp political conflicts of the depression years belong to Charles Sellers's market revolution. For it was in the Panic of 1819, Sellers believes, that the true face of capitalism was revealed. Commerce and banking represented entrapment, not liberation and opportunity; they were the tools used by an increasingly powerful monied interest to strip away the independence of the producing class. The economic crisis brought that inherent conflict of the market revolution to a head, creating a democratic groundswell in opposition to, and not in concert with, capitalism.[29]

Both Wood and Sellers use the "Era of Good Feelings" to further their larger arguments and, in the process, obscure important aspects of the tumultuous economic changes of that brief period. Wood's early Republic was the culmination of a long process of transformation, both evolutionary and revolutionary. Seen from the perspective of colonial society, the bustling "common-man" capitalism after the War of 1812 did represent liberation from constraints, at least for some, and a flowering of liberalism in the fertile soil of revolutionary re publicanism. But Wood smoothes out the rough edges of that transition. For

28. Wood, *Radicalism of the American Revolution,* especially part 3. Wood emphasizes mastery in "The Significance of the Early Republic," in Gray and Morrison, *New Perspectives on the Early Republic,* touching on Americans' efforts to control and manipulate both their environment and their culture. But his tones shifts dramatically at the end. "[N]o one seemed in control of" the "new emerging society" that "seemed to be exploding in all directions, growing helter skelter." "People now felt themselves carried along in a stream, caught up in a process that was larger and more significant than any of the individuals involved in it" (19). See especially 16–19.

29. Sellers, *Market Revolution,* and "Capitalism and Democracy in American Historical Mythology," in Stokes and Conway, *Market Revolution in America,* 311–29. The debate between Wood and Sellers echoes earlier debates between consensus and Progressive historians over interpretations of the Age of Jackson. Wood's emphasis on the capitalistic generation of economic opportunity as a manifestation of democratization is reminiscent of Richard Hofstadter, "Andrew Jackson and the Rise of Liberal Capitalism," in *The American Political Tradition and the Men Who Made It* (New York: Vintage Books, 1948), while Sellers's stark depiction of class conflict is self-consciously modeled after Arthur M. Schlesinger Jr., *The Age of Jackson* (Boston: Little, Brown, 1945).

example, he jumps from the plausible assertion that postwar Americans had come to accept their "involvement in commerce and their pursuit of individual self-interest" to the dubious claim that "by the end of the second decade of the nineteenth century there were far fewer despairing lamentations over the chaotic and commercial state of American society."[30] Missing from his account is the Panic of 1819 and all of the complications associated with the collapse of the economic boom. There was, in fact, an outpouring of "despairing lamentations" that, while not directly challenging the nation's commercial nature, did excoriate the chaos that accompanied the market revolution.

Sellers emphasizes those lamentations, tracing the roots of Jacksonian conflict back to the hard times of the early 1820s, when economic crisis exposed to the producing classes the growing power of an emerging financial and industrial capitalism. Unlike Wood, Sellers pays a great deal of attention to the economic, social, and political repercussions of the panic and sheds welcome light on a neglected topic. But Sellers draws too neat a division between the "people" and the speculating agents of the market revolution, ignoring the popular embrace of opportunity during the postwar boom. Countless ordinary Americans "speculated" whenever they bought shares in banks, took out loans, and purchased more land than they needed at higher prices than were prudent. They gambled that prosperity would continue, that bank dividends would be high, that cotton crops would pay off their debts, that settlers eager to cash in on the boom would snatch up their excess acreage. The Panic of 1819 was so devastating precisely because so many people had gambled on prosperity in one way or another during the boom and had lost out with the economic collapse.

What Americans confronted in the years following the War of 1812 was the realization that exchange was not always equal, that interdependency often meant dependency, and that the value of goods or money was ever shifting. That realization was not new, of course. Planters were aware of the fluctuations of cotton prices before the war, just as merchants and politicians were aware of specie flows and the balance of trade. What was new, though, in 1819 was the widespread belief that the excesses and instabilities of an artificial economy had created a depression that had penetrated virtually every sector of American society. The shock of the panic shook Americans' faith in the liberal promise of the Revolution: that unfettered freedom of exchange would bring prosperity and a rough equality of opportunity.[31] Many reacted by searching for scapegoats, ferreting out the artificial constraints and privileges that had corrupted the natural

---

30. Wood, *Radicalism of the American Revolution,* 327.

31. John Lauritz Larson drew my attention to this deification of a "natural" economy in America's reaction to British mercantile policy at the time of the Revolution in his comments on my paper, "The Panic of 1819 and the Political Transformations of the Era of Good Feelings," at the 1998 conference of the Society for Historians of the Early American Republic. See Matson, "Capitalizing Hope," 117–19.

system. How could there be a depression, the Committee on Manufactures asked in 1821, when "the sea, the forest, the earth, yield their abundance; the labor of man is rewarded; pestilence, famine, or war commit no ravages; no calamity has visited the people; peace smiles on us; plenty blesses the land?" Since nature was not to blame, "some deep and radical error" must have brought the "general distress" upon the country. Not surprisingly, the committee identified that error as a free-trade policy that had worked when Europe's nations were at war with one another but proved a dangerous anomaly in a post-Napoleonic world.[32] Others looked to the speculative boom following the war and blamed banks and their "rag" notes, or the character flaws of a people addicted to luxury and seduced by "golden dreams of an artificial fortune."[33] As they moved beyond blame and began to search for solutions to the depression, the central question Americans confronted was what was real, what was natural, what was solid in an economy that had proved to be so hollow.

When observers looked back to the postwar boom for clues as to what had gone wrong, their investigations led invariably to the problems of banking and trade. The common theme, whether couched in the dispassionate words of a government report or the fiery language of an economic jeremiad, was that the very artificiality of banking or trade had distorted and corrupted the natural order of the economy, leading to a false prosperity that ultimately led to depression. One anonymous essayist from New York, writing under the pen name "Seventy-Six," claimed that the liberal dispensation of bank notes during the boom had produced only "an apparent activity in business" that turned out to be "fictitious and deceptive, resembling the hectic heat of a consuming disease, not the genial warmth of substantial health." It was the public's "implicit faith in the bubbles of banking" that had kept the system afloat, but that faith had been betrayed, leaving "wise and honest Americans . . . embracing phantoms for realities, and running mad in schemes of refinement, tastes, pleasures, wealth and power, by the soul [sic] aid of the hocus pocus." Banking was like an alchemist's experiment that had gone awry, turning productive real wealth into imaginary wealth. America in 1819, "Seventy-Six" claimed, was a land of "paper gold, and paper land, and paper houses, and paper revenues, and paper government."[34] The New York convention of "the friends of national industry" lobbied in 1819 against the auction sales and government credit on the payment of duties that they claimed facilitated the flow of cheap imports into the country. American

32. "Protection to Manufactures," January 15, 1821, no. 609, 16th Cong., 2d sess., *American State Papers: Finance,* 3:595.

33. Pennsylvania Senate, "Report of the Committee appointed on the subject of the present distressed and embarrassed state of the Commonwealth," January 29, 1820, reprinted in Samuel Hazard, ed., *The Register of Pennsylvania* (August 1829), 4:138.

34. "Seventy-Six," *Cause of, and Cure for Hard Times: Containing a Definition of the Attributes and Qualities Indispensable in Money as a Medium of Commerce; and also an Investigation into the Effects of the Banking System* (New York, 1819), 4:57.

merchants were being replaced by "foreign merchants and manufacturers, or desperate speculators" who were "impelled" by their "necessities" to create new markets where none had existed before. Those foreign merchants sold "large quantities of silk, woollen, cotton, and other goods" at auction that were "less than the usual length, deficient in breadth, of a flimsy texture . . . yet so well dressed . . . that they generally escape detection till they reach the consumer, who too late discovers their inferiority."[35]

The problems of banking and trade also contributed to the emerging tensions between sectionalism and nationalism in the "Era of Good Feelings." Western antipathy toward the mercantile and financial establishment of the Northeast intensified during the hard times of the depression and found a focus in hostility toward the Bank of the United States. The continued flood of cheap imports spurred manufacturing interests, located primarily in the mid-Atlantic and northwestern states, to call in the early 1820s for higher protective tariffs and reforms in credit and auction laws. Those protectionists articulated a nationalist vision that was anathema to advocates of free trade and states' rights. No neat sectional line divided the two sides of the trade debate. Mercantile interests in the Northeast, especially in New England, opposed tariffs, while portions of the South voiced support for protection, and states'-rights localists suspicious of the nationalists' economic platform could be found in many parts of the country. But the fusion of free trade and states' rights was strongest in the South, where both an export economy and slavery faced the challenges of protectionism and the Missouri controversy. The Panic of 1819 and the problems of banking and trade heightened awareness of sectional interests, and this played a major role in the fracturing of the Republican Party into "national" and "democratic" wings in the early 1820s. Glance through Henry Clay's papers or John Quincy Adams's memoirs, as those two men handicapped the candidates jockeying for position as the election of 1824 approached, and it is evident just how much sectional identity had permeated American political consciousness. The connections between the economic dislocations of the period and the growing political strife over banking and trade deserve more attention from historians.[36]

As sectional and occupational interests fought over banking and trade during the "Era of Good Feelings," they confronted the central problem of exchange. The flow of bank notes, specie, and trade goods lay at the heart of American conceptions of prosperity and liberty and provoked questions over degrees of freedom and restriction, over what was natural and what was artificial in the economy, and over boundaries. A close reading of the discourse generated by the speculative boom and panic reveals a people coming to terms with

35. "Protection to Manufactures," December 20, 1819, House of Representatives, 16th Cong., 1st sess., *American State Papers, Finance*, 3:442.

36. Adams, *Memoirs of John Quincy Adams;* Hopkins, *Papers of Henry Clay.* See also Wiebe, *Opening of American Society,* 194–233.

sectional identities in an age of increasing economic interdependence, which in turn moved them toward different conceptions of nationalism.

The West was a troubling presence in the early years of the Republic, a reminder that centrifugal forces could threaten national union. Speculators and settlers pushed west beyond the limits of the federal government's reach, encountering the dangerous presence of powerful Indian nations and their European allies on the borders. Adventurers and politicians such as William Blount, Aaron Burr, and James Wilkinson plotted separatist schemes in the 1790s and early 1800s, manipulating settlers' fears of Indian attacks, their discontent over uncertain access to the mouth of the Mississippi River, and their alienation from the eastern seaboard and the federal government. That was especially true in the region south of the Ohio River. But the War of 1812 silenced threats of fragmentation in the southwest. Control over the Mississippi River, the displacement of European powers on the borders, the cession to the federal government of large tracts of Indian land with the promise of more to come, and a surge of patriotism all helped to solidify the nation's hold over the West. Andrew Jackson played a central role in harnessing to nationalist purposes the same expansionist impulses that had threatened fragmentation, first in his victory over the Creeks and then in his defeat of the British at New Orleans in 1815.[37]

The Panic of 1819 and the banking crisis awakened some of that old alienation and suspicion as specie flowed eastward and westerners fell more heavily into debt. Turner and Dangerfield, among others, argued that western sectional identity was forged in opposition to the eastern merchants and the Bank of the United States to whom westerners were indebted. During the depression their resentment boiled over, as western politicians lashed out against the national bank's monetary contraction, leading Thomas Hart Benton to his famous characterization of the institution as a "monster" that threatened to devour the property of the West.[38] Orramel Johnston of Kentucky agreed. He argued that the unwillingness of the Bank of the United States to part with specie was the result of "personal enmity, malice or prejudice," and that the institution, working on behalf of the eastern states, had "used their utmost endeavors to crush us in our infancy." Indiana congressman William Hendricks criticized the bank in general terms in 1819 for failing to achieve "the ends for which it was created" and for enriching "its directors and stock-jobbers, at the expense of others," but he also argued that its "depressing and monopolizing policy, in the western

37. Andrew R. L. Cayton, "'Separate Interests' and the Nation-State: The Washington Administration and the Origins of Regionalism in the Trans-Appalachian West," *Journal of American History* 79 (June 1992): 38–67; John Lauritz Larson, "Jefferson's Union and the Problem of Internal Improvements," in *Jeffersonian Legacies,* ed. Peter S. Onuf (Charlottesville: University Press of Virginia, 1993); Robert V. Remini, *Andrew Jackson and the Course of American Empire, 1767–1821* (New York: Harper and Row, 1977).

38. Dangerfield, *Era of Good Feelings,* 185; Turner, *Rise of the New West,* 106–7.

country, has borne, and is bearing, peculiarly hard on the agricultural interests of that country."[39]

Both Johnston and Hendricks, after detailing the West's bleak situation during the panic, looked ahead to a more promising future. Population was shifting westward, Johnston noted, and, with "the accumulation of steam boats in our waters," trade also would shift to "a western direction." That economic power would bring a "political preponderance" in the West's favor and "that degraded dependence and that servile submission to our eastern [brethren?] will be forever destroyed." Hendricks offered a similar vision of the future in a less vengeful tone. "The spirit of enterprize, in all parts of the Union, seems to be attracted by the fertility of our soil, and the alluring prospects of the western country." The federal government played a major role in that process. Hendricks applauded the rapid acquisition of Indian land, the "vigorous enterprize of the War Department" in pushing "our arms and military operations to the vicinity of the Rocky Mountains," and government efforts to establish a fort at the mouth of the Columbia River "and a chain of posts . . . to connect that point, with the mouth of the Missouri." All of this made possible the opening of "an extensive theatre . . . for the genius and industry of immigrants from the northern and southern States."[40]

Confidence in the bright future of the West cast new light on the relationship between section and nation. Johnston's hostility toward the East and his prophecy of future economic and political power in the West were rooted, it seems, in an intense awareness of sectional boundaries. The West might have represented the future of the nation, but the region would not lose its sectional identity; instead, it would use its newfound power to dominate the East. Hendricks's letter reveals a different kind of sectional awareness. Like Johnston, he believed that the future belonged to the West, but a West with permeable boundaries that would be shaped in large part by the actions of the federal government. Hendricks depicted an expansive West stretching to the Pacific, linked by settlers and trade like the chain of posts he envisioned dotting the rugged landscape from the Columbia to the Missouri. His was a western nationalism that, while rooted in sectional awareness, seemed to look to a future when his section would become the nation itself.

A series of letters between Treasury Secretary William Crawford and a number of western bankers during the depression years offers another layer of complication to the concept of sectionalism in the West. Two sources of alienation threatened government interests in the West after the panic: the debt owed

39. Orramel Johnston, "Chartered Rag Light, or an Impartial View of the Banking System in the United States," (Maysville, Ky., 1818), 7; William Hendricks, Indiana, February 15, 1819, in Cunningham, *Circular Letters*, 3:1046–47.

40. Johnston, "Chartered Rag Light," 6; Hendricks, February 15, 1819, in Cunningham, *Circular Letters*, 3:1046–47.

by purchasers of the public lands and the scarcity of currency. Congress moved quickly to offer relief to those who had bought high-priced land and began to reform its land policies, while Crawford scrambled to do what he could to ease pressures on debtors in the West. Since specie was so scarce, the treasury moved to identify the banks that continued to redeem in specie so that their notes could be accepted as payment in government land offices. Crawford kept up a steady correspondence with those banks' presidents, which offers a wonderful window into the financial pressures of the West.[41]

Nathaniel Ewing, president of the Bank of Vincennes in Indiana, wrote Crawford that "the present situation of the western people is distressing; they cannot get for their produce one dollar of the kind of money that will be received in payment of their debts due to the United States." The problem was that the western branches of the Bank of the United States "issue but few notes, and those few are immediately collected by the merchants and sent to the east-ward." Isolation prevented farmers from "bringing the products of their labor to its proper market," where sufficient notes acceptable to the government could be had.[42] John Sering, cashier of the Farmers' and Mechanics' Bank of Madison, Indiana, complained that his bank had "continued the payment of specie until its notes, with all western paper, were refused in payment of land; which . . . caused a general depreciation of all western paper."[43] The policies of the Bank of the United States and the national government, along with regional isolation, spurred resentment in the West and a sense of sectional grievance.

If the currency crisis of the panic highlighted the fact that the West was not fully integrated into a national trade and capital market, it also reinforced divisions within the West itself. As bank after bank in the region suspended specie payments, they confronted two problems. First, failures in one bank put enormous pressure on those still redeeming in specie, making it clear just how dependent each bank was on the notes of other western banks. The president of the Bank of Missouri wrote to Crawford in 1819 that, while they "would will-ingly receive the notes of any institution which might be named by you . . . they are too well acquainted with the situation of the western banks generally to jeopardize this institution on their responsibility." The president singled out the nearby Bank of Edwardsville, Illinois, arguing that "their paper is received with distrust, even in their own neighborhood, and passed from hand to hand as soon as possible," and thus his bank could not "give it our confidence."[44] Two years later, the president of the Bank of Edwardsville explained why his bank was

41. Malcolm J. Rohrbough, *The Land Office Business: The Settlement and Administration of American Public Lands, 1789–1837* (New York: Oxford University Press, 1968), 143.

42. Nathaniel Ewing to William Crawford, January 9, 1819, in "Banks in Which the Receipts from the Public Lands are Deposited," House of Representatives, February 15, 1822, no. 637, 17th Cong., 1st sess., *American State Papers: Finance*, 3:735.

43. John Sering to William Crawford, June 14, 1820, ibid., 739.

44. Aug. Chouteau to William Crawford, August 9, 1819, ibid., 749.

suspending specie payments. "Owing to the failure of the Bank of Missouri, and the great alarm produced in this and the adjoining sections of the country, an incessant pressure was made on this bank."[45] When Tennessee's banks suspended specie payments, their notes proved especially troublesome to north Alabama, according to Leroy Pope, president of the Planters' and Merchants' Bank of Huntsville. Eastern merchants "collected their Tennessee debts in Tennessee paper, which was then exchanged at a great discount for ours, with which they drew the specie, unless we supplied them with eastern funds."[46] A series of public meetings were convened in Huntsville in the fall of 1820 "to take into consideration the propriety of rejecting or receiving" Tennessee notes "in payment of debts and for the present crop of Cotton."[47] Competition and suspicion within the region may have undermined sectional solidarity.

Popular hostility was leveled at western banks and the Bank of the United States alike. When times were hard and debts due, the refusal of banks to redeem farmers' notes in specie was particularly galling to many. Local banks, and not just the Bank of the United States or eastern merchants, could become symbols of the monied powers, who, in many people's eyes, manipulated the economy and had caused the panic. Jesse Bledsoe attacked the banks and paper money in a speech to the Kentucky legislature. He spoke for many who believed that banks controlled the economy through their notes and could "inundate the country at one time, and parch it with drought at another," all with "a view to their own interest only."[48] While the banking problems of the West might have reinforced regional resentment toward the eastern financial and mercantile interests, they also exposed fault lines within the section itself.

The debate over tariffs and trade also complicated tensions between sectional interests and nationalist ideology. Both sides of the debate sought to identify the source of corruption in an economy that had failed to bring the prosperity and equality promised by the natural connections of unfettered exchange. Protectionists identified that force as foreign merchants and manufacturers and their imported commodities, which led them to an ardent defense of national interests. Free-trade advocates believed that the corrupting force lay in the abuses of government power represented by the tariff, which led them to emphasize the preservation of sectional interests. Both sides, however, had to grapple with the relationship between section and nation as they articulated their positions. Tariff supporters were strongest in the mid-Atlantic, northwest, and border states of the South in the early 1820s, regions that had dynamic economies based on interdependent agricultural, commercial, and manufacturing

---

45. Ben. Stephenson to William Crawford, September 26, 1821, ibid., 744.
46. Leroy Pope to William Crawford, January 21, 1819, and June 21, 1820, ibid., 762, 765–66.
47. *Alabama Republican,* September 22, 1820. See Dupre, *Transforming the Cotton Frontier,* 67–69.
48. Jesse Bledsoe, "The Speech of Jesse Bledsoe, Esq., on the Resolutions Proposed by Him, Concerning Banks" (Lexington, Ky., 1819), 20. See also Dupre, *Transforming the Cotton Frontier,* 75–97.

enterprises. This was the microcosm for their vision of a home market of distinct sections bound together by mutual dependence. Free traders defended localism and individual freedoms from the perils of national consolidation, but they offered up their own version of an expansive and powerful America. Ultimately, protectionists abandoned the revolutionary ideal of unfettered exchange for a new conception of a "natural" economy based on unlocking America's resources. The opponents of the tariff held to the old ideal, convinced that their liberties, both economic and political, and prosperity depended upon a restoration of free trade.

Protectionists often introduced the problem of trade by juxtaposing the nation's natural assets, which seemed to promise unparalleled prosperity, with the reality of depression. Henry Clay believed that the foundation of American prosperity was intact in 1824; "the land, fertile . . . as ever, yields to the industrious cultivator, in boundless profusion, its accustomed fruits, its rich treasures," while the people's "vigor" remained "unimpaired." What, then, caused "the diminished exports of native products . . . the depressed and reduced state of our foreign navigation . . . [and] unthreshed crops of grain, perishing in our barns"? Clay's answer was that for too long "we have shaped our industry, our navigation, and our commerce, in reference to an extraordinary war in Europe and to foreign markets, which no longer exist."[49] Mathew Carey, one of the most ardent advocates of economic nationalism, called the long period of profitable trade during the Napoleonic Wars a "fatal delusion," and almost gleefully noted that the plummeting agricultural prices during the panic were waking Americans from those "deceptious 'day dreams.'"[50] The Panic of 1819 gave protectionists an opportunity to expand their appeals to the depressed agricultural sector of the economy.

The conclusion of the Napoleonic Wars altered America's relationship to the rest of the world. One effect was simply the increased competition that came with peace. John W. Taylor, congressman from Saratoga, New York, described the depressed conditions of agriculture in a letter to his constituents in 1824 and used the opportunity to advocate a home market. The end of the war, he pointed out, had led to a change "in the condition of Europe, by which a million of men were converted from consumers and destroyers into producers of provisions," which in turn led to a decline in demand for American agricultural goods.[51] But peace also brought new restrictions, such as the closing of the West Indian trade and the passage of the Corn Laws excluding America grain from England, that made a mockery of the concept of free trade.[52]

49. Henry Clay, "Speech on Tariff," March 30–31, 1824, in Hopkins, *Papers of Henry Clay*, 3:684–86. See also Mathew Carey's address in *Niles' Weekly Register*, April 17, 1819, 137.

50. *Niles' Weekly Register*, June 5, 1819, 253.

51. John W. Taylor, New York, June 4, 1824, in Cunningham, *Circular Letters*, 3:1235.

52. See, for example, Congressman Ingham's speech in favor of the tariff in *Annals of Congress*, March 1816, 14th Cong., 1st sess., 1241; and "Protection to Manufactures," January 15, 1821, no. 609, 16th Cong., 2d sess., *American State Papers: Finance*, 3:606.

The principal concern of protectionists was the flow of cheap manufactured goods from abroad in the years following the war. They described an
import market as dangerously unfettered and at the mercy of foreign manipulations. England intended "to crush the infant, and as yet immature, establishments in this country" with "a flood of goods, at reduced prices," one group of
petitioners argued in 1815.[53] The House Committee of Commerce and Manufactures in 1816 believed that "foreign manufacturers and merchants" would use
"all the powers of ingenuity . . . whatever art can devise, and capital can accom-
plish, to prevent the American manufacturing establishments from striking root
and flourishing in their rich and native soil."[54] Government policies of permitting auction sales and giving credit for payment of duties aided foreign efforts
to stifle American industry. A group of merchants in New York City believed
"that our laws operate to give fugitive commercial agents advantages in this
country, which . . . transfers the trade of our country into the hands of transi-
tory strangers." Those merchants practiced "foreign frauds" by shipping goods
invoiced at low prices to lessen their taxes and then selling them to other agents
using the true, higher invoices. New practices such as auction sales worked to
the disadvantage of the "fair merchant," who built up "a long course of honor-
able dealing" only to be outmaneuvered by "strangers, bound by no ties to this
country, who bear none of its burdens, who perform no civil duties, nor any
service in peace or war," yet "are enabled to monopolize our money and our
markets."[55]

The complaints against foreign merchants and manufacturers reflected
unease over the corrupting influence of the imported goods themselves, which
were usually undersold on the American market. The seductive nature of the
commodities is evident in the complaint of American manufacturers that most
imports "are more alluring by their fashion than their use." Because consumers
were drawn to the "novelty" of the imports, which were often depicted as flashy
but poorly made, "a very great proportion of our wealth goes abroad for the
allurements which foreigners present to us."[56] Protectionists warned against
specie drains, the collapse of fledgling industries, and the inability to produce
necessities. But they also argued that the very nature of foreign trade would
erode national values. "By a too frequent open and unrestricted intercourse with
foreign nations, we imbibe their manners, contract their vices, give into their
luxuries, and lose that Republican simplicity, on which our government is based,"

53. "Prohibition of the Importation of Coarse Cotton Fabrics," Senate, December 13, 1815,
no. 455, 14th Cong., 1st sess., *American State Papers: Finance,* 3:34.
54. "Protection to Manufacturers of Cotton Fabrics," February 13, 1816, no. 469, 14th
Cong., 1st sess., *American State Papers: Finance,* 3:83.
55. "Protection to the Manufacturing and Mercantile Interests," House of Representatives,
February 4, 1817, no. 501, 14th Cong., 2d sess., *American State Papers: Finance,* 3:168.
56. "Protection to Manufacturers of Woollen Fabrics," House of Representatives, March 6,
1816, no. 476, 14th Cong., 1st sess., *American State Papers: Finance,* 3:105–6.

Congressman John Scott of Missouri argued in 1824.[57] Bank notes, in all their flimsiness and fluctuating values, came to represent the speciousness of a speculative economy driven by the hot air of credit. Imports, protectionists argued, symbolized a corrupting foreign influence that was invading the nation.

The seduction of imports bound Americans to foreign merchants and manufacturers, and this dependence could prove dangerous, protectionists argued. Baltimore's merchants called for the payment of duties in cash instead of credit in 1820 and offered an assessment of the damaging impact of imports. Like settlers who might have been seduced by easy credit and high cotton or grain prices into buying overpriced land in 1818, merchants lured by the prosperity and credit on duties bought an "immense overstock of foreign merchandise," which "soon becomes pressed, from the superabundance, into the interior—generally on extended credits." The cycle repeated itself in the interior, where merchants were "enabled to offer their merchandise on the same or more alluring credit, almost at the door of every consumer." The end result of this oversupply built on credit was consumers who, "neglecting to improve the advantages which nature has placed around them, continue to supply themselves out of the foreign stock, until debt and embarrassment have arrested the procedure." This left a chain of dependency, as "the interior of the country now stands largely indebted to the merchants of the seaport towns, while the latter are scarcely less in debt to foreign countries."[58]

Protectionists did not deny that a "natural" economy built upon the free exchange of goods would lead to prosperity and equal opportunities; they simply denied that foreign trade, in its postwar condition, was natural. European wars, the postwar restrictions, and foreign manipulations of credit and sale had placed America in an artificial world of dependency and debt.

By defining the enemy as foreigners, the protectionists took one big step toward creating a national identity. When they turned from the dangers across the Atlantic to look inward at the nation itself, their vision took on continental proportions. This was the foundation of their conception of a home market. Under the protection of a tariff, the Committee on Manufactures in 1821 claimed, trade would be "drawn to a mighty empire with a population of various habits and pursuits, embracing all the varieties of the temperate climates, fitted to the supply of all our wants." This empire was "in itself a continent," filled with "resources as yet not tried or developed" that would be "capable of furnishing boundless employment to industry and enterprise."[59] Here was the foundation of the protectionists' nationalism: the belief that the scale and resources of the

57. John Scott, Missouri, July 14, 1824 in Cunningham, *Circular Letters,* 3:1260–61.

58. "Payment of Duties in Cash," January 5, 1820, House of Representatives, 16th Cong., 1st sess., no. 565, *American State Papers: Finance,* 3:449–50.

59. "Protection to Manufactures," January 15, 1821, no. 609, 16th Cong., 2d sess., *American State Papers: Finance,* 3:616.

country could sustain an independent economy free from the fluctuations of foreign trade.

But vast stretches of territory and diversity of resources could bring conflict, division of interests, sectionalism, and fragmentation: the collapse of empire. The Committee on Manufactures admitted that "ours is a union of confederated nations" and noted that trade within the country, given "its great distance, the variety of its products, and articles of exchange," might well "be called foreign commerce." The committee countered the arguments of those who claimed that a home market was impractical and visionary by linking the character of internal and external trade. "The extent of water communication between the remoter parts is equal to the space which separates us from Europe and the West Indies," they argued, and then asked what difference there was "between the sugar of Louisiana and of Cuba; the lead of Missouri or of England."[60] Daniel Raymond, the political economist most friendly to the cause of protection, declared that the "nation is a UNITY."[61] The committee members undoubtedly agreed, at least in the political realm. But in making a case for the development of a home market, the committee came face to face with the diversity of sectional interests; what it proposed was the liberation of those distinct interests to compete freely in America, not a melding of sections into one national whole.

If Louisiana, Missouri, and other far-flung corners of the nation were as distant and diverse from each other as foreign countries, then what was to hold America together? Internal trade, the protectionists answered. Tariffs and internal improvements would create a home market, simultaneously allowing the full fruition of sectional interests and creating ties between the sections. The Committee of Commerce and Manufactures in 1816, for example, argued that sectional distinctions were natural and depended on "the climate, the population, the habits of the people, and the nature of its soil." Trade, "promoted and facilitated by roads and canals," would help erase the "prejudices, which are generated by distance," and give "the Union . . . strength and solidity."[62] Congressman David Trimble of Kentucky declared that "the perpetuity of the Union" depended on "cheap and easy intercourse, and active endless trade among the States."[63] Other expressions of protectionism hinted at the transforming powers of trade and seemed to suggest that sectional distinction could change or be muted within a home market. Daniel P. Cook of Illinois argued that "internal commerce . . . will create in each section, new interests in, and attachments to, every other section of our common country." As "local prejudices . . . subside . . .

60. Ibid.

61. Raymond, "Thoughts on Political Economy," 366.

62. "Protection to the Manufacturers of Cotton Fabrics," February 13, 1816, no. 469, 14th Cong., 1st sess., *American State Papers: Finance,* 3:83. See John Lauritz Larson, *Internal Improvement: National Public Works and the Promise of Popular Government in the Early United States* (Chapel Hill: University of North Carolina Press, 2001) for a discussion of the movement for internal improvements.

63. David Trimble, Kentucky, May 20, 1824, in Cunningham, *Circular Letters,* 3:1224.

we shall become bound together as one people, by the golden chords of interest and affection."[64] Tariffs would protect the nation as a whole, while the internal flow of trade goods would allow sections to remain true to their natural economic proclivities and foster mutual dependence within the nation.

The protectionists' vision of foreign corruption gave them a strong sense of national boundaries, within which they could give free rein to sectional distinctions. But the opponents of tariffs saw the dangers of internal corruption, and this sense of division made it difficult to reconcile section and nation. The danger facing the country during the panic was not foreign imports or even economic distress but the manipulation of those concerns by a new breed of capitalists eager to garner government privileges. The United Agricultural Society of Virginia, a coalition of country agricultural societies, mocked the rhetoric of hand-wringing protectionist memorials by stating, "we design not to harass our representatives with high-wrought pictures of distress which their wisdom could not have anticipated, and cannot remove." The panic was "inevitable" and "incurable by legislative interposition." The Virginia society located the root cause in the "transition from war to peace" and remained "convinced that our distress will be but temporary."[65] John Taylor of Caroline, in his response to the Committee on Manufactures report in 1821, noted that the government "will be implored in the names of good faith, of humanity, of honour, and of other virtues" to impose a protective tariff. But that would only lead to "abuse, monopoly, exclusive privilege, and extravagance" and intensify the transfer of property from the producing classes to capitalists.[66] The Virginia Agricultural Society of Fredericksburg pointedly began their antitariff petition in 1820 with a statement of "true republican principles" rather than a description of economic distress. They reminded Congress "that hostility . . . to partial taxation, exclusive privileges, and monopolies created by law, was the primary cause of our glorious and ever-memorable revolution."[67] To Taylor and other advocates of free trade, the enemy lay within, in a government too eager to flex its muscles and too willing to grant privileges to a rising aristocracy of manufacturers. Combined, they threatened the revolutionary promise of free and unfettered economic exchange.

Opponents of tariffs frequently used nature to draw connections between occupations or interests and sections in their petitions and essays. Both sides of the tariff debates paid homage to the great triumvirate of American occupations. "Agriculture, commerce and manufacturing are the three component parts of national industry," John Rhea told his constituents back home in

64. Daniel P. Cook, Illinois, May 30, 1824, ibid., 1229.

65. "Remonstrance Against Increase of Duties on Imports," House of Representatives, January 17, 1820, no. 570, 16th Cong., 1st sess., *American State Papers: Finance,* 3:459.

66. John Taylor, *Tyranny Unmasked,* ed. F. Thornton Miller (Indianapolis: Liberty Fund, 1992), 83.

67. "Remonstrance Against an Increase of Duties on Imports," House of Representatives, January 3, 1820, no. 564, 16th Cong., 1st sess., *American State Papers: Finance,* 3:447.

Tennessee. While "each is to be encouraged in proportion to the aid it gives to national industry," Rhea made clear that "agriculture is the principal" upon which "the other two are bottomed."[68] Nature, of course, played an important role in the distribution of those occupations. A group of Philadelphia merchants pointed out that "the natural diversities of soils and climates, and the artificial varieties of manners, habits, customs, are far better regulators of supply and demand than the wisest legislators can possibly contrive."[69] Sectionalism rooted in nature became a common point among southern tariff opponents. George Tucker of Virginia argued in 1824 that "the southern states, from their sparse population, from their laboring class being principally slaves, and their exclusive devotion to agriculture, are unfitted for engaging in manufactures."[70]

Belief in the natural foundation of sectional identity gave potency to a variety of free-trade objections to the tariff. It reinforced the sense that privileges granted to one particular interest group necessarily flowed to one particular section. Charleston's citizens argued that "injustice" of the tariff "becomes doubly great" because it did not just "transfer . . . property among the individuals of a particular division of territory . . . but some entire districts are absolutely impoverished, while others are exclusively enriched."[71] The sectional emphasis of tariff opponents also made it possible for them to portray the nationalism of protectionists as unnatural. George Tucker feared that acceptance of a tariff would force sections to "become melted down into one nation."[72] Taylor claimed that the Committee on Manufactures "endeavour to hide the effects of their policy to classes and individuals, by kneading up all of them into one mass called a nation. . . . Having created this imaginary one and indivisible being, more valuable and wonderful than the philosopher's stone, they conclude that its interest must also be one and indivisible."[73] Finally, tariff opponents argued that protectionism and the creation of a home market would violate nature by forcing occupations upon people. Accept the tariff, the congressional Committee on Agriculture argued in 1821, and "We must drive our laborers from the fields, from the beauties and bounties of nature, to those dismal and demoralizing abodes, where they sink into hopeless stupidity and penury."[74] Virginia's free-trade advocates put it simply when they argued that the true aim of protectionists was

68. John Rhea, Tennessee, May 8, 1820, in Cunningham, *Circular Letters,* 3:1116.

69. "Remonstrance Against an Increase of Duties on Imports," Senate, November 27, 1820, no. 597, 16th Cong., 2d sess., *American State Papers: Finance,* 3:545.

70. George Tucker, Virginia, June 9, 1824, in Cunningham, *Circular Letters,* 3:1244. See also Charleston's "Remonstrance Against an Increase of Duties on Imports," Senate, December 8, 1820, no. 600, 16th Cong., 2d sess., *American State Papers: Finance,* 3:565.

71. "Remonstrance Against an Increase of Duties on Imports," Senate, December 8, 1820, no. 600, 16th Cong., 2d sess., *American State Papers: Finance,* 3:563.

72. Tucker, June 9, 1824, in Cunningham, *Circular Letters,* 3:1246.

73. Taylor, *Tyranny Unmasked,* 16–17.

74. "Objections to an Increase of Duties on Imports," House of Representatives, February 2, 1821, no. 613, 16th Cong., 2d sess., *American State Papers: Finance,* 3:654.

to control agricultural production by turning farmers into factory workers. "In plain English, the hardy, independent sons of our forests and our fields are called on to consent to be starved into weavers and button-makers."[75]

The sectional emphasis of the tariff opponents would seem to leave little room for any expressions of nationalism, but their devotion to a Jeffersonian notion of "empire of liberty" forced them to articulate a national vision. Agriculture, they argued, was not just another sectional interest but the foundation of the nation. The Agricultural Society of Roanoke, Virginia, argued that in a country "like ours, reaching to every clime, and embracing every soil, with a population thinly scattered over it, agriculture is the occupation to which its inhabitants naturally look."[76] John Rhea concluded the letter to his Tennessee constituents criticizing the tariff with an optimistic prediction. "Agricultural industry is hastening its progress to the most remote regions of the west. A productive land invites cultivation, and promises a rich reward to industry."[77] Nature elevated agriculture above the other great occupations of the age and so too did the revolutionary founders. "It was once a favorite doctrine with the first republican politicians, that this country was destined to be agricultural," Isaac Thomas of Tennessee wrote in 1816.[78] Free-trade advocates positioned themselves as defenders of national virtue and the legacy of the Revolution in both their attacks on the abuses of governmental power and their protection of agricultural interests.

Free traders also offered a vigorous challenge to the protectionists' idea of a home market. To advocates of the free exchange of agricultural goods for merchandise, especially those who remembered the heyday of American shipping before the embargo and war, the prospect of tariffs and internal trade smacked of isolationism. "The nations of the earth compose one family; mutual intercourse promotes mutual interest, strengthens friendship, and enlarges the sphere of science, morality and religion," John Rhea wrote in 1821. The glories of international cooperation and advancement might have motivated free-trade advocates like Rhea, but so too did nationalism. He called the isolationism of the protectionists "a Chinese policy" that would lead "to misery and barbarism."[79] China had closed itself off from the world and become a model of impotency in the eyes of tariff opponents, especially in contrast to the power America projected into the world through overseas trade. "Compare the timid slave creeping through shallows in his clumsy junk," a group of Virginians wrote, "with the American seaman 'among the tumbling mountains of ice of the arctic circle,

75. "Remonstrance Against an Increase of Duties on Imports," Senate, December 18, 1820, no. 603, 16th Cong., 2d sess., ibid., 578.

76. "Remonstrance Against an Increase of Duties on Imports," Senate, December 22, 1820, no. 604, 16th Cong., 2d sess., ibid., 579.

77. John Rhea, Tennessee, May 8, 1820, in Cunningham, Circular Letters, 3:1121.

78. Isaac Thomas, Tennessee, April 30, 1816, ibid., 2:996.

79. John Rhea, Tennessee, March 5, 1821, ibid., 3:1143–44.

penetrating to the antipodes, and engaged under the frozen serpent of the south.'"[80] Philadelphia's merchants asked, "Can our hardy, magnanimous, and dauntless seamen, whose pursuits have heretofore exposed them to the perils of every ocean, to the vicissitudes of every clime, and enured them to that constant regimen and discipline so well calculated to fit them for all the purposes of nautical life—can *such men* . . . be converted into a set of skulking, profligate smugglers, or of sailors confined solely to the coasting trade?"[81]

Protectionists and free-trade advocates offered different visions of how best to restore a natural economy that had spun out of control in the years following the War of 1812. The tariff would create a protective wall around the nation, its supporters argued, directing capital and economic energies inward to unlock the full potential of the country's resources. Internal trade, facilitated through internal improvements, would bind sections together through exchange and allow them to retain the distinct identities of economic interests provided by nature. Free traders would open national boundaries, secure in the knowledge that unfettered trade would *naturally* promote the interests of section and nation. Their position reflected an optimistic belief in the power of America's natural resources. "The exchange of raw cotton . . . for manufactures makes Europe dependent on America, rather than America on Europe," antitariff Bostonians argued. "Ask the planter of the south which of the two is the dependent, himself or the Manchester spinner!"[82]

Many of the problems of the postwar boom and bust revolved around the issue of flow, whether of currency or goods, so it is no surprise that metaphors of water and channels dominate the writing of the period. John Williams Walker, an Alabama planter, learned of a friend's bankruptcy during the panic and feared for his own financial security. "I tremble for myself and my friends, whose heads are still above water. Some are already sunk and gone. Others are tottering—and a breach overwhelms them."[83] Jesse Bledsoe of Tennessee likened the bankers who brought the panic to "River Gods, who preside over the stream, [and] can inundate the country at one time, and parch it with drought at another."[84] Whether a flood sent by a wrathful God or a river manipulated by a powerful and corrupt monied elite, these representations are apt symbols of the sense of impotence wrought by the panic and the confusion over what was natural in an ever-shifting economy. Americans confronting the fact that the

80. "Remonstrance Against Increase of Duties on Imports," House of Representatives, January 17, 1820, no. 570, 16th Cong., 1st sess., *American State Papers: Finance*, 3:460.

81. "Remonstrance Against an Increase of Duties on Imports," Senate, November 27, 1820, no. 597, 16th Cong., 2d sess., ibid., 3:544.

82. "Remonstrance Against an Increase of Duties on Imports," House of Representatives, February 9, 1824, no. 695, 18th Cong., 1st sess., ibid., 4:469.

83. John Williams Walker to Larkin Newby, January 2, 1820, cited in Dupre, *Transforming the Cotton Frontier*, 60.

84. "Speech of Jesse Bledsoe," 20.

flow of goods or currency could be damaging in their fluctuations sought to regain a sense of mastery by restoring that flow to a "natural," beneficial state. But they disagreed on how best to achieve that goal.

Free-trade advocates like John Taylor sought to restore the revolutionary ideal of unfettered exchange. They repeatedly denigrated the tariff for forcing capital and human industry out of their natural channels. A "national surplus, like a river, can only be formed by the streamlets of individual surpluses," Taylor argued. "If these rills are diverted into other channels, the river becomes dry." Any effort to control the free exercise of individual self-interest threatened the prosperity of the entire country, free traders believed, because national wealth was simply the aggregate of individual wealth. In fact, it was the impulse to exchange "necessaries, conveniences, and especially luxuries" that generated economic growth. Taylor called that impulse the "moral steam-engine," and argued that, if left free, "its force will be sufficient to drive our commerce, our wealth, and prosperity along, in spite of all the little foreign currents . . . which may endeavour to impede them." The logic of that idea led to permeable boundaries. Why draw protective walls around a nation when its very path to prosperity and freedom was the accumulation of countless exchanges made by individuals with the rest of the world? Trust the "invisible hand" of the market, free traders urged, the myriad calculations determined by local circumstances and individual interests, to generate and channel the flow of the economy.[85]

What role did nature play in this conception of free trade? According to Taylor, nature organized "the division of agricultural labours" in order "to diffuse and equalize her blessings." Like other free-trade advocates, Taylor looked simultaneously inward and outward from his country. "Seas and rivers transfuse" the blessings of nature "throughout the world" by facilitating trade, but the United States had particular natural advantages. "Look at the Mississippi and its waters. Do we not read in this spacious map 'here are to be mutual markets?' Are not such markets already established?" Here was the juxtaposition of trade and nature. Just as the "invisible hand" of the market worked only when left alone, so too did nature grant her blessings when left untouched. The Mississippi had already created markets; agricultural labor simply had to settle the interior to take advantage of what existed. Hard times came when capitalists and ambitious politicians tampered with nature and impeded unfettered exchange, free traders argued. What was necessary was a restoration of mastery through synchronicity; if left alone, the self-interest of individuals and the blessings of nature would flow together in one stream.[86]

Protectionists were not so sure that nature could work wonders alone. Could the flow of goods be trusted when it had swelled to a flood following the

85. Taylor, *Tyranny Unmasked,* 94, 188–89.
86. Ibid., 24.

war? One congressman noted in 1816 that the tariff's critics want "to let industry pursue its natural channels," but that he preferred "to straighten and clear away the obstructions from the channels." That doctrine was part of a larger impulse to improve nature through the ingenuity, capital, and labor of man under governmental direction. "When a farmer desires to irrigate his grounds," the congressman continued, "he diverts a stream of water from its natural channel . . . and surely none will pretend that it would be better to permit these valuable streams to find their way through zigzag natural channels to the ocean, than to be thus employed for the comfort and happiness of man."[87]

In 1824 Henry Clay compared a nation without manufacturing to a keelboat "combatting the rapid torrent of the Mississippi." Despite the strength and commitment of her crew, the keelboat was mastered by the river. "How slow does the [keelboat] ascend, hugging the sinuousities of the shore, pushed on by her hardy and exposed crew, now throwing themselves in vigorous concert on their oars, and then seizing the pendant boughs of over-hanging trees; she seems hardly to move." But a nation with a manufacturing base was a steamboat "laden with the riches of all quarters of the world, with a crowd of gay, cheerful, and protected passengers, now dashing into the midst of the current, or gliding through the eddies near the shore!" This boat was master of its environment. "Nature herself seems to survey, with astonishment, the passing wonder . . . in silent submission."[88] Here was an optimistic image of controlled energy, of ingenuity conquering space for the purposes of commerce and human happiness. This vision of nation over nature, which came to be called the "American System," increasingly would alarm free traders, especially southerners enmeshed in an agricultural export economy, in the years to come.

The economic upheavals of the "Era of Good Feelings" offer a number of opportunities for further historical exploration, in part because they intersect with so many vital historiographical fields. Frederick Jackson Turner suggested that the Panic of 1819 contributed "to the forces of unrest and democratic change" in the country.[89] Since Turner's day a vast historiographical debate has emerged between historians who emphasize the persistence into the nineteenth century of republican ideals of statesmanship and civic virtue and republican fears of economic, political, and moral corruption, on the one hand, and those who stress the early development of a liberal culture that accepted individual pursuit of economic opportunity, interest-group politics, and populist styles of electioneering.[90]

87. *Annals of Congress*, March, 1816, 14th Cong., 1st sess. (Washington, D.C.: Gales and Seaton, 1834–56), 1244.

88. Clay, "Speech on Tariff," March 30–31, 1824, in Hopkins, *Papers of Henry Clay*, 3:711.

89. Turner, *Rise of the New West*, 113. For two more modern assessments of the relationship between the panic and democratization, see Ellis, "Market Revolution," and Ratcliffe, "Crisis of Commercialization," 177–81.

90. For descriptions of new styles of electioneering, see Alan Taylor, "'The Art of Hook & Snivey': Political Culture in Upstate New York During the 1790s," *Journal of American History* 79 (March

Did the Panic of 1819 contribute to republican fears of unchecked economic power? Did the virulent antibank sentiment in some regions and the demagoguery of politicians in the wake of the panic play a role in the democratization of the political culture? Governmental policies are another area worth investigating. Tariffs, internal improvements, and public land policy all underwent dramatic transformations during the "Era of Good Feelings," and no doubt the central economic crisis of the age shaped the debates.[91] State politics remains the most promising field of exploration during this period between the collapse of the first party system and the coalescence of the Jacksonian parties, since public efforts to shape economic change and transform political culture took place primarily at the state level.[92] A better understanding of the panic itself, especially the ways in which it traveled from abroad and across the nation, and its impact on particular communities and sectors of the economy, would contribute to our knowledge of the "market revolution." Finally, while excellent work has been done on the experience and meaning of debt in the 1790s and the Jacksonian period and beyond, little is understood about the intervening decades.[93] Individuals' experiences and their perceptions of the economic crisis—the causes of the panic, the meaning of debt and economic failure, the tensions between values of independence and the realities of economic interdependence—influenced political ideologies and policies in the 1820s. The Panic of 1819 offers historians a great opportunity to bridge the gaps between economic, political, and social history.

1993): 1371–96; Daniel S. Dupre, "Barbecues and Pledges: Electioneering and the Rise of Democratic Politics in Antebellum Alabama," *Journal of Southern History* 60 (August 1994): 479–512; and Dupre, *Transforming the Cotton Frontier,* 172–203.

91. Some recent works on those topics include James L. Huston, "Virtue Besieged: Virtue, Equality, and the General Welfare in the Tariff Debates of the 1820s," *Journal of the Early Republic* 14 (Winter 1994): 523–47; Larson, *Internal Improvement;* and Daniel Feller, *The Public Lands in Jacksonian Politics* (Madison: University of Wisconsin Press, 1984).

92. Wiebe argues that both popular anger at the hard times and political leaders' efforts to find solutions to the depression led to "a reshaping of the structure of political authority" on the state level. See *Opening of American Society,* 154–55.

93. Bruce H. Mann, *Republic of Debtors: Bankruptcy in the Age of American Independence* (Cambridge: Harvard University Press, 2002); Edward J. Balleisen, *Navigating Failure: Bankruptcy and Commercial Society in Antebellum America* (Chapel Hill: University of North Carolina Press, 2001). See also Scott Sandage, "Deadbeats, Drunkards, and Dreamers: A Cultural History of Failure in America, 1819–1893," (Ph.D. diss., Rutgers University, 1995).

Chapter Ten

Toward a Social History of the Corporation: Shareholding in Pennsylvania, 1800–1840

JOHN MAJEWSKI

On February 5, 1810, a large-scale melee broke out in west Philadelphia. Such disorder was common enough in America's preindustrial cities, which often seethed with political discontent and economic tension. But this melee did not involve violence between haughty Federalists and Republican plebs, or protests against the rising price of bread and other provisions, or labor disputes between journeymen workers and their entrepreneurial employers. The fracas instead centered on the ability of ordinary Americans to buy bank stock. Hundreds of angry men, eager to invest in the newly organized Mechanics' Bank of Philadelphia, went home empty-handed when the company's initial offering of twenty-five thousand shares sold out in a few hours.[1] Such intense popular interest in bank stock, as French visitor Michel Chevalier observed in 1839, became commonplace throughout America in the early nineteenth century: "In France, we queue up at the doors of the theaters; but in the United States, this year, lines of deeply anxious people form at the doors of those special places where the books for subscription to bank stock are deposited."[2]

Few investors, however, lined up at the doors to purchase stock in the Chesapeake and Delaware Canal. The canal, started

I would like to thank Lisa Jacobson for many useful comments, as well as participants of the Von Gremp economic history seminar and participants in the PEAES conference in 2001. John Larson, Cathy Matson, Richard Sylla, and Richard Wright provided particularly helpful comments. Stacy Hoffman, Shannon Magruder, Valerie Palmer, Ian Wienner, and Gina Zondorak provided excellent research support.

1. Kim T. Phillips, "Democrats of the Old School in the Era of Good Feelings," *Pennsylvania Magazine of History and Biography* (July 1971): 366–67. The bank had been chartered by the legislature in March of 1809. *Acts of the General Assembly of the Commonwealth of Pennsylvania,* session 1808–9 (Philadelphia: John Bioren, 1809), 43–51.

2. Chevalier quoted in Michel Chevalier, "Speculation in Land, Railroads, and Banks," in *Ideology and Power in the Age of Jackson,* ed. Edwin C. Rozwenc (New York: Anchor Books, 1964), 26.

in 1803, had been moribund for almost two decades when the publicist and political economist Mathew Carey took up its cause. He launched a successful movement to reinvigorate the company, embarking on a campaign to sell $300,000
worth of stock to private investors. Unlike the Mechanics' Bank, selling stock in
the canal company necessitated a lengthy and arduous public relations campaign.
Carey and other supporters of the enterprise held public meetings, published
circulars, wrote exhortatory newspaper editorials, organized ward committees,
and solicited prominent capitalists. After five weeks of hard work, Carey noted
with satisfaction that his promotional campaign had sold $360,000 worth of
shares to private investors. More than four hundred of the investors purchased
only one or two shares.[3]

The stories of how the Mechanics' Bank and the Chesapeake and
Delaware Canal raised capital represent an important opportunity for historians
of early American economic development. A large and growing literature on the
economic, social, and political impact of what has been labeled the "market revolution" has made surprisingly little effort to understand how ordinary Americans either embraced or rejected new opportunities for corporate shareholding.
Economic historians have fruitfully investigated the emergence of increasingly
sophisticated capital markets in the first half of the nineteenth century, but have
only recently begun to focus on the issue of stock ownership.[4] Scholars working in this vein sometimes assume that popular participation in stockholding
increased as improvements in transportation and communication made markets
more efficient—an assumption that ignores how political attitudes and civic
values could shape the culture of stock ownership.[5] Another literature, focused
primarily on the social history of the market revolution, asserts that an ill-
defined group of "capitalists" financed most early corporations. Such assumptions fit well with arguments that the market revolution created widespread
anxiety and political conflict. A long line of scholarship, in fact, has stressed
that nineteenth-century republican ideology frequently criticized corporations
as vehicles of corruption and privilege. Such political hostility, historians have

3. Ralph D. Gray, *The National Waterway: A History of the Chesapeake and Delaware Canal,
1769–1985*, 2d ed. (Urbana: University of Illinois Press, 1989), 35–42.

4. Howard Bodenhorn's otherwise excellent synthesis, *A History of Banking in Antebellum
America: Financial Markets and Economic Development in an Era of Nation-Building* (New York: Cambridge
University Press, 2000), ignores the issue of shareholding. Other work gives much greater attention to
the issue but fails to fully develop the social and cultural context of corporate shareholding. See, for
example, Richard Sylla, "U.S. Securities Markets and the Banking System, 1790–1840," *Federal Reserve
Bank of St. Louis Review* 80 (May–June 1998): 89–90; Robert E. Wright, "Bank Ownership and Lending Patterns in New York and Pennsylvania, 1781–1831," *Business History Review* 73 (Spring 1999),
40–60; and Robert E. Wright, *Origins of Commercial Banking in America, 1750–1800* (Lanham, Md.: Rowman and Littlefield, 2001).

5. The increasing efficiency of early U.S. capital markets is a prominent theme of Robert
E. Wright's *The Wealth of Nations Rediscovered: Integration and Expansion in American Financial Markets,
1780–1850* (New York: Cambridge University Press, 2002).

sometimes implied, must have meant that relatively few Americans owned corporate stock.[6]

The evidence here suggests that, at least in Pennsylvania, ordinary Americans owned far more shares in corporations than historians might expect. Analysis of shareholding lists filed in the official records of the Pennsylvania state government indicates that more than thirty-eight thousand individuals purchased stock in state banks, turnpikes, and toll bridges between 1800 and 1821. Thousands more probably purchased shares in canal and navigation companies, but the records are too incomplete for systematic study. Linking the long lists of shareholders to tax lists and city directories shows that that farmers, artisans, and retailers—hardly the occupations historians traditionally identify with corporate investment—readily responded to the new investment opportunities.[7] In many respects, the increase in stock ownership reflected policy decisions of the Pennsylvania state legislature, which consciously sought to "democratize" the early corporation by broadening the base of investors. A broad pool of investors not only allowed Pennsylvania's corporations to tap the savings of ordinary households, it also undermined political resistance to the corporation. It became more difficult to paint corporations as vehicles of privilege and aristocracy when many households owned shares.

The stories of companies such as the Mechanics' Bank and the Chesapeake and Delaware Canal reveal much more than a large number of eager investors. These two companies also reveal two fundamentally different investment dynamics. One was fundamentally speculative, the other focused on broader developmental goals. Investors eagerly snapped up bank stock because they believed that dividends would be large and share appreciation great. Such speculative investment reached a crescendo in 1814, when some twenty thousand Pennsylvanians purchased stock in forty-two newly chartered banks. Whereas the directors of these banks needed only to announce the time and location of stock offerings, promoters of transportation companies focused on the long-term importance of their enterprises. Carey's campaign for the Chesapeake and Delaware Canal, for example, focused on public spirit, not speculative profit. As one newspaper supporter of the canal wrote, "Every property holder, nay, every individual permanently resident here is deeply interested in promoting

---

6. This literature is synthesized in Charles Sellers, *The Market Revolution: Jacksonian America, 1815–1846* (New York: Oxford University Press, 1991), and Harry L. Watson, *Liberty and Power: The Politics of Jacksonian America* (New York: Noonday Press, 1990). For related interpretations specific to Pennsylvania, please see Kim T. Phillips, "William Duane, Philadelphia's Democratic Republicans, and the Origins of Modern Politics," *Pennsylvania Magazine of History and Biography* 101 (July 1977): 365–87; Kim T. Phillips, "The Pennsylvania Origins of the Jackson Movement," *Political Science Quarterly* 91 (Fall 1976): 489–508; Phillips, "Democrats of the Old School," 363–82.

7. The large number of small shareholders in Pennsylvania helps explain why the United States led the world in proportion of financial assets held as corporate stock. See Sylla, "U.S. Securities Markets and the Banking System," 90.

this useful undertaking; and all, that have two hundred dollars to spare, ought cheerfully to give it their positive aid and support."[8] Such language hardly intimated that speculative profits that might lead to street scuffles or long lines of eager investors.

The differing investment patterns in banking and transportation companies—speculative booms in banking, civic-minded investment in transportation companies—help historians better understand the politics of the market revolution. The intense popular interest in bank stock grated against republican sensibilities that detested rampant speculation, stockjobbers, and moneyed men. The long lines of investors, at least to republican minds, could be interpreted as symptomatic of the widespread loss of virtue and an unchecked mob mentality. Republican criticisms of bank investment took on great political significance when many banks failed in the Panic of 1819. Burned by the failure of so many banks, the legislature restricted the number of bank charters over the next decade. The great popularity of bank stock, ironically enough, contributed to a populist backlash against banks themselves, which ultimately limited the number of banks and bank shareholders.

Transportation companies, by contrast, enjoyed broader political support. Investment in this type of enterprise was portrayed not as speculation gone mad but rather as a public-spirited contribution on behalf of the community. The investment strategy behind most transportation companies—giving up short-term profits for long-term development—fit well with republican rhetoric that stressed virtuous sacrifice on behalf of the public good. That boosters could plausibly argue that transportation enterprises would benefit all property holders in a given community only added to their inherently consensual nature. Even as late as the 1850s giant companies such as the Pennsylvania Railroad had an aura of public-spiritedness that provided considerable political capital. Investment in transportation companies suggests that republican ideology and commercial expansion could be quite compatible. Pennsylvanians could readily debate banking issues within an older republican discourse suspicious of speculation, debt, and paper money, and at the same time enthusiastically endorse turnpikes, bridges, and other "public-spirited" enterprises.

The stock boom that would do so much to shape Pennsylvanians' attitudes toward banks originated, ironically, in the Pennsylvania's legislature's restrictive chartering practices. Between 1784 and 1813 the state chartered only four banks, all of them located in Philadelphia. Like most banks in the early national era, these companies raised capital from the sale of shares and then lent that capital to merchants, manufacturers, and others who needed loans. With a legal monopoly on the business of Philadelphia and the rest of the state, the four Philadelphia banks usually paid handsome dividends ranging from 8 to 12

8. Gray, *National Waterway*, 39.

percent per year. Bank shares were therefore marketable assets that could be readily sold in secondary markets. The liquidity of bank shares allowed shareholders to use them as collateral; instead of mortgaging a farm or shop to raise money, borrowers could use bank stock to secure a loan.[9] No wonder that investors would readily riot to purchase bank stock. Philadelphia banks had an enviable reputation as safe, profitable enterprises that faced little competition.

Why did the legislature adopt such a strong antichartering stance? Part of the answer lies in republican political ideology. Some Jeffersonian Democrats strongly opposed all banks as privileged corporations that fostered a "moneyed aristocracy" bent on subverting republican liberty. The "moneyed aristocracy" not only benefited from government privilege but also swindled their customers into taking bank notes of uncertain value. Too much paper money would invariably invite unhealthy speculation and lead to financial chaos.[10] Federalists believed that such charges were demagogic, but they also feared that the proliferation of too many banks would lead to an irresponsible inflation of the money supply. Federalists thus tended to support a few large banks, controlled by men of prominence and distinction who could make loans to a relatively small number of elite merchants and manufacturers.[11] Jeffersonians often opposed such institutions, but both sides could agree that restricting the number of banks was a good idea.

The ideological opposition to new banks dovetailed nicely with the economic incentives of powerful interests. Established banks feared that competition might drain their supply of specie and lower their hefty profits. As Anna Schwartz has documented, "a new institution was looked upon as a threat to the security of entrenched banking interests."[12] Those entrenched banking interests found a particularly warm reception in the state legislature, which had its own motives for restricting banking charters. In return for granting bank charters, the state government expected to receive bank shares that would pay handsome dividends. It too feared that too many banks would lower dividend payments from existing banks, which had become an important part of state revenues. Dividends from bank stock, in fact, provided approximately 40 percent of the

9. Wright, "Bank Ownership and Lending Patterns," 48. Wright shows persuasively that those who invested in mid-Atlantic banks expected "attractive yields" on their stock, which could be sold in flourishing secondary markets.

10. For Jefferson's view of banknotes, see Donald F. Swanson, "Bank-Notes Will Be but as Oak Leaves: Thomas Jefferson on Paper Money," *Virginia Magazine of History and Biography* 101 (January 1993): 37–52.

11. Drew R. McCoy, *The Elusive Republic: Political Economy in Jeffersonian America* (New York: W. W. Norton, for the Institute for Early American History and Culture, 1980), 147–48; Janet A. Riesman, "Money, Credit, and Federalist Political Economy," in *Beyond Confederation: Origins of the Constitution and American National Identity,* ed. Richard Beeman et al. (Chapel Hill: University of North Carolina Press, 1987), 131–32, 146–50.

12. Anna Schwartz, "The Beginning of Competitive Banking in Philadelphia, 1782–1809," *Journal of Political Economy* 55 (October 1947): 417.

state's total revenues between 1795 and 1825.[13] No governor or legislator wanted to be responsible for killing the state's golden goose.

The ideological and economic forces that kept a lid on bank charters, however powerful, could not keep popular discontent from boiling over. The Pennsylvania economy had a long and strikingly successful history of working with paper money, especially in the colonial period. The general loan office, for example, provided tens of thousands of farmers and other propertied households with subsidized mortgages for much of the colonial period. The loan office issued paper bills that successfully circulated as cash, easing the shortage of specie that was particularly severe in more remote regions of the colony.[14] The abolition of the general loan office, combined with the stringent limitation on bank charters, created a vacuum that private notes, branches of the four Philadelphia banks, and unchartered banking organizations could not adequately fill in the post-revolutionary era. Those most likely to support paper—and hence more banks—were farmers, artisans, and tradesmen of the interior, which formed a substantial segment of the Jeffersonian coalition. The Jeffersonian coalition would thus have to make a hard choice: either give up its republican distrust of all moneyed institutions or face the prospect of losing the main elements of its natural constituency. Historian Kim T. Phillips has usefully labeled the competing ideological factions "Old School Democrats" (to denote its traditional Jeffersonian distrust of banks) and the "New School," which was more open to banks, paper money, and credit.[15]

The War of 1812 brought these simmering ideological contradictions to the surface of Pennsylvania politics. When Pennsylvania became a staging ground for western troops and supplies, demands for more banks, more credit, and more currency rose to a crescendo. Responding to incessant political demands, the Democrats who dominated the legislature in the 1812–13 session drew up an omnibus bill that chartered thirty banks throughout the state. Much of the bill's support came from the western and central counties, which resented Philadelphia's control over the state's banking system. Although the plan passed each house by a single vote, Governor Simon Snyder—a traditional Jeffersonian ardently opposed to expanding the bank system—vetoed the measure.[16] Snyder's

13. John Joseph Wallis, Richard Sylla, and John B. Legler, "Interaction of Taxation and Regulation in Nineteenth-Century U.S. Banking," in *The Regulated Economy: A Historical Approach to Political Economy*, ed. Claudia Goldin and Gary Libecap (Chicago: University of Chicago Press, 1994), 135–36.

14. For the General Loan Office, see Mary M. Schweitzer, *Custom and Contract: Household, Government, and the Economy in Colonial Pennsylvania* (New York: Columbia University Press, 1987), 115–67.

15. Phillips, "Democrats of the Old School," 365. Although known as "Democratic-Republicans" at the national level, Pennsylvania's Jeffersonian party used the name "Democrats" in state and local elections by 1810. See Phillips, "Pennsylvania Origins of the Jacksonian Movement," 491.

16. Sanford Wilson Higginbotham, *The Keystone in the Democratic Arch: Pennsylvania Politics, 1800–1816* (Harrisburg: Pennsylvania Historic and Museum Commission, 1952), 273. For a superb account of the politics of banking, see James Richard Karmel, "Banking on the People: Banks, Politics, and Market Evolution in Early National Pennsylvania, 1781–1824," (Ph.D. diss., State University of New York at Buffalo, 1999), 169–214.

opposition stressed the fears inherent in republican ideology that moneyed institutions would inevitably "taint the purity of elections, and eventually prostrate the rights of the people." The expansion of the banks, he also argued, would create an inflationary economy that would "invite to visionary speculations; divert men from useful pursuits; damp the ardor of industrious enterprise, and consequently demoralize the community."[17] Even Snyder's republican critique, though, recognized the importance of entrenched banking interests to the state government. Snyder worried that the experiment in banking might "seriously affect the finances of the Commonwealth, which now draws a revenue, more than equal to all of its currents expenses, from the bank stock which it owns in the banks already incorporated."[18]

The legislature was unable to override Snyder's veto, but the fact that a majority of Democrats sided against their own governor foretold things to come. In response to the veto, the legislature made the bill more popular not by subtracting banks (as Snyder's message would imply), but by adding banks. In the next legislative session, the legislature passed a bill establishing forty-two new banks. Five were located in Philadelphia and its immediate vicinity, where they could provide additional competition to the more established institutions. The remaining banks, often referred to as "country banks," were scattered throughout the interior of the state. The legislature was particularly eager to expand banking in booming rural counties such as Lancaster (five new banks), Allegheny (three), Cumberland (two), and Franklin (two).[19] The legislative log-rolling inherent in the bill was part of a broader ideological trend in which overly restrictive chartering gradually became antithetical to republican political principles. Why should the legislature deny a locality in the interior its own bank when it had granted four to the merchants and financiers of Philadelphia? Such logic created inexorable demands for more charters, so that, as Gordon Wood has observed, "corporate grants for businesses virtually became popular entitlements."[20] Snyder once again vetoed the measure, but this time the legislature had the votes to override it.[21] The ultimate success of the movement to charter more banks underscores Cathy Matson's point that most Americans in the early Republic "feared abuses of banks by particular interests but welcomed the credit of state and local banking when extended widely."[22]

17. Synder's veto message was recorded in *Pennsylvania Archives,* 9th series, vol. 5, ed. Gertrude Mackinney (Harrisburg: Pennsylvania State Printing Office, 1931): 3326.

18. Ibid., 3327.

19. *Acts of the General Assembly of the Commonwealth of Pennsylvania,* session 1813–14 (Philadelphia: John Bioren, 1814), chapter 98, 154–56.

20. Gordon S. Wood, *The Radicalism of the American Revolution* (New York: Knopf, 1992), 321.

21. Higginbotham, *Keystone in the Democratic Arch,* 275, 287–88.

22. Cathy Matson, "Capitalizing Hope: Economic Thought and the Early National Economy," *Journal of the Early Republic* 16 (Summer 1996): 284.

The legislature's efforts to democratize the banking system went far beyond increasing the number of chartered banks. It also sought to make investment in banking as easy as possible. In the 1780s and 1790s, bank charters usually set the initial par value of shares between $200 and $400, which often discouraged small investors. By contrast, the charter for the forty-two new banks specified a par value of $50. Investors were required to put up only $5 or $10 as an initial payment, with the remainder paid up depending on the company's financial needs. Since many of the banks would not call for the full amount of their shares, most investors in Pennsylvania's country banks paid only $30 for a share with a par value of $50.[23] In the inflationary economy of the War of 1812, the relatively low cost of bank shares put these securities within the financial reach of many households.

Perhaps the most important charter provisions, however, specified the number of shares any one investor could initially purchase. When bank stock went on sale, an individual could purchase only two shares for each of the first five days. One could buy up to one hundred shares on the sixth day (the final day of the sale), but even that purchase constituted a tiny fraction of any bank's capital stock, which ranged in size from four thousand to twenty thousand shares.[24] To further enhance the ability of local residents to buy bank stock, all initial investors had to reside in the bank's district as specified in the charter.[25] No speculators from outside the district, therefore, could monopolize the local bank stock.

Other details of the charter enhanced the democratic ethos of the forty-two new banks. The legislative act appointed commissioners who were responsible for organizing the initial sale of shares. The legislature required that the commissioners advertise in local newspapers (in both German and English in some cases) to inform potential investors when and where subscriptions would be sold. With road travel exceedingly slow, banks made sure that their officers were scattered throughout the countryside. In 1814, for example, the Carlisle Bank advertised that investors could purchase shares in eight different locations scattered throughout Cumberland County. The advertisement made clear the intensely local nature of the enterprise. The bank sold shares not only in Carlisle, Shippensburg, and other local market towns, but also in the isolated

---

23. Sylla, "U.S. Securities Markets and the Banking System," 92.

24. The legislature granted some Philadelphia banks, which had been operating without corporate charters before the 1814 law, an exemption to this requirement. Not surprisingly, a few wealthy financiers and merchants had purchased large number of shares well over the one-hundred-share limit, among them Andrew Bayard, who purchased more than 2,900 shares in the Commercial Bank of Philadelphia. Thousands of small investors were nevertheless able to buy shares in the Philadelphia banks.

25. The broad ownership of shares had more immediate political advantages as well. A corporation representing a large number of investors—and hence potential voters—might fare better in the legislature if it needed its charter amended or extended.

rural townships of Toboyne ("at the house of Henry Zimmerman"), Tyrone ("at the house of Gilbert Moon"), and Rye ("at Clark's Ferry").[26]

Did such efforts work to expand the range of investment? The commissioners who raised the first subscription of capital left behind evidence that allows us to answer that question. Commissioners sent their lists of early stockholders and shares to the governor, who in turn issued a letter of patent to certify that the bank had raised the minimum capital required to begin operations. The stockholder lists were subsequently filed in the governor's papers. For the 1814 banks, thirty-seven of the forty-two banks filed stockholder lists that were subsequently published in the *Pennsylvania Archives* series. These lists reveal a startling boom in the ownership of bank stock. Whereas historians analyzing the distribution of stock have found companies with hundreds of stockholders, the *Pennsylvania Archives* data reveal that ten of the banks chartered in 1814 had more than one thousand investors. Most of these banks were located in Philadelphia (five area banks averaged more than 1,100 shareholders apiece) and in Lancaster country (four banks averaged more than 1,910 shareholders apiece).[27] When overlap is taken into account—investors with the same name were assumed to be the same person—more than twenty thousand individuals purchased shares in Pennsylvania banks. The average investment of these twenty thousand individuals was $363, but the very low median investment of $60 indicates that the majority of investors purchased only a few shares.[28]

It should be noted that a number of questions surround the interpretation of the *Pennsylvania Archives* stockholder lists. The lists record only buyers at the initial stock sale and offer no indication of how stockholders subsequently disposed of their shares. Could many of these buyers have been acting as informal agents for family members and business associates? Given the tight rules governing shareholding purchases—for most banks, a single shareholder could own a maximum of one hundred shares—enterprising speculators and capitalists might have quickly purchased additional shares soon after a bank had concluded its initial sale. We cannot know the extent of such practices, but even if the initial investors quickly sold their shares, the boom was nevertheless an impressive break from the previous twenty-five years, when only those residing in or near Philadelphia had the chance to buy bank stock.

The thousands of stockholders in Pennsylvania banks undoubtedly expected their investment to pay hefty dividends. The experience of the established Philadelphia banks, after all, suggested high returns for those lucky enough

26. *Carlisle Gazette,* March 25, 1814.

27. The stockholder lists are found in *Pennsylvania Archives,* 9th series, vols. 5–6. These figures do not account for overlapping investment.

28. I have assumed that investors, on average, paid 60 percent of the actual par value of their stock. The relatively high average of $363 reflected the special provisions that allowed investors in several of the Philadelphia banks to own far more than a hundred shares. See note 21 above. Average investment in the "country banks" was probably much lower.

to own stock. It would be a mistake, however, to view bank stock only from the standpoint of immediate profit. Banks in the mid-Atlantic region, historian Robert Wright has shown, often provided credit to a wide variety of borrowers, allowing small manufacturers to finance new workshops, farmers to improve their land, and retailers to expand their operations.[29] The presence of a bank would thus become a powerful magnet for attracting more people and more trade. The developmental impact of banks—which surely helped raise incomes in rural localities—might well have made the speculative boom easier to swallow, at least ideologically and culturally. Investors were enriching not only themselves but their communities as well.

As one might expect, many of the shareholders came from relatively modest backgrounds. A sample of more than seven hundred investors from five Philadelphia banks linked to the 1814 city directory is revealing. Merchants, financiers, and professionals—the occupations traditionally associated with corporate enterprise—provided more than half the capital. Through sheer numbers, though, more ordinary artisans, manufacturers, and retailers exerted great influence as well, accounting for 63 percent of the investors and 40 percent of the capital (see Table 2, p. 316). Carpenters, grocers, draymen, hatters, innkeepers, and tailors—hardly the occupations associated with wealth and prestige—made up more than 20 percent of the sampled investors.

The broad social base of Pennsylvania's banks did not save them from the ideological backlash that occurred in the aftermath of the Panic of 1819. The financial panic forced many of the country banks to close their doors forever. Of the forty-two banks chartered in 1814, only twenty-two renewed their charters in 1824.[30] For critics of banking, times could not have been better. Old-school Democrats almost gleefully reminded the public that they had predicted that the new banking system would lead to speculation and ruin. Banks and paper money, which had once had widespread popular support, were now widely scorned. An 1820 Pennsylvania senate committee sent questionnaires to various local officials to determine the causes and consequences of the Panic of 1819. A sample of the leading questions—and the responses from a state legislator from Cumberland County—showed the great hostility to the new banking system:

12. To what has the distress of your district been generally ascribed by the citizens?

Ans: Excessive speculation, and depreciated bank paper chiefly

13. Have not your merchants, storekeepers, and others, overtraded? If so, is not their overtrading to be ascribed to the facility of obtaining bank loans?

29. Wright, "Bank Ownership and Lending Patterns."
30. *Pennsylvania Archives,* 9th series, 7:6213.

Ans: They have.

20. Do you consider that the advantages have outweighed all of the evils attendant on the banking system?

Ans: The evils have far overbalanced the advantages.

23. Has a spirit of extravagance in dress, furniture and dwellings, pervaded your neighbourhood, to an extent beyond what usually results from gradual increase of wealth amongst the people?

Ans: In all, but in dress in particular.

26. What was the motive that led to the establishment of so many banks?

Ans: An avaricious desire for money, and a delusive belief that banks would make it abundant.

In case readers had any difficulty interpreting the questions, the report gave a general assessment of Pennsylvania's expanded banking system: "A bank by many was no longer regarded as an instrument by which the surplus wealth of capitalists could be conveniently loaned to their industrious fellow citizens, but as a mint in which money could be coined at pleasure, for those who did not possess it before."[31]

That concluding phrase—"those who did not possess it before"— hinted at the profound distrust of a banking system deemed too democratic for its own good. Men with too little wealth and too little standing, the report not so subtly implied, controlled the country banks, resulting in irresponsible inflation. Populists such as Andrew Jackson criticized national banks for enriching a few men through the use of special privileges and legislation. For Pennsylvania critics of the 1814 banks, the problem was precisely the opposite. In promising to enrich everybody, the extension of the banking system had set off a wave of uncontrolled speculation in which the general citizenry had been lured into the pursuit of unearned easy wealth. Such explanations were unduly simplistic, and they often played into the hands of entrenched banking interests who, fearing more competition, wished to limit bank charters for more selfish reasons.[32] Yet the apparent failure of a democratized banking system nevertheless provided critics with a powerful example of the evils of too many banks and too much paper money. The perceived need to tightly regulate the banking system created a hostile political atmosphere for new banks that would last for decades. As the Pennsylvania economy recovered, residents began to demand more banks and easier credit. The legislature began to pass piecemeal bills that chartered individual banks, most of them of quite modest capital. Yet even the banks that

31. "Cumberland County in the Panic of 1819," *Cumberland County History* 13 (Summer 1996): 42–47.

32. Historian Robert Blackson, for example, has found that "Pennsylvania bankers managed to pursue a course that moderated, rather than accelerated, the cyclical expansion during the years before the Panic of 1819." Blackson, "Pennsylvania Banks and the Panic of 1819," 358.

managed to secure legislative approval sometimes died at the governor's desk. Governor George Wolfe, for instance, vetoed the "Farmers and Manufacturers' Bank of Delaware County" in 1833. His justification for the veto rested on the experience of 1814. Wolfe vetoed the bank "to save that community . . . [from] an excited but morbid spirit of banking." According to Wolfe, experience had taught Pennsylvanians that a mania for banking and speculation would end "in a state of depression, distress, and ruin."[33] He viewed the current bill as a fore-runner to a larger expansion of the banking system, which he strongly opposed: "This bill is but of a batch of bills numbering, it is believed, not less than twenty three . . . by which it is proposed to add to the existing banking capital within the Commonwealth the further sum of six millions nine hundred and fifty five thousand dollars. It must be obvious to the plainest capacity what a state of things such an addition to the number of Banks and to the banking Capital already in operation within the Commonwealth must necessarily produce."[34]

Over the long run, such attitudes would seriously retard Pennsylvania's banking system. An 1840 government survey of banks showed, for example, that only 12,548 investors owned stock in thirty-nine Pennsylvania banks.[35] Despite higher incomes, a growing population, and improved communications, significantly fewer individuals owned stock in 1840 than in 1815. Nor did the situation necessarily improve over the course of the antebellum period. By 1860 the Keystone State had more than 9 percent of the U.S. population, but only 5 percent of the nation's banks and 6 percent of the nation's banking capital.[36] For historians, the fate of Pennsylvania's banking system testifies to the importance of political institutions in determining the direction of economic development. If political institutions made it easier for Pennsylvanians to invest in banks in the early nineteenth century, the same institutions restricted opportunities for share ownership for decades.

The critics who attacked the expansion of the state's incorporated banks said remarkably little about the growing numbers of chartered trans-portation corporations. Indeed, when the aforementioned questionnaire from the state senate asked about "the amount loaned by banks in your neighbour-hood, to road and bridge companies," the correspondent in Cumberland County replied, "Little loaned for public improvements." Was his answer a criticism of banks that refused to lend to such enterprises? Perhaps, but even more telling is how the respondent thought of turnpikes and toll bridges as "public improve-ments." Such a choice of words suggests that even bitter critics of the 1814 bank accepted and supported transportation companies. Historians must account for

33. *Pennsylvania Archives,* 9th series, 10:7762.
34. Ibid., 7763–64.
35. *Hazard's United States and Commercial Register* 2 (July 1840): 158.
36. Wallis, Sylla, and Legler, "Interaction of Taxation and Regulation," 131.

how transportation corporations, an integral element of commercial development, escaped the opprobrium leveled against banks.

Initially, they did not. Turnpikes and other transportation companies
faced the same sort of Jeffersonian opposition, couched in republican language,
that bedeviled banks. In the 1790s many Pennsylvanians believed that turnpike
and canal companies would become vehicles of political corruption. When the
first turnpike chartered in Pennsylvania, the famed Lancaster Turnpike, received
permission to operate in 1792, many farmers and other small producers reacted
with hostility and suspicio1.. In the 1793–94 legislative session, more than two
hundred petitioners claimed that the company's eminent-domain privileges "enabled an incorporated Company, engaged in a *subordinate Occupation,* to make
25 per Cent per Annum on their Capital Stock."[37] Significantly, the Pennsylvania
legislature chartered no other turnpike until 1801, when the Germantown and
Perkiomen Turnpike began operations. Even the managers of this turnpike indig-
nantly complained of "the prejudice and capricious conduct of obstinately igno-
rant persons living near the line of the road, who raised very serious opposition,
and, by every possible means, endeavored to thwart and counteract the legal
operations of the Turnpike Company."[38]

Popular opposition quickly died down, however. The Pennsylvania legislature chartered hundreds of transportation corporations in the first two decades
of the nineteenth century. Many of these projects were never built, but between
1800 and 1820 Pennsylvanians managed to fund some eighty-four turnpike companies that built eighteen hundred miles of improved roads, as well a number
of important toll bridges and navigation works.[39] In addition to a number of
local projects, Pennsylvanians built an impressive trunk line of turnpikes and toll
bridges that connected Philadelphia to Pittsburgh. If there was a residue of populist hostility directed at turnpikes and other transportation companies, it was
far too weak to hinder the rapid proliferation of new improvements.

The financial history of early turnpike corporations gives historians a
clue as to why the popular hostility of the 1790s disappeared so quickly. Promising to solidify connections between Philadelphia (America's largest city at the
time) and Lancaster (the hub of a rich agricultural region seventy-five miles
to the west), the 1792 Lancaster Turnpike seemed like a sure financial success.
Investors quickly gobbled up a thousand shares, worth $300 apiece. In Phila-
delphia 2,276 investors sought to purchase the six hundred shares allotted to the
city (the other four hundred were sold in Lancaster), forcing the company to

37. The petitions are found in RG-7, box 1, Pennsylvania State Archives, Harrisburg.
38. Albert Gallatin, "Report on Roads and Canals" (1808), in *American State Papers, Class
X, Miscellaneous* (Washington, D.C.: Gales and Seaton, 1834), 1:883.
39. Joseph Durrenberger, *Turnpikes: A Study in the Toll Road Movement in the Middle Atlantic
States and Maryland* (Valdosta, Ga.: Southern Stationery and Printing, 1931), 55.

draw names randomly.[40] Pennsylvanians who lived in the countryside undoubtedly resented a company that forced farmers to pay tolls so that urban investors
could make a fortune. Opposition thus ran deep.

As it turned out, the Lancaster Turnpike was hardly a financial success.
The company reported in 1807 that high construction costs and disappointing
revenues limited dividends to less than 2 percent per year.[41] If the Lancaster Turnpike failed to generate much in the way of dividends, other turnpikes servicing
more sparsely populated areas were bound to produce even less profit. Indeed,
turnpikes produced dividends that averaged far less than 1 percent of their capital stock. Navigation companies paid even fewer dividends than turnpikes.[42] Toll
bridges did significantly better, but their dividend rate of 5 percent was hardly a
financial windfall. These exceedingly poor financial returns disproved the entire
premise of republican opposition in the 1790s. Transportation companies did not
charge tolls on farmers and other laboring citizens to enrich a few, but rather
encouraged investment that paid little in the way of dividends or other direct
profits.

A variety of reasons accounted for the exceedingly poor financial fortunes of turnpikes. Travelers avoided tolls by taking shunpikes that avoided a
company's gatekeepers. The legislature, fearful of encouraging abuses of corporate power, prevented companies from moving their gates to combat this problem. It also forced toll keepers to calculate tolls for the exact distance traveled.
Travelers tended to underestimate their own mileage, which, as one company
sourly noted, caused "constant litigation, and the most vexatious disputes."[43]
Despite these problems, many turnpike companies still managed to earn substantial revenues, if only by charging merchants and other travelers unfamiliar
with local shunpikes. Ultimately, the worse problem for early transportation
companies was the exceedingly high cost of repairs. Turnpike companies had to
constantly resurface and repair their roads when rains turned their highways into
muddy quagmires; navigation companies found that floods and freshets often
forced them to rebuild their works; and bridge companies faced the threat of
fire, which could completely undo their projects. Rather than funnel money into
the pockets of investors, transportation companies instead spent their revenues
keeping their improvements in working order.

If transportation companies paid little in the way of direct profits, they
provided important indirect benefits. Improved roads, bridges, and rivers could
bring substantial benefits for isolated towns in the interior. Farmers could more

40. Wilbur C. Plummer, *The Road Policy of Pennsylvania* (Philadelphia, 1925), 48.

41. Gallatin, "Report on Roads and Canals," 893.

42. Louis Hartz, *Economic Policy and Democratic Thought: Pennsylvania, 1776–1860* (Cambridge: Harvard University Press, 1948), 92. Hartz reports dividends paid to the state government from invest-ment in various transportation enterprises.

43. Gallatin, "Report on Roads and Canals," 384.

easily market their surpluses; merchants and retailers could purchase manufactured goods with greater speed and reliability; tavern keepers, stable owners, and stagecoach drivers could expect to see more customers; and all townspeople and nearby farmers could receive letters, newspapers, and business correspondence more quickly and dependably. The significance of these indirect benefits should not be overstated, but the substantial decline of wagon rates during the turnpike era suggests that the external benefits were significant enough to warrant the heavy investment that Pennsylvanians made in their turnpike network.[44] Not surprisingly, contemporaries such as Henry Clay estimated that "the capitalist who should invest his money in these objects [turnpikes] might not be reimbursed three percent annually upon it; and yet society in various forms, might actually reap fifteen or twenty per cent."[45] With these high social returns in mind, politicians like Clay often supported government funding for turnpikes. Many Pennsylvanians apparently agreed, and the state legislature provided almost 30 percent of the state's turnpike capital and substantial help to many bridge and navigation companies.[46]

Government assistance, however important, cannot explain the puzzling problem of how the companies overcame the free rider problem associated with indirect dividends. In a simple public goods model, almost no turnpikes should have been built. This is especially true after the first decade of the nineteenth century, when even the most gullible investor should have known that turnpike stock was not a paying proposition. Almost any resident of a town stood to gain from the indirect benefits, whether or not he purchased the unprofitable stock. Previous research from both old and new economic history has focused on how a strong associational culture encouraged turnpike investment. Town meetings, newspaper editorials, and individual solicitations generated considerable social pressure to invest in turnpikes. Vigorous competition among towns for trade and population added a sense of urgency to such efforts. To build a turnpike or toll bridge might solidify a town's position as a regional trade depot; to fail might bring an era of economic stagnation and declining land values.[47] The booster spirit, in other words, substituted for the allure of direct profits.

44. George Rogers Taylor, *The Transportation Revolution* (New York: Rinehart, 1951), 133–34.

45. Quoted in Durrenberger, *Turnpikes*, 125.

46. Hartz, *Economic Policy and Democratic Thought*, 83–84.

47. Daniel B. Klein, "The Voluntary Provision of Public Goods? The Turnpike Companies of Early America," *Economic Inquiry* 28 (October 1990): 788–811; Daniel B. Klein and John Majewski, "Economy, Community, and Law: The Turnpike Movement in New York, 1797–1845," *Law and Society Review* 26, no. 3 (1992): 469–512; John Majewski, *A House Dividing: Economic Development in Pennsylvania and Virginia Before the Civil War* (New York: Cambridge University Press, 2000), chapters 1–2. For some of the older internal improvement literature stressing similar themes, see Oscar and Mary Handlin, "Origins of the American Business Corporation," *Journal of American History* 5 (May 1945): 22, and Carter Goodrich, "Public Spirit and American Improvements," *Proceedings of the American Philosophical Association* 92 (October 1948): 305–9.

If such a dynamic is well known in the internal improvements literature, historians have often failed to appreciate how deep the booster spirit ran in the general population. The *Pennsylvania Archives* data allow historians to calculate the widespread investment in transportation corporations. Much like banks, many transportation corporations submitted their lists of investors to the governor, which were then published in *Pennsylvania Archives.*[48] Unfortunately, either many navigation companies ignored the requirement or else their lists were lost before publication. Even when transportation companies provided lists, they were often incomplete. The state legislature required most companies to sell only a fraction of their total capital stock to qualify for a letter of patent. The Harrisburg, Carlisle, and Chambersburg Turnpike, for example, submitted an initial report listing 155 investors subscribing a total of $40,300 worth of shares. More complete company ledgers, however, list 580 total stockholders investing a total of $86,420. The *Pennsylvania Archives* data allow us to calculate the average investment, which can then be used to determine the total number of investors.[49] This procedure reveals that more than 23,000 Pennsylvanians invested in turnpikes and toll bridges between 1800 and 1821 (Table 1, p.316). Because few navigation companies left behind stockholder lists, they were excluded from the calculations. The 23,000 figure thus underestimates the total number of investors.

Such large numbers of shareholders suggest that investment in transportation companies, like investment in banks, went beyond wealthy businessmen. Analysis of shareholding patterns bolsters this impression. The average stockholding in Pennsylvania transportation companies was only $251; the median purchase was $100. Shareholders who purchased $150 or less of stock accounted for 30 percent of all private capital. In Cumberland County, located in the south-central portion of the state, local farmers and artisans provided 70 percent of the capital for two local turnpikes and a toll bridge, whereas Philadelphia capitalists were virtually absent.[50] Philadelphia merchants and capitalists, fearful of unprofitable investments in the countryside, usually invested only in companies that

---

48. *Pennsylvania Archives,* 9th series, vols. 2–10.

49. Taking overlap into account, the *Pennsylvania Archives* lists show 23,057 investors in turnpikes and toll bridges, with an average investment of $251. According to published estimates, private investors provided a total of $5.787 million in these enterprises. Dividing $5.787 million by $251 equals 23,057. This method might overestimate the number of investors if the sample average from the *Pennsylvania Archives* list is somehow too low. This appears not to be the case, as the most substantial investors purchased stock first. The sample investment average derived from the *Pennsylvania Archives* lists for the Harrisburg, Carlisle, and Chambersburg Turnpike, for example, was $260; the actual average (including all investors) was $149. The method of calculating overlap—the number of investors who owned shares in more than one company—adds another significant downward bias. Many Pennsylvania shareholders had the same name—scores of John Millers, Joseph Smiths, and other common names appear on the lists. To be on the safe side, every repeated name was assumed to be the same stockholder, so that the fifty-four John Millers investing in stock were counted as one investor.

50. Majewski, *A House Dividing,* 12–36.

served their city or its immediate hinterland. When the wealthy Philadelphia capitalist Joseph Ball died in 1823, for example, he held 484 shares of Philadelphia-
area bank stock, but only thirty-two shares in transportation companies.[51]

Investment in transportation corporations engendered none of the ideological fears that the 1814 banks had created. No mania swept the state for turnpike and toll bridge stock; investment grew steadily over several decades. Stock
in transportation companies certainly involved some degree of speculation, but
it was speculation of a much different sort from that in bank shares. Investors in
transportation companies hoped to reap the benefits of rising land values rather
than direct dividends, a much more acceptable form of speculation in the eyes of
most Americans.[52] The fact that most investors held a modest number of shares
meant that investment entailed no dramatic shifts in the investment portfolios
of most households—land still remained the primary asset for most Pennsylvanians. Ownership of transportation stock thus complemented rather than challenged the propertied independence that republican ideology valued so highly.

Even more important, transportation companies claimed political legitimacy because they provided an essentially public improvement. All property
owners—not merely those who owned stock—benefited from their works.
Investors, in fact, could justly claim that they were making significant financial
sacrifices for the public good. By the early nineteenth century, republicanism
increasingly identified the public good with a moderate degree of commercial
expansion.[53] Turnpikes, toll bridges, and navigation companies embodied the
vitality and dynamism of thriving market towns and prosperous, well-kept farms
that avoided both the poverty of squalid subsistence and the corruption of large
cities. The same improvements that carried commerce also carried news and information that kept a republican citizenry well informed about the latest political developments.[54] Transportation improvements, in short, represented the sort
of progress consistent with republican values.[55]

51. Emmett William Gans, *A Pennsylvania Pioneer Biographical Sketch, with Report of the Executive Committee of the Ball Estate Association* (Mansfield, Ohio: R. J. Kuhl, 1900), 254. Philadelphia's newspapers, not surprisingly, listed shares prices for only a small fraction of the state's corporations. Sylla
reports that newspapers listed the prices of shares for some twenty corporations in 1811; the majority
were Philadelphia banks and insurance companies, coupled with a few Philadelphia area turnpikes and
bridges. Sylla, "U.S. Securities Markets and the Banking System," table 3.

52. Historians have long noted that long-term capital gains in farms were an important
part of northern agriculture. See, for example, Jeremy Atack and Fred Bateman, *To Their Own Soil:
Agriculture in the Antebellum North* (Ames: Iowa State University Press, 1987), 262.

53. Joyce Appleby, *Capitalism and a New Social Order: The Republican Vision of the 1790s* (New
York: New York University Press, 1984), 25–50; Joyce Appleby, *Inheriting the Revolution: The First Generation of Americans* (Cambridge: Harvard University Press, 2000), 56–89; McCoy, *Elusive Republic*, 76–104.

54. See, for example, Richard John's analysis of the communication revolution in *Spreading the News: The American Postal System from Franklin to Morse* (Cambridge: Harvard University Press,
1995), 25–63.

55. All the more so in that transportation projects helped create a sense of nationalism.
Although the federal government refused to build an integrated transportation system, individual

The 1840 annual message of Governor David R. Porter forcefully highlighted the widespread support for transportation corporations. Porter was certainly no friend of corporate enterprise in general. The widespread proliferation of corporations, he declared, had "departed widely from that republican simplicity that ought to characterize a free government . . . numerous monopolies [have] been created not only to rival, but to trample down all individual enterprises." Porter called for legislative reforms that would sharply limit the number of new banks and other corporations that, to his mind, promoted only individual self-interest. Yet for all of his anticorporate sentiments, Porter recognized a class of corporations that fostered "great purposes of public utility." These included religious organizations, universities, colleges, scientific organizations, and, most significantly, corporations for the "purposes of internal communication, as turnpikes, bridges, railroads, canals, &c. &c."[56] In granting legitimacy to transportation corporations, Porter granted legitimacy to commercial development.

Significantly, Porter grouped railroads in the same class as turnpikes and canals. Despite their size and potential profitability, early railroads defined themselves as public improvements. Not only did they provide indirect benefits on a wide scale, but economic necessity and political strategy led even the largest railroads to seek capital from small investors. Take, for example, the origins of the Pennsylvania Railroad, which would eventually become one of the most powerful corporations in the country. Its promoters, desperately seeking capital, took the company's subscription books door to door throughout Philadelphia. They argued that by allowing Philadelphia to compete effectively with New York and Baltimore, the enterprise would raise land values to the benefit of all property owners, large and small. A good many investors believed the company's promoters. The railroad's 1847 annual report boasted that "out of some twenty-six hundred subscriptions near eighteen hundred are for five shares and under."[57] The same report suggested an ulterior political motive for encouraging modest investors: these small investors could make their presence felt at the polls when the city government decided whether or not to invest in the enterprise. The railroad's broad investment base, in other words, enabled the company to define itself more as a public improvement than as a private interest.

projects could receive support because they helped connect East and West. See John Lauritz Larson, "'Bind the Republic Together': The National Union and the Struggle for a System of Internal Improvements," *Journal of American History* 74 (September 1987): 363–87. For the best overview of the politics of internal improvements on the national level, see Larson's *Internal Improvement: National Public Works and the Promise of Popular Government in the Early United States* (Chapel Hill: University of North Carolina Press, 2001).

56. "Message from Governor Porter," *United States Commercial and Statistical Register* 2 (January 15, 1840): 44.

57. *First Annual Report of the Directors of the Pennsylvania Rail-Road Company* (Philadelphia, 1847), 9. The annual reports of the Pennsylvania Railroad can be found in RMG-286, PARR Records, Office of the Secretary, Annual Reports, Pennsylvania State Archives, Harrisburg.

The Pennsylvania Railroad, as one of the largest corporations of the nineteenth century, could hardly escape political controversy. That most of its capital came from Philadelphia—notwithstanding the large number of small investors who owned stock in the company—created considerable resentment in many parts of the state. Critics charged that the company exerted influence in the state legislature through bribes and other forms of corruption.[58] Yet if many Pennsylvanians opposed the PRR and its specific policies, they rarely opposed the general goal of improving transportation. After working to improve transportation links for more than a generation, Pennsylvanians could hardly turn down the potential benefits that railroads offered. Traditional associations between improved transportation and the public good proved remarkably durable over the course of the nineteenth century.

The history of shareholding in Pennsylvania helps revise several longstanding assumptions about the nature of economic change in the early nineteenth century. Contrary to the expectations of some social and political historians, shareholding in early corporations was not confined to a tiny urban elite but involved a broad occupational swath of the state. Small shareholders provided an important source of capital, especially for transportation companies. Yet the rise of corporate shareholding also confounds the predictions of economic historians, who might expect the rate of shareholding to increase naturally as the number of corporations proliferated and communications improved. The evidence suggests the opposite: shareholding in Pennsylvania may have been more popular in the first two decades of the nineteenth century than at any other time in the antebellum period, especially with regard to banking. Rather than proceeding on an inevitable upward trend, stockholding rose and fell in a boom or bust fashion, depending on economic conditions, political considerations, and investment motives.

Pennsylvania, of course, did not necessarily represent the entire United States or even its own region. The Pennsylvania experience, however, appears to have been broadly similar to other mid-Atlantic states. States such as New York, Pennsylvania, and Maryland shared important characteristics: each had a large seaboard city eager to improve links with the interior, fertile soil that supported a thriving rural economy, and numerous localities with skilled artisans and small manufacturers who might have perceived important benefits from a local bank or an improved road. Not surprisingly, most mid-Atlantic states built significant turnpike systems that relied heavily on local capital. Detailed studies of New York in particular show that the state's turnpike corporations raised most of their capital from local residents motivated by indirect benefits. Several episodes suggest that stockholding in transportation companies remained popular after the turnpike boom ended in the 1820s. Perhaps as many as thirty thousand residents

58. Hartz, *Economic Policy and Democratic Thought,* 267–85.

of Baltimore and other Maryland communities, for example, invested in the Baltimore and Ohio Railroad in the 1820s.[59] In New York, thousands of residents in upstate communities bypassed by canals and railroads invested in plank roads to improve access to outside markets. Plank roads proved to be an expensive flop, but they also demonstrated the profound importance that communities attached to improved transportation links.[60]

The religious and ethnic diversity of the mid-Atlantic states may also have encouraged corporate stockholding. Historical geographer D. W. Meinig has noted that the pluralism of these states promoted a pragmatic style of governance that tended to favor compromise among competing interest groups.[61] In the realm of corporate charters, such compromises often meant more banks, turnpikes, and toll bridges to satisfy the demands of different communities. Ethnicity and religion also formed conduits of information and capital that may have encouraged investment. The Pennsylvania shareholding data, for example, show that stockholding was especially popular in Lancaster County, home to a remarkable number of religious and ethnic communities, including English Quakers, Scots-Irish Presbyterians, and German Amish, Anabaptist, Lutheran, and Reformed congregations. Approximately six thousand individuals (or about 25 percent of the free adult population) purchased shares in Lancaster banks, turnpikes, and toll bridges. Historians have often touted "individualism" as a core value in the mid-Atlantic region. When it came to building internal improvements, however, cooperation made more sense than rootless individualism.[62] Strong community institutions, working in combination with fertile soils and the relatively equal distribution of rural property, may well have been the key to the mid-Atlantic's thriving economy.[63]

Although general data on shareholding in New England is sparse, the literature suggests a more hierarchical pattern of corporate shareholding. New England's farmers certainly invested in turnpikes and banks, but the impetus for New England's commercial expansion was more likely to emanate from a

59. Milton Reizenstein, *The Economic History of the Baltimore and Ohio Railroad, 1827–1853* (Baltimore, 1897).

60. John Majewski, Christopher Baer, and Daniel Klein, "Responding to Relative Decline: The Plank Road Boom of Antebellum New York," *Journal of Economic History* 53 (March 1993): 106–22.

61. Donald Meinig, *The Shaping of America: A Geographical Perspective on 500 Years of History* (New Haven: Yale University Press, 1986), 1:139–40.

62. James Lemon, for example, emphasized that in the colonial era Pennsylvanians "planned for themselves much more than they did for their communities. . . . As individualists, they were ready in spirit to conquer the limitless continent, to subdue the land." James T. Lemon, *The Best Poor Man's Country: A Geographical Study of Early Southeastern Pennsylvania* (Baltimore: Johns Hopkins University Press, 1972), xv.

63. Doyle's careful study of Jacksonville, Illinois, makes a similar point: "Despite all the vaunted individualism and unsettling transience of laissez-faire capitalism in the nineteenth century, it was capable of generating an intense spirit of community." Don Harrison Doyle, *The Social Order of a Frontier Community: Jacksonville, Illinois, 1825–70* (Urbana: University of Illinois Press, 1980), 62.

relatively small group of mercantile and manufacturing families.[64] The work of Philip Taylor suggests that stock ownership in New England turnpikes was far less popular and democratic than in Pennsylvania. Although local residents along the line of the projects owned most of the stock, Taylor notes that "[t]he organizers usually purchased a large share—often a majority—of the capital stock." The high price of turnpike stock in New England—which ranged as high as $400 to $1,000 per share—undoubtedly discouraged more modest investors.[65] Prominent families become even more conspicuous in financing the region's railroad network. François Weil, for example, finds that in 1831 only 238 investors purchased $1 million worth of stock in a railroad connecting Boston to Worcester.[66]

New England's banks had a similar pattern of shareholding. Naomi Lamoreaux suggests that a large number of New Englanders purchased shares of bank stock, which they expected to pay high dividends. Many of those that purchased stock often subscribed in relatively modest amounts of $100 or $200. Unlike banks in Pennsylvania and New York, however, a small group of prominent insiders, often part of a well-connected kinship network, dominated the investment decisions of most New England banks. Small shareholders, in essence, invested in the enterprises that these prominent insiders controlled. Lamoreaux shows persuasively that such "insider lending" arrangements worked well. New England banks efficiently funneled funds to small groups of entrepreneurs, who could then invest them in a wide range of diversified industries. The superior performance of New England's banking sector suggests that what small shareholders lost in terms of democracy and control relative to Pennsylvania's banks, they gained in stability and profits.[67]

Banks and transportation companies in the South displayed neither the popular appeal of Pennsylvania corporations nor the stability of New England's.

64. Winifred B. Rothenberg has found that many New England farmers owned government bonds and bank stock as early as the revolutionary era. See *From Market-Places to a Market Economy: The Transformation of Rural Massachusetts, 1750–1850* (Chicago: University of Chicago Press, 1992), 120–22.

65. Philip E. Taylor, *The Turnpike Era in New England* (Ph.D. diss., Yale University, 1934), 157–67, quote at 165. For a more local study that connects turnpike investment with merchants, see Daniel P. Jones, "Commercial Progress Versus Local Rights: Turnpike Building in Northwestern Rhode Island in the 1790s," *Rhode Island History* 48 (February 1990): 21–32. Similarly, Christopher Clark's study of the Connecticut River valley found that relatively few investors held stock in corporations even as late as the 1850s. In his words, "corporate capitalism was for the few, not the many." Christopher Clark, *The Roots of Rural Capitalism: Western Massachusetts, 1780–1860* (Ithaca: Cornell University Press, 1990), 270.

66. François Weil, "Capitalism and Industrialization in New England, 1815–1845," *Journal of American History* 84 (March 1998): 1349.

67. Naomi Lamoreaux, *Insider Lending: Banks, Personal Connections, and Economic Development in Industrial New England,* 1st paperback ed. (New York: Cambridge University Press, 1996), 52–83. See also Gordon S. Wood, "The Enemy Is Us: Democratic Capitalism in the Early Republic," *Journal of the Early Republic* 16 (Summer 1996): 306.

Southern communities certainly displayed their own brand of booster mentality and sponsored a great many of their own transportation improvements, but wealthy slaveholders dominated investment in most companies. As the largest landholders in their localities, slaveholders often had the most to gain from improved transportation and new banks. Other elements of southern society eagerly invested in these enterprises as well, but they did not have the numbers or the resources to replicate Pennsylvania's shareholding boom.[68] Slavery obviously limited the size of the southern pool of potential investors. So too did southern cultivation practices, which often relied on large swaths of uncultivated land that lay fallow for as a long as twenty years. Such techniques—which agricultural historians have labeled "shifting cultivation"—necessarily reduced southern population densities. Southern projects thus had many fewer potential investors and took much longer to organize.[69] Southern improvements, not surprisingly, depended on investments from state and local governments to a far higher degree than northern localities did.[70]

The regional differences regarding share ownership reveal a potentially rich set of comparative questions that historians could profitably explore in more detail. What regional patterns worked best to promote long-term economic development? To what extent did regional differences in investment patterns make it more difficult to develop a national plan for internal improvements? Did ordinary households in western states such as Ohio and Kentucky have the same opportunity to invest in corporations as residents of the mid-Atlantic states? That these questions have no immediate answers suggests that what might be called the social history of the early American corporation still remains to be written. Once historians dispense with the assumption that shareholding was only the province of the rich and well off, they can analyze the extent to which different groups of Americans could shape the evolution of the corporation.

68. Lacy K. Ford, for example, documents a great deal of booster activity in upcountry South Carolina, but it appears to have been far behind Pennsylvania's efforts. Lacy K. Ford, *The Origins of Southern Radicalism: The South Carolina Upcountry, 1800–1860* (New York: Oxford University Press, 1988). See Majewski, *A House Dividing,* for direct comparisons of northern and southern investment. A. Glenn Crothers makes a convincing case that bank investment permeated northern Virginia in the postrevolutionary era, but it is difficult to make the leap to all of Virginia or the South as a whole. Crothers, "Banks and Economic Development in Post-Revolutionary Northern Virginia, 1790–1812," *Business History Review* 73 (Spring 1999): 1–39.

69. John Majewski and Viken Tchakerian, "Markets and Manufacturing: Industry and Agriculture in the Antebellum South and Midwest," in *Global Perspectives on Industrial Transformation in the American South,* ed. Susanna Delfino and Michele Gillespie (St Louis: University of Missouri Press, forthcoming).

70. James A. Ward, "A New Look at Antebellum Southern Railroad Development," *Journal of Southern History* 39 (August 1973): 413.

Table 1 Investment in Pennsylvania Banks, Turnpikes, and Toll Bridges, 1800–1821

Type of Corporation	Investors in Sample	Total Capital Invested by Sample Investors ($)	Average Investment of Sampled Investors ($)	Total Private Investment in Corporations ($)	Estimated Number of Investors
Banks (1814–15)	20,126	7,310,790	363	7,310,790	20,126
Turnpikes and Toll Bridges	10,795	2,715,605	251	5,787,5457	23,057
Total (Including Overlap)	29,311	10,026,395	342	13,098,337	38,299

Sources: Samples derived from stockholder lists in *Pennsylvania Archives,* 9th series (Harrisburg, 1931). Total private investment was found in Louis Hartz, *Economic Policy and Democratic Thought: Pennsylvania, 1776–1860* (Cambridge: Harvard University Press, 1948), 84. Each category takes into account stockholders with investments in two or more companies, which is why the "Total" category is less than the sum of the "Banks" and "Turnpikes and Toll Bridges" categories.

Table 2 Occupational Holdings in Philadelphia Banks, 1814–1815

	Number of Investors in Sample	Percentage of Capital Invested	Median Holding ($)	Average Holding ($)
Merchant and Financiers	149 (18.8%)	44.7	90	709
Professionals	88 (11.1%)	7.4	90	548
Retailers	147 (18.6%)	11.7	60	341
Artisans and Manufacturers	352 (44.6%)	28.1	60	344
Miscellaneous	56 (7%)	4.2	60	318

Source: Derived from linking a sample of investors in Philadelphia banks to *Kite's Philadelphia Directory for 1814* (Philadelphia: B. & T. Kite, 1814).

Chapter Eleven

Small-Producer Capitalism in Early National Philadelphia

DONNA J. RILLING

The Philadelphia home of Horatio Melchior manifested the social and economic status a man trained to a craft might achieve in the early decades of American nationhood. In 1822 Melchior was in the prime of his career as a house carpenter, and success in constructing houses in an expanding city supported his material and social ambitions. His status rested on skilled manual labor and thus separated him from pretensions to merchant or gentleman status. His livelihood among "mechanics," or artisans, nonetheless provided his family with the amenities of genteel living. Leaning back on his "fancy lounge & cushion," or working at his secretary desk, Melchior could peruse his collection of Shakespeare's plays, any one of his three dozen other books, or his assortment of historical prints. Elegant mahogany furniture, carpeting, and serving ware announced his success to potential customers, fellow craftsmen, and friendly visitors who entered his parlor.[1]

This essay explores some of the economic means available to Melchior and fellow craftsmen in pursuing financial security and bourgeois status. It uses the experiences of Philadelphia construction tradesmen and relates their experiences to men in other crafts and retail trades to examine how artisans gained a foothold in an economy where capital-intensive businesses played increasingly central roles. Loans for housing construction fluctuated wildly between periods of economic exhilaration and periods of panic. When investors were confident, a building mechanic could borrow thousands of dollars on mortgages, and augment it by credit in labor and materials extended within the construction industry. To amass the resources to sustain and elevate their status as capable and independent men, builders were drawn to "speculative"

---

1. Horatio L. Melchior to John Wilson, Miscellaneous Book, IH1: 31 (1822), Philadelphia City Archives (hereafter PCA).

construction that promised dramatic gains but also augured great risks. They hesitated little to move into related investments, wholesale and retail ventures, and even opportunities far afield from the crafts they had learned. At each new venture they surmounted capital barriers by exploiting flexible arrangements for business ownership and production. Men in the building business were at the forefront of the "popular, entrepreneurial culture" that historian Joyce Appleby finds "permeated all aspects of American society."[2]

Transportation and communication networks (including turnpike roads, canals, railroads, postal service, and widely circulated newspapers) and a network of national and state banks opened markets regionally and nationally, and challenged producers to sell skills and wares in integrated markets. Increased concentration of capital and rising technology costs characterized the flagship industries in the early nineteenth-century economy. Extended time between capital laid out for production costs, longer and more complex chains of credit between suppliers and consumers, and slower returns of capital to producers heightened the risks of competing with producers in other regions. Consumers in rural regions and provincial towns, hungry for the comforts of more refined society, bought up many of the wares urban tradesmen and suppliers sent to them. In craft shops, workshops, home industry, manufactories and mechanized workplaces, and in industries as widely varied as textile manufacture, garment making and joinery production, men and women faced the demands of the young nation's shifting economic landscape.[3]

Historians have long debated the impact of these rapid changes on Americans, as well as the attitudes and engagement of Americans in the market economy of the new nation. For several decades, literature on men and women drawn into workshops and factories emphasized the immiserating effects that the capitalist economy exercised. Capitalists in New England's textile industry grew rich from the labor of factory workers. The experiences of factory operatives—notably Lowell's "daughters of free men"—mixed mill discipline, paternalism, and physically taxing labor with modest independence from family and farm. By the 1830s, however, low wages, immigrant labor, squalid living conditions, and

2. Joyce Appleby, *Inheriting the Revolution: The First Generation of Americans* (Cambridge: Harvard University Press, 2000), 89.

3. Paul A. Gilje, "The Rise of Capitalism in the Early Republic," *Journal of the Early Republic* 16 (Summer 1996): 159–81; George Rogers Taylor, *The Transportation Revolution, 1815–1860* (New York: Rinehart, 1951); Richard R. John, *Spreading the News: The American Postal System from Franklin to Morse* (Cambridge: Harvard University Press, 1995); Bray Hammond, *Banks and Politics in America, from the Revolution to the Civil War* (Princeton: Princeton University Press, 1957); Naomi R. Lamoreaux, *Insider Lending: Banks, Personal Connections, and Economic Development in Industrial New England* (New York: Cambridge University Press, 1994); David Jaffee, "Peddlers of Progress and the Transformation of the Rural North, 1760–1850," *Journal of American History* 78 (September 1991): 511–35; Richard L. Bushman, *The Refinement of America: Persons, Houses, Cities* (New York: Knopf, 1992); Rosalind Remer, *Printers and Men of Capital: Philadelphia Book Publishers in the New Republic* (Philadelphia: University of Pennsylvania Press, 1996).

organized labor protests belied any benevolence, republicanism, or paternalism that mill owners might have intended when they established their factories.[4]

A similar declension took place in urban crafts. Master mechanics-turned-subcontracting-entrepreneurs extracted their wealth from the sweated labor they exploited. Artisans, who formally laid claim to a political identity that accorded them status and rewarded diligent application of their skill with a modest "competence," respectability, and financial security, found their crafts "bastardized"; they were edged out by unskilled, even female or child laborers who worked for low wages at tasks that were mere slices of the product that artisans once took pride in making. Divergent responses emerged among mechanics. Journeymen identified increasingly though inconsistently with unskilled workingmen (and more hesitantly with working women) in a critique of economic individualism and its consequences for the health of the polity. Masters endorsed the liberal capitalist ideologies that befitted their status as employer-contractors (or employer-subcontractors). At critical moments in the nineteenth century, class threatened to overwhelm the identities of artisans and the claims to political and social status they demanded by virtue of their skill.[5]

Lost in this narrative is a closer examination of master mechanics and petty producers, one that does not make villains of these figures. What motivated these men and women, what constraints did they face, and what roles did they play in shaping the marketplace and the cultural values of the early Republic? Was there more consonance in economic values and behavior among these middling ranks of society and their journeymen and employees than the narrative of decline suggests? Joyce Appleby and Gordon Wood have suggested that Americans of this era were imbued with a liberal capitalist spirit that grew out of the ideological and political experience of the Revolution. The postrevolutionary

4. Robert F. Dalzell Jr., *Enterprising Elite: The Boston Associates and the World They Made* (Cambridge: Harvard University Press, 1987); John F. Kasson, *Civilizing the Machine: Technology and Republican Values in America, 1776–1900* (New York: Grossman, 1976); Thomas Dublin, *Women at Work: The Transformation of Work and Community in Lowell, Massachusetts, 1826–1860* (New York: Columbia University Press, 1979); Teresa Anne Murphy, *Ten Hours' Labor: Religion, Reform, and Gender in Early New England* (Ithaca: Cornell University Press, 1992). See also Cynthia Shelton, *The Mills of Manayunk: Industrialization and Social Conflict in the Philadelphia Region, 1787–1837* (Baltimore: Johns Hopkins University Press, 1986).

5. Sean Wilentz, *Chants Democratic: New York City and the Rise of the American Working Class, 1788–1850* (New York: Oxford University Press, 1984); Ronald Schultz, *The Republic of Labor: Philadelphia Artisans and the Politics of Class, 1720–1830* (New York: Oxford University Press, 1993); Alan Dawley, *Class and Community: The Industrial Revolution in Lynn* (Cambridge: Harvard University Press, 1976); Mary H. Blewett, *Men, Women, and Work: Class, Gender, and Protest in the New England Shoe Industry, 1780–1910* (Urbana: University of Illinois Press, 1988); Bruce Laurie, *Working People of Philadelphia, 1800–1850* (Philadelphia: University of Pennsylvania Press, 1980); Paul E. Johnson, *A Shopkeeper's Millennium: Society and Revivals in Rochester, New York, 1815–1837* (New York: Hill and Wang, 1978); Christine Stansell, *City of Women: Sex and Class in New York, 1789–1860* (New York: Knopf, 1986); Lisa Beth Lubow, "Artisans in Transition: Early Capitalist Development and the Carpenters of Boston" (Ph.D. diss., University of California, Los Angeles, 1987).

generations employed egalitarian political rhetoric to realize the radical potential of the Revolution.[6] The watershed effect of revolutionary ideology, however, need not be overstated to recognize the dynamism of the new Republic's
economy.[7] The frenetic pursuit of opportunities led "enterprising men [to knock]
against enterprising men like so many billiard balls."[8] New skills and trades rewarded able men who adapted their crafts to meet the demands of new industries such as machine building, or of innovations in existing industries such as
woodworking, textile printing, clock making, and canal building. Enterprising
peddlers and artisans persuaded rural consumers to buy merchandise that linked
them to cosmopolitan middle-class Americans.[9]

In the new Republic, energetic and aggressive Americans lived on the
edge, always courting or "navigating failure."[10] Speculation, economic reversals,
and credit shortages made engagement in the market both rewarding and risky.
In 1822, when Melchior listed the property that made his house the commodious
residence of a middle-class family, recording the material markers of affluence
must have disconcerted him: Melchior was on the brink of financial insolvency.
This essay is an opportunity to explore the financial and material foundations of
Melchior's fellow mechanics, prospective constituents of the emerging middle
class. It examines the challenges, risks, and devastation small producers faced to
encourage further exploration of the links between the perils and rewards of
material pursuits and the formation of middle-class identity.[11]

6. Appleby, *Inheriting the Revolution*; Gordon S. Wood, *The Radicalism of the American Revolution* (New York: Knopf, 1992).

7. For discussions about the market economy and similarities between the colonial and
postrevolutionary period, see especially Naomi R. Lamoreaux, "Rethinking the Transition to Capitalism in the Early American Northeast," *Journal of American History* 90 (September 2003): 437–61; Richard
L. Bushman, "Markets and Composite Farms in Early America, *William and Mary Quarterly*, 3d ser., 55
(July 1998): 351–74.

8. Appleby, *Inheriting the Revolution*, 61.

9. For important contributions to rethinking the activities of small producers, see Richard
Stott, "Artisans and Capitalist Development," *Journal of the Early Republic* 16 (Summer 1996): 257–71;
Gary John Kornblith, "From Artisans to Businessmen: Master Mechanics in New England, 1789–1850"
(Ph.D. diss., Princeton University, 1983); Lisa B. Lubow, "From Carpenter to Capitalist: The Business
of Building in Postrevolutionary Boston," in *Entrepreneurs: The Boston Business Community, 1700–1850,*
ed. Conrad E. Wright and Katheryn P. Viens (Boston: Massachusetts Historical Society, 1997), 181–
210; David Jaffee, "Peddlers of Progress"; Tina H. Sheller, "Freemen, Servants, and Slaves: Artisans and
the Craft Structure of Revolutionary Baltimore Town," in *American Artisans: Crafting Social Identity,
1750–1850,* ed. Howard B. Rock, Paul A. Gilje, and Robert Asher (Baltimore: Johns Hopkins University Press, 1995), 17–32; Remer, *Printers and Men of Capital*; Judith A. McGaw, *Most Wonderful Machine:
Mechanization and Social Change in Berkshire Paper Making, 1801–1885* (Princeton: Princeton University
Press, 1987).

10. Edward J. Balleisen, *Navigating Failure: Bankruptcy and Commercial Society in Antebellum
America* (Chapel Hill: University of North Carolina Press, 2001); see also Bruce H. Mann, *Republic of
Debtors: Bankruptcy in the Age of American Independence* (Cambridge: Harvard University Press, 2002).

11. Stuart M. Blumin, *The Emergence of the Middle Class: Social Experience in the American
City, 1760–1900* (New York: Cambridge University Press, 1989); Karen Halttunen, *Confidence Men and*

The rise of small producers like Melchior was predicated on access to credit with which they could finance real estate development. But after years of apprenticeship and an additional stint in the employ of a master craftsman, most journeymen had amassed no more than a few hundred dollars in savings. In many trades, that sum was sufficient to boost a journeyman to the helm of his own craft shop.[12] Loans from family members often added modestly to a young man's resources. Amounts derived from savings and family, however, paled beside the more extensive advances available through a variety of short- and long-term borrowing methods.

Consider the prospects of building artisans in Philadelphia. From 1809 to 1812 William Wagner employed five journeymen regularly in his carpentry shop. When employed full-time, the annual income of the men averaged $283. (The median annual income was about $276.) The highest sum a journeyman earned was $351 and the lowest was $241; these extremes reflect both different day rates commensurate with skill and modest variations in the total number of days worked. Out of their earnings Wagner's men met the expenses of board and lodging, often in the household of a more established craftsman, though not, in this case, in master Wagner's household. These expenses left each employee a little more than a third of his wages to use for clothes, washing, medical bills, tools, and a reserve fund to sustain him in periods of underemployment.[13]

Among skilled tradesmen, carpenters were high earners. Nonetheless, those who aspired to independence remarked repeatedly on the small sums they accumulated during journeywork. In contrast to the $300 one journeyman carpenter saved in the 1820s, many peers were only "about 'even with the World,'" or were actually indebted after years at journeywork. Rare was the young man who was able to squirrel away the $850 that house carpenter Michael Barron cleared over five years of journeywork in the early 1830s.[14]

Estimates of annual income ranging from $200 to $300 in the best of years diverge markedly from the level of credit craftsmen could get in periods of economic expansion. The amount a man could borrow depended on the

---

Painted Women: A Study of Middle-Class Culture in America, 1830–1870 (New Haven: Yale University Press, 1982); see also Michael Zakim, "Customizing the Industrial Revolution: The Reinvention of Tailoring in the Nineteenth Century," *Winterthur Portfolio* 33 (Spring 1998): 41–58; Michael Zakim, "Sartorial Ideologies: from Homespun to Ready-Made," *American Historical Review* 106 (December 2001): 1553–86; Toby Ditz, "Shipwrecked; or, Masculinity Imperiled: Mercantile Representations of Failure and the Gendered Self in Eighteenth-Century Philadelphia," *Journal of American History* 81 (June 1994): 51–80.

12. Laurie, *Working People of Philadelphia*, 26.

13. William Wagner, "Account Book No 3, Journeymans Wages, 1809–[1812]," Germantown Historical Society, Philadelphia; see also Donna J. Rilling, *Making Houses, Crafting Capitalism: Builders in Philadelphia, 1790–1850* (Philadelphia: University of Pennsylvania Press, 2001), chapter 5.

14. Insolvent Petitions, Philadelphia Court of Common Pleas (hereafter PCCP), PCA: James Shaw, June 14, 1830; Daniel T. Glenn, September 5, 1835; Michael Barron, March 13, 1835; see also Sebastian Root, January 15, 1841; Edgar Shivers, December 13, 1836.

confidence of the lender that he would repay it. Loans were thus tied to the capital invested in a product and its potential return. That a builder could realize a $1,450 profit on a two-house building project contributed to his ability to borrow a few thousand dollars.[15]

In boom seasons, a journeyman ready to set out on his own overcame an initial lack of capital easily. Private individuals and a small collection of institutions sought investments, and construction-related loans that returned 5 and 6 percent were among the less risky portfolio options available. Enthusiasm created wild climates as those with capital searched for borrowers. The availability of credit during these periods opened opportunities for small producers. John Munday took advantage of the ebullient economy of the 1790s to construct dwellings for low-, middle-, and high-end consumers. Munday built in anticipation of purchasers and was able to raise thousands of dollars on mortgages, short-term loans, and proceeds from concurrent construction and real estate deals. Though the causes were different from those that motivated lenders in the 1790s, the embargo and nonintercourse restrictions of 1807–9 and the subsequent War of 1812 also created would-be creditors in search of borrowers. Unable to use their capital to move goods internationally, merchants invested in construction. Capital poured into the real estate market in the form of mortgages and development contracts. Bricklayer Francis Douglass borrowed $50,000 for building projects; his indebtedness was larger than that of most building artisans but was far from unique. In the latter half of the 1820s, a decade that offered only a few alluring boomlets to builders, housepainter and glazier Warnet Myers also put together $50,000 in mortgage loans and short-term notes. He undertook the construction of sixty houses in the course of a mere two years.[16]

Munday and his peers who built on speculation (or "on spec," as they also put it) enjoyed additional aid from Philadelphia's land-tenure or "ground-rent" system. A ground-rent purchase vested legal title in the builder. It was contingent on a perpetual but transferable annual payment (fixed at approximately 6 percent of the value of the land at the time of the sale) and the development of the parcel for residences. A mortgage loan advanced by the seller (ground lord) or by another investor frequently accompanied the sale of a lot on ground rent.[17]

In practice, mortgage creditors agreed to lend builders one-third of the anticipated value of the finished house. Builders typically raised the remaining funds through an extensive network of lenders within the building crafts and

15. Joshua Sharples, Account and Day Book (1803–1809), Historical Society of Pennsylvania, Philadelphia (hereafter HSP).

16. John Munday, deposition, October 21, 1801, case of John Munday, Bankruptcy Cases, 1800–1806, U.S. District Court, Eastern District of Pennsylvania, National Archives and Records Administration, Mid-Atlantic Regional Branch, Philadelphia; Francis Douglass, June 6, 1816, Insolvent Petition, PCCP; Rilling, Making Houses, 29–36.

17. Richard M. Cadwalader, A Practical Treatise on the Law of Ground Rents in Pennsylvania (Philadelphia, 1879); Rilling, Making Houses, 45–51.

supply trades. Thus, in the early 1830s, house carpenter Daniel Glenn and his partner transformed two ground-rent purchases (and an obligation to build seventeen houses) into mortgage advances of $8,500. They met the additional approximate construction cost of $17,000 by combining exchanges in labor with other craftsmen and purchases made on credit from lumber merchants, brick makers, and other "material men." Short-term notes, notes endorsed by family members, and minor jobs undertaken during lulls in building tasks plugged remaining credit gaps.[18]

Advances or trade of labor among craftsmen in diverse construction specialties made up a critical portion of development credit. The ubiquity of artisan credit and exchanges in kind contributed to the prospects of fledgling masters. These exchanges embedded Philadelphia's building artisans in labyrinthine credit networks that functioned in complicated and surprising ways. They enabled individual masters or artisan partnerships to undertake a greater number of houses, particularly those erected on speculation, than cash payments alone would have allowed. Because their loans could be worthless when fellow artisans failed, the intensive and extensive nature of these networks encouraged craftsmen to endorse notes or otherwise assist peers who teetered dangerously close to bankruptcy. A national or local economic upset—and there were many hiccups as well as dramatic crises in the nation's early decades—often exercised a domino effect on the building community and consequently on the real estate market, as suits for debts dumped finished and unfinished houses on the auction block at depressed prices.[19]

The expense of borrowing, however, sometimes exceeded returns, and personal circumstances sometimes caught leveraged individuals overextended. Despite the mortgage advances John Munday was able to assemble, the inflation of the 1790s, although outpaced by real estate prices, forced him to borrow short-term capital at very high interest. One creditor demanded 2.5 percent per month, amounting to a staggering rate of 34 percent per annum. Accepting a high rate of interest, as Munday did, was only one way builders paid the cost of borrowing. Borrowers on notes generally paid up-front discount fees; builders complained during periods of economic instability and credit scarcity of notes "discounted at large Usurious interest." The cost of borrowing was also borne by builders who paid more when using credit than when paying cash. Purchasers able to tender cash for materials or labor paid as little as half the price demanded

18. Glenn, Insolvent Petition.

19. On the extensive use of trade credit, see George F. and Franklin Lee, Ledger, 1813–1852, Franklin Lee Papers, HSP; John and Moses Lancaster, Receipts, 1812–1836, HSP; see also Rilling, *Making Houses*, 62–65. On trade and book debt generally, see Christopher Clark, *The Roots of Rural Capitalism: Western Massachusetts, 1780–1860* (Ithaca: Cornell University Press, 1990), 30ff.; Bruce H. Mann, *Neighbors and Strangers: Law and Community in Early Connecticut* (Chapel Hill: University of North Carolina Press, 1987), 11–41; W. T. Baxter, *The House of Hancock: Business in Boston, 1724–1775* (Cambridge: Harvard University Press, 1945), 11–38.

for sales on credit. Preferred pricing for cash customers was a practice common in construction but was also employed in diverse trades and retail transactions. When upholsterer Samuel Himmelwright commenced business on his own in 1824, he was "without capital, [and therefore] purchased his stock on credit, and at an increased price." Three years later, laboring under the expense of what was in essence a high rate of interest, Himmelwright failed.[20]

Overextended finances resulted in high rates of failure among construction tradesmen when the economy somersaulted. With thousands of dollars in credits outstanding over the course of even a small housing project, reversals often proved catastrophic. In the aftermath of the Panic of 1819, for example, building artisans often lamented that they had "lost large sums of money in consequence of the great depreciation in the value of Real Estate."[21] Depreciation of goods was by no means restricted to the building community. Textile manufacturers, brass founders, morocco merchants, and shoemakers, to name a few, shared the fallout of the panic. Construction craftsmen, however, were more vulnerable than many tradesmen to the swings of the early national economy, precisely because their business compelled them to borrow large sums for long intervals. Builders availed themselves of protection under Pennsylvania's insolvency laws at a greater rate than other craftsmen. Though they made up only a fifth of the city's mechanic population, they represented one-quarter of all insolvent artisans.[22]

Family and ethnocultural connections supplied critical capital for many small-scale entrepreneurs. Philip Scranton has shown how seed capital (including skill) for textile shops was drawn from relatives and sympathetic immigrant countrymen. Likewise, for his mortgage loans, Quaker house carpenter Moses Lancaster repeatedly turned to merchants, widows, and other investors known to him through the Society of Friends. In strong markets, however, social connections had little to do with the ability of house builders to secure mortgage advances. Unknown and untested craftsmen, new to the city and to prospective lenders, were enthusiastic recipients of mortgage credit. John Munday, for example, had only recently arrived in Philadelphia in 1791 when he decided to

20. Munday, deposition: Philip Justus, June 16, 1835, Insolvent Petition, PCCP; George and Franklin Lee, Ledger; Samuel Himmelwright, 1827, Insolvent Petition, PCCP. Rosalind Remer argues that exchange accounts in book publishing functioned "much like regular cash and credit accounts, except very little money, if any, actually changed hands." The key to survival for early nineteenth-century publishers was this system of swapping, which kept the shelves of bookseller-publishers supplied with a wide array of titles. Remer, *Printers and Men of Capital,* 79.

21. William Haydock, June 10, 1819, Insolvent Petition, PCCP; see also petitions of James Ayers, June 8, 1822; Adam Burkart, October 18, 1820; Jacob Stone, September 29, 1820, PCCP.

22. Only a fraction of Philadelphia's petitions for insolvency for this period survive. Proportions were derived and compiled from Robert Desilver, ed., *Philadelphia Directory and Stranger's Guide* (Philadelphia, 1830); [Anon.], *Insolvent Register for the Last Five Years; Being a Complete List of Cases in Philadelphia Court of Common Pleas Advertised in the Newspapers* (Philadelphia, 1830); *Hazard's Register of Pennsylvania* 3 (1829): 224; 4 (1829): 85, 336; 8 (1831): 65–72; 11 (1833): 415.

engage in advance building. He immediately connected with Edward Shippen, a Pennsylvania Supreme Court justice, who lent him several thousand dollars on mortgages. A lender would generally tender money in stages as the building progressed, thus securing the loan, albeit with unfinished structures. In frenzied markets, however, lenders were often less cautious, counting complacently on the rise in real estate values to compensate for relaxed oversight.[23]

Munday plied his trade in a decade of extremes. In subsequent years, however, his artisan peers followed a similar path in their search for credit. Lenders, meanwhile, funded mortgage loans for the return on capital that these investments afforded; in bullish seasons they did so readily and in bearish ones hesitantly. Private sources—merchants, widows, estates, charitable institutions— continued to provide the greatest amount of mortgage money for building until at least the 1840s. House carpenters seeking to finance construction rarely borrowed directly from banks, which operated principally for the benefit of their own investors (who were mostly merchants, brokers, and manufacturers).[24]

To facilitate deals between borrowers and lenders (in the building business and elsewhere), a group of professionals stepped forward. A growing contingent of brokers specialized in real estate negotiations and supporting legal documentation. Through long-standing relationships built on the management of estates and rental properties, they had access to investors. Brokers used expanded print communications to attract house builders. They mediated deals between sellers and builders, whose purchases of undeveloped lots were often contingent on forthcoming credit. Advertisers attracted lot buyers with promises that they would "be accommodated with the means of building," that is, sellers or other financiers known to the broker would provide money on mortgage. The rise of brokers supported the growth of construction projects, the ability of artisan builders to gain access to capital, and the opportunities and risks of expanding their building businesses.[25]

The propensity among craftsmen to build on spec was widespread in the construction business. Ground-rent purchases (which required no initial capital) and mortgage financing from ground lords or other private lenders opened

---

23. Evidence for Moses Lancaster's financial networks is drawn from recorded mortgages in Philadelphia County; see Rilling, *Making Houses,* 15–28. Philip Scranton, *Proprietary Capitalism: The Textile Manufacture at Philadelphia, 1800–1885* (New York: Cambridge University Press, 1983); Munday, deposition.

24. Naomi R. Lamoreaux's conclusions about New England banking in this period probably describe the situation in Philadelphia's financial market as well; see Lamoreaux, *Insider Lending;* see also Anthony F. C. Wallace, *Rockdale: The Growth of an American Village in the Early Industrial Revolution* (New York: Knopf, 1978), especially 79–84, 121. Robert E. Wright argues that Philadelphia artisans enjoyed direct access to credit from the Bank of North America during the first decade of the nation; Wright, "Artisans, Banks, Credit, and the Election of 1800," *Pennsylvania Magazine of History and Biography* 122 (July 1998): 211–39.

25. *Philadelphia Gazette and Daily Advertiser,* March 6, 1804; Rilling, *Making Houses,* 57–62.

this option to craftsmen. House carpenters and other industry tradesmen regarded advance building as the definitive break from journeywork, i.e., the point at which a craftsman moved from the subordinate status of an employee working to augment the profits of his master to one where he became his own employer. This entailed taking on his own crew (initially often small) and meeting his own payroll, as well as engaging other master craftsmen for specialty labor and securing from them the best contract terms available. When John Munday decided to "try his fortune in the way of building," he engaged in a series of speculative projects that signaled his initiation into independence. Two decades later Joshua Sharples congratulated himself on his social and economic progress to master status by meticulously tabulating the cost of his first speculative project, two brick houses intended for buyers of genteel status. The house carpenter "allow[ed] a good price for [his] own work," above which he cleared more than $1,450. In addition to the salary he paid himself for his labor and superintendence, Sharples enjoyed more than a 30 percent return on the cost of building. For the two and one-half years of intermittent work (if it extended that long), punctuated by other commissioned work, Sharples netted more than twice the amount he could have hoped to get as a fully employed journeyman house carpenter. In addition to the pride that came from his elevated craft and social status were the financial rewards of independent projects. If a young master engaged in minor speculative projects could gain an annual income in excess of $580, imagine the prospects for men who undertook six, twelve, or sixty houses at a time. One master carpenter claimed that in all the years of his independence, beginning in 1826 and continuing past midcentury, his yearly remuneration was never less than $700.[26]

An income of $700 for a craftsman might appear a startling figure, particularly in light of the inconstancy of the early nineteenth-century economy and the dramatically fluctuating character of the real estate trade. But this level of income was not uncommon for skilled master artisans. The experience of another house carpenter supports the view that artisan enterprises frequently generated income in this range. While in his midtwenties and raising a young family, Daniel Glenn estimated that between 1830 and 1835 the expenses he incurred in "House & Shop rents, doctors' bills, clothing," and sundry necessities totaled at least $1,000 per annum. Glenn implied that although his family was expensive to support, he fully expected the profits from his artisan building business to cover his costs. An 1846 survey of "Some of the Wealthy Citizens of Philadelphia" revealed dozens of building craftsmen who were presumed to be worth more than $50,000 by virtue of the profits of real estate development.[27]

26. Munday, deposition; Sharples, Account and Day Book; William Eyre, March 29, 1868, Diaries, 1840–80, Friends Historical Collection, Swarthmore College, Swarthmore, Pennsylvania.

27. Glenn, Insolvent Petition; [Anon.], *Memoirs and Autobiography of Some of the Wealthy Citizens of Philadelphia* (Philadelphia, 1846).

Speculation took many forms. The house carpenter who made window shutters "in speculation" was bent on keeping his crew busy during an otherwise slack period; the master later used the joinery in his own projects or sold it to another builder. If he had prepared nothing in time for renewed construction activity, he would be forced to place an order at a sash-and-blind manufactory or to subcontract for his parts. More risky types of speculation entailed rapid property purchases and sales. In Philadelphia the ground-rent system added opportunities for trading in real estate beyond the simple buying and selling of undeveloped lots. By creating annuities payable to oneself and then selling the property, frequently after subdividing it, or by dealing in the title to collect rent charges, house carpenters were known to pocket $2,000 for a few weeks' ownership during a hot market.[28]

Investments exploiting craft knowledge and networks, such as real estate transactions for building artisans, were the most common ways artisans extended their capitalist pursuits. Some modestly successful craftsmen, or those nearing retirement (and seeking relief from manual labor), also added a supply business. House carpenters in particular became partners in lumberyards, but they embraced other entrepreneurial opportunities as well. Richard Ware identified himself as both a "Master Carpenter" and a "Hardware Merchant." In 1815 and 1818 Ware imported "a large quantity" of English hardware "for the purpose of getting such articles as were essential to him in his occupation used to furnish the houses he was putting up for sale, at the cheapest rate, instead of being obliged to pay the retail price asked at the Stores." His pursuit of speculative construction (i.e., of those "houses he was putting up for sale") thus drove Ware, like fellow craftsmen who engaged in wholesale supply ventures, to pursue new roles and take new risks in a growing economic arena. These new risks ensnared Ware, however, when the Panic of 1819 cut the value of his goods dramatically—by $11,000 by his estimate. Ware must have invested (or, more accurately, borrowed) several times that amount for his initial purchases. Clearly the ambitions of his import venture extended far beyond his own consumption and demanded that Ware sell his merchandise to fellow builders and retailers.[29]

Craft identification did not hinder builders from reaching beyond their bailiwick and entering more risky territory. Grain and flour deals in the thousands of dollars, shipping ventures with cargo valued at $12,000 and upward, and the manufacture of morocco leather were among the avenues building artisans

28. Eyre, December 18, 1850, Diaries; for an account of one such deal, see GWR8:617, MR22:70, GWR8:617, Deed Books, Philadelphia County, PCA.

29. Richard Ware, 1819, Insolvent Petition, Delaware County Court of Common Pleas, Delaware County Court Archives, Lima, Pennsylvania; on lumber yard proprietorship, see Donna J. Rilling, "Sylvan Enterprise and the Philadelphia Hinterland," *Pennsylvania History* 67 (Spring 2000): 194–217.

pursued to seize opportunities for economic expansion.[30] The inclination to push within one's craft, or to test one's mettle in unknown areas, can be spotted in diverse trades, as Joyce Appleby has shown for the nation's early cohort of entrepreneurs. Similarly, Philadelphia watchmaker George Abbott engaged "in Speculation in watches in the course of his business," apparently hoping to turn a quick profit. Thomas Record resolutely "quited his buisness" as a shoemaker with the "Idea of Making mony by Speculation." Although "unacquainted with [the] Trafect," Record did not hesitate to purchase more than one hundred head of sheep (and was able to command the resources for the deal). No doubt he reached his decision partially out of desperation, for in 1816 he was caught in the devastation of the shoemaking trade brought on by Britain's postwar dumping of goods on the American market. Numerous sporadic or long-lived forays into unallied trades raise doubt as to whether their craft had the tenacious hold on artisans that historians have assumed. The willingness of craftsmen to cross over into other ventures suggests the multiple interests and flexible identities of economic actors in the early Republic.[31]

Trades other than construction had the equivalent of advance building, although the need to take such risks was not always inherent in the craft, as it was in house construction. Rosalind Remer finds that journeymen printers joined together to engage in the speculative publishing of books. Subscribers who committed to purchasing the volume upon its appearance accorded such ventures "security" sufficient for raising credit. Echoing the refrain of young house carpenters, journeymen printers realized that spec publishing could "advance their ambitions 'much better than working journey work.'" Mirroring the method of operation of many ground-rent builders, these men required little capital, bought paper on credit, and subcontracted or commissioned the print job.[32]

The health of the real estate market contributed markedly to the ability of a journeyman building artisan to overcome barriers of entry and strike out on his own. John Munday, for instance, spent nine years at journeywork before the economy picked up in 1791–92 and presented opportunities for independent building. By contrast, contemporary Evan Lloyd worked only eighteen months as a journeyman house carpenter, benefiting from the same economic upswing as his elder colleague.[33]

30. For other adventures, see Abraham Ritter, *Philadelphia and Her Merchants* (Philadelphia: Published by the Author, 1860), 85, and *United States v. Rugan and Rhodes*, October 1818, Law and Appellate Cases, U.S. Circuit Court, Eastern District of Pennsylvania, in the noncarpentering careers of house carpenters Mark Rodes and Jacob Hentz; William Clayton, September 29, 1815, Insolvent Petition, PCCP.

31. On the grain and flour deals of house carpenter Moses Lancaster, see Rilling, *Making Houses*, 22. Insolvency Petitions of George Abbott, 1822, and Thomas Record, 1816, PCCP; see also Jacob Wood, 1826, PCCP.

32. Remer, *Printers and Men of Capital*, 5–6, 45–48.

33. Munday, deposition; Case of Evan Lloyd (1803), Bankruptcy Cases, 1800–1806, U.S. District Court, Eastern District of Pennsylvania.

While hoping for real estate markets to quicken, an artisan could further his chances for establishing an independent shop in a variety of ways. A journeyman might step tentatively and gradually into his own business by engaging in subcontracting or "jobbing" for a master builder. A contract to finish the inside carpentry of a house (or a portion of it), done on payment by the task rather than by the day, allowed the journeyman to test his abilities. It also brought the prospect of better compensation than daily wages. The more experienced men working for master carpenter William Wagner between 1809 and 1812 turned the jobbing option to their advantage. They earned from 25 to 50 percent more in annual income than fellow journeymen who were paid a daily wage. Wagner continued to call on his jobbing journeymen for occasional work at framing houses (and paid them a daily rate). But after a few years spent gaining ability, business acumen, contacts, and better earnings as subcontractors, the senior members of Wagner's crew struck out on their own.[34]

Subcontracting by masters also flourished in the building trades. Contracts to build, usually under a master house carpenter, generated the clearest form of subcontracting, that is, to craftsmen in other construction specialties. But by the second or third decade of the nineteenth century, subcontracting within trades had become increasingly common. Economic swings affected its frequency greatly. In house carpentry, for example, the tendency to subcontract "inside work" to other masters was strongest during market booms, when master builders pursued ambitious construction schedules.[35]

The specialization of trades paralleled the growth of subcontracting. Shops that held their fixed capital in joinery tools to produce window sashes, shutters, doors, and moldings, for example, became an important feature of the carpentry trade by the 1830s. Highly skilled stair builders could carry on businesses devoted exclusively to the production of stairs. House carpenters who focused on framing structures could turn to specialized shops for prefabricated parts; consistent with material and labor arrangements across crafts, house carpenters purchased joinery on credit. This commissioned or subcontracted work spread the risk of developing real estate to yet another group of lenders.

Specialization and the rise of manufactories and steam-powered factories for joinery did not spell the doom of skilled craftsmen or small producers. Craftsmen were glad to be free of some of the more tedious and repetitive tasks, which were replaced by sawing and planing apparatus. At midcentury, moreover, sash and door construction continued to demand skilled and well-paid craftsmen. In Abel Reed's prominent establishment, for example, customers placed orders

34. DSB, March term 1829, no. 291, District Court of the City and County of Philadelphia, PCA; Wagner, "Account Book"; William Wagner and Jacob Franks, Receipt Book, 1810–1817, author's collection.

35. For an in-depth discussion of subcontracting in building, see Rilling, *Making Houses,* chapter 5.

for intricate custom work. The discerning master builder William Eyre ordered standard as well as unique joinery (e.g., a complicated skylight) from Reed. Eyre's purchases from Reed replaced the labor of his journeymen only when peak out-door construction left him without "time to make [joinery] at [his] shop." The average wage of Reed's employees, moreover, compared favorably with that of journeymen house carpenters, despite the likely inclusion of unskilled or semi-skilled operatives on Reed's payroll. And although Reed had invested about $5,000 in his operation, firms with more modest pools of capital (such as the $1,000 invested by Black and Souder) were viable at midcentury.[36]

Sweated labor and gouging masters were only one possible outcome of this method of organization. In building, artisans could parlay subcontracting into flexible and remunerative operations. As the real estate industry became increasingly complex, subcontracting enabled a smaller master to combine "over-flow contracting" with a variety of commissioned and speculative work while still remaining at the helm of an autonomous shop. In the first half of the nine-teenth century, these arrangements did not relegate subcontractors to permanent second-tier status. Craftsmen who did framing or interior finishing on subcon-tracts continued to move into the ranks of master builders. Subcontracting con-tinued to ensure both entrances and flexible modes of production for young and established artisans. It did not guarantee success, of course, which hinged, among other factors, on shifts in the real estate economy.[37]

Subcontracting provided opportunities in trades other than construc-tion. Scranton has demonstrated the productive flexibility that subcontracting created among textile manufacturers. Proprietary workshops that shared prem-ises with and relied on skilled craftsmen allowed manufacturers to shift pro-duction easily and quickly. They could supply "fluctuating markets for variable goods" with smaller investments in space, equipment, and labor than would have been possible without a network of manufactories for overflow contracting. Thomas Heinrich finds that shipbuilding at midcentury relied on an extensive web of skilled craft shops located near shipyards. Shipbuilders contracted for rig-ging, sailmaking, engine building, and numerous related crafts. The versatility and diversity of these proprietary shops defrayed the amount of capital the ship-builder needed to have in hand for the undertaking. In shipbuilding as well as

36. Gregory K. Clancey, "The Cylinder Planing Machine and the Mechanization of Car-pentry in New England, 1828–1856" (master's thesis, Boston University, 1987), 30; see also Appleby, *Inheriting the Revolution,* especially 76–81; Eyre, August 8 and 10, 1850, Diaries; the average wage of Reed's employees is calculated from U.S. Census of Manufactures, 1850, using data from the Philadel-phia Social History Project "Sort by Business," University of Pennsylvania; Manuscript Return for Black & Souder, Fourth Ward, Kensington, Philadelphia County, U.S. Census of Manufactures, 1850, National Archives, Microfilm Publication T1157, Washington, D.C.

37. For a view of subcontracting as sweating, see Wilentz, *Chants Democratic,* 30–32, 122–24, 132–34. On overflow contracting, see Scranton, *Proprietary Capitalism,* 55–56. On upward mobility for subcontracting building mechanics, see Rilling, *Making Houses,* 148–50.

in textiles, Heinrich asserts, the rise of large firms "did not overwhelm the craft-shop economy but instead energized it."[38]

Partnerships, intermittent ventures, and stepped arrangements for advancement also enabled young craftsmen to become independent proprietors. Painter and glazier Thomas Lawrence "never had any property except what he earned by his labour." When he "came of age," in 1816, he worked as a journeyman, and in 1819 he formed a partnership with a fellow craftsman. Lawrence's business arrangement lasted four years, though it was not unusual for artisan partnerships to span decades.[39] Even while committed to these agreements, partners in house building engaged in other projects as sole venturers, manifesting the flexibility of partnership organization. Conversely, many builders worked on their own but cooperated now and then on specific undertakings. Partnerships that crossed building specialties—those that combined masonry and carpentry, for instance—were rare, except those that gathered craftsmen who traded labor for one limited development.[40]

The building trades also exploited stepped business organizations, whereby the status of a craftsman hovered between journeyman and master or between employee and partner; a man could be elevated to equality with associates once he had proved his worth. The more established parties to these agreements lent their weight to the firm and usually reaped uneven financial advantages as well as a reprieve from daily oversight of the venture. Evan Lloyd's agreement with his better-connected and more experienced partner allowed Lloyd one-third of the profits from a contract for construction in addition to wages for his labor. Although Lloyd brought together a crew and supervised site work, his smaller allocation reflected his mere eighteen months of experience at journeywork.[41]

In supply trades where entry costs ranged in the thousands of dollars, established principals devised methods whereby young men could gradually accumulate partnership shares. In 1822 Christopher Tennant consented to take

38. Scranton, *Proprietary Capitalism*, 55; Thomas R. Heinrich, "Ships for the Seven Seas: Philadelphia Shipbuilding in the Age of Industrial Capitalism, 1860–1900" (Ph.D. diss., University of Pennsylvania, 1992), 59–67, quotation at 67. See also Thomas R. Heinrich, *Ships for the Seven Seas: Philadelphia Shipbuilding in the Age of Industrial Capitalism* (Baltimore: Johns Hopkins University Press, 1997). On diversity of the nineteenth-century economy and its productive settings, see also Walter Licht, *Industrializing America: The Nineteenth Century* (Baltimore: Johns Hopkins University Press, 1995), especially chapter 2, and Laurie, *Working People of Philadelphia*, chapter 1.

39. Thomas Lawrence, 1828, Insolvent Petition, PCCP.

40. On the cooperation of Moses Lancaster and John Lancaster, and the subsequent division of properties, see IC2:563, IC8:6, MR5:465, MR5:466, GWR17:514, and GWR17:517, Deed Books, Philadelphia County; and Moses Lancaster, Receipt Books, HSP. For cross-craft cooperative ventures, see *Croskey v. Coryell*, 2 Wharton 223 (Penna. Supreme Court, 1837); *Hazard's Register of Pennsylvania* 10 (1832): 94; David Townsend to W. H. Brown, January 6, 1844, Chester County Historical Society.

41. Lloyd, Deposition, May 24, 1803, Bankruptcy Cases.

young Findlay Highlands into his $6,600 stonecutting business. The pair agreed
to a five-year partnership. At the close of the period Tennant was to retire and
Highlands, assuming the business had been profitable, was to buy him out. During the five-year term, Highlands was to "take charge of the business" and apply
his share of its profits toward the $6,600 value. In the interim, he was to charge
the firm with "Journeymen's wages for his labour and attendance."[42]

Similar joint arrangements that reduced the capital, equipment, and oversight that a fledgling craftsman needed to bring to a concern existed throughout the construction and construction supply trades. Lumberyard businesses,
rarely valued at less than $10,000, reveal numerous instances of the staggered
partnership succession vital to firm survival on the one hand, and to entrants
short of capital on the other. New members did not always bring capital into a
partnership; men of promise but no stake could be eased into holding a share of
the firm.[43]

The practice of leasing land and equipment, another means of over-
coming entry hurdles, was common in brick making, lime burning and marble
quarrying. Brick makers usually rented their yards and relocated them as quickly
as they extracted the superficial clay. They advanced to less populated and less
costly vicinities, where they exploited other lodes as well as spacious conditions
for drying bricks. In brick making, lime manufacture, and quarrying, landowners
usually linked the productivity of the operation (and the consequent depreciation
of their property) to the sum demanded of the tenants. Producers paid a unit price
for each brick made, each kiln of lime burned, or each perch of marble quarried.
Few stonecutters had the resources to buy a marble quarry outright, as Christopher Hocker did in 1826. Hocker paid $15,400, $7,400 in cash and the balance
in a mortgage. Low rent matched with a generous cut to the landlord could, of
course, be exploitive, but it set some craftsmen on a path to wealth. Strong building climates often held the key to success, and weak ones the route to misfortune.
Abraham Marple, who in the 1830s rented several Montgomery County kilns
to manufacture lime for the Philadelphia market, jumped at the opportunity to
add several recently vacated ovens to his operation. The landlord wondered
whether Marple would be too busy, but the lime burner insisted that he would
hire more labor and still gain by spreading the costs of his horse and wagons over
more kilns. Marple's enterprise was thriving, and he saw no need to purchase his
own sites.[44]

---

42. Exhibit (Articles of Co-partnership) to Bill of Complaint, *Tennant v. Highlands,* December term, 1822, no. 8, Equity Proceedings, PCCP, PCA.

43. Rilling, "Sylvan Enterprise."

44. *Ellis v. Lukens,* June Term 1851, no. 19, Equity Proceedings, PCCP; Case of Abraham
Weaver, OC 19967, Montgomery County Register of Wills and Orphans Court; Abraham Weaver,
RW 6958, Montgomery County Probate Records; *Wallace v. Lentz,* February Term 1845, no. 1, Equity
Cases, Montgomery County Court of Common Pleas, Montgomery County Court Archives, Norris-
town, Pennsylvania; *Fritz v. Hocker,* 4 Rawle 370 (Penna. Supreme Court, 1834); Benjamin Albertson

In other productive sectors, renting space also lowered thresholds of entry. Scranton found that many textile firms rented "apartments" or floors in mills from 1820 onward. Renting was a crucial step in the "matrix of accumulation" that Scranton postulated for Philadelphia's textile proprietors.[45] Although the tenant frequently supplied machinery, the landlord was usually obligated to supply power, including keeping a mill race clear or building and maintaining steam boilers and engines. Landowner, merchant, and gentleman-farmer Manuel Eyre constructed a mill in Blockley Township, Philadelphia, in the early 1820s, evidently with the intention of renting it for cotton manufacture. In addition to supplying it with a race, reservoir, and water wheel, Eyre commissioned the construction of a steam engine. More than a dozen years later, when fire damaged the facility, his tenant insisted that Eyre restore the engine to its condition. Keeping it fit for operation, the manufacturer asserted, was "necessary to be done to make the place tenantable as a factory."[46]

The practice of subdividing mills and workshops was not limited to the textile industry. Tenants who "carried on the business of steam engine making, boiler making, smithing & Machinist," for example, occupied the "lower part" of one establishment near Race and Fourth streets in the 1830s. The landlords followed the "Glass cutting business . . . by steam" in the upper section. When the owners dissolved their business, an additional tenant (and subsequent owner) who engaged in sawing mahogany took over their space. Subdivided facilities with shared power (sometimes the source of conflict between tenants) are much easier to verify in the 1850s and 1860s, but they probably were widespread in earlier decades.[47]

Melchior, Munday, and fellow producers needed large amounts of credit to ply their trade of house construction. Credit flowed to building mechanics in Philadelphia from family and craft networks, mortgage lenders, and short-term credit systems; builders' own successes also supplied capital for new projects. The hunger for credit was driven by an artisan's pursuit of his livelihood, which demanded an entrepreneurial—or speculative—inclination, that is, a willingness to anticipate the market in housing, to bank on a prosperous business climate, and to build without the security of an immediate customer. Entrepreneurial success in the early nation depended also upon finding ways to enter industries that had become capital intensive. Subcontracting craftsmen and suppliers of material in

to Josiah Albertson, March 23, 1838, Josiah Albertson Correspondence, Albertson Family Papers, Special Collections, University of Delaware, Newark.

45. Scranton, *Proprietary Capitalism,* 106–7, 233–35.

46. William Almond to Manuel Eyre, July 29, 1839, Blockley Cotton Factory, Acc. no. 1003, part IV-6, Manuscript Collection, Hagley Museum and Library, Wilmington, Delaware.

47. Deposition of James T. Sutton, December 31, 1840, *Vandyke v. MacFadden,* September Term 1840, no. 13, Equity Proceedings, PCCP. For post-1850, see Equity Proceedings, PCCP for *Carpenter v. City of Philadelphia and Cummings,* December Term 1855, no. 20; *McClenaghan v. Adams,* December Term 1862, no. 10; and *Shields v. Parrish,* March Term 1866, no. 4.

housing, as well as in other trades, willingly took economic chances through such arrangements as overflow work, specialized manufacture, and leased premises. Failure, whether definitive or surmountable, was an ever-present possibility in the daily operations of Philadelphia's building tradesmen—yet these mechanics repeatedly exploited market opportunities. Finding an entrepreneurial culture among artisans and small producers in the early Republic does not celebrate American liberal capitalism, but rather presents opportunities for examining how a tenuous hold on stability that was part and parcel of early entrepreneurship shaped American identities.

Chapter Twelve

The Unfree Origins of American Capitalism

SETH ROCKMAN

Unfree labor plays a central role in the economic history of colonial British North America. Although only a small fraction of enslaved Africans lived and worked in British North America, slavery animated the broader Atlantic economy in which the colonies flourished. Enslaved Africans generated wealth for the Chesapeake tobacco planters who exploited their labor, the Massachusetts fisherman who provisioned distant sugar plantations, and the Rhode Island merchants who moved goods and people between Africa, the Caribbean, and North America.[1] The European settlement of British North America also hinged on unfree labor, as roughly half the Europeans arriving before 1776 owed a term of servitude in exchange for their ocean passage.[2] Scholars are increasingly

This essay is dedicated to the late Clark Davis, who was one of its biggest supporters. For helpful suggestions and comments, my thanks go to Konstantin Dierks, Seth Cotlar, John Bezís-Selfa, Eric Foner, Joyce Appleby, Cathy Matson, Richard Dunn, and other participants in the 2001 PEAES conference, and the Los Angeles Social History Reading Group.

1. Eric Williams, *Capitalism and Slavery* (Chapel Hill: University of North Carolina Press, 1944); Barbara L. Solow and Stanley L. Engerman, eds., *British Capitalism and Caribbean Slavery: The Legacy of Eric Williams* (New York: Cambridge University Press, 1987); Philip D. Curtin, *The Rise and Fall of the Plantation Complex: Essays in Atlantic History* (New York: Cambridge University Press, 1990); Barbara L. Solow, ed., *Slavery and the Rise of the Atlantic System* (New York: Cambridge University Press, 1991); Paul E. Lovejoy and Nicholas Rogers, eds., *Unfree Labour in the Development of the Atlantic World* (Essex: Frank Cass, 1994); Robin Blackburn, *The Making of New World Slavery: From the Baroque to the Modern, 1492–1800* (New York: Verso, 1997); Colin A. Palmer, ed., *The Worlds of Unfree Labour: From Indentured Servitude to Slavery* (Aldershot, Eng.: Variorum, 1998); Russell R. Menard, *Migrants, Servants, and Slaves: Unfree Labor in Colonial British America* (Aldershot, Eng.: Ashgate, 2001).

2. David W. Galenson, *White Servitude in Colonial America: An Economic Analysis* (New York: Cambridge University Press, 1981); Richard S. Dunn, "Servants and Slaves: The Recruitment and Employment of Labor," in *Colonial British America: Essays in the New History of the Early Modern Era,* ed. Jack P. Greene and J. R. Pole (Baltimore: Johns Hopkins University Press, 1984), 157–94; Bernard Bailyn, *Voyagers to the West: A Passage in the Peopling of America on the Eve of the Revolution* (New York: Knopf, 1986); P. C. Emmer, ed., *Colonialism and*

connecting the rapid economic development of the thirteen North American colonies to the array of compulsory labor regimes that made the New World "the land of the unfree."[3]

In many accounts of American economic development, however, coerced labor loses its importance at the time of American independence. The real story after 1776 is freedom: freedom for common men and women to work when and where they wanted, to pursue their own interests free from government interference, to succeed or fail as the impartial forces of the market dictated, and to control their own destinies in a society of boundless opportunity. In the decades following the American Revolution, personal freedom coincided with the intensification of economic development (capitalism is the usual shorthand) and the expansion of political participation (democracy). Freedom, capitalism, and democracy appear as synergistic forces flowing from the inherent logic of the American Revolution. Capitalism in the early Republic is so strongly associated with democracy and freedom that its relationship to unfree labor stands unexplored, unmentioned, and ultimately unfathomed.[4]

Migration: Indentured Labor Before and After Slavery (Dordrecht: M. Nijhoff, 1986); Aaron S. Fogleman, "From Slaves, Convicts, and Servants to Free Passengers: The Transformation of Immigration in the Era of the American Revolution," *Journal of American History* 85 (June 1998): 43–76; Sharon V. Salinger, "Labor, Markets, and Opportunity: Indentured Servitude in Early America," *Labor History* 38 (Spring–Summer 1997): 311–38; Alison F. Games, *Migration and the Origins of the English Atlantic World* (Cambridge: Harvard University Press, 1999). Christopher Tomlins has disputed the quantity and significance of European indentured servitude but still finds that nearly half of Europeans arriving in British North America before 1780 owed an initial term of labor. See his contribution to this volume or his article "Reconsidering Indentured Servitude: European Migration and the Early American Labor Force, 1600–1775," *Labor History* 42 (February 2001): 5–43.

3. Philip D. Morgan, "Rethinking Early American Slavery," in *Inequality in Early America*, ed. Carla Gardina Pestana and Sharon V. Salinger (Hanover: University Press of New England, 1999), 239; Jacqueline Jones, *American Work: Four Centuries of Black and White Labor* (New York: W. W. Norton, 1998), 23–168; David W. Galenson, "The Settlement and Growth of the Colonies: Population, Labor, and Economic Development," in *The Cambridge Economic History of the United States*, 3 vols., ed. Stanley L. Engerman and Robert E. Gallman (New York: Cambridge University Press, 1996), 1:135–207; John E. Murray and Ruth Wallis Herndon, "Markets for Children in Early America: A Political Economy of Pauper Apprenticeship," *Journal of Economic History* 62 (June 2002): 356–82. The older scholarship on this front includes Richard B. Morris, *Government and Labor in Early America* (New York: Columbia University Press, 1946); Abbot Emerson Smith, *Colonists in Bondage: White Servitude and Convict Labor in America, 1607–1776* (Chapel Hill: University of North Carolina Press, 1947).

4. Gordon S. Wood, *The Radicalism of the American Revolution* (New York: Knopf, 1992); Gordon S. Wood, "The Enemy Is Us: Democratic Capitalism in the Early Republic," *Journal of the Early Republic* 16 (Summer 1996): 293–308; Joyce Appleby, *Capitalism and a New Social Order: The Republican Vision of the 1790s* (New York: New York University Press, 1984); Joyce Appleby, *Inheriting the Revolution: The First Generation of Americans* (Cambridge: Harvard University Press, 2000). Michael Zuckerman and Aaron Fogleman downplay the importance of unfreedom before and after the American Revolution in "Deference or Defiance in Eighteenth-Century America? A Round Table," *Journal of American History* 85 (June 1998): 13–97. Similarly, the contributors to the "Special Issue on Capitalism in the Early Republic," *Journal of the Early Republic* 16 (Summer 1996) pay scant attention to unfree labor as a constitutive component of capitalism.

Little is new in the notion that the United States has maximized human freedom by marrying a democratic polity to a liberal capitalist economy. Indeed, the leading figures of the postrevolutionary generation made this claim in newspapers and autobiographies, on the stump and the stage, and from the bench.[5] Alexis de Tocqueville offered confirmation in *Democracy in America,* a text that, in John Stuart Mill's words, "bound up in one abstract idea the whole of the tendencies of modern commercial society, and g[ave] them one name—Democracy."[6] By the Civil War, northerners had located freedom in the defining aspect of modern industrial capitalism—wage labor. The rhetoric of "free labor" suggested that choice, mobility, and opportunity had been the normative characteristics of American labor from the outset. The North's victory assured that slavery would thereafter be understood as an anomaly in American history, a footnote to the real story, which was all about freedom.[7]

Academic historians have enshrined this "master narrative" over the past half-century.[8] The "consensus" historians of the 1950s saw America as liberal, democratic, and middle-class from the first arrival of English colonists in the 1600s. Americans were "born equal," observed Louis Hartz, whose *Liberal Tradition in America* argued that plentiful land meant abundant freedom for a people

5. Joyce Appleby has explained that the early Republic's "connection between prosperity and democracy sealed the American imagination against a critical stance towards either." See Appleby, *Inheriting the Revolution,* 5. The idea of liberalism as a story that gained credence in repetition by a powerful and articulate segment of society appeared earlier in Steven Watts, *The Republic Reborn: War and the Making of Liberal America, 1790–1820* (Baltimore: Johns Hopkins University Press, 1987). Along these lines, see also T. J. Jackson Lears, "The Concept of Cultural Hegemony: Problems and Possibilities," *American Historical Review* 90 (June 1985): 567–93.

6. John Stuart Mill, "DeTocqueville on Democracy in America, II" in *Collected Works of John Stuart Mill,* ed. J. M. Robson (Toronto: University of Toronto Press, 1977), 18:191. See also Sean Wilentz, "The Power of the Powerless," *New Republic,* December 23 and 30, 1991, 35. Tocqueville figures largely in the arguments of those who see the market as an agent of human liberation. Newt Gingrich declared *Democracy in America* required reading for his Republican Party colleagues in the 104th Congress. American Enterprise Institute affiliate Michael A. Ledeen recently published *Tocqueville on American Character: Why Tocqueville's Brilliant Exploration of the American Spirit Is as Vital and Important Today as It Was Nearly Two Hundred Years Ago* (New York: St. Martin's Press, 2000). See Caleb Crain's review of a recent translation of *Democracy in America:* "Tocqueville for Neocons," *New York Times Book Review,* January 14, 2001, 11–12.

7. Antebellum New Englanders worked to erase slaveholding from the narratives of the northern past. By the eve of the Civil War, it seemed that slavery had always been an exclusively southern practice. See Joanne Pope Melish, *Disowning Slavery: Gradual Emancipation and "Race" in New England, 1780–1860* (Ithaca: Cornell University Press, 1998). On "free labor," see Jonathan A. Glickstein, *Concepts of Free Labor in Antebellum America* (New Haven: Yale University Press, 1991); Jonathan A. Glickstein, *American Exceptionalism, American Anxiety: Wages, Competition, and Degraded Labor in the Antebellum United States* (Charlottesville: University of Virginia Press, 2002); Eric Foner, *Free Soil, Free Labor, Free Men: The Ideology of the Republican Party Before the Civil War* (New York: Oxford University Press, 1970); Amy Dru Stanley, *From Bondage to Contract: Wage Labor, Marriage, and the Market in the Age of Slave Emancipation* (New York: Cambridge University Press, 1998).

8. Nathan I. Huggins, "The Deforming Mirror of Truth: Slavery and the Master Narrative of American History," *Radical History Review* 49 (1991): 25–48.

steeped in the lessons of Lockean liberalism and competitive individualism.[9] The ascent of social history in the 1970s and the new attention devoted to women and people of color made such generalizations difficult, but by the 1980s and 1990s scholars were once again identifying economic opportunity for some with freedom for all. While the colonial period witnessed substantive inequality (contrary to the 1950s consensus interpretation), the American Revolution ushered in a liberal society that maximized freedom via a capitalist marketplace. As Gordon Wood's Pulitzer Prize–winning *Radicalism of the American Revolution* boldly declared, the United States "would discover its greatness by creating a prosperous free society belonging to obscure people with their workaday concerns and their pecuniary pursuits of happiness—common people with their common interests in making money and getting ahead."[10]

Despite a historiographical trend that has transformed a world of unfree labor into a world of freedom in the aftermath of the American Revolution, scholars of the early Republic must recognize the continuities—if not the expansion—of coerced labor in the era's developing economy. The presumptive equation of capitalism with democracy and freedom has obscured the massive expansion of slavery in the early Republic and the contributions of that mode of production to national economic growth. Equally important, the rhetorical melding of capitalism, democracy, and freedom allows historians to dismiss unfree labor practices within capitalism as anomalies. The profitable use of enslaved labor in industrial production and the implementation of forced labor within social welfare policies, for example, indicate "contradictions" or "ambiguities" within capitalism. Such practices appear as temporary expediencies that will ultimately prove unnecessary as capitalism's inherent logic takes hold. Economic historians have tended to write as if American economic development should follow a linear progression toward a "pure" capitalism where coercion would ultimately

9. Louis Hartz, *The Liberal Tradition in America: An Interpretation of American Political Thought Since the Revolution* (New York: Harcourt, Brace & World, 1955), 309; Richard Hofstadter, *The American Political Tradition and the Men Who Made It* (New York: Knopf, 1948); Robert E. Brown, *Middle-Class Democracy and the Revolution in Massachusetts, 1691–1780* (Ithaca: Cornell University Press, 1955). "Why should we make a five-year plan for ourselves when God seems to have had a thousand-year plan ready-made for us?" asked Daniel Boorstin in *The Genius of American Politics* (Chicago: University of Chicago Press, 1953), 179. Charles S. Grant, *Democracy in the Connecticut Frontier Town of Kent* (New York: Columbia University Press, 1961), 53. See also James T. Lemon, *The Best Poor Man's Country: A Geographical Study of Early Southeastern Pennsylvania* (Baltimore: Johns Hopkins University Press, 1972). For a succinct evaluation of consensus history, see James Henretta, "Communications," *William and Mary Quarterly* 37 (October 1980): 696–97; Peter Novick, *That Noble Dream: The "Objectivity Question" and the American Historical Profession* (New York: Cambridge University Press, 1988), 332–37.

10. Wood, *Radicalism of the American Revolution,* 369. The argument that the American Revolution gave birth to a flourishing liberal society does not come from the margins of the profession. Wood's efforts garnered the 1993 Pulitzer Prize in history. Joyce Appleby, the other leading exponent of this position during the past decade, has served as president of the Organization of American Historians, the American Historical Association, and the Society for Historians of the Early American Republic.

prove unnecessary. From this perspective, the persistence of unfree labor in the early Republic merely suggests that the kinks had yet to be worked out of the system. By conceptualizing unfree labor as a paradox or a logical inconsistency within capitalism, historians enshrine freedom as the true dynamic of American economic history.[11]

This essay suggests a reorientation: The so-called "contradictions" of capitalism in the early Republic are better understood as constitutive elements of American economic development. Capitalism in this era relied less upon unfettered markets and mobility than on its relationship with the sizeable segment of the American population laboring under various forms of unfreedom. The economic history of the postrevolutionary United States simply makes no sense without slavery and coerced labor as central components.[12] The point is not that the economy of the early Republic was not truly capitalist because of its dependence upon unfree labor. Nor is the point that slavery was actually a capitalist form of labor organization because of its contribution to American economic growth. These arguments miss the larger possibilities of placing unfree labor at the center of economic history in the early Republic. For too long capitalism and slavery have been narrated as separate histories, at the cost of recognizing the contingent relationship between American economic development and unfree labor.

In the first decades of the nineteenth century, some Americans came to live in a world of economic liberalism precisely because other Americans did not. Some Americans could engage in self-making, consumerism, and enterprise because other Americans did not. Some Americans experienced boundless opportunity because other Americans did not. Economic freedom for some and economic unfreedom for others were not coincidences but were inextricably linked. We become aware of these connections only when we acknowledge the range of unfree labor arrangements that structured early-Republic capitalism.[13] To that end, this chapter will explore how slavery might be integrated into the

---

11. Historians focusing on the paradoxical relationship of capitalism and unfree labor owe a great deal to Edmund Morgan, "Slavery and Freedom: The American Paradox," *Journal of American History* 59 (June 1972): 5–29. Engaging with Morgan, Christine Daniels suggested that "slavery was not the paradox in early America . . . it was the paradigm." Christine Daniels, "Comment: Race and Class Politics of Antebellum U.S. Artisans," paper presented at the American Historical Association annual meeting, New York, January 1997.

12. Several historians have given unfreedom a key role but have not focused exclusively on issues of labor. See Howard Zinn, *A People's History of the United States* (New York: Harper and Row, 1980); Ronald Takaki, *Iron Cages: Race and Culture in Nineteenth-Century America* (New York: Oxford University Press, 1990); Edward Countryman, *Americans: A Collision of Histories* (New York: Hill and Wang, 1997); Eric Foner, *The Story of American Freedom* (New York: W. W. Norton, 1998).

13. For explicit connection between unfree labor and capitalist development, see Jones, *American Work*; Eric R. Wolf, *Europe and the People Without History* (Berkeley and Los Angeles: University of California Press, 1982); Evelyn Nakano Glenn, *Unequal Freedom: How Race and Gender Shaped American Citizenship and Labor* (Cambridge: Harvard University Press, 2002).

broader history of capitalism in the late eighteenth and early nineteenth centuries, and will catalog the persistence of other forms of unfree labor within the
emergent wage economy. But before we explore the unfree origins of American
capitalism, we must first explain how unfree labor fell out of most historical
accounts of economic development in the early Republic.

The Declining Fortunes of Unfree Labor

Joyce Appleby has noted that here, in "the most capitalistic country in the
world," historians "have a difficult time making precise just what social relations
the word, capitalism, refers to, not to mention how to characterize its development across the four centuries of American history." The story is, indeed,
"vexed."[14] The key historiographical questions have centered on the timing of
capitalism's arrival, the nature of the system it replaced, and the relative ease of
the transition from one to the other. For some scholars, capitalism informed the
very circumstances of New World colonization and was, in effect, present at the
creation.[15] Many more scholars, however, have searched for an elusive "transition to capitalism" and have applied their energies to debating whether the transition to capitalism was uncontested (and thus quickly accomplished) or whether
the transition met great resistance (and was thus accomplished slowly, piecemeal,
and perhaps incompletely). Invariably this debate has involved an evaluation of
the economy that came before (was it precapitalist, anticapitalist, protocapitalist?)
and a value judgment as to whether the results of the transition to capitalism
were positive or negative.[16] The new social history of the 1970s portrayed ordinary Americans as unreceptive to the logic of capitalist accumulation, eager to
avoid unnecessary market participation, and ultimately injured by the triumph
of market relations. In the past decade, however, historians have increasingly
argued otherwise, contending that common Americans raced into the capitalist

14. Joyce Appleby, "The Vexed Story of Capitalism Told by American Historians," *Journal
of the Early Republic* 21 (Spring 2001): 1–18.

15. William Cronon, *Changes in the Land: Indians, Colonists, and the Ecology of New England*
(New York: Hill and Wang, 1983); Stephen Innes, *Labor in a New Land: Economy and Society in Seven-
teenth-Century Springfield* (Princeton: Princeton University Press, 1983); John Frederick Martin, *Profits
in the Wilderness: Entrepreneurship and the Founding of New England Towns in the Seventeenth Century*
(Chapel Hill: University of North Carolina Press, 1991); Denys Delage, *Bitter Feast: Amerindians and
Europeans in Northeastern North America, 1600–64,* trans. Jane Brierley (Vancouver: University of British
Columbia Press, 1993).

16. To borrow from Allan Kulikoff's useful description, while "social historians" were
searching for an antimarket mentalité that resisted the transition to capitalism, "market historians" cat-
aloged the profit-maximizing behavior of eighteenth- and early nineteenth-century farmers. Allan
Kulikoff, *The Agrarian Origins of American Capitalism* (Charlottesville: University Press of Virginia, 1992),
15. The debate between the market historians and the social historians has been a heated one. See, for
example, the exchange between Michael A. Bernstein and Sean Wilentz and Winifred B. Rothenberg
in the *Journal of Economic History* 44 (March 1984): 171–78.

marketplace in search of opportunity and self-improvement. As this interpretation has gained preeminence, the relationship of capitalism and unfreedom has fallen from the picture. Because capitalism originated in the everyday aspirations of common people, the history of American capitalism necessarily appears as the history of American freedom.

To trace out this historiographical shift and its consequences, we must begin in the wake of E. P. Thompson's *The Making of the English Working Class*. Informed by labor and social history and the premise of an oppositional working-class culture, historians following Thompson recovered the efforts of American workers to resist and reject market relations. Journeymen denounced their entrepreneurial masters, who were jettisoning a timeless system of craft training and mutuality. Organizing politically and invoking their republican heritage, skilled artisans struggled to preserve their declining autonomy in commercial cities. Their rhetoric associated wage labor with a form of slavery.[17] In the countryside, farming families strove to produce household subsistence and rejected competitive market exchange that threatened their independence. Some historians have found rural communities striving against capitalism in the name of democracy as late as 1900.[18] The crowning contribution to this interpretation was Charles Sellers's 1991 tome, *The Market Revolution*, which characterized Jacksonian America as a pitched battle between urban capitalism and rural agrarianism. Sellers not only depicted these two forces as engaged in an irreconcilable *Kulturkampf* but declared that, "contrary to liberal mythology, democracy was born in tension with capitalism and not as its natural and legitimizing political expression." The ascent of capitalism in the United States required a revolution, one

17. Alan Dawley, *Class and Community: The Industrial Revolution in Lynn* (Cambridge: Harvard University Press, 1976); Howard B. Rock, *Artisans of the New Republic: The Tradesmen of New York City in the Age of Jefferson* (New York: New York University Press, 1979); Sean Wilentz, *Chants Democratic: New York City and the Rise of the American Working Class, 1788–1850* (New York: Oxford University Press, 1984); Steven J. Ross, *Workers on the Edge: Work, Leisure, and Politics in Industrializing Cincinnati, 1788–1890* (New York: Columbia University Press, 1985); Bruce Laurie, *Artisans into Workers: Labor in Nineteenth-Century America* (New York: Hill and Wang, 1989). The new labor history approach to the early Republic is surveyed in Richard Stott, "Artisans and Capitalist Development," *Journal of the Early Republic* 16 (Spring 1996): 257–71.

18. Michael Merrill, "Cash Is Good to Eat: Self-Sufficiency and Exchange in the Rural Economy of the United States," *Radical History Review* 3 (Winter 1977): 42–71; James Henretta, "Families and Farms: *Mentalité* in Pre-Industrial America," *William and Mary Quarterly*, 3d ser., 35 (January 1978): 3–32; James Henretta, *The Origins of American Capitalism: Selected Essays* (Boston: Northeastern University Press, 1991); Christopher Clark, "Household Economy, Market Exchange, and the Rise of Capitalism in the Connecticut Valley, 1800–1860," *Journal of Social History* 13 (Winter 1979): 169–89; Christopher Clark, *The Roots of Rural Capitalism: Western Massachusetts, 1780–1860* (Ithaca: Cornell University Press, 1990); Steven Hahn, *The Roots of Southern Populism: Yeoman Farmers and the Transformation of the Georgia Upcountry, 1850–1890* (New York: Oxford University Press, 1983); Lawrence Goodwyn, *The Populist Moment: A Short History of the Agrarian Revolt in America* (New York: Oxford University Press, 1978). See also the essays in Steven Hahn and Jonathan Prude, eds., *The Countryside in the Age of Capitalist Transformation: Essays in the Social History of Rural America* (Chapel Hill: University of North Carolina Press, 1985).

that in Sellers's account undercut—rather than fulfilled—the democratic promise of the American Revolution.[19]

When *The Market Revolution* appeared, it seemed perfectly plausible that a left-leaning critique of capitalism reigned historiographically supreme. Graduate reading lists and undergraduate syllabi featured texts that made the transition to capitalism appear problematic, less than inevitable, and perhaps regrettable.[20] But ultimately a different story prevailed in the 1990s, describing the early emergence of a market economy and the lack of resistance it met, particularly in the countryside. Economic historians discovered farmers' willingness to cart produce great distances for better prices and their efforts to anticipate consumer demand several seasons ahead in allocating cropland and slaughtering livestock. Such strategies resulted in price convergences in rural Massachusetts, New York, and Philadelphia after 1780. Rather than standing in the way of a capitalist economy, northern farmers were at the forefront of the kind of behavior we associate with capitalism.[21] When they complained about the market, they were not nostalgic for a premarket past but were lamenting that producers like themselves sometimes lacked the same economic opportunities as merchants and bankers. Admittedly, rural families engaged in market activity in order to meet family subsistence needs and to pursue goals of household reproduction rather than limitless profit. These goals of competency nonetheless required competition and situated rural families firmly within the marketplace; there seemed little to suggest they wanted it otherwise.[22]

19. Charles Sellers, *The Market Revolution: Jacksonian America, 1815–1846* (New York: Oxford University Press, 1991), 32. In a forum devoted to the book, Sellers further expressed hope that scholars would question the relationship between capitalism and democracy: "Nothing could be more liberating for American historians—or more salutary in this hour of capitalist triumphalism—than recognizing our own embeddedness in the liberal ideology we should be subjecting to critical analysis." For assessments of Sellers, see "A Symposium on *The Market Revolution*," *Journal of the Early Republic* 12 (Winter 1992): 475; William Glanapp, "The Myth of Class in Jacksonian America," *Journal of Policy History* 6, no. 2 (1994): 232–59; Melvyn Stokes and Stephen Conway, eds., *The Market Revolution in America: Social, Political, and Religious Expressions, 1800–1880* (Charlottesville: University Press of Virginia, 1996). See also Tony Freyer, *Producers Versus Capitalists: Constitutional Conflict in Antebellum America* (Charlottesville: University Press of Virginia, 1994).

20. Christine Stansell, *City of Women: Sex and Class in New York, 1789–1860* (New York: Knopf, 1986); Paul E. Johnson, *A Shopkeeper's Millennium: Society and Revivals in Rochester, New York, 1815–1837* (New York: Hill and Wang, 1978); Michael Merrill and Sean Wilentz, *The Key of Liberty: The Life and Democratic Writings of William Manning, "A Laborer," 1747–1814* (Cambridge: Harvard University Press, 1993); Billy G. Smith, *The "Lower Sort": Philadelphia's Laboring People, 1750–1800* (Ithaca: Cornell University Press, 1990); Morton Horwitz, *The Transformation of American Law, 1780–1860* (Cambridge: Harvard University Press, 1977); Carolyn Merchant, *Ecological Revolutions; Nature, Gender, and Science in New England* (Chapel Hill: University of North Carolina Press, 1989).

21. Winifred B. Rothenberg, *From Market-Places to a Market Economy: The Transformation of Rural Massachusetts, 1750–1850* (Chicago: University of Chicago Press, 1992); Naomi R. Lamoreaux, "Rethinking the Transition to Capitalism in the Early American Northeast," *Journal of American History* 90 (September 2003): 437–61.

22. Daniel Vickers, "Competency and Competition: Economic Culture in Early America," *William and Mary Quarterly*, 3d ser., 47 (January 1990): 3–29; Richard L. Bushman, "Markets and

It also turned out that those militant urban artisans were incipient capitalists as well. Tina H. Sheller described the Baltimore artisan as "a rational man of business" who "employed the cheapest skilled labor available, offered a variety of goods and services to meet the demands of the local market, and invested his earnings in land and buildings."[23] Gary J. Kornblith profiled Joseph Buckingham, the Boston printer who "redefin[ed] independence as adherence to an ethos of enterprise."[24] Joyce Appleby located the "popular sources of American capitalism" in the ambition of indentured blacksmith Ichabod Washburn. Bound out by his widowed mother at age nine, Washburn spent the next decade laboring to purchase an early freedom in 1818. He soon started his own company, which produced lead pipe for woolen manufactories in Worcester, Massachusetts. By 1840 Washburn had become one of the nation's largest manufacturers of iron wire. "A prototype for the American self-made man," Washburn "hitched his star to the wagon of economic development."[25] Claiming the last word in the *Journal of the Early Republic*'s 1996 special issue on capitalism, Gordon Wood identified republican "laborers" and small producers as "the main force behind America's capitalist market revolution."[26]

In broad synthetic strokes, and lucid and compelling prose, Wood and Appleby made economic development and political democratization the same story. By shedding English rule and then dismissing the aristocratic pretension of the Federalists, common Americans created a society free of the hierarchy, rank, and station that had previously stifled ambition, ingenuity, and mobility. This was, in Wood's account, what made the American Revolution radical: it demolished "two millennia" of contempt for individual ambition and created "almost overnight, the most liberal, the most democratic, the most commercially minded, and the most modern people in the world."[27] In Appleby's version, "the rate of growth in the early republic was largely set by ordinary men and women whose propensity to move, to innovate, to accept paper money, and to switch

Composite Farms in Early America," *William and Mary Quarterly*, 3d ser., 55 (July 1998): 351–74; James Henretta, "The 'Market' in the Early Republic," *Journal of the Early Republic* 18 (Summer 1998): 288; Terry Bouton, "A Road Closed: Rural Insurgency in Post-Independence Pennsylvania," *Journal of American History* 87 (December 2000): 855–87; Martin Bruegel, *Farm, Shop, Landing: The Rise of a Market Society in the Hudson Valley, 1780–1860* (Durham: Duke University Press, 2002).

23. Tina H. Sheller, "Freemen, Servants, and Slaves: Artisans and the Craft Structure of Revolutionary Baltimore Town," in *American Artisans: Crafting Social Identity, 1750–1850*, ed. Howard B. Rock, Paul A. Gilje, and Robert Asher (Baltimore: Johns Hopkins University Press, 1995), 26–27. See also Donna J. Rilling, *Making Houses, Crafting Capitalism: Builders in Philadelphia, 1790–1850* (Philadelphia: University of Pennsylvania Press, 2001).

24. Gary J. Kornblith, "Becoming Joseph T. Buckingham: The Struggle for Artisanal Independence in Early-Nineteenth-Century Boston," in Rock, Gilje, and Asher, *American Artisans*, 134.

25. Joyce Appleby, "The Popular Sources of American Capitalism," *Studies in American Political Development* 9 (Fall 1995): 445–46.

26. Wood, "The Enemy Is Us," 306–7.

27. Wood, *Radicalism of the American Revolution*, 7–8.

from homemade goods once commercial ones were available paced the expansion of farming, commerce, credit, and information." These developments attested to the "imaginative linking of political and economic liberty into a single cause of prosperity."[28] Arguing from anecdotal evidence, Wood and Appleby repudiated three decades of quantitative social history documenting rising inequality in the postrevolutionary United States. Despite receiving significant criticism for ignoring the racial and gender inequalities that structured society in the early Republic, the Wood and Appleby accounts of democratic capitalism remain highly influential among academic historians and the history-reading public alike.[29]

Historians on both sides of the "transition-to-capitalism" debate must confront the stunning evidence of economic development during the early years of the Republic. The exponential growth of canal and turnpike mileage, the proliferation of banks and corporate charters, the impact of technological innovations in milling, manufacturing, and transportation—all contributed to the emergence of a national market that linked consumers and producers across hundreds of miles.[30] Falling transportation costs and travel times opened a world of possibilities for Americans, and historians have often used such statistics as benchmarks for dating capitalism's arrival. Indeed, most scholarship on early-Republic capitalism has been content to define capitalism by its effects: an improved transportation infrastructure that facilitated the movement of goods across great distances; the rationalization of productive processes and the increased orientation of farmers, artisans, and manufacturers toward market exchange; growing links between urban and rural Americans in a common consumer culture in which rich, middling, and poor might participate; the generating of capital and a cash medium to facilitate exchange; the recognition of corporations and the sanctification of property rights (over customary rights) in statutory and common law; the cultural legitimization of self-interested behavior and celebration of the self-made man who improved his lot through hard work and delayed

28. Appleby, *Inheriting the Revolution,* 89, 253, 58–59.

29. Interestingly, some commentators have suggested that instead of celebrating the democratization of American life in the nineteenth century, Wood laments it: "No doubt that the cost America paid for this democracy was high—with its vulgarity, its materialism, its rootlessness, its anti-intellectualism" (*Radicalism of the American Revolution,* 369). Instead, his sympathies are with the Federalists and other elites who got bumped out of the way. See Joyce Appleby, Barbara Clark Smith, and Michael Zuckerman, "Forum: How Revolutionary was the Revolution: A Discussion of Gordon S. Wood's *The Radicalism of the American Revolution,*" *William and Mary Quarterly,* 3d ser., 51 (October 1994): 679–702. Wood received a more positive review in Newt Gingrich, *To Renew America* (New York: Harper Collins, 1995), 32–33. On growing inequalities, see Lee Soltow, *The Distribution of Wealth and Income in the United States in 1798* (Pittsburgh: University of Pittsburgh Press, 1989); Smith, *"Lower Sort."*

30. Carol Sheriff, *The Artificial River: The Erie Canal and the Paradox of Progress, 1817–1862* (New York: Hill and Wang, 1996); Daniel Feller, *The Jacksonian Promise: America, 1815–1840* (Baltimore: Johns Hopkins University Press, 1995); Harry L. Watson, *Liberty and Power: The Politics of Jacksonian America* (New York: Noonday Press, 1990).

gratification; and the establishment of a market in labor that allowed workers to choose their own employers, quit at will, and toil free of physical violence in exchange for wages. Although facets of capitalism appeared in Renaissance Venice and Puritan New England, this constellation of practices, institutions, and cultural ideals did not converge until the founding of the American nation.[31]

By locating capitalism in the early Republic's "culture of progress," however, historians have been blind to capitalism's underlying social relations.[32] As Michael Merrill has explained, historians err in seeing capitalism as "just an economic system based on market exchange, private property, wage labor, and sophisticated financial instruments." Instead, historians must define capitalism through the power relations that channel the fruits of economic development toward those who coordinate capital to generate additional capital, who own property rather than rent it, and who compel labor rather than perform it. In a capitalist economy, the primary mechanism for meeting and surpassing a subsistence standard of living and gaining access to additional productive property is the control of other people's labor power. In a capitalist economy, impartial market forces ostensibly set the rules of production and reproduction, but not all members of society can enter that market freely, to their own benefit, and with equal protection from its vagaries. These rules will be naturalized through cultural production and social practices, but ultimately the state serves as their enforcer and can deploy physical violence when necessary to uphold them. For those whose physical labor fuels economic development, it will be almost impossible to play by different rules, or to opt out of playing altogether, and they will have little control over the pace, structure, or remuneration of their work.[33]

---

31. Paul A. Gilje, ed., *The Wages of Independence: Capitalism in the Early American Republic* (Madison, Wis.: Madison House, 1997); Paul E. Johnson, "The Market Revolution," in *The Encyclopedia of American Social History*, ed. Mary Kupiec Cayton, Elliott J. Gorn, and Peter W. Williams (New York: Charles Scribner's Sons, 1993), 1:545–60.

32. Historians of the early Republic tend to eschew theoretical definitions of capitalism that center on social relations. Marx, Weber, Gramsci, and other social theorists rarely appear in footnotes, certainly not to the extent to which they inform the work of European historians and historical sociologists. See John R. Hall, ed., *Reworking Class* (Ithaca: Cornell University Press, 1998). At present, there is not a flourishing Marxist historiography, but see Rona S. Weiss, "The Market and Massachusetts Farmers, 1750–1850: Comment," *Journal of Economic History* 43 (June 1983): 476; John Ashworth, *Slavery, Capitalism, and Politics in the Antebellum Republic* (New York: Cambridge University Press, 1996).

33. Michael Merrill, "Putting 'Capitalism' in Its Place: A Review of Recent Literature," *William and Mary Quarterly*, 3d ser., 52 (April 1995): 322, 326; David Montgomery, *Citizen Worker: The Experience of Workers in the United States with Democracy and the Free Market During the Nineteenth Century* (New York: Cambridge University Press, 1993); William M. Reddy, *The Rise of Market Culture: The Textile Trade and French Society, 1750–1900* (New York: Cambridge University Press, 1984); Sonya Rose, "Class Formation and the Quintessential Worker," in Hall, *Reworking Class*, 133–66; James Schmidt, *Free to Work: Labor Law, Emancipation, and Reconstruction, 1815–1860* (Athens: University of Georgia Press, 1998); Robert Steinfeld, *Coercion, Contract, and Free Labor in the Nineteenth Century* (New York: Cambridge University Press, 2001).

When historians focus on the transformative effects of capitalism during the early years of the Republic—the acres of wilderness converted to production, the spread of urban fashion deep into the countryside, the pervasive
rhetoric of self-making—it is easy to lose sight of the coercion of labor. But
when historians explore the social relations of capitalism during this era, the
story necessarily looks different. At the center of any analysis of capitalism stands
"the labor question," or what Peter Kolchin has characterized as "Who should
work for whom, under what terms should work be performed, and how should
it be compelled or rewarded?"[34] The answers that emerged in the early Republic meant that the "culture of progress" would be built upon a series of exploitive
relationships. Canals did not dig themselves any more than cotton picked itself
and converted itself into shirts and pants. Early republican boosters and their historians have pretended otherwise, erasing unfreedom from the story of American
capitalism. Let us now turn to the ways in which that story might be recovered.

Slavery and American Economic Growth

The period between 1790 and 1840 witnessed the rapid expansion of slavery in
the United States. Between the ratification of the Constitution and the closing
of the Atlantic slave trade in 1808, more than 235,000 enslaved Africans entered
the new nation—almost as many new slaves in that brief twenty-year span as
had been imported between 1700 and 1780. By the 1820s slave-grown cotton
had generated fortunes for planters in the new states of the South. As millions
of new acres were brought into cultivation, cotton quickly became the nation's
most valuable export crop.[35] While arguably one of the key developments in the
economic history of these years, the emergence of the cotton kingdom is usually told as a sectional history—namely, the rise of the South. Attention quickly
focuses on southern distinctiveness and the extent to which slaveholders were
complicit with or opposed to the changes accompanying the market revolution.[36]
But no matter how frequently southern slaveholders denounced bourgeois liberalism, there can be little doubt that the slave system played an indispensable role
in the emergence of a national capitalist economy. Nor must one accept Charles
Sumner's famous accusation of a conspiracy between the lords of the loom and

34. Peter Kolchin, "The Big Picture: A Comment on David Brion Davis's 'Looking at Slavery from Broader Perspectives,'" *American Historical Review* 105 (April 2000): 468.

35. Herbert Klein, *The Atlantic Slave Trade* (New York: Cambridge University Press, 1999),
210–11; Robert W. Fogel, *Without Consent or Contract: The Rise and Fall of American Slavery* (New York:
W. W. Norton, 1989), 61–72; Jones, *American Work,* 191–218; Stuart Bruchey, *Cotton and the Growth of
the American Economy: 1790–1860* (New York: Harcourt, Brace & World, 1967); Johnson, "Market Revolution," 554.

36. Douglas R. Egerton, "Markets Without a Market Revolution: Southern Planters and
Capitalism," *Journal of the Early Republic* 16 (Summer 1996): 207–21.

the lords of the lash in order to see the simultaneous expansion of slavery and capitalism in the early Republic as no mere coincidence.[37]

Sixty years ago, Eric Williams postulated that West Indian slavery financed English industrialization. Although much criticized as an explanation of British economic development, Williams's famous juxtaposition of slavery and capitalism still warrants consideration for the United States.[38] Although southern in its location, American slavery was not "regionally restricted," and it generated wealth, defined racial and class identities, and facilitated consumerism for men and women far removed from the actual buying and selling of African Americans.[39] American capitalism flourished within a "slaveholding republic," where slavery infused the nation's politics, culture, and economy. Slavery's protection and perpetuation was of national concern.[40]

As James Oakes has observed, "behind every task assigned to every slave every day stood the mill owners and factory hands of Old and New England."[41]

37. Charles Sumner asserted this proposition at an 1848 Whig convention in Worcester, Massachusetts. See Thomas O'Connor, *Lords of the Loom: The Cotton Whigs and the Coming of the Civil War* (New York: Charles Scribner's Sons, 1968), 47; Philip S. Foner, *Business and Slavery: The New York Merchants and the Irrepressible Conflict* (Chapel Hill: University of North Carolina Press, 1941).

38. Russell Menard, "'Capitalism and Slavery': Personal Reflections on Eric Williams and Reconstruction of Early American History," in *The World Turned Upside-Down: The State of Eighteenth-Century American Studies at the Beginning of the Twenty-First Century,* ed. Michael V. Kennedy and William G. Shade (Bethlehem: Lehigh University Press, 2001), 325. Williams, *Capitalism and Slavery.* For Williams-inspired scholarship, see note 1 above. For the critique of Williams, see Roger T. Anstey, "Capitalism and Slavery: A Critique," *Economic History Review* 21 (August 1968): 307–20; Howard Temperley, "Capitalism, Slavery, and Ideology," *Past and Present* 75 (May 1977): 94–118; Seymour Drescher, *Econocide: British Slavery in the Era of Abolition* (Pittsburgh: University of Pittsburgh Press, 1977); Seymour Drescher, *Capitalism and Antislavery: British Mobilization in Comparative Perspective* (New York: Oxford University Press, 1987); Thomas Bender, ed., *The Antislavery Debate: Capitalism and Abolitionism as a Problem in Historical Interpretation* (Berkeley and Los Angeles: University of California Press, 1992).

39. David Roediger and Martin H. Blatt, eds., *The Meaning of Slavery in the North* (New York: Garland, 1998), xiii–xiv. Larry Neal argues that slavery's contribution to national wealth in the period 1790–1850 was three times as great as that made by free immigrant workers. See Neal, "A Calculation and Comparison of the Current Benefits of Slavery and an Analysis of Who Benefits," in *The Wealth of Races: The Present Value of Benefits from Past Injustices,* ed. Richard F. America (Westport, Conn.: Greenwood Press, 1990), 91–105. Robert S. Browne observes: "Any effort to assess the contribution of slaves to the economy at the time (and to present economic shares) must conclude that the United States' emergence as an industrial nation was possible only because of the massive input provided by slave labor at a time when labor was the scarce factor in the production function." See Browne, "Achieving Parity through Reparations," in America, *Wealth of Races,* 202.

40. Don E. Fehrenbacher, *The Slaveholding Republic: An Account of the United States Government's Relations to Slavery* (New York: Oxford University Press, 2001); Ira Berlin, "North of Slavery: Black People in a Slaveholding Republic," paper presented to the Gilder Lehrman Center for the Study of Slavery, Resistance, and Abolition, Yale University, September 27, 2002; Paul Finkelman, "Slavery and the Constitutional Convention: Making a Covenant with Death," in *Beyond Confederation: Origins of the Constitution and American National Identity,* ed. Richard Beeman et al. (Chapel Hill: University of North Carolina Press, 1987), 188–225.

41. James Oakes, *The Ruling Race: A History of American Slaveholders* (New York: Knopf, 1982), 53; Rachel Chernos Lin, "The Rhode Island Slave-Traders: Butchers, Bakers, and Candlestick-Makers," *Slavery and Abolition* 23 (December 2002): 21–38.

These connections between slavery and capitalism, however, began well before the American Revolution. Enslaved workers played a key role in creating the physical infrastructure of commercial exchange during the colonial period. Enslaved Africans and African Americans improved Manhattan roads, erected Philadelphia counting-houses, and manned the ships that carried goods throughout the Atlantic.[42] In New England, according to Joanne Pope Melish, slaves performed inherently valuable domestic labor that "released white males to engage in new professional, artisan, and entrepreneurial activities, thus increasing productivity and easing the transition from a household-based to a market-based economy."[43] At the same time, many of the leading families of American industrialization made their initial fortunes in the broader Atlantic slave economy. The Cabots, who erected the Beverly Cotton Mill in 1789, were deeply immersed in the so-called triangular trade; the rum they produced from West Indian molasses in turn purchased West African slaves destined for West Indian sugar plantations. One of their mercantile agents foresaw Massachusetts "coarse cloths" as a valuable commodity in "the Guinea Market." The Hazards family propelled Rhode Island to the forefront of the "negro cloth" industry, which accounted for 79 percent of the state's woolen production by 1850. The Rhode Island Browns (financiers of Samuel Slater) and the Massachusetts Lowells (key partners in the Boston Associates) also raised capital from earlier ventures in the Atlantic plantation complex.[44]

Early in the nineteenth century slave-grown cotton became, to quote Robert Fogel, "the essential raw material for hundreds of thousands of factory hands in the North and Europe. It provided employment for several million other workers in transportation, in handicrafts, and in wholesale or retail trade."[45] Northern shippers and insurers made sure that slave-grown cotton arrived safely in England. The profits they deposited in northern banks were in turn lent to southern planters seeking capital to invest in additional land and labor. When

42. Peter Linebaugh and Marcus Rediker, *The Many-Headed Hydra: Sailors, Slaves, Commoners, and the Hidden History of the Revolutionary Atlantic* (Boston: Beacon Press, 2000); Graham Russell Hodges, *Root and Branch: African Americans in New York and East Jersey, 1613–1863* (Chapel Hill: University of North Carolina Press, 1999); Leslie Harris, *In the Shadow of Slavery: African Americans in New York City, 1626–1863* (Chicago: University of Chicago Press, 2003); W. Jeffrey Bolster, *Black Jacks: African American Seamen in the Age of Sail* (Cambridge: Harvard University Press, 1997).

43. Melish, *Disowning Slavery,* 7–8, 15–21. Melish expands on Lorenzo J. Greene, *The Negro in Colonial New England* (New York: Columbia University Press, 1942), and Edgar J. McManus, *Black Bondage in the North* (Syracuse: Syracuse University Press, 1973).

44. Ronald Bailey, "'Those Valuable People, the Africans': The Economic Impact of the Slave(ry) Trade on Textile Industrialization in New England," in Roediger and Blatt, *Meaning of Slavery,* 3–31; Myron O. Stachiw, "'For the Sake of Commerce': Slavery, Antislavery, and Northern Industry," ibid., 33–44. For an elaboration, see Ronald Bailey, "The Slavery Trade and the Development of Capitalism in the United States: The Textile Industry in New England," *Social Science History* 14 (Fall 1990): 373–414; Ronald Bailey, "Africa, the Slave Trade, and Industrial Capitalism in Europe and the United States," *American History: A Bibliographic Review* (1986): 1–91.

45. Fogel, *Without Consent or Contract,* 106.

slaveholders returned their own profits to northern banks, their deposits funded loans to northern entrepreneurs. Scholars—thanks to current lawsuits seeking reparations for slavery—are only now delving into the records of individual firms to discover the financial ties between slavery and capitalism. Already northern banking, shipping, and insurance companies have had to defend their eighteenth- and nineteenth-century relationship to slavery.[46] By 1859 as much as $462 million of southern wealth accrued to the northern states annually.[47]

However, more than interregional commerce made nineteenth-century economic development a national project. Although its labor force remained in chains, the southern states developed a manufacturing infrastructure, laid railroad track, and forged iron at a rate comparable to those of France, Germany, and Austria-Hungary.[48] Only in comparison with the North or England did southern industrial development seem slow. Moreover, the behaviors associated with market revolution nationally were not absent from the nineteenth-century South, especially as slaveholders' aspirations to feudal social relations required a deep immersion in the capitalist marketplace. Slaveholders responded promptly to market signals in terms of their crop allocation and slave purchases or sales; they embraced transportation technologies like steamboats to gain marketing efficiency; they gathered information assiduously in order to rationalize production; they regulated time in ways consistent with advanced production; they created a body of law around absolute property rights; and they constructed a middle-class identity through domesticity and consumerism. Slaveholders and capitalists shared perhaps more than they would have preferred.[49]

46. Eric Foner, "Slavery's Fellow Travelers," op-ed, *New York Times*, July 13, 2000; Brent Staples, "How Slavery Fueled Business in the North," op-ed, *New York Times*, July 24, 2000; "Forum: Making the Case for Racial Reparations: Does America Owe a Debt to the Descendants of its Slaves?" *Harper's* magazine (November 2000), 37–51; Randall Robinson, *The Debt: What America Owes to Blacks* (New York: E. P. Dutton, 2000). Aetna, the Hartford insurance company, recently apologized for policies it issued in the 1850s to slaveholders against the loss of their human property. FleetBoston Financial Corporation faced a reparations lawsuit as a corporate descendant of Rhode Island's Providence Bank. Under the direction of founder John Brown, Providence Bank had financed illegal slaving voyages after Americans were prohibited from involvement in the Atlantic slave trade. Wall Street's connection to slavery remains unexplored, although New York City's effort to secede from the Union in 1860 begs the question.

47. Douglass C. North, *The Economic Growth of the United States, 1790–1860* (Englewood Cliffs, N.J.: Prentice-Hall, 1961), 114–15.

48. Fogel, *Without Consent or Contract*, 87, 103.

49. Robert Fogel contends that slaveholders created "a flexible, highly developed form of capitalism." See ibid., 64–68, 94, 109; Mark Smith, *Mastered by the Clock: Time, Slavery, and Freedom in the American South* (Chapel Hill: University of North Carolina Press, 1997); Walter Johnson, *Soul by Soul: Life Inside the Antebellum Slave Market* (Cambridge: Harvard University Press, 1999); Michele Gillespie, *Free Labor in an Unfree World: White Artisans in Slaveholding Georgia, 1789–1860* (Athens: University of Georgia Press, 2000); Keith C. Barton, "'Good Cooks and Washers': Slave Hiring, Domestic Labor, and the Market in Bourbon County, Kentucky," *Journal of American History* 84 (September 1997): 436–60.

The class relations that constituted capitalism in the North also bore the mark of slavery. As David Brion Davis has explained, "the debasement of millions of workers to a supposedly bestial condition of repetitive time appeared to liberate other human beings to take control of their destiny, to 'remake' themselves." A commodity like sugar propelled millions of Africans into unprecedented extremes of misery, while providing an opportunity for self-fashioning to an emergent middle class.[50] Slavery also did essential cultural work to legitimate wage labor. Precisely because it was not slavery, wage labor moved from a badge of unrepublican dependence at the time of the American Revolution to the hallmark of liberal freedom during the Civil War. As Stanley Engerman explains, "If slavery is regarded as a unique mode of control of individuals, this would seem to make all nonslavery appear as freedom and, therefore, to be regarded as a progressive and desirable development." As the northern public became increasingly critical of slavery in the 1850s, wage labor attained a growing acceptance.[51]

For Euro-American members of the working class, slavery provided what W. E. B. Du Bois called a "public and psychological" wage that compensated for the meager cash wages they received at the hands of capitalist employers. That bonus consisted of membership in the white race and conveyed significant privilege and status in a white-supremacist society. Ultimately, the wage of whiteness sustained race as America's primary social division and muted class antagonisms between white workers and their bosses. Following Du Bois, scholars like David Roediger have contended that "white workers could, and did, define and accept their class positions by fashioning identities as 'not slaves' and as 'not Blacks.'"[52] Obviously, capitalist labor relations emerged in other places where workers did not have recourse to a therapeutic racial identity. But without question the vitality of slavery shaped the specific trajectory of American capitalism. The enslavement of several million African Americans clearly contextualized a Workingmen's Party circular decrying "wage slavery," a Lowell striker's placard insisting that "American Ladies will not be Slaves," or an Irish maid's retort that "none but *negers* are *sarvants.*" If the satisfaction of not being a slave was enough to smooth white workers' entrance into wage relations, then

50. David Brion Davis, "Looking at Slavery from Broader Perspectives," *American Historical Review* 105 (April 2000): 455; Sidney W. Mintz, *Sweetness and Power: The Place of Sugar in Modern History* (New York: Viking, 1985); Oakes, *Slavery and Freedom,* 45.

51. Stanley L. Engerman, "Slavery at Different Times and Places," *American Historical Review* 105 (April 2000): 480; Marcus Cunliffe, *Chattel Slavery and Wage Slavery: The Anglo-American Context, 1830–1860* (Athens: University of Georgia Press, 1979); Jonathan A. Glickstein, "'Poverty Is Not Slavery': American Abolitionists and the Competitive Labor Market," in *Antislavery Reconsidered: New Perspectives on the Abolitionists,* ed. Lewis Perry and Michael Fellman (Baton Rouge: Louisiana State University Press, 1979), 195–218; Bender, *Antislavery Debate.*

52. W. E. B. Du Bois, *Black Reconstruction in the United States, 1860–1880* (1935; New York: Athenaeum, 1969), 700; David Roediger, *The Wages of Whiteness: Race and the Making of the American Working Class* (New York: Verso, 1991), 13.

slavery—simply as a negative referent—becomes essential to the development of American capitalism.[53]

Coercion and the Wage Economy

The commodification of labor was the central development of capitalism in the early Republic, as a craft economy based upon mutuality gave way to a manufacturing economy where employers and workers encountered one another at the cash nexus. While workers organized to protect their livelihoods within the new system, there seemed to be little question that labor was a legitimate market commodity. Future attorney general Caesar Rodney invoked the sanctity of unimpeded wage relations in defense of Philadelphia cordwainers facing conspiracy charges in 1806: "No person is compelled to give [workmen] more than their work is worth, the market will sufficiently and correctly regulate these matters." Likewise, the New-England Association of Farmers, Mechanics, and Other Working Men opened its 1832 constitution with the hope that "our labor may be offered and disposed of as any other article in market."[54] Indeed, political economists of the early Republic like Daniel Raymond, Theodore Sedgwick, and Henry Carey envisioned capitalists and laborers negotiating freely over the conditions of employment. This opportunity differentiated wage earners from workers trapped in servitude and divided the world of work into free and unfree labor.[55]

Historians have not been hesitant to examine the boundary between free and unfree labor. Slavery could resemble wage labor when slaveholders embraced a liberal ethos, worked their slaves in industrial production, used positive incentives to maximize labor output, and bought and sold human property without pretense of paternalism.[56] Conversely, wage labor could appear akin to

53. Eric Foner, "Workers and Slavery," in *Working for Democracy: American Workers from the Revolution to the Present,* ed. Paul Buhle and Alan Dawley (Urbana: University of Illinois Press, 1985), 20; Noel Ignatiev, *How the Irish Became White* (New York: Routledge, 1995). The scholarship on women and whiteness is thin. See Dana Frank, "White Working Class Women and the Race Question," *International Labor and Working Class History* 54 (Fall 1998): 80–102.

54. Gary Kornblith, "The Artisanal Response to Capitalism," *Journal of the Early Republic* 10 (Fall 1990): 319; David Montgomery, "The Working Classes of the Pre-Industrial American History," *Labor History* 9 (Winter 1968): 12.

55. Robert Steinfeld, *The Invention of Free Labor: The Employment Relation in English and American Law and Culture, 1350–1870* (Chapel Hill: University of North Carolina Press, 1991); James L. Huston, "Abolitionists, Political Economists, and Capitalism," *Journal of the Early Republic* 20 (Fall 2000): 487–521. See also Paul Conkin, *Prophets of Prosperity: America's First Political Economists* (Bloomington: Indiana University Press, 1980); Allen Kaufman, *Capitalism, Slavery, and Republican Values: Antebellum Political Economists, 1819–1848* (Austin: University of Texas Press, 1982); Jeffrey S. Kahana, "Master and Servant in the Early Republic, 1780–1830," *Journal of the Early Republic* 20 (Spring 2000): 27–57.

56. James Oakes, *The Ruling Race: A History of American Slaveholders* (New York: Knopf, 1982); Smith, *Mastered by the Clock;* Robert W. Fogel and Stanley Engerman, *Time on the Cross: The*

slavery in its material exploitation of unskilled workers and its reliance upon legal coercion to hinder labor mobility.[57] Historians typically use such findings to identify ambiguities in otherwise coherent—and antithetical—modes of production. But as Stanley Engerman and Robert Steinfeld have suggested, scholars should take the next step and "rethink the basic soundness of the binary opposition of free/unfree labor."[58]

By most accounts, free labor involves choice and unfree labor involves coercion. For example, free workers supposedly enter wage relations voluntarily; they *choose* to work rather than to starve. For Steinfeld and Engerman, however, if this is a matter of choice, the same could be said of a slave choosing to work rather than to incur a beating or be sold away from family. While classical economists would view the "work-or-starve" choice as the natural outcome of market forces, Steinfeld and Engerman see this dilemma as historically contingent, located in the actions of the state to narrow the range of alternative possibilities. Laws regularly constrain opportunities to pursue subsistence outside wage labor: by enforcing rules of trespass that make it impossible to produce one's own food; by deterring geographical mobility through residency requirements for the franchise or access to public welfare; by enforcing vagrancy statutes that make it illegal not to labor; by regulating entry into certain professions via licensing; by criminalizing collective labor bargaining; by providing employers with legal remedies against workers who violate terms of hire; by denying classes of workers legal standing to own property or protect property in the courts. The state defines the contours of free labor, just as it provides unfree labor with legal sanction for physical violence and public resources for suppressing uprisings and capturing runaways. Steinfeld and Engerman situate wage labor in the power relations "of law, not of nature." The "coercive content of these

---

Economics of American Negro Slavery (Boston: Little Brown, 1974); Charles Dew, *Bond of Iron: Master and Slave at Buffalo Forge* (New York: W. W. Norton, 1994); T. Stephen Whitman, *The Price of Freedom: Slavery and Manumission in Baltimore and Early National Maryland* (Lexington: University Press of Kentucky, 1997); Midori Takagi, *Rearing Wolves to Our Own Destruction: Slavery in Richmond Virginia, 1782–1865* (Charlottesville: University Press of Virginia, 1999); John Bezís-Selfa, "A Tale of Two Ironworks: Slavery, Free Labor, Work, and Resistance in the Early Republic," *William and Mary Quarterly*, 3d ser., 56 (October 1999): 677–700; Charles Steffen, "The Pre-Industrial Iron Worker: Northampton Iron Works, 1780–1820," *Labor History* 20 (Winter 1979): 89–110. For the cold calculus of the slave trade, see Michael Tadman, *Speculators and Slaves: Masters, Traders, and Slaves in the Old South* (Madison: University of Wisconsin Press, 1989).

57. On material conditions, see Peter Way, *Common Labor: Workers and the Digging of North American Canals, 1780–1860* (New York: Cambridge University Press, 1993); Matthew E. Mason, "'The Hands Here Are Disposed to Be Turbulent': Unrest Among the Irish Trackmen of the Baltimore and Ohio Railroad, 1829–1851," *Labor History* 39 (August 1998): 253–72; Smith, *"Lower Sort."*

58. Robert J. Steinfeld and Stanley L. Engerman, "Labor—Free or Coerced? A Historical Reassessment of Differences and Similarities," in *Free and Unfree Labor: The Debate Continues*, ed. Tom Brass and Marcel van der Linden (Bern: Peter Lang, 1997), 118.

practices [runs] along a continuum, rather than in terms of a single yes/no (coerced/free) decision."[59]

The asymmetry of power that structured wage labor was not lost on contemporaries in the 1820s and 1830s. Labor radicals like Seth Luther and Stephen Simpson railed against the enrichment of the wealthy on the backs of the working poor.[60] State-sponsored investigations revealed the prevalence of ear-boxing and open-handed slaps in the supervision of child factory workers.[61] The political economist Thomas Cooper captured the inequality in an imagined conversation between employer and employee: "Here I am, able and willing to work," says the worker. "Receive employment on my terms, or use your skill and strength where you please, elsewhere. The choice is in your power," responds the capitalist.[62] Cooper's conversation was telling in the employer's declaration that the exchange would be "on my terms." A free market in labor did not cost employers the ability to control their workers; it simply required a different set of tools—and perhaps a different set of workers—than had been used under the earlier system of familial labor and indentured servitude.

By most accounts, the simple logic of the market provided employers with the upper hand: economic necessity effectively "coerced" workers into selling their labor for wages. But as many legal historians have recently argued, economic pressure was secondary to legal pressure in regulating wage labor in the nineteenth-century North. The law did not create a neutral arena in which employers and workers could meet at the simple cash nexus. Instead, the wage economy took shape under a regime of judge-made law that curtailed workers' individual ability to switch employers at will and their collective ability to withhold labor from the market. Although republican jurists revised English precedents of master and servant and recognized the legal freedom of white male adults, they nonetheless ensured, according to Christopher Tomlins, "that the emerging world of wage labor would be a world riddled with important and lasting asymmetries of power." In Karen Orren's estimation, nineteenth-century

59. Ibid., 116, 121. See also Stanley L. Engerman, ed., *Terms of Labor: Slavery, Serfdom, and Free Labor* (Stanford: Stanford University Press, 1999).

60. Seth Luther, *An Address to the Working Men of New England, on the State of Education, and On the Condition of the Producing Classes in Europe and America . . .* , 2d ed., (New York: George H. Evans, 1833); Stephen Simpson, *The Working Man's Manual: A New Theory of Political Economy, on the Principle of Production the Source of Wealth* (Philadelphia: Thomas L. Bonsal, 1831). See also Edward Pessen, *Most Uncommon Jacksonians: The Radical Leaders of the Early Labor Movement* (Albany: State University of New York Press, 1967).

61. *Report of the Select Committee Appointed to Visit the Manufacturing Districts of the Commonwealth, for the Purpose of Investigating the Subject of the Employment of Children in Manufactories. Mr. Peltz, Chairman. Read in Senate, Feb. 7, 1838* (Harrisburg: Thompson & Clark, 1838).

62. Thomas Cooper, *Lectures on the Elements of Political Economy* (1829; New York: Augustus Kelley, 1971), 351. Along these lines, Michael Perelman argues that classical political economists of the late eighteenth and early nineteenth centuries espoused laissez-faire doctrines while also advocating policies that coerced workers into wage labor. See his *The Invention of Capitalism: Classical Political Economy and the Secret History of Primitive Accumulation* (Durham: Duke University Press, 2000).

labor law was so illiberal that it marked a regime of "belated feudalism." Such a characterization may seem extreme for an era when an increasing proportion of white laboring men gained access to the ballot box. However, as David Montgomery has suggested, when employers solidified power over workers in the realm of common law, they had little to fear from the expansion of the franchise. Subordination remained the lot of working people—even as personal subordination to a master gave way to impersonal subordination within a market and the liberal democratic nation-state.[63]

Even as the notion of labor as a market commodity became standard, employers continued to think of working people's labor as the property of the community as a whole. As the historian Linda Kerber has explained, one of the few "civic obligations" applying to working people within the Anglo-American political tradition was to deliver up their labor to their superiors who might best use it.[64] The Virginian St. George Tucker captured this sentiment perfectly in 1796, when he argued that society's "interests require the exertions of every individual in some mode or other; and those who have not wherewith to support themselves honestly without corporeal labour, whatever be their complexion, ought to be compelled to labour." When poorer men and women withheld their labor, they should face criminal charges as vagrants. When workers decided collectively to stop working, they ought to stand trial for conspiracy. "In every well ordered society," Tucker wrote, "and where the numbers of persons without property increase, there the coertion [sic] of the laws becomes more immediately requisite."[65]

American law circumscribed free labor in three critical ways. First, the sanction of wage forfeiture made it prohibitively expensive for workers to leave a job on short notice. American workers could not claim back wages if they did not fulfill the entirety of the stipulated term of labor. Because employers withheld pay until the completion of that term, a worker desiring a better situation elsewhere risked losing three months or more of accumulated wages. From the perspective of employers, forfeiture was "inexpensive and effective," and just as coercive as British practices of imprisonment for breach of contract.[66] Second, states brought criminal charges against workers who collectively withheld their

63. Christopher L. Tomlins, *Law, Labor, and Ideology in the Early American Republic* (New York: Cambridge University Press, 1993), 261; Karen Orren, *Belated Feudalism: Labor, the Law, and Liberal Development in the United States* (New York: Cambridge University Press, 1991); Montgomery, *Citizen Worker*; Schmidt, *Free to Work*; Stanley, *From Bondage to Contract*.

64. Linda Kerber, *No Constitutional Right to Be Ladies: Women and the Obligation of Citizenship* (New York: Hill and Wang, 1998), 51.

65. St. George Tucker, *A Dissertation on Slavery: With a Proposal for the Gradual Abolition of It, in the State of Virginia* (Philadelphia: Mathew Carey, 1796), 102.

66. Steinfeld, *Coercion, Contract, and Free Labor*; Peter Karsten, "'Bottomed on Justice': A Reappraisal of Critical Legal Studies Scholarship Concerning Breeches of Labor Contracts by Quitting or Firing in Britain and the U.S., 1630–1880," *American Journal of Legal History* 34 (July 1990): 213–61.

labor in search of better wages or conditions. Unable to locate any such cases in the colonial period, Christopher Tomlins counts twenty-three conspiracy trials in six states between 1806 and 1847. Striking shoemakers and tailors in New York, Philadelphia, and Baltimore faced prosecution as illegal combinations. Responding to the 1833 imprisonment of Connecticut carpet weavers, New England workingmen denounced "the use of the common jail in enforcing the regulations of a factory."[67] Finally, state power made it impossible for individual workers to exit the labor market. The enforcement of vagrancy statutes and trespass laws engaged the government in "policing people for the needs of a capitalist market system."[68] The early Republic's penal and welfare regimes—constructed around forced labor—offered a mechanism for labor discipline and the promise of instilling the habits of industry in the idle.[69]

As law set the parameters of free labor, employers sought out workers with the most tenuous legal standing, in particular those without access to full citizenship. Employers—who were almost always adult white men with full legal rights—used such categories as race, gender, and ethnicity in order to maximize their power over their workers. Ascriptive (or socially constructed) categories like race and gender gained a concrete reality as they determined a worker's legal standing, access to economic opportunity, and ability to opt out of labor altogether. Some workers could protect their wages in the courts, limit their hours with appeals to community standards, and even punish their employers through the ballot; other workers could do none of those things. Some workers could be physically coerced to work harder or punished for quitting early or breaking a tool. Some workers had a reasonable chance of accumulating enough productive property to withdraw from wage labor, while others faced insurmountable structural barriers to economic self-sufficiency. Whether through law, culture, or social practice, some workers were "available" to be paid less and worked more. Employers could take advantage of preexisting racial and gender inequalities that facilitated such distinctions; in turn, their collective hiring decisions could serve to reinforce those inequalities.[70]

With employers exerting power over workers of varying race, sex, ethnicity, age, and legal status, capitalism's success in the early Republic may have

67. Tomlins, *Law, Labor, and Ideology*, 128–79; Montgomery, *Citizen Worker*, 47.

68. Montgomery, *Citizen Worker*, 58; Schmidt, *Free to Work*, 53–92; Stanley, *From Bondage to Contract*, 98–137.

69. A large body of literature connects penology to the emergence of liberal capitalism. See Michael Meranze, *Laboratories of Virtue: Punishment, Revolution, and Authority in Philadelphia, 1760–1835* (Chapel Hill: University of North Carolina Press, 1996); Michael Ignatieff, *A Just Measure of Pain: The Penitentiary in the Industrial Revolution, 1750–1850* (New York: Pantheon Books, 1978); Dario Melossi and Massimo Pavarini, *The Prison and the Factory: Origins of the Penitentiary System* (Totowa, N.J.: Barnes and Noble, 1981); Michel Foucault, *Discipline and Punish: The Birth of the Prison*, trans. Alan Sheridan (New York: Pantheon Books, 1978); Richard B. Morris, "Labor Controls in Maryland in the Nineteenth Century," *Journal of Southern History* 14 (August 1948): 385–400.

70. Glenn, *Unequal Freedom*.

depended on a dysfunctional labor market in which categories of difference organized employment opportunities and wage rates. Nativism, sexism, and racism closed entire occupations to portions of the workforce and pitted groups against one another within the narrower confines of a segmented market. The workers at the forefront of capitalist wage relations possessed only nominal freedom, in many cases lacking the mobility to generate market competition. Moreover, wages did not always fluctuate with market forces when the broader culture sanctioned certain types of discrimination and deprived victims of legal recourse or the opportunity for physical relocation.[71]

Wage labor's relationship to marginal segments of the population remains a critical area for research. African Americans, for example, made up a significant proportion of manual laborers in port cities like New York, Philadelphia, and Baltimore. As street pavers, stevedores, and carters, they performed the labor that facilitated the flow of goods and commodities through the marketplace. Yet free black men worked for wages within the confines of a legal system that curtailed their alternatives. Exclusion laws kept free African Americans from pursuing opportunities in the western states and territories. Prohibitions on testimony against whites prevented free black workers from suing employers for breach of contract. As Baltimore newspaper editor Hezekiah Niles conceded, legal discrimination and public hostility kept African Americans from the "dreams of future independence which commonly lightens the white man's weary way and supports him in the severest drudgery and keenest privation."[72] Significantly, however, employers did not always seek out African American workers as the least free members of the labor pool. Employment decisions that placed black and white workers side by side or that excluded one or the other from a particular job had political and social consequences. Whatever choices employers made, the configuration of racial power within the early Republic provided them with an advantage over their workers.[73]

71. Much econometric literature seems to downplay exclusion, discrimination, and exploitation in setting the contours of the labor market. See Robert Margo, *Wages and Labor Markets in the United States, 1820–1860* (Chicago: University of Chicago Press, 2000). For a fascinating study that makes the lack of competition central to the emergence of capitalism, see Reddy, *The Rise of Market Culture*. For an overview of the debates on concepts of labor segmentation, see Ruth Milkman, *Gender at Work: The Dynamics of Job Discrimination by Sex During World War II* (Urbana: University of Illinois Press, 1987), 4–7.

72. *Niles' Weekly Register*, May 22, 1819. Harris, *Shadow of Slavery*; Hodges, *Root and Branch*.

73. "The willingness of northern industrial enterprises to hire women, families, and newcomers did not extend to African Americans. The region's industrial labor force, and its factory labor force above all, was cast firmly in whiteface." Jonathan Prude, "Capitalism, Industrialization, and the Factory in Post-Revolutionary America," *Journal of the Early Republic* 16 (Summer 1996): 251. But as Frank Towers has recently shown, Baltimore employers preferred free black workers to white immigrant ones, even when immigrant workers could be hired for a lower wage. Shipyard owners feared that "the substitution of white for black labor would enlarge the proportion of enfranchised wage earners" and thus jeopardize employers' tenuous advantage in city politics. See Towers, "Job Busting at Baltimore Shipyards: Racial Violence in the Civil War–Era South," *Journal of Southern History* 66 (May 2000): 250.

The research on gender ideology and women's labor reveals that legal bondage—organized through categories of social difference—was crucial to American capitalism. Politically disfranchised, lacking legal self-ownership, and assumed to be dependent on a male head of household, women were among the most tractable workers in the labor pool. For women, the most serious structural problem of emergent industrial capitalism was not unfettered market relations but the perpetuation of older forms of coercion and confinement. The wage economy offered women new cash-earning opportunities, but it did not create an efficient labor market where women could operate as autonomous agents. Ensconced in male households, most women lacked the physical mobility to pursue higher wages in a different locale. Social strictures prevented other women from following jobs from place to place— precisely the mechanism necessary for a free market in labor. Moreover, the underlying logic of coverture—a woman's assumed dependence within a male household—pegged wages at below-subsistence levels. Presumed to be secondary earners supplementing a family income, women garnered secondary wages. These low wages made female dependence a self-fulfilling prophecy. As Jeanne Boydston explains, "So long as principles of *feme covert* remained stubbornly embedded in the law, the growing importance of contract and free labor in the post-revolutionary United States could only put most women at a severe disadvantage."[74]

Without question, women's market labor was essential to household viability during the transition to capitalism. Midwifery, palm-leaf hat weaving, and dairying helped achieve the modest competency that rural families sought in the first decades of the nineteenth century. In urban areas, women transformed household labor into cash by taking in boarders, doing laundry for a sailor on shore leave, or finishing shirts for a tailor.[75] Capitalism transformed women's labor, but women's labor in turn proved central to capitalism's success. "Women and children comprised a major share of the entire manufacturing labor force during the initial period of industrialization," according to Claudia Goldin and Kenneth Sokoloff's study of manufacturing censuses. By 1820 women and

74. Jeanne Boydston, "The Woman Who Wasn't There: Women's Market Labor and the Transition to Capitalism in the United States," *Journal of the Early Republic* 16 (Summer 1996): 195; Seth Rockman, "Women's Labor, Gender Ideology, and Working-Class Households in Early Republic Baltimore," *Explorations in Early American Culture/Pennsylvania History* 66 (1999): 174–200; Deborah Valenze, *The First Industrial Woman* (New York: Oxford University Press, 1995); Alice Kessler-Harris, *Out to Work: A History of Wage-Earning Women in the United States* (New York: Oxford University Press, 1982), 20–72.

75. Claudia Goldin, "The Economic Status of Women in the Early Republic: Quantitative Evidence," *Journal of Interdisciplinary History* 26 (Winter 1986): 375–404; Thomas Dublin, "Women and Outwork in a Nineteenth-Century New England Town: Fitzwilliam, New Hampshire, 1830–1850," in Hahn and Prude, *Countryside in the Age of Capitalist Transformation*, 51–69; Joan M. Jensen, *Loosening the Bonds: Mid-Atlantic Farm Women, 1750–1850* (New Haven: Yale University Press, 1986); Laurel Thatcher Ulrich, *A Midwife's Tale: The Life of Martha Ballard, Based on Her Diary, 1785–1812* (New York: Knopf, 1990).

children accounted for more than 30 percent of the manufacturing workforce in the Northeast; that figure peaked at around 40 percent in the subsequent two decades.[76] From roughly 1750 onward, would-be manufacturers hatched schemes to consolidate female labor in the name of national welfare and commercial independence. As Alexander Hamilton noted in his 1791 *Report on Manufactures,* "women and children are rendered more useful, and the latter more early useful by manufacturing establishments than they would otherwise be." Hezekiah Niles praised Baltimore factory owners whose reliance upon female labor "transform[ed] some useless substance into pure gold." In New England mill villages, the daughters of yeoman farmers, followed by the wives of immigrant laborers, tended the spindles most associated with the Industrial Revolution in the United States.[77]

Women were most crucial to the emergence of capitalism in their combination of outwork and unpaid domestic labor. Entrepreneurial tailors and cordwainers subdivided production into simple and discrete components and realized great profit by paying piece-rates to women instead of wages to male journeymen. Employers of female outworkers were, in Christine Stansell's words, "at the forefront of industrialization" in the early Republic. Isolated in their own homes, female outworkers lacked the collective experience and voice that gave male journeymen political muscle and the ability to resist changes in rates or specifications. Performing this labor within the household reinforced the perception of women as secondary earners and kept their wages artificially low. A series of cultural assumptions regarding women's dependence—and not an impartial market—set the price of women's labor.[78] Those same assumptions

76. Claudia Goldin and Kenneth L. Sokoloff, "Women, Children, and Industrialization in the Early Republic: Evidence from the Manufacturing Censuses," *Journal of Economic History* 42 (December 1982): 773; Margaret S. Coleman, "Female Labor Supply During Early Industrialization: Women's Labor Force Participation in Historical Perspective," in *Gender and Political Economy: Incorporating Diversity into Theory and Policy,* ed. Ellen Mutari et al. (Armonk, N.Y.: M. E. Sharpe, 1997), 42–60; Gerda Lerner had argued this point some years earlier: "American industrialization, which occurred in an underdeveloped economy with a shortage of labor, depended on the labor of women and children." See "The Lady and the Mill Girl: Changes in the Status of Women in the Age of Jackson [1969]," in Gerda Lerner, *The Majority Finds Its Past: Placing Women in History* (New York: Oxford University Press, 1979), 24.

77. Hamilton cited in Jones, *American Work,* 161; *Niles' Weekly Register,* June 7, 1817, 227. On colonial-era efforts to put impoverished women to work in manufacturing, see Gary B. Nash, "The Failure of Female Factory Labor in Colonial Boston," *Labor History* 20 (Spring 1979): 165–88; Eric G. Nellis, "Misreading the Signs: Industrial Imitation, Poverty, and the Social Order in Colonial Boston," *New England Quarterly* 59 (December 1986): 486–507; Laurel Thatcher Ulrich, "Sheep in the Parlor, Wheels on the Common: Pastoralism and Poverty in Eighteenth-Century Boston," in Pestana and Salinger, *Inequality in Early America,* 182–200. On female factory labor, see Thomas Dublin, *Women at Work: The Transformation of Work and Community in Lowell, Massachusetts, 1826–1860* (New York: Columbia University Press, 1979); David Zonderman, *Aspirations and Anxieties: New England Workers and the Mechanized Factory System, 1815–1850* (New York: Oxford University Press, 1992).

78. Christine Stansell, "The Origins of the Sweatshop: Women and Early Industrialization in New York City," in *Working-Class America: Essays on Labor, Community, and American Society,* ed.

made women responsible for the maintenance of their families. Women converted the cash wages of other household members into meals and clothing, and performed unpaid labor such as mending and washing that would otherwise need to be purchased at market. Jeanne Boydston has found that the value of a woman's unpaid contribution to the family economy amounted to twice the cost of her maintenance and perhaps exceeded her husband's total wages. Employers could pay below-subsistence wages to men precisely because women's unpaid household labor recovered the difference. The savings in labor costs that accrued to employers fueled capital accumulation and were "critical to the development of industrialization in the antebellum Northeast." But as Boydston has observed more recently, historians still "presume [women's labor] to have existed outside of, and been largely ineffectual in, the transition to a free labor economy."[79]

Even as capitalism transformed labor into a market commodity, employers showed a continued interest in workers who themselves could be bought and sold. Although the numbers of European servants declined dramatically in the early Republic, twenty-five thousand servants and redemptioners arrived in the United States between 1776 and 1820, including 5,300 Germans in the 1810s alone. Developers of the national transportation infrastructure remained most committed to unfree labor. Importing five hundred British indentured laborers in 1829, the directors of the Chesapeake and Ohio Canal Company thought it cheaper to transport workers across the ocean than to hire from within a tight labor market. Although the C&O's canal workers were famously unwilling to abide by their contracts, their employer repeatedly asserted its claim to indentured workers. Ethnic contract labor remained central to the building of the railroads later in the nineteenth century.[80] The hope of setting slaves to industrial labor also remained strong. For example, Mathew Carey recommended in 1827 that Virginia masters put their slaves to work in textile manufactories; one hundred slaves would prove more productive than a similar number of white female

Michael H. Frisch and Daniel J. Walkowitz (Urbana: University of Illinois Press, 1983), 80. Outwork trapped women in a struggle between male journeymen and their profit-seeking masters. As a result, issues of gender were central to labor politics in the 1800s. See Mary H. Blewett, *Men, Women, and Work: Class, Gender, and Protest in the New England Shoe Industry, 1780–1910* (Urbana: University of Illinois Press, 1988); Sonya Rose, *Limited Livelihoods: Gender and Class in Nineteenth-Century England* (Berkeley and Los Angeles: University of California Press, 1992); Anna Clark, *The Struggle for the Breeches: Gender and the Making of the British Working Class* (Berkeley and Los Angeles: University of California Press, 1995).

    79. Jeanne M. Boydston, *Home and Work: Housework, Wages, and the Ideology of Labor in the Early Republic* (New York: Oxford University Press, 1990), 137–38; Boydston, "Woman Who Wasn't There," 186. On the connection between production and reproduction, see Merchant, *Ecological Revolutions;* Heidi L. Hartmann, "Capitalism, Patriarchy, and Job Segregation by Sex," *Signs* 1 (Spring 1976): 137–70.

    80. Fogleman, "Slaves, Convicts, and Servants," 75; Richard B. Morris, "The Measure of Bondage in the Slave States," *Mississippi Valley Historical Review* 41 (September 1954): 221; Steinfeld, *Invention of Free Labor,* 166–70; Howard Lamar, "From Bondage to Contract: Ethnic Labor in the American West, 1600–1890" in Hahn and Prude, *Countryside in the Age of Capitalist Transformation,* 293–324.

operatives. When Thomas P. Jones spoke later that fall to the Franklin Institute in Philadelphia, he called for new textile manufactories that employed slaves. "Why are the slaves employed?" he asked his audience. "Simply because experience has proved that they are more *docile,* more constant, and *cheaper,* than freemen, who are often refractory and dissipated; who waste much time by visiting public places, attending musters, elections, &c. which the *operative slave* is not permitted to frequent."[81]

That citizenship decreased laborers' productivity was not news to employers in cities like Baltimore and Richmond. Master artisans, shipbuilders, and manufacturers in these border cities hesitated to jettison slavery despite the growing number of free workers available in the local labor market. Enslaved workers compared favorably to free workers in productivity, skill, regularity, discipline, and cost. In seeking to stem flight and thus assure the profitability of industrial slavery, employers often paid wages to slaves and held out opportunities for self-purchase. The result was what Richard Morris called "a twilight zone of bondage" where black and white laborers collectively "dwelt in a shadowland enjoying a status neither fully slave nor fully free."[82] Once again, the suggestion is that capitalist enterprise displayed only minimal interest in the competitive labor market of classical economics. A workforce lacking physical mobility and political voice proved far more appealing.

Creating a New Narrative

This chapter has explored the absence of unfreedom from accounts of the early U.S. economy. Despite a substantial body of scholarship identifying unfree labor as crucial to American capitalism, historians have remained committed to a narrative that makes freedom the operative force in American economic development. This vision of America's past has particular resonance because it corresponds so well to how Americans conceptualize their world at the present

81. "Slave labour employed in manufactures . . . [Signed] Hamilton, Philadelphia, October 2, 1827," Library of Congress Rare Book and Special Collections Division, Washington, D.C., Printed Ephemera Collection, portfolio 153, folder 3; Thomas P. Jones, *An Address on the Progress of Manufactures and Internal Improvement, in the United States; and particularly, On the Advantages to be Derived from the Employment of Slaves in the Manufacturing of Cotton and Other Goods. Delivered in the Hall of the Franklin Institute, November 6, 1827* (Philadelphia: Judah Dobson, 1827), 11.

82. Christopher L. Tomlins, "In Nat Turner's Shadow: Reflections on the Norfolk Dry Dock Affair of 1830–1831," *Labor History* 33 (Fall 1992): 494–518; T. Stephen Whitman, "Industrial Slavery at the Margin: The Maryland Chemical Works," *Journal of Southern History* 59 (February 1993): 31–62; Barbara Fields, *Slavery and Freedom on the Middle Ground: Maryland During the Nineteenth Century* (New Haven: Yale University Press, 1985), 40–62; Takagi, *Rearing Wolves,* 17–36. In 1812 David Ross, who oversaw production at the Oxford Iron Works near Richmond, Virginia, considered slaves "ten time better than any you can hire." See Bezís-Selfa, "Tale of Two Ironworks," 679. Morris, "Measure of Bondage in the Slave States," 220.

moment. Global economic development and political democratization have been the goals of American foreign policy since the end of World War II. But the events of the past decade or so—the demise of the Eastern Bloc, the transformation of Russia, the modernization of China, and even the terrorist attacks on the United States on September 11, 2001—have confirmed for most Americans that capitalism functions as a force of human liberation. Capitalism and democracy no longer exist as modes of social organization or power relations, but as synonyms for individual choice. Increasingly, Americans understand society as a perpetual plebiscite, so that participation in the market (consumption) becomes an act of democratic expression. Freedom has nothing to do with electoral politics or self-governance and everything to do with buying athletic shoes or downloading music to an iPod. Capitalism brings choices, and choices define democracy. Our "democracy in cupidity" is by no means new, but its legitimacy has never been more secure and more consistently reinforced in op-ed columns, television commercials, and campaign speeches.[83]

The rhetorical melding of capitalism, democracy, and freedom is so central to American political discourse that many historians lack the critical distance to interrogate the relationship between capitalism and freedom in the nation's past. The story equating capitalism and freedom has been told and retold so many times that the very notion of "unfree origins" may strike some as inconceivable. An American history that hinges on unfreedom, however, need not be an exercise in self-loathing or a catalogue of atrocities. Instead, it simply recognizes that, in the words of Edward Countryman, "The glory did not come free. It had a price, and Americans ought to be comfortable enough with ourselves to recognize that the price and the glory can not be pried apart."[84] To embrace this fact opens up a far more dramatic history. Unfreedom demands contingency, creating a narrative that links freedom for some to the lack of freedom for others. The triumph of liberal capitalism in the early United States depended on unfreedom—the expansion of plantation slavery, the household subordination of women, and the legal confinement of wage earners. To acknowledge such contingencies does not deny that new kinds of freedom transformed countless lives in the early Republic. Rather, an awareness of the unfree origins of American capitalism places those freedoms in a far richer context and reminds us of their costs and consequences.

83. Thomas Frank, *One Market Under God: Extreme Capitalism, Market Populism, and the End of Democracy* (New York: Doubleday, 2000); Terry Bouton, "Welcome to the Global Economy: Rethinking Class and the American Revolution," paper presented at "Class and Class Struggles in North America and the Atlantic World, 1500–1820," Montana State University and University of East Anglia conference, Big Sky, Montana, September 2003.

84. Edward Countryman, "Indians, the Colonial Order, and the Social Significance of the American Revolution," *William and Mary Quarterly* 53 (April 1996): 362. See also Michael Meranze, "Even the Dead Will Not Be Safe: An Ethics of Early American History," *William and Mary Quarterly* 50 (April 1993): 367–78; Huggins, "Deforming Mirror of Truth."

List of Contributors

Terry Bouton is an assistant professor of history at the University of Maryland, Baltimore County. His article "A Road Closed: Rural Insurgency in Post-Independence Pennsylvania" appeared in the *Journal of American History* in 2000, and he is currently completing a book on the Revolution in Pennsylvania.

Daniel S. Dupre, associate professor of history at the University of North Carolina at Charlotte, has written *Transforming the Cotton Frontier: Madison County, Alabama, 1800–1840* (1997) and is currently researching the social, political, and cultural impact of the Panic of 1819.

David Hancock is an associate professor of American history at the University of Michigan in Ann Arbor. He has written numerous articles; among his published books are *Citizens of the World: London Merchants and the Integration of the British Atlantic Community, 1735–1785* (1995) and a study of the emergence and self-organization of the Atlantic economy between 1640 and 1815 as viewed through the lens of the Madeira wine trade.

Brooke Hunter is an assistant professor of history at Rider University. Her current research concentrates on the intersection of economic, social, and ecological revolutions in the mid-Atlantic region. She is completing a book on the grain trade during the American revolutionary era.

John Majewski is an associate professor of history at the University of California at Santa Barbara. He is author of *A House Dividing: Economic Development in Pennsylvania and Virginia Before the Civil War* (2000) and is currently writing a book on how Confederate secessionists imagined the economic future of their new nation.

Cathy Matson is a professor of history at the University of Delaware and director of the Program in Early American Economy and Society at the Library Company of Philadelphia. She has written numerous articles on the colonial and revolutionary economy, and (with Peter Onuf) *A Union of Interests: Political and Economic Thought in Revolutionary America* (1990) and *Merchants and Empire: Trading in Colonial New York* (1998). Her current research involves the comparative economic development of Philadelphia and New York, especially concerning their trade with the West Indies and new global markets during the period 1750 to 1820.

Russell R. Menard is a professor of history at the University of Minnesota and the author of many books and articles on early American economic history, including (with John J. McCusker), *The Economy of British America, 1607–1789* (1985), and *Sweet Negotiations: Sugar, Slavery, and Plantation Agriculture in Early Barbados* (forthcoming).

Donna J. Rilling, associate professor of history at the State University of New York, Stony Brook, is the author of *Making Houses, Crafting Capitalism: Builders in Philadelphia, 1790–1850* (2001). She is currently researching early industrial pollution in the Delaware Valley.

Seth Rockman is an assistant professor of history at Brown University. He is the author of *Welfare Reform in the Early Republic: A Brief History with Documents* (2003) and is currently completing a manuscript on wage labor and slavery in Baltimore in the early Republic.

Christopher Tomlins is a senior research fellow at the American Bar Foundation in Chicago and has written and edited several books, most recently *The Many Legalities of Early America* (with Bruce Mann, 2001) and *Law, Labor, and Ideology in the Early American Republic* (1993).

David Waldstreicher, professor of history at Temple University, is the author of *In the Midst of Perpetual Fetes: The Making of American Nationalism, 1776–1820* (1977), and *Runaway America: Benjamin Franklin, Slavery, and the American Revolution* (2004).

Lorena S. Walsh is a historian with the Colonial Williamsburg Foundation and the author of numerous books and articles, including (with Lois Green Carr and Russell R. Menard) *Robert Cole's World: Agriculture and Society in Early Maryland* (1991), and *From Calabar to Carter's Grove: The History of a Virginia Slave Community* (1997).

Index

Abbott, George, 328
Adapting to a New World (Horn), 168n67, 175
advance building, 317–18, 322–23, 325–27
Advice to a Young Tradesman, Written by an Old One (Franklin), 198
African Americans (free), 133, 356, 356n73
Agnew, Jean-Christophe, 92
agricultural exports
  dependence on, 64–65, 269, 278
  European demand for, 264, 267, 269, 272
  and Hessian fly, 253
  price decline of, 272
  See also staples thesis
agricultural reform, 261
  and European demand, 252, 255
  and Hessian fly, 249–52, 249n37
  strategy of Chew, 253–56
agriculture, 25, 27, 42, 122
  blended/"mestizo," 27, 110–12, 119, 121
  declension in New England, 22, 117
  diversification in, 22, 40, 47, 58
  effect of prices on productivity, 114, 121–22
  and environmental hazards, 47, 237, 240, 242
  and free-trade advocates, 289
  importance to colonial economy, 26–27, 109
  and innovation, 115–16, 121–23
  productivity of, 26, 58, 109–10, 118–19
  techniques in South, 111–12
  and wealth creation, 27, 111, 118–19
  See also farmers; Hessian fly; slovenly farmer
Agricultural Society of Roanoke, Virginia, 289
Albert, Peter, 142
American Economic Association, 1
American Economic History Association, 95
American exceptionalism, 5, 15, 26
American Historical Association, 1
American Iron (Gordon), 75
American Revolution, 147
  banking system during, 219, 231
  Franklin as propagandist, 204, 215–17
  hardships created by, 41–43
  impact on immigration, 129–30
  and labor and capitalism, 183, 187
  and Navigation Acts, 78–79
  opportunities created by, 41
  and slavery, 183–85, 189
  and "transition to capitalism," 42, 120
  See also capitalism; Franklin, Benjamin
"American System," 267, 292

"American System of Manufactures," 54, 62
"Americanus" (Franklin), 205–6
Anderson, Terry, 153–54
Anderson, Virginia DeJohn, 116, 127
Annalistes, 8
anti-Americanism, 189, 209, 209n61
antislavery, 211
  complaint against Americans, 210
  equated with anti-Americanism, 189, 209, 209n61
  and labor and capital, 201, 207
  and "Observations on the Increase of Mankind," 202, 207
  and racism, 202–4
  and revolutionary nationalism, 204, 215–17
Anxious Pursuit (Chaplin), 85
Appalachian backcountry, 149, 149n8, 163, 163n41
Appleby, Joyce, 59–60, 185, 340
  and capitalism, 235, 319, 338n10, 343–44
  and entrepreneurs, 318, 328
Armitage, David, 139
artisans, 192n21, 199, 199n36, 343. *See also* carpenters
asiento, 202
Associates of Dr. Bray, 207
"Asylum for Mankind": America, 1607–1800 (Baseler), 129
Atlantic world, 87, 252, 268
  linkage in, 97–100
  and slavery, 65, 335
  and staples thesis, 15–16
  studies of, 10, 14–17, 91, 104
Autobiography (Franklin), 189

Bailyn, Bernard, 93
  critique of, 127–29
  critique of "dual emigration," 163–64
  on "dual emigration," 161–63
  migration estimates, 177–79
  on population movements, 126–27
balance of payments, 73, 75, 267
Ball, Joseph, 310
Baltimore, 63, 271, 343, 356n73, 360
Baltimore and Ohio Railroad, 313
Bank of Edwardsville (Ill.), 281–82
Bank of England, 78, 102
Bank of Missouri, 281
Bank of North America, 220–23, 225, 228–29, 233

Bank of the United States, 45
Bank of the United States (chartered 1819). *See*
    Second Bank of the United States
Bank of Vincennes (Ind.), 281
bank notes (Pa.), 271
    insufficient to support economy, 222–23,
        233
    replaced government currency, 220–21
    and value of, 267, 270, 272
    See also specie
bank stock (Pa.), 294, 305, 312
    dividends and liquidity of, 297–98, 298n9
    ownership of, 301–3, 301nn24–25, 314
    speculative nature of, 296–97
    and state revenues, 298–300
    widely held, 296, 296n7, 312, 316
    See also shareholding
banks/banking, 45, 52–53
    and construction industry, 325, 325n24
    and Panic of 1819, 53–54, 303–5
    and Pennsylvania politics, 299–301, 299n15,
        304–5, 304n32
    privatization of, 219–20
    See also bank notes; bank stock; land banks;
        privatization
Barron, Michael, 321
Baseler, Marilyn C., 129
Battle of New Orleans, 263, 268
Beard, Charles, 4
Benezet, Anthony, 211
Benton, Thomas Hart, 279
Berlin, Ira, 138
Beverly Cotton Mill, 348
Bezís-Selfa, John, 75–76
Binns, John, 244, 251
Black and Souder, 330
"Blackamore" (Franklin), 195–96
Bledsoe, Jesse, 282, 290
blockades, 42
Blount, William, 279
Bond, Phineas, 237
Bordley, John Beale, 246, 248–49, 252
Boston Associates, 348
Bouton, Terry, 46
Boydston, Jeanne, 66, 77, 357, 359
Braddick, Michael J., 139
Brandywine (Dela.), 86, 253, 255
Branson, Susan, 67
Braudel, Fernand, 8, 10
British Atlantic World, 1500–1800 (Armitage and
    Braddick), 139
brokers (real estate), 325
Brown, Jeremiah, 260
Brown, Kathleen, 93–94

Browns, 348
Bruegel, Martin, 55–56
Buckingham, Joseph, 343
Buel, Joy and Richard, 105
bullionism, 78
Burr, Aaron, 279
Bushman, Richard, 37, 142

Cabots, 60, 348
Cadigan, Sean, 84
Calhoun, John C., 273
Calloway, Colin, 100
Cambridge Economic History of the United States
    (Engerman and Gallman), 49
Canny, Nicholas, 179
Cantwell's Bridge, 244
capital, 75
    in construction industry, 318, 333 (*see also*
        carpenters)
    in early national economy, 46, 63
    Franklin's concept of, 188, 199–201, 207
    investment by merchants, 41, 61, 322
    scarcity of, 18, 26
    for transportation companies, 308, 312
capitalism, 36, 51, 357
    "always capitalist" theory, 11, 35–37, 340
    and American Revolution, 183, 187
    and antislavery, 185, 189, 216
    as antithetical to democracy, 341–42
    commodified people, 188, 351
    definition of, 33–34, 344–45
    and democracy and freedom, 336–38,
        337nn6–7, 338n10, 361
    evolution to, 57–60
    historiography of, 340–42
    and labor of women, 357–59
    and slavery, 46, 183–85, 188–89, 346–49
    and social relations, 345, 345n32
    studies of, 11, 34–37
    and unfree labor, 68, 338–39
    See also "transition to capitalism"
Capitalism and Slavery (Williams), 183
Carey, Henry, 351
Carey, Mathew, 283, 295, 359–60
Carlisle Bank, 301–2
Carlos, Ann, 73
Carlton, David, 24–25
Carney, Judith, 114
carpenters (house), 59, 317, 319, 325
    business arrangements of, 318, 331–34
    invested in other businesses, 327–28
    and real estate development, 321–25
    sources of credit, 317, 322–25, 325n24, 333
    specialization and subcontracting, 329–30

and speculative construction, 317–18, 322–23, 326–27
wages of, 321, 326
Carr, Lois Green, 38, 73
Carroll, Charles, 250
Carson, Cary, 142
Carte, Kate, 37
Chaplin, Joyce, 85
Chesapeake, 38, 260–61
    child labor in, 137–38, 167, 171
    convict labor in, 141, 179
    creole population in, 134, 142, 156, 168–69, 168n67
    demographics of migrants to, 167–69, 167n61
    diverse economy of, 14, 24
    estimates of bound labor in, 155–56
    estimates of population, 152
    estimates of slave population, 133–35, 155
    "dual emigration," 167–68
    general migration to, 147, 152, 162–63, 166–67, 170, 174
    indentured labor in, 149, 151–56, 154n21, 169
    labor force compared with Pennsylvania, 160–61
    migration compared to New England, 166–67, 169–70
    population growth in, 168, 168n67
    servant migration to, 149, 151–53, 152n16, 167, 174–75
    servant migration compared to Delaware Valley, 171
    slave versus bound labor in, 141
    and slavery, 115, 142, 169–70
    statistical tables, 152–56
    stratification of society, 169
    studies of, 127–28, 135
    technological innovation in, 111, 115–16
Chesapeake and Delaware Canal, 294–95, 296
Chesapeake and Ohio Canal Company, 359
Chevalier, Michel, 294
Chew, Benjamin, 244, 249, 250, 253–56
child labor, 63, 164, 357–58, 358n76
    indentured, 30, 137–38, 167–68, 171
citizenship, 360
Clark, Christopher, 37, 56
Clay, Henry, 54, 62, 283, 292, 308
Clemens, Paul, 135
cliometrics, 7, 10–12
"cockpit," 211
Coclanis, Peter, 17, 24–25, 83, 85
coffee, 86
Coldham, Peter, 128

Committee on Agriculture, 288
Committee on Manufactures, 266–68, 277, 284–88
Committee on Plantation Affairs, 211
Committee on Research in Economic History, 4
commodities. See agricultural exports; staples; and names of individual crops
"competency," 11, 30, 55
    defined, 36–37
    among rural families, 342, 357
"composite" farms, 37, 55
Connecticut, 63, 94, 105
    and Hessian fly, 243, 250n39, 252–53
Conner, Samuel, 270–71
"conspicuous consumption," 3
Constitution of 1787, 219
construction business. See carpenters
"Consumer Revolution in Colonial British America" (Carson), 142
Constitution of 1787, 219
Continental Congress, 212
consumer revolution, 43, 120, 190. See also consumption
consumption, 3, 9, 108, 122
    colonial, 37–40
    and demography, 142–43
    theme of Franklin, 194–95
"Conversation between an Englishman . . . and an American, on the subject of Slavery" (Franklin), 210–11
convicts, 128
    in Chesapeake labor supply, 141, 179
    discussion of estimates, 181–82
    estimates in 18th century, 150, 150n9, 151n11, 174
    estimates in 17th century, 176
    Franklin's views on, 189, 205, 207–8, 210
Cooch, William, 259
Cook, Daniel P., 286–87
Cooper, Thomas, 353
corn, 255–56, 259–61
Corn Laws, 272, 283
cornmeal, 259–60
cotton, 61, 120–21, 272, 348
    most valuable export, 65, 269, 346
cotton gin, 121
Countryman, Edward, 361
craftsmen, 192n21, 199, 199n36, 343. See also carpenters
Craig, Michelle, 86
Craven, David, 244
Crawford, William, 280–81
Creating the Commonwealth (Innes), 101

credit, 33, 46, 55, 300
  in construction industry, 317, 321–25, 333
  crunch caused by privatization, 221, 229,
    231–32, 234–35
  in early Republic, 44–45, 48
  and land banks, 218–19, 231–32, 234–35
  and Panic of 1819, 54, 271–72, 276
  to planters, 75, 141, 169
  private banks met need for, 219–20, 303
  and supply of imported goods, 284–85
  See also specie
creole/Creolization, 15, 17, 27, 100
  in Chesapeake, 134, 142, 156, 168–69
  in New England, 165
  as source of labor, 172–73, 190
Cressy, David, 127
Crowley, John E., 142–43
Cullen, L. M., 177–78
cultural anthropology, 9, 35

dairying, 22, 58, 357
Dangerfield, George, 274, 279
Daniels, Christine, 135
databases, 7, 35, 132. See also Trans-Atlantic Slave
    Trade
Davis, David Brion, 207n55, 350
Davis, Lance, 11, 19, 73, 108, 124, 145
Dayton, Cornelia, 94
Deane, Samuel, 109–10
debt, 35, 46, 48, 199
  post-Revolution, 41, 44–45
  and privatization, 221, 233–34
  speculators in, 221, 231–32
  See also credit
Declaration of Independence, 212
Degler, Carl, 35
Delaware, 22–23, 42–43, 253, 259. See also
    Whitehall Plantation
Delaware Valley, 56
  demographics of migrants, 171
  "dual emigration," 163, 171–72
  estimates of bound labor in, 172
  estimates of population, 158
  general migration to, 147, 157, 162–63,
    170–72, 170n75, 174–75
  German and Irish migration into, 163,
    163n41, 171–72, 171n83
  immigration by nationality, 157–58, 177
  migration compared to New England, 170–71
  migration of family groups, 163, 163n40,
    170–71
  population growth, 172
  servant migration to, 149, 156–58, 160,
    171–72, 171n80, 172n89, 174–75

  statistical tables, 157–58
  See also Pennsylvania; Philadelphia
Democracy in America (de Tocqueville), 337, 337n6
demography, 31, 165, 172
  as neglected area, 117, 125–26, 133–35, 138,
    142
dependency theory, 9
de Tocqueville, Alexis, 337, 337n6
Devine, T. M., 178
de Vries, Jan, 40
Dickerson, Oliver, 79
Dickinson, John, 259
diet, 37, 108, 119, 165
Doerflinger, Thomas, 87
"domestic mode of production," 9
Douglass, Francis, 322
Douglass, Mary, 9
"dual emigration," 127, 161–65, 167–68, 171–72
Du Bois, W. E. B., 350
Dunn, Richard S., 149n8, 150
Dupre, Daniel, 54
Dwight, Timothy, 245, 252–53

econometrics, 5, 7, 10–11
economic history (survey of work prior to 1985)
  challenges to neoclassicists, 2–4, 10, 12
  criticism of new economic history, 10–12
  criticism of staples thesis, 10–11
  economics versus history, 1–2, 4–6, 5n8, 8,
    10–12
  field at crossroads, 12–13
  influence of cultural anthropology, 9
  influence of sociology, 10
  institutionalists versus neoclassicists, 3–4
  Marshallians versus non-Marshallians, 2–3
  new economic history, 5–8, 11
  new social history, 8, 10
  role of government in development, 4–5
  use of counterfactual analysis, 6–7
  use of staples thesis, 6–7, 9
economic history, colonial (survey of work since
    1985)
  Atlantic-world studies, 14–17
  comparative regional studies, 21–26, 36
  discussion of capitalism, 33–37
  lines of research on income, 18–21
  neglected areas of study, 32–33
  studies of agriculture, 27–28
  studies of labor, 28–31
  work on consumption, 37–40
economic history, early Republic (survey of
    work since 1985)
  challenges to "economic miracle" theory,
    48–51

linking history and economics, 69–70
manufacturing versus industrializing people,
    60–63
neglected areas of study, 63–64
studies of banking and economic crises,
    53–55
studies of frontier, 58–59
studies of government intervention, 52–53
studies of hinterland economy, 55–57
studies of sectionalism, 63–64
studies of southern workforce, 65–66, 68
studies of women in economy, 66–68
views of "transition to capitalism," 37, 49, 51,
    57–58
economic history, Revolution (survey of work
    since 1985)
neglected areas of study, 41–42
opportunities versus hardships of war, 41–42
views on financial revolution, 44–47
views of postwar recovery, 42–44, 48
views of "transition to capitalism," 37, 42–43
economic nationalism, 283, 285–86, 290–91
economies of scale, 7, 51
Economy of British America (McCusker and
    Menard), 12–14, 30, 107, 145
Economy of British America, question: how did
    America grow, 71–72
    "Economy of Early British America"
        conference, 73
    William and Mary Quarterly (1999), 72
    work on growth, 75–77
    work on prices, 72–74
    work on rates of return, 74–75
Economy of British America, question: what were
    effect of British mercantilism, 78–79
    work on mercantilism, 80
    work on Navigation Acts, 79
    work on smuggling, 81
Economy of British America, question: what were
    driving forces of development, 82–87
    work on commodities, 85–87
    work on staples thesis, 82–84, 86–87
Economy of British America, survey of other work,
    87–106
    Atlantic linkage, 97–100
    history versus economics, 95–97
    integrating economic and cultural history,
        97–106
    political economy, 100–103, 103n73, 104n75
    reasons for not answering questions, 89–91,
        91n41
    works combining disparate fields, 92–94
Economy of British America, survey of work on
    consumption, 142–45

areas for additional work, 144–45
interdisciplinary studies, 143
Economy of British America, survey of work on
    labor, 135–42
areas for additional work, 141–42
child labor, 137–38
coerced versus free migrations, 139–40
community studies, 135–36
gender studies, 137
Economy of British America, survey of work on
    population, 125–26
17th-century migration, 127–28
areas for additional study, 130–31
critique of Bailyn, 127–29
immigration and Revolution, 129–30
slave migration, 132–35
work of Bailyn, 126–27
work on migration, 126–35
"Economy of Early British America: The
    Domestic Sector" (1995), 19, 73
Egnal, Marc, 15, 19, 73, 87, 95
Ekirch, A. Roger, 128, 141, 178–79
Ellis, Joseph J., 185
Eltis, David, 105, 113, 139, 140
Engerman, Stanley, 124, 139, 145,
    on economic growth rate, 19, 108
    on slavery, wage labor, and freedom, 350,
        352–53
England, 17, 35, 147, 347
    and American grain, 237–38, 255, 283–84
    blamed for slave trade, 210, 213
    in Franklin writings, 202, 205–6, 213
    See also immigration
"Era of Good Feelings," 263, 266, 268, 293
    opposing views of, 275–76
    tensions during, 264–66, 278
    See also Panic of 1819
Erie Canal, 52
Evans, Oliver, 43
Ewing, Nathaniel, 281
export-led approach. See staples thesis
Eyre, Manuel, 333
Eyre, William, 330

factory workers, 63, 318–19, 353, 358
family groups (migration of), 162–64, 163n41,
    167–68, 170
farm by-production, 22–23, 26
farmers, 23, 25–26, 116, 255
    challenges to "slovenly farmer," 110–13, 118
    "competency" (see "competency")
    and diversified production, 252–56
    and environmental hazards, 47, 237, 240, 242
    and Hessian fly, 249–52 (see also Hessian fly)

farmers (continued)
in Hudson River valley, 55–56
and IOUs for grain, 223–25
and land banks, 218–19, 229–31, 234, 234n34
and "mestizo" agriculture, 27, 110–13,
    118–19, 121
"mixed farming" and "composite farms," 55
and "moral economy," 109, 119–20
and privatization, 221, 228, 233–35 (see also
    privatization)
"slovenly farmer," 109–10, 115–116, 119–20
and specie taxes, 221, 226
standard of living of, 118–19
and yeomen and planters, 65–66
See also agriculture; plantations
Farmers' and Merchants' Bank of Delaware
    County, 305
Farmers' and Merchants' Bank of Madison
    (Ind.), 281
federal government, 284
and free-traders, 282, 287, 289
influenced economic sphere, 263–64
intervention in West, 280–81, 289
Federalists, 52, 263, 343, 344n29
and banking system, 220, 222, 298
feme covert, 357
finance, 44–46, 48. See also land banks;
    privatization
Finkelman, Paul, 186
"first worldism," 5
Fischer, David Hackett, 127–28, 163, 178–79
fish and fur industries, 82–84, 84n27. See also fur
    trade
Fisher, Andrew, 250–51
Fishing Places, Fishing People (Ommer), 83–84
Flint, Wesley Pillsbury, 236
Florida, 112
flour
as export, 64, 238–39, 242, 256, 259–61
prices for, 269, 272
technology of milling, 43, 249
and white wheat, 249–50, 254
and yellow wheat, 251, 255
Fogel, Robert, 7, 348
Fogleman, Aaron, 128, 130, 175–79
Forced Founders (Holton), 93
Ford, George, 244, 254, 256
foreign markets, 25, 51. See also protectionists
Frank, Andre Gunder, 10
Franklin, Benjamin, 46, 184n3, 207
as abolitionist, 186–87, 186n9, 202n43, 211,
    215, 215n73
accused British of enslaving colonies, 184n3,
    189, 205–9, 212

Advice to a Young Tradesman, 198, 198n36
as "Americanus," 205
and artisans, 192n2, 199, 199n36
as "Blackamore," 195–96
blamed British for American slavery, 183,
    189, 211
in "cockpit," 211
colonists not responsible for slavery, 211
compared with Jefferson, 186–87
contradiction: fighting enslavement and
    owning slaves, 187, 210
"Conversation . . . on the subject of Slavery,"
    210
developed myth of American freedom, 189,
    213–214
disillusioned with imperial policy, 187, 207
epitomized Revolutionary ideals, 185–86, 189
as "Freeholder of Old Sarum," 212
Information to Those Who Would Remove to
    America, 213–14
"Invectives Against the Americans," 208
and labor theory of value, 197–99, 198n33,
    198n36
and maxims, 198–99
Modest Enquiry into the Nature and Necessity
    of a Paper-Currency, 198
"Observations on the Increase of Mankind,"
    201–5, 207, 210
and paper currency, 188, 197–98
"Petition to Pennsylvania Assembling
    regarding Fairs," 194
and Plain Truth, 201, 205
and Poor Richard's Almanack, 188, 194–96,
    198–200, 199n36
relation of antislavery, labor, and capital, 188,
    200–201, 207, 207n55
Revolution's propagandist, 217
and runaway servants, 189–90, 192–93,
    192n21, 200, 200n37
and slavery in Declaration, 212–13, 215n73
slavery as investment, 189, 202, 202n43, 211
as social commentator, 194–96
theme of social order, 194–96
as theorist of British nationalism, 204–5, 208
used antislavery to promote nationalism,
    215–16
used personae, 194–97
used racism to attack slave and convict labor,
    189, 201–5, 203n45, 207–8, 210
Franklin, James, 197
free labor, 147
Franklin mythologized, 213–14
legal work relations of, 173
replaced unfree in Pennsylvania, 160–61

slavery inefficient compared to, 189, 211
  See also migration
"free-range husbandry," 116
free-trade advocates, 278
  and government intervention, 282
  identified agriculture with nationalism,
    289
  and sectional interests, 282, 288–89
  and tariffs, 282–83, 287–88, 291
  view of protectionists, 289
"Freeholder of Old Sarum" (Franklin), 212
French Revolution, 252, 268
From Dependency to Independence (Newell), 101
"From Slaves, Convicts, and Servants to Free
    Passengers" (Fogleman), 130
frontier, 59
  Appalachian backcountry, 149, 163
  growth of, 19–20, 50
  studies of, 14–15, 25–26, 42, 58
frontier approach/thesis, 82–83, 202
"frontier exchange economy," 27, 112
fur trade, 73, 80–81

Galenson, David, 95, 146, 178–79
Gallatin, Albert, 261
Gallman, Robert, 48–49, 73
Games, Alison, 75, 127, 175
Geertz, Clifford, 9, 10
Gemery, Henry, 125, 175
gender and race, 67, 172–73, 195
  inequality in workforce, 355, 357
  studies of, 92–94, 136–37, 344
  See also racism; women in economy
Georgia, 24, 26, 136, 207
Germans, 260
  to Delaware Valley, 170
  demographics of, 171–72, 171n83
  in family groups, 163, 171–72
  migration to North America, 99, 127–29,
    156–58, 176–78, 181
  servants immigration, 180–81
Germantown and Perkiomen Turnpike, 306
Glenn, David, 323, 326
Goldin, Claudia, 357
*Good Wives, Nasty Wenches, and Anxious Par-
    tiarchs* (Brown), 93–94
Goodrich, Carter, 4–5, 52
Gordon, Robert B., 75
government regulation of enterprise, 53, 62, 80.
    See also political economy
grain cultivation, 121, 246
  and Chew, 253–56
  and Hessian fly, 239–40, 242, 251
  shift toward South, 239, 260–61

grain trade, 80, 86, 239
  and demand, 252, 255
  English ban on, 237–38
  and Hessian fly, 237–39, 247
  and milling industry, 249, 256, 259
  use of IOUs in, 224–25, 227
Grassby, Richard, 74
Great Migration, 165, 170
Green, Evarts B., 125
Greene, Jack P., 95, 118
Griffin, Patrick, 177
gross domestic product, 7, 19–20, 73, 144–45
"ground-rent" system, 322, 325–7
Grubb, Farley, 95, 128

Hamilton, Alexander, 44–45, 263, 218
  and privatization, 220, 222–23, 226–27
  and *Report on Manufactures*, 61–62, 358
Hancock, David, 16, 144
Harper, Laurence, 79
Harrington, Virginia D., 125
Harris, P. M. G., 140
Harrisburg, Carlisle, and Chambersburg
    Turnpike, 309
Hartz, Louis, 337–38
Hazards, 348
Heinrich, Thomas, 330–31
Hendricks, William, 264–65, 279–80
Henretta, James, 35–36, 41
Herndon, Ruth Wallis, 30, 138
Hessian fly, 47, 246–47
  and agricultural reform, 249–53, 249n37
  effects of, 237, 239, 250n39, 260–61
  as environmental hazard, 47, 237, 240, 242
  life cycle of, 240–42
  name, 238–39, 245–46
  origins and migration of, 242–44
  threatened economy, 236–38, 244
  See also wheat
Highlands, Findlay, 332
Himmelwright, Samuel, 324
Hirschman, Albert, 105–6
Historical Statistics of the United States, 133
History of Human Populations (Harris), 140
Hochstadt, Steve, 131
Hocker, Christopher, 332
Hoffman, Ronald, 142
Hollingsworth, Henry, 259
Hollingsworth, Levi, 250
Holton, Woody, 93
home market, 283, 285–86, 290–91
Horn, James, 127, 139, 175, 177, 179
House of Representatives Committee on
    Manufactures, 266–68, 277, 284–88

household production, 348
    in colonial economy, 22, 32
    organizing principle of work, 147, 166, 169,
        173
    primacy of, 35–35
    of women, 66–67, 357–58
housing, 108, 143. *See also* carpenters
Howe, William, 243
Hudson River valley, 22, 55
Hughlett, William, 259
"human agency," 104–6
Hume, David, 1, 204
Hunter, Brooke, 47, 86

incorporations, 63, 269–70. *See also* banks;
        transportation companies
immigration from England, 127–28, 137
    by decade, 156–57
    discussion of estimates, 176, 178–79, 181–82
    "dual emigration," 161–67
    See also migration
imperial policy/regulation
    effects of, 18, 79
    Franklin disillusioned with, 187, 189, 201–3,
        215
    and slavery, 185, 202, 207
    studies of, 102–4
indentured servitude/servants, 28, 131, 146,
        146n1, 200
    in 17th-century migration, 150, 162
    in 18th-century migration, 150, 161,
        179–82
    among children, 30, 137–38, 167–68, 171
    and colonial economy, 30–31, 146, 173, 190
    contract terms of, 148, 148n5, 152n17
    demographics in Chesapeake, 167–68
    in "dual emigration," 127, 161–63
    in general migration, 150–51, 157n28, 174
    incidence of, 30, 147, 160
    in labor force of Chesapeake, 153–56,
        154n21, 169
    and legal relations of work, 156, 166, 173
    in "metropolitan" migration, 161–62
    migration into Chesapeake, 149, 151–53, 167,
        174–75
    migration into Delaware Valley, 149, 156–58,
        160, 171–72, 171n81, 174–75
    migration into lower South, 174
    migration into New England, 149, 149n8,
        165, 174–75
    migration into New Netherlands, 174
    in Pennsylvania, 159–62
    periods of substantial migration, 148–49
    in population of Chesapeake, 152–53, 155

    in population of Delaware Valley, 157–58
    servants without indentures, 152n17, 167
    service and youth linked, 166, 171
    statistical tables, 152–56, 158–61, 181
    used to develop transportation, 359
indigo, 6, 24, 36, 85–86, 136
industrial capitalism, 3, 60, 216, 337, 357
    studies of, 183, 276
Industrial Revolution (American), 118, 358
Industrial Revolution (England), 17, 347
"industrious revolution" (de Vries), 40
inflation, 228, 271, 323
    expansion of banks led to, 298, 300, 304
*Information to Those Who Would Remove to
        America* (Franklin), 213–214
Innes, Stephen, 101
Innis, Harold, 6, 82–83, 91
"insider lending," 59
Institute of Early American History and
        Culture, 91n41
"institutionalists," 3–4
internal improvements, 52, 55, 65, 264, 293
    and booster spirit, 309, 313
    protectionists argued for, 286, 290
    in South, 315
    See also railroads; transportation companies
"Invectives Against the Americans" (Franklin),
        208
IOUs, 223–25, 224n10
Irish, 171, 178
    in family groups, 163, 171–72
    migration to North America, 127–29,
        156–58, 176–78, 181
    servant immigration, 180–81
iron-making, 75–76, 360n82

Jackson, Andrew, 263, 268, 279, 304
Jacksonians, 53–55, 264, 267, 276, 341
Jefferson, Thomas, 186–87, 213n67
    and Hessian fly, 237–38, 243–44, 246,
        251–52
Jeffersonian Democrats, 289, 298–99, 303
Jensen, Joan, 135
Jersey-Gaspé cod fishery, 83
"jobbing," 329–31
Johnson, Samuel, 209, 209n61
Johnston, Orramel, 279–80
Jones, Alice Hanson, 19
Jones, Jacqueline, 146
Jones, Samuel, 247
Jones, Thomas P., 360
Journal of the Early Republic (1996), 343
journeymen, 321–22, 326, 328–29
Junto, 192

Keimer, Samuel, 192
Kennedy, Michael, 76
Kepler, Jon, 79
Kerber, Linda, 354
Kerr, John, 266–68, 270
Kirkbride, Joseph, 246
Kolchin, Peter, 346
Kornblith, Gary J., 343
Kulikoff, Allan, 28, 80, 85

labor/labor force, 59
    and agriculture, 109, 136
    bound in Chesapeake, 141, 155–56
    bound in Philadelphia, 161
    as capital, 187–88, 198–201, 345
    and capitalism, 183, 187, 346
    of children in factories, 63, 357–58
    colonial labor, 28–29
    as commodity, 57, 187–88, 193, 351
    creole as source of, 172–73, 190
    Franklin's views on, 188, 200–201, 207
    of indentured children, 30, 137–38, 167–68,
        171
    in making of American Revolution, 183,
        187–88
    scarcity of, 18, 26
    segmented by age, gender, race, 173, 352–55
    servants in Chesapeake, 153–54, 154n21
    servants in Philadelphia, 159
    statistical tables, 154, 156, 159, 161
    system in mid-Atlantic, 190–92
    "turnover cost" of, 191–92
    of women, 63, 66–67, 137, 357–59
    See also free labor; migration; unfree labor
labor theory of value, 197–99
Lamoreaux, Naomi, 59, 314
Lancaster, Moses, 324
Lancaster Turnpike, 306–7
land, 18–19, 26, 41, 310, 337
land banks
    demand for return to, 229–31
    legislature prints money for, 231–32
    loans from, 218–19, 229, 234, 234n34
    studies of, 234–35
    See also money
Landsman, N. C., 178
Larson, John, 52
Lawrence, Thomas, 331
leasing, 332
Lemon, James T., 35
Lewis, Frank, 73
Liberal Tradition in America (Hartz), 337–38
Linebaugh, Peter, 196, 215
"linguistic turn," 12, 15

Lloyd, Evan, 328, 331
Louisiana Purchase, 271
Lowells, 60, 348
lower South, 24–25, 174
Luther, Seth, 353

Mackintosh, William, 82
Madison, James, 238, 243, 244, 261
Main, Gloria and Jackson, 73, 117
Maine, 29, 105
Majewski, John, 53
Making of the English Working Class (Thompson),
    341
males (young, single), 165, 167–68, 171–72
    in "duel emigration," 127, 161–63
Malthusian approach, 72, 82–83, 89, 117
Mancall, Peter, 107–10, 115, 119, 123
Mann, Bruce, 48
Mansfield, Lord, 211
manufacturing, 43, 60–62, 202, 247
    in "Era of Good Feelings," 267, 269–70, 272,
        292
    labor force in, 357–58
    and Navigation Acts, 18, 102
"marginalists," 2
"market revolution," 51, 56–57, 64, 295, 297
    work of Sellers, 275–76
    work of Wood, 274–75
Market Revolution (Sellers), 341–42
"Markets for Children in Early America"
    (Murray and Herndon), 138
Marple, Abraham, 332
Marshall, Alfred, 2
Marshall, John, 264
Marxist theory, 1, 3, 9, 198, 198n3
Maryland, 24, 26, 47, 80, 117
    and Hessian fly, 239–40, 253, 259–61
    migration estimates, 152–53
    See also Bordley, John; Carroll, Charles;
        Chesapeake
Massachusetts, 29, 44, 101, 164, 220
    "transition to capitalism" in, 56–57, 342
material culture, 142–44
Matson, Cathy, 80, 102, 300
Mayetiola destructor. See Hessian fly
McCloskey, Deirdre, 95
McCusker, John J., 19, 124, 144
    See also Economy of British America
McGaw, Judith, 116
McWilliams, James, 86
Mechanics' Bank of Philadelphia, 294–95, 296
Meinig, D. W., 313
Melchior, Horatio, 317, 320–21, 333
Melish, Joanne Pope, 348

Menard, Russell R., 27, 151, 175. See also
    Economy of British America
mercantile policy. *See* imperial policy
merchant capitalism, 3, 213, 215
Merchant Credit and Labour Strategies (Ommer), 83
merchants, 60–62, 87, 102
    and Hessian fly, 247, 250–51, 259, 262
    hostility toward, 265, 279, 281–82, 285
    invested in construction, 322, 324–25
    invested in stock, 303, 309
    mobilized credit, 22, 41
    overextended, 271–72
    and privatization, 220, 222, 229, 234,
        297–98
    protectionists and foreign, 282, 284–85
Meredith, Elizabeth, 67
Merrill, Michael, 35, 45, 345
"mestizo" agriculture, 27, 110–13, 118–19, 121,
    123
Metcalf, C. L., 236
Meyer, David, 44
mid-Atlantic/middle colonies, 19, 28, 58–59, 64
    banking in, 270, 272, 303
    child labor in, 138
    demand for labor in, 190–91
    farmers in, 116, 249–50, 255
    and Hessian fly, 47, 237, 244, 252
    migration to, 175
    shareholding in, 312–13
    and tariffs, 265, 278, 282
    and wheat, 64, 237, 239–40, 244, 252–53
    See also Delaware Valley; millers;
        Pennsylvania; Philadelphia; Whitehall
        Plantation
migration, 130–31
    in 17th century, 162, 175–76
    18th and 19th centuries compared, 129–30
    18th-century, by ethnic group, 176–77
    to American regions (through 1780),
        174–75
    to Appalachian backcountry, 149, 149n8, 163,
        163n41
    to Chesapeake (*see* Chesapeake, general
        migration, servant migration)
    of convicts, 181–82
    to Delaware Valley (*see* Delaware Valley,
        general migration, servant migration)
    "dual emigration," 161–65, 167–68, 171–72
    English/Welsh, 178–79, 181
    of family groups, 162–64, 167–68, 170
    general migration, 17th and 18th centuries,
        150–51
    German, 99, 177, 180
    Irish, 177–78, 180

    to lower South, 174
    to mainland (through 1780), 174–75
    "metropolitan" migration, 161–62
    "migration efficiency," 131
    to New England (*see* New England, general
        migration, servant migration)
    to New Netherlands, 174
    and population growth, 165, 168, 172
    "provincial" migration, 162
    relationship to American Revolution,
        129–30
    Scottish, 178–80
    servant migration, 149, 175–76
    statistical tables, 152–53, 157–58, 176, 181
    work of Bailyn, 126–29, 161–63, 177–79
    work of Eltis, 140
    work of Harris, 140
    See also immigration from England
Migration and Origins (Games), 175
Mill, John Stuart, 1, 337
Millar, James, 1
millers
    added new products, 259–60
    on Brandywine, 43, 47, 253, 255
    and Hessian fly, 237–39, 247, 254, 256, 262
    and wheat varieties, 249–51, 255
mixed farming, 22, 55
*Modest Enquiry into the Nature and Necessity of a
    Paper-Currency* (Franklin), 198
Money, Trade, and Power (Greene et al.), 136
money/money supply, 33
    new issue of, 220, 231–33
    and privatization, 46, 221–22, 226–28, 272
    role in Panic of 1819, 271–72
Montgomery, David, 354
moral capitalism, 37, 55
moral economy, 42, 67, 109, 119–21, 123
Morgan, George, 237n17, 245, 248–49, 250, 251
Morgan, Kenneth, 128
Morgan, Philip, 127, 138, 139, 150
Morris, Richard, 360
Morris, Robert, 218, 224n10, 233
    distrusted ordinary man, 226–27
    and money supply, 222–25, 227–28
    and stable currency, 227–28
"Morris Notes," 222, 226–27
Mount Vernon, 255
Moya, Jose C., 130
Mulcahy, Matt, 114
Mullin, Michael, 122
Munday, John, 322, 323, 324–26, 328, 333
Murphey, Archibald D., 267–68
Murray, John, 30, 138
Myers, Warnet, 322

Napoleonic Wars, 42, 60, 268, 283
    and demand for grain, 239, 252, 256
Nash, R. C., 24, 175
nationalism, 268, 280
    of Franklin, 189, 204–5, 216
    of free-traders, 289–90
    and home market, 285–86
    and international trade, 267–68
    of protectionists, 283, 285–88
    versus sectionalism, 263, 265, 278–79, 282
Native Americans, 100, 108–9, 110–12, 206n52
"natural economy," 283, 285–86, 290–91
Navigation Acts, 18, 78–79, 78n16, 102
"new agricultural history," 109, 114
New England, 56, 58, 127
    child labor in, 138
    community studies of, 35, 135
    compared to Chesapeake, 24, 166–67, 169–70
    compared to Delaware Valley, 170–71
    conflicting views of its economy, 117–18
    declension in, 22, 117
    demographics of migrants to, 165
    "dual emigration," 164–65
    general migration to, 147, 162, 174–75
    Great Migration to, 164–65, 170
    labor in, 28–29, 166, 166n56
    population growth in, 165–66
    Puritans in, 101, 164
    servant migration to, 149, 149n8, 165,
        165n48, 174–75
    and slavery, 347–48
    stock ownership in, 313–14
    women in work force, 137, 358
    See also Connecticut; Massachusetts; North
New-England Association of Farmers,
        Mechanics, and Other Working Men,
        351
New England Courant, 197
"New England debate," 120
New Netherlands, 174
New World Economies (Egnal), 87
New York, 56, 80, 102, 311, 356
    and Hessian fly, 252
    and manufacturing, 270, 272
    migration to 162
    and private banks, 220
    shareholding in, 312–13
Newcastle (Dela.), 156–57
Newell, Margaret, 101
Niles, Hezekiah, 356, 358
"non-intersection fallacy," 93
North, Douglass, 42
North/Northeast, 59, 168, 183, 261
    and banking, 270, 278

compared with South, 23–24, 32, 49, 64–65,
    314–15
economy intertwined with South, 347–49,
    347n39
farming in, 14, 22, 252–53, 342
investment by merchants, 60–61
labor force in, 358–59
wage labor in, 337, 350, 353
See also Connecticut; Massachusetts; New
    England
Notes on the State of Virginia (Jefferson), 246

Oakes, James, 347
"Observations on the Increase of Mankind"
    (Franklin), 201–5, 207, 210
Ommer, Rosemary, 83–84
Orren, Karen, 353–54
outwork, 56, 358, 358n78
Oxford Iron Works (Va.), 360n82

Panic of 1819, 53
    background of, 54, 264
    and emergence of party system, 274, 278, 292
    encouraged protectionists, 283
    impact of, 273, 276, 324, 327
    impact on banking charters, 297, 303
    and sectionalism, 278–81
    and trade and banking policies, 266–67, 272
    work of Sellers, 275–76
    work of Wood, 274–76
Panic of 1837, 55
paper currency, 299
    backed by taxes, 219, 231
    Franklin proponent of, 188, 197–98
    privately issued (see privatization)
    state-issued (see land banks)
    and war debt speculators, 231–32
partnerships, 30, 46, 60, 62
    in construction, 323, 331–32
"path dependence," 25
Pauly, Philip, 243
Pennsylvania, 22–23, 299
    bound labor force in, 158–61, 171n80
    and Hessian fly, 237, 259, 260
    labor force in, 160–61
    population in, 158
    See also bank stock; carpenters; privatization;
        transportation company stock
Pennsylvania Abolition Society, 187
Pennsylvania Archives, 302, 309
Pennsylvania Gazette, 192–93, 195, 205, 236, 249
Pennsylvania Railroad, 297, 311–12
Pennsylvania Supreme Executive Council
Peopling of British North America (Bailyn), 126

per capita income, 7–8, 43, 49
    in colonial period, 107–8, 111, 123
    estimates of, 18–21, 28
Percy, Thomas, 273
Pereira, Alfred M., 73
Perkins, Edwin, 220–21
Peters, Richard, 242–43
Peterson, Mark, 101
"Petition to the Pennsylvania Assembly regard-
        ing Fairs" (Franklin), 194
Philadelphia, 87, 135, 201, 247, 333
    and banking, 229, 271, 297–300, 302
    construction trade in (see carpenters)
    debt speculators in, 221, 233
    grain and flour industry in, 249–50, 254, 256,
        259–60
    immigration to, 156–57, 159–60, 163, 177,
        180
    population in, 159–161, 172, 172n88
    shareholding in, 302–3, 309–10, 312, 316
    statistical tables, 159–61
    workforce in, 159–61
Philadelphia County Society for Promoting
        Agriculture and Domestic
        Manufacturing, 247
Philadelphia Society for the Promotion of
        Agriculture, 247
Phillips, Kim T., 299
"picaresque unfree," 191
Pickens, Israel, 270
Pickering, Timothy, 227
Plain Truth (Franklin), 201, 205
plantations/planters, 14, 25, 65, 169, 290
    as capitalists, 36, 348–49
    and credit, 75, 141
    innovations of, 114–16, 122
    and "mestizo" agriculture, 111–12
    and recovery, 260–61
    See also Bordley, John; Carroll, Charles;
        Whitehall Plantation
plantation crops. See staples
Planters' and Merchants' Bank of Huntsville
        (Ala.), 282
political economy, 41, 52, 80
    in "Era of Good Feelings," 263–64, 266, 293
    Franklin and imperial policy, 187, 201–4,
        207, 215
    in Pennsylvania banking, 301–3, 305
    and privatization, 221, 233, 235, 270
    and Second Bank of United States, 270–72
    studies in, 97, 100–103
    and trade, 270, 284
Poor Richard's Almanack, 188, 194–96, 198–200,
        199n36

Pope, Leroy, 282
population
    free families in, 131
    growth in Chesapeake, 168, 168n67
    growth in Delaware Valley, 172
    growth in New England, 165–66
    in Philadelphia, 159–61, 172, 172n88
    servants in Chesapeake, 153–56
    servants in Delaware Valley, 157–58
    slaves in Chesapeake, 133–35, 142, 155–56
    statistical tables, 153, 155, 158–61
    work of Bailyn, 126–27
    See also creole; migration
Population History of North America (Haines and
        Steckel), 125
Porter, David R., 311
Price, Jacob, 77, 87
Price of Redemption (Peterson), 101
price series, 73–74, 140
Principles of Economics (Marshall), 2
printers, 324n20, 328. See also Franklin, Benjamin
privatization/private banks (Pa.)
    and capital base of, 223, 270–71
    citizens demand end to, 229–30
    and currency, 218–19
    led to retarded growth, 221, 224–27, 229,
        233–34
    opponents of 222–23
    as smooth process, 220–21
    and specie standard, 222
    See also Morris, Robert
probate records, 19, 40, 134, 142
Progressive institutionalists, 4
protectionists, 278
    and foreign trade, 282, 284–285
    and home market, 283, 285–86
    and nationalism, 285–87
    and "natural" economy, 283, 285
    and tariffs, 282, 285–87, 290, 292
"Protestant ethic," 3, 101
provision ground system, 114
public improvements. See internal improvements
Puritans/Puritanism, 94, 101, 164
Purdue University, 5
Purvis, Thomas, 177–79
putting-out system, 58, 61

Quakers/Quakerism, 60, 170, 201, 324

race/racism
    Franklin's view of, 189, 201–4, 210
    as social division, 350, 356
Radicalism of the American Revolution (Wood). See
        Wood, Gordon S.

railroads, 5, 7, 297, 311–12

Ramsey, David, 111

rattlesnake, 205–6

Raymond, Daniel, 286, 351

real estate, 321–23, 328

Record, Thomas, 328

Rediker, Marcus, 191, 196, 215

Reed, Abel, 329–30

Reed, Joseph, 222

Remer, Rosalind, 324n20, 328

Report on Manufactures (Hamilton), 61–62, 358

Republican Party, 264, 274, 278

Rhea, John, 287–89

Ricardo, David, 1

rice, 6, 24–25, 65, 85, 136
    and "mestizo" agriculture, 111–12

Richard Saunders (Franklin), 188, 194–96,
    198–200, 199n36

Rilling, Donna, 59

Rise of African Slavery in the Americas (Eltis), 139

Rockefeller Foundation, 4

Rockman, Seth, 63, 68

Rodney, Caesar, 351

Roediger, David, 350

Ross, David, 360n82

Rostow, Walter W., 5–6

Rothbard, Murray, 274

Rothenberg, Winifred, 44, 45, 56, 117–18

Ruggles, Steve, 117

Russo, Jean, 117, 135

Ryden, David, 114

rye, 260

safety-valve thesis, 202

Sahlins, Marshall, 9

Salinger, Sharon V., 128, 159–60

Sawers, Larry, 79

Schultz, Ronald, 197

Schwartz, Anna, 298

Schweitzer, Mary, 160

Scott, John, 284–85

Scottish Enlightenment, 1

Scranton, Philip, 324, 330, 333

"seasoning," 152, 157n28

Second Bank of the United States
    and goals of, 54, 263, 270
    hostility toward, 278–82
    monetary policies of, 264, 271–72

sectionalism, 63–64
    and currency crisis, 280–82
    and internal trade, 286–87
    and nationalism, 265, 278–79, 289
    and Panic of 1819, 264, 274
    and tariffs and trade, 282, 288–89

    and trade and banking, 266–67, 277–78
    West versus East, 279–80
    See also free-trade advocates; protectionists

Sedgwick, Theodore, 351

Sellers, Charles, 275–76, 341–42, 342n19

Sering, John, 281

Service, Elwin, 9

"Settlers and Slaves" (Horn and Morgan), 139

Seven Years' War, 33, 103n73, 204, 207

"Seventy-Six," 277

Shadow of a Dream (Coclanis), 85

Shammas, Carole, 121, 144

shareholding (Pa.)
    compared to New England, 313–14,
        314nn64–65
    compared to other mid-Atlantic states,
        312–13
    compared to South, 315, 315n68
    widespread among citizens, 53, 312, 316
    See also bank stock; transportation company
        stock

Sharp, Granville, 210–11

Sharples, Joshua, 326

Sheller, Tina H., 343

Shepherd, James, 24, 73, 75

"shifting cultivation," 315

Shippen, Edward, 325

shipping/shipbuilding, 24–25
    and agriculture, 27, 42, 65, 122, 268
    merchant investment in, 41, 60
    subcontracting in, 330–31

Shirley, William, 206

Silence Dogood (Franklin), 196

Simler, Lucy, 28–29, 118, 135

Simpson, Stephen, 353

Slater, Samuel, 348

slave trade, 132, 141, 202, 348, 349n46
    databases, 17, 73, 113, 132
    and Eltis, 105, 113
    Franklin blamed English for, 210–11
    number entering America, 151, 346

slavery/slaves, 21, 24, 26, 65, 347
    adult sex ratios of , 134–35, 139
    as anomaly in history, 337, 337n7, 339
    and Atlantic economy, 65, 66n74, 335
    and capitalism, 346–49, 347n39
    compared with wage labor, 360, 360n82
    databases, 17, 73, 113, 132
    equated wage labor with freedom, 350–51
    and expansion of, 338–39, 346
    gang versus task system, 113–14
    and labor scarcity, 156
    and "mestizo" agriculture, 111–13
    number entering America, 151, 346

slavery/slaves (continued)
  in Pennsylvania, 160–61
  population in Chesapeake, 142, 133–35, 155–56
  reliance on (Chesapeake), 115, 169–70
  slave versus bound labor in Chesapeake, 141
  South dependent on, 64–65, 185
  studies of, 28, 31
  in West Africa versus Americas, 114
  See also Franklin, Benjamin
"slovenly farmer," 109–10, 115–16, 119–20
  challenges to "slovenly farmer," 110–13, 118
Smith, Adam, 1, 44, 183–84, 184n3, 216–17
Smith, Billy, 135
Smith, Simon, 75
Smout, T. C., 178
smuggling, 81, 88
Smyth, William J., 177
snake, 205–6
Snyder, Simon, 299–300
Social Science Research Council, 4
Sokoloff, Kenneth, 357
Somerset decision, 211
South
  areas within, 23–26
  banking in, 270, 272
  and capitalism, 36, 185, 348–49
  compared with North, 23–24, 32, 49, 64–65,
    314–15
  cotton boom in, 120–21
  economy intertwined with North, 347–49,
    347n39
  and Hessian fly, 239, 260, 261
  indentured servitude in, 146–47
  industrial development in, 349
  and internal improvements, 315
  labor relations in, 65–66
  "mestizo" agriculture in, 111–12
  migration to, 162, 174–75
  shareholding in, 314–15
  specie drain in, 270–72
  and staples and slaves, 64–65, 239, 346
  tasking and provision grounds in, 27
  See also Chesapeake; slavery
South, lower, 24–25, 136, 162, 174
South Carolina, 85–86, 111, 136
specie/specie standard, 55, 284
  and bank notes, 267, 270–72
  and capital base, 223, 232, 270–71
  drain of, 221, 224, 228, 265, 267, 270–71
  led to insolvency, 221, 233–34
  opponents of, 222–23
  to stabilize currency, 222, 227–28, 270–71
  taxes payable in, 222–26, 224n10
  and West, 265, 279, 281–82

"speculative construction," 317–18, 322–23,
    325–27
"Speech of Miss Polly Baker" (Franklin), 198–99
Spring Mills (Dela.), 259
Stansell, Christine, 358
staples, 24, 121–22, 136, 239. See also staples
    thesis; names of individual crops
staples thesis, 6–7, 9
  applied to commodities, 82–87
  critics of, 10–11, 15, 87, 97
  in Economy of British America, 14, 72, 82–84,
    86–87, 90
  and linkages in economy, 6, 14
  work of Egnal, 87, 95
Steckel, Richard, 73
Steinfeld, Robert, 352–53
Steuart, James, 1
Strangers Within the Realm (Bailyn and Morgan),
    127
Strickland, William, 244, 252
subcontracting, 329–31
sugar, 36, 65, 183
  in Barbados, 115–16
  output and price of, 114, 121–22
  smuggling of, 79, 81
  and triangular trade, 113, 348
Sumner, Charles, 346–47
Sutherland, Stella H., 125
Sylla, Richard, 45, 220

"takeoff," 5–6, 7, 57. See also market revolution
tariffs, 263, 267, 270, 272
  opposed by free-trade advocates, 283,
    287–89, 291
  and sectionalism, 282, 287–88
  supported by protectionists, 278, 285–87, 290
taxes
  and insolvency, 221, 233–34
  and land banks, 219
  paper money backed by, 219, 231
  payable in specie, 221–26, 270–71
Taylor, George Rogers, 52
Taylor, John (of Caroline), 287–88, 291
Taylor, John W., 283
Taylor, Philip, 314
technological innovations, 7, 115–16, 121, 344,
    349. See also "mestizo" agriculture
tenancy, 23, 28–29
Tennant, Christopher, 331–32
textiles/textile industry, 75, 269–70, 330, 333
"thick description," 9
Thomas, Isaac, 271, 289
Thomas, Robert, 153–54
Thompson, E. P., 341